MORE CRITICAL ACCLA
(CONT'D F

"A truly outstanding work. A true Kiddush Hashem. The breadth and scope of this work is truly magnificent. Leaves one with a clear, well-balanced Torah perspective."
—*Rabbi Zev Leff, Rosh haYeshiva, Yeshiva Gedola Matityahu, Israel (full letter inside)*

"Sweeping, scholarly, hardhitting. Investigates the social, political, spiritual, medical and personal aspects of same-sex attraction. This book's single most important contribution lies in its psycho-spiritual portrait of the change process."
—*Joseph Nicolosi, PhD., Co-Founder and Past-President, NARTH; Founder & Director of the Thomas Aquinas Psychological Clinic of Encino, California; Author,* Reparative Therapy of Male Homosexuality: A New Clinical Approach, Healing Homosexuality: Case Stories of Reparative Therapy, A Parent's Guide to Preventing Homosexuality.

"A very valuable resource to educators and rabbis."
—*Rabbi Nechemia Coopersmith, Editor-in-Chief, Aish.com*

Integrates in a scholarly way the Scriptural Wisdom of the Torah, the Talmud, and Rabbinical scholars with the sound insights of many contemporary psychotherapists.
—*Rev. John F. Harvey, OSFS, Founder & Director, Courage; Author,* The Homosexual Person: New Thinking in Pastoral Care, The Cry of the Faithful: the Truth About Homosexuality, Homosexuality and the Catholic Church.

"Admirable scholarship, great insight. Persons from all religious backgrounds will benefit from this uniquely Jewish perspective and the author's willingness to address subjects like sexual reassignment surgery and homosexual parenting that are often neglected in other writings."
—*David C. Pruden, MS, Executive Director, Evergreen International.*

"Arthur Goldberg has given us all, not just Jews, a deeper, more truthful, more compassionate and more hopeful view of same-sex attraction."
—*Alan Medinger, Former Executive Director of Exodus-North America, Founder & Former Director, Regeneration; Author,* Growth into Manhood: Resuming the Journey.

"One of the most comprehensive and compassionate texts ever published on this topic."
—*Rich Wyler, Founder & Director, People Can Change.*

MORE CRITICAL ACCLAIM (CONT'D)

"Whether you agree or disagree with [Goldberg's] views, you will find them presented in a compelling, honest and forthright manner. A must read for both Jewish and Christian people dealing with unwanted SSA."
—Randy Thomas, Executive Vice President, Exodus International.

"A rare blend of compassion, scholarship and encouragement to those who take life and Scripture seriously. A wonderful read and a valuable tool."
—Joe Dallas, Founder & Program Director of Genesis Counseling of Tustin, California; Past-President, Exodus International; Author, The Gay Gospel? How Pro-Gay Advocates Misread the Bible, Desires in Conflict: Answering the Struggle for Sexual Identity, When Homosexuality Hits Home: What to Do When a Loved One Says They're Gay, A Strong Delusion, and The Game Plan: The Men's 30-Day Strategy for Attaining Sexual Integrity.

"Eloquently argues for client rights for therapeutic choice. Shows how people can change from a homosexual lifestyle to heterosexuality, drawing on recent research on the effectiveness of reparative therapy, and on the helpful religious roots of Western civilization"
—George A. Rekers, Ph.D., Distinguished Professor of Neuropsychiatry and Behavioral Science Emeritus, U. of South Carolina School of Medicine; U.S. Representative, International Federation for Therapeutic Choice.

"A landmark book. Bridges the gap between religion, psychology and public policy. I couldn't put it down."
—Richard Cohen, M.A., Executive Director, International Healing Foundation, Author, Coming Out Straight, and Gay Children, Straight Parents.

For the full text of these endorsements, please visit *www.redheiferpress.com*

LIGHT IN THE CLOSET

TORAH, HOMOSEXUALITY AND THE POWER TO CHANGE

by

ARTHUR GOLDBERG
Co-Founder & Co-Director, *JONAH*
(Jews Offering New Alternatives to Homosexuality)

Red Heifer Press

Dear Sue,

May G-d bless you for your dedication to this work and to your husband Mark. Wonderful to have met you, and I look forward to working with you!

Arthur Goldberg
1/5/11

LIGHT IN THE CLOSET: TORAH, HOMOSEXUALITY, AND
THE POWER TO CHANGE, by Arthur Goldberg.
Copyright © 2008 by Arthur Goldberg
First Edition, Second Printing
Published in the United States by Red Heifer Press,
P.O. Box 1891, Beverly Hills, California 90213-1891.
All rights reserved.

Cover design by Jorge A. Pringles (Gotham Press)
Typesetting and book design by Red Heifer Press

Library of Congress Control Number: 2008935339
ISBN: 978-09631478-9-9

HASKAMOS

(Rabbinical Approbations)

The following letters are presented in the order
in which they were received.

בס"ד

שמואל קמנצקי
Rabbi S. Kamenetsky

2018 Upland Way
Philadelphia, Pa 19131

Home: 215-473-2798
Study: 215-473-1212

July 4, 2008

Mr. Arthur Goldberg
80 Grand Street
Jersey City NJ 07302

Dear Mr. Goldberg,

Thank you for the very interesting and enlightening book "Light in the Closet". Our Sages teach us that every human being is capable of changing for the better.

Those who make the false claim that human beings cannot change their tendencies are comparing them to animals.

Indeed it may be very difficult to change one's nature, but it is definitely possible if one so desires.

Wishing you much Hatzlacha in your endeavors.

Sincerely,

S. Kamenetsky

FOUNDER & DEAN
Rabbi Noah Weinberg

DAN FAMILY OF CANADA WORLD CENTER
Jerusalem, Israel

AISH PROGRAMS
Aish.com
Aishaudio.com
Aish on Campus
Aish Productions
Discovery Production
EYAHT
Essentials
Executive Learning Center
Hasbara Fellowships
HonestReporting
Jerusalem Fellowships
Jerusalem Partners
JEWEL
Jewish Family Institute
Project Chazon
Russian Program
SpeedDating®
Spanish Division
The Jerusalem Fund
Yeshivat Aish HaTorah

AISH BRANCHES
Ashdod, Israel
Baltimore
Bat Yam, Israel
Birmingham, UK
Boston
Cleveland
Denver
Detroit
Essex, UK
Jerusalem, Israel
Johannesburg, SA
Kiev, Ukraine
Las Vegas
Livingston, NJ
London
Los Angeles
Manchester, UK
Melbourne, Australia
New York
Petach Tikva, Israel
Philadelphia
Santiago, Chile
Sao Paulo, Brazil
Scottsdale, AZ
Seattle
South Florida
St. Louis
Toronto
Washington, DC
Winnipeg, CA

July 7, 2008

To Whom It may Concern:

Aish HaTorah has successfully dealt with many young men who when they initially came to our yeshiva identified themselves as homosexuals. Our approach is to treat every Jew with the greatest amount of respect and dignity, despite the fact that they were living lifestyles antithetical to Torah.

Only G-d understands the personal situations of all individuals, and therefore, only G-d can properly evaluate the righteousness of each individual Jew. The Torah teaches us what is right and wrong, but that does not give us the license to be able to judge the worth of any individual in G-d's eyes. That is something only G-d can do.

The Gemara tells us that a person does not transgress unless a spirit of foolishness enters into him. This is the root cause for someone transgressing Shabbos and this is also the root cause for homosexuality. Therefore, homosexuality can be dealt with in the same way as any other behavior which is inconsistent with Torah.

Our sages teach us that the soul of an individual is a חלק אלוקי ממעל (literally a portion of G-d on high). G-d has made known, through the Torah, His views on appropriate sexual activity. The soul of every individual, as literally a piece of G-d, cannot have a view which differs from its true source, namely G-d Himself.

The soul of every individual realizes that homosexual behavior is not what it truly seeks, because this is a behavior which is at odds with what the soul really seeks closeness to its creator. It is the Yetzer Hara which desires inappropriate activity, and it is our mistake to identify the Yetzer Hara as who we are, because we are in actuality the soul.

This is the basis of Teshuva and correcting all inappropriate behavior. Through understanding who we really are, we come to understand what we seek. In today's world, the left, combined with the media, have waged an all-out war to convince the public that homosexual desires are natural and an expression of a person's true self. This is antithetical with Torah.

JONAH has been at the forefront working with young Jewish men to help them properly understand the roots of their homosexuality and do Teshuva through realizing that these activities do not truly represent their true selves.

I commend Mr. Goldberg and his staff at JONAH for waging this fight and the services they provide for the many individuals looking for help for this particular struggle.

Sincerely,

Rabbi Noach Weinberg

יחיאל מיכל טווערסקי
באאמו"ר הרה"צ כמוהר"ר יעקב ישראל זצללה"ה מהאָרנאָסטייפּאָל

Rabbi Michel Twerski
ב"ה

6 Menachem Av 5768
Aug 7, 2008

Dear Arthur, נ"י

It is clear from what I have read in your wonderful manuscript, that you have authored an extraordinarily compelling and literate analysis of SSA and its treatment modalities. In publishing this work you prove yourself a worthy heir to the mantle of the patriarch Abraham, who dared to speak the truth in a generation inflamed with idolatry and its twisted presentations of morality. I stand in awe of the courage manifest in bringing <u>Light in the Closet: Torah, Homosexuality, and the Power to Change</u> to the American Jewish stage. Not only because you intrepidly bare the shameless deceit of the gay lobby in its reprehensible misrepresentation of the facts of gender confusion, but far more importantly, because you offer genuine hope to those struggling with gender identity issues. To the counseling professional and layperson alike, this well-balanced and thoroughly documented presentation opens doors of understanding and optimism in judging the merits of reparative therapy. <u>Light in the Closet</u>, in my humble estimation, is a work so important that it belongs on the desk and in the hands of every Rabbi, Rosh Yeshiva, therapist, social worker, school principal, parent and most critically every SSA sufferer aspiring to make himself whole. The merit of this work is indescribably great. May G-d bless you and your efforts with the greatest success.

With every good wish for Hatzlocha, I am

Sincerely yours,

Rabbi Michel Twerski

בס"ד

Rabbi Zev Leff
הרב זאב לף

Rabbi of Moshav Matityahu
Rosh HaYeshiva—Yeshiva Gedola Matityahu

מרא דאתרא מושב מתתיהו
ראש הישיבה—ישיבה גדולה מתתיהו

D.N. Modiin 71917 Tel: 08–976–1138 טל'   Fax: 08–976–5326 פקס'   ד.נ. מודיעין 71917

Dear Friends,

Although I cannot give a general all encompassing approbation to the book "Torah, Homosexuality, and the Power to Change" due to the many and varied sources quoted some of which I cannot endorse, I feel compelled to give Mr. Arthur Goldberg a hearty "yasher kochacha" for a truly outstanding work, that is a true kiddush Hashem. The underlying theme and message of the book is totally in keeping with a true Torah perspective on how the community and individuals must view and relate to the issue of homosexuality and to homosexuals themselves. I fully endorse the message the book conveys as succinctly enunciated on page 303 "We are not suggesting that society should welcome homosexual behavior, as political correctness increasingly demands. Rather we are suggesting that society acknowledge the true intent of Leviticus 18:22, which is that those who "go astray" need to, *and have the capacity to*, return to G-d's Law; and because homosexuals are our brothers and sisters (and sons and daughters!), and because we ourselves – meaning *heterosexual* society as a whole – are far from square with the Holiness Code, we owe them encouragement, moral support and a helping hand extended in humility and brotherhood." Likewise on page 572 -" It is vitally important that the Jewish community as a whole recognize that there is no conflict between the prohibitions of the Torah and healing homosexuality. On the contrary, just as Torah commands those who are wounded or ill to heal through *teshuvah*, medicine, and counseling, so are we all prohibited from hindering their recovery through hostility, rejection, and scorn. Nor can it be countenanced that so many leaders or our communities remain in ignorance of the realities of homosexual lifestyle or of the tools and opportunities for complete healing made available through Torah, *teshuvah*, and modern psychological science. Nor can we stand idly by when those who are afflicted with SSA and "led astray" by public misconceptions are taunted, humiliated, and ostracized in the name of Torah, religion, or conventional morality."

The breadth and scope of this work is truly magnificent and it deals with every conceivable angle of this very sensitive issue and leaves one with a clear well balanced Torah perspective.

I commend Mr. Goldberg for his valiant efforts in helping those in need to make these difficult changes in life orientation; for promoting true teshuva; and for engendering understanding, sensitivity, and genuine concern, in place of scorn, humiliation, and hostility. May Hashem grant Mr. Goldberg and his organization "Jonah" the ability to continue to provide this greatly needed succor to so many pained souls who have strayed and need to be aided in finding their way back to a healthy Torah oriented sexual lifestyle.

Sincerely,
With Torah blessings

Rabbi Zev Leff

DEDICATION

With profound thanks to Hashem
I humbly dedicate this book
to the Men and Women of JONAH
whose courage and tenacity in transforming their lives
inspired me with the courage and tenacity to complete it . . .

. . . and to Ben
without whom I never would have begun it.

CONTENTS

Preface & Acknowledgments..1

Chapter 1: **Introduction** 5

Chapter 2: **Struggling Against the Current:**
Two Case Histories 19
    Case 1: Jeff...20
        Discussion..26
    Case 2: "J"..27
        Discussion..31

Chapter 3: **Defining the Problem: Gay Activism**
Versus Torah Morality..47
    Understanding the Homosexual Activist Agendas:
        the Kirk & Madsen Manifesto...49
        A Brief Look at the Born Gay Theory............................59
    Carrying the Homosexual Agenda into the
        Public School Systems...67
        The Corrupting of School Libraries................................83
    State-Sanctioned Disinformation & Censorship......................88
    Suppression of Health-Related Information............................91
    Homosexual Disaffection with Gay Politics............................96
    The Sexualization of the Media and Society..........................98
    Sexual Permissiveness Incompatible with Torah Judaism...........100
        The Jewish Individual in Crisis......................................105
    Torah Sexuality is Fundamental to Jewish Spirituality
        and to the Morality of Civilized Nations....................109
    Consistency with G–d's Plan of Creation...............................111
        The Socialist Roots of Gay Anti-Religionism................118
    Absolute Individuality & the Culture of Narcissism...................120

Chapter 4: **What Causes Homosexuality?**......................................125
    Hetero-emotional Wounds...129
    Homo-emotional Wounds..130
    Social or Peer Wounds..133
    Sibling Wounds & Other Family Dynamics..........................135
    Body-Image Wounds..137
    Heredity..138
    Temperament...139
    Sexual Abuse..140

Chapter 4 (cont'd):
    Cultural Wounds..141
    Other Factors...141
    Gender Double-Bind..142

Chapter 5: **Torah & Talmud as Primary Sources**
    For Defining Sexual Morality.......................................145
    The Basic Texts of Judaism..145
    The Oral Torah...150
    Rabbinical Law...152
    Translating the Torah into English....................................155
    PaRDes: the Four Levels of Torah Interpretation...............158
    Modern-Day, Pro-Gay Distortions....................................162

Chapter 6: **The Sexual Behavioral Prohibitions of the Torah**.......175
    Generally: the Holiness Code...175
    Sexual Purity & Civilization...179
    Adultery & Sexual Promiscuity in Contemporary Society...........182
    Prostitution & Promiscuity...184
    Male Homosexuality..185
        What does *To'eivah* Really Mean?.............................191
        Why the Commandment not to Engage in Homosexuality
          is Addressed to Men..193
        Is Homosexual Fantasy Prohibited by the Torah?..........194
    Molech (Child Sacrifice)..202
    Intercourse During Menstruation......................................205
    Obscuring of Male-Female Differences.............................206
        The Psychology of Cross-Dressing..............................210
        A *Drosh* on Deuteronomy 22:5.................................213
    Incest..215
    Bestiality...217
        New-Age Bestiality Advocates....................................221
    Masturbation..230
        Homosexuality & Masturbation..................................231

Chapter 7: **Female Homosexuality**...234
    What the Torah Says...235
    The Oral Torah...235
    The Oral Tradition: the *Sifra*..239
        Analysis..240
    The Talmud, *Yevamot* 76a...242
        Analysis..243

Chapter 7 (cont'd):
What is the Meaning of *Mesolelot*?..244
    Rashi..244
    Rambam..245
        Analysis..246
    The *Shuchan Aruch* and the *Tur*.......................................248
Further Questions..249
    Is Lesbianism Punishable?..249
        Makat Mardut...250
        Does Absence of Punishment Mitigate The Offense?
        (How Prohibited is it?) 252
        Z'nut is not a Shibboleth!..254
Pro-Gay *Halachic* Sophistry..255

Chapter 8: Sexual Reassignment Surgery................................262
Does Jewish Law Permit SRS? 267
Attempts to Circumvent the *Halachah*.....................................269
How Effective is SRS? Does SRS Accomplish
    its Intended Purpose?..270
    Jewish Tradition Rejects the Claim that SRS Can Transform
        a Man into a Woman or a Woman into Man..................271
    The Scientific View of Gender Determination:
        Does it Work for *Halachah*?...274
        More Misplaced Reliance on a Fundamental Ruling.........276
How to Perform SRS on a Torah Prohibition: Analyzing
    the Conservative Law Committee's Approval of SRS..........278
The Reform Movement "Sanctifies" SRS!................................283
How "Beneficial" are SRS Procedures?.....................................284
    Medical Risks..287
    Psychological Risks...289
Why SRS Procedures are "Experimental"..................................289
Gender Dysphoria Responds Positively to Psychotherapy..........292
Four Noteworthy Cases...295
    Michael Danielle...295
    Alan Finch...295
    Sy Rogers & Jerry Leach...296
    Conclusion...298

Chapter 9: **Leviticus 18:22: What Does *To'eivah* Really Mean?**
  Homosexuality as a Reversible Transgression....................300
  The Power of Repentance is Unlimited................................301
  Teshuvah & the Purification of Sex: a Uniquely Jewish Concept...302
  Psychological & Social Impediments to *Teshuvah*...................305
  Rabbi Bar Kappara's Talmudic Insight....….........................306
    To'eivah Contains the Possibility of *Teshuvah*..................313
    Rabbi Bar Kappara's Interpretation of *To'eivah*
      is Validated by Clinical Studies Showing
        Sexual Orientation *CAN* be Changed....................314
    Personal Testimonials Support the Clinical Findings.............318
  To'eivah as a Clinical Term for "Help Me!"........................321
  GAP (Gender Affirming Processes) Builds on
    Bar Kappara's Insight..322

Chapter 10: **To'eivah as Alienation**......................................327
  Relating to the Self: Alienation from One's Essence................328
  Alienation Between the Individual and the Community............336
    Gay & Lesbian Synagogues: an Inappropriate Response
      to Non-Acceptance by the Community.......................348
  Alienation Between the Individual & G–d……. …............353
    Sexual Idolatry & Alienation from G–d...........................359
      Envy...…......367
      An Aside on Sexual Addiction.................................368
      Sexual Politics as Idolatry.......................................370
  From Idolatry to G–d: the Way Back................................372

Chapter 11: **Teshuvah, or Return to Innocence:**
  the Jewish Process of Return, Rebirth & Healing.................376
  What is *Teshuvah?*..376
  Defining Sin..384
    Chet..388
    Aveirah..389
    Peshah...389
    Avón...389
  How Different Categories of Sin Relate to Homosexuality.........390
    Teshuvah does not Differentiate Among Categories of Sin......392
    Is There *Teshuvah* for *To'eivos?*.................................393
  Sin as Pathology...394
  Sin and Mourning...397
  Teshuvah Presupposes Freedom of Choice........................400
  How Homosexual Politics Obstructs Freedom of Choice...........405

Chapter 11 (cont'd):
Victims of Homosexual Politics Speak Out.........................413
What to Do?...418
Overcoming Homosexuality: Escalator to a New Level
  of Spiritual Awareness and Accomplishment.......................421
  Shame..425
  Recidivism..427
The *Oness* Argument: Homosexual by "Duress"......................433
  Introduction..433
  Why *Oness* Cannot Justify Homosexuality.........................434
  Some Unexpected Ramifications of the *Oness* Argument......440
G–d's Role in the Struggle to Overcome SSA.........................442

Chapter 12: "Doing *Teshuvah*" and Healing from SSA: Parallel Processes..446
Teshuvah & Refuah..446
Kapparah & Taharah..448
  Purification through Understanding..................................451
The Reparative Drive..453
Internalizing What We Learn about Ourselves........................455
Repentance of Redemption...456

Chapter 13: *Teshuvah* & Healing: Spiritual Elevation & Sexual Transformation Proceeding in Lock-Step..................458
The Book of Jonah: a Paradigm for *Teshuvah* and Healing.........460
Step 1: Regret (*Charatah*)..463
Step 2: Abandonment (*Azivah*)...467
  Abandonment through Prayer: Benefits & Limitations..........472
Step 3: Confession (*Viduy*)..474
  Confession: Catalyst for Healing......................................476
    Physical-Emotional Release as Form of Confession..........479
    "Sharing" as a Form of Confession...............................481
    Lack of Sincerity Voids the Confession.........................482
    Conflicted Confession: Confession as Prayer..................482
Step 4: Resolve (*Kabbalah*)..486
"How Long does it Take?" The Value of Time.......................487
Overcoming the Shadow Self...488
Why Band-Aid Marriages Can't Cure Homosexuality...............489
The Need for a Supportive Environment...............................492
The Four Masculine Relationships......................................494
  1. The Mentor..495
  2. The Fellow Struggler..495

Chapter 13 (cont'd):
    3. The Straight Friend who Knows..496
    4. The Straight Friend who Doesn't Know......................................498
    The Four Friends and *Teshuvah*..500

Chapter 14: **Homosexuals, "Marriage," & the Family**....................501
  Background 501
  Why Gay "Marriage" is No Marriage..507
    Duration does not a Marriage Make..511
    Out of the Closet and into the Clinic...513
  A Sober Look at "Stability" and "Duration"...................................515
  The Role of "Family" in Gay Politics..519
  Homosexual Parenting...522

Chapter 15: **What the Strugglers Have to Say: Testimonials**..........532
  Ben Newman: a Natural Leader of Men
    Steps into his Masculine Power..532
  Josh L.: One Man Shares his Thoughts
    as he Struggles Through the Process of Change.........................540
  Don M.: One Man's Escape from Personal *Gehennom* (Hell).......551
  Marshall S.: a Feminized Male Recovers
    his Gender Identity by Discovering Himself...............................556
  Daniel's & Scott's Testimony: Incorporating G–d
    into the Plan of Healing...562

Chapter 16: **Conclusion**..570

LIGHT IN THE CLOSET

Light is Torah – Megillah 16b
And Torah is Light – Proverbs 6:23

Preface & Acknowledgments

I wrote this book in order to show the emerging synthesis between traditional Judaism's view of homosexuality and the gender-affirming processes employed by the many mental health practitioners and faith-based organizations who help people affected by unwanted same-sex attractions ("SSA").

When I refer to gender-affirming processes, I am actually referring to several different psychological approaches in use within today's psychiatric community. These processes are designed to enable a gender-conflicted man or woman to develop an authentic, internalized sense of the physiological manhood or womanhood with which they were born. These various techniques include the pure psychoanalytic approach of Dr. Charles Socarides, among others, the more psychodynamic methods popularized by Dr. Joseph Nicolosi, the affective therapy approach favored by David Matheson, the integrative approach of which Dr. A. Dean Byrd has become a leading proponent, the strictly behavioral approach advocated by Dr. Jeffrey Robinson, the multi-modal treatment paradigm utilized by Dr. Norman Goldwasser, the comprehensive treatment planning model created by Richard Cohen, the religious or pastoral approach used by most faith-based ministries, and the life-coaching methodologies practiced by Rich Wyler, Alan Downing, Enrique Roman, Baxter Peffer, and Bruce

Gold.

Although each of these approaches tackles sexual reorientation through a different form of intervention and treatment, they share two critical points in common: (1) an empirically tested conviction that same-sex attraction and behavior are psychologically determined symptoms of other underlying conditions; and (2) a demonstrable track record of treatment success.

For its Judaic component, this text is based upon my own "lay" understanding of traditional Judaism. What I have learned from rabbinical scholars and spiritual leaders has been buttressed by my own independent research and thorough study of complex religious and psychological material, all in an effort to synthesize psychological and religious approaches to healing homosexuality.

As will be obvious from many of the basic premises set forth herein, my personal inclination is to accept Orthodox Judaism's views on sexuality. Nevertheless, I believe it is important to make the following disclaimer: Although I solicited and received guidance and comment from a number of Orthodox rabbis whose learning and wisdom are widely respected, I make no claim that the views I have expressed herein necessarily coincide in all respects with those of all the revered rabbinical authorities whose day-to-day judgments, responsa, and casual pronouncements guide the behavior and thinking of Orthodox Jewry worldwide. Several *rabbonim* critiqued the manuscript at various stages and offered valuable advice. I am grateful for their insights and their erudition, but the responsibility for what I have written here remains entirely my own.

Many lifelong influences, direct and indirect, theoretical and personal, were brought to bear on the writing of this book. I need to thank a number of mentors who helped educate me about SSA and provided me with the tools to help others: Richard Cohen of the International Healing Foundation, Libby Duryea of Chautauqua Alternatives, Alan Medinger of Regeneration, David Pruden of Evergreen International, JONAH facilitator Martin Pressman, Drs. Ben Kaufman, Joseph Nicolosi and Dean Byrd, all of NARTH, therapist David Matheson from the Center for Gender Affirming Processes in Jersey City, N.J., Father Donald Timone of Courage,

David Wanner of D.J. Wanner Ministries, Rich Wyler of People Can Change, Alan Downing and Enrique Roman of the JONAH Institute for Gender-Affirming Processes, and scores of others too numerous to name here, but certainly not forgotten. To all the other organizations engaged in this holy work, representing numerous faiths and denominations, thanks for being there. To Nava Rephun, a New York City therapist, thanks for introducing me to Mrs. Elaine Berk, my Co-Director at JONAH.

My father, Jack Geddy Goldberg, and mother, Ida R. Goldberg, would have been proud of my work. They are the ones who taught me the moral indignation and focus needed to oppose injustices such as that being inflicted upon those affected by unwanted SSA. Shortly before her death at age 90, my mother, evincing a motherly pride in her son's social conscience, specifically asked that I carry forth a Jewish program to help heal those afflicted with the homosexual condition. My older brother, Leonard M. Goldberg, who likewise internalized the example set by my parents, not only put up with my "rabble rousing," but has always supported and encouraged me in whatever cause I was engaged in at the time.

To my wife, Jane Elizabeth Gottlieb Goldberg, who has always been "right there" working alongside me, I cannot say "thank you" or "I love you" enough. Throughout our more than forty years of marriage, her careful attendance to the practical matters of daily living gave me the freedom to be active in ways which, with G–d's help, I hope have made a positive difference in people's lives. To my children, Ari Matthew and his wife Adina Leah, Shoshana Eve and her husband Andrew David Lee, Benjamin Saul, and Talia Akiva, and to my grandchildren, Zachary Jacob, Maya Eve, Simon Eli, Alexandra Isabel ("Ada"), Elizabeth Jada, Jared Elias, and those not yet born, all of whom I dearly love, I want to say that I hope and pray that my work will help in some small way to make the world a better and happier place for each of you to live and carry on the family tradition of helping others. To those of my friends who are struggling with SSA, the men and women of the support groups I facilitate and with whom I have been privileged to interact as they go through their healing process, thank you for teaching me so much about life. To our many fellow organizations, including the organizational members of PATH—Positive Alternatives to Homosexuality (www.pathinfo.org)—and their dedicated representatives, all selflessly striving to procure justice and assistance for those who are struggling with unwanted same-sex attractions, thank you for your support and encouragement.

To all those who generously gave of their time to review parts of the manuscript, provided scholarly guidance and invaluable advice, I thank you. These people include: my Co-Director Elaine Berk, Richard Carpenter, Richard Cohen, Rabbi David Shlomo, Rabbi Aharon Feldman, Dr. Janelle Hallman, Rabbi Joseph Y. Jacobson, Rabbi Wesley Kalmar, Rabbi Tuvia Laeb, Rabbi Leonard Levy, Rabbi Shlomo Marks, Konstantin Mascher, Alan Medinger, Dr. Allan Nahman, Dr. James Phelan, JONAH's Martin Pressman, Frank York, and Dr. Susan Shaw for her editorial assistance on the initial draft of the manuscript and for sensitizing me to the need for gender-neutral language.

To Rabbi David Shlomo, for his expert and sensitive analysis of complex issues of Jewish law; and to my editor and publisher, Sholem Gimpel, for his unwavering support, sure hand, creative ideas and organizational skill, my boundless gratitude.

I am also deeply indebted to JONAH's Martin Pressman and Elaine Berk, as well as to the many "strugglers" with whom I interact, for their constant encouragement to complete the task and get the manuscript into print. Lisa Greene, who typed and retyped innumerable drafts of this material, deserves credit for her patience and remarkable ability to understand my hieroglyphics. Finally, thanks to my friend Bill Driscoll: although happily living life as a gay man with no desire to change, Bill respects the principles of client determination, and therefore spent innumerable hours critiquing the manuscript and providing valuable insight from the point of view of a person not seeking change of sexual orientation.

To sum it all up, the help, encouragement, and insights I have received have been immeasurable. In spite of these gifts, I take full responsibility for any errors that may appear in this book.

Chapter 1:

Introduction.

We live in a time of accelerated social change. The shrinking of Planet Earth into a global village has been so rapid that civilization has lost its traditional bearings without settling on new ones. This has led, at least in the western hemisphere, to an unprecedented confusion of values, rationalized as a virtually all-permissive, "anything goes" social system founded on universal "tolerance."

If this moral relativism continues to be the lodestar of western society, our children and grandchildren may find themselves living in a world where long-cherished values of objective morality will no longer be "tolerated" by a society founded on a compulsory, acritical and indiscriminate "tolerance."

Once we throw away the compass of right and wrong bequeathed to us by ancient wisdom, we find almost everything to be subjective opinion—usually the result of a little self-indulgence and a good deal of creative rationalization. By contrast, the Jewish People have lived for well over three thousand years in accordance with a deeply rooted persuasion that morality is not some vague notion of living in a general state of rosy self-satisfaction, but a specific and intricately defined set of dos and don'ts (positive and negative *mitzvos* or "commandments") that regulate every possible aspect of public and private life. Fundamental to this world view is the recognition that over and above the common-sense reasons for these 613 Commandments there are reasons known only to the Creator of the universe, and that it is this Creator Who has ordained those Commandments for the benefit of humankind. This set of teachings, rules, and values is what defines the Jewish People, and it is known collectively as *Torah*. Its sources are the Five Books of Moses, the Twelve Books of the Prophets, the Hebrew Scriptures, the Talmud, and the rabbinical commentaries and legal compendia of our great Sages.

At the same time, there can be no doubt that the philosophy of tolerance has, by and large, made significant strides toward the definition, recognition and respecting of human and civil rights.

In this context of conflict and change, the subject of homosexuality has become an especially volatile one, particularly within the observant Jewish community. On the one hand, the gay rights movement has achieved an improved status of social, economic and political integration for male and female homosexuals, such that a great many of them no longer feel compelled to hide their sexual preferences or to live secret, fearful lives. On the other hand, the Torah, still a fundamental source for Christian moral practice, condemns the homosexual act as a *to'eivah*—an "abomination" to *Hashem* (G–d). What should an observant Jew (or, for that matter, an observant person of any other faith) do when he or she discovers that he/she, or his or her son or daughter identifies as gay? What should he or she think? How should he or she respond to questions such as: What does Judaism really say about homosexuality? Are people born homosexual? Can homosexuality be prevented or treated? Can one grow out of homosexuality? What are the causes of homosexuality? How should a synagogue respond to a new member who openly identifies him- or herself as "gay" or "lesbian" or "transsexual" or "questioning"? How should the subject be explained to children? Does Torah offer any helpful advice for a sincere and pious Jew who is struggling in secret and in anguish to overcome a forbidden sexual inclination?

The moral relativists, in league with the gay rights movement and the "politically correct", have done much to hide or misrepresent the answers, to obfuscate the issues, and, indeed, to smear traditional religion—especially Judaism—as hostile and discriminatory toward homosexuals. By doing so, they have not only fed the new antisemitism and antireligionism, but, with tragic irony, have placed many of their own in situations of unbearable ambivalence, conflict, suffering and mortal danger—by concealing the possibility of choice, of healing, and of transformation held out to them by our timeless Torah as well as by modern psychological advances. The gay activists have, in effect, turned off the light in the homosexual closet.

This book is meant to fill a void in the literature of the Jewish world. For the Jew seeking liberation from his/her homosexual fantasies and arousals, and even more for those gay or lesbian Jews struggling to free themselves from a lifestyle they know is inconsistent with their inner spiritual voices, the lack of available Torah-based resources is appalling. In fact, it is potentially catastrophic. Precious little has been written about the relevance of Torah to modern gender-affirming processes. It is critically important that the Jewish community as a whole be aware that—contrary to the conventional wisdom of the street and the campus!—gender-affirming processes have proven highly effective in transitioning persons affected with same-sex attraction ("SSA") into a stable and satisfying *hetero*sexuality. It is absolutely vital that all Jews, *B'nei Noach,* and other believers in genuine Torah values be fully informed of the powerful healing synergy that can be generated through integrating traditional Torah perspectives with the by now well-established theory and practice of sexual reorientation therapies.

For some nine years now, an organization called JONAH, Jews Offering New Alternatives to Homosexuality, has been working to achieve this vital goal. Developed by my Co-Director Elaine Silodor Berk and myself, JONAH offers outreach, counseling and referrals to gay, lesbian and sexually conflicted Jews—and their families—via a panoply of resources, including its website, www.jonahweb.org. The demand for our services has been overwhelming. Within the short span of our existence, and with a purely volunteer staff, we have grown into an international organization assisting countless individuals in many different countries. We strive to serve those struggling with SSA—them *and* their families—through a variety of support groups, both in person and via e-mail. We also maintain a growing body of information, bringing together the various resources a Jewish person is likely to need on his or her journey out of homosexuality. These resources also serve to re-educate the broader community to a truth long known but recently forgotten: that homosexuality is neither innate nor immutable. It is my fervent hope that this book will further contribute to the spreading of knowledge of the causes, nature, treatment, and *halachic* (Judaic-legal) implications of homosexuality, in a form that is easily accessible to both Jewish and non-Jewish, observant and non-observant readers.

It must be emphasized that a wealth of similarly motivated Christian-based material has been available for several years—thanks to the pioneering work of genuine heroes like Frank and Anita Worthen, Alan Medinger, Sy Rogers, Joe Dallas; and, in the secular realm, Richard Cohen, Richard Wyler, David Matheson, Regina Griggs, Estella Salvatierra, Drs. Joseph Nicolosi, Jeffrey Satinover, Ben Kaufman, Gerard van den Aardweg, and A. Dean Byrd, Christl von Holdt, the staff of Journey in Manhood, and the many others who have either treated or personally confronted and overcome "sexual conflictedness"—that miserable state of being in which one's arousals, fantasies, behavior or sexual identity conflict with one's deepest religious beliefs and values. Rather than succumb passively to the sexual mores of the period of the 1960s and onward, with its climate of sexual indulgence and experimentation, these brave souls sought help from their respective religious or cultural traditions and from whatever therapeutic models were then available. Starting in the late 1970s and early 1980s, they founded several organizations, both secular and Christian-based, to help those directly affected as well as their families and friends. For example, Exodus (an umbrella organization for Evangelicals and other Protestant ministries) was born in the mid-1970s, while Courage and EnCourage (the Catholic-based organizations founded by Father John F. Harvey) began in the early 1980s. Evergreen International, the Mormon faith-based organization, was formed in 1989 to assist members of the worldwide LDS Church deal with issues of same-sex attraction. In the secular realm, the National Association for Research and Therapy of Homosexuality (NARTH), the Inter-national Healing Foundation (IHF), Parents and Friends of Gays and Ex-Gays (PFOX), and People Can Change (PCC) also initiated ground-breaking healing strategies. Thus, when we organized JONAH a quarter-century after the earliest efforts of these pioneering organizations, we had several already-functioning models to work from.

On the other hand, we soon found it necessary, as a Jewish organization, to expand the scope of JONAH to deal with other issues of "sexual brokenness" besides homosexuality. The term "sexual brokenness" ("SB") can be conveniently defined as a condition in which a person's sexual behaviors, desires or fantasies are inconsistent with the Torah's treatment of sex as pure, holy, and the private and exclusive domain of marriage between man and woman. Professor Theresa Lantini lists 22 categories of sexual brokenness. They are: lust/fantasy, compulsive masturbation, pornography, voyeurism, exhibitionism, verbal sex, fetishism, premarital sex, adultery, promiscuity, emotional dependency, prostitution, rape, sexual abuse, pedophilia, pederasty, incest, bestiality, transvestitism, trans-sexuality, homosexuality, and addictive or anonymous sex.[1] A twenty-third category, expressly prohibited to Jews, is coitus with a menstruating woman. Behind our decision to include such cases within the purview of JONAH is our belief, supported by ancient teachings and empirical experience, that no Jew who is affected by such a condition can achieve the happiness, serenity and productive life that Torah envisions. The same can be said, in more general terms, for any person whose spiritual dimension is not completely dried up or dead. On the contrary, by ignoring such issues, affected persons condemn themselves to lives of often unbearable inner conflict—

---

1. Theresa Lantini, *One by One Pastoral Care Guide*, Pittsford: One By One (1999), 8-10.

even despite the fact that some of these behaviors are more naturally shielded from public discovery than others. The emotional pain of these individuals is not less deserving of concern and counsel. And who, besides a *tzaddik* (a wholly righteous person), can claim to be completely "unbroken," what with today's mass media increasingly enlisted in the service of sexual promiscuity?

We chose the name JONAH because we recognized parallels between the organization's work and the recalcitrant Prophet. Jonah, of course, was the Prophet commanded by G–d to prophesy to the people of Nineveh: Repent or be destroyed. But so enmeshed in guilt and sin were the people of Nineveh that Jonah could not bear to be the instrument of their salvation. In the end, however, he does prophesy, and they do repent. Read publicly in the Synagogue every Yom Kippur (Day of Atonement), the Book of Jonah stands for the greatness of G–d's mercy and love for all humankind (Nineveh was not a Jewish city!). Conversely, it also shows us the power of *teshuvah* (repentance, or returning to G–d) and reminds us that the capacity for *teshuvah* is to be found everywhere among men and women.

We also chose JONAH because we saw in the name an acronym for "Jews Offering New Alternatives to Homosexuality"—the full name of our organization. We chose these words to publicize the fact that new and refined therapies are available to those genuinely seeking to overcome one of the most common forms of sexual brokenness, that is, a sexual inclination toward one's own sex. The existence of these therapies needs to be publicized, because that information has not been freely available.

The gay rights movement has changed the landscape of our social, economic, religious, educational and family systems. "Diversity training," "sex education" (particularly in our school systems), and "anti-harassment" are new code words that have revolutionized American and other societies. No longer is marriage between a man and a woman upheld as the universal norm. Same-sex unions and homosexual behavior have come into our homes through the media (especially television), the entertainment industry, the schools, scientific organizations, and in many cases, through religious congregations of various denominations. Richard Cohen's *Coming out Straight*—a landmark book by a former gay activist insider who successfully grew from gay to straight—helps us understand "the hidden agenda, strategies, and goals of the gay rights movement" of which he was a part.[2] Because he found it so difficult to explain himself to therapists who, in his words, "didn't have a clue," Cohen embarked on a course that led him to become a leading sexual reorientation psychotherapist. In this capacity he facilitated the healing of numerous men and women, adults and adolescents, empowering them to affirm the gender of their birth.

By using the façade of "tolerance" or "civil rights" or the ruse of an alleged "scientific proof" defining homosexuality as "innate" and/or "immutable," gay activists have—particularly since the 1970s—inundated western society with propaganda carefully designed to convince us (contrary to the weight of clinical evidence) that homosexuality is simply an alternative lifestyle that must be accepted because it is genetically predetermined. Hence, the argument goes, homosexuality is immutable and therefore entitled to the same degree and kind of protection as racial and religious diversity.

Such propaganda, though praiseworthy for its success in curtailing centuries of deplorable persecution of and discrimination against homosexual men and women, has had other, equally dramatic effects—and very harmful ones—such as the vilification of religious and family life and other traditional values, the weakening of the marital bond as the foundation of society, and the deliberate corruption of young children via the introduction of gay-assertive sex education into the public school system (*see* Chapter Three).

One of the favorite psychological weapons adopted by the gay rights movement has been the use of the word "homophobic" to disparage and intimidate anyone who has a principled disagreement with the philosophy and objectives of gay activism.

---

2. Richard Cohen, *Coming Out Straight,* Winchester: Oakhill Press (2000), p. 228.

Semantically, of course, "Homophobia," should mean nothing more than an *irrational* fear of homosexuality and homosexuals. Yet the word has been used—with far-reaching consequences—by pro-gay advocates to label any man or woman conflicted over his or her SSA,[3] as well as any member of the public who has the temerity to disagree with them.

Such political usurpation of professional prestige and authority is unfortunately not exceptional. In a recent book-length critique of the mental health professions, two eminent psychologists decry the erosion of the patient-care ethic and well-established standards of scientific research by special interest groups promoting political agendas.[4] In their blistering exposé, Rogers H. Wright, founding president of the Council for the Advancement of the Psychological Professions and Sciences (CAPPS), and Nicholas A. Cummings, past president of the American Psychological Association (APA), expressly accuse gay groups within the mental health professions of insistently pressuring the APA to adopt ethical standards that limit the therapist's ability to treat SSA; to abrogate the patient's right of self-determination—especially the right of the client to determine his or her own therapeutic goals. The authors detail how political correctness has effectively altered the treatment process, redefined the parameters of permissible practice, and replaced the moral conscience of the therapist with a socially mandated barometer of "instant morality." (21)

As will be seen in Chapter Three, the success of this massive and far-reaching campaign of political correctness can be attributed to an unabashed and bluntly written homosexual manifesto which set forth a "predetermined goal of engineering a social-sexual revolution in America," and laid heavy emphasis on "strategies

---

3. *See* Case No. 2 in Chapter Two.

4. "[Gay groups within the APA] deny the reality of data demonstrating that psychotherapy can be effective in changing sexual preferences in patients who have a desire to do so." Rogers H. Wright & Nicholas A. Cummings, *Destructive Trends in Mental Health: The Well-Intentioned Path to Harm*, New York: Routledge (2005), p. xxx.

calculated to undermine the social standing of traditional religion."[5] Because of its central place in western religious tradition, Judaism has been particularly vulnerable to these attacks. Torah Judaism and other Torah-derived moral systems now stand accused, in most liberal and progressive circles, of hostile discrimination against gay men and women.

Whether out of malice or ignorance, gay propagandists have constructed an elaborate case against Judaism and its religious progeny based on the prohibitory Commandment of Leviticus 18:22—

You shall not lie with mankind as with womankind. It is an abomination.

—blatantly misconstrued by them as condemning individuals with homosexual inclinations, rather than the actual practice of homosexuality. In contrast to the English "abomination," however, the Hebrew word of the Torah has a deeper connotation of "going or being led astray" which is untranslatable in any other language; and straying implies the possibility—indeed the necessity—of *teshuvah*, of returning to the path of Torah and the Commandments.

The Torah (*i.e.*, the Five Books of Moses) and the Talmud (the Oral Law) mandate corrective action for all those whose sexual desires have led them astray, whether it be by SSA or any other form of sexual brokenness. Such corrective action can be, and has been, accomplished—and with a rate of success that is much too high to ignore—through a guided process involving professional counseling, self-discovery and a combination of gradual spiritual and behavioral self-adjustments characteristic of *teshuvah*. Thus, it is especially incumbent upon rabbinical authorities, Jewish community leaders and teachers to sensitize themselves to the issues, and to research and make available to the broader Jewish

---

5. Paul E. Rondeau, "Selling Homosexuality to America," *Regent University Law Review,* Vol. 14, No. 2 (2002), p. 443.

community a quality network of therapy, education, and support. Such an approach can offer those struggling with SSA and other types of sexual brokenness a unique and precious opportunity to restore and heal the pure souls with which they were endowed by G–d. When this is achieved, G–d's image can once again shine forth as an aspect of our sexuality.

How is this brought about? JONAH'S approach can be outlined as follows:

(1) Explore the powerful pathways to *teshuvah* taught by traditional and mystical Jewish sources;

(2) Combine these teachings with secular counseling (often called GAP for "gender-affirming processes"[6]) designed to help individuals identify and understand the missing pieces in their gender development; and

(3) Empower those individuals to choose wisely among a selection of social and practical activities specially tailored to help them fill in those empty developmental spaces and to begin taking care of long unfulfilled emotional needs.

There is an awesome similarity between *teshuvah* and the modalities of GAP. *Teshuvah* involves two levels of separation: first from the transgression itself and then from the pathways leading to transgression. GAP involves, first, cessation of the homosexual activity and, second, separation from the pathways leading to the activity. It accomplishes this separation by helping the client fulfill certain long-neglected emotional needs— deficiencies for which the inappropriate homoerotic desires are

---

6. Several names have been coined to describe this process, among them gender-affirming psychotherapy, reparative therapy, transition therapy, reorientation therapy, conversion therapy, *etc.* Regardless of the names used and the stylistic differences which they may entail, numerous individuals have reaped enormous benefit from participating in them.

only a desperate substitute. Indeed, as we shall see, in the vast majority of cases, homosexuality is a developmental adaptation caused by a number of identifiable influences working over time to create a gender-identity deficiency. There are various ways in which the process can begin, but it usually starts in very early childhood, when a boy, for example, owing to perceived rejection by his father and/or his male peers, does not break from the feminine world in which he was initially raised, and erects defensive barriers to the pain of that rejection by either detaching from or never entering the masculine world. This process may begin as early as age two or three.

While GAP evolved through clinical observation and practice, *teshuvah* is an actual *mitzvah* (commandment), derived from the Commandment to *love the L–rd your G–d with all your heart, with all your soul, and with all your might.* (Deut. 6:5-9) More precisely, *teshuvah* is a Torah-mandated process of introspection and self-correction whose purpose is to direct the individual toward a stronger, closer and deeper connectedness with *Hashem* (G–d)—a process which "takes place in the deepest recesses of the human mind and psyche."[7] The ability to perform *teshuvah* is innate within the soul of every Jew, but as a result of neglect and abuse, it often needs to be learned anew. And it *can* be learned, through study, through practice, and through becoming emotionally aware of what it entails.

In this respect, strugglers with SSA and sexual brokenness—even those who were born and raised in strictly observant families and have studied Torah and Talmud since childhood—can learn from *ba'alei teshuvah,* returnees to Jewish observance: repentance for yesterday's "strayings," combined with positive, corrective action toward a better tomorrow, in a supportive community environment, generates the inner power required to break even the most addictive of habits.

This means that a supportive community is an indispensable

---

7. Rabbi Pinchas H. Peli, *On Repentance: the Thoughts and Discourses of Rabbi Joseph Dov Soloveitchik,* Northvale: Jason Aronson (1996), p. 9.

part of the healing equation. To be wholly successful, the individual process of *teshuvah* must take place within a community that is educationally and psychologically equipped to support the efforts of an individual who has not yet attained the level of complete re-adaptation. This book is thus intended to serve a dual purpose: (1) to give hope and direction to strugglers who are still thrashing around in a closet of confusion and despair; and (2) to educate the Jewish community at large to a better understanding of the issues, and to an awareness of the great need for their guidance and moral support.

Unfortunately, the overwhelming majority of all that has been written about homosexuality (and an immense amount of material it is!) has been written about *male* homosexuality. Significantly less material is available about lesbianism. Thus, within this text, most of the examples cited are directed toward masculine issues. Nevertheless, Chapter Seven does contain a fairly in-depth introduction to the *halachic* issues raised by female homosexuality. It is an important discussion that should be of interest to female and male strugglers alike. To women readers, I apologize for the paucity of women-oriented research materials. Wherever appropriate, I have tried to include both sexes.

A word about how I came into this unusual line of work. Several years ago, I met an amazing person from Hoboken, New Jersey, who claimed he had recovered from several forms of sexual brokenness, including homosexuality, lust/fantasy, pedophilia, and addictive or anonymous sex. As a social liberal adhering to the politically correct view that people with these issues were "born that way," I was amazed to learn about his change and about the faith-based ministries that had guided him through this healing process. He gave me a book by a Jewish psychiatrist, Dr. Jeffrey Satinover, entitled *Homosexuality and the Politics of Truth*, published by Baker Books (1996). This remarkable book opened my eyes to many of the peripheral issues in orbit around a topic I knew very little about. Intrigued, I began to search out books written by "ex-gays" as well as by members of NARTH (National Association for Research and Therapy of Homosexuality), many of whom you will find quoted within the main part of this study. As I read this body of material and associated it mentally with the various gay and lesbian individuals of my personal acquaintance, I recognized several characteristics shared in common by all of them. I also realized that the vast majority of the general public, of practicing therapists, and even of homosexuals themselves, were unaware of the large quantity of available resources on the causes of and treatments for SSA. The more I read, the more I realized how much I needed to reactivate my own slumbering spirit of social activism, which had, until the not too distant past, led me to adopt any number of idealistic causes.

In fact, most of my adult life had been spent fighting for the underdog. In college, during the 1960s, I had organized and participated in numerous civil rights organizations and activities including sit-ins, freedom rides, and sundry other acts of protest. I was actually hanged in effigy on my college campus for advocating civil rights for Black Americans. In the 1970s, I became involved in the struggle to secure equal access to housing for all Americans. I co-founded the National Leased Housing Association (NLHA), a major advocacy group for low-income housing. In the 1980s, my attention shifted to the Jewish and other Refuseniks seeking to escape from the oppressive, totalitarian regime of the Soviets. In response to their plight, I organized the Committee for the Absorption of Soviet Emigrees (CASE) and the CASE Museum of Russian Contemporary Art.

On the threshold of the 21st Century, I realized that another group of individuals—men and women dealing, at one level or another, with the challenge of SSA were suffering an incredible injustice in that they were commonly being denied some very basic freedoms. Among them:

(1) the right to receive, without interference from others, life-giving information about the existence and effectiveness of various gender-reaffirming methods and therapies;

(2) the right to seek, unimpeded, treatment for sexual disorientation; and

(3) the right freely to choose to change their sexual orientation so as to match their physiological gender.

Such interference with fundamental rights offends the dignity and humanity of these men and women. Isolated and alone, unaware that help, healing and support are within reach, many of these strugglers do not know which way to turn. They are told by the gay activists, "You can't change;" by ultra-conservatives, "You are loathsome;" and by the majority of psychologists and psychiatrists, "Accept your gay feelings and act upon them—even though this might be in conflict with your internal values."

Such attitudes are not merely wrong. They are contemptible, immoral, irresponsible, and potentially lethal.

Chapter 2:

Struggling Against the Current:
Two Case Histories.

Years of insidious lobbying and disinformation by the gay rights movement have helped create a social climate that is increasingly unhealthy—in fact downright dangerous—for homosexuals in general, and in particular for those who are uncomfortable with their homosexual fantasies or behavior, or who are uncertain about their sexual orientation. In later chapters we shall examine the severe risks to physical and mental health associated with the gay lifestyle. At this point, however, we present two case histories to illustrate how the "normalization" of homosexuality, by interfering with patient's rights and freedom of choice in regard to sexual therapy, can give rise to situations that, on the individual human level, are the very opposite of what the movement claims it is working to achieve.

In Case No. 1, we meet a young man whose ardent desire to leave the gay "scene" is defeated—with tragic consequences—when his gay companions ridicule his desperate attempt to learn about gender-affirmative processes. In Case No. 2, a young boy who is clearly uncomfortable with his SSA is denied the option of changing sexual orientation, only to be treated for "internalized homophobia" by his gay-affirmative psychiatrist—with very questionable results.

Case 1: Jeff.

A desperate young homosexual dies of a drug overdose after his gay "friends" ridicule him for considering a program of gender affirmation or reparative therapy under JONAH's guidance.

A few years ago, I responded to a phone inquiry from a young man who identified himself as Jeff, age 20. Jeff described his attempts to alleviate his recurrent depressive episodes by engaging in sex with other men, often on a purely anonymous and impersonal basis. These sexual exploits gave him a transient endorphin high that left him feeling empty, used, and more depressed than before. Intellectually, Jeff recognized how futile and self-degrading his conduct was. He understood that most of his partners saw him as a mere sex object. He found it humiliating when the men in the gay bar referred to him as "fresh chicken meat" or "the boy toy." Nevertheless, his unbearable loneliness kept calling him back for more. Using sex with other men to fill an agonizing void in his life, Jeff found himself locked into a pattern he despised, yet didn't know how to break out of. He sounded desperate.

Jeff's story was not unusual. I had heard many similar stories as the first responder to JONAH's hotline. Jeff had been sexually active with men since he was a fifteen-year old sophomore in a Sephardic Jewish day school. His first sexual experience was mutual masturbation with a male classmate who had initially approached him with an offer of friendship. Because he had always felt uneasy around boys his own age, Jeff initially welcomed his friend's interest. He actually thought that such sexual interaction was part of what friendship was all about.

Jeff wanted me to know that he had "always felt different" from most other boys. In grammar school, he had been smaller and weaker than the others. After puberty, he perceived the lack of hair growth on his face and body as setting him apart.

Jeff's father was a hard-working immigrant from the Middle East who worked tirelessly to earn a living for his large family. Although he recognized that his father occasionally reached out to him, he had a hard time meeting his father's academic expectations, and never felt as comfortable with Dad as he did with Mom or his several sisters.

Because of his religious upbringing, Jeff grew more and more conflicted about his sexual behavior, until finally, during his 17th year, he sought guidance from his *Rosh Yeshivah* (literally, "Head of the *Yeshivah*") or school principal. The *Rosh*, a rabbi of considerable learning and authority, responded with a moralistic lecture: Jeff was violating a clear Torah prohibition by indulging in an activity considered abominable by G–d. Moreover, since any pre-marital sex was forbidden, it was doubly wrong to engage in sex with another man. Furthermore, continued the rabbi, by engaging in mutual masturbation, he was "spilling seed" (another Torah prohibition) and thus destroying a potential human life.

This conversation only confirmed what Jeff had already suspected—based, as he himself told me, on his (erroneous) understanding of the Hebrew word *to'eivah* ("abomination") in Leviticus 18:22: he was an abominable person, and G–d was punishing him by consigning him to a living hell.

Shaken by his meeting with the *Rosh Yeshivah,* Jeff promptly withdrew from the sexual liaison, but resumed the relationship after an abstinence of only a month or two. Guilt ridden, yet unable to desist, he sought guidance once again, this time not from a rabbi but from his high-school counselor—a licensed social worker with a Master's Degree. The counselor took an entirely different approach: Jeff was being overly harsh on himself; he needed to understand that he was born this way, and that by accepting himself as "gay," he would come to realize that G–d created certain men and women like him as "special people" with unique challenges.

Soothed by these reassurances, Jeff resumed the liaison in the belief that he need no longer feel guilty. Yet the conflict persisted, and the sexual activity left him emotionally "torn up" and unhappy with himself.

Subsequently, when Jeff learned that his friend was "doing other guys," they had a falling out. However, the very next Shabbos, at the *mikveh* (ritual bath), he met an older man who offered him his friendship. After Shabbos was over, Jeff's new "friend" took him to a gay bar in Brooklyn. A new, young face in this milieu, Jeff was solicited by many and enjoyed the attention. There he met a young man (a boy in his twenties) with whom he engaged in his first anal intercourse. Thereafter, this gay bar became Jeff's *Motzoei Shabbos* (Saturday-night) hang-out, and Jeff became part of Brooklyn's underground "gay crowd."

Jeff's induction into the gay *demimonde* did nothing to alleviate his internal conflict. On the contrary, by the time he called us, he was in a "double bind," and desperate to find a way out.

Jeff learned about us through an article he read in an Orthodox newspaper—*Jewish Voice and Opinion*—that explained how JONAH works with men and women conflicted about their sexuality, providing resources for those seeking to change their sexual orientation. Jeff had never heard of such a process, nor would he ever have learned about it in his gay hangout or in the Sephardic community in which he lived. Incredulous, but at his wits' end, Jeff was willing to try anything.

After I had calmed him down a bit, I told him in no uncertain terms that, from all I had been taught, Leviticus 18:22 spoke to his behavior, not to him as a person. I referred him to the Talmudic elucidation of that Biblical verse, deriving the word *to'eivah* from the Hebrew words *to'ei attah bah*, meaning "you have strayed, or been led astray, in it."[1] I suggested to him that he had actually been led astray—first by his *Rosh's* lack of understanding and compassion for his plight, and then by his counselor's gross misconceptions about homosexuality. Most important of all, I explained how his own unfilled emotional needs for male

---

1. Talmud, *Nedarim* 51a.

bonding—legitimate needs inherent in every normal male child—could have led him down the path to a kind of substituted fulfilment via this unwanted sexual activity.

I went on to outline what psychological research had discovered about homosexuality: that "homosexual" men are born inherently *heterosexual,* that their homosexuality is the result of some developmental problem which, however deeply rooted, can be resolved through the resumption of their psycho-social and psycho-sexual growth. I assured him that this reprise of emotional development can be achieved through a binary program of guided *teshuvah* (a Hebrew word meaning a "return" or a "turning," but often translated simplistically as "repentance") in combination with a program of specialized psychotherapy and group support.

I told Jeff of the hundreds of men and women known to me personally, of the thousands more comprising the membership of "ex-gay" organizations, and of the countless others known to psychological research, who were able to grow out of their SSA with the help of such spiritual and psychological guidance. I explained to him how this hybrid therapy enabled SSA strugglers to confront their underlying emotional problems holistically—that is, on four distinct but interrelated levels: cognitive (head), emotional (heart), experiential (body), and spiritual (soul)—thus ensuring that the transformation, when completed, is integral and all-pervasive, affecting every aspect of the subject's personality.

Calmer now, Jeff seemed genuinely interested in my exposition, interjecting several times that what I was saying made sense to him. In response to my questions, Jeff spoke freely about his childhood and adolescence. His story presented a very familiar pattern. I was able to show him how his homosexuality was very likely determined by a confluence of factors including (1) his perceived early rejection by his father; (2) his compensatory excessive attachment to his mother; (3) his hypersensitivity and resultant rejection by his peers; (4) his poor physical self-image (feeling too short and fat), derived from and contributing to his feelings of inferiority and inadequacy; and (6) his having been sexually abused by an older boy during pre-adolescence. I explained to him in particular how his feelings of isolation and alienation from his peers could have led to an intense envy of other boys and how this envy can become eroticized and sexualized with the onset of puberty.

Jeff was astounded. How could I have possibly known so much about him? Was I psychic? I explained to him that I had worked over the past several years with dozens of men in analogous circumstances, and had verified for myself what has long been known to others in the field: men who are sexually attracted to other men often fit a recognizable profile. The real question was whether Jeff wanted to change his sexual orientation. If so, I was ready to provide him with a list of resources he would need to accomplish this. Jeff replied with a resounding yes, pleading for the "silver bullet" that would liberate him from the agony that had plagued him for years. I cautioned him that there were no "silver bullets," and that just as his homosexuality had developed out of a conjunction of influences working over time, so would he need time to unlearn the behaviors he had acquired—time to grow into his authentic masculine self.

As our dialogue progressed, I emphasized that the first and most important key to change was motivation: the desire to change must either consciously or unconsciously outweigh the perceived "benefits" of pursuing the homosexual practices. In other words, in order to change his behavior, Jeff would first have to be clear *both* about what satisfaction that behavior was giving him *and* what it was costing him. Only then could he make a meaningful decision to change.[2] "Being clear about the satisfaction" meant understanding the original, unfulfilled needs for which the substituted behavior was striving to compensate, thereby enabling Jeff to engage the cognitive, emotional, behavioral and spiritual aspects of healing.

Intrigued, the young man wanted to know more. I referred him to several websites, including our own. I reeled off a list of suggested reading—books and articles by men who had

---

2. *See* Andrew Weil, M.D., *8 Weeks to Optimum Health*, New York: Fawcett Columbine / Ballantine (1997), p. 9.

successfully left the gay lifestyle, or by therapists who had successfully treated people with unwanted SSA. I told him that whenever he felt ready, he would be welcome to join our group support meetings as well as our Internet Listserv. Finally, I recommended several therapists whose methods and abilities I respected and trusted. After taking down his contact information, I asked him to stay in touch and keep me informed about his progress.

As our phone conversation drew to a close, Jeff seemed excited about all this new information. He told me that this was the first time he had ever heard those issues discussed in a straightforward, logical fashion. It all made sense to him, but everything I had told him was totally contrary to what his social milieu and the media had taught him. My "counter-cultural" message had given him a real sense of hope—an emotion he had not felt in several years.

About two or three weeks later, Jeff called again. He sounded more depressed than the first time, and I told him so. He concurred, and proceeded to repeat some of the conversations he had had in the interim at his favorite Saturday night hangout. In a word, Jeff's "friends" had ridiculed the whole concept of reparative therapy, calling it "snake-oil science" and cautioning him not to be taken in by the so-called "religious right." They had tried to convince Jeff that being gay was like being Black or being born with blue eyes. Gayness was something that couldn't be changed. They had sneered at his efforts to share the new information he had gleaned from our talk and from the books and websites to which I had steered him. In short, having failed to arouse the only support system he had ever known to an interest in his new project, Jeff felt more confused than ever. Distraught and dismayed at their complete lack of respect for our program, he now saw no escape from his misery. I implored him to speak with some of our men who were well on the road to recovery. I gave him their phone numbers and made him promise to call them. I pleaded with him to contact one of the therapists I had recommended. Finally, I urged him to get immediate help for his depression.

Generally, when I give these references to an individual, the people to whom I refer that individual contact me to let me know that they have heard from the person I have sent them. When a week or two had passed without news from or about Jeff, I became very concerned. I started to make inquiries. Subsequently, through our network in the Brooklyn Community where Jeff resided, I learned that this young man had died of a drug overdose. Apparently, Jeff accomplished this tragedy shortly after a sexual encounter with a man about fifteen years older than himself.

Discussion.

What happened here? Clearly, Jeff didn't want to be gay, but, like so many others, he had been thoroughly brainwashed into believing that there was no way to change. Grasping at straws, he contacted JONAH, and to his amazement, discovered that the straw might actually turn out to be a life raft. Incongruously, instead of immediately following up with JONAH's leads and recommendations (such as meeting with some of JONAH's "success stories"), he first ran to his favorite gay bar to seek the approval of his crowd. Why? And when the latter, not surprisingly, showered him with ridicule and challenged him with questions he could not possibly have known how to answer, why did he abandon all hope?

While some might argue that Jeff's pathological vulnerability to peer pressure as well as his unreasonable expectation of support from the very peer group least likely to offer it lessen the illustrative value of his case, the truth is just the opposite. The intensity and irrationality of Jeff's reliance on what may have been the only support system he had ever known are common if not typical features of the gay gestalt. Such features derive from the exacerbated sense of insecurity and inferiority frequently found at the root of a gay person's homosexual development. Indeed, homosexual attraction is commonly a compensatory response to the emotional trauma of perceived rejection by a same-sex parent and/or peers during childhood and adolescence. The easy acceptance and fluidity that characterize social relations within the gay community serve in part to compensate for the powerful feelings of loneliness, sadness, and isolation that characteristically accumulate in the psyche of SSA individuals. Remember, however, that Jeff was deeply conflicted over his SSA and homosexual activity. Thus Jeff's case, extreme as it may be, is genuinely representative of the extraordinary peril in which an individual can find himself when, emotionally or philosophically at odds with his own "acceptance" group, he must rely on that same "acceptance" group for the very support he needs in order to separate from it. Having experienced the futility of seeking advice and support from his religious community, fearful of acting independently, and unable to face the prospect of renewed loneliness and isolation that he feared awaited him in "straight" society, Jeff had no alternative but to turn to those he had already "betrayed" by expressing his desire to leave. By seeking their approval and encouragement, Jeff placed himself in an untenable position. Perhaps in his own mind, Jeff saw himself as attempting to rescue his peer group along with himself—the prisoner redeeming his captors, as it were. Hence Jeff's naïve—even delusional—attempt to disseminate his new-found "gospel" among those most primed to reject it.

The result was as disastrous as it was predictable. Rebuffed and humiliated by his only "friends," his fragile new hopes dashed to pieces, and he himself lacking the courage to act on his own, Jeff needed only one more "proof" to convince himself of the utter hopelessness of his situation and of his utter failure as a human being. The "proof" came in the guise of a last sexual encounter of a kind he inwardly abhorred, yet felt powerless to refuse. Thus, it is probable that the drugs that killed him were meant to dull the agony of a pain that he perceived as inescapable.

Case No. 2: "J".

A fourteen-year-old boy identifying himself as having SSA, but expressing a profound aversion for gay sex undergoes four years of treatment for "severe internalized homophobia"—without being informed of his right to choose alternative treatment for unwanted SSA.

The following is a précis and discussion of an article by James Lock, M.D., Ph.D., then Assistant Professor, Department of Psychiatry at Stanford University School of Medicine,[3] describing his treatment of "J" over a four year period. The patient was a fourteen-year old boy when referred to Dr. Lock by the child psychiatrist initially consulted by J's parents.

Away from home for the first time, J had initially done well at the prestigious prep school where his parents had enrolled him. However, he soon grew despondent, calling his parents daily and begging to come home. This, they eventually permitted, enrolling him in a local high school, where his despondence increased. His mother found him "moody, withdrawn, extremely hostile and alternatively very needy." (203) She was unable to discover the reason until he finally confessed his belief that he was gay. Apparently regretting his confession, J subsequently threatened to run away or commit suicide. He also reported feelings of isolation, sadness and anger, and experienced trouble sleeping. He blamed his family for his inability to develop "other social or emotional supports."

J's family described him as temperamental and physically uncoordinated. Notwithstanding her difficulty controlling him, his mother doted on him. His father, an emotionally distant personality, stayed aloof from the entire family, and especially from his son J. Though family therapy was conducted concurrently with J's individual sessions (the exact time-frame is not specified), J's father did not become actively involved until J struck his mother and sister.

In the early phase of his individual therapy with Dr. Lock, J disclosed some limited homosexual fantasies, but was uncomfortable discussing them. He was more willing to share his general impression of gay males, whom he described as "sexual, effeminate, and as preying on younger men." (205)

---

3. "Treatment of Homophobia in a Gay Male Adolescent," *American Journal of Psychotherapy,* Vol. 52 (Spring, 1998), pp. 202-14.

Although the therapist clearly recognized that many of the boy's issues were rooted in his feeling rejected by his father, resulting in a longing for genuine male bonding (205), Dr. Lock apparently did little or nothing to help J find a way to actualize and fulfill his legitimate emotional needs, choosing instead to focus on resolving J's purported "internalized homophobia." Thus, when J expressed a "deeply ambivalent" interest in a local gay teen support group (it is not clear whether the therapist actually referred him), Dr. Lock evidently encouraged him to attend, with predictably negative results:

> [H]e felt he had little in common with other gay teens there. [They] were not attractive enough, masculine enough, were from a different socioeconomic background, and were not as educated as he. [. . .] Intellectually, he rejected the idea of gay equaling feminine, but he was also intolerant of those gay males who were effeminate. This was 'not me' as he put it. (205)

Far from helping, the support group actually aggravated J's condition. The therapist reported that after attending the gay teen group, J developed "feelings of hopelessness, worthlessness, passive suicidal ideation, increased confusion, and worsening anxiety. He also had worsening problems with sleep, appetite, and concentration." (205-6)

Although he craved acceptance by "normal" boys at school (some of whom he found attractive), J undermined his own chances for acceptance by deliberately "coming out" to his classmates. Dr. Lock characterized this act as "premature" and "only symbolic," by which he apparently meant solely an attempt by J at defining his social identity rather than a full-fledged declaration of sexual identification.[4] J's gay-assertiveness further jeopardized his peer relations and increased his isolation. Indeed, during his junior year, J complained to his therapist that "coming out" to his peers was undermining his desire to be accepted by

---

4. In my experience, this premature "coming out" is often a misguided gambit to attract attention and sympathy.

"normal" boys. Finding himself associating exclusively with girls, J worried that this would harm him in some way. Unfathomably, the therapist concluded that the support of the girls was "helping him make better progress in peer relations overall." (209)

Although Dr. Lock writes that he sometimes encouraged the use of "reading materials, movies and so forth" (209) (in other words, pornography) as a way of familiarizing the patient with his or her homosexuality, he apparently refrained from doing so in this case, explaining that "many are so uncomfortable with their homosexuality that they cannot tolerate reading or seeing movies with homosexual themes until there is some resolution of the most vexing elements of their self-hatred." (209)

Somewhere between age 14 and 16 (the exact age is not specified), J had his first physical encounter—initially limited to "petting episodes"—with a man in his late twenties. (208) These were half-hearted trysts that aroused little interest in J and left him feeling disappointed and depressed. In fact, after one such episode led to J's having an orgasm, he felt so alienated ("empty, unhappy and dissociated" (208)) that he broke off the relationship. Despite J's starkly negative description of the affair, ("he felt dissociated and distant from himself") the therapist's assessment was that J's attempt to engage in homosexual sex was "premature because he was still quite homophobic." (208)

After two solid years of therapy designed to break down J's "homophobia" and induce him to accept his homosexuality, Dr. Lock reports that J developed "definite symptoms of depression, including sleep, appetite, concentration, and other difficulties." (210) The therapist prescribed Sertaline, but J's response, though "positive," did not prevent him from developing "a number of somatic symptoms." (210) In fact, J's scholastic performance declined, and he began to skip school, as well as some therapy sessions.

During J's senior year at school, we are told, "J had a tumultuous fall quarter with continuing struggles . . . evidenced by more social avoidance, increased feelings of shame, and intermittent depression. He began missing therapy sessions once again and some minor self-destructive behavior occurred." (212) Despite the patient's worsening condition, Dr. Lock persisted for another year in his attempts to reinforce J's homosexuality. By the end of that year, J terminated his regular sessions with Dr. Lock and left for college. According to Dr. Lock, J's mood improved during his last semester of high school, with J participating in various school activities and enjoying a trip with his father to visit various campuses. Yet his longing for an "intimate relationship" with a man remained unfulfilled as he grew weary of purely sexual encounters. Here is how the doctor summarized J's prospects:

> One of the more difficult areas for J was the ongoing identification with being gay for the rest of his life. He was troubled by patterns of failed gay relationships, purely sexual relationships, and had difficulty separating his stereotyped assumptions from his own coming out process that had entailed certain aspects of this. Helping J understand that some parts of being a gay person required experience of these kinds, but that being gay was not limited to them will continue to be a task for J as he grows. This longer-term perspective is a characteristic feature of work with adolescents in the last phase. It can be a risky time if a great deal of internalized homophobia remains because such a long-range view can lead to hopelessness. Many gay suicides occur in this transition. (213)

Discussion.

One of the great divides separating gender-affirming or reparative therapists from those of the gay-affirmative school involves how they approach a client who combines SSA with a strong repugnance for homosexual activity and the gay lifestyle. Generally speaking, the gay-affirmative therapist sees SSA as normal, healthy, and genetically determined. Hence, the invented term of "internalized homophobia" to cover persons expressing aversion to their own SSA. To the gay-affirmative therapist, the client's "problem" is not his SSA, but rather his inability to fully embrace it; and the solution is to treat him for "internalized homophobia."[5]

The gender-affirming or reparative therapist (as opposed to the gay-affirmative therapist) sees the problem in a totally different light. He or she views the SSA as an *unhealthy* response to severe emotional pain. Thus, his or her focus is to change the response by helping the client identify and resolve the sources of that pain. He or she may even help him explore the subconscious sources of his ambivalence towards his SSA. By addressing the *source* of the client's emotional pain as the ultimate *source* of his homosexual fantasies, arousals, identity and/or behavior, practitioners of the gender-affirming process are able to attack the operative causes of the client's homosexual tendency, thus enabling the client to grow emotionally, under the guidance of the therapist, in harmony with his physiological gender. Thus, in a case like J's, a gender-affirming or reparative therapist, rather than attempting to "cure" their client's aversion to homosexual behavior, would deal directly with a panoply of issues such as those expressed by J: hopelessness, feelings of worthlessness, depression, shame, suicidal ideation, *etc.*

---

5. It is questionable whether clinical internalized homophobia exists. George Weinberg, an American psychologist who long advocated the normality of the gay/lesbian community coined the term "homophobia" in the late 1960s. He discussed the term at length in his 1972 book, *Society and the Healthy Homosexual*. To understand how broadly this term is now defined by gay activists and their allies, *see* <http://psychology.ucdavis.edu/rainbow/html/ihptems.html>, which suggests that if you have SSA and can identify with the following statements, the "pathology" of "internalized homophobia" is indicated: (1) I have tried to stop being attracted to members of my own sex. (ii) If someone offered me the chance to be completely heterosexual, I would accept the chance. (iii) I wish I weren't lesbian/bisexual/gay. (iv) I feel that being lesbian/bisexual/gay is a personal shortcoming for me. (v) I would like to get professional help in order to change my sexual orientation from lesbian/bisexual/gay to straight. (vi) I often feel it best to avoid personal or social involvement with other lesbian/bisexual/gay individuals. (vii) I feel alienated from myself because of being lesbian/bisexual/gay. (viii) I wish that I could develop more erotic feelings about those of the opposite gender.

J's case does more than just serve to illustrate this therapeutic divide. It illustrates how ideological bias can affect the judgment of a well-respected therapist, even blinding him to the clear indications of a treatment strategy gone seriously awry. From the very beginning, Dr. Lock chose to ignore strong signs that this young teenager, behind his "symbolic" mask of over-assertive (or "premature," as Dr. Lock calls it) gay identification, may have been profoundly unsure about his sexual identity. From the beginning, Dr. Lock stubbornly discounted the boy's repeated expressions of aversion to homosexual activity (an aversion that resurfaces consistently throughout the therapy!), attributing them to "internalized homophobia"—a condition that the therapist feels duty-bound to cure. From the beginning, Dr. Lock stolidly refrained from exploring the deeper significance of the boy's fantasies, of his "premature coming out," of his longing for an "intimate" (*i.e.*, loving) relationship—despite noting in passing the boy's extreme loneliness and isolation, his alienation from his father, and his deeply frustrated need for normal male bonding. Was it not possible that J's homosexual fantasies were the product of a sensitive child who was experiencing an attachment failure with respect to his father, an emotional enmeshment with his mother, self-image wounds about his body and lack of physical coordination, and same-sex peer wounds? In other words, the therapist seems deliberately to have disregarded the possibility that J's homosexual fantasies represented a need to console other parts of his life in which he was experiencing intolerable stress, emotional pain, and deep grief—all of which could have been dealt with therapeutically, as the gender-affirming therapists routinely do.

On the contrary, the therapist (apparently based on his unexplained belief that "high school social dynamics support homophobia") (209) does nothing to help integrate the boy into normal, age-appropriate social activities such as team sports, camping, hiking, dance classes, photography clubs, and the like, ignores the obvious significance of his patient's worsening mental and physical symptoms, offers no discussion of the boy's classification as a "gifted student" or of the difficulties that can involve, and implicitly views as an indicator of treatment success the patient's more frequent involvement in unwanted homosexual activity.

Indeed, the list of purported successes achieved at termination of therapy is clearly one-sided and unsupported by any objective discussion. Here are the positive indicators listed by Dr. Lock:

(1) "J's mood brightened [and he] became more active in school activities;" (212)

(2) his relationship with his father was "much improved;" (212)

(3) he "sought out a college that was accepting of gay students and wrote about these issues in his essays for admission [and] was accepted into his first choice of colleges." (212)

(4) "J needed therapy a good deal less and was performing well in all areas of his life." (212)

(5) "He still did not have an intimate relationship, but was beginning to better understand what it was he was looking for." (212)

If, however, we examine these alleged "successes," most of them seem far less significant in light of J's behavioral patterns. Indeed, comparing point by point:

(1) J shows a fairly steady cycle of upbeat mood change whenever he is about to enter a new chapter in his academic career, undergo a "change of scenery," or escape from a long-time oppression. ("The ongoing stress of high school and his sense that it would never end was a major component of [his depression].") (210) Such impending crossroads seem to elicit in J a brief period of hopeful expectation, followed by devastating disappointment and depression.

(2) The one truly positive development here is the improvement in J's relations with his father. However, this warming seems most likely to be the result of the ongoing family therapy (presumably with a different therapist) and of J's ensuing revision of his former perception of paternal rejection. (206, 207, 208)

(3) J's choice of college based on sexual policy hardly paints him as either emotionally mature or secure in his sexual identity.

Moreover, J's advance "coming out" on his college applications rings an ominous bell, reminding us of J's premature "coming out" in high school. Dr. Lock does not discuss to what extent this new declaration, too, might be "symbolic."

(4) As for J's needing therapy "a good deal less," only a few lines further down, Dr. Lock characterizes this purported improvement as "failing to show up" for several sessions, and as "a possible attempt to avoid working on our termination." (213) J had skipped sessions before, when he was prescribed Sertaline for his serious depression. The repetition of this behavior could well indicate that, now, too, all was not smooth sailing for J— notwithstanding his seemingly upbeat mood.

(5) J has been clear and vocal all along about his desire for an "intimate" bonding relationship with other men and his distaste for purely sexual encounters. Dr. Lock does not explain why he regards this perception as an achievement of therapy. Rather, the point to be made is that even though Dr. Lock is now fully aware of J's idealization of homosexual love, he seems less than forthcoming when it comes to preparing J for the painful realities of homosexual relationships.[6]

In brief, so far as we can see from this study, in no way did Dr. Lock ever examine the youth's expressed feelings of discomfort with his same-sex attractions as a case of ego-dystonic homosexuality (*i.e.,* unwanted SSA). The possibility that the boy's aversion to being homosexual may have been a perfectly natural manifestation of his incompletely determined sexuality appears to have been totally ignored by the therapist, who assumes conclusively throughout the treatment that the boy is fundamentally homosexual.

To put it another way, Dr. Lock saw J's SSA as natural and the

---

6. Homosexual pairing is rarely sexually monogamous. *See, e.g.,* David P. McWhirter and Andrew M. Mattison, *The Male Couple: How Relationships Develop,* Englewood Cliffs: Prentice Hall, Inc. (1984), p. 285: "The majority of couples in our study, *and all of the couples together for longer than five years,* [emphasis added] were not continuously sexually exclusive with each other." *See also* Chapter 3, below, for further discussion.

homosexual fantasies simply as an expression of genuine gayness. Were these assumptions justified? To put the question in more general terms: does the fact that a person has homosexual fantasies make that person gay? This question relates to all areas of sexual fantasy, and is profound and complex, because, as Freud established,[7] the fantasy may originate in something entirely unrelated to the person's sexuality. For Dr. Lock, however, the only problem was the boy's alleged "homophobia," which the therapist diagnosed based on the sole fact that the boy came to him with homosexual fantasies combined with a profound aversion for acting them out! In his report, Dr. Lock never asks *why* J was either lukewarm or turned off about "acting them out." Was it not possible that J's gay fantasies were untrue to his "real self"—his spiritual intuition, his conscience? Or does Dr. Lock's school of thought regard such entities as meaningless or imaginary?

Not only did Dr. Lock's treatment begin with a conclusory premise (namely, that J was in fact gay) that by any standard should have been the *end result* of a thorough investigation, but the treatment was *limited* to "helping" him express his assumed homosexuality. Such a narrow-beam approach is in itself highly questionable. In the words of Dr. Norman Goldwasser, Director of Horizon Psychological Services in Miami Beach:

> In general, psychological and personality disorders can be seen as phenomena that are multi-faceted in their complexities, reflecting the reality that who we are and how we function are not simplistic, unitary concepts. Rather, we are complex beings, and our thoughts, behaviors, personality and styles, as well as our sexual arousal patterns, are complex and multi-faceted, as

---

7. Freud proposed that the male homosexual's difficulties stemmed from the formation of an overly strong "erotic attachment" to mother, which was "favored by too much love from the mother herself" and reinforced by the "retirement or absence of the father during the childhood stages." Therefore the individual would gain such anxiety as to interfere with his taking a woman as a love object. See "The Dissolution of the Oedipus Complex," in J. Strachey (ed.) *The Standard Edition,* Vol. 19, London: Hogarth (1924), pp. 12-68.

well. Consequently, therefore, it stands to reason that any treatment paradigm that aims to heal psychosexual disorders should reflect their multi-faceted nature. *Treatment approaches that focus on one aspect of a person's difficulties, or narrowly address only behavior symptoms, fail to comprehensively resolve the totality of the presenting problem.*[8] (Emphasis added.)

Perhaps most distressing of all is that nowhere does it appear that any consideration—whether by the parents or by the therapist—was given to the boy's own choice of therapy: "How do you wish the therapist to help you? How would you describe the ideal outcome of your therapy? Do you feel you need help in expressing or actualizing your homosexual fantasies, or do you wish to be rid of them?" Such questions strike one as basic intake, but no one seems to have posed them. Thus, without the minor client's informed consent, or, for that matter, the informed consent of his parents, the therapist embarks on a program of insistently and insidiously attempting to overcome the client's dogged resistance to becoming a practicing homosexual.

To that extent at least, Dr. Lock appears to have been partly successful. At termination of therapy, the client's anxiety about his homosexual self-identification and occasional sexual activity is reportedly considerably diminished. Yet, as Dr. Lock himself summarizes, "One of the more difficult areas for J was the ongoing identification with being gay for the rest of his life." (213) It is certainly legitimate to question the value of a therapeutic approach that leaves us with *no conclusive indication* that the subject's mental health has significantly improved after four years of treatment! On the contrary: while the facts as reported are open to

---

8. Norman Goldwasser, "The Use of a Multi-Modal Interdisciplinary Team Approach with Reparative Therapy," NARTH Conference, November, 2005. According to Dr. Goldwasser's presentation, his method involves "multiple modalities . . . preferably by an interdisciplinary team of clinicians who work collaboratively and interdependently to help the individual achieve his or her therapeutic goals."

some interpretation, Dr. Lock himself cautions that the "longer-term perspective" of a case like J's is "risky . . . if a great deal of internalized homophobia remains," (213) and may lead to hopelessness and suicide. (213)

Was this result inevitable? We don't think so. J was apparently never given the opportunity to explore the various conditions that might have contributed to his gay self-identification, such as J's alienation from his father, his enmeshment with his mother, his mistreatment by same-sex peers, his shame over his own body image and poor physical coordination, his giftedness and his sensitivity—all of which are clearly recognizable as factors commonly contributing to the development of SSA. In fact, J's case is essentially—and in virtually every detail—a classic text-book example of the experience of a great many homosexual males.[9]

On the other side of the coin, the therapist does not report any attempt to reinforce J's positive attributes—his giftedness, for example, or his sensitivity and idealism in regard to human relationships and sex—attributes in which J might justly have been encouraged to take pride. Nor does the therapist mention any effort to help J overcome the significant difficulties inherent in communicating with classmates, many of whom would have been less gifted and less sensitive than he. Nor was J's distaste for gay sex ever examined in reference to J's basic value system—religious or moral—with which such a lifestyle may have been completely incompatible. Nor again does there appear to have been any attempt to determine whether J's revulsion for homosexual activity might have been a protective defense mechanism activated by J's unwanted homosexual fantasies. Nor was the possibility

---

9. For a full discussion of the empirical causes of SSA and homosexual behavior, *see* Chapter 4, below. These contributing causes are often seen in conjunction with homosexuality, as has been known to various cultures since ancient times. *See,* for example, the popular 17th-century Chinese Novel, *The Red Chamber Dream*, in which the anonymous author follows the hero's character development from his early rejection by his father.

ever seriously considered that these fantasies arose out of a need to palliate the intolerable stress, emotional pain, and deep grief engendered by J's frustration with his family and social environment.

Had Dr. Lock explored such issues with his client, it should not have interfered—at least according to Dr. Lock's own ideology of homosexual immutability—with J's ultimate transformation into a "healthy," non-homophobic homosexual; but it might have paved the way to self realization for one very confused and tormented young man. Nevertheless, the gay-affirmative philosophy itself refuses to admit of such exploration. True to form, J's therapist chose to see J's SSA as incontrovertible evidence of homosexual identity, and all the other issues as artifacts of homophobia. If the boy's negative feelings towards gay men and gay sex could be overcome, the other issues would somehow fade away!

If Dr. Lock were some kind of fringe radical, we might simply dismiss J's story as an isolated example of what can happen when an unfortunate subject walks into the wrong office. But Dr. Lock is a well-respected psychiatrist, fairly representative of the mental health professional community.[10] The *American Journal of Psychotherapy,* in which Dr. Lock's article originally appeared, is a well-regarded, mainstream professional periodical for psychotherapists.[11] Indeed, Dr. Lock's approach to treating J's condition is quite typical of a substantial sector of the mental health community (including psychiatrists, psychologists, and social

---

10. James Lock, M.D, Ph.D., is a board-certified child and adolescent psychiatrist whose research interests include eating disorders in adolescents, mood disorders in adolescents, and developmental issues of gay and lesbian youth. He is now a Professor of Psychiatry and Behavioral Sciences at Stanford U. School of Medicine, where he directs both the Stanford Child and Adolescent Eating Disorder Program and the Comprehensive Pediatric Care Unit at Lucille Packard Children's Hospital. When he wrote this article, he was an Assistant Professor at Stanford.

11. Founded in 1939, the *American Journal of Psychotherapy* (*AJP*) describes itself as a leader in the publication of eclectic articles for all psychotherapists.

workers).[12] Contrary to the oft-touted claim that gay-affirmative therapists are prepared to explore *all options* with their clients—including the possibility that they may be more comfortable with a heterosexual lifestyle, or that their SSA may be a behavioral or emotional response to certain unfulfilled needs—the plain fact of the matter is that all too often gay-affirmative therapists ignore the expressed or implied wishes of their clients with regard to their therapeutic goals. What has happened, in essence, is that political correctness in regard to homosexuality has substantially eroded the right of a patient to be fully informed of all treatment options and to determine his or her own therapy.[13] Yet medical ethics demands

---

12. In a letter dated October 16, 2006, and addressed to Norman B. Anderson, Ph.D. Executive Vice President and Chief Executive Officer of the American Psychological Association, Melanie Spinks, a former lesbian, writes:

> [. . .] Almost ten years ago, I didn't know that I had stepped into a politicized issue. I was simply a woman with an unwanted homosexual orientation wanting to improve my life by dealing with identifiable contributing factors pressing me into a way of adaptation that was ironically leading me further from what I craved—connection with women. I sought help from licensed mental healthcare professionals in dealing with these issues with the goal of shifting my orientation. But I was literally laughed to scorn. Finding no one respecting my desires, I set about reading everything I could get my hands on in the stacks of medical school libraries and the like. Nearly a decade later, I have experienced the shift to a heterosexual orientation along with an exponential improvement in overall well-being. Had I had the help and support of trained professionals of the APA, how much sooner could I have experienced the settling of the past and the attainment of the goal I now enjoy? People like myself have been politicized out of getting the help we desire by the one-sided arguments presented by the gay lobby. They do not speak for everyone who faces sexual identity issues. Please grant us your serious and thoughtful consideration as the APA makes decisions regarding the treatment of those with unwanted homosexual orientations in the future. We need unbiased research in this area and your professional care. (Published with the author's permission.)

13. I offer two additional examples in support of this statement: Alex, a 23-year-old Jewish man, called the JONAH hotline after emergency room doctors told him that he was gay. The doctors so concluded because Alex was experiencing

that mental health professionals *enhance,* rather than inhibit, the client's right of self-determination by making the client aware of all alternative forms of counseling and treatment—including gender-affirming (as opposed to gay-affirmative) processes.

Although Dr. Lock's article purports to describe some of the problems posed by the presence of "homophobia" in a gay adolescent, we suggest that it more clearly illustrates the additional pain and misery that can flow from the therapist's uncritical adherence to the ideology that homosexuality is innate, immutable, and incurable. Indeed, rather than help the patient understand, validate and actualize his or her resistance to gay feelings or fantasies, the goal of gay-affirmative therapy is, as Dr. Lock explains, to utilize "supportive and homosexual-affirming techniques" (202) (such as pornography and sexual experimentation) to break down that resistance, and "to integrate personal aspects of self with gay group identity." (214) In other words, change the client's personal value system to fit his presumed homosexual condition!

---

an obsession about penises. The obsession started after his father ridiculed the size of his (Alex's) penis—an experience that left Alex with severe emotional trauma. Over the phone, Alex stated that he had always identified as heterosexual, never entertained fantasies about homosexual sex, and had never even considered acting out with another man. Nevertheless, because of his obsession with penises, the physicians advised him to seek therapy and learn to accept being gay. This, despite being aware of the nature of the abuse Alex had suffered.

In a comparable situation, therapist Erik Bohlin reported on a 19-year-old male client who had been hospitalized for cutting behaviors. While at the hospital, the client told the staff psychiatrist about his occasional SSA fantasies, explaining that he had never acted upon them and that he had always identified as heterosexual, as homosexuality was against his religious and moral principles. The psychiatrist advised Bohlin's client that he (the client) was gay and that "homosexuality is hard-wired," adding that he was "tired of hypocritical gay men who put down other gay men." Other hospital staff members also advised the client that he was gay. According to Bohlin, this client was "truly egodystonic," and experienced increased shame and suicidal ideation as a result of the hospital staff's comments.

It is interesting to consider for just a moment what this "personal value system" might be. To avoid using terms like "conscience" or "spiritual awareness," or "true self," or "sense of duty"—terms that might not be sufficiently "scientific" for some psychologists (Dr. Lock refers to them neutrally as "personal aspects of self") (214)—let us briefly examine this hypothetical entity from a purely functional point of view. In that light, we might define a "personal value system" as something that induces a person to enlist in the armed forces despite the risk of getting killed; or persuades a couple deeply in love not to get married—despite the heartbreak—because of religious differences; or inspires a person to get involved in a political or social cause at the sacrifice of what little free time is left over from his or her job; or to adopt an orphaned child after years of hard striving to reach a certain level of economic ease and leisure time, or to become a teacher despite the low pay and high aggravation. In other words, whether such "values" are "real" or "imaginary," they are *powerful,* and their power comes from their ability to give *meaning* to a person's life. So when a therapist encourages a resistant SSA client to live his fantasies and enjoy them at the cost of his or her "personal value system," that therapist is actively working to degrade the *meaningfulness* of that client's life.

At this point, it is hard not to wonder how J might have fared if he had gone with a different therapist—one who believed in gender-affirming processes. For one thing, a reparative therapist would likely have approached J as someone caught in a "gender double bind."

> The essence of this gender double bind is that a man is not OK with being a man, and he is not OK without being a man . . . . One side of his psyche says, "I am a man." But the other side says, "But I am not accepted as a masculine person, so I am not really a man."[14]

---

14. David Matheson, *Four Principles of Change: A Supplement for the Journey into Manhood Weekend,* 2003, pp. 3-4.

Other reparative therapists might have suggested that J's SSA arose from a conflict between his masculine self-assertion and his shame—the "anticipatory shame concerning the fear of punishment or expulsion for his gender self-assertion."[15]

So prominently do the dynamics of gender double bind and anticipatory shame figure in the formation of male homosexuals,[16] that one of the key objectives of gender-affirming processes and reparative therapies is to encourage the client to cultivate intimate but non-sexual bonding relationships with others of the same sex. As the client gains self-confidence with regard to his masculinity, positive, non-sexual relationships with other males become increasingly attainable. In turn, this achievement strengthens the client's internalized sense of masculine sufficiency and helps take him out of the gender double bind and the shame posture.

Would J have been happier on such a path? Would his treatment have been more successful? Sadly, we'll never know. What we do know is that in the course of his treatment for "internalized homophobia," J experienced continued depression, confusion, apathy, hostility and self-destructiveness. Could it be that J's worsening anxiety, hopelessness, and suicidal fantasies were due to confusion over why he was letting himself be pushed into a form of sexual expression that repelled him? Apparently, Dr. Lock did not consider that possibility, since his training, his reputation, and a large part of professional and public opinion all required that J's worsening condition be due to his "homophobia"—in other words, to his deep-seated and irrational fear of sexual relations with other men!

Consider the following: here is J, still legally a minor, tormented by homosexual fantasies, yet hesitant to engage in gay sex. Should he be encouraged to do so? Even forgetting that J is a

---

15. *See* Dr. Joseph Nicolosi, "The Next Step in Treatment of Ego-Dystonic Homosexuality," Paper delivered at NARTH Convention, November 12, 2004.

16. A not too dissimilar dynamic exists for female homosexuals, but gender-reversed. *See* Chapter 4, below, *passim* and text there at note 16.

minor: should someone stating discomfort with his own sexual fantasies be induced by his therapist to put them into practice? Remember how Dr. Lock reported J's first sexual experiences: "When these culminated in J's experiencing an orgasm and afterward feeling empty, unhappy, and dissociated, he decided to end these encounters and stopped his trips to the city." (208) Remarkably, Dr. Lock's conclusion was simply that the boy's venture into homosexual sex was "premature because he was still homophobic." (208) Rather than characterize the boy as "still homophobic," shouldn't J's reaction to his sexual encounter have signaled to the therapist that J's reservations might have had a strong moral basis or at least that he had encountered some intolerable incongruity with his personal value system? After J attended the gay teen group, he had commented, "This was not me." Later, after another man had brought him to climax, J felt "dissociated" and "distant from himself." What does this mean? It probably means that J said to himself, "J wouldn't have done what I just did. Therefore, I can't be J. I must be someone else." Was this not an enormous clue that J had done something to himself that was devastating to his personal sense of who he was?

Something else bothers me about Dr. Lock's explanation of J's starkly negative reaction to homosexual activity. If someone is acrophobic, yet manages to climb to a considerable height, he usually feels at least partly exhilarated at having triumphed over his fears. If someone is claustrophobic, yet successfully uses an elevator to get to an upper floor, he or she usually feels a sense of accomplishment combined with his/her feeling of relief. Why, then, would a homophobic homosexual feel merely "empty, unhappy and dissociated" (208) after his first sexual encounter? What was there about this experience that confirms that J was either homophobic or homosexual? And how does the experience support Dr. Lock's conclusion that "the therapist working with a homophobic gay male in the middle phase [14-16 years old] can assist the patient . . . [by supporting] the appropriate exploration of same-sex romance and sexual interactions"? (208) Given that the "middle phase" occurs during the patient's minority, there is obviously a very fine line between "assisting the patient" and corrupting the minor.

What I personally find especially distressing about this case is the plain fact that J consciously recognized his own isolation from other boys and sought guidance from his therapist on how best to obtain the desired "peer validation." He complained about "coming out to peers because it undermined his wish to be accepted by 'normal' boys at his school." (209) He complained about his social contacts at school being limited "exclusively with girls." He worried about being "relegated to girl status" (J's words). Notwithstanding these appeals, Dr. Lock appears to have done little or nothing to help his young patient make friends with heterosexual males or to learn how to better relate to them. Instead, he concluded, apparently without basis, that his reliance on female friendships was helping him "make better progress in peer relations overall"—a conclusion that was later belied by evidence of "more social avoidance" (*see* page 31, above) during J's senior year. (209) A treatment plan more consistent with the patient's stated wishes would have involved strategies for him to associate and identify more completely with his same-sex peers, without regard to their sexual identity. (And, maybe it would have been useful to provide an athletic coach to improve J's physical coordination!)

There is yet another disturbing aspect to Dr. Lock's approach, and it touches an area where ideological affiliation can impinge on one's professional integrity. The therapist states, "[J] was troubled by patterns of failed gay relationships, purely sexual relationships, and had difficulty separating his stereotyped assumptions from his own coming out process that had entailed certain aspects of this." (213) Were J's impressions of the homosexual lifestyle nothing more than "stereotyped assumptions?" Patterns of failed relationships and purely sexual encounters are part and parcel of the gay lifestyle for an overwhelming majority of gays (*see* note 6, this chapter, and note 53 in Chapter 3, at pp. 91-2). Both J's "stereotypes" and his personal experiences were close enough to gay reality for J's apprehensions to be taken seriously. The therapist, however, is not about to validate the accuracy of his client's perception. Instead, he counsels "a longer-term perspective," suggesting that being gay "required experience[s] of these kinds, but...was not limited to them." (213) However, it seems difficult to justify such a point of view when, as Dr. Lock himself warns, a "longer-term perspective" often leads to despair and suicide in cases where the client's "homophobia" has not been substantially resolved. (213)

Still, why Dr. Lock should finger "homophobia" as the operative factor in gay despair and suicide is not explained. The human soul craves love, understanding, and good faith on a reciprocal and enduring basis. J seems quite miserably cognizant of the sordid future that most probably awaits him on the gay scene, and one wonders whether "homophobia" is really a significant factor in either J's unhappiness or in the abnormally high rate of suicides among gay men and women (*see* Chapter 3, below, at pp. 91 and note 58 at p. 94).

J's case study, published as something of a success story in a prestigious medical journal, should raise a red flag regarding the choices that must be made by those seeking help for their unwanted SSA. Clearly, the patient *must* interview and research the prospective therapist exhaustively for such particulars as his or her beliefs regarding same-sex attraction, homosexuality and homophobia, personal value systems, the goals, methods, and possible outcomes of his or her therapeutic approach, and his/her primary indicators of success and failure. In short, the prospective client must become thoroughly acquainted, not only with the expertise and experience of the therapist being considered, but—no less important—with the therapist's value system and psychiatric or psychological philosophy.

To put it more specifically, the client must *first of all* ascertain where the therapist stands on the issues of homosexuality and patient's rights. The choice the prospective client is about to make could well prove to be not only about gender-identity but a life-or-death decision.

Chapter 3:

Defining the Problem: Gay Activism versus Torah Morality.

In the last chapter we saw how two individuals who sought help for their SSA were led astray by the misinformation and disinformation that is rife within both the gay community and society at large. "Jeff" died of a drug overdose after being browbeaten into believing that he would never be able to change his unwanted same-sex attractions. "J" was inappropriately treated for a politically concocted pathology called "internalized homophobia." "Don M.," whom we shall meet later on (*see* Chapter 15, pp. 551-56) was nearly driven to suicide by his culturally induced conviction that he was fated to live out his life as a homosexual. In a devastating letter addressed to the APA, Melanie Spinks (*see* Chapter Two, note 12) described the ridicule she endured from the psychological profession when she sought treatment for her unwanted SSA.

Central to the propaganda behind such travesties is the pseudo-scientific postulate that a gay gene exists and that therefore homosexuality is biologically fated. A well-researched and insightful book entitled *My Genes Made Me Do It!* surveys how strongly the premise of "biologically fated" has affected not only personal decisions, but professional, social, and governmental policy.[1] Such influence, claim the authors, has led to (i) the adoption, by many in the psychiatric, psychological and other counseling professions, of attitudes promoting patients' unreserved acceptance of their homosexuality; (ii) a trend in the legislative and judiciary bodies toward the creation of special homosexual rights and privileges (such as same-sex marriage, civil unions, and gay-couple child adoption, *etc.*); (iii) the ordination of openly practicing homosexuals; (iv) the introduction into the public school system of highly controversial sex-education programs that openly promote homosexual behavior by incorporating "homosexual concepts" into all curricula,[2] as well as the overtly growing presence of college campus, high-school, and even grammar-school (!) associations of homosexual students (gay and lesbian student clubs); (v) the increasing prominence of pro-gay messages in the press and news and entertainment media; and (vi) heavy social pressure on ambivalent homosexuals to conform to the norms and expectations of a "liberated," gay-affirmative society. (N. & B. Whitehead, 8)

Western society in general has not only ignored these challenges, but has wholeheartedly invested in the premise that sexuality is genetic, ingrained, inborn, and unchangeable. The result is obvious: the plight of the homosexual, born into a condition he wrongly

---

1. *See* Neil and Briar Whitehead, *My Genes Made Me Do It!: A Scientific Look at Sexual Orientation*, Lafayette: Huntington House (1999), p.8.

2. *See, e.g.,* "Mission Statement of the Gay, Lesbian, Straight Education Network (GLSEN)," <http://www.glsenco.org/ About%20Us/our_mission.htm>; and George Archibald, "N.E.A. Groups Protest Award to Gay Studies Activist," *Washington Times,* July 3, 2004, http://www.washingtontimes.com/functions/print.php?storyID=20040702-115950-5378r. For further discussion of this issue, *see* below, this chapter.

believes he cannot change any more than an African-American can change the color of his skin, becomes a *cause celèbre*, and judicious movement towards social acceptance is transformed into a massive campaign for "civil and human rights of gay Americans."

How did this happen? How could virtually all of western society buy into an unfounded hypothesis that is actually disproved by the multitude of studies, beginning with Freud,[3] that document verified changes of sexual orientation, and by the growing numbers of homosexuals who have been successfully and enthusiastically transitioned into heterosexual life?

Understanding the Homosexual Activist Agendas: the Kirk & Madsen Manifesto.

In an interesting article in the *Chicago Sun Times,* columnist Mark Steyn notes how language has been an important weapon in furthering the homosexual activist agenda. "In the old days," says Steyn,

> there was "sodomy": an act. In the late 19th century, the word "'homosexuality" was coined: a condition. A generation ago, the accepted term became "gay": an identity. Each formulation raises the stakes: One can object to and even criminalize an act; one is obligated to be sympathetic toward a condition; but once it's a fully fledged 24/7 identity, like being Hispanic or Inuit, anything less than wholehearted acceptance gets you marked as a bigot . . . . The transformation of a "crime against nature" into a co-equal civic identity within little more than the span of one human lifetime is one of the most remarkable victories ever achieved by any minority group in the Western world. A minority that didn't even exist in a formal sense a century ago has managed to overwhelm and overhaul

---

3. *See* Sigmund Freud, *Three Essays on the Theory of Sexuality,* in J. Strachey (ed.), *The Complete Works of Sigmund Freud* (Standard Edition), Vol 7, London: Hogarth (1905), pp. 135-243.

a universal societal institution thousands of years old.[4]

It didn't happen by magic. Indeed, a masterful public relations campaign orchestrated by the "pride extremists" (a phrase coined by John McKellar, the openly gay founder of HOPE—Homosexuals Opposed to Pride Extremism) has achieved "a transformation in public morals consistent with widespread abandonment of the Judeo-Christian ethics upon which our civilization is based. Though hailed as progress," continues McKellar, "it is really a reversion to ancient pagan practices supported by a counter-culture restatement of gnostic moral relativism."[5]

Not surprisingly, Rabbi Samuel H. Dresner, author of a probing book on the mores of the American family, agrees:

> [The homosexual activist movement] launched the most successful public relations campaign in the history of the nation [and] in little more than a decade homosexuals have moved from pariahs to cultural heroes. During this period, Americans have not only come to accept homosexuality as an inevitable phenomenon in our society, but also as a legitimate "lifestyle" deserving of affirmation as well as tolerance.[6]

So sure of themselves were the strategists of this movement that, as one communications expert remarked, they actually envisioned that a decision to legitimize homosexuality would ultimately be made "without society ever realizing that it has been purposely conditioned

---

4. Mark Steyn, "There's No Stopping Them Now," *Chicago Sun Times*, July 13, 2003, p. 35; <http://www.suntimes.com/output/steyn/cst-edt-steyn13.html>.

5. John McKellar, "There's HOPE For the World," Speech delivered March, 2003, posted on the Classical Anglican Net News website, <http://www.anglican.tk/modules.php?name=Content&pa=showpage&pid=225>.

6. Rabbi Samuel H. Dresner, *Can Families Survive in Pagan America?* Lafeyette: Huntington House (1995), p. 28.

to arrive at a conclusion that it thinks is its own."[7]

This subliminal agenda was actually the brainchild of two Harvard-trained social scientists, Marshall Kirk and Hunter Madsen. Using well-known psychological principles and coast-to-coast networking, Kirk and Madsen laid out a meticulously calculated, step-by-step plan for manipulating society into adopting a set of ideas and perceptions that would change the way America looked at homosexuality. Their objective was "to force acceptance of homosexual culture into the mainstream, to silence opposition, and ultimately to convert American society" through manipulation and control of the public discourse. (Rondeau, 447)[8] That they succeeded beyond their own expectations is obvious to anyone who sticks his head out the front door.

How did the myth of a so-called "gay gene" become so prevalent as to be taken for granted at virtually every level of society? How did the belief that homosexual sex is equivalent to heterosexual sex take root so deeply? As recently as the 1970s and '80s, the intellectual elite of the gay activist movement began to elaborate detailed plans for selling the normalization of homosexuality through the mass media and other channels. In the mid-'80s, two critical articles by

---

7. Paul E. Rondeau, "Selling Homosexuality to America," 14 *Regent U. Law Review* (2002), p. 485; posted at <www.Jonahweb.org>.

8. Their success can be measured by the American public opinion polls which show a gradual but continuous increase in the acceptance of homosexuality as a legitimate alternative lifestyle. In 1982 only 34% of Americans approved of homosexuality. In 1992, the number had increased to 38%; by February, 1999, to 50%, and by 2001 to 52%. A significant factor in changing public opinion has been the growing acceptance of the myth that homosexuality is genetic—a basic premise of the Kirk and Madsen plan. *Compare* a 1977 Gallup poll showing Americans believing by a four-to-one ratio that environment was the most prevalent factor in causing same-sex attractions, with 2001, when, according to another Gallup poll, at least 50% of Americans believed in the existence of a "gay gene." Charles Moore, "A Calculated Agenda of Moral Subversion," *Western Catholic Reporter,* June 7, 1999; and Frank Newport, "American Attitudes Toward Homosexuality Continue to Become More Tolerant," *Gallup News Service,* June 4, 2001.

Kirk and Madsen—the latter writing under the pseudonym of Erastes Pill—appeared in homosexual periodicals, in which the authors set forth preliminary versions of their plan.[9] By 1989, Kirk and Madsen (the latter writing this time under his real name) had expanded the initial articles into a full length book entitled *After the Ball: How America Will Conquer its Fear and Loathing of Gays in the 90s.*[10] In it, they chronicle a February, 1988 "war conference" held by 175 leading gay activists convened outside of Washington, D.C. The purpose of the conference was to lay the groundwork for the next phase of the gay revolution—the ultimate "battle for [the] hearts and minds of America." How? By means of a carefully calculated, "unabashedly subjective and one-sided . . . national propaganda effort." (*After the Ball*, 163)

The media campaign that emerged from this conference might have been masterminded by Sun Tzu himself, the great Chinese military theoretician who, more than two thousand years ago, authored the first known treatise on the *Art of War*. Indeed, quoting Sun's famous precept, "Those who have supreme skill use strategy to bend others without coming to conflict," (172) Kirk and Madsen outline a public relations agenda deliberately engineered to drastically alter American attitudes toward homosexuality without any one ever realizing what was going on. The authors set forth eight graduated tactics purposefully adopted by the "war conference" and cannily designed subliminally to persuade "straight" America that "the gay alternative" is legitimate, acceptable, and good. (172-192) These eight tactics or stages can be summarized (in order) as follows:

---

9. Marshall Kirk & Erastes Pill, "Waging Peace: A Gay Battle Plan to Persuade Straight America," *Christopher Street*, No. 95 (1985); "The Overhauling of Straight America," originally published as a two-part essay in *Guide*, Vol. 8, Oct.-Nov. 1987, pp.7-14; and <http://www.abidingtruth.com/_docs/resources/8142838.pdf>.

10. Marshall Kirk & Hunter Madsen, *After the Ball: How America Will Conquer its Fear and Loathing of Gays in the 90s,* New York: Doubleday (1989).

1. Communicate with others at their own level while curtailing gay "self-expression."

2. Appeal to the "ambivalent skeptics" or the "muddled middle."

3. "Desensitize" people to the subject by constantly talking about gayness (but hide the negative aspects).

4. Keep the message focused on gay issues (don't fight for other causes).

5. Portray homosexuals as victims, not as threats to the status quo.

6. Give potential supporters a cause they can relate to, such as anti-discrimination; don't ask them to support the practice of homosexuality per se.

7. Make gays look good: portray them as Everyman and Everywoman.

8. Make opponents look bad: portray them as evil and victimizing.

According to Kirk and Madsen, each of these eight tactics had to be handled in such a way as to accomplish three things at once:

A. Employ emotionally powerful images so as to "desensitize," jam, and/or convert the undecided and the confused.

B. "Challenge homohating beliefs and actions on a (not too) *intellectual* level."

C. Gain access to the type of public media that "would automatically confer legitimacy" upon the message, while making sure that the message remains "both subtle in purpose and crafty in construction." (172-73)

Now let's examine each of these eight points in turn.

1. Communicate with others at their own level while curtailing gay "self expression."

The plan was eminently logical. The first item on the gay agenda would be to convince straights that in spite of the key differences in sexual orientation, gays and straights "speak the same language [and] share enough ideas and values so that dialogue can proceed in a meaningful and fruitful way." (174)

At the same time, gays were warned to curtail their "self expression," which Kirk and Madsen defined as outlandish dress, prurient speech, and radical politics: "What is healthy for the individual isn't necessarily healthy for his community." (174)

2. Appeal to the "ambivalent skeptics" or the "muddled middle."

The second principle recognizes the economics of persuasion. Resources are more productively used when directed at convincing the malleable and the undecided than when squandered on the fanatically opposed. Conversely, why waste precious time and money trying to convince those who need no convincing—*i.e.,* the movement's non-gay supporters? "War Conference" theoreticians had calculated that each of these three groups—supporters, undecideds and opponents—comprised approximately one third of the total population. If the middle third could be won over, reasoned the ideologues, a major gay victory was assured.

3. "Desensitize" people to the subject by constantly talking about gayness (but hide the negative aspects).

The third principle was aimed to help get straights to "view homosexuality with neutrality rather than hostility." (177) As phrased by Kirk and Madsen, "You can forget about trying right up front to persuade folks that homosexuality is a *good* thing. But if you can get them to think it is just another thing—meriting no more than a shrug of the shoulders, then your battle for legal and social rights is virtually won." (177) To accomplish this "shoulder shrug," the movement would have to talk nonstop about homosexuality in a neutral yet supportive way.

> The free and frequent discussion of gay rights by a variety of persons in a variety of places gives the impression that homosexuality is commonplace. (177) [...] Constant talk builds the impression that public opinion is at least divided on the subject, and that a sizable block—the most modern, up-to-date citizens—accept or even practice homosexuality. (178)

Kirk and Madsen foresaw that incessant talk about "gay rights" as an "abstract social question" would obviate the need for any serious discussion of the real issues of homosexuality. Hence, avoidance of the real issues was an essential corollary to the "Keep Talking" stratagem. Indeed, the authors stress the need for the homosexual community to hide the grim realities of homosexual behavior from straight America, to limit any discussion about what gay sex really involves, and to refrain from admitting the negatives of the gay lifestyle. "In the early stages of the campaign," write Kirk and Madsen, "the public should not be shocked and repelled by premature exposure to homo*sexual* behavior itself. Instead the imagery of sex per se should be downplayed, and the issue of gay rights reduced, as far as possible, to an abstract social question." (178) As phrased by the authors in the earlier article, "First let the camel get his nose inside the tent—and only later his unsightly derriere." ("The Overhauling of Straight America," 9)

Once the desensitization campaign has been successfully completed, then any perceived negatives attached to the condition—including, presumably, the camel's "unsightly derriere"—can be attributed to the distorted projections of a few recalcitrant, neurotic "homophobes" and their pathological revulsion for what has already been accepted by society at large as a natural variant of the sexual urge.

Kirk and Madsen recognized that, without further definition, "constant talk" would be powerless to "quell the religious heebie-jeebies felt by many Ambivalent Skeptics and played upon by the Intransigents." (178) To remedy this deficiency, they advocated the following measures "to confound the homohatred of the moderately religious:" (179)

> **i. Muddy the Moral Waters:** The talk should strive to "muddy the moral waters" by "publicizing support by moderate churches and raising serious theological objections to conservative biblical teachings . . . ." (179)
>
> **ii. Undermine Religious Authority:** The talk should seek to "undermine the moral authority of homohating churches over less fervent adherents by portraying such institutions as antiquated backwaters, badly out of step with the times and with the latest findings of psychology." (179) The authors cite the example of the proponents of divorce and abortion, both of whom won significant victories over "the atavistic tug of Old Time Religion" by focusing on "the mightier pull of Science and Public Opinion." (179)[11] To that end, the authors urge gays to forge an "unholy alliance" (179) with scientists, moderate religious leaders, and opinion makers against the more recalcitrant religious groups.

The growing acceptance of gay ordination and gay "marriage" within the less traditional sectors of Christian and Jewish congregations may give some indication of how well these tactics have succeeded.

4. Keep the message focused on gay issues: don't fight for other causes.

Gay strategists were concerned lest the movement embroil itself

---

11. The example cited by the authors is no longer persuasive. A 2002 study reported the following results from the decline of the two-parent, married-couple family over the past 30 years: "poverty, ill-health, educational failure, unhappiness, anti-social behavior, isolation and social exclusion for thousands of men, women, and children." Rebecca O'Neil, "Experiments in Living: the Fatherless Family," *Civitas,* Sept., 2002; <http://www.fathersforlife.org/divorce/chldrndiv.htm>.

in extraneous causes. "We have no natural allies," write Kirk and Madsen, "and therefore cannot rely on the assistance of any group. We have only tactical allies—people who do not want barbarous things done to us because they fear the same thing may someday be done to them."[12] (181) Therefore, the authors advise fellow gays to stay clear of other marginalized groups and their causes, lest they become associated in the public perception with such groups, thus "[reinforcing] the mainstream's suspicion that gays are another microfraction of the lunatic fringe." (181) Conversely, gays are advised to align themselves "with large mainstream groups that can actually advance our interest (*e.g.,* the Democratic party, the National Organization for Women, or the Presbyterian Church)." (182)

5. Portray homosexuals as victims, not as threats to the status quo.

Another part of the war plan articulated by Kirk and Madsen was to portray homosexuals as victims of hatred and prejudice while simultaneously vilifying their opponents by comparing them to the Ku Klux Klan and the Nazis (*see* stratagem No. 8, below). The authors recommend the use of "graphic pictures of brutalized gays, dramatizations of job and housing insecurity, loss of child custody, public humiliation, *etc.*" (184) The authors recognized that in order to prevail in the arena of public opinion, "gays must be portrayed as victims in need of protection so that straights will be inclined by reflex to assume the role of protector. [. . .] For that reason, we must forgo the temptation to strut our gay pride publicly to such an extent that we undermine our victim image." (183) For Kirk and Madsen, this meant that "cocky mustachioed leather-men, drag queens, and bulldykes would not appear in gay commercials and other public presentations." (183-84) Neither would NAMBLA, or other extreme

---

12. By the term "natural allies" Kirk & Madsen mean people who support gays for what they are rather than because of "the way we are treated."

fringe elements of the gay movement.[13] Kirk and Madsen had made the same point in their earlier magazine article: "[S]uspected child-molesters will never look like victims" (*Guide,* 8)

Films like the Academy Award winning "Philadelphia"—purportedly the first Hollywood movie to confront the issue of AIDS discrimination—both exacerbated gays' own self-image of victimhood and exponentially augmented outside sympathy for their cause.[14]

Thus, Kirk and Madsen counsel that homosexuals portray themselves as victims of circumstances who "no more chose their sexual orientation than they did, say, their height, skin color, talents, or limitations." (184)

Indeed, given the central role to be played by gay victimhood in the homosexual revolution, it was predictable that gay strategists would espouse the theory that homosexuals are "born that way"—in

---

13. NAMBLA is the acronym for North American Man/Boy Love Association. Their website home page proclaims, among other things, that "Freedom is indivisible. The liberation of children, women, boy-lovers and homosexuals in general, can occur only as complementary facets of the same dream." On a different page, we read, under the title, "Is Harry Potter Gay?", by emu [sic] Nugent: "Gay literature is everybody's literature, all boys need to read about homosexuality, and children and young people have as much right to read and hear what they want as anyone else. [. . .] Gay kids' books, like gay boys, are on their way out of the closet." <http://216.220.97.17/>. NAMBLA's lesser-known sister organization NAWGLA, the North American Women/Girl Lover Association, has similar goals: "'Why should a woman have to wait until she turns eighteen or twenty-one to be sexually active with other women? [. . .] If a woman is interested in having a cross-generational lover, I cannot think of one good reason—apart from the threat of persecution—why she should deny herself such a relationship." Pat Califia, <http://www.inoohr.org/lesbianpedophilia.htm>.

14. This 1993 award-winning film portrayed an AIDS-stricken homosexual fired by his law firm because of his medical condition, and the small-time black lawyer who represents him in his wrongful-termination lawsuit. The film observes the lawyer as he transforms from anti-gay bigot to sympathizer once he draws the intended parallels between the gay rights movement and the African-American struggle for civil rights.

other words, that their sexual orientation is already *determined* at birth—whether or not there existed any scientific basis for such a claim. Revealingly, Kirk and Madsen stress the need for homosexuals to stand behind the "Born Gay" theory—even *though the authors themselves recognize its invalidity:* "For all practical purposes, gays should be considered to have been born gay—*even though sexual orientation, for most humans, seems to be the product of a complex interaction between innate predispositions and environmental factors during childhood and early adolescence.*" (184) (Emphasis added.)

A Brief Look at the "Born Gay" Theory.

The need to portray gays as victims is thus inseparably linked to the "Born Gay" hypothesis. Jan Clausen, a former leader of New York's lesbian community (later expelled by her comrades for marrying a man), details how gay advocates developed this "born gay" fictive science as a tactic to influence public perceptions of sexual identity: "fuelled by the prestige of contemporary genetic science, the craze for biological explanations of all sorts of human behavior has given boost to 'born that way' theories of erotic attraction."[15] Such pressure from "determinist" quarters, as well as "high profile campaigns for basic rights for gay men and lesbians" resulted in "obsessive media coverage of scientists' efforts to identify possible biological influences on sexuality," which, as the author herself acknowledges, were "commonly reported in oversimplified terms that foster notions of genetic determination not claimed by the researchers themselves." It bears stressing that as of the date of this publication, *no genetic earmark distinguishing homosexuals from heterosexuals has been identified.* So far as science has been able to discover, homosexuals and heterosexuals are genetically indistin-

---

15. Jan Clausen, *Apples & Oranges: My Journey Through Sexual Identity*, Boston & New York: Houghton Mifflin (1999), p. 235.

guishable.[16] Moreover, as noted in a highly respected journal of

---

16. Not one of the researchers commonly cited by gay activists has reported anything even close to proving the genetic nature of sexual orientation. Not one study claiming results favorable to the "gay gene" theory has ever been replicated under the scrutiny of rigorous experimental controls. The three most cited studies are not only seriously flawed, but the authors themselves have admitted that those studies should not be cited as proof of the gay gene theory. For example:

(1) Dean Hamer claimed his study showed a statistically significant correlation between homosexual orientation and the genetic sequence of the top of the X chromosome. His study has been widely criticized for lacking a control group and for a statistical methodology that, according to charges by a former research colleague, was flawed by data selectively chosen to enhance Hamer's thesis. Even Dr. Hamer admitted that "These genes do not cause people to become homosexuals ... the biology of personality is much more complicated than that." *Time,* April 27, 1998, cited in Chad Thompson, *The Homophobia Stops Here: Addressing the Ex Gay Perspective in Public Schools,* Des Moines: InQueery (2004), p. 10.

(2) Michael Bailey and colleagues conducted numerous studies in an attempt to show a statistically significant concordance of homosexuality in identical twins. Since identical twins share the same gene pool, the existence of a "gay gene" should have produced a near 100% rate of concordance. However, the highest percentage ever tabulated was just over 50%. When Bailey tried to replicate his findings with an Australian population of twins, his new study showed homosexuality concurring in less than half the number claimed in his original study. Dr. Neil Whitehead has extensively analyzed these studies. *See* <www.mygenes.co.nz>.

(3) In an attempt to show that sexuality is hard-wired into the brain via the hypothalamus, Simon LeVay examined the corpses of 19 homosexuals who died of AIDS complications and compared them with a group of 16 male and 6 female corpses he *presumed* were heterosexual. His debatable conclusion noted a difference in the size of a specific neuron group (INA H3). His results, too, could never be replicated. Shortly after the study's publication, an openly homosexual reporter correctly observed, "It turns out that LeVay doesn't know anything about the sexual orientation of his control group." Critiquing LeVay's claim that "he knows his control group are heterosexual because their brains are different from HIVer corpses," the same commentator jibes, "Sorry, doctor; this is circular logic. You can use the sample to prove the theory or vice versa, but not both at the same time." Michael Botkin, "Salt and Pepper," *The Bay Area Reporter,* September 6, 1991, pp. 21 and 24, as quoted in Anton M. Marco, "Gay Marriage," <http://www.narth.com/ docs/marco.html.>. LeVay himself is on record as stating: "The most common mistake people make in interpreting my work" is either that "homosexuality is genetic" or that it can prove "a genetic cause for being gay." *Discover,* March, 1994, as cited in Thompson, *supra,* p. 9. Hence, in spite of the

medicine, "[F]rom an evolutionary perspective, genetically determined homosexuality would have become extinct long ago because of reduced reproduction"[17]

6. Give potential supporters a cause they can relate to, such as anti-discrimination; don't ask them to support the practice of homosexuality per se.

Consistent with the need to emphasize gay victimhood while drawing attention away from homosexual practices themselves, Kirk and Madsen advise that "[the gay movement] should not demand explicit support for homosexual practices, but should instead take anti-discrimination as its theme." This stratagem is as inseparably linked with Stratagems 7 and 8, as it is part of 6. Indeed, the purpose of this directive is obviously to make the movement's opponents look

---

torrents of propaganda about claimed differences in the wiring of "homosexual" versus "heterosexual" brains, no credible evidence has yet been found to support such claims. As Masters & Johnson conclude, "no serious scientist" would apply the "simple cause-effect relationship" of the genetic theory of homosexuality. Wm. Masters, Virginia Johnson, Robert Kolodny, *Human Sexuality,* Boston: Little Brown & Co. (2d ed. 1985), p. 411.

Notwithstanding the flaws in "gay gene studies," and thanks to the constant bombardment of misinformation and disinformation by the media, the myth of a "gay gene" has seeped into the public consciousness. (*See above,* note 8.) For example, after the 1993 publication of Dr. Hamer's study, the *New York Times* headlined, "Report Suggests Homosexuality is Linked to Genes," while the *Wall Street Journal* trumpeted, "Research Points Toward a 'Gay' Gene." Two later headlines in the *New York Times* illustrate the ongoing effort to keep the theory alive: "Study Reveals New Difference between the Sexes, *New York Times,* March 17, 2005, p. A25; and "For Gay Men, Different Scent of Attraction," *New York Times*, May 10, 2005, p. 1.

17. Miron Baron, "Genetic Linkage and Male Homosexual Orientation," *British Medical Journal,* Vol. 307 (Aug. 7, 1993), p. 337, cited in Peter Sprigg and Timothy Dailey (eds.), *Getting It Straight: What The Research Shows about Homosexuality,* Family Research Council, Washington, D.C. (2004), p. 13.

so bad that average Americans will want to dissociate from them. In America, the anti-discrimination theme always has great potential for winning. "Fundamental freedoms, constitutional rights, due process and equal protection of the laws, basic fairness and decency toward all of humanity—these should be the concerns brought to mind by our campaign." (187)

Just how effective this tactic has been can be gauged from the way in which the mental health professions succumbed to it: in 1973, in what was intended as a statement of the inherent decency and humanity of the profession, the American Psychiatric Association removed "homosexuality" from the nomenclature of mental health disorders. The next day, worldwide headlines simplistically blared "Doctors Declare Homosexuality Normal." Subsequently, other mental health professional associations, such as the American Psychological Association in 1974, followed the Psychiatric Association's lead.

From a reading of the history of the debate in both APAs, it is clear that the decision was never based on any scientific re-evaluation of the evidence, but rather was linked almost entirely to political pressure from the gay activist movement. In other words, the declassification of homosexuality from the list of mental pathologies should not be viewed as an "approximation of scientific truth" but rather as "an action demanded by the ideological temper of the times."[18] The motivating force behind the decision was the demand for equal rights, for human rights. And who is against human rights?[19]

---

18. Ronald Bayer, *Homosexuality and American Psychiatry: The Politics of Diagnosis,* Princeton U. Press (1987), p. 4. *See also* Wright and Cummings, *op. cit.,* and the material found in Chapter 11, pp. 403 ff." And *see Responsum* of Rabbi Leonard Levy, *Same Sex Attraction and Halakhah,* Appendix I, "The Clinical Experience of Dr. Nicholas Cummings," pp. 29-33, <http://www.rabbinicalassembly.org/law/new_teshuvot.html >.

19. In an e-mail dated Nov. 28, 2006, Dr. Nicholas Cummings, past president of the American Psychological Association indicated to me that his sponsorship of the resolution to remove homosexuality from the DSM in 1974 was premised upon his belief that the APA's classification of homosexuality as a disease had resulted in

Of course, the issue of human or civil rights has nothing to do with whether homosexuality is "normal" or "abnormal." Is it permissible, under our laws, to penalize or discriminate against those who may be justifiably classified as outside the norm—simply because they have characteristics which are atypical of the majority of society? The shining principle of American Constitutional law is surely that all human beings are entitled to equal treatment under the law. Moreover, it is a universal principle of jurisprudence that just laws imply an underlying freedom to choose between what is

---

homosexuals being denied equal treatment under the law. During his forty-four years of private practice in San Francisco, Dr. Cummings principally served gay and lesbian clients (while simultaneously serving as Chief of Mental Health for a California HMO where he supervised over 900 psychologists, psychiatrists, and social workers). Dr. Cummings estimates that while he helped 80% of his clients adjust to their same-sex orientation, he was able to help the remaining 20% *successfully* change their orientation to heterosexual. Dr. Cummings attributes this success to his scrupulous honoring of the patient's right of determination.

Dr. Cummings also reaffirmed his commitment to the principle that political beliefs should never be promoted as science when the scientific evidence does not exist to support them:

> My early resolutions [on gay issues] were intended to spark research in the area, and every one of my resolutions included that the APA would promote and even sponsor such research. My appointing the First Task Force on Gay & Lesbian Issues was to be just that. A task force to investigate, research, find evidence, and make subsequent recommendations. Unfortunately, the portions of my resolutions requiring research were conveniently forgotten and lost in history. Several years after my initial resolutions, I confronted the APA as to why absolutely no attempt at research was made, and I was completely stonewalled. All my resolutions (except the one on diagnosis, which I thought was inappropriate absent research that homosexuality is a disease) were meant for APA Internal use, not as proclamations to the public. The Leona Tyler principle [which authorized the] APA [to] speak to the public only when evidence justified proclamations, has been essentially trampled. [...] It was not long after my well-intentioned efforts that the APA went completely one-sided on gay issues, and any push for adequate research evidence was met with hostility and charges of homophobia . . . .

permitted and what is forbidden. Our repugnance for discrimination is based—very fundamentally—on the recognition that race, color, and physical or mental handicaps are generally not matters of choice. Given the anti-discrimination thrust of the gay movement, it was inevitable, as discussed above at Stratagem No. 5, that the hypothesis of a genetic cause for homosexuality would be seen as indispensable to it, and would be adopted as its central tenet.

7. Make gays look good: portray them as Everyman and Everywoman.

Gay strategists recognized that in order to demonize the "straight" opposition (*see* Stratagem No. 8, below), the image of "gay victim" must first be presented in as favorable and sympathetic a light as possible. This would heighten the contrast between the oppressed and the oppressor. As Kirk and Madsen write, "[S]trongly favorable images of gays must be set before the public. The campaign should paint gay men and lesbians as *superior*—veritable pillars of society. Yes, yes, we know, this trick is so old it creaks." (187-88). This was to be done by drawing on (a) famous homosexuals in history, and (b) gay celebrities in the contemporary media. (Evidently, the list of documented homosexual greats was not big enough for them, for they substituted a number of hypothetical ones (188) for their greater shock value!)

In a revealing passage, Kirk and Madsen explain why historical gay figures are so useful to the movement:

> [F]irst, they are invariably dead as a doornail, hence in no position to deny the truth and sue for libel. Second . . . the virtues and accomplishments that make these historic gay figures admirable cannot be gainsaid or dismissed by the public, since high school history textbooks have already set them in incontrovertible cement. By casting its violet spotlight on such revered heroes, in no time a skillful media campaign could have the gay community looking like the veritable fairy godmother to Western civilization. (188)

As far as the celebrity endorsements were concerned, the logic behind this tactic was the same as any other advertising campaign. The point was to get the average American to say to himself, "I like and admire Mr. Celeb; Mr. Celeb is queer and/or respects queers; so either I must stop liking and admiring Mr. Celeb, or else it must be all right for me to respect queers." (188-89)

8. Make opponents look bad: portray them as evil and victimizing.

Now, however, comes a significant switch. The tables are to be turned: the average American must be induced to dissociate himself from the opponents of homosexuality. Time to go on the offensive. Apparently, Kirk & Madsen believed that only so much could be achieved through a campaign of positive reinforcement. Once that plateau was attained, the campaign was to be turned negative, and the opponents of the gay movement were to be attacked and vilified. For Kirk and Madsen, this technique was "the clincher." Thus they made it the final step of their envisioned media campaign for gay rights.

Clearly, strategists Kirk & Madsen were saving the best for last: "[T]he best way to make homohatred look bad is to vilify those who victimize gays." (189) However, *the word "victimize" is so loosely applied as to include almost anyone who disagrees with any aspect of the homosexual movement.* Indeed, as we have seen in "J's" Case History (Case No. 2) in Chapter Two, the pseudo-medical term "internalized homophobia"[20] has become the weapon of choice for discrediting all those who, for whatever reason, have reservations about the gay agenda or any part of it. Some may remember how Dr. Laura Schlessinger's TV show was cancelled as a result of a

---

20. Significantly, though the APA expunged homosexuality from their Diagnostic & Statistical Manual of Mental Disorders ("DSM"), "homophobia" has never been added to the list! The phrase "internalized homophobia" is meaningless jargon: all phobias are "internalized," or they would not be phobias! Moreover, by definition, a phobia is an *irrational* fear, not a rationally-based disagreement!

concerted campaign by gay activists resentful of her conservative stance on sex and fearful of her growing popularity. It should be noted that similar tactics were used with particular gusto and refinement by Karl Marx and his followers in their ideological battles with rival socialist theorists. Other notable targets of this vitriolic gay rights stratagem include Dr. Joseph Nicolosi and Richard Cohen, both well-known therapists with long records of helping gay strugglers.[21]

Another, more visual and more visceral technique of vilification was through a time-honored propaganda shtick called the "bracket technique." Kirk and Madsen, cleverly enough, suggest juxtaposing images of ranting "homohaters" (for example, an unctuous, beady-eyed Southern preacher pounding the pulpit against "those perverted, abominable creatures") alongside photos of badly beaten gay victims.[22] This technique, however, is particularly dangerous in

---

21. Both Nicolosi and Cohen were ridiculed in Wayne Besen's book, *Anything but Straight: Unmasking the Scandals and Lies Behind the Ex-Gay Myth*, San Francisco: Harrington Park Press (2003). in chapters bearing the titles "Nicolosi's Nonsense" and "Radical Richard." The present author, too, has had a taste of this medicine. When a "sexpert" columnist for *Time Out New York* lambasted two letter writers for expressing disaffection for the gay lifestyle and for seeking advice about settling down with someone of the opposite sex, I sent in a letter suggesting that the columnist should have at least discussed the option of changing sexual orientation and listed some of the available resources. The columnist featured my letter in his column, but, instead of addressing the substantive issues raised, chose to respond with a personal attack on my character, message, work, and qualifications. "S***-shower," "creepy," "ignoramus," "moral bankruptcy," and "psychological pathology" were among the terms used! See *Time Out New York*, No. 451, May 20-27, 2004. Subsequently, in *Genre Magazine*, this same columnist listed me as "the most ingeniously insidious" of "the 15 most dangerous people to gays," for being "so seriously delusional about the ability of gays to change." Jaime Bufalino, "Evildoers: *Genre* Takes Aim at the 15 People, Places & Things that Pose the Biggest Threat to Gay Life as We Know it," *Genre Magazine*, June, 2004, p. 84.

22. The original magazine article was more direct on this point than the book.: "Our goal here is twofold. First, we seek to replace the mainstream's self-righteous pride about its homophobia with shame and guilt. Second, we intend to make the anti-gays look so nasty that average Americans will want to disassociate themselves from such types. The public should be shown images of ranting homophobes whose

malicious hands. A pro-gay documentary film about homosexuality within the Orthodox and Hasidic Communities used a number of poignant personal "stories" to generalize, ridicule and denigrate Orthodox attitudes to homosexuality. The film won huge acclaim in the gay and lesbian and secular Jewish media as well as a major grant from Steven Spielberg's Righteous Persons Foundation. The film used the "bracket" technique very effectively when it showed several apparently chassidic individuals angrily protesting against gays, and then contrasted that segment with footage of decent, harmless, and likeable individual gays who had allegedly been "victimized" by Orthodox Jewish religious persecution.[23]

Carrying the Homosexual Agenda into the Public School Systems.

When Kirk and Madsen and the "War Conference" were plotting to "Undermine Religious Authority" (see Stratagem No. 3 above), they couldn't have foreseen that the greatest blow to the moral authority of one of the major Churches would come from its own priests under a snowstorm of accusations of widespread pederastic

---

secondary traits and beliefs disgust middle America. These images might include: the Ku Klux Klan demanding that gays be burned alive or castrated; bigoted southern ministers drooling with hysterical hatred to a degree that looks both comical and deranged; menacing punks, thugs, and convicts speaking coolly about the 'fags' they have killed or would like to kill; a tour of Nazi concentration camps where homosexuals were tortured and gassed."

23. The context of this "protest" footage was obviously cut. Such demonstrations have occurred in response to deliberate provocations such as gay-pride parades through religious neighborhoods. The movie "Trembling Before G-d" did more than just denigrate Orthodox attitudes towards homosexuality: it completely and deliberately suppressed any positive references to the possibility of change. Instead of pointing to the remarkable success of gender-affirming processes, the producers of the film chose to focus on various ludicrous remedies allegedly prescribed by the Orthodox for overcoming homosexuality—such as, for example, "eating figs and dates."

abuse. Ironically, however, the homosexual movement was hardly in a position to benefit from the scandal. The image of a priest using the authority of his office and his vestments to commit sexual battery on trusting young boys and youths does little for the homosexual image that the movement hopes to project. In actuality, however, while most homosexual activists publicly deny that homosexual males want access to young boys or that lesbians want access to young girls, it is well documented that "many homosexual groups around the world are working aggressively to lower the age of sexual consent."[24] Some of these groups have been fully transparent about their motives. Former California State Assemblyman Steve Baldwin reports that a Netherlands homosexual organization (COC), commenting on the success of that campaign in their country, crowed:

> The liberation of pedophilia must be viewed as a gay issue . . . ages of consent should therefore be abolished . . . . [B]y acknowledging the affinity between homosexuality and pedophilia, the COC has quite possibly made it easier for homosexual adults to become more sensitive to the erotic desires of younger members of their sex, thereby broadening gay identity.[25]

Baldwin adds that "Homosexual leaders repeatedly argue for the freedom to engage in consensual sex with children, and blind surveys reveal a shockingly high number of homosexuals [who] admit to sexual contact with minors. Indeed, the homosexual community is

---

24. Frank York & Robert Knight, "Homosexual Behavior and Pedophilia," <http://us2000.org/cfmc/pedophilia.pdf>. Mexico, the Netherlands, Argentina, Chile, and Columbia have lowered the age of consent to 12; Spain, to 13, and Italy, Iceland, Hungary, Austria and Canada, to 14. *See* Sam Kastensmidt, "International Sex Laws May Affect U.S. Policy," Jan. 17, 2005, <http://www.reclaimamerica.org/PAGES?NEWS/newspage.asp/story=2366>. In England, the campaign to lower the age of consent is led by two homosexual organizations, Outrage! and Stonewall.

25. Steve Baldwin, "Child Molestation and the Homosexual Movement," 14 *Regent U. Law Review,* No. 2 (2001-2002), p. 278.

driving the worldwide campaign to lower the legal age of consent." (268)

In our own United States, as far back as 1972, the National Coalition of Gay Organizations included in their "gay rights platform" a demand to "repeal all laws governing the age of sexual consent."[26] (Baldwin, 277, *citing* York & Knight, 3) Here, too, this campaign has won substantial gains, and further inroads may be

---

26. The *Journal of Homosexuality*, one of the leading American academic journals in the mainstream homosexual world, published a special double issue entitled *Male Intergenerational Intimacy*, extolling sex between male adults and minors. Baldwin cites examples of the ideas to be found therein, *e.g.*: "[P]arents should view the pedophile who loves their son 'not as a rival or competitor, not as a theft of their property, but as a partner in the boy's upbringing, someone to be welcomed into their home.'" (Baldwin, 274) Another example cited by Baldwin is from a 1995 article in *Guide:*

> We can be proud that the gay movement has been home to the few voices who have had the courage to say out loud that children are naturally sexual, that they deserve the right to sexual expression with whoever they choose .... [...] Instead of fearing being labeled as pedophiles, we must proudly proclaim that sex is good, including children's sexuality .... We must do it for the children's sake. (Baldwin, 274)

Ironically, the pedophilia lobby has been careful to "dignify" their objectives under the cloak of generic sexual liberation for children. One representative book argues for the decriminalization of pedophilia and the legitimization of "intergenerational intimacy" as a lifestyle choice. Judith Levine, *Harmful to Minors: The Perils of Protecting Children from Sex,* U. Minnesota Press, 2002. Levine believes that "adults owe children not only protection and a schooling in safety but also the entitlement to pleasure." (Introduction), and that "[w]hen we are ready to invite children into the community as fully participating citizens ... [t]hat will be the moment at which we respect their sexual autonomy and agency and realize that one way to help them cultivate the capacity to enjoy life is to educate their capacity for sexual joy." (224) ("Sexual autonomy" is a favorite buzzword employed by NAMBLA, the North American Man/Boy Love Association.) Indeed, argues the author, "Sex is not harmful to children. It is a vehicle to self-knowledge, love, healing, creativity, adventure, and intense feelings of aliveness. There are many ways even the smallest children can partake of it." (225)

expected.[27]

In this regard, it is interesting to note that according to Avert, an organization that, among other things, provides homosexuals with legal guidelines facilitating sexual activity with minors,[28] courts in 21 states have either repealed or struck down as unconstitutional age-regulatory laws as applied to gay or lesbian sex between an adult and minor, while analogous laws pertaining to heterosexual sex were left intact.[29] Similarly, eleven American jurisdictions are listed as having repealed laws setting a minimum age for minors to engage in gay and lesbian sex—while retaining laws prohibiting sex between underage males and females.[30] In 16 states, the age of consent is purportedly the same for both sexes, irrespective of the type of sex involved.[31] In only three states is there a higher age of consent (18) for gay or lesbian sex

---

27. Sam Kastensmidt (*see* note 24, above) worries that the U.S. Supreme Court, in deciding age-of-consent cases, will consider social trends in foreign law, as it did in *Lawrence vs. Texas* (Texas anti-sodomy law struck down). Kastensmidt refers to an article by a current Supreme Court Justice (Ruth Bader Ginsburg) that (prior to her appointment) called for lowering the age of consent to 12! *See* "Sex Bias in the U.S. Code," *Report of the U.S. Commission on Civil Rights* (April, 1977).

28. For their chart, "Worldwide Ages of Consent," listing by state and country the minimum ages of consent for homosexual and heterosexual sex, *see* <http://www.avert.org/aofconsent.htm>. The following statistics are taken from that source.

29. These 21 states are listed as: Alabama, Arkansas, Florida, Idaho, Kansas, Kentucky, Louisiana, Maryland, Massachusetts, Michigan, Minnesota, Mississippi, Missouri, North Carolina, Oklahoma, South Carolina, Tennessee, Texas, Utah, Virginia, and Wyoming.

30. These states are listed as: Arizona, District of Columbia, Delaware, Hawaii, Iowa, Nebraska, North Dakota, Ohio, Rhode Island, South Dakota, and Vermont.

31. These states are listed as: Alaska, California, Colorado, Connecticut, Georgia, Illinois, Indiana, Maine, Montana, New Jersey, New Mexico, New York, Oregon, Pennsylvania, Washington, and Wisconsin.

than for heterosexual sex (16).[32] Puerto Rico is reportedly the only U.S. jurisdiction where homosexual sex—gay or lesbian—is illegal.[33]

Had the "gay rights" advocates confined themselves to disseminating objective and accurate information about homosexuality, much might have been said in favor of educating young adolescents toward the ability to make intelligent and informed choices in regard to their developing sexuality. However, rather than provide fair and unbiased information, over the last two decades the "gay rights" advocates have worked tirelessly behind the scenes to proselytize, indoctrinate and intellectually seduce children through the very public school system whose duty it has traditionally been to protect and foster their morality. In many school districts throughout the nation, elementary, middle and high schools have been transformed from community-oriented centers where moral, civic and scholarly values were instilled and nurtured, into carefully guarded precincts for the counter-cultural transformation of young and adolescent children.

Indeed, often without the parents' full awareness of what is going on (many of these programs expressly warn teachers not to let students take class materials home with them), "sex education programs" throughout the USA, Canada and Europe, have swept all educational levels from kindergarten on up. These "sex education programs" have less to do with "education" than with indoctrination.

Consistent with the gay movement's stated goals of deconstructing family life, these programs have as their common, stated objective the "re-education" of youth to a full acceptance of gay and

---

32. Nevada, New Hampshire, and West Virginia.

33. Note, However, that in regard to Puerto Rico the minimum age for consensual heterosexual sex is listed as 14.

lesbian homosexuality as legitimate, "alternate lifestyles," available to any and everyone for experimentation and selection. So blatant is this purposeful, behind-the-door meddling with the sexuality of children sent to school to learn "reading, writing and 'rithmetic," that many people are shocked to realize that some of this material has been in school systems for 35 years or more.[34] *About Your Sexuality* is a good example. Published by the Unitarian-Universalist Association and prepared by one Deryk Calderwood, this program includes slides, audiocassettes, and printed materials. The package is designed for

---

34. A major issue in the battle over sex education in the public schools involves what rights, if any, parents retain over the education of their children. *See* Bret Kaplan, "Can The State Distribute Condoms to Children in Schools Without Parental Consent?" 23 *Rutgers L. Rec.* 3 (1999), <http://www.lawrecord.com/oldsite-re20050412/articles/vol23/232rlr/23rlr3.html>. According to another law review article, New York City school children receive a pamphlet entitled "A Teenager's Bill of Rights," which states: "I have the right to decide whether to have sex and who [*sic!*] to have it with." Judith A. Reisman, "Crafting Bi/Homosexual Youth," *Regent U. Law Rev.*, Vol. 14 (2002-02), p. 325.

The 2002 *Elementary and Secondary Education Act Reauthorization,* Title VIII, Part E, Sec. 8513 prohibits funds authorized under the Act to be used "to develop programs designed to promote or encourage sexual activity, whether homosexual or heterosexual." However, the exceptions appear broad enough to dilute or nullify the effect of the statute.

A number of jurisdictions have passed parental notification laws under which parents may "opt" their children into or out of sex-ed programs. It is doubtful, however, whether such laws are respected by school authorities. In Silver Lake, Massachusetts, school officials ordered 9th grade students in a freshman health class to keep from their parents a book that advised: "You may come to the conclusion that growing up means rejecting the values of your parents." Similarly, New York City school children receive a pamphlet entitled, *A Teenager's Bill of Rights,* which instructs young readers that "I have the right to decide whether to have sex and who [*sic*] to have it with." The pamphlet does not mention parents, or the age at which a minor may consent to sex, or what constitutes statutory rape. And, in Manomet, Massachusetts, when an 8th grade health class student complained that the material handed out by his instructor violated his parents' beliefs, the instructor replied, "if you have trouble with your parents, tell me and I'll handle them." *See* <www.article8.org>. The lesson for parents is clear: maintain vigilance over what your children are being taught.

presentation to grades as young as junior high school (ages 12-14). A promotional flyer claims that *"About Your Sexuality* has been used extensively across the continent by religious organizations: Protestant, Catholic, Jewish and others; public and private schools; junior high, senior high, and colleges; and by community organizations including: YMCA, YWCA, Planned Parenthood affiliates, youth agencies, adolescent shelters, public and private health care organizations, *etc."* (Dresner, 37)

Rabbi Dresner surveys this material in his book, *Can Families Survive in Pagan America?* He rates the material "contemptuous of conventional morality" and "as explicit as any X-rated movie." (36) It is worth looking at Rabbi Dresner's run-through of the contents:

> First there is the specific warning to teachers which reads: 'Caution: Participants should not be given extra copies of the form to show to their parents or friends. Many of the materials of this program, shown to people outside of the content of the program itself, can evoke misunderstanding and difficulty.'

Next, Rabbi Dresner lists (36-7) several features of "About Your Sexuality" that might conceivably "evoke misunderstanding and difficulty" if disclosed to "parents or friends:"

➤ "Color Slides of heterosexual and homosexual couples engaging in a variety of sex acts, including oral and anal intercourse. In these slides, nothing is left to the imagination. Sex organs and penetration are explicit."

➤ "Instructions to the teacher, suggesting what to do if youngsters are repelled by color slides of homosexual acts: 'You might compare any negative responses concerning the difficulty of accepting same sex lovemaking with the difficulty some people experience in watching a birth film for the first time. It is a natural part of life, but we aren't used to seeing it. It may take some time to appreciate and enjoy the beauty of the experience.'"

➤ "Testimonials from homosexuals indicating their satisfaction with the life they lead," including graphic descriptions of their sexual practices.

➤ "The argument that homosexual experiences in youth actually help heterosexuals to adjust to sexual relations with members of the opposite sex in later life."

➤ "Two slide segments which in turn depict a naked boy and a naked girl, while the audio portion tells the audience how each subject masturbates. In film sequence, the boy tastes his own semen, and male viewers are subtly urged to do likewise."

As emotional as Rabbi Dresner's reaction to this material may be, his description leaves no room for doubt that this "educational program" is far more than a clinical, precautionary introduction to sexual awareness. It is in fact an open invitation to underage boys and girls to experiment with masturbation and sexual and homosexual intercourse, an introduction to pornography, and an outright plea to children of unformed judgment to consider gay sex as if it were nothing more than a breakfast cereal: "Try it. You'll like it."

About Your Sexuality is far from an isolated instance. On April 30, 2005, at a Brookline, Massachusetts High School conference sponsored by GLSEN (Gay, Lesbian Straight Education Network) an "educational" pamphlet entitled *A Little Black Book* was distributed to children as young as 13. This pamphlet was partially sponsored by government agencies such as the Massachusetts Department of Public Health and the Boston Public Health Commission. Open to the first page, and this is what you will read:

> Is this a great time to be gay or what? We are faced with important challenges every day like the right to marry, homophobia, coming out, STDs [*i.e.,* sexually transmitted diseases] and HIV/AIDS, but queers have never enjoyed more visibility and acceptance than

today. The Boston area is a good place to be young and queer . . .

As might be expected from this introduction, *A Little Black Book* is really a sexual "how-to" manual complete with explicit pornographic material. While the pamphlet makes some attempt to explain the health risks involved in various sexual activities (explicit photos show how to apply condoms)—and thus qualify for government funding as an "age-appropriate HIV-prevention program"—*A Little Black Book* actually minimizes the danger of unrestrained sexual activity, and ultimately advocates certain potentially dangerous sexual behaviors. For example, on pages 24-25, under the heading "How Safe is Dat?" (note the patronizing use of street slang here!), the authors advise impressionable young teens about the hazards of what they genteelly term "Mutual Jerking Off:" "Jerking off together can be a hot and safer way to have fun. This is a safe activity for HIV. Some STDs can be transmitted by touching, but all-in-all, this is a pretty low-risk, boys!"

A Little Black Book also offers "advice" regarding the use of "sex toys:"

> Sharing toys can be fun, and fortunately they are easy to keep clean. A good idea is to put condoms on your toys, replace the condom between users, and use lots of lube. If you don't have any rubbers, clean those toys well with lots of soap and hot water. There is some risk of hepatitis, herpes, warts and parasites.

Condoms are recommended as the be-all and end-all recipe for "safe sex." This topic is addressed several times within the booklet. On the "Handy-Dandy Condom Guide" page, the booklet lists "5 reasons why condoms are still a queer boy's best friend," but scoffs outright at the concept of sexual abstinence of any degree or kind! Thus, the pamphlet advises: "Condoms are still the most reliable protection against STDs a gay boy can have (next to abstinence, but how much fun is that?)" Aside from the fact that *A Little Black Book* was at least partially paid for with tax dollars (has it sunk in yet?) the "safe-sex" advice it purveys may not be altogether reliable. According to Dr. John R. Diggs, Jr., a noted physician from South Hadley, Massachusetts who has written widely on the health risks of homosexuality,

> The brochure is patently wrong—Mass Department of Health, where are you?—when it states that STDs are dramatically diminished by condom use. The National Institute of Health reviewed widespread data that showed that there is an absence of convincing epidemiological data that condoms prevent the transmission of herpes, syphilis, chlamydia, human papilloma virus, and chanchroid. The rates of anal cancer caused by HPV infection are very high and can be fatal. Condoms have not been shown to significantly reduce this risk. The standard condom is not built to withstand the increased friction associated with anal sodomy. Even with [vaginal] intercourse the slippage and breakage rates approach 10%.[35]

It might appear that, for better or worse, *A Little Black Book* is only attempting to promote "safe sex" techniques to those who are already sexually active. But just what is this pamphlet promoting when it proposes:

> Condoms allow you a certain freedom that can be a great selling point if you're cruising the park and you don't want to spray spunk on your new polyester shirt, or if you and your boy have to make that 7 o'clock movie?

What a great state-sponsored education for your young teenage son!

In the same vein, and without any clue to the reader that multiple sex significantly increases the risk of sexually transmitted diseases, we read the following philosophical insight in the section entitled "Peace of Mind" (No. 4):

---

35. <http://www.article8.org/docs/news_events/glsen_043005/conference.htm>.

> The next best thing to having sex with another guy (or guys) is remembering it. When those memories are jumbled up with fear and guilt about not using condoms, it's a real drag. Condoms can give you the freedom to reflect on the pleasure of your past encounters instead of being obsessed with your next HIV antibody test.

More important information for inquiring young minds: "Developing a social life and interpersonal communication can be very rewarding, and for better or worse, the bars have been a nexus of gay life for ages." Thus, the booklet recommends several Boston area "bars and clubs for the discerning queerboy." Three examples will suffice to indicate the type of off-campus "education" being promoted:

➤ "Campus/Manray . . . Dancing, young guys and those who like young guys."

(Just how young?)

➤ "Paradise . . . Strippers dancing on the pool tables and bonking their heads on the overhead lights, porn on the television, the old, the young. Something for everyone."

➤ "Eagle . . . Old school, cruisy, sex-charged late at night. Varied crowd is unpretentious."

Outrageous as it may be, *A Little Black Book* is nothing extraordinary: public and private schools are wallowing in sex "education" courses. The educational establishment, steeped in "moral" (or perhaps, more accurately, *amoral*) relativism and political correctness, carries the message of the homosexual rights movement under the banner of tolerance, diversity, and (yes!) school safety and hygiene. As Rabbi Dresner writes:

> Public school officials claim they are obeying the Constitution by refusing to teach traditional sexual morality in school, though they

are perfectly willing to teach other moral values, such as tolerance. They claim that the idea of confining sex to marriage is . . . a 'religious' notion, rather than one of those beliefs that are virtually universal. (Dresner, 37)

Much of the media lends voice to this ideology of sexual revisionism, and California, too, is in the forefront. *The San Francisco Chronicle*, for example, reported that "Gay activists and others are making uneven but gradual gains against 'homophobia' in high schools, but they're already looking toward the next frontier: middle and elementary schools."[36] That is old news. Indeed, the "next frontier" has already been crossed—big time. Today, numerous pro-gay organizations are delivering the message of gay sex as an alternative lifestyle to elementary schools—*including kindergarten!* The Gay, Lesbian, Straight Educational Network (GLSEN), defines its mission as "changing schools and school culture around LGBT [*i.e.*, lesbian, gay, bisexual, transgender] issues and people,"—a goal which, it says, includes "holding diversity seminars for teachers and students and ensuring that *only positive discussions* about homosexuality are allowed into elementary school discussions, *including kindergarten.*"[37] (Emphasis added.)

The extent of the movement's seemingly hypnotic power over the

---

36. Elizabeth Bell, "Teaching Tolerance Before Hate Takes Root: Schools Differ on When–and If–They Should Tackle Homophobia," *San Francisco Chronicle,* March 13, 2000, p. A21.

37. George Archibald, "NEA Groups to Protest Award to Gay Studies Activist," *Washington Times,* July 3, 2004, <http://www.washingtontimes.com/functions/print.php?StoryID=20040702-115950-5378r>. GLSEN's executive director, Kevin Jennings, makes no secret of their strategy that "making schools safe is strongly tied to ensuring that classrooms are inclusive of LGBT themes . . . . We immediately seized upon the opponents' calling card—safety. We knew that, confronted with real-life stories of youth who had suffered from [*i.e.,* because of] homophobia, our opponents would automatically be on the defensive. This allowed us to set the terms of the debate." Candi Cushman, "Unsafe at Any Grade," *Citizen Magazine,* Dec., 2002, <http://www.family.org/cforum/citizenmag/coverstory/ a0023411.cfm>.

bureaucracy of education can be gauged from the inroads it has made in the legislatures of the various states of the Union. Two California state laws are illustrative. The first, AB 1785, strongly encourages pro-homosexual education at all public schools and *at all grade levels, including kindergarten.* The second, AB 1931, provides taxpayer-funded grants to take children on "field trips to teach them "diversity" and "tolerance of homosexual activities."

Consistent with this legislation, the *kindergarten-through-sixth-grade students* at Park Day School in Oakland, California were treated to presentations on gay and lesbian life by 45 speakers described as "the Bay Area's Gay Movers and Shakers." These reportedly included an eleven-year-old boy, Ben Ruffman-Cohen, described as the child of a lesbian couple. Addressing the school's *first-graders,* Ben is reported to have described for them what it is like to grow up in a lesbian household: "[I]magine how much you love your mom and then double that. That's my life."[38]

After being subjected to these harangues, the students were given homework assignments to write essays about famous homosexuals and to write "Dear Abby"-style letters to imaginary gay children who had been teased on the playground. They were also instructed to decorate their classrooms with rainbow flags and pictures of Melissa Etheridge, a known gay celebrity activist, and her partner.

The *second-through-sixth-grade* children in Novato (Marin County), California's Pleasant Valley School and San Ramon Elementary School were subjected to pro-homosexual performances staged in the auditoriums of the schools *without a parental notice or consent.* The play was performed by a Los Angeles-based educational theatre company called "Fringe Benefits," whose stated purpose is "to

---

38. Meredith May, "Teaching the Reality of Gay Life," Oakland School Kids Learn a Rare Lesson," *San Francisco Chronicle,* March 10, 2002, p. A23. *See also* "High School Teachers Promote Homosexuality to Captive Audience," http://www.pacificjustice.org/resources/news/ focusdetails.cfm?ID=PR050202a, posted February 2, 2005.

generate understanding and compassion . . . to generate sociopolitical activism . . . to dismantle the conventional theatre frame . . . [and] to de-essentialize cultural and gender identities." The play, entitled *Cootie Shots: Theatrical Inoculations Against Bigotry,* is primarily concerned with sexual orientation and gender issues. Since its first performances in California schools, it has been used as an "educational tool" in numerous other states as well.

A homosexual parents group at the Buena Vista *Elementary* School in San Francisco created a program incorporating both *Cootie Shots* and a children's book entitled *Jesse's Dream Skirt.* One of the skits features a transsexual boy in the hero's role. The boy wears a dress and high heels and talks approvingly about cross-dressing. The poem around which the skit is constructed includes the lines:

> *So let them say I'm like a girl!*
> *What's wrong with being like a girl?*
> *And let them jump and jeer and whirl*
> *They are the swine, I am the pearl!*
> *And let them laugh and let them scream!*
> *They'll be beheaded when I'm queen!*
> *When I rule the world! When I rule the world!*
> *When I rule the world, in my mommy's high heels!*

Another skit highlights a female character who runs off with a princess instead of a prince. Educators in the Bridgeport, Connecticut school system were so enamored of *Cootie Shots* that they made it part of their permanent curriculum and asked the teachers of all 26 classes in one particular school, *from Pre-K to 8th grade*, to either show the play or use it as a model for other gay-affirmative performances.[39]

---

39. *See* Dana Williams, "Cooties: from the Playground to the Stage," <http://www.tolerance.org>, May 30, 2003; "Parents Sue School District Over 'Cootie Shots'" *Education Reporter,* <*http://www.eagleforum.org,*> *April, 2002;* Joseph Tomaselli, *"Age of Innocence at Risk,"* Dec. 22, 2005, <http://www.hernandotoday.com/MGBROQ7IJHE.html>. Other plays with homosexual themes and simulated sexual activity are now commonplace in schools. *Postcards*

In a February 18, 2002 interview on Fox News Network, Brad Dacus, President of the Pacific Justice Institute, pointed out how these skits use the guise of "preventing harassment" to actively and aggressively model and promote homosexuality. This same tactic was used in April of 2002, when the Board of Education of the Hayward Unified School District (California) approved a new policy allowing homosexual employees of the District to discuss their homosexuality with students during classroom hours in order to promote "a safe environment for LGBTQ [lesbian, gay, bisexual, transgender, and questioning] students and staff." The Board's resolution encourages an "age appropriate district curriculum" offering "positive images of LGBT people in the classroom and [discussion of] alternative family configurations."[40] The resolution further encourages teachers to include homosexual figures in their instruction, and to use books with homosexual characters, such as *Heather Has Two Mommies*, as reading material. Under the resolution, neither the school nor the teacher is obligated to notify parents about such instruction, nor are parents given any power to opt their children out of such programs. A number of examples from the other coastline of America are equally instructive.[41]

---

from Paradise, performed at Stone Bridge High School in Ashbury, Virginia (Loudon County School District), featured a high school football star who discovers he is gay. At the end of the play, this character asks the audience: "Am I a little too much like you for your own comfort? Do you hate me because you see a little of me hiding in you?" Jim Brown, "Lawmaker Calls Pro-Homosexual Play Typical Public School Propaganda," <http://headlines.agapepress.org>, Feb. 14, 2005.

40. Diana Lynne, "Brave New Schools: Coming Out in Class," *World Net Daily*, May 29, 2002; and Jim Holman, "Teachers Come Out," *San Francisco Faith News*, July-August, 2002, p. 6, <http://sffaith.com>. Other examples abound. A mother with a *2nd-grade* son and a *4th-grade* daughter at Washington Elementary School in Winslow, Arizona was shocked to see pro-gay posters throughout the school. The poster displayed women "who were going to kiss or had just kissed." Jim Brown, "Mom Wants Pro-Homosexual Poster Out of Ariz Elementary School," *Agape Press,* Jan. 28, 2005, <http://headlines.agapepress.org>.

41. The Massachusetts examples were taken from John Haskins, "It's 1984 in

First-graders in Brookline, Massachusetts were subjected to what the *Boston Globe* termed—without any intended irony—a "sex-change counseling session:" a transsexual proudly explained to these small children how his penis was cut off in order to become a woman. A school-wide assembly in a Needham, Massachusetts High School featured a girl rhapsodizing about lesbianism and describing her first lesbian kiss. Even though a state law required teachers to inform pupils of their right not to attend the assembly, no such information was provided. Another *first-grade class* in Massachusetts heard their teacher explain to them that he loves another man the same way their parents love each other. As in the California cases cited above, this classroom instruction was inspired by the regularly held professional development workshops that coach gay elementary school teachers how to discuss their homosexuality with schoolchildren. (Heterosexual teachers rarely tell their students about their family life, nor are they compelled to by board of education resolutions. So why is it imperative for gay and lesbian teachers to inform children about their private lives?)

In some instances, all pretense of tolerance training and egalitarian "sensitization" is simply thrown out in favor of outright recruitment. Pamphlets prepared for distribution to the (underage) students of a Framingham Massachusetts high school queried: "If you haven't slept with someone of the same sex, how do you know you wouldn't like it? Is it possible you merely need a good gay experience?" Freshman students in Silver Lake, Massachusetts were exposed to a "health" text that counseled: "Testing your ability to function sexually and give pleasure to another person may be less threatening in the early teens with people of your own sex." (As already indicated, Massachusetts is listed among those states whose laws setting the minimum age of consent for sexual conduct address

---

Massachusetts—and Big Brother is Gay," *Insight,* January 7, 2002, <http://www.insightmag.com >, and from *Reports of the Massachusetts Parents Rights Coalition,* including the June, 2001 and November, 2002 issues.

or apply to *only heterosexual* acts. *See* text and notes 29 and 30, at page 70, above.)

A Massachusetts workshop held in March 2001 for both teachers and students included "Addressing GLBT [*i.e.,* gay, lesbian, bi-sexual, trans-gender] Issues in Pre-Schools, Daycare, and Kindergartens: A Networking Summit and a Chance to Share Experiences."

The Provincetown, Massachusetts School Board voted to begin teaching *preschoolers* about homosexual lifestyles! Obviously persuaded that Affirmative Action policies for hiring African-Americans—a social group once enslaved and with a long history of being discriminated against—applied equally well to homosexuals, the Board also supported legislation mandating hiring preferences for "sexual minorities." Susan Fleming, superintendent of the Provincetown Schools, reportedly announced that in addition to having *kindergarten* students hear from the parents of homosexual children, students in *grades 1 through 3* would be taught that not all families contain a mother and a father. Noting that the school system is the appropriate "laboratory for social change," she proudly proclaimed, "[We] are going to be a change agent." How this change was to be accomplished was by "being able to talk about family structures other than the heterosexual."

The Corrupting of School Libraries.

This "social change"—perhaps more accurately termed sexual brainwashing of schoolchildren—is being implemented not only via legislation and board of education policies, but also by direct pressure on library associations, teachers unions, parent-teacher associations, *etc.* For example, GLSEN has been pressuring schools to stock their libraries with books and instructional materials which they contend promote diversity, safer schools, and, of course, tolerance of homosexual activities. To further this goal, in March 2000 GLSEN offered grants amounting to $15,000.00 per school to help school libraries acquire books on GLSEN's recommended reading list. Their "selected bibliography" for children assures us that GLSEN wishes to provide "an honest look at the experiences of LGBT youth."[42] Another strongly pro-gay organization, PFLAG (Parents and Friends of Lesbians and Gays) has a similar recommended reading list.[43]

It is illuminating to examine some of the books being foisted on children in public schools under the pretense of promoting "safer schools." *Rainbow Boys*, a work of fiction by Alex Sanchez, tells the story of three 17-year-old boys who explore their homosexual desires and describe their sexual activities—all while making propagandist assertions at opportune moments.[44] On page 78, for example, one of the boys declares: "It's not a choice, you're either born gay or you're not." On page 103, the mother of one of the boys questions him: "What about the ex-gay groups that claim that homosexuals can change?" The boy's answer: "Those groups are full of fakes. Besides, I wouldn't want to change, even if I could. I'm finally starting to like who I am." These two comments are inserted deliberately to disinform and mislead youthful readers. As emphasized above, no study has ever proven the existence of a gay gene. (*See* text and note 16, at pages 59-60, above.) Moreover, "Those groups" are full, not of "fakes," but of decent, courageous, sincerely motivated men and women who invest enormous emotional energy toward regaining the full potential of their physiological gender and natural sexuality. If some of them were to fail in the attempt, that should hardly define them as "fakes"! However, a great many of these individuals (some of whom are profiled in the present work) have genuinely succeeded in changing their sexual orientation. This fact alone demonstrates very clearly how false the book's contentions about immutability really are. It also demonstrates how even those who self-righteously trumpet

---

42. GLSEN *"Selected Bibliography of Books for Children and Young Adults with LGBT Characters and Themes,"* (2002), p. 3, <http://www.glsen.org>.

43. See PFLAG "Recommended Reading List," <www.pflag.org>.

44. Alex Sanchez, *The Rainbow Boys,* New York: Simon & Schuster (2001).

"tolerance," "human dignity," and "civil rights" are not above resorting to the old group smear.

It goes without saying that nowhere on GLSEN's and PFLAG's recommended reading lists can we find the hundreds of books written by gender-affirmative or reparative therapists, or by ex-gay heterosexuals testifying to the reality and the success of sexual reorientation.

Rainbow Boys' propaganda is not limited to factual misinformation. A calculated effort to romanticize homosexual intercourse and entice the reader is obvious. This is how Sanchez describes the experience of a 17-year-old boy who has just had "unsafe" anal intercourse with a 29-year-old man he has met via the Internet: "Nelson [the 17 year old] looked down at the soft blond hair and broad shoulders of the man he let inside of him . . . He'd never felt anything so incredible in his life. Then he remembered the condom, or lack thereof." (148-49). Later, Nelson relates his experience to a new friend, who is 19 years old and HIV infected:

> "What if I got infected? Just my luck! The first time I got laid!"—
> "I hope not," Jeremy said. "But if you did, it's not the end of the world . . . . Nelson, I wouldn't wish this on anyone. If I could go back, I'd do things differently. But in many ways, this has helped me grow up. I see things a lot more clearly now. I know what is important." (168)

On the next page, Jeremy, the HIV-infected youth, explains what is "important." He will tell Nelson that he, Jeremy, does not have sex often enough but that when he does have sex, he uses condoms in an attempt to be safe! Another 17-year-old observes, while sharing a pornographic magazine, "I always get hard looking at men." (51)

I cannot refrain from mentioning that while I was reviewing *Rainbow Boys* in the Hoboken, New Jersey Public Library, the Young Adults Librarian suggested "another wonderful book to read" on the same topic: David Levithan's *Boy Meets Boy*. Incredibly, it describes the life of a boy who first "identified" himself as gay *at age five—*

with some "timely" help from his teacher!

> I've always known I was gay, but it wasn't confirmed until I was in kindergarten. It was my teacher who said so. It was right there on my kindergarten report card: "Paul is definitely gay and has very good sense of self. [...] I have to admit I might not have realized I was different if Mrs. Benchly hadn't pointed it out. I mean, I was five years old. I just *assumed* boys were attracted to other boys. Why else would they spend all their time together, playing on teams and making fun of girls? [...]*[45]*

Another item on GLSEN's "selected" list for children is a non-fiction book with the contentious title of *Two Teenagers in Twenty*.[46] The title is an allusion to the book's irresponsible claim that 10% of the population is gay or lesbian.[47] (Most researchers in this field agree

---

45. David Levithan, *Boy Meets Boy*, New York: Alfred A. Knopf (2003), p. 8.

46. Ann Heron (ed.), *Two Teenagers in Twenty: Writings by Gay and Lesbian Youth*, Los Angeles: Alyson Books (1995).

47. This perpetually repeated claim was subsequently exposed as false, as even the gay lobby has conceded. In their Friend of the Court Brief filed in the "the Texas sodomy case" before the U.S. Supreme Court, 31 gay-activist or pro-gay organizations (including the Jewish Anti-Defamation League, the Human Rights Campaign, National Gay and Lesbian Task Force, PFLAG, Gay & Lesbian Advocates & Defenders, National Center for Lesbian Rights, Pride at Work: AFL-CIO, Alliance for Full Acceptance, *etc.*), "finally admitted that their claim that 10% of the population is 'gay' is false." Frank York, "Exposed; the Myth that 10% Are Homosexual," <http://www.traditionalvalues.org/urban>. *See Lawrence v. Texas*, 539 U.S. 558 (2003). The Brief (p. 16, note 42) adopts the percentages cited in Edward O. Laumann *et al., The Social Organization of Sex: Sexual Practices in the United States*, U. of Chicago Press (1994): 2.8% of males and 1.4% of females identify themselves as gay, lesbian, or bisexual—clearly a total percentage of gay self-identification that aggregates to less than 3%. Though conceding in effect that the 10% number is bogus, the authors of the Brief could not resist inflating the actual numbers by including minors (male and female) from the age of 9 years and up—many of whom were almost certainly victims of sexual abuse as opposed to voluntary partners. While proposing the figures of 4 million and 2 million, respectively, for male and female homosexuals, they neglect to cite the Laumann

that approximately 1% of women and 2% of men are homosexual.) In her preface, the editor states with some satisfaction: "This new book, I believe, gives a realistic sense of what life is like for gay and lesbian teenagers." (8) The first story, by Rachel Corbett, a 16-year-old lesbian from Madison, Wisconsin, sets forth her gratitude to two lesbian neighbors she met around her age of puberty: "[They] made me aware of my sexual orientation, and I thanked them." (12) Rachel explains, "The two women and their children made me aware of a new type of life that I hadn't really known existed. I began to realize that I wanted to live a life like theirs . . . not like the one my parents lived." (12)

Another contributor to this book is a 15-year-old runaway and school drop-out (D.B. from New York City) who relates how "In December, I met this guy named Reggie, who was twenty-three. I met him hanging out in the subway station . . . He spent the night with me a few times, which was okay, but when I started coming in late to work, I was asked to leave." (81)

Yet another contributor, a young girl, informs us:

My name is Nicole, and I'm a lesbian. I'm twelve years old. I know you people think I'm young, but I know how I feel. I never liked any

---

study (also referred to as the *National Health and Social Life Study*) for its finding that "only 0.9% of men and 0.4% of women reported having only same-sex partners since age 18, a figure that would represent a total of only 1.4 million Americans as homosexual." (York)

boys. But I've liked a lot of girls. At first, I thought it was wrong, because I didn't know any other gays . . . . I came out to my big sister when I was ten. (167)

And then there is 16-year-old Bill Andriette, from Levittown, N.Y., who lectures that "for gay liberation to have any value for youth, people must be reminded, preferably in *fifth- or sixth-grade sex education classes,* that gay is not only good, but probably a part of most sexual make-ups." (171)

If you find these quotes shocking, just remember that they are only a small, random sampling of the hundreds of books, pamphlets, films and other materials that have been absorbed—with taxpayer dollars—into the school systems for the distinct purpose of radically impacting the sexual consciousness and behavior of children—*typically without the knowledge or consent of their parents!* Yet the examples we have cited are fully representative of the kind of propaganda that the homosexual rights movement—and their well-meaning but badly misinformed allies—have, through intimidation, secrecy, ignorance, apathy and deception, foisted on public schools throughout the United States.

State-Sanctioned Disinformation and Censorship.

Indeed, if some sex education materials misinform because the authors themselves have been misinformed, others knowingly suppress relevant facts that contradict, challenge, or belie their claims. An award-winning video entitled *It's Elementary: Talking About Gay Issues in School* documents several students discussing lesbian and gay issues. Among the individuals featured in this video is Noe Gutierrez, a young man who "came out" when he was sixteen. The video shows him answering questions from middle school students about what it feels like to be gay. Eight years later, the film was still being shown, but in the interim, Mr. Gutierrez had resolved his sexual identity issues and had decided to leave the gay world. Wishing to give other people the benefit of his experience in changing his lifestyle. Gutierrez informed the makers of *It's Elementary* that he no longer identified himself as gay, and requested that an acknowledgment of that fact be added either to the video or to its accompanying literature. Not surprisingly, it wasn't.

When Gutierrez heard that the Montgomery County (Maryland) Citizen's Advisory Committee for Family Life and Human Development was planning to show the video, he asked the Committee to inform the audience that he had subsequently changed his sexual identity. Gutierrez's request was one of basic honesty: if *It's Elementary* was still being used to present a particular viewpoint about gay life, viewers should be apprised that Gutierrez no longer identified with the views expressed in the film, and now considered himself heterosexual. Gutierrez's request was simple, and it would have cost the Committee nothing to honor it. Moreover, as a government committee, they very arguably had an ethical duty to inform the public of a fact that had a direct bearing on the contents of the video and on the audience's ability to evaluate its overall significance. Yet the Committee refused to make the requested announcement. In fact, though Gutierrez often speaks to audiences about his change, he has been virtually excluded from the schools that screen *It's Elementary,* as well as ignored by the mainstream media.[48]

Gutierrez's experience accurately reflects the state of the culture. While gay and lesbian advocates are frequently invited to address school assemblies and classes, former homosexuals—men and women eager and qualified to speak to students about their journey back from homosexuality—are most often excluded. Rarely if ever are they granted the opportunity to tell their vitally significant stories to the young people whom the school boards claim to be educating about homosexuality. So, too, are psychologists, psychiatrists, and other therapists and health professionals with expertise and

---

48. *See* Throckmorton, "Hiding Truth from School Kids: *It's Elementary* Revisited." <http://www.drthrockmorton.com>. Gutierrez later asserted that his sexuality is a private matter, and that he no longer seeks to be heard by either side.

experience in healing SSA denied any access (let alone "equal access!") to public schools and colleges across the country—denied access *solely on the basis of their (politically incorrect) professional opinion that homosexuality can be overcome.*

The message that homosexuality is neither inborn nor unchangeable—a message fully supported by scientific research and authenticated by personal experience—has virtually been censored by the boards of education and the media. What published criticism there is comes almost exclusively from religious and grassroots organizations that oppose the various sexual-political agendas. The video *It's Elementary* is a case in point. A *New York Times* movie review acclaimed it as "educational and aimed at helping parents untangle fact from fiction concerning homosexual people,"[49] However, Family Friendly Libraries labeled the movie a "bait and switch vehicle," and complained that while, on the surface, it asked viewers to respect gay *people,* in reality it preached acceptance of homosexuality itself. According to the reviewer, "'indoctrination' was not too strong a word to use to describe what was really going on." Indeed, as one young member of the audience reportedly remarked after viewing the film: "'It's kind of like vegetables; you don't know [you'll like it] until you try.'"[50] Similarly, a reviewer for Fathers For Life wrote: "What struck me first about the film was the manipulative, indeed almost Maoist, techniques used by the teachers."[51] Kirk and Madsen would have been proud.

In truth, such "educational" materials rarely if ever discuss the seamier details of the homosexual lifestyle. That is exactly what Kirk and Madsen meant by keeping the camel's "unsightly derriere" outside the "tent." Needless to say, none of these "educational

---

49. <http://www.movies2.nytimes.com>.

50. <http://www.fflibraries.org.>.

51. O'Leary, *"'It's Elementary': Talking About Gay Issues in School,"* <http://www.fathersforlife.org>.

programs" gives any voice at all to the obvious fact that male coupling is simply *not* the equivalent of the male-female relationship in any physical, ethical, or moral sense; and of course, few, if any, such programs offer truthful and adequate coverage of the special health risks associated with homosexual behavior.

Suppression of Health-Related Information.

Rarely, if ever, will you find a discussion of the fact that the suicide rate (including attempted suicides) is *six times higher* among homosexual men than among heterosexual men; or that more than two thirds (67%) of all AIDS cases in the U.S. are attributable to homosexual behaviors; or that more than 78% of homosexuals have had a sexually transmitted disease, as compared to 7.5% of all Americans (including both homosexual and heterosexual individuals.)[52] Rarely, if ever, will these "educational" materials discuss the fact that sexual fidelity is exceedingly rare among homosexual men,[53] or explain how such promiscuity relates to disease and

---

52. Except for the last figure, which was taken from a study based on 1998 data (*see* "Sexually Transmitted Diseases," <http://www.culture-of-life.org>), these statistics were provided by the International Healing Foundation. *See also* "Ten Things Lesbians Should Discuss with their Health Care Providers," and "Ten Things Gay Men Should Discuss with their Health Care Provider." *Gay and Lesbian Medical Association Press Releases,* July 17, 2002. An excellent survey of the health issues related to homosexuality can be found in Dr. Timothy Dailey, "The Negative Effects of Homosexuality," *Family Research Council,* Feb. 19, 2005. <http://www.frc.org>.

53. A 1984 study by two gay researchers confirmed the lack of sexual monogamy in male gay couples. Of the 156 male couples studied, all of whom were in a relationship lasting more than 5 years, "[all] incorporated some provision of outside sexual activity in their relationships." "Fidelity [was] not defined in terms of sexual behavior, but rather by the emotional commitment to one another." David P. McWhirter, M.D. & Andrew M. Mattison, M.S.W., Ph.D. *The Male Couple: How Relationships Develop,* Englewood Cliffs: Prentice Hall (1984) pp. 242-5. Numerous studies, principally by gay advocates, confirm the statistical rarity of monogamy in gay coupling. Even Kirk and Madsen acknowledge that "the cheating

violence in the homosexual community, or how it impacts the physical and emotional health of gay men.

Reliable studies have compiled a considerable amount of data showing that the gay lifestyle (or, perhaps, more accurately, deathstyle) can be extremely detrimental to one's emotional and physical health. Of course, the author of this book does not by any means intend to deny or hide the fact that heterosexual promiscuity can be just as damaging to one's body, mind, and spirit.[54] Nevertheless, it is no myth that people who engage in homosexual activity show a higher incidence of depression, anxiety, and drug, alcohol and tobacco abuse, even in nations and cultures where homosexual behavior is widely accepted and approved.

A woman physician member of the Gay and Lesbian Medical Association who serves as a director of a community health project expressed "fright" as she warned in a gay publication that

---

ratio of 'married' gay males, given enough time, approaches 100% . . . . Many gay lovers, bowing to the inevitable, agree to an 'open relationship,' for which there are as many sets of ground rules as there are couples." (*After the Ball,* 330) Another gay writer confirms that "there is more likely to be a greater understanding of the need for extramarital outlets between two men than between a man and a woman." Andrew Sullivan, *Virtually Normal,* New York: Vintage Books (1996), p. 202. In a 1991 study of 900 gay men, Dr. Martin Dannecker, a homosexual German "sexologist" found that 83% of those involved in "steady relationships" had numerous sexual encounters outside the partnership over a one-year period. <http://forever.freeshell.org/gayprom/htm>. A Dutch investigation found that men in steady homosexual relationships had from 6 to 10 partners a year outside the principal partnership. Maria A. Xiridou, Ronald A. Geskus, *et al.* "The Contribution of Steady and Casual Partnerships to the Incidence of HIV Infection Among Homosexual Men in Amsterdam," AIDS 17(7) May 2 (2003), p. 1038.

54. A study of sexually transmitted infections by Dr. Shahul Ebrahim *et al.,* published in *Sexually Transmitted Infections,* vol. 81 (2005), pp. 38-40, attributed 20 million adverse health consequences and 1.3% of all U.S. deaths in 1998 to risky sexual behaviors. According to the authors, this was three times the rate in other wealthy nations. *See* Jeanne Lenzer, "One in 100 U.S. deaths is related to sexual behavior," BMJ, Feb. 5 (2005), <http://www.bmj.com/cgi/content/full/330/ 7486/ 276-e>.

current data show that we do experience a number of heightened risk factors. By comparison to heterosexual women, lesbians are more likely to be overweight—84% vs. 80%—to be significantly overweight (obese)—30% vs. 20%—to smoke cigarettes—42% to 28%—to drink alcohol—72% vs. 55%—and to have an alcohol problem—5% vs. 2.5%. [Such risk factors] will likely show us to have higher rates of heart attacks, strokes, breast cancer, lung cancer, emphysema . . . ."[55]

Indeed, according to figures provided by the International Healing Foundation, the average life span of lesbians is only 49. Male homosexuals, too, live on average only until 42. Another authoritative study concluded:

In a major Canadian center, life expectancy at age 20 years for gay and bisexual men is 8 to 20 years less than for all men. If the same pattern of mortality were to continue, we estimate that nearly half of gay and bisexual men currently aged 20 years will not reach their 65th birthday. Under the most liberal assumptions, gay and bisexual men in this urban center are now experiencing a life expectancy similar to that experienced by all men in Canada in the year 1871.[56]

The argument used by the extremists in the gay and lesbian community to rebut these unchallenged statistics is that they reflect disorders resulting from "internalized homophobia" and anti-gay bias. This argument deserves to be addressed head-on. In the first place, it bears emphasizing that discrimination and even persecution do not inevitably lead to neurosis and illness. For example, Jews, as a group, have experienced horrific persecutions throughout the ages, yet, as a group, Jews have emerged physically healthy and psychologically

---

55. Dawn Harbatkin, MD, "Lesbians and Women Who Partner With Women: Taking Charge of Your Health," *NYC LGBT Pride Guide* (2005), p. 86.

56. Robert S. Hogg, *et al.*, "Modeling the Impact of HIV Disease on Morality in Gay and Bisexual Men," *International Journal of Epidemiology*, Vol. 26 (1997), pp. 657-61.

well-balanced, with natural life expectancies reflecting the norm of the society in which they live.

More significantly, a 2001 study conducted in the Netherlands, where same-sex marriage is legal and homosexual behavior is public and socially accepted, belies the claim that homosexual ills can be laid at the "homophobic" doorstep of the straight world.[57] The authors surveyed approximately 6,000 sexually active persons. Men and women who had engaged in any same-sex activity in the prior 12 months were classified as homosexual. These same men and women showed a significantly higher incidence of both psychological and psychiatric disorders *in nearly every category measured.* Among the factors identified by the authors as contributing to this mental health differential between homosexuals and heterosexuals were loneliness, infidelity between gay partners, and pervasive promiscuity.

The Netherlands study was one of three important studies published in the *Archives of General Psychiatry* that confirmed previous findings showing men and women engaging in same sex behavior to have significantly more psychiatric problems than heterosexual men and women.[58] Commenting on the 1999 studies, J. Michael Bailey, author of the controversial "gay twin studies" (*see* note 16, above, this chapter), commented:

> These studies contain arguably the best published data on the association between homosexuality and psychopathology, and both converge on the same unhappy conclusion: homosexual people are

---

57. T.G.M. Sandfort *et al.*, "Same-sex Sexual Behavior and Psychiatric Disorders: Findings from the Netherlands Mental Health Survey and Incidence Study," *Archives of General Psychiatry,* 58 (2001) pp. 85-91. *See also,* Neil. E. Whitehead, Ph.D., "Homosexuality and Mental Health Problems," <www.narth.com/docs/whitehead.html>.

58. The other two papers are D.M. Fergusson, *et al.,* "Is Sexual Orientation related to Mental Health Problems and Suicidality in Young People?" *Arch. Gen. Psychiatry,* Vol. 56 (1999), pp. 876-80; and R. Herrell *et al.,* "Sexual Orientation and Suicidality: a co-twin control study in adult men," *ibid.,* pp. 867-74.

at substantially higher risk for some forms of emotional problems, including suicidality, major depression, and anxiety disorder, conduct disorder, and nicotine dependence .... The strength of the new studies is their degree of control.[59]

In even the most materialistic, morality-neutral society, health considerations alone would counsel against state sanctioning of the new-age gospel of homosexuality as a fully equivalent, alternative lifestyle. Yet under the rainbow cloak of "multiculturalism," "diversity training," "tolerance," "civil and human rights," "anti-harassment," and even "school safety and hygiene," (!) we are witnessing the mass corruption and physical and emotional destruction of America's youth.[60] Children barely into puberty—not to say barely out of the playpen—are being actively indoctrinated, enticed and recruited—and right under the noses of their parents—into a high-risk lifestyle of promiscuity, pornography, and physical and spiritual degradation—a lifestyle, as we have seen, that is closely linked statistically to a broad variety of physical and mental disorders, addictions, and early death.[61]

---

59. "Commentary: Homosexuality and Mental Illness," *ibid.*, pp. 876-80.

60. Continued reliance on the rubric of "school safety" is extremely disturbing in light of the growing number of reported incidents of sexual violence allegedly perpetrated by lesbian gangs against female classmates. *See e.g.,* John Henry Western, "Lesbian Gangs Raping Young Girls, Some Attacked in School Washrooms," *Life Site News.Com,* July 3, 2007, <http:// www.lifesite.net/ idn/2007/jul/07070303.html>; "Students Fear 'Lesbian Gang' at School," NBC 10 Philadelphia, Feb. 18 & 19, 2004, <http://nbc10.com/news/2857417/detail.html>; "The Oppressed Become the Oppressor," Eyewitness News CW30 (Memphis, Tennessee), March 9, 2007, <http://blip.tv/file/165392/ >.

61. Some parents and students have begun to fight back in the courts. Three cases are especially worthy of note.

(1) In *Hansen and Martin vs. Ann Arbor School District*, 293 F. Supp. 2780 (2003), Detroit Federal Judge Gerald Rosen upheld the right of a Christian student to have her orthodox Catholic religious views expressed in opposition to the one-sided "information" disseminated by her Michigan high school. The court found

Homosexual Disaffection with Gay Politics.

Not all homosexuals, of course, are comfortable with the gay activist agenda. In a letter to the *Wall Street Journal* (May 26, 1993), Mark Dennis, a homosexual who opposes the intrusion of gay politics into the educational system, wrote: "Some of us are deeply embarrassed by the gay agenda, which plans the end of 'breeders' (heterosexuals) through a takeover of public education." Tammy Bruce, an avowed lesbian who disagrees with the gay establishment's agenda, is indignant that "the radicals in control of the gay estab-

---

that the clergy selected by the school for a panel discussion of religious views on homosexuality were exclusively pro-homosexual. In doing so the school district violated the student's constitutional rights to freedom of speech, equal protection of the law, and the Religious Establishment Clause.

(2) In *CRC and PFOX v. Montgomery County Public Schools*, No. 05-1194 (D. Maryland, May 5, 2005), Federal District Court Judge Alexander Williams, Jr. issued a temporary restraining order directing the Montgomery County Public Schools to suspend implementation of a planned revised health education curriculum. The court found that the school board had chosen to "present only one view on the subject—that homosexuality is a natural and morally correct lifestyle—to the exclusion of other perspectives." The court held that the revised health curriculum, incorporating as it did the gay agenda's viewpoint to the exclusion of other views, constituted a prohibited form of "viewpoint discrimination" in violation of the First Amendment. "Viewpoint discrimination consists of state action in which 'there is no ban on a general subject matter, but only on one or more prohibited perspectives.' When government restrictions 'target not subject matter but particular views taken by speakers on a subject,' the violation of the First Amendment is all the more blatant. Viewpoint discrimination is thus an egregious form of content discrimination."

(3) In *Parker et al. vs. Hurley et al.*, David Parker sued the town of Lexington, Mass. and school officials after the latter had him arrested for trespass for refusing to leave school premises upon the peremptory conclusion of a private conference he had called to protest the school's refusal to allow him to "opt out" his 6-year-old son from class "sexuality" lessons promoting gay unions and gay parenting. The U.S. District Court dismissed the complaint (474 Fed. Supp. 2nd 261, aff'd, 1st Cir., 07-1528, Jan. 31, 2008). The case has been appealed to the U.S. Supreme Court. *See* <www.article8.org>, and <http://www.townhallcom/opinion/johnleo/2005/10/02/158916.html>.

lishment want children in their world of moral decay, lack of self-restraint, and moral relativism. Why? How better to truly belong to the majority (when you're really on the fringe) than by taking possession of the next generation?"[62]

Canadian John McKellar leads a group called HOPE (Homosexuals Opposed to Pride Extremism). In March 2003, he gave a speech before a group of parents, school officials, media, and academics, in which he vigorously disputed the wisdom of allowing gay activists to introduce their agenda into the portals of primary and secondary educational institutions. "One could fairly and legitimately ask . . . who authorized [gay] lobby groups to bring their self-serving agenda and their cultural angst in the schools."[63] And, "How thoroughly have these activists been qualified and scrutinized?" Characterizing the membership of such special interest groups as "mostly . . . wounded and resentful individuals who should be receiving counseling and compassion, rather than trying to dispense it," McKellar warned:

> Introducing kindergarten and grade one students to alternative behaviors and lifestyles is *psychological pedophilia*. You don't have to engage solely in physical contact to molest a child. You can diddle with their minds and their emotions. And this is exactly what some of my radical brothers and sisters are up to. And this is exactly what a disheartening majority of educators, school trustees and teachers unions endorse. (Emphasis added.)

---

62. Tammy Bruce, *The Death of Right and Wrong*, New York: Three Rivers Press (2003), p. 88. *See also* her article, "Protect New York's Children from the Gay Elites," *Front Page Magazine,* July 31, 2003, <http://www.frontpagemag.com/Articles/ReadArticle.asp?ID=9165>, and <http://theroadtoemmaus.org/RDLb/22SxSo/PnSx/HSx/BruceTam%20lesbian.htm>.

63. John McKellar, *"There's HOPE for the World,"* Address, REAL Women, March, 2003, and <http://www.theroadtoemmaus.org/RdLb/22SxSo/PnSx/HSx/MckellarJ%20HOPE01.htm>. *See also* McKellar's August 2003 address, *ibid.*

> [. . .]
>
> Spare me the tolerance and compassion bunkum. Just leave the kids alone and let them enjoy their short period of innocence and sexual latency. Then when they approach puberty, balance the pop-culture bombardment with messages of abstinence, discipline and self-control.
>
> [. . .]
>
> You don't need gay activists to teach young people love and respect for one another. And you certainly don't want young, impressionable minds forever inculcated with a victim and entitlement mentality.

McKellar's criticism of the radical mindset of the gay pride leadership is not without sensitivity to the traumatic origins of gay militancy. Indeed, he observes with perspicuity:

> I have often expressed the unfortunate, but undeniable truth, that the number of times one was called "faggot" in the schoolyard is directly proportional to the stridency of one's activism [. . .] When you fancy yourself an oppressed minority—particularly one that is based on a basic human drive and compulsion—you become obsessed with increasing your numbers and mainstreaming your behavior. You try to evoke guilt and intimidation by incessantly reiterating banal epithets, such as "hate," "homophobia," "intolerance," "teen suicide," and "self-esteem." You quickly discover that the optimum way to ensure future supporters to your cause and ideology is through the minds of the young. You skillfully master the techniques of invoking sympathy, hiding the truth and presenting a sanitized portrait of gay life.

The Sexualization of the Media and Society.

McKellar's précis of the radical gay agenda is wholly consistent with Kirk and Madsen's "war plan." Yet it still boggles the mind how the educational establishment could embrace a policy so obviously and so egregiously wrong-headed and wrong-hearted, one that hurts the very people (our youth) that the activists and the educational establishment claim to be helping. How could this happen?

To answer this question, it is necessary to look at the 9th item on the Kirk-Madsen agenda. That item is not actually there in black and white. It is too big. No special interest group could implement such a plan. However, the homosexual movement did not have to implement it. It was done "for them." The "sexualization" of the media (in the broadest sense) has had an enormous impact on society at large, and has given a tremendous impetus to the liberalization of sexual mores. It is as though the ubiquitous use of sex in advertising, movies, television, and fashion—sex as entertainment, sex as economic incentive, sex as substitute for thought, for communication, for edification—has given a green light and public blessing to the unashamed use of sex as a crass commodity of self-gratification.

There is no question but that this trend is and has been principally *heterosexual* in origin and it is only by riding the crest of this commoditization of sex that the homosexual movement could have gotten where it is today. It is only in a culture where sexual gratification is valued more than physical and emotional well-being that the pursuit of the former can occur to the total neglect of the latter. It is only in a society where political, economic, cultural and religious leaders have lost their moral grip on *themselves* that a gay-affirmative agenda like the one we have been examining could insinuate itself into our public schools—with virtually no opposition.

A prime symbol of this sexual Cultural Revolution has been an adult magazine called *Playboy*. First published in December, 1953, this monthly magazine features photographs of female models posing nude, as well as short fiction and articles on sports, fashion, and consumer goods. The magazine grew into a New-York-Stock Exchange-listed international enterprise comprising several other media. While *Playboy* generally adhered to certain self-defined standards of "good taste," the magazine's success gave rise to several less restrained imitators such as *Penthouse* and *Hustler,* and inspired a gradual but relentless chain reaction of relaxed modesty in film, television, and mass-market literature. Accordingly, *Playboy's* founder Hugh M. Hefner views himself as a cultural icon who radically changed the social values and mores of America.[64]

Bizarre as it may seem, so mainstream did *Playboy's heterosexual* agenda become that no less sober an organization than the Jewish Anti-Defamation League (ADL) presented Hefner with their 1980 First Amendment Freedoms Award!

In a blistering editorial, conservative Catholic columnist William Buckley wondered how any organization steeped in Jewish self-awareness could applaud the purveyor of a philosophy that "measures human worth by bustline and genital energy," or the creator of a magazine based on "nude women, jokes about copulation, and advice on how to seduce young girls."[65]

Sexual Permissiveness Incompatible with Torah Judaism.

It should be obvious to anyone who knows the least thing about Judaism that the lifestyles advocated by such contemporary "prophets" as Hugh Hefner and Kirk & Madsen are totally inconsistent with traditional Jewish life. "Judaism has always maintained that there are fundamental standards and ideals that are normative, and without them we have chaos, 'each man doing what is right in his own eyes,' the situation prevalent in the days of the

---

64. In an interview published on the internet, Hefner declaimed: "I think life is meant to be celebrated, sexuality is part of that, that is why I played a part in changing sexual mores, and why in the '60s the *Playboy* philosophy changed the views and values in America. *Playboy* was a big part of the sexual revolution." <http://designboom.com/eng/interview/hefner/html>. In the interview, Hefner named Viagra and "the Pill" as the two most important inventions of the second half of the twentieth century.

65. William Buckley, "Come Undressed," *National Review*, October 3, 1980, p. 1221.

Biblical Judges (Jud. 17:6, 21:25) . . . ."[66]

Less obvious in today's climate of sexual permissiveness is that any lifestyle based on self-gratification and sexual excess is inconsistent with a genuine aspiration to spiritual growth and enlightenment. How can one advance in the path of spirituality when one is enslaved by one's own physical desires and passions and entangled in a web of reciprocal sexual exploitation? Spirituality, or the devoted quest for the deeper meaning of life and of the universe, demands a focus away from one's bodily appetites and cravings. This principle has been fundamental to all the world's great religions, and can be found in the practices of many surviving aboriginal or pre-industrial cultures. Judaism was the first religion to articulate this principle clearly, accomplishing this by making the laws of human conduct paramount over bodily desires and needs.[67] The pathway of a strictly observant Jew is meticulously laid out for him by the Torah, which, as articulated by the Talmud and the various Codes of Jewish Law, addresses every minutest aspect of a person's life—from the rigorous demands of daily prayer and scriptural and Talmudic study all the way down to the detailed particulars of personal hygiene and social and sexual conduct.[68]

---

66. Rabbi Robert Gordis, *Love & Sex: a Modern Jewish Perspective,* New York: Farrar, Strauss Giroux (1978), p. 94.

67. In Judaism, a person's physical instincts and passions are to be consecrated to the service and love of G–d. "Sexual impurity . . . leads to the deadening of the holiest human instincts." Rabbi Dr. J.H. Hertz, *The Pentateuch and Haftorahs,* London: Soncino Press (1970), p. 492. "Thus, sex outside of marriage is regarded as the mere satisfaction of one's lust. In the context of marriage, however, it becomes a veritable *mitzvah,* a religious act, a counterpart of the love, gratitude and oneness that are also essential ingredients of our spiritual life and our relationship with G–d." Rabbi Jeffrey M. Cohen, *1001 Questions and Answers on Rosh Hashanah and Yom Kippur,* Northvale: Jason Aronson (1997), p. 173. *See also,* Dennis Prager, "Why Judaism Rejected Homosexuality," <www.lukeford.net/Dennis/indexp22.html>.

68. A minor tractate of the Talmud, *Derech Eretz* ("Proper Conduct") sets forth

Because the Torah is so very clear about the inconsistency of homosexuality with G–d's law of creation, gay rhetoric, as previously noted, has resolutely smeared traditional, Bible-mandated views of sexuality as inhumane, shameful, and outmoded. A central theme of this anti-Biblical, and in some cases anti-Judaic, propaganda, has been the use of the Hebrew word *to'eivah* (translated as "abomination" in the King James-based versions, or "abhorrent," or "a perversion" in other versions) in the Biblical verse,

> *You shall not lie with mankind as with womankind: it is to'eivah.(Lev.18:22)*

However, as we have already hinted in Chapter One, *to'eivah* has a deeper connotation of "straying or being led astray" that cannot be conveyed by any single word. That connotation is crucial to a correct interpretation of the Hebrew text as well as to a genuine understanding of the Torah attitude to homosexuality. The gay movement, however, insouciant of philological distinctions in the Hebrew text, continues to portray religious Jews and the faithful of other traditional religions as gay-hating enemies and oppressors of homosexual men and women.[69] Moreover, gay strategists have made it an express part of their "war plan" (*e.g.*, item 3b of the Kirk and Madsen manifesto) to denigrate and undermine religious institutions, tradition and authority.

That such attitudes and measures have been largely accepted by

---

what is considered to be traditional propriety, good manners, and proper etiquette in Jewish society. "Table manners, cleanliness, seemly clothing, food and drink, manner of walking, proper bearing in an argument, even proper conduct in the toilet are considered in these tracts." Helen Latner, *The Book of Modern Jewish Etiquette*, New York: Schocken Books (1981), p. 4.

69. The converse is also true: many on the so-called "religious right" have, in equal ignorance, wrongly banished the homosexual from the pale of salvation, healing and recovery.

the gay community is both tragic and unjustified. What is true is that Jewish law requires both men and women to observe *tz'nius* ("modesty") in all their activities: Orthodox Jews, in deference to the laws of *tz'nius,* are generally reluctant to discuss sexual matters in public. They are also antagonized by public displays of sexually provocative behavior, whether heterosexual or homosexual, that expose impressionable children, students and men and women of all ages to dress and conduct deemed undesirable by the observant community. For the same reason, they are sorely put off by the attempts of gay activists to turn homosexuality into a political issue.

For their part, gay activists have seized on this vulnerability of the Orthodox as a way to provoke them to the kind of behavior they, the gay lobby, can use to denigrate and discredit the Jewish religion (again, item 3b on the Kirk-Madsen agenda). Hence the repeated attempts by the international gay lobby to hold a "gay pride" parade in Jerusalem—and so much the better if that outrages Christians and Muslims too!

In all fairness, it must also be said that, while observant Jews are obligated to refer questions pertaining to sexual intimacy to a *rav* (a rabbi who is an acknowledged expert in Jewish law), rabbinical expertise on the subject of homosexuality has been sadly wanting. All too few rabbis understand either the causes of, or the remedies for, the homosexual condition. In Chapter Two, we saw in Jeff's Case an example of this kind of insensitivity and unpreparedness and of the terrible damage it can lead to.

Because Jewish tradition generally sees *all* sane behavior as a matter of free choice, Jews who "choose" to manifest their homosexual desires publicly are seen as apostates or rebels, and thus suffer the consequence of some degree of ostracism from Jewish life. Nevertheless, if observant Jews have any feeling toward homosexuals themselves, it is surely compassion rather than hatred. In fact, a Jew is required to show compassion toward *all* living beings. If a Jewish homosexual turns to another Jew—any Jew, not just a rabbi—for help in finding a way out of his homosexuality, the Torah indisputably forbids turning him/her away.[70]

According to *halachah*, however, compassion does not mean condoning or remaining silent in the face of another's errors. The commandment *Neither shalt thou stand idly by thy brother's blood* (Lev. 19:16) has been interpreted as imposing a moral duty on every Jew affirmatively and compassionately to come to the aid of his or her fellow who has fallen in harm's way—be the harm physical, emotional, spiritual, or even economic or financial.[71]

By contrast, the non-traditional outgrowths of Judaism, such as Reform and Reconstructionist, (both of which embrace the gay activist thesis that homosexuality is immutable and neither harmful nor unnatural), have responded to social and political pressure by virtually expunging the Levitical prohibition against homosexual behavior. These two movements hire openly declared gay and lesbian rabbis for their pulpits and authorize their rabbinates to officiate at homosexual "marriages" and civil unions. Most recently, even the Conservative Movement has attempted to develop a "new age" theology that redefines sexual morality in a way that legitimizes the theory and practice of homosexuality.[72] Meanwhile, the Orthodox

---

70. In his foreword to Rabbi Chaim Rappaport's *Judaism and Homosexuality*, London: Vallentine Mitchell (2004), p. ix, England's Chief Rabbi Jonathan Sacks writes: "Just as the Torah asks of the homosexual to wrestle with his or her sexual desires . . . so too it asks the rest of us to understand his or her plight . . .[We] have special reason to be on our guard against attitudes, words, and behavior that give needless offense or in any other way add to the trauma of those already fraught with internal conflict . . . Jewish law and teaching condemn in the strongest possible terms those who shame others." *See also* the remarks of the Lubavitcher Rebbe, in "Rights or Ills," *Sichos in English,* posted at <www.jonahweb.org>.

71. *See* Maimonides, *The Commandments,* vol. 2, *Negative Commandments,* London: Soncino Press (1967), p. 276-77 and note p. 277.

72. *See, e.g., Responsum* to the (Conservative Movement's) Committee on Jewish Law and Standards, by Rabbis Elliot Dorff, Daniel Nevins, & Avram Reisner, "Homosexuality, Human Dignity and Halakhah," <http:// www.rabbinicalassembly. org/law/ new_teshuvot.html>, permitting *non-anal* (!) sexual activity between men, female homosexuality, commitment ceremonies for gay and lesbian couples, and

community stands firm, also bearing the brunt of politically correct criticism and opprobrium.

The Jewish Individual in Crisis.

The twenty-first century finds the Jew in a very awkward position, bombarded by myriad contradictions and inconsistencies. It doesn't matter whether we are talking about a religiously observant man or woman, or someone from the ranks of secularized Jews whose value structure is, nevertheless, still premised upon traditional Jewish precepts. In his Introduction to the *Artscroll Siddur,* Rabbi Nosson Scherman elaborates:

> [A Jewish individual's] religious teaching and Torah study tell him that G–d is the Creator not only at the birth of the universe, but every day and every moment; yet his news reports tell him constantly of more and more new frontiers conquered by science. His soul tells him that Heaven is a spiritual concept beyond his grasp, but he sees his fellow men walking in space . . . . He learns a morality of eternity, but he lives in a society preaching the here and now.[73]

How does a Jew handle these and other wrenching contradictions? Rabbi Dr. Moshe Meiselman, former Director of Academic Programs

---

advocating the ordination of gay and lesbian rabbis. The Committee adopted this position and two others diametrically opposed to it, and left it to each individual rabbi which *halachah* to choose! According to one of the Committee members (who, along with three others, resigned in protest) "[Dorff *et al.'s*] decision was arrived at entirely independent of *halachic* reasoning, and . . . the defensibility of their after-the-fact reasoning was not relevant to them. The decision simply had to be as it was. . . . [T]he permissive position validated by the law committee was really outside the *halacha* framework . . . ." Rabbi Joel Roth, "Gay Ruling Outside the Halachic Framework," *Jewish Standard,* December 15, 2006, p. 20.

73 *The Artscroll Siddur* (Renov Edition), Brooklyn: Mesorah Publications, Ltd., (1988), p. xviii.

at Yeshiva University, Los Angeles, and author of one of the first book-length treatments of feminism from a Jewish perspective, suggests that most contemporary Jews will respond by choosing one of three main courses of action: (1) become a nominally observant Jewish secularist; (2) retreat into piety and no longer address outside issues; or (3) "integrate the goals and values of the Torah into one's personality and acquire them as his own."[74] Abandoning one's Jewish identity and devoting oneself entirely to worldly pursuits is an unfortunate fourth choice taken by some Jews, and one which underscores how difficult it can be to resolve such conflicts.

Let us elaborate on Rabbi Meiselman's paradigm. The nominally observant Jewish secularist adopts the goals and values of the broader society in which he/she was raised and educated, while still utilizing certain Jewish traditions to help define his/her identity and direct his/her day-to-day actions. Meiselman suggests that such a resolution makes Judaism "nothing but shallow formalism." (*Jewish Woman*, xv)

The fourth category, the Jew who has rejected his tradition, can also be viewed as being ultimately related to the first category. Hence, the secular Jew who has altogether rejected Jewish observance has concluded (albeit erroneously) that a three-thousand-year-old legal code can't be relevant in today's changing world. On the other hand, he/she has not yet typically found a moral/ethical framework to replace the heritage he/she has abandoned. He/she is still searching, and the answers he/she finds very likely leave him/her unsatisfied, frustrated, confused, and hungry for "something spiritual."[75]

---

74. Rabbi Dr. Moshe Meiselman, *Jewish Woman in Jewish Law*, New York: Ktav Publishing House (1978), p. xvi.

75. The new secular divinity before which they kneel cannot truly nourish their innermost spirit. As Rabbi Dresner observed, "Most modern Jews have discovered a puzzling truth. No license has replaced the law; no symphony, the Psalms; no chandelier, the Sabbath candles; no opera, Yom Kippur; no country club, the synagogue; no mansion, the home; no jaguar, a child; no mistress, a wife; no banquet, the Passover seder; no towering metropolis, Jerusalem; no impulse, the joy of doing a *mitzvah;* no man, G–d." (Dresner, 329)

The "pietist" in Rabbi Meiselman's example is a spiritual type, devoted to Torah study, prayer, and the performance of *mitzvos*. He/she may appear to be untroubled by worldly contradictions, but in fact, he/she handles such issues by ignoring them. He/she can succeed in this only by living a sheltered life, isolated from or oblivious to the surrounding world. However, as the *midrashic* commentaries clarify (*see, e.g.*, the incident of the twelve spies in *Numbers* 13-15), such a path is not favored by Torah. The Torah desires that humankind sanctify the world by *regulating* it—by being in the world and of the world while conducting oneself in the manner prescribed by G–d. Judaism is a "this world" religion: yes, there is an *Olam Habah* (the Next World), but in that world of spirit, we cannot do *mitzvos,* or praise G–d with living tongue. Indeed, the whole of human existence is the province of the Torah. The foundation of Torah is the belief in One G–d , a G–d of justice, truth, law, modesty and holiness, an awesome, eternal, uncreated G–d of pure spirit, the Creator of the universe.[76] And just as that universe, in Jewish belief, obeys physical laws devised by the G–d who created it, so Jews believe the Torah—a word which literally means "teachings"—was given by G–d for the regulation and guidance of humanity. It is important to understand, however, that while Orthodox Jews regard the Torah as the revealed word of G–d, most Conservative and Reform Jews view the Torah as the words of human beings, though divinely inspired. Consequently, and notwithstanding the fundamental difference between these positions and the conflicts which derive from them, all denominations of Judaism see the Torah as an inexhaustible storehouse of wisdom from which to draw inspiration, strength and direction.

Nowhere are the contradictions between Jewish teachings and today's cultural climate more evident—or more profoundly confusing to the individual—than in the area of sexual morality and conduct.

---

76. *See, e.g.,* Ezekiel, 45 and 46; and Hertz, *Chumash,* London: Soncino Press (1981), p. 1002.

> The sexual revolution, the highly erotic content of films and television shows, and the general breakdown in the traditional structure of the family have led to a moral crisis among our young people. . . . If their parents bother to tell them that sex outside of marriage is a sin, society at large is voicing a much more permissive message: Sex is O.K.—as long as you and your partner mutually agree and if you take precautions to avoid pregnancy and sexually transmitted disease. (Dresner, 34-5)

It is in this area, perhaps more than in any other, that the various restrictions of Torah law are challenged by the current secular ethics of Pleasure, Fun and Excitement as the ultimate good and the principal objective of every human activity.

Moreover, while the secular ethic views the repression of sexual desires as harmful and dangerous, Torah sees sex in general as an enormously powerful force of nature that needs to be harnessed and controlled in order to realize its full potential for good. Indeed, so powerful is this force of nature, and so widespread and sudden, in our time, has been its fraudulent rise to a position of moral authority, that the prospect of being able to achieve near-total "sexual liberation" without undue risk of severe social sanctions has become one of the most difficult temptations a thoughtful individual can face.

While a devoutly practicing Jew may respond to such temptations differently from the less observant, or from the secular Jew who governs his actions more or less by his own lights, no person who is at all conscious of his Jewish heritage can feel completely untouched by the issue. Thus, not unlike American society as a whole, only perhaps more intensely, Jewish American society is torn—both inside and out—by a values conflict—or, more appropriately, a "culture war" in which the specific sexual restrictions of the Torah[77] are challenged

---

77. The sexual restrictions fall into three main categories: forbidden liaisons (of which homosexual union is only one of several), forbidden times (for example, marital intercourse is to occur only during certain times of the month), and forbidden conduct (principally, promiscuity and wasteful emission.)

by a moral relativism in which the only sacred criterion is "mutual consent": "So long as two or more consenting adults want to _____ (fill in the blank) with each other, then it's nobody else's business to interfere." This "playboy" philosophy of life not only scoffs at deferred or selective gratification in general—particularly where sex is concerned—but also tends to be *extremely lenient* when assessing the presence of "mutual consent"—so lenient, in fact, as to justify the art of seduction: "Yes, she resisted me at first, but in the end she yielded gratefully, so it's OK, and, by the way, also another notch in my belt."

Torah Sexuality is Fundamental to Jewish Spirituality and to the Morality of Civilized Nations.

The egocentric hedonism typified by *Playboy* is directly antithetical to the Torah's promise of spiritual and physical well being that is inherent in the careful regulation of one's relations with G–d, humanity and nature. That promise rests on two fundamental conditions: (1) that we accept G–d's authority and decisively reject forbidden conduct, attachments and desires; and (2) that we recognize that even the most ordinary Jew has within him or her the strength and the power to turn away from temptation and wrongdoing and do what is right—in other words, that everyone has the power to elevate him- or herself to a higher spiritual plane.

This is the essence of the "priestly law" set forth in the Book of Leviticus, whose purpose is summed up in G–d's Commandment to "sanctify yourselves and be holy," (Lev. 11:44; 20:7, *etc.*)[78] As will

---

78. *See* Chapter 6, pp. 173 ff., for a discussion of the "holiness laws" of the Hebrew Bible. "Judaism addresses the human being as it finds him . . . seething with animal passions, ridden with negative character traits. [It is] through the agency of those Divine tools of refinement that are the commandments," whether positive or negative, that "the Torah beckons man to exchange his obsession with sensuality, his pettiness, self-centeredness and worse for a world of spiritual grandeur and ultimate meaning . . . Judaism's battle is forever pitched [against] the human being's desire to eschew growth and change [and thus to] remain static in the face of G–d's

be explained in more detail in Chapter VI, the "Priestly Law"—the commandment to be holy, and the instructions how to accomplish this—is meant for all of humanity, and not just for the Priests!

> *For this commandment which I command you this day, it is not too hard for you, neither is it far off.* (Deut. 30:11)

There is nothing secret, nothing arcane, nothing exclusive, about Jewish holiness. The Priests, the Levites and the Israelites all study the same laws. The Torah does not ask us to endure painful tests of physical endurance—to walk through burning coals, or to endure weeks of cold, thirst, and hunger alone in the wilderness. It asks us to do "that which is good and right *in the eyes of the L–rd your G–d*," (Deut. 12:28) and not "every man whatsoever is right *in his own eyes*." (Deut. 12:8)

In the context of sexuality, in even the most private, and intimate of marital settings, where passion and desire are viewed as positive and essential, the Levitical laws require vigilant attention to details of time, conduct and circumstances. Awareness, self-control, and moderation are seen as the keys to attaining not only "holiness" and "purity," but happiness, fulfilment, and *shalom bayis*—the peace of the home.

---

summons to greatness." Eytan Kobre, "Judaism, Nature and Homosexuality," *Forward,* Jan. 2, 2001, [Op. Ed. Page], <www.forward.com/issues/2001/01.02.02/oped3.html.>

Thus, Judaism, as opposed to an unbridled lifestyle that values sexual excitement and physical gratification as the highest good,[79] offers a code of behavior and a system of values that call upon men and women to exert themselves to meet a set of behavioral and philosophical standards that empower the spirit, the will, and the intellect to overcome the potentially destructive forces of habit, selfishness and unrestrained physical desire. In other words, Judaism decisively rejects what Rabbi Maurice Lamm calls "the accepted justification for casual sex or an adulterous affair: 'It makes me happy'".[80]

Consistency with G–d's Plan of Creation.

---

79. Not even Epicurus, the famous Greek thinker whose philosophy became identified, in later ages, with the pursuit of physical pleasure, would have respected such a base vision of human morality.

80. Rabbi Maurice Lamm, *The Jewish Way in Love and Marriage*, Middle Village, NY: Jonathan David Publishers, Inc. (1980), p.25.

All well and good, say the critics of traditional Torah Judaism: but why not substitute another set of laws more in keeping with the times? We often hear statements like "We are no longer living in the Dark Ages." Or, "No one gets trichinosis from pork any more: now we have the FDA to regulate food." And, finally as to sexual issues, "If two guys want to sleep together, why not let them?" "What, you're going to send policemen into the bedroom?" "There's enough suffering in the world. Do we need to make it worse by inhibiting our sexual drives?" Etcetera, etcetera.

Such abysmally ignorant criticisms, along with tired, worn-out epithets such as "legalistic" and "obsessive" have been leveled at Judaism for many centuries. And granted: viewed from the outside, from a position of ignorance (or more to the point, from the accumulated distortions that constitute the popular wisdom), a moral/legal system such as the Jewish Torah may appear arbitrary and haphazard. It is only when the edifice is carefully examined from the inside that the coherence, logic, wisdom, structure and overwhelming spiritual significance of the whole emerges. The beholder begins to perceive an internal architecture of intricate complexity but also of compelling consistency—not just with itself, but with the whole universe. As phrased by Rabbi Dr. Jonathan Sacks, Chief Rabbi of England,

> One of Judaism's fundamental beliefs is that the G-d of revelation is also the G-d of creation. There is, in other words, a deep congruence between the life we are called on to lead (revelation) and the universe in which we are called on to live it (creation). Judaism is neither an abandonment *of* the world nor an abandonment *to* the world, but a struggle to establish G-d's presence *within* it. To put it another way, Judaism is neither a renunciation of pleasure (asceticism) nor an amoral pursuit of it (hedonism) but a way of life that *sanctifies* pleasure by dedicating it to G-d and to the wider values of the Covenant as a whole.[81]

---

81. Chief Rabbi Jonathan Sacks, Forward to Rabbi Chaim Rapoport, *Judaism and Homosexuality*, London: Vallentine Mitchell (2004), p. vii; "Sex and Struggle,"

(Emphasis added)

Rabbi Meiselman explains this concept further:

The story of creation, as viewed by Jewish tradition, establishes G-d not only as the One who brought the physical universe into being, but also as the source of moral law. The *Midrash* tells us that the moral and physical worlds are not independent of each other. G-d created the physical universe with a moral purpose. Just as a builder does not build randomly, but proceeds from a prearranged plan to achieve his desired end, so G-d had a plan when he created the physical universe. Our tradition teaches that the moral principles of the Torah were the prearranged plan which determined the patterns of physical creation. The laws of the Torah, tradition continues, preceded physical creation. To realize the moral end of creation, man was fashioned to serve as that being who would bring moral order into the universe. There is, hence, no contradiction between the laws of the Torah and human nature. The G-d of nature and the G-d of the Torah are one. (*Jewish Woman*, 3)

---

reprinted in *The Jewish Chronicle* (London), June 23, 2003.

What was this "moral purpose" for which G–d created a universe? What was the motivation behind the Plan of Creation? Mystical Jewish sources explain that G–d, as an infinite fountain of lovingkindness, desired to create living beings upon whom He could bestow His love. To house these beings, He created a world of base, inanimate heavy matter, and gave them the task to make that world harmonious, pure, spiritual and holy, so that it could become a dwelling place for G–d. Because He endowed these beings with the freedom to choose between good and evil, G–d shared His Plan of Creation (the Torah) with them, so that they would be able to choose correctly.[82]

Thus, assuming—as Torah revisionists would have us believe—that we were free to pick, choose and replace one Torah law with another—for example, a law that says homosexuality is OK—before doing so, we would have to inquire: will the new law fit into the overall Plan?

Applying this approach to the case in point: What about homosexuality? Does homosexuality fit into the Plan of Creation? Rabbi Barry Freundel, former Chairman of the Ethics Committee of the Rabbinical Council of America, answers:

---

82. The great philosopher of Judaism, Moshe Chayim Luzzato, who lived during the first half of the 18th century, explained: "G–d's purpose in creation was to bestow of His good to another. [. . .] G–d's wisdom, however, decreed that for such good to be perfect, the one enjoying it [*i.e.,* man] must be its master. [. . .] Man must earn this perfection, however, through his own free will and desire. If he were compelled to choose perfection, then he would not actually be its master, and G–d's purpose would not be fulfilled. It was therefore necessary that man be created with free will." *The Way of G–d,* Jerusalem: Feldheim (1988), pp. 37, 39, 45. According to Chabad chassidism, however, "the ultimate purpose for the creation of the [spiritual and physical] worlds was that 'G–d desired to have a dwelling place in the lower worlds.' He desired that Divinity be revealed [even on the material plane] below by means of man's divine service of subordinating and transforming his physical nature." (Bracketed text in the original.) Rabbi Yosef Yitzchak Schneersohn (the Previous Lubavitcher Rebbe), *Basi LeGani: Chassidic Discourses,* Brooklyn: Kehot Publication Society, 1990, p. 3 (citing *Tanchuma, Parshas Bechukosai,* sec. 3).

Homosexuality . . . is maladaptive and inappropriate. Depending upon one's theory, it may indicate arrested development, poor family structure, early trauma, frustration of the purpose of creation, disruption of the basic family structure, unnatural behavior, *etc.* But whatever the case, *it constitutes activity that will diminish an individual's capacity to fulfill, in his own life, G‑d's expressed plan for creation. As such, this individual cannot achieve his full potential as a human being.*[83] (Emphasis added.)

Another modern rabbinical scholar, Rabbi Baruch Ha-Levi Epstein, focusing on the unnaturalness of the homosexual act itself, characterizes it as a going astray or a leading astray from the foundations of creation.[84] Succinctly stated, Rabbi Epstein cites the standard argument that because the physical anatomy of male/female is so obviously complimentary and designed for the purpose of procreation, the homosexual liaison defies the natural functionality of the human sexual apparatus.[85] Traditionally, however, the congruence

---

83. Rabbi Barry Freundel, "Homosexuality and Judaism," *Journal of Halacha,* Vol. XI (Spring), 1986, p. 80; <www.jonahweb.org>. The quoted passage is followed by a pertinent observation: "We are told by the Talmud that G–d does not play tricks on His creations. Particularly as the area of sexuality is an area of such deeply personal implications to any individual, it is difficult to imagine G–d creating a situation wherein those who feel themselves to possess a homosexual orientation cannot change and are consequently locked in a living prison with no exit and no key. Therefore, some method or methods must exist to successfully change the sexual orientation of motivated individuals." Freundel cites the more than 70% success rate documented by M.F. Schwartz & W.H. Masters, "The Masters & Johnson Treatment Program for Dissatisfied Homosexual Men," *American Journal of Psychiatry,* Vol. 141 (Feb., 1984), pp. 173-81.

84. Rabbi Epstein's characterization of the homosexual as being led "astray" by his same-sex attractions echoes the Talmudic interpretation of *to'eivah* (Nedarim 51a). As we have already stated, this Talmudic understanding will be discussed in later chapters.

85. Rabbi Norman Lamm, "Judaism and the Modern Attitude to Homosexuality," *Encyclopedia Judaica Yearbook 1974,* Jerusalem: Keter Publishing House (1974), p. 198, citing Rabbi Baruch Ha-Levi Epstein, *Torah Temimah* to Lev. 18:22.

of heterosexuality with G–d's plan of creation is based upon more that just the physical complementarism of the male and female bodies, or its obvious relevance to the Commandment of *P'ru ur'vu* ("be fruitful and multiply"). That congruence unifies the masculine and feminine energies into a unity which harmoniously balances the physical and spiritual worlds, and that balance is an aspect of holiness.

Torah teaches that man and woman were originally created as a single being in whom masculine and feminine attributes were united, as they are in G–d:

> *And G–d created man in His own image, in the image of G–d He created him; male and female He created them. And G–d blessed them; and G–d said to them: "Be fruitful, and multiply and replenish the earth . . . . "* (Gen. 1:27-28)

And again,

> *In the day that G–d created man, in the likeness of G–d He made him; male and female He created them, and blessed them and called their name Adam, in the day when they were created.* (Gen. 5:1-2)

It was only later (Gen. 2:21-22) that G–d separated Adam into two distinct beings. Thereafter, G–d recognized that man should not be "alone," (Gen. 2:18) and thus G–d determined that man and woman should be reunited. *He brought her to the man.* (Gen 2:22). A tripartite covenant is thus created (man, woman, and G–d): the man and the woman become one and whole once more, but this time in a manner sanctified by the fulfillment of a unique *mitzvah* in which each of the three has a special interest and an essential role: the procreation of humanity.[86] Thus, in Jewish teaching, the

---

86. *See,* generally, Rabbi Abraham R. Besdin's study of Rabbi Joseph B. Soloveitchik, *Man of Faith in the Modern World: Reflections of the Rav,* Hoboken:

complementarism of male and female is not just a physiological and biological fact, but a profoundly spiritual bond between G–d and humanity; and the frustration of that bond—whether by homosexuality, onanism or celibacy—is not just a physical annihilation, but a spiritual misfortune that not only affects the human members of the covenant and their unborn children, but disrupts the balance of civilization and, ultimately, of the entire universe.

For a Jew, as for any other Bible-educated person, frustrating or circumventing the divinely ordained complementarism of male and female negates a lot more than the institutions of marriage and family: it negates the very purpose for which the world was created. Without human beings to receive G–d's lovingkindness, there is no reason for Him—being of pure spirit—to dwell in a lowly world of matter. Without subjects to serve Him, there is no kingdom for G–d to rule over. Yet, according to our teachings, it is not G–d's nature to retire into Himself in a state of ecstatic solitude. The commandment of *Pru u r'vu* ("Be fruitful and multiply") was the very first commandment given after the creation of the universe, a commandment whose purpose was the perpetuation not only of the generations of Adam and Eve, but of the blessings that accompanied their creation.

Ktav Publishing House, Inc. (1989).

The Socialist Roots of Gay Anti-Religionism.

It is precisely these holy attributes of physical and spiritual blessing pertaining to marriage between man and woman that radical gay activists and their allies must denigrate in order to advance their agenda. Thus, gay anti-religionism stems from the anti-bourgeois aspects of socialist theory, rather than strictly from its atheist foundations. The avowed aim of militant gay theorists is quite literally to destroy and overthrow the sexual morality inherited from the Torah in favor of a kind of sexual socialism. To do this, they reason, religion need only be revised, not abolished. The family, however, is another matter. (*See* Chapter 14, *below*, pp. 519-22)

Of course, the idea of abolishing the procreative family as a social unit is an ancient one, going back to Plato's *Republic* and reappearing at intervals throughout the history of socialist theory and experimentation.[87]

However, the anti-family plank in the radical gay activist platform is plainly consistent with Marxist ideology. In the *Communist Manifesto*, Karl Marx and Friedrich Engels had called for the abolition of marriage and family, which they viewed as oppressive institutions.

> On what foundation is the present family, the bourgeois family, based? On capital, on private gain. In its completely developed form this family exists only among the bourgeoisie. But this state of things finds its complement in the practical absence of the family among the proletarians, and in public prostitution. The bourgeois family will vanish as a matter of course when its complement vanishes, and both will vanish with the vanishing of capital.[88]

---

87. For example, the Oneida Community, established in New York State in 1848, instituted "compound marriage," whereby "[e]very woman in the community was the wife of every man. They called monogamy 'selfish love,' and defined it as 'that exclusive and idolatrous attachment of two persons for each other.'" W.E. Woodward, *A New American History,* New York: Garden City (1938), p. 420.

88. Robert C. Tucker, *The Marx-Engels Reader,* New York: W.W. Norton & Co.

Marx and Engels had argued for free love, in which every man would have sexual access to every woman. This became a fundamental principle of Communist ideology. In a classic Communist text, we read:

> The workers' state needs new relations between the sexes, just as the narrow and exclusive affection of the mother for her own children must expand until it extends to all the children of the great, proletarian family, the indissoluble marriage based on the servitude of women is replaced by a free union of two equal members of the workers' state who are united by love and mutual respect. In place of the individual and egoistic family, a great universal family of workers will develop, in which all the workers, men and women, will above all be comrades. This is what relations between men and women, in the communist society will be like. These new relations will ensure for humanity all the joys of a love unknown in the commercial society, of a love that is free and based on the true social equality of the partners.[89]

As in the Communist literature, radical gay rhetoric is rife with

---

(2nd ed., 1978), p. 487.The American Communist Party has apparently reconciled itself to the continuity of the family unit. Its Party Program for 2006 says nothing about abolishing it. <http://www.cpusa.org/article/static/758/>. Even the Revolutionary Communist Party (USA) has declined, with amusing linguistic contortions, to identify itself with militant gay calls for the abolition of the family unit: "We, as Maoist revolutionaries, want to liberate all of human expression and social relations from the weight of thousands of years of traditional (oppressive) morality and institutions. [. . .] [W]e also understand that it is not possible for anyone to fully predict what forms sexual expression might take in socialist and then in communist society (and what the social 'meanings' and significance of various practices might turn out to be in these new social contexts)." "On the Position on Homosexuality in the New (2001) Draft Programme," <revcom.us/margorp/ homosexuality.htm>. The previous Party Program of the RCP viewed homosexuality as a symptom of bourgeois capitalism. *See ibid.*

89. "Communism and the Family" (1920), in Alix Holt (ed. & trans.), *Alexandra Kollontai: Selected Writings*, Westport: Lawrence Hill (1977), pp. 259-60.

calls for the elimination of the family structure. The following, by Michael Swift, is typical: "[T]he family unit—spawning ground of lies, betrayals, mediocrity, hypocrisy and violence, will be abolished. The family unit, which dampens imagination and curbs free will, must be eliminated."[90]

It may be true that gay moderates, concerned that such rhetoric will "play right into the hands of the homohaters," (Kirk and Madsen, 361) have repeatedly urged their more militant colleagues to tone down the anti-family language; but according to Kirk and Madsen, Michael Swift's diatribe is "fairly representative of the line taken by gay media radicals—angry people, perhaps damaged by emotionally sick families and blinded to the family's good side, who feel compelled to turn their fear and loathing into a sort of social philosophy of absolute individuality." (361)

Absolute Individuality and the Culture of Narcissism.

This gay radical mantra of "absolute individuality" or "exaggerated individualism" is part of a larger trend in society described by Rabbi Dr. Norman Linzer as "a culture of narcissism."[91] Rabbi Linzer sees this trend as an outgrowth of the exaggerated importance society has come to attach to "self-realization and individual fulfillment." Linzer can't be far off the mark when he suggests that this "deification of the self . . . creates conflict in the family and breeds its dissolution." (24).

On a broader societal level, individual autonomy, independence,

---

90. Michael Swift, "For the Homoerotic Order," *The Gay Community News*, February (1987), pp. 15-21, quoted in Kirk and Madsen, *After the Ball*, p. 361, and Dresner, *Can Families Survive?*, p. 30. Like Marx and his followers, Swift also wants to abolish religion: "All churches who condemn us will be closed. Our only gods are handsome young men . . . . For us, too much is not enough." (*After the Ball,* 361; Dresner, 30).

91. Rabbi Norman Linzer, Ph.D., *The Jewish Family: Authority and Tradition in Modern Perspective*, New York: Human Science Press, Inc. (1984), pp. 24, 156.

self realization, the right to choose, the right to privacy, the right to be different, the right to express oneself—all of which, in the appropriate context, are laudable and worth striving for—have instead become slogans for the meaning and purpose of life. Each individual—from childhood on—is continually exalted as a unique personality endowed with special, one-of-a-kind qualities; each is exhorted to pursue his/her own personal pleasure—not as a reward for some worthy achievement, but purely as a privilege of that purportedly unique individuality. This distorted vision of "The American Dream" has created an environment where "to live for the moment is the prevailing passion—to live for yourself, not for your predecessors or posterity." (Linzer, 156) Nor even, for that matter, for one's country or community! "We are fast losing the sense of historical continuity, the sense of belonging to a succession of generations originating in the past and stretching into the future." (156) "Family relationships are more tenuous, as marriage partners expect each other to fulfill unrealistic demands; parents and children function on different wave lengths, with each absorbed in a separate world. Singlehood is a preferred value to marriage, and marriage is valued without parenthood." (174) Divorce is routine and sex without marriage, whether casual or cohabitant, is commonplace. Carryings on of the most private and personal kind, reason not too long ago for shame and elaborate secrecy, are now flaunted. People talk openly and in the media of their own extramarital affairs, boast of their sexual exploits, joke ubiquitously about masturbation, read, view, exchange and discuss pornographic materials (even TV celebrity critics publicly praise movie scenes of explicit sexual depiction!) and take pleasure from watching "reality" shows where their fellow men and women humiliate themselves and each other in front of a TV camera. A new breed of "how-to" sex manuals, which unabashedly teach fetishism, sadism, masochism, oral and anal sex, are sold in bookstores.[92]

---

92. Ruth La Feria, "The new manuals: more sex, less 'joy,'" *New York Times,* May 29 (2005), Section 9, pp. 1-2.

Sexual imagery is used to sell everything from jeans to toothpaste, and every new movie and TV season brings a flood of new sexually oriented material of ever escalating prurience, tastelessness, and violence. All this in an atmosphere of intolerance and hostility towards any legitimate criticism.

How does all this affect the lives of people trying to live a life of decency and morality, or the lives of Jewish parents and children trying to live a life of Torah and *Mitzvos*? First and foremost, under the constant barrage of sexual images, the commandment to keep one's thoughts holy is either violated or exposed to violation. For the mature person, the guard is weakened, and the individual is seduced into a laxity that can evolve into actual misconduct. For the child, who naturally looks everywhere and sees everything—even without understanding what he or she sees, a seed is planted that will germinate and interfere with his/her spiritual and psychological development.

With the exception of the *tzaddik* (the totally righteous person), every person—Jew or gentile—living in western society is confronted on some level with the socially fabricated fantasy that true happiness is to be found "on the outside" in a world of complete and unrestrained sexual freedom. Second, the naturally tense dynamics of the parent-child relationship are exacerbated. The child gets glimpses of a world of sensual temptations from which he is then barred by parents, Yeshiva teachers, spiritual leaders, and the Torah itself. In the larger society, the propagation by the media—books, magazines and magazine covers, newspaper, TV, movies, billboards—of an ideology of sexual indulgence baited with sexual imagery has created a culture of sexual obsession in which constant arousal is doomed to continual frustration: the partner can never be sufficiently attractive, the foreplay never sufficiently passionate or uninhibited, the climax never sufficiently intense, the fulfillment never complete, the relationship rarely satisfactory or enduring, and the reality of intermittent or protracted loneliness irremediable except by resort to the "three Ps:" prostitution, promiscuity, and pornography.

Indeed, the constant challenge to match unrealistic expectations with unachievable experiences has triggered a pandemic in which the pain of deep personal frustration and unhappiness can only be assuaged by the various forms of escapism which have been made available to us—all of which are treacherously addictive and destructive of the body and the soul. Perhaps because we live in a secular culture where spiritual messages are relegated to the personal sphere of church and preacher, or perhaps because it is human to take comfort in numbers, or yet perhaps because certain theorists have dignified the syndrome with the philosophical terminology of existentialism, the symptoms of this societal unhappiness—the loneliness, the vague and nagging emotional pain, the dysfunctional relationships, the failed marriages, the recourse to drugs and alcohol, the sexual deficiencies (and their pharmaceutical remedies), the pornography and masturbation, the sexual experimentation by middle and high-school children—have all attained the status of normalcy.[93] And of course, male and female homosexuality is also

---

93. Kids are experimenting with sex at younger and younger ages. Sexual activity, including oral sex, mutual masturbation, nudity and exposure as well as intercourse, has dramatically increased among middle-school students ages 10 to 14. One thirteen year old reportedly told the *New York Times* that when, in the 3rd grade, he began watching the TV program "Beverly Hills 90210," he "wanted to try what they were doing in the show." So, together with his friends, they began developing a schedule for sexual initiation. "By third grade, they were familiar with slang terms for masturbation and oral sex. By fourth grade, they were playing kissing games with the girls. In the fifth grade, they were dating; in sixth, French kissing and petting. By seventh grade, they had done oral sex and some had had intercourse. By the ninth grade, one boy reported, 'It's just one big spree of going all the way.'" Mona Charen, "Just Something to Do," <http://www.jewishworldreview.com/cols/charen041200>. Karen S. Petersen in *USA Today* (November 16, 2000, Nov. 16, 2000, Sec. LIFE, p. 1) reports that as many as one third of all middle school girls have performed oral sex on boys. According to Dr. Dean Edell of healthCentral.Com, many young teens who engage in oral sex don't believe they are having sex: 27% of the 10,000 teenagers answering the magazine survey described oral sex "as a fun thing to do with a guy." <http://www.health central.com/drdean/408/44577.html>. *See also* Anne Jarrell, "The Face of Teenage Sex Grows Younger," *NY Times,* April 3, 2000, Section 9, p. 1; Kim Painter, "The Sexual Revolution Hits Junior High," *USA Today,* March 15, 2002, Sec. A., p. 1.

"normal."

The origination of homosexuality in severe and early emotional pain and its relation to the individual narcissism fostered by the culture of narcissism will be discussed later, in Chapter Four. But whereas the gay lobby is hard at work trying to convince the state legislatures that this climate of profligacy and misery is healthy, enlightened and normal, the legislation of the Torah was "enacted" to promote the happiness, fulfilment and physical and mental well being of both the individual and society. It is this foundation for healthy living that radical homosexual activism is trying to destroy.

As we have commented elsewhere in these pages, the gay "rights" movement has made a fundamental contribution to public awareness of the many serious issues surrounding homosexuality, thus making possible the rescue of countless homosexual men and women from discrimination, blackmail and violence. On the other hand, today's culture of acritical acceptance of homosexuality and the oppressive climate of political correctness have created a new prison of darkness for those homosexuals who are either genuinely interested in changing their sexual orientation or seriously confused or conflicted about their same-sex attractions.

None of the foregoing would have any practical meaning if those afflicted by homosexuality and other sexual issues had no real possibility of growing, healing and changing. They do, but the culture we live in doesn't want us to know that, and has done everything in its power to keep us from finding out.[94] In the following chapters, we shall discover how Torah Law, Jewish insights into spiritual cleansing (*teshuvah*), and modern psychology converge in a way that has made healing from homosexuality a reality for thousands of thankful men and women.

---

94. "Part of the homosexual agenda is getting people to stop considering that conversion is even a viable question to be asked, let alone whether or not it works." Michael Glatze, *World Net Daily,* July 3, 2007, <http://wnd.com/news/article.asp?articleID=56481>. Michael Glatze is the former editor of the newspaper, *Young Gay America,* and a former homosexual and gay advocate.

CHAPTER 4:

What Causes Homosexuality?

In the last chapter, we explained the fallacies of the "born that way" theory. The tactical success achieved by this fictive science has given rise to a new and fallacious public perception of sexual identity in which homosexuality is considered a genetically-based—and therefore perfectly legitimate—alternative form of sexual expression. By painting those who justifiably reject this perception with the most opprobrious colors of reactionism, proponents of the new "gospel" have muzzled dissent, suppressed relevant information, and stifled debate, thus making possible the legislative and regulatory enactment of adventurous social policies tending to the complete normalization of homosexuality. The primary victims of these machinations, besides the innocent schoolchildren indoctrinated by public school systems across the country, have been the strugglers: men and women with unwanted homosexual tendencies who have cried in vain for help in ridding themselves of their SSA, and languished in misery, believing that no such help was available.

But if, in contradiction to the "gay gene" hypothesis, homosexuality is not "immutable and unchangeable" (and, generally speaking, it is not!), what are the factors that can cause a person to develop SSA? What kinds of stresses are sufficient to prevent a person from identifying with his or her birth gender?

Our Torah-inspired program for healing from homosexuality is based on a carefully observed and thoroughly studied connection between certain types of early emotional trauma and the later development of SSA, homosexual behavior and identification as gay.

Among those who are experienced in helping individuals grow out of homosexuality, there can be little if any dispute that early disidentification from (or perceived rejection by) a same-sex parent and/or peers can lead to "defensive detachment" from one's physiological gender.

Defensive detachment typically occurs when one ceases to identify with one's birth gender in order to protect oneself from the pain of rejection and ridicule by one's gender role models. As phrased by recovered lesbian Erin Eldridge,

> A boy gains confidence in his own masculinity from his father and his [male] friends. If he fails to bond with his father or peers, he might fail to identify with the masculine role. If a girl fails to identify with her mother, she may lack the confidence needed to feel secure in the feminine role. She might avoid feminine peer groups because she feels estranged from them. Her interests in activities that are not commonly considered feminine can contribute to feelings of alienation from many of her female peers.[1]

If what Eldridge says is true, then gender identification is basically a learning process. Alan Medinger, one of the pioneers of the ex-gay movement, writes, "Male homosexuality is, at its core, a

---

1. Erin Eldridge, *Born That Way?* Salt Lake City: Deseret Book Co. (1994), p.38.

matter of undeveloped manhood . . . true healing requires that we grow—even as adults—into our manhood."[2] What this means is that homosexuality is not simply a matter of misdirected sexual interest: it involves a fundamental lack of gender definition at the root of one's self-identity.

Nevertheless, to say that homosexuality is typically associated with certain types of childhood experiences, or with an underdeveloped sense of gender identity, is not to say that wounds or debilities of this type will always give rise to homosexuality. Many individuals have encountered such problems from early childhood on, yet have *not* developed SSA. Indeed, problems with gender identity can lead to other forms of sexual brokenness, such as "Opposite Sex Attachment Disorder" (OSAD). OSAD represents the inability to be emotionally intimate with members of the opposite sex. A male might become a "skirt chaser" or a rapist. A female might develop nymphomania or a compulsive attraction for men with obvious character flaws. Other examples of OSAD are heterosexual pornography, compulsive masturbation, and fetishism.

Another important *caveat* to bear in mind when considering the relationship between early emotional trauma and homosexuality is that the wounding may not always correspond to objective reality, but may have taken place solely in the subjective perception of the child. It is axiomatic that the perceived wounding may not have been intended, but may have only been interpreted as such, existing only in "the story I tell myself" about what occurred. Nevertheless, to the one who feels "it happened the way I saw it," it is real and requires attention just as if it really happened. A simple example might be a daughter who perceives maternal abandonment when mom suddenly takes a job to make ends meet in the household.

---

2. Alan Medinger, *Growth into Manhood*, Colorado Springs: Shaw Books / Waterbrook Press (2000), p. xii. Hence, acknowledging the lack of full gender identification with one's birth gender is a critical factor in beginning the process of healing from SSA and other characteristics of homosexuality.

So what then are the real causes of SSA and homosexuality? Obviously, we need to look more closely at the various factors contributing to a full-blown manifestation of this condition or emotional adaptation. In doing so, we need to keep in mind that no single factor has been found that will invariably lead to homosexuality. It is only when the totality of potential variables fall together in some requisite pattern or constellation that a subject will begin to experience same-sex attraction. "A single factor does not cause a Same-Sex Attachment Disorder," cautions sexual reorientation specialist Richard Cohen. "It is the confounding of several variables that will lead an individual to experience same sex attractions."[3]

Moreover, as Dr. Van den Aardweg explains, "these factors are not the strict causes of homosexual longings but only *precipitating factors* which create a certain predisposition."[4] This predisposition is in turn affected by the environment in which one lives, and by the events and opportunities of one's daily life. We might compare the variables that contribute to homosexuality to a combination lock. All combination locks share a similar construction, yet the specific combination of numbers required to open each lock is unique. In much the same way, which factors predominate in generating homosexual tendencies depends on the individual as well as the circumstances. When the constellation of variables fall together in a certain pattern *and* when the individual's "Achilles heel," so to speak, is his or her gender identity, then he or she will at some point start experiencing same-sex attraction.

---

3. Richard Cohen, *Coming Out Straight,* Winchester: Oakhill Press (2000), p. 28. Note that the terms "Same-Sex Attachment Disorder," ("SSAD"), and "Opposite-Sex Attachment Disorder" ("OSAD") were coined by Cohen. As a former homosexual, Cohen believes the acronym "ssad" more accurately describes the homosexual condition than "gay."

4. Gerard J.M. Van den Aardweg, *On the Origins and Treatment of Homosexuality: A Psychoanalytic Reinterpretation,* Westport: Praeger Publishers / Greenwood Press, Inc. (1986), p. 65.

Richard Cohen (28-53), lists ten of the most common factors contributing to same-sex attraction in individuals. Some of their descriptions overlap. The brief overview of these factors which follows is meant to help the reader understand how same-sex attraction may come about. It is one of psychiatry's most basic tenets that understanding is the first stage of recovery. As Cohen urges, "By addressing each of these issues, by uncovering their meaning and impact, the individual may heal and fully recover the ability to experience his/her own gender identity and a sense of self-worth." (29) Naturally, the severity of the wound and the length of time it has been allowed to suppurate are among the several factors that will affect the duration and intensity of the healing process.

1. Hetero-emotional wounds.

This factor typically involves a lack of separation, individuation, or differentiation from the opposite-sex parent, often owing to an abnormally close or, conversely, a particularly troubled or distant, relationship with that parent. Such departures from the normal bonding process between mother and son or father and daughter can lead to homosexuality or lesbianism, heterosexual promiscuity, prostitution or compulsive recourse to prostitutes, impotence, or simply an inability to relate to a spouse or partner of the opposite sex. (Cohen, 29)

A different hetero-emotional wound may involve sexual abuse. On the other hand, sexual abuse, obviously, need not be perpetrated by a family member in order to leave a devastating mark on gender identity. For example, a lesbian might owe her condition to a physical or emotional trauma inflicted by a male upon her in childhood or adolescence. The victim, in her desire to protect herself from further sexual, emotional, mental, and/or physical abuse by a male—or even from reliving the pain of a traumatic disappointment or rejection, may turn to other women for comfort, love, and understanding. In her memoir of induction into and recovery from lesbianism, Erin Eldridge reports:

> Real problems began at the age of nine when an older boy in the neighborhood sexually molested me. I felt a little funny about it but went along because I liked the attention and enjoyed the touching. The fact that I found pleasure in those experiences would come back to haunt me, serving as proof that I was guilty and bad. (Eldridge, 6-7)

Not surprisingly, the same emotions of pleasure and guilt often characterize the reaction of a boy who was victimized by an older male. When this results in later development of homosexuality in the victim, the male victim will tend to seek a repetition of the experience, whereas the female will often seek comfort in the arms of other women.[5]

2. Homo-emotional wounds.

Many reparative therapists believe this to be *the most significant factor* in the development of what may later manifest as same-sex attractions.

> In the heart of every man or woman who experiences same-sex desires is a sense of detachment from his or her same-sex parent. [...] Experiences of detachment, which occurred in the first years of life, are locked deep in the unconscious mind. This is why many homosexual individuals say, "As long as I can remember, I felt different." (Cohen, 36)

This sense of detachment can develop in a number of different ways. A small boy, for example, may perceive his father as aloof or uninterested. Conversely, the child may take on a timid and fearful manner because dad is over-dominant or too forceful. In other cases, the talents and interests of the child and parent may simply be a mismatch. Sometimes small acts of neglect or

---

5. Edward O. Laumann, *et. al.*, *The Social Organization of Sexuality: Sexual Practices in the United States,* U. of Chicago Press (1994), p. 344.

withholding of love can be damaging even though the effect may not be obvious. On the other hand, severe emotional, physical, or even sexual abuse may exist.

For the male, detachment from the father can have profound consequences. The small boy subconsciously creates a deep sense of ambivalence toward the rejecting father: "I need you, but I perceive that you hurt or rejected me, so stay away, but come close and hold me, but don't, because it hurts me too much." This is exactly what psychologists mean by "defensive detachment" or "attachment strain." Such ambivalence toward the father can act as a lifelong block against full masculine identification—unless the child is somehow able to work through the ambivalence. By rejecting his primary source of masculine identity, the future gay male essentially rejects his own core gender identity. However, the longing for bonding with the father, the child's desperate need to be accepted and approved by same-sex role models and peers remains unfulfilled. When puberty sets in, this need is sexualized and manifests as a sexual attraction to other boys.

No less critical for boys than identification with the father is individuation from the mother. Obviously, if this does not occur, the masculine identification process is bound to be disrupted.

Of course, individuation from the mother is also necessary for a girl's normal psychological development. She, too, must separate and individuate during early stages of development, but, in contrast with boys, will continue to identify with her mother, her primary feminine role model. (Cohen, 38) However, as noted by Carol Ahrens, a psychologist with many years' experience working with lesbians, when the individuation from her mother fails to complete, a tendency to lesbianism may result.

> Independence comes when we have received enough affection and reassurance to build our confidence, and so we begin to depend less on others to care for us and we learn to take care of ourselves. Whenever I see a woman who is emotionally dependent on another woman, I know that she has not been able

to successfully complete this process of independence.[6]

Excessive female bonding or over-dependence is a key factor in lesbianism, as even the Sages seem to have intuited. Indeed, the Talmud draws such an inference in its analysis of why the father of the Talmudic Sage Shmuel prohibited his virgin daughters from sharing the same bed. (*Shabbos* 65a-b) (Nevertheless, the Talmud concludes that what Shmuel's father actually feared was that such contact might lead to sexual dependency in general.) The psychology of lesbianism clearly involves emotional dependency on the other woman. According to Dr. Ahrens, this state of mind goes considerably beyond what is commonly experienced:

> Emotional dependency is a state in which a woman feels totally reliant on another woman for safety and functioning. I'm not talking about the normal need we all have for close friendship and intimacy. I'm talking about a virtual obsession with another woman, one that leaves you hooked as surely as though you were hooked on a drug. When a woman is emotionally dependent, she feels as though she literally cannot exist without the object of her dependency. She needs constant reassurance from the other woman, consistent displays of affection, and large quantities of time with her. (204)

(The idolatrous aspect of this dependency is discussed in Chapter 10, at pages 359-67.)

As might be expected, however, boys have an extra developmental task that girls do not have. From age one-and-a-half to three, boys must not only separate and individuate from their mother, but also be initiated into the world of the masculine by his father or other significant male role model. Cohen suggests that if

---

6. Dr. Carol Ahrens, "Emotional Dependency and Lesbianism," in Joe Dallas, *Desires in Conflict: Answering the Struggle for Sexual Identity,* Eugene: Harvest House Publishers (1991), p. 205.

no male role model is available to the male child by the time he reaches three years of age, his gender identity may already be compromised. "This is a critical time for the son to bond with his father or other men." (*Coming Out Straight,* 38)

How does a baby boy lose this precious bonding opportunity? Cohen lists three common scenarios: "(1) the mother continues to cling to her son; (2) the father is unavailable or abdicates responsibility to the mother, or (3) the son perceives rejection from the father." (38)

3. Social or peer wounds.

This factor has to do with a child's strong sense of being different from other children. He might regularly have been on the receiving end of particularly cutting name-calling and other put-downs, or possibly he was ostracized as a "goody-goody" or the "teacher's pet." Perhaps he shied away from rough and tumble activities with other boys, or preferred the quiet play of girls with whom he happened to be familiar. "Bookish" boys are particularly vulnerable, with non-athleticism often leading to "sportsphobia" and an inability to bond with others in team sports. Lack of hand-eye coordination often accompanies the sports component in male peer wounds.

Conversely, girls may be subject to social mockery if they are too athletically inclined or heavily involved in physical activity. For Dr. Van den Aardweg, peer rejection is even more significant a factor than the lack of a masculine role model during infancy. In fact, Van den Aardweg sees same-sex peer wounding as far and away the most significant contributor to same-sex attraction.

> The strongest association, then, is not found between homosexuality and father-child and mother-child relationships, but between homosexuality and *peer relationships.* [. . .] It should be made the *prime suspect* in any explanation of homosexuality [. . .] Feeling less masculine or feminine as compared to same-sex peers is tantamount to the feeling of *not*

belonging.[7] (Original emphasis.)

Even some gay mental health professionals believe that when healthy, non-sexual bonding occurs, homosexual orientation is avoided. Indeed, the psychological research team of McWhirter and Mattison conclude that the earlier boys experience same-sex attraction, the stronger the indication that they "apparently failed to make close-knit associations with other boys, and thus their developing ego formation was not influenced by the powerful molding forces of peer conformity."[8]

In our view, the peer wound often occurs as an "add-on" to the defensive detachment the boy may have already "acquired" from Dad and the enmeshment he may already have with Mom. He may withdraw from same-sex peers just as he may have already detached from the same-sex parent.

The majority of individuals afflicted by same-sex attraction experience both a great loneliness and a profound sense of alienation from others of the same sex. In response to their isolation, such individuals commonly develop a "complex" of either inferiority or superiority—either "I am not as good as the rest of them," or "I am better than they." As a "defense mechanism," such rationalizations are, of course, a total failure, only adding further grounds for rejection. In his many years of treating homosexuals, Van den Aardweg found that feelings of inferiority, in one variant or another, were "evident in every male homosexual I have analyzed." (*Battle for Normality,* 64) According to Van den Aardweg, this feeling of inferiority is "psychophysical"—that is, it pertains to both physical and mental aspects of virility. (64) Not only does the homosexual man feel "inadequate in those things he associated in his youth with 'being a

---

7. Gerard J.M. Van den Aardweg, *The Battle for Normality: A Guide for Self-Therapy for Homosexuality,* San Francisco: Ignatius Press (1997), pp.41, 48.

8. David P. McWhirter & Andrew M. Mattison, *The Male Couple: How Relationships Develop,* Englewood Cliffs: Prentice-Hall, Inc. (1984), p. 136.

real man,'" but he is often paralyzed with fear; hence "he does not dare to fight—physically as well as psychologically." (64)

This could explain why so many gay men dread taking the steps necessary to grow out of homosexuality, thus neutralizing what motivation they may have to change sexual orientation. It also helps us understand Jeff's tragic failure to follow through with the contact information I gave him (*see* "Jeff's Case," in Chapter Two).

4. Sibling Wounds and Other Family Dynamics.

A young boy who bears the brunt of emotional, mental, physical, and/or sexual abuse from his siblings may develop a poor self-image and disidentify with his physiological gender. In a later chapter (Chapter 15), one of our strugglers (Scott) will relate how from the age eight he was sexually abused by his older brother, and how this adversely affected his self esteem.

Less dramatically, it often happens that a boy will perceive that, for example, his younger brother is favored by Daddy and there is no room in the relationship for anyone else. Hence, the older boy defensively detaches from the father *and* the brother, subconsciously stating that if they don't want him, he does not want to be like them. In the case where a sister has assumed the role of "princess," the boy may emulate her in an attempt to gain greater attention. The converse may be true where the girl perceives her brother as the family's favorite.

Another dynamic that has been found to reinforce defensive detachment from the father is the situation where the young son becomes an emotional surrogate husband for the mother. Suppose, for example, that the boy fails to bond with the father and compensates by over-bonding with the mother. Suppose the mother, too, is so emotionally deprived by her husband, and so emotionally needy, that she reaches out to her son for the kind of emotional support more properly provided by a spouse. Such a dynamic will very likely precipitate or reinforce the son's defensive detachment from dad. Mental health professionals use several terms to describe this situation: "emotional incest," "surrogate spouse," and "adultified child" are common examples. In such cases, the son absorbs his mother's emotional frame of mind. When she is lonely, she confides in him; when she is angry, she yells at him; when she feels like a failure, she projects her unhappiness and disappointment onto him. This typically results in one of two possible scenarios: (1) The more he identifies with Mom and internalizes female behavior, the more inadequate he will feel as a male; (2) The boy will project his mother's neediness onto other women and grow to avoid intimacy with women.[9]

Parenting styles, too, have been found to have a determinative effect on the way children form intimate relationships in adulthood and on the "attachment quality" of those relationships.[10] For example, homosexuality has been tied to "ambivalent/inconsistent" parenting in a dynamic which Dr. Joseph Nicolosi calls a "triadic narcissistic family pattern."[11] In this scenario, the child is pulled

---

9. For information on this topic, *see* Dr. Patricia Love, *The Emotional Incest Syndrome: What to do When A Parent's Love Rules Your Life,* New York: Bantam Books (1990); and Jeff Konrad, *You Don't Have to Be Gay,* Hilo: Pacific Publishing House (1998), pp. 256-60.

10. For example, Hazen and Shaver's 1987 ground-breaking study ("Romantic love conceptualized as an attachment process," *Journal of Personality and Social Psychology,* Vol. 52 (1987), pp. 511-24) found that a warm/responsive parental style generally produced children who were self-confident and secure in their attachments in both infancy and adulthood. Conversely, a cold/rejecting/unresponsive parental style typically produced children who avoided close attachments. The products of ambivalent/inconsistent parenting formed anxious/ambivalent attachments characterized by neediness and insecurity about their partner's feelings. Wayne Weiten & Margaret A. Lloyd provide percentages of the general population reflecting the three alternative attachment styles. Secure Adults (55%), Avoidant Adults (25%), and Anxious-ambivalent or preoccupied adults (20%). *Psychology Applied to Modern Life: Adjustment in the 21st Century,* Belmont: Tomson & Wadsworth (8th ed., 2006), p. 253.

11. Dr. Joseph Nicolosi, *Reparative Therapy of Male Homosexuality: A New Clinical Approach,* Northvale: Jason Aronson, Inc. (1997), pp. 78-80.

into the dynamic of discord surrounding the parents, and is thus forced to choose between them and to identify psychologically with one or the other parent. For example, the boy may be tied to his mother by guilt and alienated from his father through hurt and anger, while losing touch with his own needs. A variant of this dynamic occurs when the child is taunted, teased or ridiculed by members of his own family—a pattern that, as explained by David Matheson in his Supplement for the "Journey into Manhood" weekend—can literally "shame" a child into homosexuality.[12]

Interestingly, the long-term damage caused from such moments does *not* come directly from the pain experienced at the time the shaming occurs. Rather, the harm develops by way of a defense mechanism that enables the child to survive the pain and embarrassment of the moment: the future struggler learns to disconnect from his feelings. This may lessen the pain, but because the child's feelings of hurt and anger are repressed rather than expressed, they get buried—literally stored—within the tissues and sinews of the body. Each time the abuse occurs, the boy more deeply internalizes his unacknowledged pain and shame, thus reinforcing his sense of inferiority and worthlessness. Ultimately, the child, now adolescent or adult, sees everything—including himself—through the lens of his self-devaluation. He disconnects from his "self" and experiences difficulty either perceiving or meeting his own authentic emotional needs.[13]

5. Body-image wounds.

---

12. David Matheson, *Four Principles of Change: A Supplement for the Journey into Manhood Weekend,* Private publication (2002-07). Obviously, the same applies to peer ridicule or to any shaming experience.

13. According to modern kinesthesiological theory, this storing of unprocessed emotional trauma in the tissues of the body can create severe physical and organic problems as well. Thus it is very possible that various types of body-centered therapies, such as chiropractic, acupuncture, massage, *etc.,* can enhance gender healing. Unfortunately, little research has been done in this area.

Whether real or perceived, negative peer or parental reactions to a child's physical attributes can cause great pain leading to low self-esteem and feelings of physical inadequacy. The child grows up thinking of him- or herself as unattractive, or too short, too tall, too fat, too thin, or, for example, as having too large a nose or ears. In a word, because of childhood taunts, for example, he or she may reach adulthood with a self-image that has no relation to his or her actual appearance—which, in reality, may be very attractive.[14] Such feelings of self-disparagement can seriously affect one's gender identification. On the JONAH listserv, our strugglers discussed the embarrassment they felt about maturing physically. For example, while some men found underarm hair attractive because it represented masculinity to them, others felt ashamed of their underarm hair, because, as one contributor wrote,

> My body was showing me very clearly that I was a *male* and there was really no way to deny it. However, *inside,* I don't think I really felt I was a male. Thus, the hair was like an unwanted testimony to my maleness. I also think, that for me, the more I was aware I was male, or in any way felt I was male, the more I felt threatened. I was either separating from my mother, something I think was very scary, or resisting identification with my Dad, something that intimidated me, or both. I was emotionally stuck in-between as if I was androgynous.

Another struggler spoke of shaving off much of his body hair in order to counteract a feeling of maturity, while a third struggler expressed embarrassment over his pubic hairs.

6. Heredity.

---

14. Body image wounds usually do not occur in isolation. A typical pattern for a male homosexual involves, first, detachment from Dad, then, in early childhood alienation from peers, and finally unhappiness over his own body image. In sum, he distances himself from his own gender.

As we have emphatically pointed out, no evidence of a "gay gene" has yet been found. On the other hand, it appears there may be certain inheritable characteristics which may predispose some people to internalize emotional hurts more easily than the average person. For example, he or she may be "oversensitive" or have a brooding, melancholic disposition. In truth, it is not at all clear whether even suchlike characteristics are inherited genetically or acquired via the parental role model. In any case, it is not the event, but the response to the event, not the reality but the perception of reality, that determines the course of gender development. Nor should it be excluded that SSA can sometimes be transmitted behaviorally from one generation to another. In other words, "learned." Richard Cohen proposes that this is what is implied by Exodus 34:7, where G–d describes Himself, among other holy attributes, as " . . . visiting the iniquity of the fathers upon the children, and upon the children's children, unto the third and to the fourth generation." The Hertz *Chumash*,[15] too, comments that this verse relates to the chain of consequences arising from the sins and misdeeds of the previous generation. Incestual sexual abuse and child-beating are two commonly cited examples of pathological behavior transmitted within the family system.

7. Temperament.

Closely related to heredity concerns are certain positive temperamental characteristics or "gifts," which may or may not be inherited. If not properly validated within the family environment, these special qualities may cause the child to be shunned by other children, making him or her feel excluded and "different." This may lead or contribute to same-sex attraction. Such characteristics might include hypersensitivity, artistic talent, esthetic fastidiousness, gender-nonconforming behaviors—a more masculine

---

15. Rabbi Dr. J.H. Hertz, *The Pentateuch and Haftorahs,* London: Soncino Press (1981), p. 365.

female, a more feminine male—or a medical condition requiring special care and great expense. Also, a submissive nature, as in a child who complies or withdraws, rather than speak up, is a temperamental characteristic which potentially creates detachment. Nicolosi refers to this aspect as the "good little boy syndrome."

8. Sexual Abuse.

Even one episode of sexual abuse can leave a child scarred for life with feelings of powerlessness and extreme vulnerability. Abuse victims learn to fear and distrust others, even those who are closest to them. Clinical studies show that surprisingly high percentages of homosexual adults were sexually abused as children. At a Therapeutic Seminar in 1998, Dr. A. Dean Byrd, a therapist in Salt Lake City and Professor of Medicine at the University of Utah Medical School, presented a study entitled "Understanding and Treating Homosexuality." In it, he summarized numerous findings indicating that as many as 90% of the homosexual women and 75-80% of the homosexual men surveyed had been sexually abused during childhood by men—many of whom had themselves been abused as children. Studies show that boys victimized by older men are at least seven times more likely to identify as homosexual, and four times more likely to be currently engaged in homosexual activity, than non-victims. (Cohen, 43) Other studies cited by Cohen find "a statistically strong correlation between childhood sexual abuse and homosexual activity in adolescence and adulthood." (Cohen, 43) As we saw above (p. 130), Erin Eldridge felt that her sexual abuse at age 9 by a male turned her away from men and fostered her lesbianism. The opposite typically results when the abuse victim is a boy: male victims turn to other males. A man in our JONAH recovery group reported having endured constant sexual abuse by his older brother from the age of 8 to 16.

Many boys are so desperate to bond with older males that their vulnerability is apparent to the abuser. Child abusers learn to recognize the child who harbors this unmet homo-emotional need.

"The insidious nature of abuse is that it first begins as emotional intimacy and later becomes sexual." (Cohen, 43) The boy craves masculine attention and initially views the touching as innocent and evidencing affection. Cohen writes that a male child who is disidentified with his dad and over-identified with his mom is more susceptible to abuse by an older male.

9. Cultural wounds.

These are influences which molest the mind and the spirit. They include pornography or other sexually less explicit but highly suggestive entertainments or ads and commercials which appear on TV, the movies and the Internet and in various other media outlets. In addition, the culture of political correctness, the bias in our schools and school boards, the repetition ad nauseam of myths and lies propagated with the goal of normalizing a pathological condition born out of emotional distress—all these tend to confuse children about their sexuality. As noted by John McKellar (in Chapter 3, p. 97), "educating" elementary- or middle-school-age children about sexual practices may constitute "psychological pedophilia." It is beyond dispute that cultural indoctrination—pro-gay propaganda and the climate of political correctness draws sexually insecure people into the homosexual lifestyle. This factor is discussed in detail in Chapters 3 (pp. 67-88, 98-100, 105-109, 120-24) and 11 (pp.405-416).

10. Other factors.

A variety of other miscellaneous factors can further push a child over the precipice into homosexuality: divorce, a death in the family, adoption, or immigration to an unfamiliar culture. If a child learns that he or she was "unwanted," or conceived by accident, or born in spite of an attempted abortion, it may result in a devastating loss of self-worth that can lead to a reckless disposition to experiment with sex, drugs and/or alcohol. Yet another factor involves disenchantment with religion and rejection of G–d. A young man tormented by SSA can feel abandoned by G–d: "G–d betrayed me. He made me gay and his disciples preach an absolute truth which makes me feel like an abominable creature. His rules cannot therefore apply to me." Dr. Carol Ahrens cites trauma, emotional dependency and feminist politics as factors frequently encountered in the etiology of lesbianism.[16]

Gender Double-Bind.

While the emotional harm caused by any one of, or any combination of, the above-indicated factors, may or may not of itself lead to SSA and homosexuality, a key element in triggering the transformation is what some psychologists refer to as the "gender double bind." In psychological jargon, the classic "double bind" is a situation in which the child finds himself punished by a parent or other authority figure for expressing him- or herself. For example, the child feels hurt and wants to cry, but is told not to; or the child is angry and is warned to control his/her rage. Of course, when children reach a certain age, it is appropriate that they begin to learn to control their emotions. But barring a small child from expressing him- or herself can impair the child's resilience to life's challenges, stilt his/her emotions and prevent him/her from developing the capacity to deal authentically with his/her own feelings. Thus, when confronted by the internal emotional conflicts of puberty, the child lacks the emotional skills necessary to resolve them.

The double bind can have sexual ramifications when the emotional impasses created by this type of imposition are gender-significant, or made to appear so—as, for example, when a boy is scolded for crying because "crying is what little girls do." Psychotherapist David Matheson describes the "Gender Double

---

16. Dr. Carol Ahrens, "Childhood Trauma and Female Sexuality," and "Emotional Dependency in Lesbianism," (two chapters) in Joe Dallas, *Desires in Conflict: Answering the Struggle for Sexual Identity,* Eugene: Harvest House Publishers (1991), pp. 185-214.

Bind," as a dynamic where boys, for example, are taught that it is bad to be a boy. "If they assert their masculinity, they are punished. If they abandon it, they experience a deep sense of loss which, lacking any help from the environment to absorb, they repress and cover up—often through sexual behavior." (*Four Principles*, 3-4)

The essence of this male-gender double bind is that it just hurts too much to be a man, and it hurts too much not to be a man. Thus, the boy detaches from his "manhood"—his maleness—to shield himself from unbearable pain (defensive detachment). However, the detachment also hurts: an essential part of himself has been excised—"lost." The boy still longs for what he has given up. As the boy goes through puberty, he begins to desire physical union with another boy or adult male as a means of recovering the manhood that he has renounced. The need is essentially emotional, but is perceived and expressed as sexual. "The greater the detachment from feelings, thoughts, and needs in the present, and the greater the detachment from the unresolved wounds and unmet needs of the past, the greater or more intense the desire will be for homosexual relations." (Cohen, *Coming Out Straight,* 53)

Once we recognize the full import and emotional impact of the factors outlined above, the role of a "gay gene"—even assuming there were one—appears significantly less determinative. Certainly, we do not deny that genetic factors very likely play a determinative role in the physiological virility of a man—his hairiness, musculature, strength, physical endurance and testosterone level, *etc.;* but many male homosexuals display these outward signs of healthy sexual vitality (and many lesbians all the attributes of nubile and fertile femininity).[17] Thus, it still appears that sexual attraction is primarily an *acquired,* not an inherited

---

17. Remember that body-image wounds (point 5, above, in text) often have nothing to do with *actual* physical appearance, but rather with the struggler's *perception* thereof. For further discussion of this issue *see* Father John F. Harvey, *The Truth About Homosexuality*, San Francisco: Ignatius Press (1996), p. 313; and Dr. Richard Green, *Sissy Boy Syndrome and the Development of Homosexuality,* Yale U. Press (1987), p. 77.

characteristic.[18]

Notwithstanding the foregoing, gay advocates still argue the very opposite—that a person's genetic make-up is what causes homosexuality, and that the emotional factors described above are the *result!* In other words, arguing from a false premise to a false conclusion, they claim, for example, that what causes defensive detachment from same-sex parent and peers is the purported anti-gay bias—or "homophobia"—that, they maintain, pervades our society.

This is quite simply a reversal of cause and effect. The classic event patterns associated with developing homosexuality generally occur *well before* any manifestation of same-sex attraction. Essentially, the same histories are found in homosexuals raised in a gay-tolerant society like the Netherlands as are found in more conservative regions like the American South. Indeed, much of "J's" Case (*see* Chapter 2, above) is absolutely consistent with the experiences of a great many homosexual males from all over the world. Many strugglers reading this chapter will have recognized the same patterns in their own personal lives. It is our hope that this knowledge will restore to them the personal autonomy and right of self-determination that gay politics has taken away from them.

Indeed, by fostering the myth that homosexual drives are "genetic" or "biological" or otherwise predetermined (and therefore "immutable and unchangeable"), and by blaming "homophobia" for *causing* homosexuality (a charge that is increasingly hard to support, in view of society's enormous investment in "normalization"), the "gay rights" movement has contributed to the present social climate of ignorance, suppression, and disinformation that is not only *not* "liberating" to homosexuals, but on the contrary positively oppressive to the many individuals among them who are undecided, conflicted, or profoundly disillusioned with the "gay" lifestyle.

---

18. Evidence of this can be seen in the GLBT's addition of the letter "Q" in an attempt to bring "Questioning" (undecided) individuals into their fold.

CHAPTER 5:

Torah and Talmud as Primary Sources for Defining Sexual Morality.

The Basic Texts of Judaism.

The Torah of the Jews, containing the familiar books of Genesis, Exodus, Leviticus, Numbers and Deuteronomy, not only records the origins of the Jewish Nation; it also provides the basis of Jewish Law.

While the term "Torah," in Jewish tradition, is often used generically to indicate the whole body of Jewish learning, "*The* Torah" refers specifically to the Scrolls of the Law, containing the Five Books of Moses. The Torah, or Pentateuch (Greek for "Five Books"), as it is often called by Christian scholars, is the foundation stone of all Jewish religious, moral and social teaching. The Torah is also the primary source of Christian doctrine, and, in its Christianized version (the "Old Testament"), the primary source of the religious, moral, and ethical foundation of western civilization.[1]

---

1. The Hebrew name for what Christianity calls the "Old Testament" is the *Tanach,* an acronym formed from the first letters of its three divisions: *Torah*

Thus it is essential not only from a Jewish perspective, but from a universal (and certainly a therapeutic) one, that our understanding of homosexuality, and of sexuality in general, be consistent with Jewish tradition—in other words, with the Torah views and interpretations expressed, argued, elaborated, and handed down by authentic normative Jewish scholarly sources. Such are the sources we are referring to when we refer in this book to "Jewish Tradition" or "Jewish Teaching," *etc.*

One reason that we make a distinction between "Torah" (Jewish Teaching) and "*the* Torah" (the Scrolls of the Law) is that Jewish Tradition holds that there is much more to the Five Books than meets the eye. In other words, there is an "oral" Torah that is inseparably linked to the written text of the Scrolls. When we say "inseparably linked," we mean that the written Torah cannot be fully understood without the explanations provided by this Oral Torah.

Indeed, Jewish Tradition holds that as G–d was dictating the "Written Torah" to Moses upon Mount Sinai, He explained the meanings and implications of every verse, as well as the rules of Torah interpretation, so that Moses in turn would be able to apply the Law consistently and correctly—and also teach it to future

---

(Teachings), *Nevi'im* (Prophets), and *Kesuvim* (Scriptures).

The Torah consists of the Five Books of Moses: *Bereishis, Shemos, Vayikra, Bamidbar,* and *Devarim,* (Genesis, Exodus, Leviticus, Numbers and Deuteronomy). In book-bound form (as opposed to the handwritten Scrolls), these five books are generally referred to as *Chumash* (meaning "five-fold"), rather than "the Torah."

Nevi'im has two parts: *Nevi'im Rishonim* (First Prophets), consisting of Joshua, Judges, First and Second Samuel, First and Second Kings, Isaiah, Jeremiah and Ezekiel; and *Nevi'im Acheronim* (Latter Prophets), consisting of Hosea, Joel, Amos, Ovadia, Jonah, Micah, Nahum, Habakkuk, Zephaniah, Haggai, Zechariah and Malachi.

The first part of *Kesuvim* contains Psalms, Proverbs and Job. The middle section consists of the five *Megillos* (scrolls): Song of Songs, Ruth, Lamentations, Ecclesiastes, and Esther. The concluding section is comprised by Daniel, Ezra, Nechemiah, and Chronicles.

generations. Moreover, G–d stipulated that these supplementary explanations were for oral transmission alone, not to be written down. Thus, while the contents of "The Torah" were to be preserved and transmitted in writing, the rules and methods for understanding and implementing it were to remain an "Oral Torah," to be meticulously handed down from teacher to student and from generation to generation, but never committed to writing. Rambam names forty generations in this chain of oral transmission, from Moses to the redactors of the Babylonian Talmud,[2] and we refer to them collectively as "the Sages." In the words of Nosson Scherman in his introduction to the Stone Edition of the Hebrew Bible, "It is unprecedented in human history that any tradition could be kept intact orally for so long . . . and it is with us still, in the Talmud, the *Midrash*, the Codes, and the primary commentaries of the ages."[3]

We may not know G–d's reason's for imposing this separate but parallel transmission of written and oral Torah, but one consequence is clear: each arm of our Holy Tradition confirms and authenticates the other as it completes it. The fact that we are able to interpret the Written Torah coherently, consistently, and at such great distance of time testifies to the unity and authenticity of its tradition, and to the faithfulness of its content—including, in particular, Exodus's account of the giving of the Torah at Sinai.

Thus, it is no coincidence that those who propose new and strange interpretations of the Written Torah generally deny both the historicity of the Exodus and the integrity of the Oral Tradition. Yet, as Rabbi Scherman points out, "Even a cursory reading of the Torah proves that such a tradition *had* to exist, that there is much more to the Torah than its written text." (Scherman, xxiii) Three

---

2. Maimonides, *Mishneh Torah, Yesodei HaTorah: Introduction to the Mishneh Torah,* Rabbi Eliyahu Touger, ed., New York: Moznaim Publishing Corporation (1989), pp. 22-25.

3. Rabbi Nosson Scherman,, *The Chumash (Stone Edition)*, Brooklyn: Mesorah Publications, Ltd., 1994, p. xx.

examples (there are thousands) will serve to illustrate:

1. As is well known, the Torah prohibits work on the Sabbath. However, the written Torah never tells us what "work" actually means, nor what activities are included in or excluded from that category. What kind of "work" are we supposed to refrain from on the Sabbath? Anything that demands physical or mental exertion? Or may we do whatever we like as long as it's done for pleasure? Does it become "work" only if we are paid for it? Are we permitted to carry a feather on the Sabbath, but not a load of bricks? How is one to know? And, how could G–d expect us to keep His Commandments without telling us precisely how?

In fact, the *Oral* Torah gives us a very clear definition of what constitutes "work" on the Sabbath, and what does not. However, a person who limits him/herself to the Written Torah cannot possibly discover what that definition is, and will always be in danger of violating the Sabbath. If he/she wishes to learn what he/she may or may not do on the Sabbath, he/she *must* turn to the Oral Tradition.

2. The Torah tells the Jews to bind "these words which I command you today . . . upon your hand," and to wear them as "frontlets between your eyes." (Deuteronomy 6:5-9) But how are we to fulfill these Commandments? Are they to be taken literally or figuratively? Exactly which words is the Torah referring to, and how are we to "bind" them on our hand? And what are "frontlets?" What do they look like? What are they made of?

Again, the Oral Tradition tells us in great detail what the Torah is referring to: two leather boxes of prescribed dimensions, worn during prayer, one on the arm, one over the forehead, the latter box divided into four compartments, the former box undivided, each box made from the hide of a kosher animal, and each threaded with leather straps. These little boxes—or *tefillin,* as they are called—have to be constructed in a very particular way. Each must contain specific Torah verses written with special ink on little scrolls of kosher parchment arranged in a carefully prescribed manner. If any one of these several dozen rules and regulations for making *tefillin* happen to be overlooked, the *tefillin* are considered invalid, and one who even inadvertently wears such *tefillin* has not fulfilled the *mitzvah* of *tefillin*.

3. Our third example is a case in which a passage in the Torah has commonly been misinterpreted (and also severely criticized) by those who are totally unfamiliar with the Oral Law. In an oft-quoted passage (Ex. 21:24-25), the Torah declares,

> *But if any harm shall follow, then you shall give life for life, eye for eye, tooth for tooth, hand for hand, foot for foot, burning for burning, wound for wound, stripe for stripe.*

Taken at face value, this passage seems to require the courts in certain cases of unintentional injury to impose an equal measure of *physical* retribution upon the perpetrator—namely, an eye for an eye, a tooth for a tooth, *etc.* That understanding, however, is simply wrong. The Oral Tradition explains that the penalty is not a retributive physical punishment. Rather, the perpetrator must pay monetary compensation. How much? For the loss of an eye, whatever amount is considered an "eye's worth"—in other words, the value that custom and the courts have assigned to that particular type of injury.

Why then does the Torah say "eye," and not "the value of an eye?" The great medieval commentator Sforno explains that here the Torah is teaching us a spiritual lesson: the perpetrator has in fact rendered *his own person* liable for the loss of an eye. It does not mean that his eye must actually be put out. Other commentators might offer a different explanation of why the Torah chose to say "eye" when it really meant "money;" but no one disagrees with the basic law: the penalty imposed by the Torah is financial, not physical.

From the above, we can perhaps begin to see that to interpret and apply the words of the Torah correctly—that is, in conformity with authentic Jewish tradition—requires a lot more than just familiarity with the written text. It is a complex process requiring a profound mastery of the Oral Tradition, constant study, and conscientious reliance on acknowledged *halachic* authorities. Let us now briefly survey the state and structure of this Oral Tradition in the form in which it has reached us today.

The Oral Torah.

It must be stated at the outset that this "Oral Torah" is no longer strictly "oral." Nearly two thousand years ago, in one of the most fundamental developments of Judaism since the giving of Torah at Sinai, the Oral Tradition was committed to writing. The process of compiling that Tradition was begun at the instigation of Rabbi Yehudah the Prince shortly after the end of the first century of the common era. Rabbi Yehudah took this drastic step lest the Oral Tradition be utterly lost in the wake of the destruction of the Second Temple by the Roman armies—a disaster which entailed the exile of a great part of the Jewish People, and the slaughter and dispersal of many of the great rabbis of the time.

Foremost among the new compilations was the *Mishnah*, which became the basis of all subsequent explications and codifications of Jewish Law. Written in a shorthand Hebrew suitable for committing the laws to memory, the *Mishnah* provides a kind of snapshot of how the Oral Torah was remembered at that time. However, because its style is so tightly condensed, to understand it correctly requires careful analysis. Thus, the study of *Mishnah* assumed early on the form of discussion and debate. Records of such discussions were kept by the Torah academies of Babylonia, which had become the center of Jewish life in exile, and somewhat later, as Jewish life began to revive in Judea, by the academies of Jerusalem. Thus were born the Babylonian and Jerusalem Talmuds, in which each chapter of the *Mishnah* is followed by a "lesson" or "study" (*gemara*) of how it was analyzed and interpreted by the greatest rabbis of the day. Together, *Mishnah* and *Gemara*, comprise the monumental, multi-volume work collectively known as the Talmud.

The Talmud is the primary repository of the Oral Law and the ultimate source of all Jewish legal codes. Thus, observant Jews look to Talmudic interpretation as timeless and definitive. Nothing contained therein is considered to have been stated in groundless speculation or casually included. Essentially, the Rabbis of the Talmud engage in "explicating the Torah and applying its principles to everyday existence."[4] They expound upon, interpret, construe, argue and explain the deepest and most hidden meanings of the words of the Torah. "Employing their methods of interpretation," writes one popular scholar, "[they] were able to penetrate to the deeper sense that lies beneath the letter, and in consequence, to find in the Scripture the loftiest conceptions of G–d's character and man's duty..."[5]

On another level, the substance of the Talmud can be separated into two distinct and characteristic components: *halachah* (law) and *agadah* (homily)—also called *midrash*. These two components are often intertwined, and it is important to explain how and why we distinguish between them, and what value we attribute to each. *Halachah* deals directly with the details of the *Mitzvos* ("Commandments") as they affect the life of the Jew. Literally, *halachah* means "a way of going or walking" or "a way of living." Thus it implies "a manner of conducting oneself so as to walk in G–d's ways." If the *Mitzvos* can be compared to statutes, then *halachah* might be compared to case law—a compendium of the many thousands of decisions handed down by qualified judges and which define what we may or may not do under various circumstances.

Agadah, on the other hand, consists of

> history, stories, fables, legends, prayers, meditations, reflections, religious discourses, exegetical remarks, allegory, ethical, moral and metaphysical teachings and maxims, theosophical and philosophical discussions, and scientific observations of anatomical, anthropological, ethnographical, physiological,

---

4. Reuven P. Bulka, *One Man, One Woman, One Lifetime,* Lafayette: Huntington House (1995), p. 12.

5. Rabbi Dr. Isidore Epstein, *Judaism: A Historical Perspective*, Baltimore: Penguin Books (1959), p. 132.

medical, physical, astronomical and mathematical character.[6]

Homiletic in style, the *agadic* (or *midrashic*) portions of the Talmud are intended to be instructive, explicative, and illustrative of Torah and *halachah,* but are not necessarily to be understood literally or viewed as definitive or legally binding.

Rabbinical Law.

There is another source of Jewish law which we need to mention. In addition to constituting the living repository of the Oral Torah, the Sages (starting with the Prophets), and later, the Great Sanhedrin, or "Great Court," had broad power, within the strict confines of Torah Law, to pass necessary laws and execute judgment. As Moses commands (Deuteronomy 18:15):

The L–rd your G–d will raise up for you a prophet from among you, one of your brothers, like me; to him you shall listen;

and (Deut.16:18):

Judges and enforcement officers for your tribes shall you make for yourselves in all your cities which the L–rd your G–d gives you: and they shall judge the people with righteous judgment.

and (Deut. 17:11):

According to the Torah which they shall teach you, and according to the judgment which they shall tell you, you shall do; do not stray from the word that they shall tell you, whether to the right or to the left.

---

6. Rabbi Philip Blackman (ed.), *The* Mishnayoth, *Tractate* Berachoth , New York: Judaica Press (rev. ed. 1977), p. 11.

Thus, as Rav Steinsaltz phrases it, "Everything done or decided by the sages over the centuries derives from the fact that the Torah authorized the judges of each generation to create laws and render justice to the people of Israel, from the days of the prophets to the last days of the Second Temple."[7] However, in light of the Commandment (Deut. 13:1):

Everything that I command you, take care to do it: you shall not add to it, nor diminish from it.

and (Deut. 4:2):

You shall not add to the word which I command you, nor shall you take away from it, so that you may keep the commandments of the L–rd your G–d which I command you.

the legislative power was limited to laws fostering the proper observance of the *Mitzvos*, to *ad hoc* or emergency decisions, to enactments of temporary duration, and to the decreeing of festivals and fasts based on the *divrei sofrim* ("the words of the Scribes"). For example, with respect to assuring proper observance, the Early Prophets instituted the two-day observance of Rosh Hashanah in order to prevent neglect of the Holy Day out of uncertainty as to when the new moon made its first appearance.

Similarly, invoking the applicable *divrei Sofrim*, the Sages decreed the post-Torah Festivals of Purim and Hanukka, as well as various communal fast days, to ensure thanksgiving and repentance at the appropriate times.[8]

---

7. Rabbi Adin Steinsaltz, *The Essential Talmud*, (Chaya Galai, trans.), Northvale: Jason Aronson (1992), p. 126.

8. Note, however, that the Sages are never considered an independent source of legal authority. Their authority can only be viewed as derived from the Torah. Thus, it is theoretically impossible to interpret a rabbinical law in a way that contradicts or overturns a provision of the Torah or an established *halachah*.

The disbanding of the Sanhedrin in 358 C.E. put severe limitations on the ability of the Rabbinate to promulgate new laws and execute judgments. Indeed, the primary legislative activity of the great rabbinical scholars since that time has been the development of *halachah* in pace with the ever-changing conditions of history, culture, and technology. Such new *halachos* (for example, the identification of an incandescent light-bulb with fire, in connection with the Torah prohibition of lighting a fire on Shabbos) become universal not by virtue of imposition from "above," but by voluntary adherence to the decisions of the greatest and wisest of the rabbinical scholars applying universally acknowledged principles of Torah, established *halachah*, and clear and unequivocal logic.

Regarding the judicial power, after the disbanding of the Great Sanhedrin, Jewish Tribunals (*battei din*) consisting of one or three judges (or, in some cases, regional councils of qualified rabbis) continued—and still continue—to administer justice and monitor the public safety in religious communities throughout the Land of Israel and the Diaspora. However, the growth over the centuries of powerful gentile kingdoms with sophisticated juridical systems significantly curtailed the judicial autonomy of their resident Jewish communities. Thus, it became no longer feasible to enforce observance or punish transgression as was practiced in Biblical and medieval times. Although various forms of social and economic pressure are still available to a *Beis Din,* in the last analysis, the willingness of the people to accept the authority of *poskim* (*halachic* decisors) and *dayanim* (judges of the *Beis Din*) depends—as no doubt it always depended—on the reputation of the rabbis in question for justice, scholarship, and piety, as well as on the strength of the following of each.

Thus, until the Sanhedrin is re-established, Judaism lacks a

Similarly, though there may be several competing views as to the interpretation of a Torah commandment or verse, no such interpretation can contradict or negate the Oral Tradition.

single high official body or person who is empowered to speak and act with ultimate legislative, judicial, or doctrinal authority for the entire People. Among the great sages of our time (the *Gedolei Yisroel*) each has his following, who scrupulously abide by his example and his rulings. Nevertheless, owing to the high degree of legal articulation found in the Talmud, the Codes, and the Commentaries, as well as to the deeply ingrained respect for tradition and custom, regional and sectarian differences among the Orthodox are largely confined to modest variations between stricter and more lenient views, and minor variations in regional custom and liturgical practice.

Translating the Torah into English.

As explained above, Torah represents both "the Divine Teaching given to Israel and the Message of Israel to mankind." (Hertz, *Chumash*, 1) It is of critical importance to recognize that this Teaching and this Message were originally written in Hebrew (the *Tanach*), and in Aramaic (the Talmud): not in English, Greek, or Latin.

The explication of just the original Hebrew of the Torah has given rise to an enormous body of interpretative literature. Imagine the problems that arise on translating the Torah into other languages! No matter what the original language, translation rarely (if ever!) conveys the full complexity and depth of meaning of the original text. However, with the Hebrew of the Torah, this difficulty is magnified many times over. Here is how the author of a much-loved survey of Jewish history and practice explains the problem:

> The Torah was given to Israel in the holy tongue together with a prescribed method for interpreting its words, verses and letters; thereby eliciting the wide range of meaning which inheres in them. By contrast, one who seeks to translate the Torah into a foreign tongue will find that there is no language whose words

are as rich in possible connotation as is the holy language.[9]

To the above, one could add, "or whose words, even were they as rich, could evoke the same or parallel connotations!"

> What then does such a translator do? He forsakes all the treasures of interpretation, allusion, and esoteric meaning contained in each word, and translates only the literal meaning. If one translates the Torah into another language, he is therefore like one who makes of the Torah an empty vessel; empty of its entire wealth of meaning which is the essence of Torah. He is left with literal meaning alone. How impossible is such an effort therfore, for those who love the Torah and know its greatness. (Kitov, 319)

The problem does not end there:

> At times the literal meaning of a particular verse or word is also in doubt and allows for alternate meanings. Which is to be chosen? (319)

In other words, we have to understand that words cannot be divorced from their narrative, linguistic, historical and exegetical contexts. Johann Gottfried Herder, the 18th-century German poet and philosopher, declared that it would be worthwhile to study the Hebrew language for ten years just to be able to read Psalm 104 in the original!

Obviously, it doesn't take ten years to learn enough Hebrew to be able to read Psalm 104! What did Herder really mean? In his introduction to his modern translation of the Torah, Rabbi Aryeh Kaplan describes the only legitimate approach to Torah translation: "The translator must not only analyze the text very carefully, but he must also study all the works that interpret it."[10]

---

9. Eliyahu Kitov, *The Book of Our Heritage: the Jewish Year and its Days of Significance* (trans. N. Bulman), Jerusalem: Feldheim (1978), Vol. 1, p. 319.

10. *The Living Torah: The Five Books of Moses and the Haftarot*, New York,

What Rabbi Kaplan is saying is that to be genuinely successful, the translator's approach must be not only contextual but *holistic*. The challenge lies in conveying not only the sense of the words themselves, but the meaning *behind* the words. To do this requires more than a mastery of the language. It requires an intimate knowledge of the entire culture.

Indeed, it was precisely because of the virtually insurmountable difficulties inherent in the task of translating the Torah that the Rabbis originally forbade its rendition into other languages. As Rabbi Kitov explains, "[T]here are many passages in the Torah which, if translated literally, would be misunderstood by the gentiles, and would cause them to deride our Torah's sanctity." (319) Thus, it was only at the command of King Ptolemy II Philadelphos of Hellenistic Egypt that seventy-two learned rabbis (the "Seventy" of the Septuagint version)[11] were forced to convene in Alexandria to translate the Torah into Greek—a development that caused much grief and dismay among the Jews of the time, and is still remembered by many as a day of repentance and fasting.

Moreover, it is generally acknowledged among Biblical scholars that, even on the level of literal meaning, the classic translations of the Jewish Bible are not accurate in every respect. This is due not only to the many archaisms whose meanings would have been clear to readers of bygone centuries but are no longer understood by present-day readers, but also, in part, to the "collusion" of the "Seventy," who deliberately substituted certain mistranslations rather than expose the Torah to the abuse of its opponents and the derision of the ignorant.[12] Several significant departures from the Hebrew original are also attributable to

---

Jerusalem: Moznaim Publishing Corporation (1981), p. vi.

11. The title *Septuagint* derives from the Latin word for 70: *septuaginta*.

12. The Talmud, *Megillah* 9, reports that though the 72 elders were forced to work independently in separate chambers, their versions turned out to be identical in all respects—even where they departed from the literal translation.

deliberate tampering by later Christian editors. The King James Version is a case in point. As Rabbi Aryeh Kaplan noted, "Although a superb scholarly work, this translation is not rooted in Jewish sources, and often goes against traditional Jewish teachings." (*The Living Torah,* v)

For our own purposes, then, the translation of key words and phrases must be clearly understandable to the contemporary reader in their authentic significance—a requirement that often calls for an interpretative, rather than a literal, translation. Thus, even the most literal translator cannot altogether avoid being an interpreter. Consider, for example, three alternative translations of Genesis 4:7, where G–d tells Cain that he has the power, if he so chooses, to overcome his evil inclination: *"timshol bo"* is variously translated as, "rule over it," "dominate it," and "conquer it." The distinctions between, "rule over it," "dominate it," or "conquer it," are not as subtle as they may seem.

Such interpretative decisions, however, must be consistent with the Oral Tradition, which, as previously indicated, is understood to be definitive. Thus, in proposing the textual interpretation which constitutes the central theme of this book, we will be seen to have relied on the Talmud itself, as well as on the expertise of recognized rabbinical scholars of unimpeachable credentials.

PaRDeS: the Four Levels of Torah Interpretation.

Torah is the light that illuminates the darkness of the world. Just as things look different in the light of dawn, in the sun of midday, and at sunset, so Torah reveals different things when viewed at different angles. In our Tradition, there are four distinct levels of meaning in the Torah. They are called: *P'shat, Remez, Drosh* and *Sod,* referred to collectively by their acronym—*PaRDes* (or *Pardes*), which is also the word for "Orchard."[13] The word "Paradise" derives from *Pardes.* Like the layers of an onion, each

---

13. Talmud, *Chagigah,* 14.

level of *PaRDeS* reveals a deeper aspect of Torah wisdom. Rabbi Yehoshua Karsh, writing on the website of the Torah Learning Center of Chicago, describes *PaRDeS* as "a hierarchy of planes of Torah understanding."[14] Let us briefly examine each plane in turn.

P'shat is the plain meaning of the text. It is the starting off point of Torah study. Its function is to lead us somewhere else. Rashi explains that even this simple level of meaning must be based on text and context. This may not always correspond to what the lay reader takes to be the literal meaning. To cite the example discussed above (at page 149), Exodus 21:24 ("eye for an eye, tooth for a tooth, *etc.*") is one of the most commonly misunderstood phrases in the Bible. That is because the general reader looks at it as though that passage existed in a vacuum. However, in the context of several other Torah passages, as well as in acknowledgment of the Oral Tradition, it is clear that the phrase does not call for retaliatory mutilation, but rather for monetary compensation. Why then does that passage use the words it does? As explained earlier, the *p'shat* conveys a spiritual message that needs to be distinguished from its practical intent as explicated by the Oral Law.

Remez ("hint") refers to the level of allusive implication—the allegorical meaning of the *p'shat*. One example of *remez* is found in the first word of the Torah: *B'reshis*. The simple meaning (*p'shat*) is "In the beginning." However, on the level of *remez,* the Vilna Gaon said that *b'reshis* alludes to the ritual of *pidyon haben* (redemption of the first born), because *b'reshis* is also an acronym for the words of the Commandment: *ben rishon acharei shloshim yom tifdeh*— "the first son you shall redeem after thirty days."

Drosh is a homiletic lesson derived from the *p'shat.* We gave an example of *drosh* when we referred to Sforno's interpretation of "eye for an eye" (*see* above, page 149): the verse comes to teach us that when a person injures a limb or organ of another out of

---

14. <http://www.torahlearningcenter.com/html/karsh14.html>.

carelessness, the negligent party has actually rendered himself liable to replace that limb or organ *out of his own body* (but since that is impossible, he must pay compensation).

Sod is the mystical or esoteric meaning concealed in the words of the text. An example of *sod* can be found in reference to the Holiday of *Chanukah* (Hanukka). *Chanukah* is not a Biblical holiday, because it commemorates a post-Biblical event: the Jewish victory over the Greek armies of Antiochus in 156 B.C.E. and the rekindling of the Menorah in the Holy Temple on the 25th day of the month of Kislev of that year. But where did the Sages get the authority to institute this extra-Biblical Holiday? Doesn't the Torah command (Deut. 13:1),

All this word which I command you, that you shall observe to do; you shall not add thereto, nor take away from it?

However, the Sages noted (among other things) that the 25th word of the Torah (counting from *B'reshis*) is *Ohr*—"light"—and that this word appears in the third verse. They saw in this a prophetic allusion to the lighting of the Menorah on the 25th day of the 3rd month (Kislev).

The *PaRDeS* schematic should *not* be understood to imply that there are only four possible interpretations for any passage of the Torah! On the contrary, there is a tradition that for any Torah passage under examination there are 600,000 possible interpretations *for each of the four levels* of interpretation—*p'shat, remez, drosh and sod!*[15] Nor does this mean that the Commandments themselves are "open to interpretation" as to whether and how and to what degree we are to observe them! The Oral Tradition distinguishes very clearly between the process of mining the Torah for insight and understanding on the one hand, and, on the other hand, the process of establishing the *halachos!* That

---

15. *See, e.g.*, Aryeh Kaplan (trans.), *MeAm Lo'ez*, Vol. 6, New York: Moznaim (1979), p. 104.

process is extremely well defined and fully structured. Legal determinations may only be made strictly within the bounds of tradition and precedent. These rules and traditions are part of the Oral Law: they may not be abrogated or modified except as permitted within the accepted guidelines of the Law itself. It cannot be stressed often enough that, as mentioned earlier, the details and requirements of every mitzvah were given at Sinai along with the written Torah, and they are indelibly fixed in the Oral Tradition.[16]

Thus, the Commandments themselves are not "open to interpretation"—however carefully reasoned—where the reasoning is divorced from the traditional understanding of the text. Unfortunately, as will be seen below, gay activists and their allies have attempted to develop a new, "pro-gay theology"—one in which the *halachah* is "liberated" from its moorings in Talmud and set adrift upon the high seas of human whims and crafty rationalizations. "When it comes to *halachah*, there is only one truth. For whereas Torah is G–d's wisdom, which . . . allows for different opinions, *Halacha* is [not intellect, but rather] G–d's will . . . ."[17]

This does not mean that *PaRDes* cannot uncover layers of *meaning* in a commandment. The words in which a *mitzvah* was given can and do have *additional* layers of meaning, and uncovering those layers can give us insights into the reasons why a certain *mitzvah* was given, or what *kavanah* (mental state) we should strive for when doing the *mitzvah,* or what we can hope for as a reward for performing the *mitzvah.* Likewise, the circumstances surrounding the giving of a *mitzvah* might serve to indicate the proper behavior in a related context; or might allude to another verse, or to some past or future event. All these things can teach us

---

16. Maimonides, *Mishneh Torah,* Vol. 1, (Rabbi E. Touger ,ed., trans.), New York: Moznaim (1989), p. 92.

17. Rabbi Naftali Silberberg (ed.), <http://www.askmoses.com/qa_print.html?h=417&o=2703&pg=2>.

something about Him Who "sanctified us with His Commandments and commanded us"[18] to do them.

What we do have to remember is that we may not draw any *halachic conclusions* from the additional layers of meaning that we purport to have discovered. When it comes to the Law, speculation regarding the *meaning* of and *reasons* for a commandment remains just that—speculation; and that is not an appropriate basis for deciding matters of law in any system of jurisprudence.

Modern-Day (Pro-Gay) Distortions.

Let us depart from the formidable gates of *halachah* to return for a brief moment to the Garden of Eden. In Genesis 3:1 we find the serpent asking the woman, "Did G–d really say that you may not eat from any of the trees in the garden?" According to rabbinic understanding, this "statement expressing surprise and incredulity" has the objective "of creating doubt in the reasonableness of the Divine prohibition." (Hertz, *Chumash,*10) Pro-gay apologists are fond of challenging G–d's words through a similar ruse. Like the Biblical serpent, they question whether the Bible really says such and such, or meant something else that is entirely extraneous to the Oral Tradition. Or they question whether the Torah would have given us the same commandments, had they been given to us in our own "enlightened" time and at our present "advanced" state of civilization. Like the serpent in the Garden of Eden, their prime objective is to create doubt or disbelief. "Would a loving G–d really demand that someone committing a homosexual act be put to death?" Often this question is wrapped in a thick cloak of Moral Outrage: *"What kind of a G–d would require that homosexuals be put to death!"*

Of course, to ask such questions, one has to ignore (whether through ignorance or design) a substantial portion of talmudic and *halachic* writing that clarifies the terms and conditions under

---

18. The standard formula for the blessings which precede the performance of various *mitzvos.*

which a transgressor may be executed. In actuality, the penal system of the Torah was designed to ensure that the death penalty would rarely, if ever, be applied. According to Rabbi Norman Lamm, "Usually, the Biblically mandated penalty was regarded as an index of the severity of the transgression, and the actual execution was avoided by the strict insistence upon all the technical requirements...."[19] Such requirements included forewarning the potential culprit in a very specific manner, the testimony of at least two competent eyewitnesses, rigorous cross-examination of all witnesses (the witness's testimony is taken separately but must match down to the minutest detail), and the use of numerous "trick" questions calculated to disqualify even the most reliable witness.

In short, the "ultimate penalty" was almost never carried out. "Having legitimized the penalty in principle, the *Halakhah* invoked and practiced it with extreme caution."[20] The Talmudic sage, Rabbi Eleazer ben Azariah, opined that a Sanhedrin that imposed the death penalty *even once in seventy years* was "overzealous!"

The *Sanhedrin* was the Supreme Court of the Judaic judicial system. Consisting of 71 rabbis chosen from the greatest Torah sages of their generation, it was the only Jewish Court authorized to adjudicate capital cases. Thus, with certain exceptions limited to a minor *Sanhedrin* of 23, no other *beis din* (Jewish tribunal) had

---

19. Rabbi Norman Lamm, "Judaism and the Modern Attitude to Homosexuality," *Encyl. Judaica Yearbook* (1974), pp. 194, 203. Note the similarity with Sforno's interpretation of "eye for an eye." (*See* above, p. 149). Rabbi Lamm's analysis is quite likely derived from Maimonides' evaluation of the relative severity of various transgressions. Rambam suggests that the severity of the offense can be inferred from the kind of penalty that applies. In other words, the most serious transgressions are punishable by a form of execution, while the less severe infractions comport lesser consequences—for example, lashes. *See* Rambam's *Commentary on the Mishnah, Avot* 2:1.

20. Rabbi Basil F. Herring, *Jewish Ethics and Halakhah for Our Time*, New York: Ktav Publishing House & Yeshiva U. Press (1984), p. 156.

the power to sentence a person to death. But the *Sanhedrin* was dissolved after the destruction of the Holy Temple, and nearly two thousand years have passed since then, during which *no* Jewish court has had the power to issue a death sentence.[21] Without a *Sanhedrin*, the penalty for capital offenses—such as homosexual conduct, child sacrifice (Lev. 20:2), cursing one's parents through mention of G–d's name (Lev. 20:9), adultery (Lev. 20:10), certain forms of incest (Lev. 20: 11-12), sexual relations with the mother of one's wife during the daughter's lifetime (Lev. 20:14), and bestiality (Lev. 20:15-16)—is Divine retribution (*kares*).

In portraying the G–d of the Jews as a cruel tyrant who demands the execution of those who violate His laws, gay activists have taken up an old and disreputable canard. For it is clear from all Torah sources that G–d is anything but a harsh and unforgiving judge who demands strict enforcement of absolute laws and never considers the mitigating circumstances of the transgression or the contrition of the transgressor. In our sacred Tradition, His compassion is everywhere in evidence, and repeatedly—even constantly—acknowledged. The "Thirteen Attributes of Mercy" recited daily in the *Tachanun* (Confessional Prayer) is perhaps the most comprehensive example:

> *L–rd, L–rd, benevolent G–d, compassionate and gracious, slow to anger and abounding in kindness and truth, He preserves kindness for two thousand generations, forgiving iniquity, transgression, and sin, and He cleanses.* (Ex. 34:6-7)[22]

According to our Tradition, it is not punishment that G–d

---

21. In 1961, in a one time exception to Israeli *secular* law, a specially constituted secular Israeli court condemned the Nazi Adolf Eichmann to be hanged for having ordered and supervised the liquidation of approximately one million Jews.

22. *Siddur Tehillat Hashem* (Bilingual Ed.), (Rabbi Nissen Mangel, trans.), Brooklyn: Merkos l'Inyonei Chinuch (1995), p. 62.

wants of His children, but *teshuvah*—repentance, and a mending of ways. Indeed, that is the great lesson of the Book of Jonah; that is the purpose of Yom Kippur, the "Day of Atonement." *Hashem* wants us to go into the depths of our soul, examine our deeds and misdeeds, awaken our shame and remorse, and resolve to improve. He wants us to come closer to Him through the study of His Torah and the keeping of His Commandments. He is ready to meet us more than half way by strengthening our resolve and helping us overcome our spiritual doubts and perplexities.

Clearly, however, such a view does not well suit the politics of the gay lobby, for that would mean conceding that even the prohibition of homosexual sexual activity was decreed out of G–d's love and mercy.

And it is here that the Morally Outraged have attempted to assume the robes of a *Posek*—a revered decisor of *halachic* questions. Indeed, reformist camps have twisted the four levels of interpretation into a purported license to liberalize, bowdlerize, and even de-legitimize the Commandments as they see fit. In other words, they seize upon the example of the Sages—devout rabbis skilled in the techniques of *PaRDeS*—as a pretext for re-interpreting the Commandments in an unauthorized way that "allows" them to compromise with the "dictates" of our times— exactly what the Torah expressly prohibits:

And that you go not about after your own heart and your own eyes, after which you use to go astray. (Num.15:39)

Closely allied with the camp of the Morally Outraged is that of the Moral Relativists. They concoct a G–d who is not evil and cruel, but merely confused and indecisive. "If G–d gave us these feelings," they ask, "how can it be wrong to express them?" In their view there are no absolute standards. All is relative. While they do not shrink from teaching G–d "Morality 101," they offer no real guidance to humanity: nothing done out of "love" for a fellow human being is to be condemned; nothing that does not harm someone else is to be considered sinful. However, the relativists do not tell us how we can ever be sure that we are acting out of love rather than selfishness, or ego, or lust, or power. Again, how can we ever know whether what we are doing to another person will harm him/her or not? Who is to decide what is harmful? The person who wishes to do it, or the person to whom it will be done? The moral relativists see themselves in a kind of Garden of Eden before the Fall. There is no Tree, no Forbidden Fruit, no Knowledge of Good and Evil. In fact, there is no such thing as "good" or "evil"—period! Everything is just neutral, natural, and "OK".[23]

One typical variant of this approach is the Gift from G–d Theory: "Since most homosexuals did not 'choose to be gay,'" goes the argument, "their homosexuality must be a 'gift from G–d.'" The founding co-president of the first gay and lesbian synagogue in America asserts, "G–d loves His children, G–d has created us, G–d has had a hand in our life styles."[24] But with the same logic one could also—and more aptly—cry out, "G–d, You have created me out of your love, and out of Your love You have created my imperfections so that I may overcome them; in Your lovingkindness, please grant me the strength and the will to overcome my limitations and my defects and so win merit in Your eyes." Indeed, Jewish Tradition teaches that through our own faith,

---

23. *See* Rabbi Norman Lamm, "The Arrogance of Modernism," Chapter 5 in Rabbi Lamm's *The Royal Reach: Discourses on the Jewish Tradition and the World Today,* New York: Feldheim (1970), pp. 36-42. This new order of morality has been characterized as a form of "cultural Marxism" in which "the patriarchal social structure would be replaced with matriarchy; the belief that men and women are different and properly have different roles would be replaced with androgyny; and the belief that heterosexuality is normal would be replaced with the belief that homosexuality is normal." J.J., "Political Correctness: More Insidious and Dangerous Than Most Realize, Say Writers: True Purpose is the Complete Eradication of Traditional Western Culture." May 19, 2005, <http://www. lifesite.net/ldn/printerfriendly.html>.

24. Quoted in Erwin L. Herman, "A Synagogue for Jewish Homosexuals," CCAR Journal, Vol. XX (Summer, 1973), p. 38.

G–d grants each of us the opportunity to overcome adversity and challenge; and that through our own faithfulness, He provides us with the courage to face our fears, walk through our pain, and come out whole.

Most Moral Relativists prefer to cloak themselves in the guise of an evolved, socially conscious and morally-based philosophy rooted in hallowed western, Judeo-Christian ideas. For example, one Reform rabbi declared, "While Leviticus is a legally based argument for Jewish law, there are Jewish values that infuse our entire understanding of the Torah that some would argue, as I would, are more important."[25] Another proclaimed, "G–d is more concerned in our finding a sense of peace in which to make a better world than He is in whom someone sleeps with."[26] The former of these rabbis apparently believes in the existence of amorphous "Jewish values" that have somehow managed to escape being articulated by all-encompassing Jewish Law. The latter-mentioned rabbi might be advocating a sexual free-for-all—provided we all drink organic tea and meditate!

How convenient! How does a mortal human presume to know what concerns G–d most? Where does a rabbi get the idea that a Jew is permitted to "choose" among the *Mitzvos* on the basis of their presumed relative importance? In our Tradition, G–d has already figured out which *mitzvos* are needed to perfect the world, and He commanded us in the Torah to do them, specifically so that we might achieve that result.

More insidious—because proffered in the guise of traditional Talmudic scholarship—is the approach taken by some Conservative rabbis who claim not to be rejecting tradition, but merely to be "reinterpreting" it—as, *e.g.*, Rabbi Daniel Grossman: "Those who have interpreted the Leviticus passage [18:22] as

---

25. Rabbi Joshua Lesser as quoted in "Sodomy Ruling: Love It or Hate It," *Jewish Standard,* July 4, 2003, p. 25, col. 2.

26. Herman, 38. One would like to ask the author if G–d becomes more concerned where the "sleeping" involves, *e.g.*, pedophilia, necrophilia, or bestiality.

banning gay sexual unions have taken it out of context. The passage actually prohibits [only the] male and female cultic ritual prostitution practiced by certain people as a sacred ritual during biblical times."[27] Another commonplace is the suggestion that Leviticus 18:22 solely prohibits "a man from sexually penetrating (or being penetrated by) another man anally."[28]

Gay activists and their academic cohorts eagerly tout the claim that Jonathan and David were homosexual lovers while Ruth and Naomi were lesbian lovers.[29] Besides the psychological short-sightedness of ignoring—or pretending to ignore—the potential depth and intensity of non-erotic love associated with true friendship, neither of these "theories" finds any basis whatsoever in the primary texts or in the tradition of interpretation. Another misleading contention is that Sodom was destroyed *not* because of its sexual practices, but because of its legislation outlawing

---

27. Debra Rubin, "What is the role of Gays in the Jewish Community?" *The Jewish State,* July 21 (2000), p. 8. In pre-Israelite Canaan, ritual prostitution (male and female) was a common component of idolatrous worship. All forms of prostitution including ritual) are outlawed by Deut. 23:18. If Lev. 18:22 were really referring to ritual prostitution, wouldn't the Sages have known that long before Rabbi Daniel Grossman of Adath Israel, Lawrenceville, N.J. "discovered" it?

28. Rabbi Steven Greenberg, *Wrestling with G–d & Men,* Madison: U. Wisconsin Press (2004), p. 85.

29. . *E.g.:* Christopher A. Hubble, *L–rd Given Lovers: the Holy Union of David & Jonathan,* Lincoln: iUniverse, Inc. (2003); Thomas Marland Horner, *Jonathan Loved David: Homosexuality in Biblical Times,* Philadelphia: The Westminster Press (1978); Rick Brentlinger, *Gay Christian 101—Spiritual Self-Defense for Gay Christians,* Pace: Salient Press (2007); Trevor Dennis, "Lesbians and Gays are the Bible's Greatest Lovers," *The Guardian,* Oct. 14, 2006, http://www.guardian.co.uk/ comment/story/0.1922480.00.html; Heather Hendershot, "Holiness Codes and Holy Homosexuals: Interpreting Gay and Lesbian Christian Subculture," *Camera Obscura* 45, Vol. 15, No. 3 (2000), pp. 150-93; Dr. Patrick M. Chapman, "Homosexuals in the Bible: Ruth and Naomi?" http://www.rainbowcenteroly.org/ rjo/rjo0509/ThePast.htm>. *Etc. ad inf.*

hospitality to strangers. While technically accurate, it is only half the story. The Torah views Sodom as the epitome of anti-social "civilization," and its homosexual practices as a fitting and obvious indicator of its antisociality. Certainly, nothing in the Biblical narrative of Sodom either justifies or condones the sexual behavior of its inhabitants. On the contrary, when describing their antisocial behavior, it is precisely their homosexuality, along with their violence, that the Torah places into evidence.

Other critics of the Torah are less disingenuous, openly espousing the path of the Biblical rebel, Korach. "For me, the choice is clear," declares the leader of a Los Angeles gay and lesbian temple.

> I could not be guided by laws which seemed profoundly unjust and immoral. I believe, and I teach my congregants, that Jewish law condemns their way of life. But I teach also that I cannot accept that law as authoritative. It belongs to me, it is part of my history, but it has no binding claim on me. In my view, the Jewish condemnation of homosexuality, is the work of human beings—limited, imperfect, fearful of what is different, and, above all, concerned with ensuring tribal survival. In short, I think our ancestors were wrong about a number of things, and homosexuality is one of them.[30]

Along the same lines, another Reform clergyman proclaims that "men and women have the right to their natural desires."[31] The irony of these positions is that it is precisely because we humans are "limited, imperfect," that we need to adhere to the guidelines set down by the Torah, for they confer spiritual perfection and

---

30. Janet Marder, "Jewish and Gay," *Keeping Posted*, Vol. 32 (Nov., 1986), p. 2, <http://www.betham.org/kulanu/marder.html>.

31. PFLAG [Parents and Friends of Lesbians and Gays] *NYC Newsletter*, Mar/Apr, 2001, p. 5. Whether homosexuality is a "natural desire" is questionable. It is perhaps more properly defined as an "emotional adaptation."

unlimitedness on beings whose spiritual potential is weighted down with "natural desires" that tend to interfere with our serenity, our judgment, and our relationships, and, if uncontrolled, can become all-consuming.

In truth, there is nothing new about ignoring the Oral Tradition. In Hellenistic times (332-31 B.C.E.), the Saddukees, rejected the Oral Tradition, basing themselves strictly upon their own understanding of the written Torah. Even if one were to say that their intentions were pure and that they aspired to observe the Commandments faithfully, they significantly altered the character of Jewish observance. Similarly, the Karaites of a later age (10th century), rejected the Talmud and developed their own *halachah*. As influential as those sects may have been in their time, they were never able to establish themselves as authentic currents of Jewish tradition. Eventually, they died out.

Naturally, everyone is free to invent his/her own personal value system or philosophy; but how honest is it to label it "Jewish" when basic Jewish sources expressly say quite the opposite? Moreover, while it may at first seem legitimate to ask rhetorically, "Why should love between two consenting adults be considered wrong?" the rhetoric is grossly deceptive. Indeed, there are many ways one could answer that question.

First, the very basis of Torah is that consensual relations between one person and another affect many more than just those two persons. Such relations involve a whole circle of people, and even G–d Himself. (Wouldn't that be why marriages are generally celebrated in public and by a representative of the clergy?) Can two "consenting individuals" consent on behalf of all those other persons too?

Another answer is that "love between two consenting adults" isn't necessarily wrong, *provided it is expressed in the appropriate manner*. Fraternal or filial or parental love, for example, is not only acceptable, but laudable.

A third answer is that even if we accept that the love uniting a particular gay couple is genuine, deep and committed, does that make their actions any more moral than the love of two people engaged in adultery or incest?

A fourth—and perhaps the most important—response is, what does a person's "consent" actually entail? Is the consent wholehearted, or is only one part of the person's psyche (or body?) doing the consenting, while the other part is cowed or drugged into silence? Under what circumstances does a person's "consent" truly represent his or her fully informed and rational decision? For example, most relativists would probably agree that it is wrong to take advantage sexually of a man or woman who is unambiguously "willing" but obviously intoxicated. But isn't any condition that interferes with responsible decision-making analogous to intoxication? When the moral relativists talk of "consensual" sex, are they not really saying "con-*sensual*"?

The four answers set forth above are precisely the answers that Torah holds out to men and women who have the conscience and the courage to question their desires and their actions. Author and talk-show host Dennis Prager observes, "We live at a time when many people feel that because universal standards can cause pain to some individuals, the standards should be dropped."[32] But how effective is a diet, for example, when you indulge whatever craving happens to overwhelm you? How solid is a building when construction standards are lowered? There is a purpose underlying our observance of Torah, and that purpose is the optimal care and maintenance of the human body and soul as well as of the community of human beings.

All this word which I command you, that you shall observe to do; you shall not add thereto, nor diminish from it.
(Deut. 13:1)

Why must we not add to or diminish G–d's Commandments? Lest we harm ourselves—our mind, our body, our soul, and the

---

32. Dennis Prager, "Judaism, Homosexuality and Civilization," *Ultimate Issues,* April-June 1990, pp. 20-21.

society in which we live.

> *See, I have set before you this day life and good, and death and evil,* etc. (Deut. 30:15)

In this connection, recall the words of the Prophet Isaiah, who warns us,

> *Woe unto them that call evil good, and good evil; that put darkness for light and light for darkness; that put bitter for sweet, and sweet for bitter!* (Isaiah 5:20).

Similarly, the *Shulchan Aruch, Orach Chaim* 110, sets forth a prayer that is to be recited before entering a *Beis Medrash* (study hall) to study Torah. It states in relevant part, "I pray that I should not proclaim the impure pure or the pure impure, the permitted forbidden or the forbidden permitted."

This admonitory theme continues throughout the *Tanach*, including the very Prophets whom the reformists like to hold up as a "humanizing" influence upon Judaism—as though Judaism, without the Prophets, were an "inhuman" religion; as though the Prophets themselves were not scrupulously careful in their keeping of the *Mitzvos!*

> *Remember His covenant forever, the word which He has commanded to a thousand generations* . . . . (I Chron. 16: 8-36)

Or, similarly, in the *Mishnah* (*Avos,* 1:11):

> *Sages, be careful with your words, for you may incur the penalty of exile and be banished to a place of evil waters (heresy), and the disciples who follow you there will drink and die (spiritually), and consequently the Name of Heaven will be desecrated.*

To repudiate these precepts, so fundamental to Judaism that even the reformists will rarely admit that that is what they are doing, is not merely antithetical to every authentic Jewish source; it is self deception. Yet repudiating is exactly what they have done. Their arguments (those outlined above and many others) play fast and loose with text, tradition, history, and logic—all in a desperate attempt to fashion a pro-gay theology that will satisfy political correctness and accommodate the growing power of the gay lobby and their media friends. Such an approach has little in common with the Saddukees and Karaites of ancient times, whose approaches, though rejected by the Tradition, were both intellectually honest and morally uncompromising.

The Oral Tradition considers the written Torah to be infinite and the process of Torah interpretation to be endless. However, the rules for interpreting the Torah and for deriving the *halachos* have been established for millennia—certainly since the *mishnaic* period, when the Oral Law was first written down. A disciplined, Talmudic approach to the concise, condensed and pregnant language of the Torah is thus key to unlocking the treasures secreted in its verses, words, and letters. *Chiddushim* (new insights) need to be consistent with the Oral Tradition as compiled in the Talmud and as codified throughout the later traditional sources. The Commandments set forth in the Torah are for all time and for all generations. They can't be repealed, revised, or invalidated. Nor can they be interpreted out of existence.

Nowhere are the limitations on Torah interpretation more crucial than in the area of sexual morality. For, as attested by the records and relics of virtually all the great civilizations known to history, the "regulations of the relationship between the sexes" are the very foundation of civilized society.[33] Thus, it is important to

---

33. In his classic study, *Sex and Culture* (London: Oxford U. Press, 1934), British anthropologist J. D. Unwin, chronicled the historical decline of 86 primitive and civilized societies over 5,000 years of history. Unwin discovered—quite contrary to his personal philosophy and inclination (p. vii)—a distinct correlation between increasing sexual freedom and social decline. He claimed to have found no instance where a society retained its creative energy

remember that the whole purpose of the sexual laws is to avoid the unbridled licentiousness which leads to the disintegration of society.

> The object of these precepts concerning sexual conduct is . . . to diminish sexual intercourse, to restrain as much as possible indulgence in lust and [to teach us] that this enjoyment is not, as foolish people think, the final cause of man's existence. (Maimonides, *Moreh Nebuchim*, III, 35)

Thus, the challenges of living in sexual propriety apply to every Jew, not just homosexuals, and to every person, not just Jews. For a man or woman burdened with an "irresistible" attraction for the opposite sex—or with any other variety of sexual brokenness—it is no easier to avoid self indulgence than for a gay man or woman to shun same-sex contacts and fantasies. Certainly, no Jew, no person, has the right or the authority to amend the Torah to allow for his or her own (or other persons') special sexual "needs." To believe the contrary might be soothing, but it is plainly delusional.

---

after abandoning "absolute monogamy." Unwin theorized that when social or moral regulations forbid indiscriminate satisfaction of sexual impulses, the sublimated sexual impulses are channeled into a "social energy" that builds society. Several other academicians such as Historian Arnold Toynbee and Harvard sociologist Pitrim Sorokin likewise affirm that sexual restraints (such as set forth in the Torah) promote cultural progress and, further, cultures that postpone rather than stimulate sexual experiences are most prone to progress. *See also:* Arnold Toynbee, "Why I Dislike Western Civilization," *New York Times Magazine,* May 10, 1964, p. 15. Pitrim Sorokin, *The American Sex Revolution,* Boston: Porter Sargent (1956); Carl W. Wilson, *Our Dance Has Turned to Death,* Carol Stream: Living Books-Tyndale House Publishers, Inc. (1979); Konstantin Mascher, "Is Sex A Private Matter Only? Sex, Sublimation and Its Effect on Society—An Introduction to the Work of J.D. Unwin," Paper delivered at 2005 NARTH Annual Conference, and "The Erosion of Monogamy—What History Tells Us about Sexual Codes and Cultural Development," Paper delivered at 2006 NARTH Annual Conference.

CHAPTER 6:

THE SEXUAL BEHAVIORAL PROHIBITIONS OF THE TORAH.

The Torah prohibition of homosexual intercourse is neither "homophobic" nor discriminatory against homosexuals. In fact, homosexuality is only one of several sexual behaviors outlawed by the Torah. In today's climate of sexual permissiveness, it would be natural to ask: Why this apparent "obsession" of Torah—and of religion in general—with behaviors that most people regard as private and personal?

To answer this question, we must start with the Torah itself.

Generally: The Holiness Code.

Chapter 19 of Leviticus begins with the phrase,

> *And G–d spoke to Moses, saying, "Speak to all the congregation of the children of Israel, and you shall say to them: You shall be holy, because I, the L–rd, your G–d, am holy.'*

By this language, the Jewish People—and all of humankind[1]—are bound by an unconditional command to "be holy." By striving to comply with this command, we are in effect seeking to emulate G–d, for, as He informs us in the second verse, He is holy. The command tells us to be holy, like our G–d.

What does this powerful, awesome request mean? The words are clear enough, but the Commandment itself is rather vague: What, exactly are we being commanded to do? And what connection, if any, is there between this Commandment which launches Leviticus Chapter 19 and the catalog of sexual prohibitions found immediately preceding in Leviticus Chapter 18?

As we explained above in Chapter Five, in order to tap into the meaning of this verse, we must turn to the Oral Tradition and classic commentary. A famous *midrash,* quoted by Rashi, asks:

> . . . and why was the section that lists sexual prohibitions juxtaposed to the section that begins, "And you shall be holy"? The *midrash* answers: It is in order to teach you that wherever you find boundaries that guard against sexual impropriety, there will you [also] find holiness. And, whoever guards himself from sexual impropriety is called a *Kadosh* ["holy"]. (*Midrash Yalkut Shemoni, Parashat Kedoshim*)

Rashi also explains the actual *words* of the Command:

> *Speak to all the congregation of the children of Israel:* This teaches you that this section was said in front of the entire

---

1. Technically, Lev. 18 is addressed exclusively to the Jewish People. However, the Commandments contained therein correspond, with minor exceptions, to the Laws of Marriage contained in the Noahide Laws, which apply to the whole of humankind.

assemblage, for the reason that much of the Torah's foundations depend on what is stated here.

You shall be Holy: You should separate yourselves from [potential] sexual impropriety and transgression, as wherever you find boundaries that guard against sexual impropriety, there will you [also] find holiness. (Rashi on Lev. 19:2.)

What we learn from these insights is that (1) something called "holiness" attaches to those who avoid sexual impropriety, (2) sexual purity constitutes one of the principal foundations of the Torah (and hence, as we have seen, of all of Creation), (3) it is our duty to keep ourselves sexually pure, and (4) in some way the universe depends on our honoring that duty. Or, as Rabbi Dresner succinctly restates it, "the first lesson of holiness is to remain sexually pure."[2]

The question still remains: If G–d has just commanded a whole list of sexual prohibitions, and observance of those prohibitions is deemed equivalent to holiness, why was it necessary for G–d to command, "you shall be holy"? One possible answer, as suggested by Rabbi Hertz, former Chief Rabbi of the British Commonwealth, is that sexual purity is only one of three components comprising the holiness commanded by G–d. Therefore, the prescription for "purity" alone is not enough to ensure holiness.[3] Hence G–d's reminder: *You shall be holy.*

Another, more obvious, explanation is that while the sexual

---

2. Rabbi Samuel H. Dresner, *Can Families Survive in Pagan America?* Lafayette: Huntington House Publishers (1995), p. 145.

3. Rabbi Dr. Joseph D. Hertz, *Pentateuch and Haftorahs* (2nd ed.) London: Soncino Press (1981), p. 685. The suggestion is based on his reading of *v'hatzne'a lechet* in Micah 6:8: "What doth the L–rd require of thee, but to do justly, and to love mercy, and to walk humbly with thy G–d?" According to Rabbi Hertz, *v'hatzne'a lechet* means "and walk in purity," instead of "and walk humbly" as in the conventional translations. Thus, the Prophet Micah (750-690 B.C.E.) was teaching that what G–d requires of us is justice, mercy and *purity*.

prohibitions are *negative* Commandments—things we must *not* do, the Holiness Commandment constitutes an *affirmative duty* to be holy, so that when we take the sometimes difficult step of refraining from a prohibited action toward which all our hormones, instincts, lusts and deep-seated hangups are driving us, we should know that by making this seeming sacrifice, *we are in fact rendering ourselves holy.* Indeed, this is what both Rashi and the *Midrash Yalkut Shemoni* tell us, if we go back and read those excerpts again.

There is yet another very important difference between the negative and positive aspects of the Holiness Code. Without the positive Commandment to be holy, the negative Commandments leave us with the potentially loathsome burden of forever saying no to a *yetzer hara* ("evil impulse") fueled by one of the most powerful forces known to human nature: sexual desire. Therefore, the Torah gives us a positive Commandment *to be holy*—to build around ourselves a perimeter of holiness, a refuge and a sanctuary for body and soul in which to create a synergetic partnership with G–d. The Commandment to be holy is thus directed, not to our individual *deeds,* but to a whole *way of life*—a way of life that strengthens us spiritually and psychologically while limiting our exposure to the seductions of the "pagan" world. This in turn allows us to accomplish three things: (1) we strengthen the formation of good and healthy habits; (2) we limit our opportunities for transgression; and (3) we provide for ourselves a supportive environment for resisting temptation.

In the context of same-sex attraction, this means a directive not only to resist and remove oneself from temptation and develop a network of social and emotional support, but also actively to confront the underlying emotional and psychological issues that gave rise to the condition in the first place. For an individual raised or converted to religious observance, not to deal with those underlying issues can mean finding oneself in a perceived situation of no exit ("double bind")—of desiring with all one's heart to practice G–d's commandments while being unable to control one's baser longings for a prohibited sexual activity.[4]

Sexual Purity and Civilization.

Is Leviticus 18 asking too much? Is the Torah being unrealistic when it commands us to be holy? Actually, the Torah is being very realistic. The Torah recognizes that the sex drive is one of the most powerful forces influencing human behavior, affecting both the individual and the society in which he/she lives. The Torah acknowledges that all prohibited sexual acts are within the potential range of human sexual expression, and recognizes, that if left uncontrolled and unchanneled, any one of these prohibited activities could bring civilized society to the point of disintegration and collapse, thus undermining the very purpose of Creation.

For that very reason, G–d ordained and defined the marital relationship as a controlled and beneficial outlet for this powerful and potentially destructive force. Within the sanctity of the marriage relationship and its prescribed rules, Torah views sexual enjoyment as the right of both partners, passion as healthy and spiritual, the arousal of mutual desire as praiseworthy, and intercourse as a *mitzvah* (*i.e.,* fulfillment of a Torah duty).

As a noted American rabbi observed, "Nowhere is the distinctiveness of Jewish ethics more impressively implemented than

---

4. "A corollary issue for many is a sense of religious or spiritual identity that is sometimes as deeply felt as is sexual orientation. For some it is easier, and less emotionally disruptive, to contemplate changing sexual orientation, than to disengage from a religious way of life that is seen as completely central to the individual's sense of self and purpose." Dr. Douglas Haldeman, "Gays, Ex-Gays, Ex-Ex-Gays—Examining Key Religious, Ethical, and Diversity Issues" (symposium paper), American Psychological Association Annual Meeting, Washington, D.C., August 7th, 2000 (quoted in Linda Ames Nicolosi, "Some gay advocates acknowledge reorientation therapy as a legitimate option: Simon LeVay joins Douglas Haldeman in qualified support," <http://www.narth.com/docs/legitimate.html>). Dr. Haldeman is a gay-identified therapist and a member of the APA Taskforce on Enhancing Diversity.

in connection with sex and marriage."[5] Rabbi Dr. Hertz wrote that humanity defiles itself by indulging in forbidden sex and through neglect of marital restrictions.

> Whenever sex is withdrawn from its place in marriage and separated from its function as the expression of reverent and lawful wedded love (whereby its quality is completely changed), the person concerned is defiled. The Rabbis deem sexual immorality the strongest of defilements, cutting man off from G–d. (*Pentateuch*, 493)

Indeed, the Torah expressly implicates the sexual immorality of the Canaanites as one of the main reasons G–d took the land away from them and transferred it to the Israelites:

---

5. Roland B. Gittelsohn, *The Modern Meaning of Judaism,* Cleveland: Collins (1970), p. 97. Rabbi Gittelsohn was the first Jewish chaplain ever appointed to the United State Marine Corp. He rose to national prominence because of a bigoted attempt to ban delivery of his eloquent interfaith eulogy in 1945 concerning the battle for Iwo Jima.

> *Do not become contaminated through any of these abhorrent acts* [to'eivos]; *for through all of these the nations that I expel before you became contaminated. The Land became contaminated and I recalled its iniquity upon it; and the Land disgorged its inhabitants. But you shall safeguard My decrees and My judgments, and not commit any of these abhorrent acts. For the inhabitants of the Land who are before you committed all these abhorrent acts, and the Land became contaminated. Let not the Land disgorge you for having contaminated it, as it disgorged the nation that was before you. For if anyone commits any of these abhorrent acts, the people so doing will be cut off from among their people. You shall safeguard My charge not to do any of the abominable customs that were done before you and not contaminate yourselves through them; I am Hashem, your G–d.* (Lev.18:24-30)

When the Torah warns us in Lev. 18:24-30 not to contaminate ourselves "through any of these abhorrent deeds" and reminds us that the prior occupants of the land are being expelled because of their abhorrent sexual practices, it is referring to widespread manifestations of sexual excess and moral corruption (some of them historically documented) that brought down entire peoples and cultures.[6] Hence, the "paramount duty of [sexual] purity and self-control." (Hertz, 488—quoting Rabbi Hermann Adler) These prohibited acts include adultery, fornication, bestiality, various degrees of incest (both consanguineal and non-consanguineal), male homosexuality (Lev.18:22), female homosexuality (lesbianism) (Lev. 18:3),[7] and

---

6. English anthropologist J.D. Unwin (*see* above, Chapter 5, p. 173, note 33) noted that "In human records there is *no instance* of a society retaining its energy after a complete new generation has inherited a tradition which does not insist on pre-nuptial and post-nuptial continence." He saw "no exception to these rules." *Hopousia: The Sexual and Economic Foundations of a New Society*, London: George Allen & Unwin (1940), pp. 84-5, 89.

7. Regarding the source of this *halachah,* opinions differ. *See* below, Chapter 7.

gender confusion (cross dressing) (Deut. 22:5). Many of these prohibitions still define American sexual morality—if not always as a code, at least as a frame of reference. The corresponding transgressions may range from a social gaffe to a lapse of moral judgment to a statutory violation.

Adultery and Sexual Promiscuity in Contemporary Society.

While, as we have said, many of the Torah's sexual prohibitions still hold moral and legal force within American culture, adultery (meaning consensual intercourse by a married man or woman with someone other than his or her wife or husband), though clearly proscribed by Torah law and Christian traditions, has gained in social acceptability. Though adultery remains a valid ground for divorce in some states, many jurisdictions, such as California, now refuse to consider any allegation of "wrongdoing" as a basis for legal divorce (hence the term "No-Fault Divorce").[8] Almost all the criminal statutes pertaining to adultery have been repealed.

The gradual erosion of age-old legal sanctions surrounding adultery is symptomatic of a sexual revolution that has radically transformed the concept of love into "a splendid experience more magnificent than morality,"[9] and sex into a sport without boundaries

---

8. Until the early 1960s, divorces meant "broken homes." Few today would use this judgmental language to describe what has unfortunately become commonplace. Likewise, cohabitation without the benefit of marriage has become a prevalent social condition, viewed neither as a stigma nor a moral compromise, but on the contrary as a socially acceptable alternative to marriage.

9. Denis De Rougemont, *Love in the Western World*, New York: Doubleday (Anchor Books) (1957), pp.286-87. This classic work explores the psychology of love as set forth in seven centuries of western literature, postulating that the only true passionate love is adulterous love. DeRougement believed romantic love cannot exist in marriage—a thesis contradicted by many famous historical (not to mention Biblical) examples, as well as my own personal experience and that of numerous friends and relatives.

or rules.[10]

Fornication (defined as sex between unmarried partners), once outlawed by many states, is now known as "sexual liberation," or "free love" and has achieved virtually complete social acceptance. It has become an essential element—if not the main theme—of almost any book, film or TV drama one can think of. Glamorized by the media and by celebrities, pre-marital and extra-marital affairs no longer carry the stigma of social disapproval or moral opprobrium.

Over the last forty years, we in America have seen myriad examples of plays, films, and TV shows evincing (overtly or covertly) envy and admiration for men and women engaging in adultery or promiscuity. Bernard Slade's famous play (later adapted into the movie) *Same Time Next Year* ran for years on Broadway. The award-winning movie *The Bridges of Madison County* (1995) won the ASCAP Award for "Top Box-Office Film" of 1996.[11] The ever-re-running TV serial (adapted from Candace Bushnell's novel), "Sex and the City," spotlights four professional women in their 30s and their big-city sexual escapades as they search for the "perfect orgasm" and "Mr. Right"—in that order.

What lessons are learned from such shows? What do they teach us

---

10. The May 19, 2003 American Psychiatric Convention sponsored a symposium to discuss removing pedophilia and a host of other paraphilias from the next edition of the Diagnostic Statistical Manual ("DSM")—the psychiatric manual of mental disorders. Linda Ames Nicolosi, "Should These Conditions Be Normalized? American Psychiatric Association Symposium Debates Whether Pedophilia, Gender-Identity Disorder, Sexual Sadism Should Remain Mental Illnesses," <www.narth.com/docs/symposium.html>.

11. In *Same Time Next Year* a man and a woman, each married to another, meet by chance at a country inn. After spending the night together, they agree to meet again the next year. This continues for some 25 years, during which time each discovers the other as a genuine soul-mate. In *The Bridges of Madison County,* a lonely farmer's wife is attracted to a photographer on assignment to photograph bridges in a rural landscape. The two fall in love while the wife's husband and children are away at a county fair. The affair awakens emotions and awarenesses that the lovers had believed lost or superfluous.

about self respect, honoring commitments and personal boundaries? The four sirens of "Sex and the City" may be sympathetic and amusing, but their affairs—however kooky or disillusioning—are romanticized and prized. Sex is portrayed as a desirable but short-lived commodity typically spoiled by attempts to transform it into a meaningful relationship.

Of course, it is true that many plays, movies and TV shows often express a nostalgic regret for lost innocence and tarnished integrity. Nevertheless, the focus on casual sex is obvious and obsessive, and this alone would be enough to promote the acceptance of adultery and sexual promiscuity—not because it is right, but because it is "natural" and "normal": "Everybody does it." The sad truth is that it has taken an AIDS epidemic to reawaken some members of society to the concept of sexual abstention prior to marriage, and sexual fidelity during marriage. Perhaps, then, the sexual prohibitions of the Torah are not as irrelevant as the popular culture tends to portray them. Let us examine them one by one.

Prostitution and Promiscuity.

The Torah prohibits indiscriminate sexual intercourse. Thus any sexual activity outside of marital relations transgresses Divine Law.

Deuteronomy 23:18 states:

There shall not be a kadeisha among the daughters of Israel, and there shall not be a kadeish among the sons of Israel.

Kadeisha and *Kadeish* are unusual words, dependent upon the Oral Tradition for their meaning. Rashi, at Deuteronomy 23:18, explains these terms as follows:

Kadeisha: [a woman who is] promiscuous, dedicating herself to be readily available for promiscuity.

Kadeish: [a man who is] available for male intercourse.

Although some commentators argue that this prohibition applies solely to prostitution or ritual prostitution, it actually prohibits a man or woman from having intercourse without being married to each other.[12] Both Rambam and Rashi make it clear that any such intercourse is by definition "prostitution" or "licentiousness." According to Rambam, the reason for prohibiting unmarried intercourse is given in Leviticus 19:29, by the words: ... *lest the land fall into harlotry, and the land become full of lewdness.* Similarly, as the *midrash* (*Genesis Rabbah* Chapter 26) says on Deuteronomy 23:18, "Rabbi Joshua Ben Levi said: G–d is forgiving in the case of every sin except sexual promiscuity"—another indication that promiscuity is what is targeted by this Commandment.

Male Homosexuality.

As opposed to lesbianism—a complex question requiring detailed analysis (see discussion below, Chapter 7)—homosexual sexual activity between males is explicitly prohibited by the Torah:

You shall not lie with a man as one lies with a woman: it is a to'eivah ["abomination"]. (Lev. 18:22)

The penalty prescribed by the Torah is extraordinarily severe :

A man who lies with a man as one lies with a woman, they have both done an abomination [to'eivah]; *they shall surely be put to death, their blood is upon themselves.* (Lev. 20:13)

What do these words mean? What is the basis for this Commandment? Which other Torah verses can contribute to its

---

12. Although the words *kadeish* and *kadeishah* are linguistically related to the Akkadian *qadissu* denoting the cultic prostitutes common to various idolatrous religions, there is no evidence whatsoever, whether Biblical, historical, or archeological, that prostitution ever played a role in Jewish ritual observance.

understanding? All parties to the ongoing debate about homosexuality agree that these questions must be addressed. The Talmud ascribes the origin of these laws to the Biblical verses narrating G–d's creation of woman out of the flesh and bone of Adam (Gen. 2:21-23). *On account of this,* says the Torah,

> *a man shall leave his father and his mother and shall cling to his woman, and they shall be one flesh.* (Gen. 2:24)

Although some modern commentators take this verse to be little more than "the origin of marriage or of sexual union or both,"[13] the Talmud, in *Sanhedrin* 58a, expressly interprets this as an implied prohibition of homosexual intercourse. As it explains:

> "**And shall cling**—*but not to a male.*

Rashi clarifies further: "This prohibition against homosexuality is derived from the fact that man was commanded to 'cling' to his mate. This, though, is not possible with a male mate . . . ." Why not? One possible answer is that the woman was taken *out of the man's flesh.* Thus, when he *clings* to her, his flesh is restored to him, and they indeed become *one flesh.* If a male were to cling to another male, there would be "two fleshes." Each of the two fleshes would be incomplete. By this interpretation, a man and a woman form a single composite being—one that is created from two complementary beings.

Rashi also provides a second understanding: *one flesh* alludes to the conceiving of a child, "who combines the flesh of the father and mother." In the same vein, the Talmud, *Sanhedrin* 58a, comments

---

13. Richard Elliott Friedman, *Commentary on the Torah,* San Francisco, Harper Collins, (2001), p. 20.

that the phrase *one flesh* excludes animals because of the obvious procreative incompatibility. By the same logic, other male humans are likewise excluded.

Nevertheless, when Rashi says that a man cannot *cling* to a male mate, it is possible that he is alluding to the inherent instability of the homosexual relationship. Indeed, as we saw in Chapter Three (above, at pp. 91-2, 94, and n. 53 at p. 91), sexual promiscuity and relational instability are primary components of male/male homosexual coupling.[14] This, too, would preclude the possibility of the relationship being one of "clinging."

It is a basic tenet of Judaism, exemplified by Rabbi Avraham Ibn Ezra[15] in his commentary on *Sefer Vayikra* (Lev. 18:22), that G–d's will is expressed in the biological design of the human being. The complimentarity of the male and female physiology by itself suggests the proper scope of sexual pairing, to the exclusion of all other possible combinations. Any other expression of the sexual drive, such as through homosexual coupling, Ibn Ezra considers not only unnatural (*i.e.,* inconsistent with the basic physiological design of the male and female human), but an outright negation of the Creator's will.

Thus, some modern commentators have seized on the physical incongruity of male-male sex to argue that Leviticus 18:22 only forbids anal sex between males. The *halachah* decisively rejects this interpretation. As stated by Maimonides in his *Mishneh Torah* (Laws of Prohibited Relations, 21:1):

Whoever has physical contact with any of the forbidden partners,

---

14. Gay activists Kirk and Madsen, extensively quoted in Chapter 3, admit in *After the Ball*, p. 330, ". . . [T]he cheating ratio of 'married' gay males, given enough time, approaches 100%. . . . Many gay lovers, bowing to the inevitable, agree to an 'open relationship,' for which there are as many sets of ground rules as there are couples."

15. Rabbi Ibn Ezra, the 12th-century scholar and poet, believed in the compatibility of science and religion, and argued that rationality was inherent in revelation.

whether through genital contact, or sexually motivated hugging, and kissing, and has pleasure due to this closeness of flesh, [has committed a Torah Prohibition] and is to be given Torah-ordained lashes, as it says (Lev. 18:30), "that they should not do according to these *to'eivos*" [including, but not limited to, the *to'eivah* of homosexuality], and (Lev. 18:6.), "Do not approach to uncover the nakedness." What this means is that we are forbidden to engage in acts that might lead to the uncovering of one's genitals.

What Rambam is saying here is that it is not only illicit intercourse that is forbidden, but also any other type of erotic contact. All male-male sexually stimulating activity—and not just male-male anal intercourse—is prohibited by the Torah.[16]

Homosexual relationships are never mentioned in the Torah in anything but extremely negative terms.[17] Sodom and its neighboring cities of the plain were destroyed (Gen. 18:20 ff.) because of the sins of their inhabitants—sins which included homosexuality and homosexual rape, as we learn from the Biblical account in Genesis 19:4 ff. as well as robbery, as the *Midrash* (*Genesis Rabbah,* 50:7) informs us. However, the midrashic tradition points to a more critical concern: that it was not merely the odious nature of these crimes that so offended G–d, but the fact that such practices were perpetrated

---

16. Rabbi Betzalel Naor interprets Rabbi Abraham Issac Hakohen Kook (1865-1935), the first Ashkenazi Chief Rabbi of mandatory Palestine as suggesting that the *halakhah's* reluctant allowance of "occasional acts" of male to female anal intercourse between a husband and a wife is a concession to married males with homosexual drives, permitting them a substitute outlet for a prohibited desire. Rabbi Betzalel Naor, "Rav Kook on Homosexuality," <www.orot.com/hms.html>.

17. One of the explanations of the cause of the Flood was G–d's dissatisfaction with the widespread homosexual activity. When the Torah says that each species corrupted its way, it is referring to improper sexual relationships. When Noach got drunk, at least one Talmudic opinion explains that Ham forced Noah to engage in a homosexual act. *See* Sanhedrin 70A where Rab and Shmuel differ, one maintaining that Ham castrasted Noah while the other maintains he had homosexual relations with him.

with the sanction of the law![18] In other words, homosexuality, among the other offenses, had been elevated to the dignity of an approved social institution. It was this wholesale inversion of justice (itself a clear violation of one of the Seven Laws of Noah!), and not simply the practice of homosexuality, that induced G–d to destroy Sodom and Gemorrah with fire and brimstone.

Commenting on the relevance of this *midrash* to our own time and place, Rabbi J. David Bleich suggests that, "removal of the odium associated with a transgression is potentially more serious a matter than the transgression itself. . . ." (*Bioethical Dilemmas,* 133) In other words, though moral laxity can never be prevented by laws alone, once our laws change to accommodate or promote immorality—so that practices known to be harmful to society are transformed into "protected rights" or "protected forms of expression"—then we find ourselves in a position of moral equivalence to Sodom and Gomorrah.[19]

Certainly, one purpose of Leviticus 18:22 is to prevent the elevation of homosexuality into a legally recognized social institution.[20] Looking at today's socio-cultural climate, we can see that there is legitimate cause for concern. Gay activists and their allies

---

18. *See, e.g.,* Rabbi Isaac Arama's commentary in *Akeidat Yizhak. Bereishit Rabbah* 50:10.

19. There is nothing new about this phenomenon. For example, the institution of brother-sister marriages in Hellenistic Egypt is well documented. At the time of the Exodus, "Sexual excesses among the Canaanite population had not only ceased to be considered abominations but had, in fact, become sanctioned by custom or religious cult. They had become 'statutes' or 'institutions'. Rabbi Samson Raphael Hirsch, *The Pentateuch,* Rabbi Ephraim Oratz (ed). New York: The Judaica Press (1986), p. 450. *Compare* Isaiah 24:5: "They have . . . changed the ordinance." In other words, "They have changed the law into the opposite; *i.e.,* they have elevated immorality to become law." Rabbi Hirsch, on Lev. 18:30.

20. *See* Spero, *Handbook of Psychotherapy and Jewish Ethics: Halachic Perspectives on Professional Values and Techniques,* Jerusalem: Feldheim (1986), p. 162.

have covered much ground pushing homosexuality into the social and even religious mainstream.[21] As we saw in Chapter Three, the homosexual *ménage* has already achieved, in many quarters, the status of a legally recognized domestic arrangement. The intention—indeed, the trend—is now to go beyond the judicial and legislative victories achieved in health care benefits, joint child-custody and support, *etc.,* and move toward acquiring for gay and lesbian unions the same legal status as traditional marriage.

The rallying point for this push is, and has been, "discrimination against homosexuals." However, as is evident from the text itself, when the Torah uses the word, *to 'eivah*, it is condemning a *behavior,* not an individual. We emphasize this crucial point because our goal in this work is not to deprive homosexuals of fundamental human and civil rights, but to reassure those who are afflicted with SSA (and society as a whole), that according to authentic Jewish tradition, homosexuals are indeed people of worth; and that, through *teshuvah,* they can still draw close to G–d, and through appropriate gender-affirming processes, reacquire their inherent gender sexuality. Feelings of depression and hopelessness are all too common within the gay community. As a society, we need to hold out to SSA-affected

---

21. For those who disagree with this agenda, the concept of holiness also mandates that individuals take principled stands on these issues. By incorporating the Holiness Code into our everyday civic and communal life, concerned individuals can affect the direction of society and make a difference in our culture.

men and women the assurance that we are there for them to assist them and encourage them in their process of emotional and spiritual growth. They were led astray by their own emotional pain and by society's callous indifference to their plight. They should not have to labor under the cruel misconception that they, as individuals, are considered "abominations" either by G–d and His Torah or by human society! As will be seen below, the language of Lev. 18:22 may be looked upon as an affirmative statement to the effect that persons struggling with SSA retain the power to overcome their pain, grow out of homosexuality, and emerge as a whole and holy person whose sexuality can express itself in the manner sanctioned by G–d.

What Does *To'eivah* Really Mean?

First, it may be helpful to recognize that although *to'eivah* has traditionally been translated as "abomination," some newer bilingual editions of the *Chumash* (Pentateuch) employ the word "abhorrence." "Abhorrence" has a more objective, less judgmental meaning, perhaps more consistent with the many places in *Tanach* where G–d's abundant compassion for His creatures is very clearly in evidence. *Webster's Deluxe Unabridged Dictionary* (2nd ed.) defines "abhorrent" as "contrary to," or "repugnant to" someone, or "inconsistent with" something. Certainly, G–d views homosexual behavior as both "contrary to" and "inconsistent with" His Plan of Creation. It is a behavior to which He has expressed "extreme opposition" and "repugnance."

"Abomination," on the other hand, carries a significantly stronger connotation of opprobrium. *Webster's* defines it as something "very hateful, detestable, loathsome, odious to the mind, offensive to the senses." Thus, translating *to'eivah* as "abomination" may reflect human feelings rather than G–d's. After all, there are many things in the world of nature, for example, that arouse horror and disgust in the mind of this or that person; but does G–d, Who created them, necessarily find them disgusting?

Whichever way we choose to translate the Hebrew word, the fact that sex between men is *to'eivah* has no bearing on G–d's readiness to accept the sincere *teshuvah* (return) of the penitent. The L–rd is always ready to welcome back an individual who performs *teshuvah* and completely expiates his or her sin.

In this connection, it behooves us to reflect briefly upon a noteworthy comment reported in the Talmud (*Nedarim* 51a). Though really an aphorism pronounced in circumstances that to us might seem informal, the comment was made in the tradition of authentic Torah interpretation (*PaRDeS*), and adds a far deeper dimension to the meaning of *to'eivah*. Moreover, considering that the source of this aphorism was one of the great Sages of the Talmud—Bar Kappara—sitting in the immediate presence of Yehuda haNasi (the leader of the Sanhedrin and the creator of the *Mishnah!*), it should be obvious that the remark must be taken in extreme earnest.

What Bar Kappara says is that the word *to'eivah* "means" or "suggests" or "derives from" the words, *to'ei attah bah*, or "you [*attah*] are straying [*to'ei*] through it [*bah*]. By this aphorism, Bar Kappara proposes a popular etymology for the term *to'eivah*—one which suggests that those who engage in homosexual behavior are "straying" or have been "led astray."

Bar Kappara's aphorism is a fine example of the *drosh* level of Torah interpretation, and is much more in line with a holistic Torah perspective than the narrow readings of the literalists. Bar Kappara is saying that homosexuality is a deviation, a departure from the proper path—a view that suggests that the proper path can be regained. This accords well with the great medieval commentators known as *Tosafos*, who comment *ad loc.*, "They leave aside their wives in favor of intercourse with males." Another great medieval sage, Rabbeinu Nissim (RaN), says similarly: "They set aside heterosexual intercourse in favor of male intercourse." Implicit in both these comments is that returning to heterosexuality always remains an option: "leaving aside" or "setting aside," the operative verbs in the above comments, implies the possibility of resuming, or "taking up again"—of going back to what was left or set aside.

The rest of this chapter, as well as Chapters 9 and 10, will further elaborate on the deeper meanings of *to'eivah*, and will introduce the concept that the spiritual workings of *teshuvah* and the recovery processes offered by the healing professions are interconnected and run along parallel tracks (*see* Chapters 11-13 for an in-depth discussion). We will also discuss the gender-affirming processes ("GAP")[22] espoused by the National Association for Research and Therapy of Homosexuality (NARTH).

Why the Commandment not to Engage in Homosexuality is Addressed to Men.

Although women, too, are enjoined from homosexual activity (*see* Chapter Seven, below), the express prohibition contained in Leviticus 18:22 is directed to men, not women. What accounts for this? Men and women obviously have a great deal in common; but they also differ in many other ways than anatomically and physiologically. Indeed, there are many distinctions between the male and female personalities. As Rabbi Soloveitchik observes, "There is a man-personality and a woman-personality. They are two individualities with unique existential experience."[23] Rav A. Y. Kook explains that men are more easily led astray from G–d's Plan than are women. A man has "the distinct disadvantage of being limited to the narrow limitations of his spiritual and physical make-up." A woman, however, "can aspire to fulfill G–d's will without turning astray," thanks to her superior receptivity and involvement in process more than in action.[24]

---

22. The term GAP is an acronym for Gender-Affirming Processes, as well as a symbol for the developmental *gap* that characterizes the etiology of same-sex attraction. As explained in the Preface, these processes include "reparative", "conversion," and "reorientation" therapies.

23. Rabbi Joseph Soloveitchik, *Family Redeemed*, David Shatz & Joel B. Wolowelsky (ed.), Brooklyn: Toras HaRav Foundation (2000), pp. 67-8. Gender differentiation is also discussed in Dr. John Gray, *Men are from Mars, Women are from Venus: The Classic Guide to Understanding the Opposite Sex.* New York: Harper Collins (1992).

24. Rabbi A.Y. Kook, *Olas Ras Rayoh,* pp. 71-2, as quoted in Rabbi Yaakov Haber, "Gender," *The Pardes Project,* Part I, p. 32.

It is for this reason that the prohibition of Leviticus 18:22 is directed to the male of the species, whose energy, if "left in a state of chaos ... will necessarily become destructive." (Rav Kook, in Haber, 32) This insight can be corroborated by statistics showing that male homosexuality not only occurs twice as frequently as lesbianism, but also is generally far more promiscuous and carries greater health risks. (*See* Chapter Three, *above,* at pp.91-2 and notes 52 & 53.)

Is Homosexual Fantasy Prohibited by the Torah?

One question that many strugglers ask is whether repression of behavior—without an alteration of their sexual fantasies or "sexually indulgent rumination" (Spero, 45)—complies with Leviticus 18:22. As we shall see in the discussion below, opinion is divided. My own view, based on extensive experience as Co-Director of JONAH, is that "complete healing" requires the total elimination, or at least a drastic reduction, of "forbidden" fantasizing. Given that it is a *mitzvah* of the Torah to "take care of your health" (Ex. 21:19; Deut. 15:4, Deut. 22:2), it appears to me that mere repression of the behavior does not amount to full compliance with this prohibition. This all the more so, since, as we shall see, the achievability of healing on all levels of sexual re-adaptation (including fantasy and arousal) has been conclusively demonstrated.[24a]

Not everybody would agree with the above. Focusing upon the oft-stated principle that "acting in accordance with biblical and rabbinic law is the Jews' central obligation,"[25] Rabbi Michael Gold, a noted Conservative pro-family rabbi, argues, "Jewish law is

---

24a. *See, e.g.,* Dr. Joseph Nicolosi, *Healing Homosexuality: Case Studies of Reparative Therapy,* Northvale: Jason Aronson (1993), pp. 213-14, 216-17; Richard Cohen, *Coming Out Straight,* Winchester: Oakhill Press (2000), p. 126; Dr. Peet Botha, *Homosexuality: Questions and Answers,* Kranskop: Khanya Press (2005), pp. 44-6.

25. Dennis Prager & Joseph Telushkin, *The Nine Questions People ask about Judaism,* New York: Simon & Schuster (1981), p. 78.

concerned not with the source of a person's erotic urges nor with inner feelings, but with *acts*."[26] Thus, writes Rabbi Gold, "the Torah forbids the homosexual act, known as '*mishkav zachar*,' but has nothing to say about homosexuality as a state of being or a personal inclination."(138) Moreover, he states elsewhere,

> Nowhere does the Torah forbid homosexual orientation for either men or women. If an individual has erotic feelings towards his or her own gender but chooses never to act on those feelings, that person has broken no law of the Torah. The concern is with action, not thoughts or intentions.[27]

Rabbi Reuven P. Bulka, a noted Orthodox rabbi and psychologist who served as a member of the NARTH Advisory Board, agrees: "The Torah does not condemn orientation; it condemns behavior. Someone who is attracted to the same sex is not within the framework of biblical proscription until actually acting upon this inclination."[28]

The opposite point of view is expressed by psychologist Rabbi Moshe Halevi Spero, who believes that "*Halakhah* forbids not only the act of homosexual intercourse, but also considers abnormal or deviant the broader homosexual *relationship,* psychological orientation, and life-style." (*Handbook,* 149) Again, "[I]t would also be incorrect to conclude that *halakhah* does not obligate the homosexual to seek modification of his general sexual orientation as long as it is not expressed behaviorally." (160) Rabbi Spero cites Maimonides for the view that repentance does not only apply to "acts committed" but also to a person's "inappropriate personality traits (*de 'othra 'oth*)." (160) As he explains, "there is no behavior without

---

26. *Does G–d Belong in the Bedroom?* Philadelphia: Jewish Publication Society (1992), p. 11.

27. Rabbi Michael Gold, *G–d, Love, Sex, and Family*, Northvale: Jason Aronson, Inc. (1998), p. 191.

28. Rabbi Reuven J. Bulka, *One Man, One Woman, One Lifetime,* Lafayette: Huntington House (1995), p. 39.

its psychic, affective counterpart."(46) Thus, suggests, Rabbi Spero, "homosexuality as a state of being, while not punishable according to the express biblical criterion, is no less subject to *halakhic* accountability and to possible characterization as sin or sickness." (160) Accordingly, he believes that a gender-identity deficit creates a corresponding "intervention prerequisite for *teshuvah.*" (160) Indeed, as will be seen in Chapters 11-13, sincere *teshuvah* activates a person's ability to change his or her very nature and inner being.

Gender Affirming Processes (GAP) seek to go beyond the simple repression of the behavior or the letting go of a "gay" identity. It looks to heal the wounds underlying an individual's homosexual orientation. As one recovered homosexual testifies,

> We discovered the path to healing as we came to understand that *our homosexual feelings were not the problem but were actually symptoms of deeper, underlying problems and long-buried pain that usually had little or nothing to do with erotic desire.* Rather, they [the feelings] had to do with our self-identity, self-esteem (especially our gender esteem), relationships and spiritual life. Once we discovered and healed the underlying pain, the symptoms of homosexuality took care of themselves.[29]

The numerous studies referenced throughout this book, including Dr. Robert Spitzer's dramatic announcement at the 2001 American Psychiatric Association (APA) Convention, independently confirm the ability of men and women with same-sex attraction to change multiple indicators of sexual orientation—including the two critical internal aspects: fantasy and arousal.

Noted Chassidic writer, Rabbi Simon Jacobson, observed that the Torah describes man at the moment of creation not as a creature of intelligence and feelings, not as a being who is born and dies, but rather as a being with a "divine persona" who was created in the "divine image." Being created in G–d's image means that we as persons are capable of changing our essential selves, a change

---

29. Rich Wyler, <www.PeopleCanChange.com>.

significantly deeper than a mere change of behavior. "The Divine is a source of constant energy flowing from the Essence of it all. It is dynamic and alive, and always open to change."[30] Because "we are not human beings on a spiritual journey [but rather] spiritual beings on a human journey," Jacobson affirmatively believes that a person can change his or her sexual orientation: "'*Nurture,*'" writes Rabbi Jacobson, "can actually rewire our very '*nature.*'" (E-mail, May 13, 2005)

Thus, while it is true that the legal definitions of almost all the Torah's Commandments are generally concerned with regulating actions rather than thoughts, nevertheless, the ultimate purpose of such regulation is to bring the individual (and the world) to higher levels of perfection—specifically including perfection of thought. Obviously, that does not mean that merely thinking the right thought about a *mitzvah* is the same as actually *doing* the *mitzvah*. In fact, given the choice of having a "good thought" or doing a good deed without any accompanying "good thoughts," doing the deed is preferable. The Commandments require *action,* not just "good thoughts." Similarly, one cannot commit a transgression without actually having done something. Merely thinking about stealing, for example, does not create legal liability, just as "wanting" to give money to the poor does not fulfill the *mitzvah* (commandment) of *tzedakah* (charity).

When it comes to homosexuality, it is clear that the Torah forbids actions, not a state of being. That does not mean, however, that harboring thoughts or fantasies of homosexual activity is inconsequential or that it is permitted. In his helpful comments to an early draft of this work, Rav Aharon Feldman, Dean of Baltimore's Ner Israel Rabbinical College, cited Numbers 15:38-39 as textual proof that "it is forbidden by Torah law to permit lewd thoughts to enter our minds," for such thoughts can lead to action.[31] The Ramban

---

30. Rabbi Simon Jacobson, e-mail, "Can We Change Our Personalities?" May 13, 2005.

31. Numbers 15:38-39 commands men to wear *tzitzis* ("fringes" or "tassels") "so

(Nachmanides) comments on these same verses that they command us to not permit our desires and feelings to lead us astray.[32]

Indeed, all the classical authorities agree that a person is not allowed to have improper fantasies or willingly to put him- or herself into a situation that would lead to improper fantasies. If, while walking down the street, one suddenly comes upon a situation that triggers improper thoughts, one's *halachic* obligation is to cross the street and distract oneself by thinking about some other matter. If one were instead to dwell on the improper thoughts, the person would then be committing the transgression mentioned by Rabbi Feldman, that is, the *aveirah* of indulging in lewd thoughts.

To give a more specific example, if the struggler is out for an evening stroll, he or she should choose a place other than the local gay bar district. If the person is in the gay bar district already, having just stumbled upon it, the obligation is to go quickly to some other neighborhood, before his or her thoughts are compromised. The same would be true of avoiding pornography which is so easily available on the Internet.

Similarly, it would seem that if someone is simply unable to control his or her improper thoughts (even if he or she is able to refrain from doing the *action*) then that person would have to take reasonable steps to obtain the kind of help and counsel that would enable him or her to do so. Within the context of homosexuality, it would be appropriate to suggest that an individual with such involuntary fantasies or arousals seek psychological help from therapists skilled in treating same-sex attraction issues.[33]

---

that you may look upon it and remember all of the Commandments of the L–rd, and do them; and so that you not follow after your own heart and your own eyes, after which you go astray." *See also* Rashi on Numbers 15:30: "The heart and the eyes are the agents of sin—the eye sees, the heart desires, and the person executes" (*citing Midrash Tanchuma* and *Midrash Bamidbar Rabba* 10:2).

32. Ramban, *Commentary on Torah* (Rabbi Dr. Charles B. Chavel, ed.), New York: Shilo Publishing House, Inc. (1971), p. 156.

33. No one is immune to unholy thoughts or fantasies. Many JONAH clients have struggled with same-sex sexual fantasies without ever acting upon them. Some try to

At this point, however, we might be excused for asking: If there is no *halachic* liability for *thinking,* why is it so important to avoid lewd thoughts? Provided we do not allow our fantasies to lead us into prohibited *acts,* why should we not be permitted to fantasize about them, as long as we find such fantasies pleasurable and stimulating? The short answer is that such thoughts are harmful to the person who harbors them, interfering in that person's relationship with G–d—the Source of the person's spiritual essence and awareness—with others, and with himself. To restore that relationship to its pristine state, it is necessary to perform *teshuvah*—"repentance." The Jewish liturgy contains several prayers concerning both the sinfulness of forbidden sexual fantasy[34] and its amenability to *teshuvah*. On *Yom Kippur* (the Day of Atonement), for example, Jews ask G–d to forgive, pardon and grant atonement for their collective transgressions. Included among the lengthy list are: "the sin we committed against Thee by evil thoughts . . . by evil impulse. . .by levity of mind . . . by a confused heart"—all of which confirm that thoughts and fantasies are included within the purview of transgression and *teshuvah*. Indeed, as

---

repress these feelings by diverting their attention, reading a biblical verse, or praying. Although often effective in the crisis of the moment, such "repression" techniques are usually ineffective as a long term solution. However, by changing the way we look at, and behave toward, ourselves, G–d, and the world, we can radically change our dreams, thoughts, fantasies, and emotional responses. I call this "replacement" (as opposed to "repression")—a process of internalized self transformation that characterizes the spiritual state of *teshuvah*. Such an approach can so profoundly change one's inner being that the unwanted lust-fantasies disappear or significantly diminish. By learning to readjust distorted perceptions of ourselves and our relations with others, by acquiring a new mastery over the way we think and act, we gain the ability to reprocess with a totally different energy the stimuli that trigger our emotional and sexual responses. What makes this possible is the fact that, as was explained in Chapter Four, same-sex attraction is an adaptive response to stimuli that have nothing to do with sex.

34. We must emphasize that, *halachically,* it is *not* forbidden to entertain, in the appropriate circumstances, sexual fantasies about one's spouse. On the contrary, the Sages were well aware that such fantasy is an essential ingredient of a successful marriage.

our Sages teach, "The beginning of sin is the murmuring of the heart." (Talmud, *Derech Eretz, Zuta* 6).

The following examples show how the duty of guarding one's thoughts is rooted in the Commandments, even though the legal aspect of these examples may only concern an action:

(1) Deut. 23:10. *When you go out as a camp against your enemies, you must avoid everything evil.* This refers to the duty of the Congregation of Israel to maintain itself free of "both personal and moral pollution." (Hertz, *Pentateuch,* 847)

(2) Lev. 11:44-45, Lev. 20:7, Lev. 20:26 and Num. 15:40. The commands:

Sanctify yourselves; be holy; remember My Commandments...

are impossible to honor without (i) freeing oneself of unholy thoughts, (ii) focusing one's mind on holiness, and (iii) internalizing the desire for holiness so that it becomes akin to a physical need.

The view that lewd thoughts are unholy in themselves can be substantiated by a passage in the Talmud (*Avodah Zarah* 20b; *Ketuboth* 46a) in which Rabbi Pinchas ben Ya'ir warns men, "Do not think illicit thoughts in the day and come to nocturnal emission of seed." The nocturnal emission is, of course, involuntary, yet *halachah* considers this event to be unholy, and attaches liability to it. The unholiness of the event must come from somewhere—namely the unholiness of the thoughts. And since one provoked this action with these thoughts, it is hardly an excuse that the action was "involuntary," occurring during sleep. In fact, one might even say that the person "called on himself" to have the emission.[35]

Ample rabbinic commentary (in the Talmud and other sources) underscores the need to guard against sinful thoughts. For example, (*Yoma* 29a) "The thought of sin is worse than the actual sin."

---

35. For further discussion of this subject, *see* pp. 231-34, *below*.

Maimonides writes (*Moreh* 3:8) that to engage in sinful thought is to sin with the "noblest portion of the self." Obviously, all this applies regardless of whether the context is homosexual or heterosexual.

It needs to be said here that—as Rav Feldman, cited above, points out—the *halachah* recognizes a distinction between "dwelling on lewd thoughts" and "spontaneous fantasy." According to Rav Feldman, fantasy and behavior are not equivalent when the fantasy is *involuntary*: thoughts which one does not actively bring upon oneself are *not* forbidden. Some modern theorists appear to disagree. Rabbi Spero, for example, as previously noted, holds that "there is no behavior without its psychic, affective counterpart." (*Handbook*, 149) The converse would also seem to apply: there is no psychic, affective activity without its behavioral counterpart. Thus, he concludes, any distinction between fantasy and behavior introduces "a psychologically as well as halakhically inaccurate dichotomy."[36] (159)

In brief, Rabbi Spero disagrees with those rabbis and psychologists who make a distinction between "active and passive homosexuality," or between "latent and manifest homosexuality." For Spero, fantasy is "synonymous" with behavior:

> Both *Halakhah* and psychology subscribe to the belief that fantasy—the stuff of dreams, 'passive' homosexuality, or of homosexual 'tendencies' inferred from projective testing and so

---

36. Underlying Rabbi Spero's position is the premise that "involuntary fantasies" are actually blocked when the desire for holiness is properly internalized.

forth—is also behavior. From the psychological viewpoint, fantasy and behavior are synonymous *to the degree* that each is but a different form of expression of psychodynamic impulses, wishes, or conflicts. (160)

Notwithstanding all of the above, it is nevertheless still true that, as the Alter Rebbe (founder of the Chabad-Chasidic movement) teaches, when an improper thought comes into one's mind, the sinfulness that attaches to that thought can be converted into *kiddushah* (holiness) by diverting our attention to a verse of Torah or *Tehillim* (Psalms), for example, or to a Talmudic exposition.[36a] This would seem to reconcile the apparent contradiction between the two positions we have just outlined: were the "spontaneous fantasies" not "forbidden," we would be deprived of the opportunity of performing the significant *mitzvah* indicated by the Alter Rebbe. On the other hand, since the fantasies arise *of themselves* (that is the meaning of "spontaneous") liability does not attach to the *individual* until he or she begins to dwell on them.

Although such "diversion" techniques might otherwise be criticized as "repressive"—and therefore ineffective in the long run—their mystical component and specific association with Torah and *Mitzvos* renders them comparable, rather, to what I call "replacement" (*see* note 33 above, this chapter), which goes to the complete transformation of the inner being.

Female Homosexuality.

This subject is discussed separately in Chapter Seven.

Molech (Child Sacrifice).

Leviticus 18:21 says:

36a. Rabbi Schneur Zalman of Liadi, *Likutei Amarim Tanya* (Bi-lingual, Revised Ed.), Brooklyn: Kehot (1984), Chapter 27, pp. 115-117.

And you shall not give any of your seed to set them apart to Molech; neither shall you profane the name of your G–d. I am the L–rd.

According to our Oral Tradition, this Commandment prohibits child sacrifice. The fact that it does so within the context of a listing of sexual prohibitions or illicit relations (called *arayos* in Hebrew) has given rise to a great deal of discussion. It is also noteworthy that Leviticus 20:2-5 expands the dire punishment allotted to the individual who gives his offspring to Molech, to *any one who fails to prevent this from happening.* For in doing this terrible deed the individual has "[defiled] My sanctuary" and "[profaned] My holy Name."

Two questions immediately arise. In the first place, what is the connection, if any, between these two passages and the sexual prohibitions of Leviticus 18? In other words, why does the Molech prohibition appear where it does—right in the middle of a list of illicit sexual relations? Second, we know that the abominable cult of Molech was not performed in the Holy Temple of the Jews—*i.e.*, the "Sanctuary" of Hashem: how then, does sacrificing to Molech "defile My Sanctuary?"

Turning to the latter question first, Rashi holds that "My Sanctuary" refers here to "the Assembly of Israel which is sanctified to G–d." In other words, as Rabbi Avraham Fisher explains, "*Mikdash* (sanctuary) does not always refer to 'The Sanctuary,' a place of holiness; it can also mean a sanctified thing, such as in sacrifices (as in Lev. 21:23) or the people of Israel (as in our verse Lev. 20:31)"[37] Thus, Rashi implies that the sacrifice of a child tarnishes the entire community in which such a crime is permitted to take place. Similarly, Sforno opines that the community is harmed because the offending individual has "banished the Divine Presence" from the

---

37. Rabbi Avraham Fisher, OU Torah Insights Project, May 3, 2003, *Parshat Kedoshim* 5763, <www.ou.org/torah/ti/5763/kedoshim63.htm>.

midst of the people.[38] Why? Because, as Rambam explains, apart from the several fundamental transgressions involved (murder, idolatry, profanation of Hashem's Sanctuary, *etc.,*) children are the fulfilment of the Commandment *P'ru ur'vu* ("Be fruitful and multiply"), hence, a source of blessing to the entire community; if, however, the fruit of that procreation is destroyed, the community is deprived of that blessing.

In the same vein, some modern scholars aptly suggest that Molech was inserted into the chapter on sexual immorality because his cult targeted innocent and defenseless children. Thus Molech can be seen as a symbol for the sexual abuse of children. Indeed a salient feature of both pedophilia and the cult of Molech is the willingness to sacrifice the life of a child for the sake of gratifying one's own desires. Our discussion of homosexual propaganda in the public schools in Chapter 3 showed quite graphically how sexual immorality, whether homosexual or heterosexual, vilifies not only the individual but also society as a whole. Children are supposed to be a source of blessing to the entire community, but if their innocence, their outlook, their hopes, their selfhood, are sacrificed by the society in which they live, for the sake of greater sexual "freedom," then that society, in effect, sacrifices those children to Molech. As previously noted, the Spirit of G–d touches every person. By defiling a child, the abuser defiles G–d's sanctuary within that child, and violates the sacred responsibility with which we have been entrusted to guard that sanctuary.

Thus, it is reasonable to suggest that Leviticus 18:21 and 20:2-5 encompass more than just the hideous practice of child-sacrifice. It seems quite plausible that the prohibition includes not only the practice of pedophilia—but also the systematic efforts of various special interest groups to "educate" and legislate children into potential fodder for any form of sexual activity which robs them of their autonomy and innocence. Indeed, the child victim is very likely dragged by the perpetrator's lust into his or her own cycle of

---

38. Sforno, *Commentary on the Torah* (Rabbi Raphael Pelkowitz trans., ed.), Brooklyn: Mesorah Publications (1997), p. 575.

homosexuality and abuse.[39]

Author Dennis Prager suggests that the Torah juxtaposes child sacrifice with male homosexuality because both of these *aveiros* (transgressions) involve a kind of death: child sacrifice ends the children's physical lives, while homosexuality prevents the child victims from enjoying their full spiritual, emotional, and procreative potential. As Prager clarifies, citing the Talmud (*Yevamot* 63b): "He who does not engage in propagation of the race is as though he had shed blood."[40]

Intercourse During Menstruation.

The concept of shedding blood is significant in the context of another sexual prohibition: the Torah expressly forbids sexual intercourse with a woman during her time of menstruation (*niddah*). To this sexual moratorium, the Rabbis added seven more days as a safety zone, counting from the cessation of the blood, as well as additional precautionary days of abstinence on days when the onset of bleeding might be expected. It is clear that this *mitzvah* is principally directed at the marital relationship.[41] Jewish Law intervenes in the

---

39. Sexual abuse of minors often leads the victim to subsequent homosexual involvement. *See* Bill Watkins & Arnon Bentovim, "The Sexual Abuse of Male Children and Adolescents: A review of Current Research," *Journal of Child Psychology and Psychiatry* 33 (1992), p. 216. The authors reviewed the research on sexual abuse of male children and found that "one effect is the development of homosexual tendencies. . . . [A]dolescents attributed the onset of their homosexual desires to having been victimized by an older male."

40. Dennis Prager, *Judaism, Homosexuality, and Civilization*, reprinted in Dr. Chrystl Von Holdt, *Striving for Gender Identity*, Reichelsheim: German Institute for Youth and Society (1996), p. 30.

41. Lev. 18:19, Maimonides, Negative Commandment 346. *See also* Lev. 12:2-6 dealing with the abstinence required for a woman after childbirth. A woman after childbirth is ritually unclean like a *niddah* (menstruant) and has a proscribed period of abstinence time before indulging in sexual relations with her husband.

bedroom in this manner to reinforce the sanctity of the marriage by imposing self-restraint on the libido—as well as to enhance the physical "chemistry" between the marital partners. The *niddah* laws are thus viewed as a way of strengthening both the spiritual and the physical bonds of marriage.

Other possible rationales for this *mitzvah* include the desire to avoid: the mixing of semen with menstrual blood (life with death), the wasting of seed, disrespecting the procreative purpose of sex, disturbing the woman during her process of spiritual purification,[42] causing pain, discomfort or embarrassment to the woman or revulsion to the man.[43]

Obscuring of Male-Female Differences.

The Torah prohibits Jews from wearing garments that are specific to the opposite sex.

> *Male garb shall not be on a woman, and a man shall not wear a woman's garment, for anyone who does so is* to'eivah *to Hashem.* (Deut. 22:5)

The reason for this prohibition, according to traditional commentators, is to prevent intermingling of the sexes that would lead to promiscuity. Presumably, masquerading as a member of the opposite

---

42. Although this Commandment has been observed principally by Orthodox Jews, some nontraditional Jewish feminists have created a resurgence of interest in observing the *niddah* laws, including the use of the *mikveh* (a bath for ritual purification) as a way to repudiate their sex-object status, and as a proud demonstration of their womanhood. *See* Susan Weidman Schneider, *Jewish and Female; Choices and Changes in Our Lives Today*, New York: Simon & Schuster (1984), p. 207, and Diana Stevens, "Coming of Age: the Growth of the Conservative Mikveh Movement," *The United Synagogue Review* (Fall, 2001), p. 17.

43. *See* Robert A.J. Gagnon, *The Bible and Homosexual Practice: Texts and Hermeneutics,* Nashville: Abington Press (2001), pp. 137-38.

sex would make it easier to enter the opposite sex's social circle for the purpose of seeking a sexual opportunity. Similarly, a homosexual might masquerade as a woman in hopes of getting close to "straight" men. Either way, once the Torah forbids it, it doesn't matter what a person's motivation might be for transgressing. Even if one's purpose has nothing at all to do with sex, it is still forbidden. Thus, the general concern of this prohibition appears to be the maintenance of proper behavioral boundaries between the sexes.

There is also a more specific dimension to this prohibition—an aspect not often spoken about in the traditional sources. Clothes generally project the outer image of one's inner personality and feelings. The prohibition against cross-dressing could also be directed specifically toward the maintenance of gender distinctiveness—in other words, toward the avoidance or obscuring of male-female differences. (Gagnon, 109, 135, and 156)

While this interpretation is not as explicit in Jewish sources as it might be, Rabbi Menachem Mendel Schneerson, the Lubavitcher Rebbe, notes that Deuteronomy. 22:5 extends well beyond the appropriateness of garments and clothing, applying "not only to the clothes we wear but also to the way we present ourselves."[44] This simple yet remarkable insight (reflected also in the popular saying, "clothes make the man,") might explain why here in Deuteronomy 22:5, in contrast to Leviticus 18:22 (the prohibition of homosexuality), the Torah calls the person *to'eivah,* as opposed to the *act*: in this case, the "act" and the person become one!

In a separate *Sichah,* Rabbi Schneerson emphasizes that gender distinctiveness in no way implies inequality: Torah, certainly, assigns different roles to men and women. But different does not mean unequal, equality is not sameness. In the divine plan for creation, men and women have distinct, diverse missions, which work in harmony, complementing one another and bringing the divine plan to fruition.

---

44. Rabbi M.M. Schneerson, "*Sicha: 6 Tishrei 5745,*" *Sichos in English,* <http://www.sichosinenglish.org/books/partner-in-the-dynamic-of-creation/07.html>.

The role of one is neither higher nor lower than the other's: they are simply different. Torah says emphatically that the diverse missions of men and women does not mean inequality. Just as Torah commands that "A man shall not wear a woman's garment," so equally it commands, "A man's garment shall not be on a woman." It is clear from the Rebbe's words that gender separation means gender fulfillment: Neither men nor women carry out their G-d given tasks or achieve self-fulfillment by imitating the other.[45]

Christian scholarship, too, has recognized that the prohibition against cross-dressing is directed at the "concern for maintaining lines of distinction in maleness and femaleness." (Gagnon, 156) The Evangelical Alliance declares quite unambiguously that

> The strength of the Hebrew word [*to'eivah*] translated as 'abomination' indicates that in the sight of G-d such practices [cross-dressing] were fundamentally incompatible with the identity of G-d's people, and therefore it remains likely that Deuteronomy 22:5 is intended to signify a reaffirmation of the distinctiveness between two created sexes to be maintained.

This is consistent with Rambam's having codified this law in the *Mishneh Torah,* in the part that deals with Idol Worship (*Hilchos Avodah Zarah* 12:10), rather than in the chapter dealing with the Sexual Prohibitions (*Sefer Kedushah, Hilchos Issurei Bi'ah*). In fact, continues the Alliance, "[T]he cross-dressing prohibition was introduced to prevent involvement on the part of Israelites in contemporary Canaanite religious rituals of the day, which involved swapping of sex roles and cross-dressing."[46]

Indeed, the theme of "separation" is fundamental to the Jewish way of life, beginning with Abraham's separation from his country, his kin, and his father's house. As noted by one perceptive

---

45. Rabbi M.M. Schneerson, "Women: Equal Rights," *Sichos in English,* <http://www.sichosinenglish.org/essays/70.html>.

46. Evangelical Alliance Policy Commission, *Transsexuality,* London: Whitefield House (2000), p.47.

commentator from a Canadian *kollel,*

> [S]eparation is critical to the creative act; in Genesis, G–d separates [*vayavdeil*] light from dark as the first act of creation. If we didn't make separations and the world was allowed to lose all differentiation it might revert to *tohu vavohu,* the primordial chaos of Genesis.[47]

The same commentator, relying on the wisdom of Rashi, further informs us:

> Holiness is about separation, and this theme is found throughout the Torah . . . . Jewish laws specify separating meat from milk, pure from impure, men from women . . . .

Indeed, we can see that the cross-dressing prohibition is found among a series of *mitzvos* (Deuteronomy 22:9-11) having to do with separation: separation of plantings, of draft animals, of wool from linen, of spaces (the fence around the edge of the roof)—and, with Deuteronomy 22:5, of men from women.

Even the *mitzvah* of chasing off the mother bird (*Lo tikach ha'eim*—"You shall not take the mother") when taking the eggs or hatchlings has to do with the theme of separation. The placement of this commandment (Deut. 22:6) *immediately after* the cross-dressing prohibition (Deut. 22:5) is extremely intriguing, because as we saw in Chapter Four, homosexuality and other gender confusions are closely and consequentially related to the inability of a young boy properly to separate from the world of the feminine (usually represented by the mother). "A boy gains confidence in his own masculinity from his father and his [male] friends. If he fails to bond with his father or peers, he might fail to identify with the masculine role."[48] Thus we

---

47. Baruch Sienna, "Lessons for Today: This Week's Parsha: Commentary on Lev. 8:30," <http://www.kolel.org/pages/5765/tzav.html>.

48. Erin Eldridge, *Born That Way?* Salt Lake City: Deseret Book Co. (1994), p.38.

might say that the *mitzvah* of chasing off the mother bird alludes to the father's responsibility to help the male child through the sometimes difficult transition to the world of the masculine. The consequence of neglecting this *mitzvah* is confusion of gender.

Indeed, in the world of male homosexuality, the donning of female clothes and other female appurtenances assumes a variety of meanings but all essentially attempt to blur the lines of distinction between the sexes as a way of achieving a certain type of satisfaction that is not only physical but also psychological.

The Psychology of Cross Dressing.

Let us take a closer look at this phenomenon. Michelle (Michael) Danielle, a fully recovered homosexual "transz" (transsexual) who spent years as a drag queen and show-business female impersonator tells us:

> [T]he gay society is divided up into many different areas—just like normal society. There are drag queens, transsexuals, transvestites. They all wear women's clothes. One [the transvestite] does it for sexual reasons. The other [the drag queen] does it for fun. He likes to dress up and run the streets. The other [the transsexual] does it because he feels more comfortable that way . . .[49]

---

49. Marie S. Rice, *Michelle Danielle is Dead,* Nashville: Jonathan Publishers (1985), p. 34. Terry Weir, *Holy Sex,* New Kensington: Whitaker House (1999), pp. 297-98, defines the different forms of transgenderism. A transvestite is "someone who dresses in clothing of the opposite sex for purposes of sexual stimulation;" (298) "drag queens are homosexual men who dress as women to entertain others or because they have some transsexual inclinations. Drag queens do not have erotic feelings about dressing as women because they are sexually attracted to men." "Drag Kings are women who dress as men for the same reasons." (298) "Transsexuals, on the other hand, have convinced themselves that they have somehow been born with the body of the wrong sex. They usually begin by assuming the dress and mannerisms of the opposite sex. Transsexuals, whether male or female, who show early gender dysphoria are invariably homosexual." (297). *See also* Albert Allgeier and Elizabeth Allgeier, *Sexual Interactions*, Lexington: D.C. Heath & Company (1995), pp. 640-51. The Torah prohibition applies to all three categories: transvestites, drag queens or kings, and transsexuals. *See also* comment in <http://jewishsf.com/content/2-0-/module/displaystory_id/4986/format/print/

Danielle's autobiography evidences many of the causes of homosexuality we described in Chapter Four. Danielle tried hard to be a "good little boy," but found in grade school, that the other boys didn't want to be his friends, and by junior high school, he had serious problems relating to the other male students. He hated gym class. He felt he was puny and was ashamed that he couldn't measure up to the other boys. His uncle sexually abused him. His desire to retain a feminine energy in his persona pushed him to shower attention on his mother and use her as a sexual role model. While a teenager, he began wearing jewelry and woman's make-up. He not only became a female impersonator in show business in order to generate a sense of acceptance, but also a "dench queen," which he defines as "a white sissy who goes with black guys." (18)

As Danielle involved himself more and more heavily in drugs and alcohol, he began to bottom out. Eventually, Danielle realized that "the gay scene was a means of escape from reality or responsibility" and a "mask to hide behind." (27) Noting that for him, "Gay is . . . utter confusion," Danielle sums up his past struggles with remarkable perspicacity. "[E]ven though I was a homosexual, I was running [away] from the homosexual [identity] into the straight world by pretending to be a woman, so I would be accepted by society." (34)

Ultimately, Danielle chose to step out of his false self and reclaim his authentic self by reaffirming the gender of his birth.

Alan Medinger, an early leader of Exodus, who had successfully traveled the road to recovery, shares his own valuable perspective:

> When looking at gay men, we often see someone who at the level of his deepest feelings has no sense that he is a man. Cross-dressing, or campy talk, might make him feel like one of the girls, but, in truth, he is neither a man nor a female but rather a little boy who evidences emotional immaturity.[50]

---

edition>.

50. Alan Medinger, *Growth into Manhood: Resuming the Journey,* Colorado Springs: Waterbrook Press (2000), p.178.

Rich Wyler, another man who was able to heal the emotional wounds which led him to homosexually addictive behavior, reports that, feeling alienated from the male world, he often found comfort in female identification, whether in companionship or in dress. "Many of us learned to identify with women and girls as our sisters, our buddies and, inadvertently, even our role models. Our sense of girls as the 'same sex' and boys as the 'opposite sex' was reinforced." (www.peoplecanchange.com)

Danielle referred to life as a drag queen as being "all illusion—deception to the nth degree." He came to understand, that he, like Peter Pan, was a boy who never grew up and was thus stuck in perpetual adolescence.[51]

There is a deep psychological overlap between homosexuality and cross dressing. Noted psychologist, Rabbi Dr. Moshe Spero suggests that homosexuality itself is "a sexual masquerade, indicating an erroneous or inauthentic state of existence." (*Handbook*, 167) In Danielle's case, the sexual masquerade was a psychological defense he raised during childhood as a protection against emotional harm from his same-sex peers. Later, as an adult, Danielle gradually learned that these very defenses not only cut him off, but also alienated him from the world of men. Nevertheless, his defenses enabled him to initially (a) convince himself of the correctness of his homosexual orientation, and (b) rationalize a behavior pattern he otherwise knew to be wrong. As he himself states in his assisted

---

51. The "Peter Pan syndrome" actually refers to an acknowledged psychological profile that explains many of the emotional issues discussed by Danielle. Its general characteristics include irresponsibility, anxiety, loneliness, and sex role conflicts. *See* Dr. Dan Kiley, *The Peter Pan Syndrome: Men Who Have Never Grown Up*. New York: Avon Books (1983).

autobiography,

> It [homosexuality] deeply affects the mind as well as the body of the afflicted one, until he refuses to see the abnormality of his actions. He builds up mental defenses to convince himself that although not normal, it is all right for him to deviate from the natural. (Rice/Danielle, 122-123)

A *Drosh* ("Lesson") on Deuteronomy 22:5.

Perhaps we can now suggest an answer to a question we have postponed asking until now: Why do we find the prohibition against cross dressing in Deuteronomy, rather than in the Holiness Code of Leviticus? The answer may be that the Holiness-Code prohibitions concern behaviors that are generally of a *private,* even secret nature; whereas cross dressing is intrinsically a social and *public* act. (Obviously, this is not to say that it is never done in private.[52]) The private (*i.e.,* sexual and homosexual) component of cross dressing was already dealt with in Leviticus 18:22. It remained for Deuteronomy 22:5 to address the social or externalized aspect in a passage devoted to the individual's relations with his or her social and natural environment.

However, there may be something more. We suggested (above, pages 209-10) a possible reason for the placement of the cross-dressing prohibition immediately *before* the *mitzvah* of chasing off the mother bird. May we now suggest a reason why the cross-dressing prohibition comes immediately *after* the *mitzvah* of the fallen beast of burden (Deut. 22:4)? Here is the text of that *mitzvah:*

> *You shall not see your brother's ass or his ox fallen down by the way and hide yourself from them; you shall surely help him to lift them up again.*

The Baal Shem Tov taught that the "ass" alludes to our "animal"

---

52. An example would be the male fetish of secretly wearing feminine underwear.

nature (as opposed to our spiritual side). Thus, says the Ba'al Shem Tov, when we see ourselves faltering under the weight of the Commandments, we must come to the aid of our "animal" nature by uplifting and refining it—not through guilt and self-mortification.[53] Accordingly, the proximity of the cross-dressing prohibition to the foregoing suggests that when we see our fellow beings faltering under a similar weight (in this case, the burden of gender confusion) we have a moral duty to come to their assistance—not through reproach and castigation, but by "lifting them up" and helping them with loving support through the process of healing.

Through his mastery of Torah and psychology, the Lubavitcher Rebbe, Rabbi Menachem Schneerson understood very clearly the kind of emotional defenses Michael Danielle mentioned in his autobiography, and stressed the moral imperative of helping such a person reclaim his or her authentic self. In a 1986 *Sichah* ("Talk") of the Rebbe's, entitled "Rights or Ills," Rabbi Schneerson was explicit:

> [W]e must keep in mind that the vehement and vociferous arguments presented by a patient, that he is really well and that his condition is a healthy instinct—or at least not destructive, do not change the severity of the 'ailment.' In fact, this attitude on the part of this individual indicates how serious his malady really is for this person, how deeply it has penetrated into his body and psyche, and how perilous for him it really is. *And so, special action must be undertaken to heal the person and save his life. And again, there is no insult at all, no disrespect involved, only a true desire to really help.* (Emphasis added.)[54]

---

53. Rabbi M.M. Schneerson of Lubavitch, *Hayom Yom... "From Day to Day": an Anthology of Aphorisms and Customs, Arranged Acording to the Days of the Year Assembled from the Talks and Letters of the Rebbe, Rabbi Y.Y. Schneersohn of Lubavitch*, Brooklyn: Otzar Hachassidim Lubavitch (5754), p. 23.

54. <http://www.jonahweb.org/cms/e/index.php?option=content&task=view&id=100&Itemid=33>.

Sexual Reassignment Surgery.

This subject is discussed separately in Chapter 8.
Incest.

Leviticus 18 also prohibits sexual intercourse between men and women related in various degrees by birth or marriage. Whereas the origins of the marriage taboos of many different peoples and cultures are to be found in genetic and economic factors, the incest prohibitions of the Torah are also very much concerned with guarding against sexual license. Indeed, family relations, by their very nature, furnish many opportunities for transgressing in the privacy of the home or behind the screen of domestic familiarity.

By and large, the sexual revolution—some of whose "accomplishments" have provided the stimulus for this book—has not focused to any great extent on liberalizing the boundaries of incest. As evidenced by the Woody Allen scandal of a few years ago, Western society remains, in general, ostensibly opposed to such liberalization.[55] Thus we feel no compelling need to elaborate at length on this subject. For our present purposes, it will suffice to list the prohibitions and mention a few salient points that may have

---

55. Nevertheless, even here, cracks in the edifice have begun to appear. A recent *Time Magazine* article queries, "Should Incest Be Legal?" (Michael Lindenberger, April 5, 2007, <http://www.time.com/time/printout/ 0,8816,1607322,00.html>). After all, Belgium, Holland and France have decriminalized incest, and Sweden permits half-siblings to marry. And even though the U.S. Supreme Court in *Lawrence v. Texas,* 539 U.S. 558 (2003). held that states are barred from making private sexual conduct a crime, it has yet to apply that holding to incest between consenting adults. *Boston Globe* columnist Jeff Jacoby informs us, "Your reaction to the prospect of lawful incest may be 'Ugh, gross.' But personal repugnance is no replacement for moral standards. For more than 3,000 years, a code of conduct stretching back to Sinai has kept incest unconditionally beyond the pale. If sexual morality is jettisoned as a legitimate basis for legislation, personal opinion and cultural fashion are all that remain." *Boston Globe,* May 2, 2007, <www.boston.com/news/globe/editorial_opinion/oped/articles/2007/05/02/lawful_incest_may_be_on_its_way/>.

escaped the common notice.

The Torah sets forth a broad principle that a man may not make sexual advances "to any that is near of kin to him." (Lev. 18:6). The particulars are spelled out in verses 7-18 of Leviticus 18, which forbid sexual relations with one's close blood relatives, such as one's mother, sister, daughter, grand-daughter, father's sister, or mother's sister, as well as with one's relatives of affinity, such as the wives of one's blood relatives or the blood relatives of one's wife. The Sages extended some of these prohibitions. For example, while the Torah forbids marrying one's mother (Lev. 18:7), the Rabbis of the Talmud extended this concept to prohibit marriage with the grandmother and great grandmother (*Shulchan Oruch, Even HaEzer*, 15:2).

Because the family is the foundation of Judaism's religious culture, the Torah sets up additional boundaries to protect even those family members who are genetically unrelated, such as one's daughter-in-law (Lev. 18:15) or step-mother (Lev. 18:8). The Torah recognizes that family relations are sufficiently delicate without allowing matters to be complicated by the addition of a sexual component. The matter is further compounded when the participating relatives are of the same sex: the transgressors would be liable to two penalties—one for homosexuality and one for incest. Their act involves two separate and distinct transgressions and each carries its own penalty. (Talmud, *Sanhedrin* 54a).

Indeed, the most common and destructive among the incestuous relationships involves the sexual abuse of child relatives. Many of JONAH's clients tell of having been abused during childhood by a parent, sibling, uncle, or other close relative. In such cases, horrific long-lasting consequences can result. One man with whom I worked carried into his 50s a total inability to establish a loving relationship with anyone unless sex was involved. This devastating emotional deficiency he learned from his father, who began sexually abusing him at age four, and from his mother, who sexually infantilized him until his mid-teenage years. By the time this man reached puberty, he had totally internalized the belief that sex was the only kind of love in existence. It is firmly established in the psychological literature that childhood incestuous relationships can cause an adaptive pattern of promiscuous homosexuality from adolescence onward.

Thus, to abuse a child for sexual gratification is to violate that child in body and mind and soul at an age when all three are defenseless. When the perpetrator is a family member, the offense is compounded by an utter betrayal of the sacred trust reposed in him or her by the child and by the social contract that honors the privacy and sanctity of the family. So precious does the Torah hold the sexual inviolability of a human being, that a person is required to resist sexual aggression even at the cost of his or her life or the life of his or her assailant. (Talmud, *Sanhedrin* 74a)[56]

Bestiality.

Leviticus 19:19 prohibits mating an animal with an animal of a different species:

You shall keep my statutes. You shall not let your animals mate with a different species.

---

56. This is one of the sole three exceptions to the law of *pikuach nefesh*, which requires a person to transgress a Commandment rather than allow himself to be killed. The other two exceptions are idol worship and murder. In other words, if forced under threat of death to engage in illicit sexual relations, to worship idols, or to commit murder, a person is required to resist to the point of death.

More specifically, Leviticus 18:23 prohibits sexual relations between humans and animals (bestiality):

Do not perform any sexual act with an animal, since it will defile you. A woman shall [likewise] not give herself to an animal and allow it to mate with her. This is tevel.

Similarly, Deuteronomy 27:21:

Cursed be he that lies with any kind of beast.

The word *tevel* in Leviticus 18:23 is generally translated as "confusion" or "perversion." However, some commentaries translate *tevel* with an elaborate phrase. For example, the brilliant 20th-century rabbi, Aryeh Kaplan, translates *tevel* as "an utterly detestable perversion," while Rabbi Abraham Ibn Ezra, the great 12th-century exegete, translated it as a "destructive perversion."[57]

Rashi suggests two alternative meanings for the word *tevel*: (1) It means prostitution, incest, adultery, or depravity, as in the verse (Isaiah 10:25): "My anger is against their depravity" (*tavlitam*); or (2) it refers to the mixing or intermixture (*blilah*) of the seed of a human with that of an animal. The term *tevel* is similarly used (Lev. 20:12) to characterize the conduct (forbidden by Lev. 18:23 and 20:12) of a man who has sexual relations with his son's wife. Here, the connotation of "confusion" is more evident: if the child of such a union resembles both father and son, it will be impossible to know (short of DNA testing!) who the real father is.

When asked for his interpretation of *tevel,* Bar Kappara responds (Talmud, *Nedarim* 51a) that it is as if the Torah were asking "Is there any *tavlin* (spice) in it (this cohabitation)?" In other words, according

---

57. Rabbi Aryeh Kaplan, *The Living Torah*, Brooklyn: Moznaim Publishing Corporation (1981), p.599.

to one explanation of Bar Kappara's response, "Why does she abandon one of her own kind and go to an animal?"[58] Another cited interpretation of Bar Kappara's comment suggests that Bar Kappara means "Relations with a different species is like a food that is only edible through seasoning that overpowers the taste. There is no real connection possible with an animal at all."[59] In other words, such a union is "unappetizing" in the extreme.

Ultimately, however, there is a more significant aspect to this prohibition—one that highlights a critical distinction between humans and animals. According to our Tradition, humans were endowed at the moment of Creation with a Divine soul (*nefesh elokis*):

Then the L–rd formed man of the dust of the ground, and breathed into his nostrils the breath of life; and man became a living soul. (Gen. 2:7)

Animals, however, were created differently; they were created by the word of G–d:

---

58. RAN (Rabbeinu Nissim ben Reuben of Gerondi [1320-80 C.E.]), *Nedarim* 51a.

59. Rabbi Hersh Goldwurm (ed.), *Tractate Nedarim,* Brooklyn: Mesorah Publications (2000), 51a.

> *And G–d said: "Let the earth bring forth the living creature after its kind, cattle, and creeping thing, and beast of the earth after its kind." And it was so.* (Gen. 1:24)

Thus, unlike humans, animals were not endowed with a divine soul. The soul of an animal is called *nefesh habehamis*—an "animal soul." Human beings, too, have an animal soul, characterized by all the physical needs and appetites of the body; but these are opposed, monitored and tempered by the spiritual needs and longings of the Divine soul that ennobles humankind.

A related distinction is that only human beings were created in the image of G–d:

> *And G–d created man in His own image, in the image of G–d He created him.* (Gen. 1:27)

The animals were not created "in the image of G–d," but "each after its own kind." (Genesis 1:20-26) In simple terms, this means that there is a level of *kiddushah* ("holiness" or "G–dliness") in a human being that is simply lacking in even the most intelligent, loyal and affectionate of animals. Thus, for a man or a woman to couple (*i.e.*, to join sexually) with an animal debases the divine soul within them and degrades their basic humanity.

In Jewish tradition, human sexual activity is limited to marriage between a man and a woman.

> *Therefore a man shall leave his father and his mother and shall cleave to his wife and they shall become one flesh.* (Gen. 2:24)

As previously noted (*above*, pp. 186-87) the Talmud interprets *they shall become one flesh* as excluding both wild and domesticated animals "because they do not become one flesh with a man." (*Sanhedrin* 58a)

New-Age Bestiality Advocates.

Of course, for those who reject G–d or Torah, there is basically no essential difference between humans and animals. The distinction is purely one of degree: humans are "more evolved," "more intelligent," "more advanced:" nothing more than "animals with big brains." This, they argue, is hardly enough to endow humans with a unique or special moral value. For many "New-Age" spiritualists and philosophers, better to have sex with an animal (provided the animal enjoys it) than to eat it!

For example, Peter Singer, Professor of Bioethics at Princeton University, teaches that if the world can disregard "the nonsense found in the Judeo-Christian tradition," the Torah prohibition against bestiality will eventually fall, just as the bar against homosexuality has fallen.[60] Since sex with animals has always existed, suggests Professor Singer, it too must be normal. Bestiality is fine, according to Singer, as long as you do not hurt the animal! (Consequently, Singer cautions people against sex with chickens because such activity will always result in the death of the chicken.)[61]

---

60. It is interesting to note that the Torah prohibition of bestiality (Lev.18:23) follows *immediately after* that of homosexuality (Lev. 18:22). The two forbidden relationships share several traits in common: each stems from severe emotional deficits that interfere with the development of normal attractions for and relations with the opposite sex; neither is suitable for conception, each diverting the sexual drive from any possible procreative result. Each subverts and disparages the Commandment *Be Fruitful and Multiply* and G–d's Plan of Creation. Note that Torah does not discourage lawful marital relations where conception is known to be "medically impossible." This is because the cohabitation is essentially suitable for procreation. The mating of human and animal subverts the procreative purpose of sex. *See* Moshe ben Nachman ("Ramban" or "Nachmanides"), *Commentary on Sefer Vayikra*, 18:22 (Rabbi Charles Chavel trans.), New York: Shilo Publishing House, Inc. (1974), p. 267.

61. Peter Singer, "Heavy Petting: Midas Dekker's *Dearest Pet: On Bestiality*" (book review), *Nerve,* March, 2001. To the same effect, a *Seattle Post Intelligencer* columnist ridiculed a proposal to outlaw bestiality in Washington State. Robert L.

This brave new vision of sexual morality was seconded by none other than Ingrid Newkirk, Co-founder and President of PETA (People for the Ethical Treatment of Animals):

> If a girl gets sexual pleasure from riding a horse, does the horse suffer? If not, who cares? If you French kiss your dog and he or she thinks it's great, is it wrong? We believe all exploitation and abuse is wrong. If it isn't exploitation and abuse, it may not be wrong.[62]

Despite Newkirk's attempt (four years later!) to clarify this statement,[63] her position—and consequently PETA's—remains ambiguous. Though she condemns "all bestiality," it is still unclear whether "bestiality," for Newkirk, excludes what she calls "non-assaultive sexual contact" between humans and animals. Such an exclusion would constitute a cagey endorsement of "non-assaultive" zoophilia.

By contrast, other "animal rights" organizations, like the Humane Society of the United States (HSUS), unequivocally condemn *any kind* of human-animal sexual contact and classify any such contact as either "sexual molestation" or "animal sexual abuse" *per se*.

> [Advocates of animal-human sex] defend their sexual abuse of animals as 'consensual,' claiming it benefits their 'partners,' and

---

Jamieson, Jr. argues that since practices such as masturbation, oral sex, and gay sex —once considered wrong—are now "normal," why worry about human-animal copulation, as long as the animal isn't injured. *See also* Wesley J. Smith, "Horse Sense: the Debate in Washington State about Bestiality is actually a fight over human exceptionalism," *Weekly Standard*, Aug. 31 2005; <http://www.weeklystandard.com/content/public/articles/000/000/005/ 985pgwjh.asp?pg=1>.

62. Sarah Boxer, "Yes, But Did Anyone Ask the Animals' Opinion?" *New York Times*, June 9, 2001 (Arts Section).

63. Alexander Rubin, "PETA, Perverts & Horses," *Canada Free Press*, July 21 (2005) <http://www.canadafreepress.com/printpage.php>.

characterize their behavior as 'loving.' The rationalizations used to justify their actions are the same as those used by pedophiles, and, as in the case of pedophiles, the claimed motivations don't matter to the victims.[64]

HSUS also unequivocally condemns the proliferation of bestiality "resources" available both in book form and on the web.[65] Drawing comparisons with human rape and pedophilia, HSUS notes that such trends foster "the eroticisation of violence, control, and exploitation."

> Bestiality may be considered cruel even in cases when physical harm to an animal does not occur (this is similar to the case of adult sexual activity with a child where consent is presumed to be impossible). This is because animals are unable to be fully informed, communicate consent, or speak out about their abuse.[66]

Most "animal rights" organizations rightly dismiss as nonsense the idea that animals are capable of consent to sexual activity with humans. In the language of one New York State organization,

> Relationships of unequal power cannot be consensual. In human-animal relationships, the human being has control of many—if not

---

64. *Animal Sexual Abuse Fact Sheet,* February (1999) <http://www.nmanimalcontrol.com/aco_fo/sex/abuse>.

65. These include detailed how-to-guides and "even [includes] a model letter for an animal abuser to use to 'come out' to his/her friends and relatives." *Animal Sexual Abuse Fact Sheet,* February, 1999, <http://www.nmanimalcontrol.com/aco_fo/sex/abuse>.

66. HSUS Animal Sexual Abuse Fact Sheet, quoting Dr. Frank R. Ascione, "Children Who are Cruel to Animals: A Review of Research and Implications for Developmental Psychology," *Anthrozoos,* Vol. 6 (1993), No. 4, pp. 226-47. Dr. Ascione is a world-renowned developmental psychology researcher and professor of Psychology and Family and Human Development at Utah State University.

all—of the aspects of an animals' well being. [. . .] Bestiality is the model case of circumventing consent on the one hand, while confusing affection for consent on the other.[67]

Similarly, Dr. Piers Beirne, Professor of Criminology and Legal Studies at the University of Southern Maine notes that "for genuine consent to sexual relations to be present . . . both participants must be conscious, fully informed and positive in their desires."[68]

The foregoing sources may be relying too heavily on the premise that animals have no genuine means of communicating their consent or objection in a language readily understood by humans. Indeed, many pet owners, dairy farmers, shepherds and stable grooms, *etc.* claim to enjoy a deep, intuitive understanding of their animals' moods and wishes and would disagree that their animals are incapable of consent. Moreover, animals generally have no problem signifying their objections to treatment they find undesirable, yet no ethical problem arises when we override their objections. Most cats, for example, object to being bathed, yet we bathe them. Dogs put up a great fuss when we take them to the vet. Sheep and cattle do not go willingly to the slaughter. Is all this abuse, too? Logically, zoophiles ask, "How is sex different?"

Perhaps owing in part to the difficulties experienced by the unsophisticated public in answering questions of this kind, the idea of animals as potential sex partners is becoming more and more mainstream. Not long ago, the *New York Times* reviewed a "new breed" of explicit how-to sex manuals (published by Doubleday-Broadway) that overturned publishing boundaries previously respected by mainstream publishers. These manuals offered textual and pictorial instruction in such paraphilias as bestiality, fetishism,

---

67. <http://www.pet-abuse.com/pages/animal_cruelty/bestiality.php>.

68. Dr. Piers Beirne, "Rethink Bestiality: Towards a Concept of Interspecies Sexual Assault, *Theoretical Criminality,* Vol. 1 (1997), p. 3.

sado-masochism, and others. "The publishers maintain that these are service books at heart, maybe even beneficial. 'We're not publishing to shock,' said Kristine Poupolo, a senior editor at Doubleday Broadway, "... I like to think we are improving people's lives.'"[69]

There is no question but that such ill-conceived ideas row in the wake of the gay rights movement and the clamorous successes it has achieved,[70] or that such trends are favored by a climate of sexual permissiveness and moral relativism that equates sexual pleasure with the ultimate good.[71] Hence, for Ms Poupolo, "improving people's lives" appears to mean more sex and more *kinds* of sex.

According to Jewish Tradition, however (and with all deference to Doubleday-Broadway's altruistic motivations!), the way to improve people's lives is to encourage them to learn and keep the ways of peace and well being, rather than to instruct them in the performance of sexual aberrations. The Torah establishes clear boundaries of

---

69. Ruth LaFeria, "*The New Manuals: More Sex, Less 'Joy'*," *New York Times*, May 9, 2005, sec. 9, pp. 1-2.

70. Most gay activists would dispute any connection between "gay rights" and emerging calls to legitimize bestiality. However, to zoophiles, the fight for societal acceptance logically follows the trail blazed by the gay movement. From my own observation post as a spokesperson for traditional sexuality, the successes of the gay movement appear to have opened up a whole Pandora's box of paraphilias all clamoring for recognition and respect.

71. There is nothing new under the sun. Already in the late 1940s, Alfred Kinsey (himself a homosexual and pedophile) strove to legitimize bestiality, suggesting that since the incidence of sex with animals closely parallels (claimed Kinsey) that of prostitution and homosexuality, bestiality should not be classified as a paraphilia. In a series of scathing books and articles, Dr. Judith Reisman has effectively lifted the veneer of respectability that formerly surrounded Kinsey's research, exposing falsified statistics and bogus behavioral data. Despite its critical debunking as unscientific and misleading, Kinsey's research is still cited with glee by sexual devotees of all kinds. *See* Reisman's *Kinsey: Crimes and Consequences*, Crestwood: The Institute for Media (2000), <www.drjudithreisman.com>.

sexual behavior. For Jews, "establishing boundaries," means respecting the differences between sacred and profane, permitted and forbidden, pure and impure, men and women, human and animal—because that is the way of peace and well-being, and it is through inner peace and physical and mental well being that a person develops his or her fullest potential.

When Rabbi Ibn Ezra interpreted *tevel* as a "destructive perversion," he was undoubtedly aware that, aside from the great spiritual harm, bestiality is a high-risk behavior with adverse consequences to both human and animal.[72] Veterinarians and researchers explain how infections ("zoonoses") may be transmitted from animals to humans via activities that expose humans to the blood and bodily fluids of their animal victims.[73] Obviously, the animals are subject to corresponding injury and infection. Despite claims by zoophiles of a "loving" rapport with their animal paramours, bestiality often occurs in conjunction with acts of sadistic brutality.[74] Pet-abuse.com describes some of the injuries to which the animals are exposed. (*See* note 67, *above.*)

---

72. There are numerous examples of injuries going both ways. In 2005, a Washington State man died from internal injuries he sustained while having sex with a horse. Wesley J. Smith, "Horse Sense: the Debate in Washington State about Bestiality is actually a Fight over Human Exceptionalism," *Weekly Standard,* Aug. 31 (2005), <http://www.weeklystandard.com/content/public/articles/000/000/005/985pgwjh.asp?pg=1>.

73. Loretta Kowal, *Recognizing Animal Abuse: What Veterinarians Can Learn from the Field of Child Abuse and Neglect. Recognizing and Reporting Animal Abuse: A Veterinarian's Guide,* Washington, D.C.: American Humane Association (1998).

74. A Superior, Minnesota man was convicted on two occasions for killing animals for the purpose of having sex with their carcasses (a horse in April 2005 and a deer in March, 2007). Anna Kurth, "Man Faces Probation in Animal Abuse Case." The Daily Telegram, March 20, 2007 <https://secure.forumcomm.com/ superior/articles/ index.cfm?page> and <http://americansfortruth.com/the-bible-churches-glbtq/a-what-does-the-bible-say-about-ho...>.

Consistent with Ibn Ezra's definition, zoophilia has also been associated with severe emotional stunting. Dr. Andrea M. Beetz, a German research psychologist specializing in human-animal interactions, suggests that zoophiles are typically individuals who cannot succeed in the challenges posed by human relationships and often reject human society altogether. Through this mentality, they lose all hope of obtaining mutually satisfying sexual pleasure and in turn any hope of equality in their sexual relationships. She compares zoophiles/bestialists to necrophiles and pedophiles because they derive pleasure from the defenselessness of the victim or animal. Just as those who engage in pedophilia and necrophilia attempt to satisfy their sexual lust by taking advantage of an innocent victim, so too does the zoophile/bestialist. Beetz believes that human-animal sex is not only cowardly but also destructive of a part of the animal's spiritual essence that belongs to it simply by virtue of its being an animal.[75]

Beetz touches on an essential point that calls to mind the famous dictum, "G–d created animals for their innocence." Even if it were possible for an animal to "consent," the act of bestiality is always an assault upon its innocence. This should be no less obvious to secularists than to the observant. When animals mate or hunt, it is not for pleasure or recreation, but in blind obedience to the laws of natural necessity. In the Torah view, when an animal is removed from its natural pattern of behavior by being made to copulate with a human, it can no longer fulfill the purpose for which it was created: it becomes unfit for food or any other purpose. It must be destroyed.[76] The human participant, too (with the procedural limitations already described—*see above,* Chapter 5, pp. 162-64) is liable to execution.

---

75. Andrea Beetz Ph.D.: *Love, Violence, and Sexuality in Relationships between Humans and Animals*, Aachen: Shaker Verlag GmbH (2002) section 5.2.7.

76. The same is true for an animal that has killed a human being. Ex. 21:28-32.

> *And if a man lie with a beast, he shall surely be put to death; and you shall slay the beast. And if a woman approach unto any beast, and lie down thereto, you shall kill the woman and beast; they shall surely be put to death; their blood shall be upon them.* (Lev. 20:15-16).

Thus, in Jewish law, there is no way in which a sexual act between an animal and a human can be condoned as non-injurious to the animal. Such an act constitutes a deadly assault on the spiritual essence of the animal, depriving it of its claim to life.

Is this *halachah* cruel to animals—especially to the unwilling animal participant? We think not. The *halachah* provides additional discouragement to those who might otherwise contemplate sinning in secret. The *shochtim* (ritual slaughterers) had (and still have) great expertise in detecting those defects that would disqualify an animal from consumption, and sexual abuse is more easily detected in the animal than discoverable in the act.

Though not endowed with the breath of the Creator, animals still have various levels of *kiddushah* (holiness) that rendered them fit for sacrifice in the Holy Temple (the kosher mammals and birds), marked for redemption (a first-born donkey—Ex. 13 :13), or protected from abuse (all animals).[77] Indeed, when G–d gave humanity dominion over animals, He appended two important exclusions, prohibiting (1) cruelty to animals, and (2) sex with animals. G–d's love for all animals is evident from all the *halachos* and commandments that pertain to them. A few examples: we may not sit down to eat before feeding the animals in our charge (*Gitten,* 62a), nor may we acquire an animal if we lack the means to provide for it (*Yevamot,* 15:3). We may not muzzle an ox while it is working in the field (Deut. 25:4).

---

77. "It is only in our day that legislation at long last forbade cruelty to animals. Until the middle of the nineteenth century, it was nowhere illegal—except in Jewish law." (Hertz, *Chumash,* 854)

nor yoke it with an animal of a different species (Deut. 22:10).[78] On *Shabbos*, the animals are as much entitled to rest as humans (Exodus 20:10, Ex. 23:12, Deut. 5:14), while the *Sh'mitta* (Sabbatical) year is likewise designed for the benefit of *thy cattle, and for the beasts that are in the land.* (Lev. 25:7) The complex laws of slaughter are expressly designed to spare the animal unnecessary pain and suffering. Remember how Balaam was severely rebuked for striking his donkey (Num. 22:32).[79] Consistent with the foregoing, where an animal lacks the ability to defend itself from the sexual advances of humans, the Torah provides severe laws to keep it out of harm's way.

When G–d wished to place boundaries between different categories of Creation, He distinguished the latter with clearly discernible signs. There is virtually no conscious human being who is unable to distinguish between a person and an animal. To the

---

78. *See* Ibn Ezra on Deut. 22:10 ("You shall not plow with an ox and an ass together"): "The Lord had compassion on all His creatures, insofar as an ass does not have the strength of an ox."

79. Rabbi Yaakov Ben Asher (1270-1340) suggested that when Balaam's female donkey asked him, *Am I not your ass on whom you have ridden . . . ?* she was really reminding Balaam that he had had bestial relations with her. Ben Asher derived this interpretation from the *gematriah* (numerical value) of the Hebrew words for "you rode upon me," which is the same as for "you mated with me." *See* Rabbi Chaim HaQoton, "Abominable Relations," <http://rchaimqoton.blogspot.com/2006_01_01_archive.html>.

obviously physical signs are added undeniable biological and moral distinctions. These differences, too, are apparent to any thinking person. To ignore them is to transgress against both G–d *and* nature.

Masturbation.

Although the Torah does not expressly forbid it, traditional Judaism strictly prohibits masturbation by males, regarding it as equivalent to the killing of a human being.[80] The Hebrew term for masturbation is *hashchatas zera*—the willful destruction of seed.

The prohibition appears to originate from the narrative of Onan in Genesis. The Torah tells us that Jacob's son, Yehudah had three sons, Er, Onan, and Shelah. Er married Tamar. After Er died:

> *Then Yehudah said to Onan, 'Go to your brother's wife, and perform the duty of a brother-in-law to her and raise up offspring for your brother.' But Onan knew that the offspring would not be his; so when he went in to his brother's wife he spilled the semen on the ground, lest he should give offspring to his brother. And what he did was displeasing in the sight of the L–rd, and he slew him also.* (Gen. 38:7-11)

Note, however, that the story also involves the serious *aveirah* ("sin") of evading the obligations of a contracted levirate marriage. Thus there is a question whether the prohibition of masturbation is implied in the Torah or rabbinically decreed. Since the prohibition is not expressly stated in the Torah (*lav miyuchad*), a *Beis Din* (Jewish Tribunal) has no power to impose any punishment for this transgression. As explained in Chapter Seven (at pp. 252-54, *below*),

---

80. *Niddah* 13a and 13b. *See* Maimonides *Mishneh Torah, Hilchot Issurei Biya* 21:18. To the same effect, *see* also *Shulcan Aruch, Even HaEzer* 23:5.

this limitation does not lessen the severity of the offense. On the contrary, according to some authorities,[81] it is punishable by *kores* ("excision"), which means punishment by decree of Heaven.

Despite the enormity of the transgression, it can be rectified, according to Kabbalistic teaching, "by means of true repentance and intense *kavanah* ["concentration"] during the recital of the *Shema* at bedtime . . . ." (*Tanya*, 29) According to the Alter Rebbe, this unique amenability to repentance explains (for reasons beyond the scope of this book) why masturbation is not listed among the forbidden coitions. (*Tanya*, 31)[82]

Homosexuality and Masturbation.

Do homosexual persons engage in masturbation more widely than heterosexuals? Does masturbation give rise to undesirable emotional, behavioral consequences?

Based on his pastoral experience of more than a quarter of a century of counseling both homosexual and heterosexual individuals, Father John Harvey, the founder of the Catholic ex-gay ministry (Courage), notes that homosexual persons engage in masturbation to a far greater extent than heterosexuals, in part because homosexuals generally have greater difficulty achieving

---

81. Rabbi Schneur Zalman of Liadi, *Likutei Amarim Tanya* (Bi-lingual, Revised Ed.), Brooklyn: Kehot (1984), *Igeret haTeshuvah*, Chapters 1-2, p. 347

82. The Alter Rebbe also describes various penitential procedures "to urge on and expedite the conclusion of [the sinner's] atonement"—in other words, to restore him to G-d's favor. (*Tanya, Igeret haTeshuvah*, Chapters 1-2, p. 347)

authentic intimacy and friendship than heterosexuals.[83] Psychologist Gerard Van den Aardweg agrees: "Many homosexual men and women are addicted to the practice of masturbation, which chains them to their immature interests and sexual ego-centeredness." (*The Battle for Normality,* 127)

Masturbation is typically a crucial link in an obsessive cycle of fantasy-masturbation-orgasm-depression that forms the basis of an addiction pattern. Masturbation most often involves the use of pornography. The use of such images enables the compulsive viewer to free himself from the vulnerability and uncertainty that go along with human relationships, thus alleviating his sexual anxiety. Through such practices the masturbator temporarily escapes from his loneliness, emptiness, and need for intimacy. As one of my strugglers described it, "Masturbation in our case is just a cover for bad feelings, a way to run to 'escape' from the darkness and loneliness of our daily life. A sign of our brokenness." The masturbator may be able to numb these feelings temporarily, but only at the cost of habituating himself to staying physically and emotionally detached. In this process, the masturbator (1) learns to associate intimacy with mere sexual excitement, while dissociating sexual attraction from the risks of communication, rejection and disappointment which characterize genuine human relationships; (2) cultivates an unrealistic and unhealthy expectation of sexual fulfillment on demand; and (3) grows more and more detached from his legitimate needs for genuine intimacy and companionship. In simple terms, as is often the case

---

83. Father John Harvey, *The Truth About Homosexuality: The Cry of the Faithful*, San Francisco: Ignatius Press (1996), p. 161.

with homosexuality, masturbation becomes a crutch, the habitual use of which diminishes the ability to walk.

Thus, "The habit of masturbation . . . renders many homosexual persons vulnerable to promiscuity. First, fantasy and masturbation, then cruising the haunts, and later, finding someone for a one-night stand." (Harvey, 162).

Although western medicine (including the psychological professions), has expended—with the hearty assistance of the media—much effort in proclaiming masturbation normal, natural, and beneficial,[84] most traditional cultures condemn the practice. The JONAH program for the sexual reorientation of SSA individuals discourages masturbation as a "substitute" for homosexual activity. As the struggler we quoted above advised a fellow struggler, "What is important is to replace masturbation with something healthy, such as sports, being with friends, or having sex with your wife." As we shall see in later chapters, adding holiness to one's life through Torah and *Mitzvos* can empower one to break the "chains" of masturbation and other destructive cycles.

---

84. It may come as no surprise that the Reform and Conservative movements have succumbed to these ideas, permitting masturbation (in moderation), both "as a means of sexual release" and "as a way to learn about one's body."

CHAPTER 7:

Female Homosexuality.

We have already observed that the Torah does not appear to harbor an express prohibition of lesbianism. The gay-affirmative literature has been quick to seize on this apparent omission for its own purposes. For example, Steven Greenberg (dubbed by the media as the "first openly gay Orthodox rabbi") writes: "Unlike its very strong reference to sex between men, the Torah gives no hint that sex between women is a particular problem."[1] Not only is this statement highly misleading, but Greenberg's use of the phrase "no hint" is extremely questionable. In the first place, a prohibited behavior need not be explicitly stated in the Torah: an implied prohibition would be just as authoritative. Second, Rabbi Greenberg is surely aware that several weighty authorities hold that there is indeed a Torah prohibition against lesbianism; and third, Rabbi Greenberg presumably knows that this authoritative view is based on Leviticus 18:3. Of course, Rabbi Greenberg would like to show that the prohibition against lesbianism was "made up" by the Sages. However, even if that were

---

1. Rabbi Steven Greenberg, *Wrestling with G-d and Men: Homosexuality in the Jewish Tradition,* Madison: U. Wisconsin Press, (2004), p. 88. Despite the media's practice of identifying him as "Orthodox," Orthodox institutions have virtually unanimously disassociated themselves from Greenberg and his interpretations.

true, it would still make no difference in terms of actual practice: *halachah* and Talmudic interpretations are unanimous that lesbianism is forbidden.

What the Torah Says.

Let us now explore how this *halachah* is derived. In Leviticus 18:3, we read:

Do not perform the practice of the land of Egypt in which you dwelled; and do not perform the practice of the land of Canaan to which I bring you, and do not follow their traditions.

The Torah is clearly telling us that we are forbidden to follow the "practices" and "traditions" of ancient Egypt and Canaan. To follow their "practices" or their "traditions" would indisputably violate a Torah prohibition. The question is, what "practices" and "traditions," specifically, does the text have in mind? The Torah is telling us to refrain from doing something, but the text itself leaves us pretty much in the dark as to what that something might be. To find out, we must turn to the Oral Law, and that requires a small digression.

The Oral Torah.

We have already seen (in Chapter Five, *above,* pp.146-50) that the Oral Law is a necessary companion to the Written Law of the Torah. Let us now take a closer look. Many verses from the Torah call upon the Jews to do or refrain from doing something, but omit to specify what it is we must do or not do. For example, ritual slaughter of animals is indicated in Deuteronomy 12:21, where the Commandment is to slaughter the appropriate animals "as I have commanded you." However, *nowhere in the written Torah do we find a description of how to do it.* This clearly suggests that the requisite comprehensive details must have been communicated elsewhere. In Chapter Five, we cited various other examples—such as the *tzitzis* ("fringes"), the *tefillin* ("prayer phylacteries") and the *melachos* ("labors") that are forbidden on the Shabbos—that testify to the existence of an Oral Tradition. An additional proof can be found in the fact that in some places in the Torah text, the Tradition calls for a different word from that actually written in the Scrolls to be read aloud during the public readings. These substituted words are footnoted in the *Chumashim* (printed texts) but nowhere are they marked in the Scrolls, which antedate *Chumashim* by several centuries.

The existence of an oral tradition is acknowledged in all the main *halachic* literature. For example, the *Sifra*, a *halachic* compilation dating from the earliest period of Rabbinic interpretation, states outright that the Jews received two Torahs at Mt. Sinai—one written, and one oral. This teaching emanates from the language of Leviticus 26:46:

> These are the statutes and judgments and teachings *["Toros"]* which the L–rd made between Him and the children of Israel on Mount Sinai by the hand of Moses.

The Sages commented that the use of the plural *Toros* ("teachings," but also "Torahs") is a "hint" (*remez*) at the existence of both a written and an oral law.

As previously explained (in Chapter Five, *above,* at p.150), the Oral Tradition survives today in written form, in the Talmud and the *midrashim*. Narrating its own history, the Oral Tradition teaches that the Oral Law was transmitted in a direct line from Moses to Joshua to the Elders to the Prophets to the men of the Great Assembly. It was then recorded in the Babylonian and Jerusalem Talmuds. These great compendia of oral tradition are written in a free-ranging style, recording discussions and debates that cover the range of Jewish Law, Philosophy, and Ethics. While these monumental compilations form the basis of our knowledge of what the Torah means and how to carry out its Commandments, their size and their style make them unsuitable—in the hands of all but the most brilliant and learned scholars—for use as a manual for practical *halachah*. The needs of ordinary scholars and working people called for the reduction of the

Talmud to a more "user-friendly" format. Hence the composition, during the Middle Ages and Late Renaissance, of various *halachic* compilations that codify in a clear and systematic way the decisions of the Talmud.

Jewish tradition is virtually unanimous in regarding these later compilations as the primary sources of Jewish Law. These three major codes are the *Mishneh Torah* of Rambam (Maimonides) (1135-1204), the *Arba'ah Turim* (the *"Tur"*), compiled by Jacob Ben Asher (1269-1340), and the *Shulchan Aruch*, compiled by Joseph Caro (1525-1572).

The codification of the Oral Law has led to one inescapable result: by definition, any attempt to present a "Traditional Jewish Approach" must necessarily be consistent with what is written in these codes. They represent the authoritative precedent for all later applications of Torah Law to any given case or situation. These works not only reflect the tradition; they also define it.

The traditional approach to Torah jurisprudence has been to study not just the general rules that may be derived from these texts, but to examine each and every word with the greatest of care. The traditional scholar's working assumption has been that all of these works—especially that of Rambam—were written with utmost precision, every word carefully selected. Thus, the key to understanding the implications and ramifications of every *halachah* lies in analyzing carefully and conscientiously the meanings and connotations of its language, even to the point of inquiring diligently why one word was chosen over another. Needless to say, in quoting passages from these sources, we shall endeavor to adhere to the same exacting standards.

It is also important to note that many of the terms used in these sources have a very specific technical meaning that would be immediately apparent to any experienced Rabbinic scholar, but might nevertheless throw off or confuse others who are not sufficiently grounded in this type of scholarship.

Why should all this be of concern to the reader of this book—and why are we putting this section right in the midst of a discussion about female homosexuality? The reason is simple: the attitude of

Jewish Law towards lesbianism has been misrepresented in much of the material that is commonly available to English-speaking lay readers. Indeed, such material is generally polarized at two extremes, neither of which is consistent with the traditional understanding. Citing the perceived lack of a specific Torah prohibition against lesbianism, gay-affirmative ideologues are quick to assert that lesbianism is permitted. At the opposite pole are those who condemn not only the behavior but also the individuals involved. At the same end of the spectrum are those who claim that Leviticus 18:22 and 20:13—which on their face are limited to *male* homosexual behavior—apply equally to female homosexuality. We do not believe that any one of these opinions accurately reflects the authentic *halachic* view.

Please understand: we do not wish to dictate what a person may or may not believe, nor do we seek to deny others the right to voice their own opinion. However, when one undertakes to speak in the name of Jewish Tradition, clearly, one's reasoning must be based on traditional Jewish sources.

Moreover, it is obviously of critical importance that such sources be read *correctly*. Clearly, a proper understanding of the sources rests on a correct decoding of rabbinic phraseology and terminology. Hence, it behooves us to apply something of what we learned in Chapter Five about reading Jewish texts to the specific passages that pertain to our topic. The importance of this excursion will become evident later, as we critique one of the most frequently cited articles on lesbianism. Though written by a professor of Jewish studies, and widely available on the internet,[2] the article will furnish us with an excellent example of how unfamiliarity with the traditional language and method of *halachic* exegesis can lead to an utter distortion of the Law.

A similar example could be made of Steven Greenberg's book, (*Wrestling with G–d and Men*), in which arguments justifying lesbianism are likewise founded on what we believe to be totally

---

2. *See, e.g..*, <http://www.utoronto.ca/wjudaism/journal/vol1n1/ v1n1zeid. htm>.

incorrect readings of fundamental texts. Indeed, virtually the entire liberal establishment persists in misreading (and mistranslating!) the source material in such a way as to justify the claim that sex between women is actually *permitted* under both Biblical and Rabbinic Law!

In rejecting this claim, we shall not only set forth all the arguments step by step, but we shall also lay out and explain the actual source material, so that you, the reader, may decide for yourself.

The Oral Tradition: the *Sifra*.

As we have previously explained, the Oral Tradition is the authoritative source for decoding the written Torah. When the primary text comes from Leviticus, our first recourse is normally to the *Sifra*, which, like Leviticus, is principally occupied with the Priestly laws.[3] Although the core of this text developed in the mid-third century C.E.—several centuries before the Talmud—it contains layers of later additions and emendations. Consisting of a *midrashic*-style, verse-by-verse (and sometimes word-by-word) commentary, the *Sifra* records legal traditions from the school (among others) of Rabbi Akiba, who lived nearly 2,000 years ago. This is what the *Sifra* (9:8) says regarding Leviticus 18:3:

> ***Do not perform the practice of the land of Egypt in which you dwelled; and do not perform the practice of the land of Canaan to which I bring you [and do not follow their traditions].***

Could it be that you are not to build buildings or plant crops as they do? Rather, the Torah writes, *"do not follow their*

---

3. The name *Sifra* is Aramaic for "Book," a name which first became associated with this compilation during the Gaonic period (600-1000 C.E.). Later commentaries refer to it as *Torat Kohanim* ("The Torah of the Priests") or *Sifra D'vei Rav* ("Book of the House of Rav").

traditions." This must refer to practices that are long established amongst them, their fathers, and grandfathers. And what would they do? A male would "marry" [*noseh*] a male, a female a female, a man a woman and her daughter, and a woman two males. That is why it says, "*their traditions.*"

Analysis.

The *Sifra* begins by implicitly asking the question that we posed at the beginning of this section: What "practices" does the Torah have in mind when it tells us that we are forbidden from following the "practices" of ancient Egypt and Canaan? Obviously not planting or building! Rather, it had to do with their "practice," or custom, of males "marrying" males, females "marrying" females, males "marrying" females and their daughters, and a female "marrying" two males.

We might ask, parenthetically, how did the *Sifra* know about these practices of ancient Egypt and Canaan? Of course, the Torah is very clear that the reason G–d drove out the Canaanite nations from Canaan was that their customs and traditions were the exact opposite of the Holiness Code of Leviticus 18:

> *Do not defile yourselves in any of these [abominations], for in all these [abominations] the nations are defiled, which I cast out from before you. And the land was defiled, therefore I did visit the iniquity thereof upon it, and the land vomited out her inhabitants.* (Lev. 18:24-25)

Curiously, however, the Holiness Code does not expressly mention the *ménage à trois* mentioned by the *Sifra* ("a female 'marrying' two males"). This suggests that Rabbis of the *Sifra* knew about this aspect of pagan "practices" from sources independent of the Torah. And in fact, the licentiousness of Egypt and Canaan is independently documented in the writings of various historians of classical antiquity.[4] This fact needs to be noted, because there are those who would feel more comfortable if the Holiness Code were an arbitrary list of prohibitions concocted by some uptight rabbis, and the "abominations" of Egypt and Canaan were a fiction.

For our purposes, however—that is, for purposes of establishing what is permitted and what is forbidden—when the *Sifra* uses the word *noseh* (which we translated as "marry"), we must ask, what does the word *noseh* really mean in this context? The published translations alternate between "marry" and "take," "marry" being the more frequent choice. That being so, does the word denote actual marriage, sanctioned by ritual ceremony and public record, or is *noseh* only a euphemism for sexual relations? (Note that the same ambiguity exists in English as well as other modern languages. For example, contrast, *e.g.*, "Do you take this woman to be your lawfully wedded wife?" with, "he took her.")

Let us assume for a moment that *noseh* in the *Sifra* refers to the sexual act of "taking": the *Sifra* can't be implying that a bona-fide marriage would "cure" the stigma of unmarried homosexual relations, for in that case, the *Sifra* would not have used a word like "*noseh*"—which means literally "marry!" On the other hand, if we understand *noseh* to mean "marry" in the legal sense, surely the *Sifra* is not suggesting the converse—namely, that homosexual relations (whether casual or ongoing) are OK as long as *not* "sanctified" by marriage!

---

4. *See* Chapter Six, note 19, and *e.g.*, Herodotus, *The Histories*, (Aubrey B. Selincourt trans.), New York: Penguin (1954), p. 92; Raymond O. Faulkner, *The Ancient Egyptian Pyramid Texts*, Oxford U. Press (1969), p. 56; J.E. Manchip White, *Ancient Egypt*, New York: Thomas Y. Crowell (1953), p. 122; Lisa Monniche, *Sexual Life in Ancient Egypt*, New York: Routledge & Kegan Paul (1987), pp. 106-15; Henri Frankfurt, *Kingship and the Gods: a Study of Ancient Near Eastern Religion as the Integration of Society and Nature*, U. Chicago Press (1948), pp. 296-9 and 330-31; E.O. James, *Myth and Ritual in the Ancient Near East: an Archeological and Documentary Study*, London: Thames & Hudson (1958), pp. 114-22 and 130-31; Samuel Noah Kramer, *The Sacred Marriage Rite*, Bloomington: U. Indiana Press (1969); Jack Conrad, *The Horn and the Sword: the History of the Bull as Symbol of Power and Fertility*, Westport: Greenwood (1973), p. 84.

Common sense alone should compel us to conclude that when the Torah forbids us to follow "Egyptian and Canaanite practices," it is prohibiting even isolated incidents of homosexual activity—irrespective of gender.

Nevertheless, let us pursue the matter, and see what the principal sources can contribute in regard to our specific question: Are female-female relations prohibited altogether, or only when they become stable or formal? The question is a serious one, because when the Talmud says (*Sanhedrin* 108a) that even the generation of the Flood did not legalize homosexual "marriages," it is said as much in praise of that generation as in disparagement of later ones. For an answer, we shall look first to the Talmud and then to the *Rishonim* (literally "First Ones"), *i.e.,* the legal codes known as the *Mishneh Torah* and the *Shulchan Aruch.*

Talmud, *Yevamot* 76a.

This is the most extensive discussion in the Talmud of female-female sexual activity. Although this passage does not immediately tell us whether lesbianism is permitted or forbidden, it does establish the basis for further discussion by giving us a technical term (*mesolelot*) that seems to refer to lesbianism. The issue addressed here is whether a woman who has engaged in this practice is qualified to marry a *cohen* (priest) or not. The background is that a *cohen* may not marry a woman who is classified as a *zonah*. The discussion is legalistic and technical rather than based upon any kind of moral judgment:

> ***Yevamot* 76a: Rav Huna says: Women who are *mesolelot* with one another are disqualified from marrying a *cohen*. [But] even Rabbi Elazar, who holds that an unmarried male who had sexual relations with an unmarried female—[even] without matrimonial intent—renders her thereby a *zonah*, disagrees. The disqualification arises only where a male was involved; but where it is a woman, it is only *p'ritzut* [and not *z'nut*].**

Rav Huna uses four technical terms that need to be explained before we proceed further.

Mesolelot refers to some as yet undefined activity that, engaged in by women, is considered *p'rizut.*

Zonah. Usually mistranslated as "harlot" or "prostitute," this term has no direct counterpart outside of the language of Torah. In the context of this Talmudic passage, it refers to the legally defined class of females who, as a result of having committed certain sexual improprieties, are not eligible to be married to a priest. A *zonah* would be subject to additional restrictions, and—as we shall see—if already married, would no longer be permitted to cohabit with her husband, whether he were a *cohen* or not. In this passage, the issue is only whether she would be eligible to marry a *cohen.*

Z'nut is the abstract noun form of *zonah*; it is what the *zonah* has done.

P'ritzut is usually translated as "licentiousness." Literally, it means "breaking of boundaries."

Analysis.

What Rav Huna is saying is that women who engage in this activity acquire the status of a *zonah,* thereby becoming ineligible to marry a *cohen.* Rabbi Elazar disagrees. In his opinion, their behavior is *p'ritzut* (lewdness), but not *z'nut:* since such women do not acquire the status of a *zonah,* they are free to marry a *cohen.* Rabbi Elazar's rationale appears to be technical: there was no male penetration. The fact that Rabbi Elazar is strict in the matter of male-female fornication gives added weight to his more lenient view of women who are *mesolelot.*

Note that the Talmud is not saying here that *p'ritzut* is not prohibited; it is only saying that, of itself, it does not disqualify a woman from marrying a *cohen*. Note also that whatever *mesolelot* really means, the Talmud does not appear to give any significance to the formality, frequency, or duration of this activity.

What is the Meaning of *Mesolelot*?

The next step in our investigation is to ask, what does *mesolelot* actually mean? In other words, precisely what activity is the Talmud referring to as disqualifying a woman from marriage with a *cohen*? *Mesolelot* is a verb participle. It refers to a certain action that the women are *doing*. The Talmud is not calling anybody names; it is merely indicating what certain women do. Hence, translating this term as "prostitute" or "harlot", as is commonly found in modern treatments of the subject, is grammatically and lexically wrong.

Various commentaries throughout the centuries have attempted to define exactly what being *mesolel* consists of. However, the general consensus is that it refers to certain kinds of non-permitted erotic behavior that involves at least one female and no male penetration.[5] Indeed, in his commentary on the Talmud, Rashi, the preeminent Talmudic commentator, defines the term as follows:

Rashi on *Yevamot* 76a: *HaMesolelot.* In the manner of heterosexual intercourse. They rub their genitals against one another. This is also the meaning when this term is used in *Sanhedrin* 69b, in the case of a woman who is

---

5. *Mesolel* is also used in *Tosefta, Sotah* 6:7 and *Gittin* 8:8, as well as Talmud, *Sanhedrin* 69b, to refer to a woman who is *mesolel* with her young son. *See* the important list of sources cited by Rabbi Chaim Rapoport in *Judaism and Homosexuality,* London: Vallentine Mitchell (2004), pp. 142-5.

mesolel with her young son.

There, too (*Sanhedrin* 69b), the issue is whether this type of activity disqualifies a woman from marrying a *cohen*.

It is now clear from Rashi's explanation of *mesolelot,* that the activity in question, when practiced among women, is homosexual—*i.e.,* lesbian, and that what counts is the kind of action—not the kind of relationship in which it occurs.

Let us summarize the argument so far: (1) We learn from the *Sifra* that sexual practices (such as those of Egypt and Canaan) are prohibited. However the *Sifra's* use of the ambiguous word *noseh* ("marries/takes") leaves some residual doubt as to whether even casual relations are prohibited, or only long-term, formalized relationships. (2) *Yevamot* 76a tells us that the activity engaged in by women who are *mesolelot* with each other is *p'ritzut* ("lewdness" or "licentiousness"), but does not disqualify them from marrying a *cohen.*(3) Rashi, at *Yevamot* 76a, defines being *mesolelot* as genital contact with a woman, without male penetration. Rashi's comment also indicates that whether the contact takes place in a casual or formal relationship is irrelevant. We learn from this that a better way of translating *noseh* in the *Sifra* might be "take" rather than "marry."

Let us now see what Maimonides has to say on the subject.

Rambam: *Mishneh Torah:* Laws of Forbidden Sexual Relations, 21:8

Distilled from the entire Talmud, Rambam's *Mishneh Torah* is one of the prime codifications of practical *halachah.* Its author was a master of precision. His *halachic* works are meticulously scoured for the nuances written into its every detail. In the Section called Laws of Forbidden Sexual Relations, Rambam says:

[Laws of Forbidden Sexual Relations, 21:8]: Women who are *mesolelot* with one another: It is forbidden [*assur*]. This is the practice of Egypt about which we were warned [*shehuzharnu*], as it is said: [Lev. 18:3] "Like the practice

of the Land of Egypt you shall not do." The Sages said [*Sifra*, on Lev. 18:3—*i.e.*, the *Sifra* we have just examined]: "What did they do? A man takes a man, a woman takes a woman, and a woman takes two men." Although this practice is *assur* [forbidden], there is no *malqin* ["whipping"] for it, since there is no *Lav Miyuchad* ["specific prohibition"]. And, there is no *biyah* ["intercourse"] at all.

Consequently, they [*i.e.*, such women] are not forbidden to marry a *cohen* because of *z'nut*, nor is a wife forbidden to her husband because of this [practice], for it is not considered *z'nut*. However, it would be proper to give them [*i.e.*, such women] *Makat Mardut* [a "flogging of rebellion"], since they have performed a forbidden act.

A man should be strict with his wife in regard to this matter and bar women known for this practice from visiting her, and her from visiting them.

Analysis.

The section begins by telling us that the act of being *mesolelot* is *assur* (forbidden). By itself, the term *assur* does not tell us whether the practice is "forbidden by the Torah" or, alternatively, "forbidden by Rabbinic Decree." However, we begin to see the answer in the very next sentence, for the term *shehuzharnu* ("which we are warned against"), is a *halachic* term that usually indicates a transgression on a *Torah* level. And in fact, immediately following, Rambam quotes the Negative Commandment of Leviticus 18:3. It is now apparent that— at least according to Rambam—the practice of being *mesolelot* is *prohibited by the Torah*. In other words, it is a Torah-based prohibition, not a rabbinic one.[6]

Rambam then cites the "Sages" of the *Sifra* (the same *Sifra*, 9:8

---

6. The opposite view, argued by the great Posek, Rabbi Moshe Feinstein, is, because of its intricate complexity, beyond the scope and purpose of this exposition. *See* the detailed discussion in Rapoport, pp. 143-45, notes 17 and 18.

which we examined above), which he quotes in abbreviated form, to teach us what were the practices of Egypt and Canaan that the Torah warns us not to do.

Next, Rambam informs us that, despite being prohibited by the Torah itself, the practice of "being *mesolelot*" is not punishable by *malqin* ("whipping")—a punishment that could only be imposed by a *Beis Din*—a Jewish Tribunal. The reason for this exemption, Rambam tells us, is *Lav Miyuchad,* meaning that *the Torah does not specifically identify the prohibited conduct.* Rambam is referring here to the rule is that no Torah-mandated punishment may be imposed unless the Torah expressly spells out the conduct it is prohibiting. Leviticus 18:3 refers to the "practices" of Egypt and Canaan in general terms, but does not specificy *which* practices. Thus, by citing this rule, Rambam is telling us that the transgression of being *mesolelot* carries *no Torah-mandated punishment.*

Rambam now notes that despite the sexual nature of this transgression, it does not technically constitute *biyah* (sexual intercourse). The implication here is that if this practice did involve *biyah,* it might indeed be punishable by whipping—not for transgressing Leviticus 18:3, but, for example, for prostitution, which *is* a *specific* Torah prohibition. (*See Mishneh Torah,* "Laws of Sexual Prohibitions," 18:2).

Rambam then explains why the woman who is or was *mesolel* would still be allowed to marry a *cohen:* as reprehensible as her behavior might be, it still does not constitute *z'nut,* which requires actual intercourse with a *man* or boy from a category forbidden to her. Rambam adds that she may also stay with her husband, since, as has just been noted there has been no intercourse with another male.

Now Rambam tells us that women who do such things deserve *makat mardut*, which means, literally, "flogging of rebellion." In other words, while there is no Torah-decreed punishment, Rambam cites a Rabbinically ordained punishment, called *makat mardut,* which would sometimes be meted out for "rebellious" behavior. Note also that Rambam's exact words are *vera'ui lehakotan makat mardut* ("It *would be* proper to flog them with strokes of rebellion"), which might imply that in the case of *mesolelot,* and for whatever reason, *makat mardut* were either not ordinarily administered, or else were discretionary rather than compulsory. This will be discussed further in a subsection (*Makat Mardut*) below.

In the final paragraph, Rambam tells us that it is the husband's responsibility to see to it that his wife does not become involved with this behavior. This recalls a passage in the Talmud (*Shabbat* 65a-b) which reports that one of the Sages was careful not to let his daughters acquire the habit of sleeping together in the same bed (*but see above,* Chapter Four, p. 132.)

The *Shulchan Aruch* and the *Tur*.

As noted earlier, the *Mishneh Torah* of Maimonides has been accepted as one of the two paramount authorities in Jewish Law for over the past 800 years, the present day included. The other universally accepted authority, the *Shulchan Aruch,* compiled by Rabbi Joseph Caro, not only incorporates Maimonides' pronouncements concerning female homosexuality, but even adopts his actual *language.*

> ***Shulchan Aruch (Even HaEzer* 20:2): Women who are *mesolelot* with one another: It [this practice] is forbidden. It is from the [Torah] verse regarding the practices of the Land of Egypt, that we derive that it is forbidden from the Torah.**
>
> **It would be proper to flog them with *makat mardut* ["Flogging of Rebellion"], since they have performed a forbidden act.**
>
> **A man should be strict with his wife in regard to this matter and bar women known to engage in this practice from visiting her. And, he should prevent [his wife] from visiting them.**

The *Tur* (compiled by Rabbi Jacob Ben Asher), the *halachic* predecessor to *Shulchan Aruch,* also essentially quotes Maimonides, but adds that the woman who engages in such practices "receives *lindotah*. That phrase translates as, "She receives a writ of social ostracization." Note, however, that Rambam, who precedes the *Tur*, says nothing about *lindotah*, and neither does the *Shulchan Aruch*, which succeeds it. These omissions from the two main *halachic* authorities seem to indicate that this punishment was never universally applied to lesbianism, and that by the time of the *Shulchan Aruch*, *lindotah* may have been abandoned altogether.

Whatever some modern scholars may have to say about it, we have so far seen that both of the great and universally accepted *halachic codes* (*i.e.*, Rambam and the *Shulchan Aruch*) agree that lesbianism per se is prohibited. Moreover, not only do both the *Shulchan Aruch* and the *Tur* adopt the actual language of the *Mishneh Torah*, but we see also that they accept Rambam's characterization of lesbianism as a Torah-based prohibition.

Further Questions.

Assuming, with some justification, that we have established that lesbianism is in fact prohibited by the Torah, does that necessarily mean that it was prohibited in practice? After all, Rambam seems to imply that, in practice, at least, there is no punishment of any kind for this transgression. Might it not have been tolerated? So it is legitimate to ask, how prohibited can something be if there is no punishment for it? This question really has two components: (1) Is lesbianism punishable according to *halachah?* (2) If it is not punishable, as Rambam seems to imply, to what degree, if any, does that mitigate the severity of the offense? Let us look at these two questions in turn:

(1) Is Lesbianism Punishable?

Rambam says very clearly that "there is no *malqin* [whipping] for [lesbianism] . . . ." *Malqin* (or *malkut*) is a Torah ordained punishment (Deut. 25:2-3), and Rambam gives two reasons for the exemption: *lav miyuchad*, and absence of *biyah*. *Lav miyuchad* is legal shorthand for the rule that when the Torah prohibits something in a general category without specifying the particular, there is no

Torah-prescribed punishment for that act. In the case of lesbianism, the Torah prohibits "the practices of Egypt and of Canaan," but leaves it to the Oral Tradition to specify what those practices are. This is a clear example of *lav miyuchad*.

The second reason given by Rambam is that "there is no *biyah*." *Biyah* is the legal term for male-female intercourse, which the Torah (Deut. 23:18, Lev. 19:29) *specifically* forbids between a man and a woman who are not married to each other. Indeed, as Rambam says elsewhere, "Contravention of this prohibition . . . is punished by whipping." Since there can be no *biyah* between two women, *biyah* cannot serve as grounds for punishing lesbianism.

At this point, as if by afterthought, Rambam adds something rather curious:

However, it would be proper to flog them with *makat mardut* ("flogging of rebellion"), since they have performed a forbidden act.

This seems to imply that Rambam disapproves very strongly of lesbianism, but finds no basis in the law for actually flogging those who practice it. Let us take a few moments to understand what Rambam is saying.

Makat Mardut.

When Rambam says that "*it would be proper* to flog them with *makat mardut*," he is referring to a punishment not commanded by the Torah, but administered on rabbinical authority. This type of flogging is generally applied where the infracted *mitzvah* is *d'Rabbanon*—i.e., of Rabbinic origin, as opposed to Torah-mandated. The phrasing Rambam uses here is striking, in that, of the 134 times he employs the term "*makat mardut*" in his *Mishneh Torah*, only in one other case does he say, **"It would be proper to administer *makat mardut*."** The other 132 times, Rambam says, **"And we *hit* them with *makat mardut*."** Given the Rambam's reputation for deliberate and meticulous wording, this exceptional phrasing cannot be regarded as haphazard. As mentioned above, it seems to mean that lesbianism was not ordinarily subject to this punishment, though, as Rambam suggests, it ought to be.

This is confirmed by Rambam's comments on the *Mishnah* (*Sanhedrin* 7:4), written when he was much younger:

And likewise, that ugly act that occurs among women as well, bringing a woman upon another woman, it is a *to'eivah*, but there is no punishment for it, neither from the Torah nor from the Rabbis.

Thus, it appears that, while it would be proper to punish such women with *makat mardut*—because "they performed a transgression,"[7] punishment was not actually carried out, since there was no precedent for doing so. Rambam does not give us the reason for this anomaly, but we can speculate that since such women were still permitted to their husbands—even to a *cohen*—the Jewish Courts were careful to avoid jeopardizing a marriage that might still be viable.[8]

In summary, the sources we have examined show that although lesbianism is prohibited by the Torah, it is not—according to the majority and most authoritative view—punishable either by the Torah or by the rabbis. In fact, as the Rambam makes clear, the lesbian is

---

7. Although Rambam uses the term *to'eivah* in this early comment to *Sanhedrin* 7:4, he avoids that term in his discussion of lesbianism in the *Mishneh Torah*—the work of his maturity. The reason might be that Rambam eventually came around to the view that when the Torah calls the practices of Egypt and Canaan *to'eivos*. (Lev. 18:24-30), it is referring exclusively to the *specific* prohibitions listed in Lev. 18.

8. *See,* for example, what Rambam says in regard to a man who secludes himself with a woman who is forbidden to him: "An exception is made with regard to a married woman. Although it is forbidden to enter into privacy with her, if one does enter into privacy with her, lashes are not administered lest a rumor be initiated that she committed adultery, *etc.*" (*Mishneh Torah,* Laws of Prohibited Sexual Relations, 22:3)

not even deprived of her marital status:

> **A woman would not be prohibited to her husband on account of [her having been *mesolel*], as this does not fall within the [technical category of] z'*nut*.**

In other words, since this is not *z'nut*, the woman is permitted to her husband, even if he is a *cohen!*.

So now we must ask, if it can't be punished, is it really prohibited, and, if so, to what degree?

(2) Does Absence of Punishment Mitigate the Offense? (How Prohibited is it?)

The Torah way is founded on the acceptance of G–d as the absolute Sovereign and Judge. To a genuinely pious Jew, the judgment of Heaven is something as real as the judgment of an earthly tribunal. The same is true of punishment. Sometimes earthly punishment—however justly deserved—cannot be administered without causing or risking an injustice. In such a case, Torah (the Oral Tradition) withholds punishment. We saw, for example (pp. 249-50, above) that in the case of *lav miyuchad*, the Law will not have someone whipped for transgressing a prohibition that is not expressly set forth in the Torah. Similarly, in the case of a married woman secluding herself with a man not her husband, the rabbis declined to administer *makat mardut* lest that should foster rumors that the lady had committed adultery.[9]

This is not to say that we always understand the reasons why punishment would be unjust. Nor does it mean that the transgressor will not ultimately receive her due. Indeed, our Tradition teaches that when the *Beis Din* is unable to punish a transgressor, the matter goes before the Heavenly Tribunal. Thus, in some instances, it is Heaven that will administer the punishment, not humankind. What this means

---

9. See Note 8, above, p. 251.

in terms of the present discussion is that the ability or the authority of the *Beis Din* to mete out a punishment is not necessarily an indicator of the seriousness of the transgression.[10] The following two examples may illustrate:

(1) Suppose someone goes into a stationery store, takes a pencil off the rack, and snaps it in two. He has committed a transgression judicable in a *Beis Din* and will be compelled to pay a certain amount—say 25 cents—to the owner of the store.

(2) Now suppose the same man spreads a false rumor about the same store owner, causing him to lose not just a single pencil, but his reputation, the love of his family, and his business? The degree of damage is much greater than the loss of a pencil. Yet, a *Beis Din* might very well be powerless to order him to pay even a single penny.

---

10. If this be so, why must we view the death penalty mandated for homosexuality as an indicator of the severity of the transgression? The answer is that whether a *Beis Din* has the authority or not to impose a punishment may be a technical or practical matter (Does the *Beis Din* have jurisdiction over the transgression? Do the witnesses qualify? Was there proper warning? Is the prohibition express or implied? *Etc.*); whereas a punishment mandated by G–d Himself is by definition scaled to an absolute measure of justice and morality. *See* Chapter Five, pp. 162-64.

How could this be? The reason is technical, turning on whether the misdeed involves *direct causation,* which is actionable in a Jewish court, or *indirect causation,* which is not actionable. Moreover, while breaking a pencil is considered an *action,* speech, *per se,* is *not* considered an action, and therefore cannot be the basis of a proceeding in a Jewish court.

Do these technicalities barring a remedy for defamation mean that Jewish law does not prohibit defamation? Or that destroying someone's reputation is morally less objectionable than breaking someone's pencil? Of course not! As a matter of fact, defamation of character is considered one of the greatest sins in Jewish Law, one from which it is almost impossible to do *teshuvah* ("repentance"). It's just that Jewish law places certain precautionary limitations on the *Beis Din's* power to act. This does not mean that the perpetrator will never have to answer for his misdeed, or that the victim will never be compensated: it simply means that the matter will be handled by a Heavenly court instead of an earthly one.

The same is true for lesbianism. We cannot conclude from the absence of punishment that this practice is not "really" prohibited, or that it was meant to be tolerated, or that the offense is not severe.

Z'nut is not a Shibboleth!

In addition to the foregoing, the fact that the lesbian is not classified as a *zonah* is also not to be taken as a mitigating factor. Consider, further, that a woman who engaged in sexual relations with an animal would also not be considered a *zonah*: the transgression does not fit the legal parameters of *z'nut.* Accordingly, such a woman would not be disqualified from marrying a *cohen.* Moreover, it is possible for a woman to acquire the status of a *zonah* through no fault of her own. The reasons are technical, and beyond the scope of this discussion. Suffice it to say that whether or not a particular transgression is categorized as *z'nut* has no bearing on the severity of the offense. *Z'nut* is simply not a moral shibboleth, and its presence or absence is not some magical barometer of morality or immorality.

Pro-Gay *Halachic* Sophistry.

In our personal view, the primary sources we have just examined express unequivocal condemnation of female homosexual behavior. Moreover, traditional-minded Jews (and not just the Orthodox) are virtually unanimous in the belief that female homosexuality is strictly forbidden by Jewish Law.[11]

However, in deference to the vigorous efforts from other quarters to present a radically different conclusion, I propose that we now examine a treatment of this subject that has been widely circulated and is frequently cited for the proposition that lesbianism is *halachically* acceptable. Dr. Reena Zeidman, Professor of Jewish Studies at Queens University in Kingston, Ontario writes that her survey of the primary sources (the very sources we have just examined) led her to "two major conclusions." Her first conclusion is that "lesbianism is nowhere explicitly prohibited." Zeidman's second conclusion is a bit more complicated and needs to be quoted in full. "Lesbianism," writes Dr. Zeidman,

> is solely addressed with respect to issues of marriage, and whether it should be considered harlotry with respect to marriage to priests, and within the traditional marriage relationship. At issue is the wife's mark of independence from her husband and the effect this has on family life. Even *Sifra,* in the passage quoted above, refers to women 'marrying' other women—not women having relationships

---

11. *See* for example, Rabbi J. David Bleich, "Lesbianism is included in the Biblical admonition against participation in the deviant sexual practices associated with the Egyptians and Canaanites of antiquity, but it is not a capital offense." Rabbi J. David Bleich, *Judaism and Healing: Halakhic Perspective*, New York: Ktav Publishing House, Inc. (1981), p. 69; Rabbi Basil Herring, *Jewish Ethics and Halakhah for Our Time*, New York: Ktav Publishing House, Inc. (1984), p. 184; Rabbi Maurice Lamm, *The Jewish Way in Love and Marriage*, Middle Village: Jonathan David Publishers, Inc. (1980), p. 67; Rabbi Chaim Rapoport, *Judaism and Homosexuality*, London: Vallentine Mitchell (2004), p. 105: "[L]esbian sex remains forbidden and whatever the severity involved—as a negative commandment—must be avoided in all circumstances . . . ."

with others outside the boundaries of the archetypal family. Bonding between women, sexual or otherwise, is not addressed.[12]

If the author of those words is correct, then it would seem that we have totally misread our texts. Let us examine Dr. Zeidman's arguments, starting with her interpretation of Rambam in *Mishneh Torah*, "Sexual Prohibitions," 21:8.

Maimonides posits, as no talmudic text or commentary does, that the force of lesbianism is crouching at the door, ready to snare one's spouse.

This sentence appears to have been inspired by Rambam's statement that

A man should be strict with his wife in regards to this matter and bar women known to engage in this practice from visiting her. And, he should prevent [his wife] from visiting them.

Apparently, Zeidman feels that everything Rambam says in this section was motivated by the husband's fear of losing his wife to another woman. Would Zeidman feel the same way, one wonders, about a husband protecting his wife from predatory men? In any case, Dr. Zeidman's assumption about Rambam is pure speculation, and the evidence she offers to support it is a gross misreading of the texts:

Bavli [the Babylonian Talmud] *Yevamot* classifies lesbianism as *prizut*—literally, "breaking out" or "going out." Maimonides thus seems to draw on the *Bavli* and extrapolate that the spouses in question are going out to meet, or conduct liaisons with, lesbians. But as to the identification of these latter women—their marital status, age, relationships—we do not know. All we can posit is that

---

12. Dr. Reena Zeidman, "Marginal Discourse: Lesbianism in Jewish Law," *Women in Judaism: A Multidisciplinary Journal;* <http://www.utoronto.ca/wjudaism/journal/vol1n1/v1n1zeid.htm>.

the community is aware of this "danger" and must be on guard against it—not only, as we must realize, for matters of priestly lineage and status, but also and perhaps more importantly in Maimonides' view, to protect one's marriage.

It is true that *Yevamot* 76a classifies lesbianism as *p'ritzut* and, further, that *p'ritzut* could be translated literally as "breaking out," but Zeidman is going way out on a limb to suggest that Rambam reads *p'ritzut* as an allusion to the wife's leaving home to "go out to meet, or conduct liasons with, lesbians," or to the wife's "breaking away from her husband." As we explained before, *p'ritzut* means "lewdness" or "licentiousness"—"breaking out" of the *boundaries of moral law*. Nowhere in the entire rabbinical literature does it mean anything else! As we might expect, no proof is adduced for Zeidman's startling new theory: her interpretation is purely conclusory—and, as we have just seen, based on a serious misreading of the Talmudic text.

How does Dr. Zeidman support her radical, new proposal? Let Dr. Zeidman answer that question herself:

> This last suggestion [namely, that Maimonides understands *p'ritzut* as a "breaking away" from home and husband] is supported by Maimonides' claim that the spouse in question is to be flogged for disobedience (*mardut*); that is, that she is considered a rebellious wife, a *moredet*. Rambam here employs the technical term for sexual rebellion in a marriage.

In the first place, Dr. Zeidman's statement that according to the Rambam the "spouse in question is to be flogged for disobedience" is completely specious. The *halachah* here is directed at "women who are *mesolelot* [*i.e.*, who practice lesbianism] with one another"—not just at married women![13] Second, as we have seen, Rambam never

---

13. Remember that the *activity* involves a female engaging in non-permitted erotic behavior that does not include male penetration. Nowhere does Rambam say that a person engaging such activity deserves to be punished for being a *moredet*, a "rebellious wife." Moreover, as the Rambam himself expressly states, the *Sifra* to which he referred is talking about *marriage Egyptian style*—"the practice of Egypt

says that they are "to be flogged!" On the contrary, Rambam says very emphatically that "*it would be proper* to flog them"—implying that they are *not* to be flogged!

More to the point, while it is true that *moredet* and *mardut* are philologically cognate, they mean two entirely different things. As we have seen, *makat mardut* is a rabbinically prescribed punishment for "rebelling" against a rabbinic decree. The "rebellion" is against Rabbinic Law, not against one's husband! The proof is that *makat mardut* may be given, for example, to someone who ate an egg from a non-kosher bird, or who harassed an emissary of the *Beis Din;* but nowhere is *makat mardut* prescribed for rebellious wives! Is Dr. Zeidman suggesting that a woman who eats a non-kosher egg is to be punished for a sexual offense (against her husband, no less)?[14]

Proceeding with her analysis, Dr. Zeidman pursues her methodology of misconstruing the primary texts to support her thesis. Dr. Zeidman informs us that the *Tur* adds a novel piece of information:

> Jacob ben Asher [author of the *Tur*] introduces one piece of information novel to him: "The woman is not prohibited to her husband sexually but is considered as if she is in a state of menstrual impurity." Unfortunately, commentary is silent on this particular

---

about which we were warned," and not "kosher" Jewish marriage. Finally, there is no limitation to married women in the key sentence of the Rambam: "However, it would be proper to give *them* [such women] *makat mardut*, since *they* have performed a forbidden act." (Emphasis added).

14. If Zeidman were correct, then *makat mardut* could only be meted out to a married woman—a premise which is plainly false: *see, e.g.,* Rambam, *Mishneh Torah,* Laws of Illicit Relations, Chapter 22, *Halacha* 3, prescribing *makat mardut* for a man who secludes himself with a woman who is forbidden to him. Must we then classify such a man as a "rebellious wife?" An even more devastating counter-point against Dr. Zeidman's thesis is the fact that wives who are legally deemed to be "rebellious wives" (a technical term) do *not* receive *makat mardut*. There are over 130 places in the *Mishneh Torah* where Rambam prescribes *makat mardut*. But nowhere does the Rambam prescribe *makat mardut* for a *moredet*, a "rebellious wife!"

innovation, but the *Tur* suggests that her sexual acts place her in a state of impurity analogous to her monthly cycles—she is to be distanced from her husband and then readmitted to his life after, we can assume, twelve days.

Were this true, it certainly would be quite novel! Not only does the *Tur* not say what Dr. Zeidman attributes to him, but no one else does either. (That should explain why "commentary is silent.") What happened here is that Dr. Zeidman has confused *lindotah* (from the root word *"nidui,"* a form of social ostracism) with *"niddah,"* which means "in a state of menstrual impurity." Let us recall what we wrote earlier in this chapter, when we summarized the very same passage from the *Tur* that Dr. Zeidman purports to translate (*see above,* pp. 248-9):

> [T]he woman who engages in such practices "receives *lindotah.*" That phrase translates as, "She receives a writ of social ostracization."

The literal meaning of *lindotah* is "to ostracize her." The term refers to a legal sanction directed against the errant woman in order to get her to conform to community standards. It has absolutely nothing to do with her state of ritual purity or impurity, or whether her husband is permitted to have relations with her or not. In fact, under Jewish law, assuming that she is not *niddah*, her husband remains *obligated* to engage in sexual relations with her notwithstanding the fact that she is under a decree of social ostracism!

The extent of Dr. Zeidman's error can be surmised from another passage of the *Tur* (*Evan HaEzer,* 187):

> Outside of the Land of Israel, the court is not empowered to collect fines. However, lest the sinner get off scot-free, and lest the Jewish People become careless about causing damage to others, the later rabbis are obliged *lindoto* [masculine form of *lindotah*] until he reaches a monetary settlement with the one he had damaged.

Let the reader be the judge: does the *Tur* mean here that the errant gentleman is to be turned into a menstruant woman, or does it mean that he is to be subjected to a decree of social ostracism?

Armed with her new misreading, Dr. Zeidman seeks to reinforce her original hypothesis: It all comes down to the Rabbis getting together to chastise a wife for daring to "break away" from her husband's control. She is to be punished by being treated as though she were *niddah*—in a state of menstrual impurity![15]

Although Dr. Zeidman has once again wildly misunderstood a basic term of Rabbinic Hebrew, she uses her "novel" interpretation as a basis for offering a proposal that bears absolutely no relationship to what the *Tur* was saying:

> It may be proposed that the *Tur* wants to place the transgression as some sort of ontological act, one that is involuntary [*i.e.*, like menstruation], but can be resolved through placing the wife in a position where she is aware of her error.

Evidently, Dr. Zeidman would like to garner support for the idea that lesbianism is "natural," and that even Jewish Law, which, in Zeidman's view, penalizes a woman for the "ontological" [sic] and "involuntary act" of menstruation, considers the woman's same-sex activity as no worse than her monthly cycle. Indeed, in her conclusion, Dr. Zeidman criticizes what she perceives as the "fictional ideal of the nuclear family, which belies the fluidity and variability of actual family structures," as well as the "inordinate amount of privilege and legal support" for the traditional household. Moreover, she encourages the further questioning of long-standing assumptions that place lesbianism outside Jewish tradition. "The point of such questioning," she adds, with no doubt unintended irony, "is that it would allow scope within the traditional texts for new readings."

---

15. For an explanation of *niddah*, *see* Chapter 6, pp.205-6.

At this point, it might be amusing to summarize Dr. Zeidman's thesis in light of what we can read between the lines:

> Rambam's personal sexual insecurities led him to misinterpret the Talmud's term (*p'ritzut*) for a harmless "escapade" or detour from contemporary social norms as rebellious behaviour threatening the repressive institution of marriage and the husband's control over his wife—hence his status within the male-dominant, female-oppressive community. Rambam therefore advocated punishing her behavior with the punishment known as "the flogging of the rebellious wife," so that the wife would return meekly to her natural condition of obedient and obliging servant to her husband. The *Tur*, however, notes that, while she remains permitted to her husband, the lesbian act she has committed confers upon her, in the eyes of the Rabbis, the status of a menstruant woman, requiring her to be quarantined from her husband for twelve days, after which she re-enters the state of ritual purity and her husband's bed—as the Rabbis are imagined to believe—a chastened and wiser woman. The fact that Jewish Law treats the lesbian as a menstruant underscores, notwithstanding its inherent male-chauvinism, its underlying recognition that lesbianism is a natural, "ontological act" [sic!] over which the woman has no control.

As we have just seen, Zeidman's thesis has no discernible relationship to the realities of textual interpretation or of Jewish Law. In fact, the errors that Dr. Zeidman has fallen into would be quite comical, were they not tragically typical of the many harmful misrepresentations of Torah and Judaism being disseminated through the internet, media and print, in the name of social progress, sexual liberation and political correctness.

Chapter 8:

Sexual Reassignment Surgery.

Sexual reassignment surgery ("SRS") commonly referred to as "sex change operation," involves the physical removal or alteration of the sex organs as well as hormone injections to alter secondary gender characteristics such as body hair, breast size, and voice timbre.[1] Many hundreds of sex-change operations are performed every year in the United States alone and thousands more worldwide. The subjects of these surgeries are men and women suffering from deeply ingrained gender-identity issues (gender

---

1. Radical surgical procedures on male-to-female transsexuals include removal of the penis and scrotum, bilateral orchiectomy (removal of the testicles), vaginoplasty (creation of artificial vagina), estrogen hormone injections, and perhaps a tracheal shave (reducing the tracheal cartilage commonly called the Adam's apple) and sometimes even pelvic reconstruction. Female-to-male surgery includes a radical mastectomy, a total hysterectomy (removal of the uterus and ovaries), testosterone injections, and in rare cases, an artificial construction of a penis (phalloplasty) or enlargement of the clitoris (metaidoioplasty). Phalloplasty merely creates an imitation penis that lacks sensitivity and will not become erect without a stiffening device. Metaidoioplasty allows the clitoris to extend further out, and it shapes the enlarged clitoris to look more like a small penis. The length of the metaidoioplasty-enlarged clitoris would still be insufficient for intercourse.

dysphoria) typically (but not always), involving SSA and/or homosexuality, and generally stemming from many of the same factors that contribute to SSA.

Tragically, instead of exploring the option of addressing their gender identity issues through psychotherapy, transsexuals, by and large, have chosen to march off to the SRS clinics to the drumbeat of "gender liberation" and all the cliché tunes and riffs of the gay propaganda machine: "Transsexuality is a natural variant of the human condition; we were born that way; nothing can be done psychologically to change us; *etc., etc.*" The pro-gay lobby has not been slow to expand its political base by taking up the cause of transsexual people and incorporating it in their own.

Neither has this coalition hesitated to induct small children into the transgender "lifestyle." For example, an organization called TransYouth Family Advocates, one of a broad variety of support groups that have sprung up to encourage children to "come out" as transsexual, claims that children as young as five years old have the ability to recognize their identity as transsexuals![2] Through the

---

2. "8-Year Old Boy Returning to Class as a Girl," *World Net Daily*, March 3, 2008, <http://www.worldnetdaily.com/index.php?pageId=55892>. This claim is belied by the many known cases attesting the contrary, including the following, provided by a clinical professor of pediatrics at the University of California, San Francisco to Dr. Michelle Cretella, Chair of the Sexuality Committee of the American College of Pediatricians. Influenced by the gay affirmative environment of San Francisco, and relying on a book (American Academy of Pediatrics, *Caring for Your School Age Child: Ages 5-12: the Complete and Authoritative Guide,* (Edward L. Schor, ed.), Elk Grove Village: Bantam Dell Pub. Group, 1999), which claimed "[B]efore their third birthday they are easily able to label themselves as either boy or girl as they acquire a strong sense of self. By age 4, children's gender identity is stable, and they know they will always be a boy or a girl.," the parents of a 5-year-old boy who exhibited all-around effeminate behavior (including dressing as a girl, adorning his hair with barrettes and bows, playing with dolls, preferring the company of girls rather than boys, *etc.*) and repeatedly demanded that his penis be cut off, sought advice on transitioning their son to the female sex. Fortunately, the MD they consulted was a member of the American College of Pediatricians (not to be confused with the prior-mentioned American Academy of Pediatrics!) who, agreeing with its views, began by systematically identifying

usual methods of disinformation and intimidation, schools have been compelled to accommodate such "self-identifying" children by providing unisex bathrooms, allocating public funds for "transsexual education," and instituting commemorative celebrations such as "Transgender Days of Remembrance."[3]

As usual when it comes to political correctness, the broadcast and print media have lent this parade the full weight of their sympathetic coverage, and often their wholehearted support. On her April 23, 2007 show, Barbara Walters interviewed a six-year old boy who at age five had "come out" as a girl with the full support of his parents. On August 31, 2004, Oprah Winfrey highlighted an eleven-year-old desiring to change gender.[4]

---

the environmental and medical factors that could have caused the child's condition. Upon examination, the child was discovered to be suffering from phimosis, a painful condition preventing retraction of the foreskin. After successfully treating the phimosis, the physician referred the family to a child behavorial psychologist who recommended that the father cut off his long pony tail, spend more bonding time with the boy, and that both parents avoid primping the boy's two-year-old baby sister in the boy's presence. The therapist also prescribed play therapy, using power rangers, superheroes, trucks, and other masculine toys. In less than 6 months, the boy showed increased comfort with traditional masculine activities and identified more closely with Dad. Subsequent follow up found the boy playing with other boys, rejecting female dress and behavior, and generally following the normal psychosocial growth patterns of a boy. There is no question that if this child had been brought to a gay-affirmative physician, he or she would have diagnosed him as "an anatomically born boy who self-identified with the feminine gender," because of his "continuous and consistent behavior pattern," and thus would have qualified either for sexual reassignment or an appearance on a Barbara Walters Special.

3. One example: when an eight-year-old boy in Colorado sought to return to class as a girl, the school district used taxpayer resources to "educate" students and parents about transgenderism. *World Net Daily,* Feb. 8, 2008.

4. It boggles the mind how supposedly intelligent and educated people can seriously entertain the idea that a pre-pubescent or pubescent child can have the either the capacity or the maturity to make such a life-altering choice! On that score, recent studies with magnetic resonance imaging (MRI) by investigators at

Transgendered individuals have even appeared on a network TV show as competitors for "top transgender model." Similarly, the "human-interest" pages of the newspapers and news weeklies are full of articles designed to create sympathy for this little understood category. One example: the *New York Times Magazine* (March 16, 2008, p. 37) featured an article about a lesbian from Chappaqua (Westchester County, NY), who, with the encouragement of her girlfriend, decided to have "top surgery" done during her freshman year in college. The article concluded with her statement, "I want to be accepted as a transman—my brain is not gendered. There's this crazy gender binary that's built into all of life, that there are just two genders that are acceptable. I don't want to have to fit into that."

The trend has even given rise to a new support literature, not unlike that catering to purportedly "gay" or "lesbian" boys and girls. Books with titles such as "Mom, I Need to be a Girl," by Just Evelyn, "Finding the Real Me," edited by Tracie O'Keefe and Katrina Fox, and "Made in [G–d]'s Image," by Ann Thompson Cook and the Dumbarton United Methodist Church, are just a few examples of the new literature available to help guide "transsexual children" and their well-intentioned parents through the complex process of transition.

A whole new terminology has arisen to denote the child victims of this mentality: "gender variant," "gender queer," "gender non-conforming," "gender-fluid," "omni-sexual," and

---

the National Institute of Mental Health, UCLA's Laboratory of Neuro Imaging, and Boston's McLean Hospital, show that the critical areas of the brain (the frontal lobes and the amygdala) related respectively to goal-oriented rational thinking and the ability to distinguish among the emotions, are not fully developed until the mid-to-late twenties. *See, e.g.,* J. Giedd, J. Blumenthal, N. Jeffries, F. Castellanos, H. Liu, A. Zijdenbos, T. Paus, A. Evans, and J. Rapoport, "Brain Development During Childhood and Adolescence: A Longitudinal MRI Study,*" Nature Neuroscience,* Vol 2, No. 10, (1999), pp. 861-63; D. Yurgelun-Todd, "Inside the Teen Brain," *Frontline Interview* (2002), <http//www.pbs.org/wgbh/pages/frontline/shows/teenbrain/interviews/todd.html >; and Elizabeth Williamson, "Brain Immaturity Could Explain Teen Crash Rate," *Washington Post*, Feb. 1, 2005, p. A1.

"cross-gender." There can be no doubt that transsexuality, with the surgical, hormonal and psychological treatments that it entails, has become a "culturally driven" phenomenon (as one disillusioned transsexual phrased it), that promotes the sex-change industry[5]

---

5. With an entire infrastructure consisting of clinics, clinical support staff, surgeons, endocrinologists, pharmacists, psychiatrists, psychologists, social workers, *etc.,* a new, booming "industry" has developed in various countries around the world. Perhaps foremost among them is Thailand, which offers various "medical tourism" packages attractively priced for SRS customers. *See, e.g.,* Margie Mason, "Thailand's sex-change Industry," *Seattle Times,* Sept. 3, 2006; and "A Thai Junket for a Sex Change," http://www.healthmedicaltourism.org/Blogs/The_Shabana_Medical_and_Dental _Tourism. . .>. *See also,* "Thais to Perform First Live Sex Change Operation," <http://www.chinadaily.com.cn/english/doc/2004-12/10/content_399282.htm>. In the United States, Trinidad, Colorado has become the "sex change capital of the world." James Brooke, "Sex-Change Industry a Boon to Small City," *New York Times,* November 8, 1998.

The profit potential is obviously enormous. The windfall for the insurance industry is less obvious. According to Marcus Arana, a San Francisco Human Rights Commissioner, through 2005 that city collected $5.6 million in increased premiums from city employees to cover the benefit, but paid just $183,000 on 11 claims for different surgeries over the same period. With eleven campuses and a combined student body of nearly 200,000, and over 100,000 faculty/staff employees, the University of California provides sexual reassignment coverage through their Kaiser Permanente health plan. Not surprisingly, HealthNet of California has publicly stated its willingness to provide such coverage to the employees of any private company or municipality that requests it. Many U.S. corporate employers—including Ford, General Motors, Microsoft, Bank of America, Wachovia, Goldman Sachs—now provide complete or partial sex change benefits with their health plans. We suggest that "altruism" (however misguided) is not the only factor involved. Where national health plans—such as those of Brazil, Canada, Denmark, Germany, and Holland—provide SR coverage, the wallet is clearly the taxpayer's. Even U.S. taxpayers—who as yet have no nationally or state-funded universal healthcare—pay for others' sex change procedures through various Medicaid programs, and, in some states, prisoner health plans. *See, e.g.,* Chris Bull, "Benefit of Transition: San Francisco, California, to Offer Employees Sex-change Benefits," *The Advocate,* June 5, 2001; John Ireland, "He Shoots, She Scores," *In These Times* (June 27, 2007), <http://www.inthesetimes.com/article/continued/3232/ he_shoots_she_ scores/>, p. 2; Andrew Ross Sorkin, "Another Goldman Perk: Sex Changes," *Deal Book* (Feb. 8, 2008), <http://dealbook.blogs.nytimes.com/ 2008/02/08/

because the culture permits it, does all it can to accommodate its human byproducts—defenseless children included—and indeed "glorifies" it in the media, with virtually no public discussion of its moral, ethical, or religious implications.

Does Jewish law Permit SRS?

Surgical procedures involving removal of the testes are expressly forbidden by Torah law:

> *You shall not offer to the L–rd that which has its testicles bruised or crushed, or broken, or cut. Neither shall you do this in your land.* (Leviticus 22:24)

According to the Sages of the Talmud, this verse does not just refer to the animal sacrifices; it prohibits the emasculation of both animals and humans.

The Talmud (*Shabbos* 110b) clarifies the meaning of the clause:

Neither shall you do this in your land

as: "neither shall you do this [*i.e.*, castration] to yourselves."[6]

The Sages dispute whether this particular prohibition (Lev. 22:24) applies to women as well as men but the *halachah* (*i.e.,* Jewish Law) is clear: women are included in the prohibition. Both are forbidden to engage in attempts to change gender.[7] Thus, the

---

another-goldman-perk-sex-changes/>; http://money.cnn.com/2008/ 02/08/news/ companies/gender.fortune/ index.htm>, *etc.*

6. *See* Rambam, *Mishneh Torah, Hilchos Issurei Bi'ah* 16:10, and *Sefer haMitzvos (Negative),* No. 361.

7. Rambam says only: "A person who castrates a female, whether a human or other species, is not [subject to punishment]." However, the *halachah* takes this to mean that, though female castration is prohibited, lashes are not given,

Shulchan Aruch (*Even HaEzer* 5:11) states:

> It is forbidden to destroy the procreative organs of a human, animal, or bird....

Regarding human castration, Deuteronomy 23:2 provides a severe additional sanction:

> *He that is crushed or maimed in his privy shall not enter the Assembly of G–d.* [8]

Shall not enter the Assembly of G–d is understood as prohibiting a man who is thus maimed from marrying a Jewish woman.[9]

Moreover, as we saw previously in Chapter 6, Deuteronomy 22:5 prohibits males and females from wearing jewelry, clothing, and accessories commonly associated with the opposite sex. If merely wearing a garment associated with the other sex is forbidden, it would seem to follow all the more that making physical changes (whether by chemical or surgical means) to one's body in order to "pass" as a member of the opposite sex is

---

because the prohibition is not expressly stated in the Torah in regard to women (*lav miyuchad*). *See* Chapter Seven, *above*, pp. 249-50.

8. The King James Version lists this particular prohibition as Deuteronomy 23:1 and translates it: "He that is wounded in the stones, or hath his privy member cut off, shall not enter into the congregation of the Lord." According to the Catholic Church, "[P]ersons who claim to have had their sex changed may not marry or be ordained." John Norton, "Vatican Says 'Sex-Change Operation' Does Not Change a Person's Gender," *Catholic News Service,* Jan. 14, 2003, *cited in* Dr. Richard P. Fitzgibbons, "The Desire for a Sex Change: Psychiatrist Says Sex-Change Surgery is a Collaboration with a Mental Disorder, not a Treatment," <http://www.narth.com/docs/desiresch.html>.

9. Maimonides, *Mishneh Torah, Kedushah, Hilchot Issurei Bi'ah,* 16:1. One who is maimed in the privies may marry a convert to Judaism, or a freed maidservant.

prohibited as well.[10] In other words, any attempt to develop physical attributes typically associated with the opposite sex is forbidden.

Owing to the nature of cross-gender behavior, this prohibition is violated every time the activity is initiated, and for as long as it continues. For example, SRS candidates are typically required to spend a year or two "training" for their prospective role as a member of the opposite sex, by cross dressing, taking hormones, and practicing the appropriate gestures and mannerisms. Thus, each time the candidate does any of these things constitutes a violation of Deuteronomy 22:5, and the violation is continuous.

Attempts to Circumvent the *Halachah*.

Rambam explains (*Sefer HaMitzvos, (Negative)*, Nos. 39 and 40) that the very reason for this prohibition is to prevent a man or woman from mingling surreptitiously with the opposite sex. Thus, one might be tempted to think that the obstacle of Deuteronomy 22:5 would disappear if it were shown that SRS really does change the subject's gender: if "James" has really become "Jan," then (so goes the reasoning), it is neither scandalous nor sinful for Jan to mingle with other women. *Note well:* the *halachah* rejects this argument: "Deuteronomy 22:5 is not limited to the wearing of apparel . . . but encompasses *any action* uniquely identified with the opposite sex...." (emphasis added). For example, a man is prohibited from dying his hair—a practice typically associated with women—even though it is not something that a man does to pass himself off as a woman. (Bleich, 100) Accordingly, "A procedure designed to transform sexual characteristics violates the very essence of this prohibition." (100)

---

10. Such is the opinion of Rabbi Meir Amsel, *Ha-Ma'or,* Kislev-Tevet 5733. *See* Rabbi Dr. J. David Bleich, *Contemporary Halakhic Problems,* Vol. 1, New York & Hoboken: Ktav (1977), p. 100.

For that reason, those who advocate sex-change surgery seek a way around the prohibition against sexual mutilation (Lev. 22:24) on grounds of medical necessity. Indeed, Jewish Law recognizes that certain prohibitions, under certain circumstances, may be subordinated to preserving the life, health and well-being of a patient. For example, surgical removal of cancerous testicles or ovaries, in the appropriate context, would clearly fall under the medical exception; but whether the same exception applies to SRS is a more intricate question. However, to get to that question, it is first necessary to cross the threshold inquiry: does SRS actually accomplish the desired gender change?

How Effective *is* SRS? Does SRS Accomplish its Intended Purpose?

These threshold questions are of paramount importance in relation to Jewish Law and medical ethics. If the subject is a Jew, and his or her underlying gender remains unaffected by the procedure, then the subject will be committing a grave *aveirah* (sin) every time he/she dresses as, mingles with, "has sex" with, or marries, a member of the "opposite" sex. Further, since Jewish Law assigns different *mitzvos* and different ways of observing *mitzvos*, to men and to women, gender must be unambiguously established before the subject can know which religious obligations apply. For example, what are his/her obligations with respect to, *e.g.*, *davening* (*i.e.*, "praying") with a *minyan* (quorum for daily prayers), *davening* at set times, studying Torah, resolving where to sit in *shul, etc.* And, in the case of a female-to-male transsexual, how do we handle the matter of circumcision? As long as the gender of the subject remains *halachically* in doubt, the subject would appear to be relegated to a "no-man's land" in which proper Torah observance is nugatory.[11]

More generally, if the procedure is not fully effective, the subject, whether Jewish or non-Jewish, may be left in a social "no-

---

11. *See* discussion in Bleich, pp. 104-5.

man's land" in which he/she finds him-/herself excluded from and rejected by both sexes.[12]

Finally, in evaluating the effectiveness of SRS, account must also be taken of the potential harm that could stem from the operation and subsequent treatments. The risks must be weighed against any perceived benefit. Moreover, if an alternative remedy for gender dysphoria exists that is more effective and less dangerous than surgery, then even a secular, pragmatic approach (let alone a religious one) would seem to dictate discarding SRS as a viable option.

Jewish Tradition Rejects the Claim that SRS can Transform a Man into a Woman or a Woman into a Man.

While surgery on the genitals, chest and face can alter one's external appearance, it can not deliver genuine anatomical structures of the opposite sex. Nor can it provide bona-fide sexual functioning of either sex. In fact, sex-change surgery eliminates major aspects of normal sexual functioning and eradicates any possibility of reproduction. Thus, from a functional point of view, "sex-change" surgery does not really change sex. As Rabbi Bleich (103) observes, "There is at least one early source which apparently declares that a male cannot acquire the status of a woman by means of surgery." Indeed, Ibn Ezra, in his commentary on Leviticus 18:22 (the Holiness Code), quotes Rabbeinu Chananel, who declares that "intercourse between a normal male and a male in whom an artificial vagina has been fashioned by

---

12. For a glimpse into the surrealist possibilities of gender confusion, *see* "A Lesbian Group which Refused a Transgender Doctor Entry to an Event Says her Attendance Would have had an Impact on the 'Intimacy' of the Meeting," *Adelaide Now,* October 4, 2007, <http://www.news.com.au/adelaidenow/story/0,22606,22527404-2682,00.html>. The doctor, a Sydney-based, male-to-female transgender psychotherapist involved in a long-time lesbian (*sic!*) relationship, sought admission to a lesbian seminar. Denied entry, he/she brought an action for discrimination before the Equal Opportunity Tribunal!

means of surgery constitutes sodomy. This would appear to be the case, according to Rabbeinu Chananel, even if the male genitalia were removed." (Bleich, 103)[13]

Much has been made, in the GLBT ("gay-lesbian-bisexual-transsexual") and so-called progressive camps (including, most recently, the Committee on Jewish Law and Standards of the [Conservative] Rabbinical Assembly) of two *halachic* decisions that appear on the surface to contradict Rabbeinu Chananel's view. To follow the argument, it is necessary to understand that normally Jewish Law requires that an estranged spouse must obtain a *get* (divorce, or bill of divorcement) in order to remarry.

In the earlier of these decisions, Rabbi Yosef Pelaggi (19th century) concluded—partly on the basis of the traditional formulaic language of the *get*—that a *get* would *not* be necessary to dissolve a marriage contracted prior to "an occurrence" in which the wife acquired the sexual characteristics of a male *"in every way" ("bakol, mikol, kol"*), and became *"a complete man" (ish g'mur veshalem)*. In other words, assuming that "something happens" which *effectively* changes the wife into a man, it is unnecessary to petition for divorce in order to dissolve a marriage contracted prior to the "happening."

In the later decision, Rabbi Eliezer Waldenberg, the eminent *Dayan* (rabbinic judge) known as "the Tzitz Eliezer," considering a male-to-female transition (*Tzitz Eliezer* X, No. 25, ch. 26, Sec. 6, and XI, No. 78), concluded that a *get* would not be necessary in order to permit a woman to marry another man, where her former husband "has become a woman (as in a famous [SRS] case that occurred in Europe two years ago)."

Note that both these rulings *assume a priori* (*i.e.,* without any evidentiary inquiry) that a change of gender (from female to male, and from male to female, respectively) has actually taken place. Indeed, Rabbi Pelaggi *posited* a case in which the woman, "in every way," turned into "a complete man." Similarly, The Tzitz

---

13. For a detailed analysis of this view, *see* Bleich, 103, note 10.

Eliezer *assumed* that in a certain "famous" case of sex-change surgery, the man *really did* "become a woman."[14] The implication that the pro-SRSers would like to draw from these decisions is that, as far as *halachah* is concerned, SRS effectively changes the gender status of the patient. This is exactly what the Conservative Jewish Law and Standards Committee attempted to do in their 2003 *Responsum.* To squeeze from Rabbi Pelaggi's and Rabbi Waldenberg's rulings—which were clearly limited by their own assumptions—a *general principle* that "Therefore sex change does change the sex status of the person,"[15] is frankly ridiculous. Hello? Wasn't that the *premise* of Rabbi Pelaggi's hypothetical? Wasn't that the *assumption* of Rabbi Waldenberg? By what chariot and horses of fire did these *assumptions* become transformed into a *conclusion*? Through what contortions did a hypothetical premise turn into a finding of fact? This is Houdini logic!

It seems to me particularly significant that in explaining the rationale of his ruling, Rabbi Waldenberg, the *Tzitz Eliezer,* cites the example of *Terumat haDeshen,* No. 102, which asks whether the wife of the Prophet Elijah would be permitted to remarry.[16] Elijah, as is known from 2 Kings 2:11, did not die, but ascended bodily into heaven. *Terumat haDeshen* rules that Elijah's wife could remarry. Clearly, this conclusion was not based on the supposition that Elijah was still alive, for if so, it would follow that his wife could NOT remarry. Nor was it based on the opposite supposition, for that would contradict what the Scripture tells us. The ruling was premised on the *fact* that Elijah was transformed into a *Malach* ("angel")—a state in which, *by definition,* he could

---

14. As Rabbi Bleich (103) observes, "Rabbi Waldenberg . . . cites no evidence whatsoever for this view."

15. "Status of Transsexuals," *Responsum,* Committee on Jewish Law and Standards of the Rabbinical Assembly (2003), p. 4.

16. Jewish Law requires that a man or woman who was previously married submit proof of a *get* or of the spouse's death in order to remarry.

not continue as a husband. The implication is that the *Tzitz's* ruling was based on the bald *fact* that the husband had been emasculated and was holding himself out to be a woman—not on the *assumption* that he had really and truly turned into a woman!

In any case, both Rabbi Pelaggi's and Rabbi Waldenberg's rulings were limited to a situation where a purported sex change has already occurred (as we have seen, attempting to bring about a sex-change, whether through surgery or other means, is *apriori* categorically forbidden!).[17] The narrow question under examination was whether the subject's spouse may remarry without a *get*.[18] Thus, the rulings of Rabbis Pelaggi and Waldenberg cannot be taken out of context and generalized into an overall *halachic* view of the efficacy of SRS. Indeed, subsequent authorities have taken the position that SRS can have no effect on one's legal gender.[19]

The Scientific View of Gender Determination: Does it Work for *Halachah*?

This view is supported by modern medical science. Indeed,

---

17. Even sex-change advocates will readily admit that this is so. As stated emphatically by noted SRS advocate Beth Orens, a self-styled "Orthodox trans woman:" "[T]he significance of [Rabbi Waldenberg's] responsa applies only to post-op transsexuals. There is no implication that actually undergoing hormone therapy and surgery are permissible." "Judaism and Gender Issues: the Responsa of the Tzitz Eliezer on Transsexuality," <http://members.tripod.com/~suelong/tzitz.html>.

18. There is also an analogy here to what in secular law would be called estoppel, suggesting that where a marriage is disrupted by SRS performed on one of the spouses, *halachah* will not suffer the transsexual spouse to invoke his/her marital status in order to prevent or hinder the remarriage of the forsaken spouse.

19. Rabbi Michael J. Broyde, "The Establishment of Maternity & Paternity in Jewish & American Law," Appendix, p. 5, note 287, *citing* F. Rosner & M. Tendler, *Practical Medical Halacha,* p. 44 (1980), in *Jewish Law Articles,* <http://www.jlaw.com/Articles/maternity_appendix.html>.

rejecting the view that how the SRS patient sees him- or herself subjectively can affect his or her legal status, one scholar argues compellingly that a person's chromosomes are the decisive factor in determining his or her sex.[20] A chromosome is a unit of gene-carrying material found in the nucleus of a cell. Every human cell contains 23 pairs of chromosomes, two of which are sex chromosomes. The sex chromosomes come in two varieties, called "X" and "Y." The egg of the female contains a pair of X chromosomes, and the sperm of the father contains an XY pair. When the chromosomes combine in the fertilized egg, they form a new pair of chromosomes, either XX (yielding a female zygote) or XY (yielding a male zygote). Thus, gender is genetically determined by the chromosomes. (To date, no surgical, chemical, or other method has been discovered by which to "change" the gender of an individual at the chromosomal level.)

On the other hand, recourse to gene testing may not always be practical or one-hundred-percent definitive. Genetic defects can sometimes (albeit rarely) interfere with normal development, giving rise to an "intersex" baby with both male and female characteristics, or, as we shall see below, with the chromosomes of one sex but the gonads or genitalia of the other. (Staver, 39). It seems reasonable that laboratory analysis should be reserved for those situations where ordinary means do not suffice.

Perhaps with that very consideration in mind,[21] the Rabbinical Assembly rejected the view that one's chromosomes should as a rule determine one's *halachic* gender, and concluded summarily that "[E]xternal [sex] organs determine the sexual status of a person."

---

20. Mathew Staver, "Transsexualism and the Binary Divide: Determining Sex Using Objective Criteria" (September 14, 2006) p. 38, *bepress Legal Series.* Working Paper 1756. <http://law.bepress.com/expresso/ eps/1756>.

21. The rationale invoked by the Committee of Law & Standards of the (Conservative) Rabbinical Assembly was the purported principle that "*Halakhah* has always been macroscopic and not microscopic." There is no such principle in *halachah.*

In reaching that decision, however, the Rabbinical Assembly's Committee of Law & Standards (hereinafter referred to as "the Committee) made it clear that by "external sex organs" the Committee was referring to the artificial organs created by surgery. Moreover, in invoking the Tzitz Eliezer as authority for their ruling ("The position of Rabbi Waldenberg on this issue best fits the *halakhic* system, and therefore is the acceptable one for us."), we believe that the Committee was being deliberately specious.

> The argument that is based on the statement of Rabbenu Hananel [*see above,* pp. 271-72], that sex change is naturally impossible, may have been true in his time. It certainly is possible today. His position could very well change if he saw the results of hormonal and surgical treatment. Therefore to base one's position on such grounds seems implausible. (*Responsum,* 9)

Clearly, neither Rabbi Chananel nor Rabbi Waldenberg ever considered the artificial and partially functional organs created by SRS. To base a *halachic* ruling on the pure speculation that a revered *posek* (*halachic* decisor) "could very well change his position" is not only specious but intellectually dishonest. All the more so in light of the highly questionable statement that "[sex change] certainly is possible today"—yet another assumption magically transformed into a conclusion by result-oriented "logic."

More Misplaced Reliance on a Fundamental Ruling.

We have already seen (*above,* pp. 272-74) by what twisted logic the Conservative movement concluded that SRS changes the *halachic* gender status of the patient. As we have shown, this proposition is not proven by the decisions cited as precedent by the Committee: their conclusion merely adopts, without any evidence, critique or analysis, *the hypothetical assumptions* on which those rulings were based.

The Committee chose to bolster its ruling with another opinion by Rabbi Waldenberg—this one a real case actually presented to him for his *halachic* consideration. The case concerned an intersex baby who, though genetically male, and devoid of internal sex organs, possessed a female vagina.[22] The vagina was normal in appearance, except for a lump imbedded in one of the labia that proved to be a testicle. Removal of the testicle would permit the child to develop as a girl, albeit sterile. The question before the *Posek* was whether surgery was *halachically* permitted, and if so, which gender should the surgery attempt to suppress?[23] In ruling that removal of the testicle was permissible, Rabbi Waldenberg stressed that "even if we were to do nothing and leave the child 'as is' the child would be considered a female. That is because the external genitalia that are visible are the ones that determine gender for *halakhah* . . . ."[24] (*Responsum,* 8)

Relying on this latter statement by the Tzitz Eliezer, the Conservative Law Committee chose to base "[its] position that

---

22. Intersex births in the United States are extremely rare. According to Mathew Staver (40), they account for less than two out every one hundred thousand (.0018%) of the population. *See* note 20 above.

23. The question of *halakhic* permissibility is not really distinguishable from that of the medical advisability of "surgically assigning femaleness to male newborns who at birth had malformed, sexually ambiguous genitalia and severe phallic defects." In a 2004 widely quoted article on surgical sex, Dr. Paul McHugh, psychiatrist in chief at the Johns Hopkins Hospital from 1975-2001, reports on a study by Dr. William G. Reiner (a member of his staff) which found that "such re-engineered males were almost never comfortable as females." Paul McHugh, "Surgical Sex," *First Things* (Nov. 2004), pp. 34-8, <http://www.firstthings.com/ftissues/ft0411/articles/mchugh.html> *See also New England Journal of Medicine* (Jan. 22, 2004). However, it is clear from Rabbi Waldenberg's *responsum* that the possibility of such negative consequences was as yet unreported, and that the Rabbi could not have considered them.

24. As will be shown in the text, we believe that Rabbi Waldenberg's language is entirely consistent with traditional *halachic* views on gender. Nevertheless, a number of Orthodox rabbis and medical professionals disagree with Rabbi Waldenberg's rule *as commonly interpreted,* characterizing it as a "dissenting view" or "minority position."

recognizes a change in sex status...on the concept that one's sex status is determined by the external genitalia"—adding that "This has been forcefully advocated by Rabbi Waldenberg." (9) In invoking the authority of Rabbi Waldenberg, however, the Committee neglected to consider that the Tzitz Eliezer was referring to the specified case of a person possessing *naturally formed* genitalia, and *not one whose genitalia had been surgically constructed.* Granting that Rabbi Waldenberg's "external and visible" principle is the *halachah,* the question still remains which "external genitalia" does the *halachah* look to when determining the sex status of an SRS patient? Should the *halachah* look to the natural, pre-op genitalia, or to the artificial ones constructed by the surgeon? The Committee never bothered to ask that essential question! Clearly, Rabbi Waldenberg's ruling was based on the *pre-op* status of the baby's genitalia, which were "similar to a female." There was no penis, only "in one of the lips of the vagina ... a lump shaped like a testicle." By what "surgical operation" did the Committee transmute that ruling into a precedent for classifying a male-to-female transsexual as a woman, or a female-to-male transsexual as a man?

For the Tzitz Eliezer, the primary question was whether the surgery would be permitted in the first place, given the prohibition of Leviticus 22:24. Thus, Rabbi Waldenberg stressed that the child was already sterile, and hence that the surgery would have no effect on its reproductive capacity. Yet the Committee failed to perceive any meaningful difference between operating on a sterile person for the ostensibly beneficial purpose of resolving a physical ambiguity in genitalia that were nonetheless obviously female, on the one hand, and, on the other, mutilating a sexually and reproductively functional person affected by a primarily mental (as opposed to physical) disorder!

How to Perform Reassignment Surgery on a Torah Prohibition: Analyzing the Conservative Law Committee's Approval of SRS.

As flawed as is the Law Committee's analysis of transsexual gender status, they did at least devote several pages to a discussion of the *halachic* sources. By contrast, virtually *no such discussion* is accorded to their treatment of the issue of *permissibility*. Indeed, the complex problem of getting around the prohibition of Leviticus 22:24 (... *neither shall you do this in your land*) is relegated to an "appendix" of less than a single page! In part, this may be due to the provisional nature of their decision.

> SRS can be justified on the following arguments which are based on treatment for a mental condition. However, for these arguments to be considered, reliable medical studies must verify that SRS is beneficial for people suffering from gender dysphoria.

Certainly, the Committee is to be congratulated for suggesting that, for them, whether SRS is beneficial is an open question; and also for declining to entertain claims of a genetic origin of transsexuality. Notwithstanding the caveat, however, the Law Committee seems quite content to dispose of the matter of permissibility with a few ambiguous and highly misleading pronouncements. Indeed, intoning the mantra of "the good of the patient," they claim that

> SRS is being done for the patient's betterment and health, and therefore would be permissible, just as it would be permissible to help treat a physical ailment. We have permitted other procedures for mental ailments and have said that the mental illness is to be treated in the same way as a physical one. Therefore SRS may be permissible and the prohibition against castration can be overridden in this case.

This is a remarkable example of kangaroo logic. By this argument, one could justify amputating a healthy leg in order to "cure" a person affected with apotemnophilia (also known as Body Integrity Identity Disorder)—a sexual fetish involving amputation of one's own healthy limbs!²⁵ Indeed, noted medical ethics professor John Kenyon Mason opined that "as long as you say that people can have a sex change for what is a severe psychological disease then it is difficult to say you cannot have an amputation for this form of severe psychological disease."²⁶

Note also that initially the Conservative Law Committee seems to be looking at the problem from inside the patient's head: "For them," they write, SRS is all being done for their "betterment and health." By the second sentence, however, the Committee appears to be speaking in its own name: "We have permitted . . . [and we] have said . . . ." Apparently, in the Committee's logic, having permitted something in the past justifies permitting something totally different (and indeed unprecedented!) in the future:

> We have permitted other procedures for mental ailments and have said that the mental illness is to be treated in the same way as a physical one. Therefore SRS may be permissible and the prohibition against castration can be overridden in this case.

"Therefore," concludes the Committee, "SRS *may be* permissible, and the prohibition against castration *can be* overridden in this case." (Emphasis added.) Note the finessing from

---

25. Not unlike the belief that a woman is trapped in a man's body or vice-versa, apotemnophiles believe they are disabled individuals trapped in a fully-abled body. Dr. Walter Everaerd quotes a patient of his as telling him, "Just as a transsexual is not happy with his own body but longs to have the body of another sex, in the same way I am not happy with my present body, but long for a peg leg." Walter Everaerd, "A Case of Apotemnophilia: A Handicap as a Sexual Preference," *Am. J. Psychotherapy,* Vol. 37, No. 2 (April, 1983) p. 286

26. Gerard Seenan, "Healthy Limbs Cut Off At Patients' Request," *The Guardian* (February 1, 2000), <http://www.guardian.co.uk/uk_news/story/0,3604,237010,00.html>. Dr. Paul McHugh ruefully observed, "[S]ome surgeons and medical centers can be persuaded to carry out almost any kind of surgery when pressed by patients with sexual deviations, especially if those patients find a psychiatrist to vouch for them." McHugh, Sexual Surgery at p. 37.

potentiality to possibility: "May be permissible" seems to refer back to the appendix's opening caveat: if "reliable medical studies...verify that SRS is beneficial . . . ." However, the very next clause lends itself to a categorical interpretation: "the prohibition . . . *can be* overridden in this case." (Emphasis added.) *"In this case?"* One might well ask, "In *which* case?" Is the Committee referring to the fulfillment of a *condition* (in the case that medical studies verify that SRS is beneficial), or to the *sha'alah* (*halachic* inquiry)—the hypothetical "case" being deliberated by the Committee)?

Note, however, that there is no actual "case" before the Committee. The Committee was not asked to consider whether Jewish Law permits SRS. The question presented to the Committee was: *"What is the sexual status of a person who has undergone SRS? Can SRS redefine the basic status of male and female?"* That is why the question, "Is SRS permissible *a priori*?" is discussed separately, in an "appendix." Indeed, the Committee framed its appended discussion of permissibility on the condition that the "beneficialness" of SRS be reliably attested:

> However, for these arguments to be considered, reliable medical studies must verify that SRS is beneficial for people suffering from gender dysphoria.

That, according to the opening statement of the appendix, is the only circumstance in which "the prohibition against castration can be overridden," and the only condition on which

> [h]ormonal treatment *would* also be permitted and *would not* transgress the prohibition of wearing the garments of the other sex . . . .

However, by this juncture, the Committee seems very conveniently to have forgotten its own stated parameters. No longer does it appear to be speaking according to the terms of its opening statement. Rather it appears to be issuing a theoretical ruling:

"[T]he prohibition . . . *can be* overridden in this case," and "Hormonal treatment *would* also be permitted and *would not* transgress the prohibition of wearing the garments of the other sex...." Indeed, as if to make sure there is no misunderstanding of the Committee's intention, the authors pointedly add: "since it is a case of 'for the good of the patient!'"

At this point, it is difficult to conclude that the Conservative movement was not trying to ramrod the "beneficialness" of SRS down the throats of its congregants. Indeed, not only has the appendix waved a magic wand over what had been the professed need for "reliable medical studies," transforming the unfulfilled need into a fulfilled condition, but the authors have built their argument upon a blatant misrepresentation of a fundamental source! Indeed, they tell us that *Talmud, Pesachim 25a* is their authority for their pronouncement that "there are no restrictions on what type of medicine may be used to heal a patient." Unfortunately, the passage they cite says quite the opposite! It asks, "When is it that there are no restrictions?" and the answer given is: "When the patient is in danger!" In other words, the only time there are no restrictions on the type of medicine being used is *when the patient is in danger.* Otherwise, we are *not* permitted to set aside Torah prohibitions such as Leviticus 22:24 and Deuteronomy 23:2—even though the patient feels that the "cure" would be to his benefit!

At this point, there can be no doubt that the Committee has understood that, in spite of its protestations about the prerequisite need for "reliable medical studies," it has given a *halachic* ruling. Accordingly, it closes with a kind of disclaimer:

> However due to the lack of studies about the long term effectiveness of SRS in dealing with gender identity disorder, we would recommend at this time that we counsel those who ask us for the *halakhic* opinion concerning this type of treatment, to consider the lack of sufficient studies that document the beneficial results of this treatment, and how this relates to our *halakhic* decisions.

This is a far cry from the Committee's initial caveat. Let's look at it again:

> SRS can be justified on the following arguments which are based on treatment for a mental condition. However, for these arguments to be considered, reliable medical studies must verify that SRS is beneficial for people suffering from gender dysphoria.

To summarize: the Committee opens by stating that it lacks a basis for ruling on the issue. It then purports to tell us how it would rule if a basis existed, but, fudging the condition, actually rules. It then tells us (blatantly *misstating* the Law), that "there are no restrictions on what type of medicine may be used to heal a person"—implying that, so long as the purpose is to heal, the "beneficialness" of SRS is a given. It then concludes by recommending that, when congregants ask if SRS is permissible, Conservative rabbis should tell them, "Yes it is, but 'the *beneficial results* of this treatment' [*sic!*] are not sufficiently *documented* and that could have an impact on our decision to permit it."

The Reform Movement "Sanctifies" SRS!

Not wishing to be outdone by the Conservative movement, or to wrestle with *halachic* opinions, yet no less desirous of ingratiating itself with the spirit of the times, the Reform movement took the drastic step, in August, 2007, of officially approving sexual reassignment surgery by "sanctifying" it in the form of three new "blessings," to be recited before and after sex-change surgery![27]

---

27. *See* Reform's new, 500-page, revised version of *Kulanu: A Program for Implementing Gay and Lesbian Inclusion.* The "blessings" were conceived and composed by Reform rabbi Elliot (formerly Eliza) Kukla, who reportedly came out as a transgendered person around the time she was ordained. The first "blessing" is apparently meant to be recited before initiating hormone treatments

How "Beneficial" are SRS Procedures?

Much propaganda has issued from the pro-GLBT lobby to the effect that surgery effectively relieves the suffering caused by gender dysphoria. However, there is little genuine public debate on this topic, nor, generally speaking, does the public get to read about the unfortunate consequences experienced by many who opt for the surgery out of confusion over their gender or sexual orientation.

The most obvious danger is that after the operation the person will change his/her mind and discover him- or herself irretrievably and vitally maimed.[28] One study notes that as few as 39% of those who have had phalloplasty are happy with the result, leaving 61% dissatisfied. The same study found 9% of male transsexuals

---

preparatory to surgery; the second, upon commencement of surgery, and the third, upon completion of the same. This may rightly strike the reader as bizarre: As Rabbi Bleich comments: "Quite apart from the unwarranted assumption regarding divine approbation implied by this phraseology, it may be objected that in the absence of any liturgical formulation pertaining to "transformation" the proposed texts do not constitute rabbinically ordained formulae and hence cannot serve as valid substitutes for statutory blessings." (*Contemporary Halachic Problems*, Vol. 1, p. 105)

28. In one of the more famous cases, this very point was brought poignantly home by tennis-star Renée Richards (formerly Richard Raskind), who has often expressed second thoughts over her 1975 sex-change surgery ("Better to be an intact man functioning with 100% capacity for everything than to be a transsexual woman who is an imperfect woman." Renée Richards, as quoted in "The Lady Regrets," *New York Times*, Feb.1, 2007), and has warned others not to "hold [her] out as an example to follow." Renée Richards, "The Liason Legacy," *Tennis Magazine*, March, 1999. Richards has also criticized the 2004 decision of the International Olympic Committee, to allow transsexuals to compete, as "a particularly stupid decision." ("The Lady Regrets") For more "regret" cases, *see* Lynn Conway, "A Warning for Those Considering MtF SRS" (March 16, 2007), <http://ai.eecs.umich.edu/people/conway/TS/Warning.html>.

unhappy with their vaginoplasty.[29] Leslie Lothstein, a noted specialist in transsexual psychology, alludes to a reported 68%-86% success rate in transsexual surgery, but warns against uncritical acceptance of such figures, given the lack of sufficient follow-up data.[30]

However, prior to closing the SRS Center at Johns Hopkins, Dr. Paul McHugh, psychiatrist-in-chief at Johns Hopkins Hospital from 1975 to 2001 and Director of its Department of Psychiatry and Behavioral Science, directed staff psychiatrist and psychoanalyst Jon Meyer to perform just such a follow up. Accordingly, Dr. Meyer endeavored to track down every patient who had undergone SRS at Johns Hopkins. Prof. McHugh summarizes what the Meyer study found:

> [M]ost of the patients . . . were contented with what they had done and . . . only a few regretted it. But in every other respect, they were little changed in their psychological condition. They had much the same problems with relationships, work, and emotions as before. The hope that they would emerge now from their emotional difficulties to flourish psychologically had not been fulfilled. [. . .] With these facts in hand I concluded that Hopkins was fundamentally cooperating with a mental illness. We psychiatrists, I thought, would do better to concentrate on trying to fix their minds and not their genitalia. ("Surgical Sex," 35)

---

29. James Barrett, "Psychological and Social Function Before and After phalloplasty," *International Journal of Transgenderism,* No. 2 (1998), <http://www.symposion.com/ijt/ijtc0301.htm>, *citing* Tsoi's Singapore study (1980, 1992, 1993).

30. Leslie M. Lothstein, Ph.D, "Sex Reassignment Surgery: Historical, Bioethical, and Theoretical Issues," <http://www.susans.org/reference/lothsrs.html>.

Accordingly, Prof. McHugh ordered the clinic closed in 1979.[31] Reflecting on his action, Prof. McHugh confided:

> I have witnessed a great deal of damage from sex-reassignment. The children transformed from their male constitution to female roles suffered prolonged distress and misery as they sensed their natural attitudes. Their parents usually lived with guilt over their decisions—second-guessing themselves and somewhat ashamed of the fabrication, both surgical and social, they had imposed on their sons. As for the adults who came to us claiming to have discovered their 'true' sexual identity and to have heard about sex-change operations, we psychiatrists have been distracted from studying the causes and natures of their mental misdirections by preparing them for surgery and a life in the other sex. We have wasted scientific and technical resources and damaged our professional credibility by collaborating with madness rather than trying to study, cure, and ultimately prevent it.

The Meyer study is not unique. A 2004 review of more than 100 international medical studies of post-operative transsexuals by the Aggressive Research Intelligence Facility (ARIF) of Birmingham University in England found no robust scientific evidence that SRS is clinically effective: "There is no conclusive evidence that sex change operations improve the lives of transsexuals, with many people remaining severely distressed and even suicidal after the operation...."[32] The ARIF review reported that up to 20% of

---

31. Dr. Meyer's study found that most of the male cases fell into one or the other of two different groups. One group consisted of guilt-ridden homosexual men who saw sex change as a way out of their moral anguish over their homosexuality. The other group consisted of usually older heterosexual or bisexual males who had found intense sexual arousal in cross-dressing. As they matured, they felt the need to add more authenticity to their costuming and—often with encouragement from their friends—sought SRS in order to accomplish this. (See McHugh, *Sexual Surgery*, p. 38)

patients in the United States and Holland regret changing sex. The same study also cited a 1998 study by the Research and Development Directorate of England's National Health Service for data showing attempted suicides among SRS patients to be as high as 18%. (Batty, "Sex Changes")

As SRS enthusiasts will no doubt argue, 20 dissatisfied patients out of a hundred also means 80 who are "content." But according to the Meyer study cited above, "content" does not mean improved: ". . . they were little changed in their psychological condition. They had much the same problems with relationships, work, and emotions as before." We leave it to the reader to decide whether a rate of 80% "success" by this measure is enough to warrant sexual reassignment—especially given the dramatic and largely irreversible consequences of "unsuccess." Indeed, it is undisputed that the procedure involves significant medical and psychological risks—even for those who are presumably "happy" with their new gender.

Medical Risks.

A recent study revealed that major complications can occur during and after the surgery. Intrauterine complications can develop after hysterectomy (Staver, 46, and note 182). In one study, out of 66 patients studied, six developed "severe wound infections," three, rectal lesions, three, necrosis of the glans, and one, necrosis of the distal urethra.[33] Staver observes that "One of the most common and gruesome risks of a male-to-female SRS is a rectovaginal fistula which also includes a very high risk of

---

32. David Batty, "Sex Changes are not Effective, say Researchers," Society Guardian, (July 30, 2004) <http://society/guardian.co.uk/mentalhealth/story/0,8150,1272093,00.html>.

33. Staver, 47, *citing* S. Krege *et al., Male-to-female Transsexualism: A Technique, Results and Long-term Follow-up in 66 Patients, BJU International,* Vol. 88 (2001), pp. 396-402.

infection."[34] Less drastic complications are frequent.[35]

Hormone therapy, which generally precedes and follows the surgery, is hardly less problematic.

> Hormonal treatment of the female-to-male and male-to-female transsexuals can cause a number of dangerous side effects, [including] water and sodium retention, increased erythopoiesis, decreased carbohydrate tolerance, decreased serum high-density lipoprotein (HDL) cholesterol, liver enzyme abnormalities . . . obesity, emotional or psychiatric problems, and sleep apnea.[36]

Impaired vascular reactivity in genetic females may result from prolonged administering of androgen therapy at high dosages.[37] In male-to-female transsexuals, androgen treatments can cause recurrent myocardial infarction. Based on a study of 303 male-to-female transsexuals undergoing estrogen hormone treatment, pulmonary embolism, cerebral thrombosis, myocardial infarction, prostatic metaplasia, and breast cancer were not uncommon side effects of the hormones.[38] Testosterone can present special

---

34. Sarah, *Notes on Gender Transition: Living With a Rectovaginal Fistula* (1996; editor's note, 2000) <http://www.avitale.com/Rectovaginal_Fistula.html.> "Symptoms include intrusion of intestinal fluids, gases and feces into the vagina, and often intestinal distress."

35. Staver, 47, *citing* S. Krege *et al.*, "Male-to-female Transsexualism," According to Staver, thirty-six percent of the sample developed meatal stenosis, *i.e.* a narrowing of the urethra, which can cause difficulty urinating.

36. Staver, 45, *citing* Walter Futterweit, "Endocrine Therapy of Transsexualism and Potential Complications of Long-term Treatment," *Archives of Sexual Behavior*, No. 27 (1998), pp. 209-18

37. *See* Robyn J. McCredie *et al.*, "Vascular Reactivity is Impaired in Genetic Females Taking High-Dose Androgens, *Journal of the American College of Cardiology*, No. 32 (1998), pp. 1331-35.

38. Staver, 46. *citing* H. Asscheman *et al.*, "Mortality and Morbidity in Transsexual Patients with Cross-Gender Hormone Treatment," *Metabolism*, Vol. 38 (1989), p. 869.

problems to post-mastectomy or mastopexy patients.[39]

Psychological Risks.

The psychological impact of the surgery on transsexual patients has been much discussed in the medical literature. One study reported general satisfaction among a group of post-SRS female to male transsexuals, yet suggested that one half of their number experienced suicidal ideation.[40] Less ambiguously, a 1989 study reported "The number of deaths in male-to-female transsexuals was five times the number expected, due to increased numbers of suicide and death of unknown cause."[41] A study of transsexual satisfaction in 1965 showed that more than 33% attempted suicide post-surgery, and more than 25% appeared to have a schizoid or personality disorder.[42] A 1981 study cited by Susan Jacob-Timm showed that 24% of male-to-female surgeries resulted in dissatisfaction.[43]

Why SRS Procedures are "Experimental."

---

39. Staver, 47, *citing* Shadow Morton *et al., Notes on Gender Transition, FTM 101: The Invisible Transsexuals* (revised 1997), <http://www.avitale.com/FTM101.htm>. "With testosterone comes body hair. The chest hair that grows in around the sutures and incisions can, at the very least, be incredibly annoying, and in the extreme can be ingrown and even cause infection."

40. Barrett, "Psychological & Social Function," *citing* Pauly (1981) quoting an oral address by Lothstein. <http://www.symposion.com/ijt/ijtc0301.htm>.

41. Staver, 46, *citing* Asscheman *et al.,* "Mortality and Morbidity," 869.

42. Staver, 60, *citing* Susan Jacob-Timm, *Ethical and Legal Issues Associated with the Use of Aversives in the Public Schools: the SIBIS Controversy, School Psychology Rev.* No. 25 (1996), p. 191.

43. Staver, 61, citing Susan Jacob-Timm, p. 191.

As Staver concludes, "Sex-reassignment surgery is an experimental and likely unethical treatment because it dramatically increases health risks while showing no objective evidence of curing the . . . gender identity disorder." Dr. Lothstein offers an additional reason, despite her belief that "there is evidence suggesting that some gender dysphoric patients benefit primarily from sex reassignment surgery. [Citation] *The problem is how to identify these patients.*" (47) (Emphasis added.)

> As long as sex reassignment surgery remains a viable treatment modality, it is reasonable to ask how one determines which patients will most benefit from sex reassignment surgery. Currently the selection criteria available are informally culled from clinical guidelines established by the various gender identity clinics nationwide. [...] In order for these guidelines to be effective one would have to ensure that sex reassignment surgery was done only by skilled surgeons in highly selected university-based clinics that could provide follow-up. (Lothstein, "Sex Reassignment Surgery")

The procedures are experimental, not because the surgical techniques have not been perfected (obviously, they haven't), but because there is no reliable way to control or predict the ultimate effect on the patient, and no way to fully reverse or correct the operation if the patient is disappointed with the results. Indeed, without impugning the technical skills of the plastic surgeon, no one can predict the ultimate outcome of an SRS intervention.

In my personal opinion, to expose a patient to the physical and mental health hazards such as those outlined above—without reliable guidelines for selecting the likeliest candidates—is a form of human experimentation that defies *halachah* and turns its back on medical ethics. As Mathew Staver observes in his fundamental article,

> Part of the ethical code of the helping professions is that treatment must have beneficiance and the patient has the right to treatment with the least drastic alternative. Beneficiance or

responsible care means that psychologists engage in actions that are "likely to benefit others, or at least do no harm. (Staver, 60, *citing* Susan Jacob-Timm, "Ethical Issues")

Medical Ethics Professor Arthur Caplan of the University of Pennsylvania agrees: "It's absolute, utter lunacy to go along with a request to maim somebody." Commenting that such surgery would violate the Hippocratic Oath, Dr. Caplan emphasized that the issue was "not just about 'do no harm.' It's also about whether [such persons] are competent to make a decision when they're running around saying, 'Chop my leg off.'"[44] Dr. Caplan was referring to apotemnophilia; but does substituting "genitals" for "leg" make a difference?

Apparently not to Dr. Norman Spack, a pediatric endocrinologist at world-renowned Children's Hospital Boston, and founding head of its new Gender Management Service Clinic ("unique in the western hemisphere," boasts the Hospital). According to an interview published in the *Boston Globe,* this clinic administers puberty-blocking drugs to children (optimally aged 10-12 for a girl, and 12-14 for a boy) to help them adapt more easily to prospective sex-change surgery! The drugs purportedly also aid in diagnosing the "true" gender identity of the children: "Sexual identity is fixed at three years old," claims Dr, Spack. "If a girl starts to experience breast budding," continues the doctor,

> and feels like cutting herself, then she's probably trans-gendered. If she feels immediate relief on the [puberty blocking] drugs, that confirms the diagnosis. [. . .] The biggest challenge is the issue of fertility. When young people halt their puberty before their bodies have developed, and then take cross-hormones for a few years, they'll probably be infertile. You have to explain to the patients [*sic!*] that if they go ahead, they may not be able to have children. When you're talking to a twelve-year old, that's a heavy-duty conversation. Does a kid that age really think about

---

44. Randy Dotinga, "Out on a Limb," Salon.com (Aug. 29, 2000), <http://archive.salon.com/ health/ feature/2000/08/29/amputation/index.html>.

fertility? But if you don't start treatment, they will always have trouble fitting in. And my patients [*sic!*] always remind me that what's most important to them is their identity.[45]

Perhaps not surprisingly, the interview says nothing about warning these children that the treatment they are being asked to consent to is wholly experimental, as defined above.

Gender Dysphoria Responds Positively to Psychotherapy.

Research indicates that transsexuals who regret their decision to undergo SRS tend to share certain characteristics in common, such as "inadequate family support, inadequate self-support, [and] inappropriate physical build."[46] Not surprisingly, these characteristics remind one of the causal factors we cited in Chapter Four as contributing to homosexuality. In other words, very plausibly, the characteristics that contribute to the "regret" of post-op transsexuals are the very same ones that contributed to their gender dysphoria in the first place. Alan Finch, a former transsexual who had his male-to-female reassignment reversed, observes:

> For the majority of patients, gender identity disorders are secondary to other identifiable psychological problems or situational factors that may resolve in time or through psychotherapy. The view held by the majority of the medical profession is that surgical intervention for treatment of individuals whose gender identity disorders are of a psychological or emotional origin is unethical, illusory, and become culturally driven, ineffective to the resolution of

---

45. Pagan Kennedy, "Q & A with Norman Spack: a Doctor Helps Children Change their Gender," *Boston Globe,* March 30, 2008, <http://www.boston.com/bostonglobe/ideas/articles/2008/03/30/qa_with_norman_spack/?page=1>.

46. Staver, 60, *citing* Susan Jacob-Timm, "Ethical and Legal Issues Associated with the Use of Aversives in the Public Schools: the SIBIS Controversy," *School Psychology Review,* No. 25 (1996), p. 190.

underlying causes of gender confusion and should not be promoted.⁴⁷

Dr. Lothstein is even more categorical: "[T]he disorders of gender dysphoria are primarily psychological disorders." ("Sex Reassignment Surgery") Indeed, one study cited by Staver actually ascribes gender dysphoria to "an excessive identification of patients with their mothers, and the inability of these mothers to permit their sons to separate from their mother's bodies—resulting in an etiology of mother-infant symbiosis and absent fathers."⁴⁸ Sound familiar? (*See* Chapter Four, above.)

In brief, transsexuality (like homosexuality) is very persuasively a secondary condition to other identifiable psychological issues that may be resolvable over time and through gender-affirming processes (GAP).⁴⁹ Many transsexual persons suffer from a variety of personality or mood disorders set forth in the Diagnostic & Statistical Manual of Mental Disorders (DSM). Some contributing factors to gender dysphoria lie at the root of other pathologies. Those factors include (as we saw in Chapter Four) family dysfunctions, sexual abuse or incest, lack of ego development, social and environmental conditions, object losses or separations, other psychopathologies, and finally general stress situations such as the break up of relationships, aging, or inability to function in appropriate masculine or feminine roles.⁵⁰ Indeed, as

---

47. Gender Menders: Social outreach of the Gender Identity Awareness Association (GIAA), <http://home.vicnet.net.au/~gendmend/Facts.htm>.

48. Staver, 59, *citing* Kenny Midence & Isabel Hargreaves, "Psychosocial Adjustment in Male-to-Female Transsexuals: An Overview of the Research Evidence," *Journal of Psychology,* No. 131 (1997), p. 602.

49 Stephen Levine, and L. Lothstein, "Expressive Psychotherapy with Gender Dysphoric Patients," *Archives of General Psychiatry* (August, 1981), p. 924.

50. *See* Leslie Lothstein, Howard Roback, "Black Female Transsexuals and Schizophrenia: A Serendipitous Finding?" *Archives of Sexual Behavior* 13:4

one descriptive essay on the subject aptly phrases it, "Sometimes the desire for sex reassignment is simply a cry for help, an expression of psychological pain stemming from a long history of anxious attachments, generalized anxiety, social phobia, intimacy dysfunction, depression, loneliness and despair."[51]

Some investigators even suggest that the desire for SRS is closely related to other body-image disorders, such as anorexia nervosa, bulimia, cutting behaviors, and even apotemnophilia.[52] Drawing a compellingly apt comparison between transsexualism and anorexia, Prof. McHugh, comments:

> It is not obvious how this patient's feeling that he is a woman trapped in a man's body differs from a feeling of a patient with anorexia nervosa that she is obese despite her emaciated, cachectic state. We don't do liposuction on anorexics. Why amputate these poor men's genitals? Surely the fault is in the mind, not in the member.[53]

Professor McHugh recalls how a colleague of his, a plastic surgeon, complained to him one day, "Imagine what it's like to get up at dawn and think about spending the day slashing with a knife at perfectly well-formed organs, because you psychiatrists do not

---

(1984), p. 371 and Michael Ross and William Walters, *Transsexualism and Sex Reassignment*, Oxford: Oxford U. Press (1986), p. 1.

51. Walter Bockting and Eli Coleman, "A Comprehensive Approach to the Treatment of Gender Dysphoria" (abstract), *Journal of Psychology and Human Sexuality,* Vol. 5, No. 4 (1992), pp. 131-153. <http://www.haworthpress.com/store/ArticleAbstract.asp?sid=LB231GR9H64R9KTUSDV4HQKHUF5A5UAF&ID=77632>.

52. *See* Staver, pp. 62-8 for a discussion of apotemnophilia and its unsettling relevance to transsexualism.

53. Paul R. McHugh, *Psychiatric Misadventures,* <http://www.lhup.edu/~dsimanek/mchugh.htm>

understand what is the problem here but hope surgery may do the poor wretch some good." ("Psychiatric Misadventures")

Four Noteworthy Cases.

Let us now look at SRS from the vantage point of those who have actually confronted it. Their stories are all the more important in that you will not likely hear them from the clinics where these surgeries are performed.

Michael Danielle.

We have already met Michael (formerly "Michelle" Danielle) described earlier Chapter Six (*see above,* pp. 210-11). Danielle's psychiatrist in Memphis, Tennessee referred him to a transsexual center for testing. The verdict: "You are a good candidate for a male to female sex change." Fortunately for him, after beginning the hormone treatment, Danielle had a religious experience from which he gleaned an insight that virtually saved his life. "No longer did I think of myself as a woman trapped in a man's body. I knew I was a man. All those years I had been deceived and believed a lie. Now I could walk in truth and say, I am a man and proud of it."[54] His sex change "was not an operation. It was a transformation!" (Rice/Danielle, 101) Such transformation enabled him to become happily married, have children, and rebuild his previously shattered internal identity

Alan Finch.

Australian Alan Finch was not so fortunate: he went ahead with the procedure. After the surgery, he came to realize that his alleged gender identity problem stemmed from other psychological issues that he had in the meantime successfully resolved. He thus reverted

---

54. Marie S. Rice, *Michelle Danielle is Dead,* Nashville: Jonathan Publishers (1985) p. 59.

to living life as a male, the gender of his birth, and had a second round of surgery. He proclaims that the key to dealing with the issue is to work with the psyche, not the body; to rebuild the patient's damaged and incomplete internal identity, rather than perform the kind of drastic surgery that damaged him for life. He believes that the medical team who performed his SRS committed malpractice and he has sued them. Ultimately Finch became a leader of Gender Menders, a support service that helps those who, like Finch, were misdiagnosed and sent to a sex-change clinic. Finch rejects the notion that a transsexual is "a woman trapped in a man's body" or "a man trapped in a woman's body." As Finch mentioned to me in conversation, this notion has been transformed into such a cliché that transsexuals themselves can no longer be sure whether they actually feel that way, or whether they are merely repeating a socially implanted mantra.[55]

Sy Rogers & Jerry Leach.

Two other men besides Finch whom I have had the privilege of knowing personally had similar experiences of being advised to undergo sex change operations (and beginning the process) but ultimately found it inconsistent with their religious beliefs.

Sy Rogers exclaims with wonder, "Imagine—me married! Only three years before my wedding day, I was a transsexual. At least that's what my psychiatrist called it." In 1978 Sy concluded that his only chance to find love, acceptance and an end to his inner pain would be to shed his "failed male identity." He went to

---

55. There are a host of articles about Alan Finch. Among them are: "Double Sex-Change Patient to Sue" (Sept. 15, 2004), <http://www.smh.com.au.articles/ 2004/09/15/10949276634658.html?=storylhs>; "Australian Story:" Boy Interrupted, <www.abc.net.au/austory/content/2003/s934839.htm>; Christine Hogan, "Man who became woman wants to be a man again," *The Sun-Herald* (Aug. 31, 2003), <www.smh.com.au/articles/2003/08/30/1062194756832 .html>.

two specialists who diagnosed him as a transsexual eligible for sex reassignment surgery. After undergoing preparatory therapy for two years, he was scheduled to have the surgery performed at Johns Hopkins Hospital in Baltimore. Rogers began having doubts right before the surgery. As he stated, "I gradually realized the operation could only change my 'packaging.' It wouldn't change me." He prayed to G–d for guidance: "G–d, please show me what to do. I'm so confused. If You don't want me to pursue this sex change, then show me. I'll do what You want." Sy's prayers were answered. Three days later, thanks also to Prof. McHugh, Johns Hopkins announced it would no longer perform sex reassignment surgery. Rogers took this a sign from G–d. Unfortunately, the hormone regime left residual effects. "Though I dressed in men's clothing and had short hair, the residual effeminate mannerisms, high voice, and all the results of female hormones caused many people to mistake me for a girl." Nevertheless, he went on to become a major leader of Exodus, the Christian faith-based ministry. He concludes, "Our marriage is not [only] proof of my recovery from perversion and compulsion. Rather it is one of the most beautiful evidences of a human life made whole...."[56]

Jerry Leach reported that dressing as a woman gave him excitement, sexual pleasure, and a temporary escape from his hated existence as a man. Unlike Michael Danielle and Sy Rogers, both of whom, prior to their spiritual rebirth, thought of themselves as homosexuals and transsexuals, Jerry was never sexually attracted to men. He enjoyed women and being among women. He began to believe he was really "a woman trapped in a man's body," and

---

56. Sy Rogers, "Man in the Mirror," <http://www.anotherway.com/pages/sy_r.html>. Sy's story is very similar to that of "Mickey," reported in Mathew Staver's Law Review article (47-48), cited above, at note 20. Mickey had spent 2 and 1/2 years taking hormones and learning to live as a woman when the hospital where he was scheduled for SRS stopped doing the procedure. Mickey continued to live as a female, but "through a series of events and therapy," gradually regained his natural gender identity, fell in love with a woman, and initiated "a happier and more stable life."

assumed a second personality that he called "Jennifer." To him, acting and dressing like a woman was his escape from stress and self-hatred. Jerry began to consider the possibility of sex-reassignment surgery. He began taking female hormones under the direction of medical specialists. However, as a married man with children, Jerry became anxious about possibly losing his family if he went through with the surgery. He decided to go to a religious psychologist for different counseling. As he progressed in his new counseling program, his perspective changed. "I had believed many lies. G–d had not made a 'mistake' in creating me with a male body. [...] There was not a woman inside my body, longing to be expressed. I had become addicted to certain forms of behavior in order to nurture that fantasy. I had chosen to abandon my manhood, one of G–d's good gifts to me." Going through the various steps of a gender-affirming process, Jerry came to "see the man G–d created me to be. No longer must I be seen as Jennifer. My real identity is contained in the name I proudly answer to: Jerry."[57]

Jerry has gone on to become a noted counselor in treating others with gender identity issues.

Conclusion.

In summary, we humbly suggest that the *halachah* is *not* divided on this issue. SRS, for purposes of alleviating transsexual anxiety in a physically normal male or female, is forbidden, and no medical justification has yet been shown to exist. From so much as is now known, the procedure is dangerous, potentially harmful, of doubtful value or benefit, and emphatically contrary to medical ethics. Moreover, alternative and less drastic means of providing relief and a cure are available in gender-affirming processes (GAP) which—as we hope to show in this book—offer holistic

---

57. Jerry Leach, "Jennifer or Jerry," <http://www.anotherway.com/pages/jherry_1.html>.

approaches not only to resolving gender dysphoria, but to fully reintegrating the shattered personality of the affected individual.

Regarding the status of the post-operative transsexual, there appears to be no question that, for carefully specified reasons, and in the limited situation of a marriage terminated *de facto* by SRS, the *halachah* "recognizes" the gender of reassignment. However, we humbly suggest that such recognition amounts to nothing more than acknowledging that sex-change surgery has taken place, and has annulled the marriage—not that the surgery actually changes the patient's gender![58] Nothing in the language of the Tzitz Eliezer or Rabbi Pelaggi warrants extending their rulings to recognize (even *post facto*) the legitimacy of transsexualism. *No published opinion by any Orthodox scholar permits sex change surgery for reasons of gender dysphoria. No published opinion by any Orthodox scholar recognizes the post-operative gender status of the patient for any other purpose than dispensing with the need for a get.*

---

58. The confusion over this issue has had the most serious consequences. The *Jerusalem Post* (May 8, 1998, p. 8) reports the case of Bracha, an Orthodox Jewish male who, despite his stated knowledge of the *halachic* prohibitions, deliberately underwent SRS on the mistaken assumption that Rav Waldenberg's rulings would at least enable him to be "a female in the eyes of *halacha*." As we believe we have demonstrated, such an assumption is groundless.

Chapter 9.

Leviticus 18:22:
What Does *To'eivah* Really Mean?
Homosexuality as a Reversible Transgression.

To'eivah, (commonly translated as "abomination" or "abhorrent") is a word loaded with far-reaching personal and social implications.

The word appears in several different contexts in *Tanach* (Torah, Prophets and Writings) and Talmud,[1] all of them concerned with detailed interactions between the human and the Divine. However, its most familiar—and powerful—association is in Leviticus 18:22, as a characterization of the male homosexual act. In that specific context, the term *to'eivah* can be read as transmitting an urgent spiritual imperative while simultaneously providing instruction and support for the redemptive process of growth. Our Tradition teaches us that the Torah records G–d's actual words and contains not a single superfluous letter. Thus it is highly significant that the male homosexual act is the only prohibited activity to which the Torah

---

1. *See* Robert A.J. Gagnon, *The Bible and Homosexual Practice*, Nashville: Abington Press (2001) pp. 118-19 for a listing.

applies the label *to'eivah* twice—that is, in two separate places.[2]

Some might therefore conclude that this transgression is so great that those who have committed it are pariahs, irrevocably condemned to a life of rejection and dishonor. However, it is hardly controversial to state that such a view is *totally inconsistent* with traditional Jewish teachings.

The Power of Repentance is Unlimited.

However we choose to understand the term *to'eivah*, the Torah expressly recognizes the inherent power of a human being: (a) to repent for any past transgression, and (b) to refrain from such prohibited activity in the future. In fact, this lesson is among the very first that we learn from the Torah. When Cain falls prey to resentment against his brother Abel, G-d chastises him in the following terms:

If you behave well, shall it not be lifted up? If you behave not well, sin crouches at the door; and lusts for you, but you can rule over it. (Gen. 4:7)

The *Targum* (the traditional Aramaic version of the Torah found in most standard *Chumashim*) translates Genesis 4:7 as follows:

If you will amend your ways, your sins shall be remitted; but if you will not amend your ways, your sin awaits you until the day of judgment, for you will be punished if you do not repent; but if you repent, you will be forgiven.

---

2. *See* Rabbi Basil Herring, *Jewish Ethics and Halakha for Our Time*, New York: Ktav Publishing House, Inc. and Yeshiva U. Press (1984), p. 185, 195, citing R. Moshe Feinstein, *Iggerot Moshe,* New York: *Orah Hayyim* (1973) Vol. 4, p. 115. Rabbi Samuel Edels comments that homosexuality is the only form of sexual misconduct to which the Torah applies the term *to'eivah*. Rabbi Bezalel Noar, *Rav Kook on Homosexuality,* <www.orot.com/hmsfoot.html>, note 22, citing *Hiddushei Agadot MattaRSHA, ad loc.* and Rabbi Yosef Hayyim of Baghdad, *Den Yehoyada, Sanhedrin* 82a.

Teshuvah and the Purification of Sex: a Uniquely Jewish Concept.

The repentance to which the *Targum* refers is a uniquely Jewish concept called *teshuvah*, or "returning." The "returning" is to G–d and His ways, as set forth in the Torah. *Teshuvah* involves all the faculties of the body, mind and emotions in a "remedial process of purification."[3]

The purification of the human sex drive has a spiritual significance in Jewish teaching that cannot be overemphasized. Remember that the Torah itself cites the sexual *to'eivos* of the Canaanites as the prime reason for their expulsion from the Holy Land. Jewish teaching calls upon humankind to serve G–d even through sex:[4]

All my bones say, "Lord, who is like you?" (Ps. 35:10)

The rabbis teach that this verse obligates us to praise G–d with *all* parts of our body. Thus in Judaism's view, the moral development of humankind is largely predicated upon the refinement of the sexual drive through moderation and self-discipline. As phrased by Rav Soloveitchik, "Judaism singled out sexuality as the most crucial drive upon whose redemption the whole religious destiny of man depends."(*Family Redeemed,* 78)

Indeed, as we have seen, Deuteronomy 12:29-31 warns the Children of Israel not to engage in the idolatrous practices of the nations expelled from the Land of Israel.[5] Verse 31 describes these

---

3. Rabbi Joseph Dov Soloveitchik, *The Family Redeemed: Essays on Family Relationships,* New York: MeOtzar HoRav (David Shatz and Joel B. Wolowsky, eds.) (2000), p. 77.

4. "Jewish Law is not concerned simply with how we pray or how we treat our fellow but also with how we work, dress, eat, drink, or have sex." Rabbi Michael Gold, *Does G–d Belong in the Bedroom?* Philadelphia: Jewish Publication Society (1992), p. 2.

5. *See* also Lev. 18:24-30. Rabbi Micha Berger, "*Bemachashavah Techilah,*" <http://www.aishdas.org/mesukim/5764/kiSeitzei.pdf>, suggests, "Perhaps the

practices, identified with the Canaanite religion, as *kol to'eivas Hashem asher sonei,* or "everything abhorrent to *Hashem* (G–d) that *Hashem* hates." The Israelites were thus charged with "the duty of extermination"[6] of these practices. For the most part, Christianity accepted this duty along with the authority of the Bible. Both Jews and Christians have traditionally understood that when something is classified as a *to'eivah,* it is a measure of how deeply abhorrent that something is to G–d. The word raises a red flag that is difficult, if not impossible, to ignore. Though harsh in its implications (and perhaps owing to its very harshness), the terminology used in Leviticius 18:22 has, without a doubt, inhibited many men and women with same-sex attractions from acting out their fantasies.

Harry M. is just one example. Harry was one of JONAH's clients who never acted upon his SSA desires. A Reform Jew, and one of JONAH's strugglers whose deep psychological work enabled him to complete his growth into manhood, Harry told me in private conversation why he never became a practicing homosexual:

> The simplicity and poignancy of G–d's statement clearly forced me to reconsider. It created a boundary that I simply would not cross. This self-imposed limitation enabled me to ignore society's urgings to identify as gay and prevented me from acting out my homosexual fantasies. Everyday, I thank G–d for creating such a bright line over which I would not step.

Of course, among those who act out their male homosexual fantasies, many believe that the Bible (and, in particular, what the

---

common reason for labeling these activities as *to'eivah* is that they are associated with the cultures of the neighboring idolatrous peoples. This notion of it being the unacceptable behavior of another people is reinforced by its first usage in *Chumash*. The Egyptians were unable to eat bread with the Jews 'because it was a *to'eivah* to the Egyptians.' *Bereishis* [Genesis] 43:32. Also, we find that they could not tolerate our shepherding, 'for it is a *to'eivah* of Egypt, all shepherds of flocks.' *Bereishis* [Genesis] 46:34; *See* also *Shemos* [Exodus] 8:22."

6. Rabbi Dr. J.H. Hertz, *The Pentateuch and the Haftorahs,* London: Soncino Press (1981) (cited hereinafter as Hertz, *Chumash*), p. 804.

Bible says about homosexuality) is irrelevant and outdated (*see* Chapter 5, above, at pp. 162-70). They claim to be untroubled by it. Others, not quite so cavalier about dismissing the significance of a moral institution that goes back all the way to Abraham (*circa* 3,800 years ago), invariably wind up in a state of internal conflict. They feel torn between the desire to actualize their sexual urges and the irrepressible consciousness that, by doing so, they are going against not only the moral basis of Western Civilization, but against the very core of their being.

We believe—in fact, we are certain!—that many in this latter group can find help through the spiritual practice of traditional Jewish *teshuvah*, combined with the latest gender affirming techniques. Jewish tradition teaches that a person retains the ability to modify his or her behavior, no matter how grievously he or she may have transgressed. Not only does the individual retain the power to change his or her entire behavior pattern (in other words, not only the performance, but the temptation), but there is no spiritual blemish that cannot be completely washed away, no wound that cannot be healed.

Where does this cleansing and healing power come from? It comes from an intense and heartfelt regret, combined with a decisive rejection of past misbehavior and an unshakable resolve to return to the proper path—no matter how arduous that may seem—and an unwavering faith in *Hashem* as a boundless storehouse of spiritual strength, comfort, and guidance. Indeed, in discussing this power to heal a soul torn and shattered by desire and guilt and sin, Rav Soloveitchik compares *teshuvah* to the Ingathering of the Exiles that, according to the Torah and the Prophets, will precede the coming of *Moshiach*—the Jewish Messiah:

> His [the sinner's] capabilities, his spiritual powers, his emotions and his thoughts are without internal cohesion; he has no single axis around which his personality revolves. For such a person repentance leads to 'the ingathering of the exiles," meaning the reunification and concentration of the personality which has been shattered to smithereens as a consequence of sin.[7]

---

7. Pinchas H. Peli, *On Repentance: The Thought and Oral Discourses of Rabbi Joseph Dov Soloveitchik,* Northvale: Jason Aronson, Inc. (1996), p. 306-307. "The

Innumerable Torah sages have expounded on the virtually infinite power of *teshuvah*. Rabbi Yochanan said: "*Teshuvah* is so great that it has the power to annul a person's guilty verdict."[8] Rabbi Yochanan was referring not to an earthly tribunal, but to the verdict of the Heavenly Court—in other words, a sentence of death by Heavenly Decree!

Psychological and Social Impediments to *Teshuvah*.

Alas, the vast majority of humankind is unaware of the tremendous power of *teshuvah* and of the ability of even the most ordinary individual to tap into it. In particular, many gay men and women perceive themselves as beyond salvation—as social rejects eternally condemned and despised by G-d, the Bible, and human society. This tragic self-perception only augments their alienation from "straight" society and from G-d; it also compounds their misery, shame and anger, causing greater internal resistance to changing their sexual disorientation. By internalizing this shame, the person condemns him- or herself "because of an unfulfilled norm, an unrealized ideal, an aspiration which did not come true, or a wrong of which one is guilty." (Soloveitchik, *Family Redeemed*, 83) What often occurs as a result of this flawed and distorted perception is that such persons bar their own way back: they act—or remain "stuck"—in ways that inhibit their own recovery.

Of course, the other side of the coin is that gay perceptions of discrimination and prejudice are frequently well-founded, reflecting bitter personal experience. Nor are gays alone in misunderstanding the sense and intent of the Biblical prohibitions. Straight society is hardly less likely than gays to misconstrue Leviticus 18:22 in a way that paints homosexuals as "abominations" hateful to G-d. Spurned

---

Ingathering of the Exiles" refers to the return of the Jewish People to the Land of Israel from the four corners of the earth.

8. *Ein Ya'akov* (Avraham Ya'akov Finkel, tr. & ed.), Northvale: Jason Aronson, Inc. (1999), p. 247.

by straight society, but often feeling "safe" and comfortable among gays, many homosexuals—perhaps most—have little incentive to consider changing their sexual orientation. Indeed, "political correctness" only exacerbates their isolation and loneliness by fomenting a climate where "changing" is considered impossible or dangerous.

Nevertheless, it is not simply a matter of encouraging homosexuals to give change a chance. We are dealing with a society that historically has shown itself to be cruel, discriminatory and vindictive toward gay men and women—a society that, owing to the swing of the pendulum, has now entrenched itself in the equally perilous notion that gay is okay, natural, and healthy. The challenge—and it is a formidable one—is to reach out to those homosexually oriented individuals who wrongly see their situation as either emotionally unresolvable or spiritually acceptable—and to do this in a way that doesn't foster sexual permissiveness or trample basic freedoms.[9]

Every individual has the power to unlock the doors of his or her own emotional prison by taking positive, redemptive steps—both religious and secular—that culminate in radical and dramatic change. Such a course is all the more difficult, however, when the society at large fails to reach out to those of our fellow men and women who are affected by SSA. If we perpetuate a pattern of rejection—a pattern experienced by many SSA individuals since early childhood—we as a society can only add to their already unbearable emotional hurt and push them further away. In this regard, all of us, as a civilized society—let alone as a Community of Torah and *Mitzvos*—must do *teshuvah* for transgressing the Commandment, "You shall love your fellow man as yourself." (Leviticus 19:18)

We are not suggesting that society should welcome homosexual *behavior,* as political correctness increasingly demands. Rather we are suggesting that society acknowledge the true intent of Leviticus 18:22, which is that those who "go astray" need to, *and have the capacity to,* return to G–d's Law; and because homosexuals are our

---

9. Ironically, many of those who rail against gays are just as ignorant as the pro-gay lobby of the fact that change of sexual orientation is possible. In this way, these two polar opposites are indeed strange bedfellows!

brothers and sisters (and sons and daughters!), and because we ourselves—meaning *heterosexual* society as a whole—are far from square with the Holiness Code, we owe them encouragement, moral support and a helping hand extended in humility and brotherhood.

A community that regards itself as moral and G–d-conscious, yet shies away from raising up one who has caved under the weight of a great and hidden emotional pain, not only perpetuates their plight but also commits a terrible *chillul Hashem*—a desecration of G–d's Holy Name.

Rabbi Bar Kappara's Talmudic Insight.

In a later chapter, we will discuss how this redemption from the *to'eivos* of Canaan can be accomplished through the remarkable process of psychological change and spiritual renewal that is *teshuvah*. Now, however, calling upon what we have learned about traditional methods of Jewish interpretation (*PaRDeS—see above*, Chapter 5, pp. 158-62), I would like to show how the deeper meanings behind the term *to'eivah* point towards this redemptive process of growth.

The Talmud itself provides a key by which homosexual strugglers can unlock the door of darkness in which they have closeted themselves. Indeed, tractate *Nedarim* (*Vows*) of the Babylonian Talmud offers a visionary interpretation of *to'eivah*, using a Hebrew word play. At this point, it bears reiterating that the Talmud is the repository of an oral tradition that dates back to the giving of the Written Torah at Mount Sinai. As stated by one of the great Torah Sages of our time, "The Talmud is the central pillar supporting the entire spiritual and intellectual edifice of Jewish life."[10]

One of the greatest sages of the earlier period of the Talmud was Bar Kappara. The Talmud quotes him often, referring to him as "the great sage." He lived about 1800 years ago (200 C.E.) and was part of the inner circle of the Sages who compiled the *Mishnah*. Bar

---

10. Rabbi Adin Steinsaltz, *The Talmud: The Steinsaltz Edition: A Reference Guide*, New York: Random House (1989), Introduction.

Kappara's first name is not known with certainty,[11] but his last name (or patronymic) is curiously symbolic, given the context in which we are going to cite him. The Hebrew word *"kapparah"* (homophonous with Kappara) literally means "atonement." It is the final step in the process of repentance and transformation known as *teshuvah*. As noted, *teshuvah* begins with the decision to change and—if one completes the process successfully—culminates with *kapparah*, atonement. With the attainment of *kapparah,* the spiritual debt incurred through the *aveirah* (sin) is fully paid off. In other words, not only is the penitent forgiven, but the record of his or her transgression is expunged: the slate is wiped clean. In the context of SSA, *kapparah* enables the penitent to regain the gender of his or her birth.

Although a jovial and sympathetic figure with a fine sense of humor, Bar Kappara was not one to speak lightly. "Aside from his prominence in *halakhah,*" writes historian Gershom Bader, "Bar Kappara was famous for his expositions, and his clever interpretations and deductions from Biblical passages were repeated in the academies of Palestine and Babylonia." (Bader, 401). The Talmud relates several anecdotes concerning the relations between Bar Kappara and Yehuda *haNasi* ("Yehuda the Prince")—the "Chief Justice" of the Jews of Babylon and the Head of all its Jewish Academies.

The incident that interests us here occurred at the wedding of Rabbi Yehudah's daughter to the wealthy Ben Elasha. Bar Kappara challenged Rabbi Yehudah with three riddles based on three sexual prohibitions from Leviticus 18. The first riddle was, "What is the meaning of the word *to'eivah* in the verse, 'You shall not lie with a man as one lies with a woman; it is a *to'eivah.'"* Bar Kappara refuted every explanation proffered by Rabbi Yehuda. Finally, Rabbi

---

11. Gershom Bader, *Encyclopedia of Talmudic Sages,* Northvale: Jason Aronson (1988), p. 401, notes that he is alternatively referred to in the Talmud by the first names of Simeon, Eleazer and Abba.

Yehudah asked Bar Kappara to give his own interpretation. Before answering, Bar Kappara insisted that Rabbi Yehuda's wife pour a cup of wine for her husband and that the *Nasi* join the dancing. Afterwards, Bar Kappara explained: "This is what the Merciful One is saying in His Torah: '*To'eivah: to'ei attah bah*—You are straying with this cohabitation."

Our first puzzled reaction to this anecdote might be, "What a strange setting for wordplay on homosexuality! A wedding? And not just any wedding, but the *Nasi's* daughter!" And why was this story so significant to the editors of the *Gemara* that they would set it down among their *halachic* debates? The story doesn't end there, however, and the continuation sheds more light on Bar Kappara's meaning. Indeed, Bar Kappara follows suit with two more puzzles, one addressing the prohibition of incest and the other the prohibition of bestiality! Concerning the latter, which the Torah characterizes as *tevel, i.e.,* "confusion" (Lev. 18:23) Bar Kappara interprets the phrase *tevel hu* to stand for *tavlin yesh bah?*—meaning, "Is there any *tavlin* (spice) in this cohabitation?" The term "spice" is used here as a euphemism for sexual attraction—something that is inherently lacking between a human being and an animal. As the Sages commented, "How can a person do something like that?" (*Ein Ya'akov,* 410)

Concerning the sin of incest, the Torah characterizes it as *zima,* ("wickedness" or "wanton, licentious union"). (Lev. 18:17) Leviticus 18:17 prohibits a man from having sexual relations with the daughter or granddaughter of his wife. The same term is used in Leviticus 19:29 in connection with the sin of supplying women for illicit purposes. Bar Kappara proposes *zima* as an acronym for the phrase, *Zo, mah hi?* Or, "This child, what is she?"

Bar Kappara's interpretation hints that prostitution and incest— besides producing offspring of dubious parentage, also deprive such offspring of valuable rights and legal status. Further, the effect of incest is often to destroy the family unit. "The Torah forbids incest because it is seeking to protect families," writes Rabbi Michael Gold, in a book that every Jewish mother and father ought to read.[12]

---

12. Rabbi Michael Gold, *G-d, Love, Sex, and Family,* Northvale: Jason Aronson, Inc. (1998), p. 183.

We can see now that there is a common thread running through these three riddles of Bar Kappara. The thread has to do with the effects of promiscuous sex upon marriage and society. The very reason that these three prohibitions carry such severe warnings (*to'eivah, tevel, and zima,* respectively) is to admonish the Jewish people not to be drawn into the destructive sexual and cultic-sexual practices of the pagan nations. As Rav Soloveitchik observes, "Promiscuity is perhaps the most abhorrent phenomenon of the heathen world against which the Bible fought." (*Family Redeemed,* 25)Another common thread uniting these three transgressions is that they are all avoidable, all correctable. If one clears one's head, there is no *tevel* (confusion); if one keeps the *Mitzvos,* there is no *zima* ("debauchery" or "licentiousness"). Similarly, if one embraces one's gender identity, one will not "stray" into homosexuality. Indeed, in construing the word *to'eivah* as he does, Bar Kappara treats the term as the shortened form of *to'ei attah bah,* with the subject *attah* ("you") understood, meaning "you err in it." (*Nedarim* 51a) Less literally, one could also translate, "you have been led astray regarding it," "you have gone amiss," or "taken a wrong course," "fallen from grace," "gotten lost," "erred," or "been deceived."[13]

What is Bar Kappara really trying to say with this interpretation? Rabbi Basil Herring, Executive Vice President of the Rabbinical Council of America, notes that the classical commentaries (Rashi, Rosh and Tosafos) understand Bar Kappara's homiletic play on *to'eivah* "to refer to the undermining of marital life by the homosexual abandoning his familial relationships to pursue such illicit relationships." (Herring, 184) This reading is clearly supportive of the reason why these matters were raised at a wedding feast. If a married man engages in homosexual activity, he compromises the bond of trust between husband and wife while simultaneously destroying the emotional foundation and integrity of the family unit.

---

13. The English translation of Bar Kappara's insight is gender-neutral. However, in Hebrew, the word *to'eivah* is feminine. Since the prohibition of Lev. 18:22 is directed specifically toward the man, some commentators suggest that the feminine ending, in Bar Kappara's interpretation, indicates that the male is "straying from her." See *Ein Ya'akov,* p. 410.

The great Talmudic exegete, Rabbenu Nissim (known as RaN), suggests that the straying indicated in *to'ei attah bah*, means that they "turn away from heterosexual relations and seek relations with men." (*Ein Yaakov*, 410) Other commentaries expresses concern about the amount of time a gay married man spends away from his family owing to his homosexual pursuits. His family members—particularly his children—will be led astray by the loss of his masculine presence. The homosexual adulterer thereby violates his obligation to be an appropriate role model within the family structure. Along the same lines, Rabbi Shlomo Riskin, Chief Rabbi of Efrat, Israel, stated in the much-discussed film, *Trembling Before G–d* (2001):

> Interestingly enough, the Talmud explains '*to'eivah*' as *to'ei attah bah*—you're making a mistake through this thing. You're making a mistake because it does not lead to the kind of normative family life which the Torah sees as being the fundamental building structure of a good and holy society.

Rav Kook, on the other hand, understands *to'eivah* to mean that a male who engages in homosexual intercourse simply strays from the course of nature.[14] Rabbi Basil Herring concurs that "such activity goes astray from the foundations of creation and of nature." (184-5)

Other sources, such as *Pesikta Zutarti*, understand the wordplay in more basic terms of going against the first of all the Commandments G–d gave to human beings (*p'ru ur'vu*—"be fruitful and multiply"): "You stray thereby, for it does not result in procreation."[15]

Rabbi David Eidensohn suggests that "straying" refers to the homosexual struggler getting lost in the process of growing up. "In general, homosexuality is a sexual style of the traveler: seeking but not finding. Some homosexuals go from partner to partner, meeting utter strangers in the street, mating without any delicacy . . . . This is more than sin. This is the soul adrift in pain."[16] The same writer

---

14. Rabbi Bezalel Naor, "Rav Kook on Homosexuality," <www.orot.com/hms.html> (1998), citing the *Torah Temimah* (Vilna: 1904) at Lev. 18:22.

15. *Rav Kook on Homosexuality*, citing the *Pesikta Zutarti*, <www.orot.com/hmsfoot.html> (1998), footnote 24.

stresses that "you are lost in it" implies a societal obligation to help those lost strugglers "find their way back."

Dismissing outright those gay apologists who argue that Bar Kappara was actually trying to say that homosexuality is not really such a big deal—merely a simple bit of straying from the path of the straight and narrow—Rabbi J. David Bleich, one of the foremost contemporary scholars of Jewish Law argues that "A person burdened by homosexual orientation 'goes astray' if he believes such activity to be acceptable because it does not appear to him as an abomination."[17] Thus, insists Rabbi Bleich, Bar Kappara's wordplay is pointedly "directed to homosexuals who feel no repugnance regarding their conduct." (132) In other words, "going astray" means permitting oneself to rationalize away the profound repugnance of the activity that is so emphatically expressed by the Torah.

In an inadvertent tribute to the power of Bar Kappara's maxim, a prominent gay activist who presents himself as a "gay Orthodox rabbi," urged, in a public debate with this author,[18] that Bar Kappara was "simply a court jester" who offered these wordplays "merely for their comic value." That someone would not hesitate to publicly trivialize the words and dignity of a great Talmudic Sage—while holding himself out as a Torah-observant rabbi (!)—speaks volumes about the length to which some gay activists are prepared to go in order to justify their political agenda. How ironic that such a person should ridicule in this crude manner a *halachic* attitude toward homosexuality and homosexuals that holds out so much hope, humaneness, compassion and relief. Considering who Bar Kappara

---

16. Rabbi David Eidensohn, "Homosexuality and the Holy Law," Gender Central (March 5, 2002), <www.sinaicentral.com>. Rabbi Eidensohn further suggests that the "Gay Lobby wants to remain 'lost' and [thus] declares that nobody can return from homosexuality.... Central to their program is that (a) no gay *can* change and (b) no gay *should* change. Both are lies." <www.sinaicentral.com/kedusho/The%20Orthodox%20Homosexual.htm>.

17. Rabbi J. David Bleich, *Bioethical Dilemmas: a Jewish Perspective*, Hoboken: KTAV Publishing House, Inc. (1998), p. 134.

18. Rabbi Steven Greenberg, during a panel discussion with the audience following a 2002 Miami, Florida showing of *Trembling Before G-d*.

was, and to whom he was speaking, Bar Kappara's "jests" are certainly not to be taken lightly. Rather, his words were meant to honor and exalt the *mitzvah* of marital sex.

To'eivah Contains the Possibility of *Teshuvah*.

The significance of Bar Kappara's interpretation cannot be underestimated. Bar Kappara understood that when one pursues an erotic interest in the wrong gender, it is in error—a straying off the right path. But in the Jewish view, errors can be corrected. Sins can be repented of. Expiation and redemption are always available. Rabbi Adin Steinsaltz, one of the leading Torah sages of our time, observed, "All forms of *teshuvah,* however diverse and complex, have a common core: the belief that human beings have it in their power to effect inward change."[19] In "doing *teshuvah,*" one empowers oneself to correct one's errant behavior and come closer to G–d. It is, however, a process: "one cannot extricate oneself all at once from both the inward and outward consequences of one's actions." (4) "In this sense, the principle of *teshuvah*—that no matter what the starting point, no matter how far gone the sinner, penitence is [always] possible—is itself an important source of reawakening and hope. (6) The principle of *teshuvah* is the possibility of change.

In fact, Rav Steinsaltz's analysis is directly relevant to the SSA struggler. The Rav teaches that there is no irredeemable situation. The force, direction, and coherence of one's healing is "largely determined by the clarity and strength of the initial recognition of the past. (6) Further, without recognizing the feelings of inadequacy one may have internalized, "no amount of intellectual sagacity can change a person's behavior." (5) Thus, he concludes, "When *teshuvah* is seen as a process of complete self-transformation, nothing could be more difficult; yet nothing could be easier than the momentary resolve that

---

19. Rabbi Adin Steinsaltz, *Teshuvah: A Guide for the Newly Observant Jew,* Northvale: Jason Aronson, Inc. (1987), pp. 3-4.

set the process going." (7) There comes a moment when the struggler can choose to embark on this journey of change. "From that point on, his steps will be carrying him toward a different destination. The turn itself is accomplished in a second. Yet the new path, like the one abandoned, is long and arduous."(7)

When Bar Kappara characterized homosexuality (*to'eivah*) as errant behavior, he was implying that there *is* a way back, and that the repentant person can find it by seeking insights into the misperceptions that led him/her astray. This concept is critical to Judaism. Without it, it would have been pointless to give the Torah to human beings. Only the *malachim*—the angels, who are incapable of sin—would have qualified to practice Judaism!

Classic commentators, including Rambam, compare the intentional violation of a Torah prohibition to a rebellion against G–d, to an act of total heresy (in Rambam's example, idol worship). Nevertheless, if the perpetrator does *teshuvah,* Judaism considers such violation to have been nothing more than a "mistake"—the work of a confused heart and a "spirit of folly"[20]—and in Judaism a "mistake" is something that can, and must, be rectified.

In that regard, it is significant that in expounding on the *to'eivah* of homosexuality, Bar Kappara refers to G–d as "the Merciful One." Gay activists and their allies often refer to the G–d of Israel as a stern, harsh judge, deficient in the attributes of love, forgiveness and mercy. By expressly referring to G–d as "the Merciful One," Bar Kappara is surely reminding us that the G–d Who commanded Leviticus 18:22 is a G–d of kindness and mercy, Who desires and favors *teshuvah,* strengthening the resolve of those who choose to follow Him, clearing the road to healing for those who genuinely seek well being, and relieving the suffering of those whose pain has become unbearable.

Bar Kappara's Interpretation of *To'eivah* is Validated by Clinical Studies Showing Sexual Orientation *CAN* Be Changed.

Gay activists have so thoroughly commandeered public opinion, that the belief that homosexuality is immutable and unchangeable has

---

20. "A man does not sin unless a spirit of folly enters into him." Talmud, *Sotah* 3a.

become deeply rooted in western society. True, no one denies that it is possible for a homosexual to *suppress* his or her gay or lesbian behavior. However, when it comes to internal sensory experiences like fantasy and arousal, gay activists insist that change is simply not a viable option. Thus, political correctness does not tolerate the view that homosexuality is an errant behavior for which corrective action is possible—or necessary.[21] This is why a Jewish gay activist can publicly dismiss Bar Kappara's teaching as the antics of a "court jester." And since there can be no repentance without change and reformation, gay activists and the public at large can openly scoff at the idea that *teshuvah* can have a meaningful role in the psychological treatment of homosexual issues.

Of course, if it could be shown that many individuals have successfully changed their sexual orientation from same-sex to opposite-sex, that would certainly tend to validate Bar Kappara's teaching. Therefore it behooves us to briefly summarize a few of the many studies and personal testimonials conducted and published over the past 50 years, documenting cases of change in sexual behavior, identity and attraction, from homosexual to heterosexual.[22]

New Direction Ministries in Toronto, Canada, collected and critiqued 31 clinical research studies published in books or academic journals between 1952 and 2003. (<www.pathinfo.org>) The most striking point in their analysis is the consistency of evidence, over a 50-year period, showing that sexual orientation is flexible and homosexuality is reversible.

Commenting on his 2002 article entitled "Initial Empirical and Clinical Findings Concerning the Change Process for Ex-Gays," Dr. Warren Throckmorton, a professor of Psychology at Grove City College, concluded:

> My literature review *contradicts* the policies of major mental health organizations because it suggests that sexual orientation, once thought to be an unchanging sexual trait, is actually quite flexible

---

21. *See* Gallup Poll figures cited in Chapter 3, above, note 8.

22. *See* <http://www.pathinfo.org> for a selection of sources.

for many people, changing as a result of therapy for some, ministry or others, and spontaneously for still others."[23] (Emphasis added.)

In another article, Throckmorton refers to his own clinical practice: "I have assisted clients who were, in the beginning of mental health counseling, primarily attracted to those of the same gender but who declare they are now primarily attracted to the opposite gender."[24] He reviews several (but clearly not all) modalities of therapy that have successfully enabled clients to transition from primarily homosexual to primarily heterosexual—including behavioral approaches such as non-aversive classical conditioning, systematic desensitization, assertiveness training and other social skill building, and cognitive approaches (including the rational-emotive-behavior therapeutic approach of Albert Ellis), as well as various religiously oriented approaches.

But perhaps the most interesting of all is a landmark 2001 study by Dr. Robert Spitzer, a noted psychiatrist who played a pivotal role in the 1973 removal of homosexuality from the *Diagnostic Statistical Manual* ("DSM"), the psychiatric manual of mental disorders. Dr. Spitzer thus came to be viewed by gay activists as one of their staunchest allies. However, in a stunning reversal, Spitzer's 2001 study demonstrated that his formerly gay subjects did have a measurable ability to successfully change the four critical variables of sexuality: sexual fantasies, arousals, identity, and behavior.[25] Spitzer interviewed 143 men and 57 women who for many years had had a

---

23. "Gay-to-Straight Research Published in APA Journal," <http:www.narth.com/docs/throckarticle.html>. *See also* Warren Throckmorton, "Initial Empirical and Clinical Findings Concerning the Change Process for Ex-Gays," *Professional Psychology: Research and Practice,* Vol. 33 (June, 2002), p. 242-8.

24. Warren Throckmorton, "Efforts to Modify Sexual Orientation: A Review of Outcome Literature and Ethical Issues," *Journal of Mental Health Counseling,* Vol. 20 (Oct. 1998), No. 4, pp. 283-305.

25. Dr. Robert Spitzer, "Can Some Gay Men and Lesbians Change Their Sexual Orientation? 200 Participants Reporting a Change from Homosexual to Heterosexual Orientation," *Archives of Sexual Behavior,* Vol. 32, No. 5, Oct., 2003, pp. 403-17.

predominately homosexual attraction (defined as at least 60 on a 100-point scale of sexual attraction) and who, after therapy, had experienced a shift to heterosexuality of at least 10 points, lasting five years or more. Spitzer found that the *average* level of reported homosexual attraction among his 200 interviewees dropped, from 90 (on the 100 point scale) in the year before they started therapy, to 19 in the year just prior to the interview. He also noted that 19% of the respondents reported *complete* change—that is, no lingering homosexual thoughts, fantasies or desires—while 60% met Spitzer's criteria for "good heterosexual functioning," that is, never or rarely having same-sex thoughts during heterosexual sex.

Spitzer's earlier conviction that sexual orientation was immutable, and his established reputation as an influential voice for the pro-gay lobby, attest to the reliability of his conclusions. Indeed, in a statement that angered many of his former allies, Spitzer acknowledged: *"Some people can and do change. Like most psychiatrists, I thought that homosexual behavior could not be resisted, and that no one could really change their sexual orientation. I now believe this to be false."*[26] (Emphasis added).

Spitzer's study addressed another critical aspect of the amenability of homosexuality to therapy. Responding to the unsubstantiated claim of gay activists and their allies that gender affirming processes may cause harm (including attempted suicide, depression, emotional trauma, and a host of mood and anxiety disturbances) to its participants, Spitzer showed that not only was there *no evidence of harm,* but "to the contrary, they [the study participants] reported that it was *helpful in a variety of ways beyond changing sexual orientation itself.*" (414) (Emphasis added.) In other

---

26. Dr. Spitzer received a great deal of personal abuse after publishing the 2001 study. Many of his colleagues were outraged by what they perceived as his abandonment of a strictly pro-gay politically correct position. In an interview with Douglas Leblance, published in *Christianity Today* (March 29, 2005), "Therapeutically Incorrect Atheist Psychiatrist Argues that Gays Can Change," <http://www.ctlibrary.com/ct/2005/April/20.94.html>, he reported, "I remember when it [the survey] first appeared in the media, I got a letter from, I think, a dean of admissions at Columbia. He wrote me that it was just a disgrace that a Columbia professor should do such a thing. Within the gay community, there was initially tremendous anger and a feeling that I had betrayed them."

words, when counselors worked to help clients seeking change of sexual orientation—as opposed to imposing gay-affirmative counseling techniques—the clients reported significant benefits to their mental health overall. Dr. Spitzer, for example, found that many of his participants were very depressed *prior* to their change therapy and were *much improved afterwards*. In a documentary film, *I Do Exist*, Dr. Spitzer summarized: "The majority of the subjects reported moderate to severe depression before they went into therapy and there was marked change. Very few were depressed when we saw them."

The numbers are telling: 42% of men and 47% of women were clinically depressed *prior to* entering reorientation therapies. *After counseling* for change, only 1% of the men and 4% of the women continued to experience depression. And, because he independently found "considerable benefit" and "no harm" as the result of reorientation therapies, Spitzer advocated a change in the American Psychiatric Association's policies. He recommended that the APA stop applying a double standard—namely, actively encouraging gay-affirmative therapy to confirm and solidify a gay identity, while discouraging reorientation therapy for those with unwanted SSA.

Personal Testimonials Support the Clinical Findings.

Clinical studies that survive the withering peer scrutiny that follows publication in respected scientific journals carry great weight of themselves. However, it is only when supplemented by personal testimony that these cold statistics come truly alive.

Ben Newman is a former homosexual sex addict. He will tell us his story in Chapter 15. In an article entitled "Change is Real," published on his website (www.peoplecanchange.com), Newman writes of himself and his fellow strugglers:

> Is change really possible? Absolutely! We testify from our own personal experience that we have experienced profound change in our sexual identity, behavior, interests, and desires—change that has brought us great peace and satisfaction.

Jeff Konrad spent four years living with his gay lover. His courageous exploration of the power to change, his dedicated study of homosexuality, and the insights he acquired into the root causes of his own same-sex attractions gave him all that he needed to change his sexual orientation.

> I didn't seek help for some time because I thought it was impossible to change. I believed the myth, "once gay, always gay." Severe depression and dissatisfaction with my homosexual lifestyle—particularly my inherent insecurities and jealousies—brought me to an exhaustive study of homosexuality, more specifically, a study in the formation of gender identity.
>
> I immersed myself in books, seminars, and counseling. Then I sifted through all this information and discerned what was true and practical from what was purely theoretical and technical. As I applied this new understanding, I found the freedom I so desperately sought. It began with understanding the *root causes* and gaining insight into the *real problem.*
>
> Through healthy introspection, I was able to pinpoint these root barriers in my life that blocked proper fulfillment of legitimate same sex needs. For instance, I was overly sensitive. I felt unlovable, inadequate, insecure and inhibited. My self-image, on a scale from one to ten, was on the negative side of zero! I also was lazy. I lacked any motivation to change and was afraid of trying.
>
> By bringing these root issues to the surface, I began working through past hurts, misconceptions and my wrong responses. I no longer felt I was a helpless victim of past circumstances . . . .
>
> Being gay is an acquired identity, an identity brought about through the misinterpretation of events and its subsequent responses. Many of my childhood experiences were beyond my control, but my responses were my own choices. An inappropriate response to a situation here, another one there—eventually they all added up to a distorted image of myself . . . and, for me a homosexual identity. Since homosexuality is an acquired identity, it makes sense that you can choose to change your identity. As adults we can choose to respond to things in a healthy and mature manner rather than reacting in childish and foolish ways . . . .
>
> "Once gay, always gay?" That is what I used to think. Not any more. Finding the true causes of my homosexual orientation gave me the spark, the hope, I needed to find the real me and relieve my inner turmoil . . . .
>
> I'm not just talking about behavior or surface stuff. I'm talking about deep down change. I no longer have the feelings, desires,

temptations, orientation, or identity of the past.[27]

Like Konrad, sexual reorientation specialist Richard Cohen had been actively homosexual, and he, too, found the motivation and the resources to reclaim his natural sexuality:

> People told me that I was born this way and the thought of changing was impossible and therapeutically contraindicated. Phooey! [A]nyone can do whatever he wants if he has a burning desire, makes a plan, gets support, and goes for it.... I have the unique position of having been the client and now the therapist. I not only struggled with unwanted homosexual desires, I struggled equally in trying to find professionals who understood my condition and how to help me heal. It was so difficult to explain myself to therapists who did not have a clue.[28]

David, a JONAH struggler living in Israel, e-mailed me to say:

> A person in my support group made a poignant point to me when I complained 2 weeks ago about being in a rut. He answered my question, "Is change really possible" strongly in the affirmative by reminding me of my own personal experience since I began this process 8 months ago. I must admit change HAS occurred. On bad days, I try to deny it. But then I realize how I have *changed* . . . being more open with people, or more relaxed with a woman, or taking bigger risks, or working-out with great energy, or just simply being less neurotic. When I realize what has transpired, I know that healing/growth HAS occurred. No way to deny it.
> One more thing—I heard in the name of Rav Dressler, *zt'l* (he was talking about spiritual growth) . . . "When you are not going up, you are going down." Amazing huh? No such thing as static. No such thing as being in holding mode. So that's my message to me/us today—gotta keep pushing forward with therapy & posting & reading & reaching out etc., because if we are not going up we are

---

27. Jeff Konrad, *You Don't Have to Be Gay: Hope and Freedom for Males Stuggling with Homosexuality Or for those Who know of Someone Who is*, Hilo: Pacific Publishing House (1998), pp. 11-12.

28. Richard Cohen, *Coming Out Straight,* Winchester: Oakhill Press (2000), p. xiii.

going down.

Instead of giving in to the delicious, somewhat dramatic notions of responding to questions such as "Is there ever an end to this?" Or "Why am I not presently attracted visually to women?" I have—more or less—decided to stick to *going up* stuff; not euphoria, but rather *to do the work you gotta do*.

To'eivah as a Clinical Term for "Help Me!"

Based on the real-life experience of thousands like Konrad, Cohen, and David, a growing number of medical professionals— among whom noted psychologist Rabbi Dr. Moshe Halevi Spero— believe that *to'eivah* is best understood when viewed as an ailment that cries out for corrective action. This view makes a lot more sense than the current socio-political agenda that seeks to promote homosexual interests by overturning the moral foundations of civilized society. As Rabbi Norman Lamm, Chancellor of Yeshiva University in New York City, explains in a feature article in the *Encyclopedia Judaica,* homosexuality is a pathology that originates from certain developmental traits (*e.g.,* passivity, dependence, and phobic tendencies), and the APA's declaration of normality was politically motivated.[29] Rabbi Basil Herring neatly summarizes: "In [Rabbi Lamm's] view, there are sufficient clinical traits that would render homosexuality to be a pathology that simply cannot be turned into health by a majority vote." (Herring, 188)

Whether we call it a "pathology" or not, with clinical assistance, a program of gender affirmation can help overcome the underlying emotional blockages causing same-sex attraction. Hence the need for intervention at the psychological level.[30] Dr. Spero's pioneering work in gender-affirming psychoanalysis seeks to combine *halachic* ethics with modern psychotherapy by specifically focusing on Bar Kap-

---

29. "Judaism and the Modern Attitude to Homosexuality," *Encyl. Judaica Yearbook* 1974, Jerusalem: Keter Publishing House (1974), pp. 194-205.

30. *See* Rabbi Dr. Moshe Spero, *Handbook of Psychotherapy and Jewish Ethics: Halakhic Perspectives on Professional Values and Techniques,* Jerusalem: Feldheim (1986), p.167.

para's lesson. For Dr. Spero, *to'eivah* is above all a clinical term: "[T]he value of *to'eivah* as a religious concept would be to indicate pathological status." (*Handbook*, 167) In other words, for Spero, *to'eivah* means, "This is pathological: you need help."

GAP (Gender Affirming Processes) Builds on Bar Kappara's Insight.

What kind of intervention can best help a person struggling with SSA? What prescriptions are available? What enables the corrective action to take place? Several modern psychotherapeutic strategies have evolved. They all build on the premise that homosexuality involves a series of erroneous choices (conscious and subconscious), and that by rectifying the errors, the condition can be overcome. Since there is no one methodology preferred by all sexual-reorientation counselors, I have termed these several approaches collectively as "gender-affirming processes" (GAP). Some strugglers thrive under pure psychoanalytic therapies, while others find psychodynamic, behavioral, cognitive, EMDR (Eye Movement Desensitization and Reprocessing), group, or religious approaches most applicable to their particular needs. Throckmorton's 1998 article (*see* note 24, this chapter, at p. 316, *above*) concluded that the strength of GAP lies in its diversity of approach. However, Throckmorton found that the most successful modalities for modifying patterns of sexual arousal share certain characteristics in common. These include (1) increasing assertiveness, (2) addressing the acquired fear of relationships with others (3) developing gender-appropriate social skills (4) maintaining motivation, and (5) garnering social support for sustaining change.

Dr. Joseph Nicolosi, co-founder of the National Association for the Research and Therapy of Homosexuality (NARTH) and a clinical psychologist in private practice in Encino, California, has popularized the most widely known approach, which he calls "Reparative Therapy." In his landmark books, Nicolosi explains his belief that reparative therapy provides the patient with an opportunity to finally complete those unfinished childhood tasks that are essential to normal growth and the attainment of full adulthood.[31]

According to Dr. Nicolosi, the majority of his homosexual clients suffer from a syndrome he calls "gender-identity deficit." (*Reparative Therapy,* 211) The underlying foundation of homoerotic attraction is a deeply ingrained sense of the incompleteness of one's own sexuality. The gay person's lack of gender integrity is the so-called Achilles heel through which his or her emotional pain attacks the psyche, the body, and the spirit. The central postulates of reparative therapy, as articulated by Dr. Nicolosi, are:

(1) gender identity—the gender with which the subject identifies—determines his or her sexual orientation (211); and

(2) one tends to sexualize or eroticize the gender with which one doesn't identify. (211)

A central part of Dr. Nicolosi's method is to help the client discover the *reasons* behind his or her misplaced gender identification. Once the client understands that the misplacement arises out of a deprived need for normal bonding with a same-sex parent and/or same-sex peers, he or she is ready to learn how to fulfill that need in a normal, non-sexual manner.

> Reparative therapy works on issues from both the *past* and the *present*. . . . Like all psychotherapies, reparative therapy creates a *meaningful transformation*. This meaningful transformation is the result of the client's gains in insight. When he comes to see the true needs that lie behind his unwanted behavior, he gains a new understanding of this behavior. His unwanted romantic attractions are demystified. He begins to perceive them as expressions of legitimate love needs—needs for attention, affection, and approval

---

31. *Healing Homosexuality: Case Studies of Reparative Therapy*, Northvale: Jason Aronson (1993), and *Reparative Therapy of Male Homosexuality: a New Clinical Approach,* Northvale: Jason Aronson (1997).

from other men—which were unmet in childhood. He learns that such needs indeed *can* be satisfied, but not erotically." (*Healing Homosexuality,* 213)

Another way of looking at this gender deficit was developed by therapist David Matheson and Life Coach Alan Downing (currently Director of Counseling and Group Support Services at the JONAH Institute for Gender Affirmation) as part of a "The Journey Begins" group protocol that I co-facilitated.[32] Matheson and Downing hypothesize that OSA men (*i.e.,* opposite-sex-attracted men, as opposed to SSA men) experience identity-congruence between their "concept of self" and their "concept of gender." Even if these concepts of self and gender are not in complete alignment in an OSA man, they nevertheless overlap sufficiently to allow him to orient himself sexually as a man. On the other hand, the SSA man perceives a significant incongruity between his concepts of self and gender. Because his sense of self falls short of his "vision" of the ideal man, the SSA man creates certain "gender imperatives," *i.e.*, those physical or emotional characteristics he feels he must acquire in order to be the man he envisions.

Another aspect of congruity that must be considered is the emotional "charge" that attaches to gender. When one's "gender affiliation needs" (*i.e.,* a man's innate and cultural needs to connect with men and masculinity) are congruent with one's "gender relations experience" (the sum of a man's actual experiences with other men and the interpretations he gives those experiences), then OSA (opposite sex attraction) is more likely to result. When there is no such congruence, one's ability to engage in gender-affirming relationships is limited, and the individual experiences what Moberly and Nicolosi refer to as "defensive detachment."[33] If one or the other of these two components (self and gender on the one hand and gender needs and gender experience on the other) manifests congruence (*i.e.,* if one's concepts of self and gender are in alignment, or if one's

---

32. Unpublished protocol materials created by David Matheson, L.P.C. and Alan Downing, revised October 4, 2006, presented in Jersey City, New Jersey.

33. See Elizabeth R. Moberly, *Homosexuality: a New Christian Ethic,* Cambridge (Eng.): James Clarke & Co. (1983), *passim;* and Nicolosi, *passim.*

gender affiliation needs are consistent with one's gender-relational experiences), then the probability of SSA is reduced. Matheson and Downing believe that this explains why so many OSA men are able to avoid a homosexual identity despite poor relationships with their fathers or same-sex peers. They further postulate that when both sides of the model are out of alignment, then the likelihood of SSA is greatly increased.

To overcome these gaps, say Matheson and Downing, the SSA man needs to broaden both (or at least either):

(1) his sense of self; and

(2) his concept of what constitutes masculinity.

At the same time, the SSA man needs to gain greater congruence between his (1) gender affiliation needs and (2) his actual relational experiences (or, more precisely, the stories he tells himself about them). Therapeutically, this involves examining one's personal history in order to heal past wounds, and at the same time to adopt new perceptions and behaviors in order to move forward.

To summarize Matheson & Downing's theory: when the concepts of self and gender, on the one hand, and/or the concepts of gender-affiliation needs and gender-relational experiences overlap significantly, a man has a greater probability of an OSA orientation. When one or the other (or both) of these concept pairs diverge significantly, an SSA orientation is more likely to develop. When therapy succeeds in creating "gender congruity" and "gender connection" (or at least one of them), the male client can resume his interrupted gender-emotional growth into manhood at least to some significant degree.

Both Nicolosi and Matheson-Downing recognize the need to access the client's physiological responses during the therapy in order to release emotional pain stored in the muscular-skeletal systems. We are talking here about a process that demands considerable courage and commitment. No one is saying that it is easy. On the contrary, it can be, at times, emotionally very arduous. But those who have gone through it have also described it as "amazing," "transcendent," "awesome," and "something I never imagined could be possible." Indeed, those who choose to engage in GAP will find it—to borrow a phrase from Rav Soleveitchik—"a passional experience born of bewildering and painful events, of struggle and combat with one's self and others. In a word, it is a heroic performance attained only when one's life story becomes an *epos,* a narrative of great and courageous action." (*Family Redeemed,* 74)

Chapter 10:

To'eivah as Alienation.

As discussed in the previous chapter, a key Talmudic understanding of the biblical word *to'eivah* ("abomination" or "abhorrent") provides us with the perspective that a person who engages in homosexuality is straying or has been "led astray." Implicit within this understanding is a simple fact: one who goes astray retains the ability to find the way back. Thus the SSA struggler, may be viewed as someone who (owing to his or her own skewed perceptions) has fallen into an error which is correctable and into a peril from which he or she can be delivered.

We have seen, in Chapters Four and Six, that the etiology of SSA involves a process of alienation on three distinct levels: one's self, one's social surroundings (including family), and, frequently, one's religious beliefs. Hence, the struggler who is determined to confront his or her SSA—to understand it in order to transcend it—will most often need to retrace this process of alienation on the three distinct levels on which it occurs: the self, society, and faith. Of course, in "real life" these levels are closely intertwined. However, to understand more clearly how they interrelate, it is convenient to examine each level separately. So let us now explore what this means in terms of how SSA individuals generally relate (1) to themselves, (2) to others in the broader community, and (3) to G–d.

Relating to the Self: Alienation from One's Essence.

Therapists generally concur that SSA individuals tend to suffer from an extraordinary degree of alienation from the self. Strugglers typically feel that they are and have been, in a sense, unfaithful to the way they were created—specifically in regard to gender identity. They often create deep-seated beliefs that they are inherently unlovable, unacceptable, inferior, or in some other way unworthy. As explained in our last chapter, most strugglers internalize a "gender incongruity." A man who perceives himself as gender incongruent generally experiences two essential conflicts: (1) his vision of himself differs dramatically from his archetype of the ideal man; and (2) his personal relational experiences with other men go far afield from his core needs for gender affiliation. Thus a gender shame becomes part of the psyche of such a person—a belief that something is fundamentally wrong—in males, for example, either with masculinity in general or with their own masculine identity, or both.

We saw in Chapter Four that this dissociation from one's natural gender typically stems from early childhood perceptions of rejection by same-sex parent and/or peers. Dr. Maria Valdes, the legendary practicing psychologist and academician who has been treating and healing SSA strugglers for over 30 years, explains that

> In homosexuality, there is a disidentification with self, with the person one is. The person is body and soul at once with a specific physiological sex, either male or female. If the gender is not developed with the physical sex, a basic unmet need is established in the individual for which he is not responsible at all. The need for gender identity will remain until it is met."[1]

---

1. Dr. Maria Valdes, "Holistic Treatment Procedural Model for Treating the Homosexual Condition," in Rev. John F. Harvey, *The Truth about Homosexuality: The Cry of the Faithful,* San Francisco: Ignatius Press (1996), p. 363.

Self-acceptance is often predicated upon external acceptance by others, and in particular, same-sex peers. Dr. Richard P. Fitzgibbons, a practicing psychiatrist and prolific author with an impressive track record in healing persons affected with ego-dystonic homosexuality, amplifies: "The need for male acceptance is essential for the development of a positive male identity, and it precedes the adolescent stage of development. If self-acceptance is not attained through peer affirmation, rarely will a boy find himself attracted to girls."[2] Dr. Gerard Van Den Aardweg, author of several books on homosexuality, and, since 1963, a clinician in private practice in Holland, emphasizes that the lack of peer affirmation (leading to same-sex peer wounds) is a most critical variable leading to homosexual identification.[3]

The distorted self-perception of the SSA individual causes him or her to disconnect even further from his/her authentic self—creating at the same time a surrogate self or false persona. When people become self-alienated in this manner, they find it difficult to relate to others "objectively," *i.e.,* in a manner consistent with most people's perceptions. Their reactions to the behavior of others will be skewed by wrong conclusions, misinterpretations, imaginary problems, pseudo-solutions, evasions, counterproductive defenses, and/or inhibitory responses. Viewing others through the prism of their own projections and transferences, they will distance themselves from those others and from their natural social environment. Remember: these "others" may be perfectly innocent of any desire to reject or ostracize them! Nevertheless, because this self-inflicted ("defensive") detachment from self and society is *perceived* as imposed on them by "the others"—and therefore as undeserved, discriminatory, and

---

2. Dr. Richard P. Fitzgibbons, "The Origins and Healing of Homosexual Attractions and Behaviors," in Harvey, pp. 313-14, note 1.

3. This is equally true for lesbians as it is for male homosexuals. *See, e.g.,* Gerard Van Den Aardweg's, *The Battle for Normality: A Guide for (Self) Therapy for homosexuality,* San Francisco: Ignatius Press (1997).

unjust, such individuals ultimately also turn angrily away from the social order, G–d, and religion.

Van den Aardweg describes in detail the inferiority complex and emotional infantilism generally prevalent among homosexuals. According to Van den Aardweg, the typical homosexual is a highly insecure person who feels a deep disappointment at any real or imagined lack of affection or appreciation. When the outcome of a self-comparison with others or with his own perception of ideal-self is negative, the individual feels "hurt, slighted, wronged, less loved, given less respect and appreciation than the real or imaginary others."[4] Whether this negative self-image is based on body image wounds (*e.g.,* too fat, too thin, too tall, too short) or detachment from others of the same gender, or any other underlying causes of emotional wounding, the alienation from self becomes real, creating a mindset in the individual that he is not accepted by, and does not belong among his own peers. "[T]he consequential emotional reactions are, among other things: shame, loneliness, self-deprecation and naturally, sadness or anger." (Aardweg in Holdt, 96) In turn, the negative self-image which emerges affects the homosexual individual in his proverbial Achilles heel—that is, his sense of gender identity.

---

4. Dr. Gerard Van den Aardweg, "The Homosexual Inferiority Complex," in Dr. Christl Ruth Von Holdt, *Striving for Sexual Identity,* Reichelsheim: The Reichenberg Fellowship (1996), p. 95.

Male homosexuality is, at its core, a problem of insufficient masculine identity. The male acquires a sense of gender emptiness. He has somehow skipped over the process of maturing from early childhood to full manhood. As recovered homosexual Alan Medinger describes it, male homosexuals are basically just men who have withdrawn from masculinity because "[they] found the process too difficult or too painful."[5] As we learned in Chapters Four and Six, this alienation or estrangement from self may be caused by detachment from Dad, enmeshment with Mom, same-sex peer wounds, body-image issues and/or by any number of other contributing factors. No matter what the causative factors may be, the bottom line is that the boy's emotional growth into manhood was placed on hold. Meanwhile, the other components of the boy's personality continue to grow and develop; but without the guidance of proper gender awareness, he literally "strays" into SSA.

Thus, when such an individual wakes up "lost"—*led astray* by drives and circumstances beyond his control, even beyond his complete awareness—and wants to find the way back, the first thing he needs to do is to resume his growth into manhood. Medinger describes this step with poignant accuracy:

> Now, fifteen, twenty, or forty years later, if you want to resume your growth, you will have to venture back out into that world of men and boys. Essentially you are going to have to develop your manhood in the same way that young boys do, through a process of learning, testing, failing, getting back up and testing again, and finally succeeding. *We grow into the fullness of our manhood by doing the things men do.* (Medinger, 8)

Based on his own personal experience of overcoming homosexuality and helping scores of others do the same, Medinger

---

5. Alan Medinger, *Growth into Manhood: Resuming the Journey,* Colorado Springs: Waterbrook Press (2000), p. 7.

believes that to conquer the forces driving one toward homosexuality, one needs "to seek to live out the inner man." (Medinger, 149) This "inner man" is the core of manhood that exists deep within even the most feminized male.

> The healthy, solid man is the same person at every level. The stereotypical homosexual man, however, is "layered." Buried deep within him is the person G–d created him to be. Resting above that is the frightened boy, the man who feels he has little worth. This is the area where the wounds and the pains reside, the quivering jellied layer. To cover it up and avoid feeling the pain, he creates the next layer, a hard but brittle layer of fantasy, defense, and denial. Then there is the outermost layer, the one that interacts with the world, the one he wants people to see. It is often gifted and attractive, sometimes flamboyant or highly accomplished.
>
> All men are susceptible to creating an image that covers up deep insecurities, but in many homosexual men the center quivers so much and the shell is so brittle that they spend an extraordinary amount of energy maintaining the outermost man. Occasionally the shell does crack and the fearful man leaks through, but the most 'successful' homosexual man is the one who manages to live almost totally out of the outermost man. (Medinger, 149)

Jungian therapist Diane Eller-Boyko, herself a former lesbian and now a happily married mother of two children, tells how her typical lesbian client's mother wounds lead to self-alienation and hinder her feminine self-identification:

> Mothers who cannot honor the feminine in their own natures become unavailable, dull, depressed, angry, compulsive—living by neurotic rituals which they use in order to fill the empty core of their being. The daughters are wounded by this. And so the daughters carry on this wound to the feminine spirit for yet another generation.[6]

---

6. Dr. Joseph Nicolosi, "Touching the Feminine Soul: Interview with Diane Eller-Boyko," <www.jonahweb.org>.

Observing that "In falling in love with another woman, [the lesbian woman] is really seeking to connect with herself," Eller-Boyko counsels her lesbian clients to become aware of their "outer lives," and of how that facade insulates them from their feminine core. (Nicolosi, "Eller-Boyko")

> That is where the nourishment will come from. Instead of looking for another woman, I'm trying to connect her with that reservoir within herself. When she has been filled up by the feminine, she will find the nourishment she needs within her own depths. Only when she has been nourished by that deep connection, can a woman move on to connect with the masculine.
>
> [. . .]
>
> With another woman, she will have only the illusion of wholeness. The shadow, representing those real developmental needs that were never met, will continue to haunt her. (Nicolosi, "Eller-Boyko")

In seeking to discover the source of the emotional pain that leads to homosexuality, we find loneliness and isolation near the top of the list. "Since loneliness is one of the most painful of all life experiences," explains psychiatrist Richard Fitzgibbons,

> significant amounts of energy are expended in attempting to deny the presence of this debilitating pain. As a result, many individuals have no conscious awareness that they struggle with this deep emotional wound. Understandably, many men and women with these painful emotional wounds of loneliness may prefer believing that they are homosexual rather than face their terrible inner sadness.[7] (311)

---

7. Fitzgibbons also concludes that the extraordinary promiscuity prevalent in the homosexual lifestyle stems from the participants' inability to fill an inner loneliness from childhood and adolescence. It becomes compensatory behavior.

Fitzgibbons identifies several situations in which inner loneliness can lead to homosexuality.

> Some adults who are very frustrated and lonely because they have not yet met the right person to marry retreat into homosexual behavior in an attempt to seek relief from their loneliness. Married persons may engage in homosexual acts as a result of stress and loneliness in their marriage. Also, the sadness and loneliness that occur after the ending of a marriage or a serious heterosexual relationship may result in homosexual behavior because these individuals are fearful of becoming vulnerable to someone of the opposite sex. In my clinical work I have seen this pattern occur more frequently in women. (310-11).

Rich Wyler describes very well how "defensive detachment" feeds on itself and increases one's sense of loneliness and isolation.

> Fearing men, feeling like we could never measure up, being overly sensitive and easily hurt, we built walls around ourselves to protect ourselves from further hurt. "They can't hurt me if I reject them first," we told ourselves, intuitively. And, in so doing, we unknowingly increased the isolation and detachment we so desperately needed. Reparative therapists call this "defensive detachment"—defending against anticipated rejection and hurt by detaching or distancing ourselves preemptively.[8]

Wyler's heart-rending confession illustrates very effectively how alienation from self begins with, and overlaps with, alienation from others. This is especially clear when the detachment begins in infancy or very early years, for the sense of self is not yet fully developed in small children, who identify with their mother and father long before

---

8. <peoplecanchange.com>.

they develop a full awareness of themselves.[9] It follows that when the early child-parent relationship is disturbed, the child may have problems developing his or her own identity—quite apart from any gender issues per se.

In an insightful 1965 essay, Rav Soloveitchik, founder of the Modern Orthodox Movement, observes that the lonely individual does not seek to externalize himself into the world, but rather to internalize the world into himself.[10] Although the Rav was not writing of homosexuality at all, the observation certainly fits one aspect of homosexuality. Indeed, whereas in normal heterosexual pairing, "opposites attract" (not only sexual opposites, but opposite personalities: the exotic becomes erotic!), each partner finding desirable in the other those characteristics perceived as different from or complementary to him- or herself; in SSA individuals, the desire to internalize—fueled as it is by loneliness and dejection—reaches a level of outright envy and idolization. Indeed, many SSA individuals subconsciously believe that through intimate physical contact between two same-sex bodies he or she could internalize the physical attributes or personality traits of the other.[11]

---

9. Freud suggested that an infant's emotional ties to his/her parents are the foundation for later relationships. Subsequent research on the outcomes of early attachment has been consistent with Freud's idea. Reparative therapists strongly believe that the process of identification with the father is supposed to occur somewhere between the ages of two and three. When it does not occur, the child is at risk of developing subsequent homosexual attractions.

10. Rabbi Joseph Dov Soloveitchik, "The Lonely Man of Faith," *Tradition* (1965), Vol. 7, no. 2, pp. 3-65. *See also,* Rabbi Dr. Norman Linzer, *The Jewish Family: Authority and Tradition in Modern Perspective,* New York: Human Science Press (1983).

11. The psychological process involved is analogous to that of cannibals who, desiring to "internalize" the strength of a defeated enemy, would eat the fallen warrior.

This is not to say that the internalization paradigm does not apply to heterosexual attraction, but only that, in SSA individuals, the attraction stems from a painful sense of gender deficiency within oneself; whereas in the heterosexual, it derives (at least in its sexual component)[12] from a fully developed and untroubled identification with one's natural gender needs and responses.

The foregoing clarifies—at least in part—why the SSA individual is drawn to someone of the same sex. Through sexual intimacy, he (or she) unconsciously endeavors to acquire and internalize the masculinity (or femininity) that he or she perceives unconsciously as an agonizing emptiness within him- or herself.

Alienation between the Individual and the Community.

The second level of alienation involves the relationship between the SSA man or woman and the community in which he or she lives. Obviously, there are two basic aspects to this relationship: how the SSA individual interacts with the community, and, correspondingly, how the community handles this interaction. An individual's relationship to others within the community often depends upon a common value structure—a "community of values." If the community shuns or excludes the person, the resultant marginalization will be damaging both to the individual and to the community as a whole—to

---

12. Thomas Mann's famous novella *Tonio Krüger* is a classic illustration of the intense attraction commonly felt by a shy and sensitive youth for a shallow, extroverted and fun-loving girl.

the individual, because acceptance and approbation is necessary to his or her emotional growth and well-being, and to the community, because by ridding itself of the "dissonant" individual it has also deprived itself of his or her potential contribution to the welfare of the whole.

In early childhood, the pre-homosexual child often distances him- or her self from others by defensively detaching from his/her social environment. Earlier in this chapter, Rich Wyler explained the concept of defensive detachment as "defending against anticipated rejection and hurt by detaching or distancing [oneself] preemptively." Thus, for the SSA person, the way back—the way to experience authentic connection with others—means stepping out of isolation, speaking one's truth, and learning to recognize the totality of one's being while relating to others. He or she will also learn to create proper boundaries in his/her relationships.

It is important to remember that although defensive detachment and SSA develop as defenses to unbearable pain, their palliative effect is ephemeral and, in the long run, counterproductive. Charles W. Socarides, M.D., a founder of NARTH (National Association for Therapy and Research of Homosexuality) and author of numerous books and articles on homosexuality, tells us just how "effective" these defenses generally are:

> Despite a decrease in societal condemnation, most homosexuals suffer from a sense of inferiority and guilt over their disability due to the infantile fears which have isolated them from the social-sexual relationship of the majority. This remains a constant and deep-rooted source of shame, humiliation, inferiority, and discontent.[13]

The personal testimony of one of JONAH's strugglers supports this conclusion:

---

13. Dr. Charles Socarides, *Homosexuality,* New York: Jason Aronson (1978) p. 419.

> During the past several years I just kinda felt lost and alone, never quite feeling part of any community. It was hard never feeling part of the Jewish community cuz of the gay things I was doing and the feelings I was feeling. But also never feeling fully comfortable in the gay community, cuz I'm guessing my soul didn't want to be there. Most of all, just not having contact with my family, and not having a good relationship with them made me feel even more disconnected from who I am and where I belong in the world.[14]

The degree of resistance to change is one measure of how deeply internalized is one's homosexuality. To break down that resistance, the struggler needs to overcome the defensive detachment that is obstructing his/her personal relationships. Dr. Lawrence J. Hatterer views this as a central point of the style of gender therapy he advocates in his classic textbook:

> [D]istorted interpersonal relationships with people do provoke resistance to change, and learning about them is vital. The therapist has to know about the patient's daily personal life to assess just how much resistance to change is related to his everyday activity with people.[15]

Of course, the main barrier to healing is typically the subject's ironclad conviction that his or her present *mis*perceptions are accurate—that his or her outlook, feelings and opinions correspond to reality. This resistance starts to break down, however, once the struggler starts to appreciate that his or her SSA feelings are nothing more than a compensatory surrogate for legitimate gender-need fulfillment. By replacing homosexual fantasy and longing with healthy same-sex bonding (thus genuinely fulfilling legitimate gender-needs of attention, affection and approval from other same-

---

14. Email to author, dated November 3, 2004.

15. *Changing Homosexuality in the Male*, New York: McGraw Hill Book Co. (1970), pp. 124-5.

sex peers and gender role-models), rather than simply attempting to repress or deny those needs or to palliate them with homosexual activity, the struggler will achieve completion of his or her psychosexual development. He/she will no longer allow him- or herself to be led astray and will begin the journey to sexual wholeness. The master key to achieving this is learning how to relate authentically to members of one's own sex in a non-sexual manner.

Drawing on his 17 years of experience treating homosexual clients, Dr. Hatterer describes just how this can occur:

> [R]esistance [to change] breaks when [the male patient] has contact with people who help him solidify his heterosexual identity and way of life. One person or several people can help the patient over the line. A stable male heterosexual friend or friends, contact at work with people who value his maleness on a daily basis, and/or a woman or women who react to his maleness help cut through resistance to change . . . . [. . .] [Such therapeutic relationships] always counteract his resistances to change, and they dissipate hidden, repressed or expressed feminine identifications. (124)

According to Dr. Hatterer, experiences—both past and present—which bolster identification with heterosexual values favor change and constitute leverage in overcoming resistance. Such positive encounters are internalized by the male struggler as genuinely fulfilling legitimate needs, such as:

> (1) the need for a close and warm non-erotic relationship with a male; (2) the need for warmth and intimacy with his family; (3) a desire to relate successfully to, and have his own family; and (4) a desire for a stable life devoid of transiency. (124)

Increased confidence with non-erotic same-sex relationships—at whatever level of interaction—brings other advantages, in that it helps build an empathetic awareness of others which is most often lacking in homosexual liaisons. Indeed, pronounced egocentrism or narcissism is a common feature of the gay/lesbian gestalt. Noting that

"Judaism rejects the joy of physical gratification when it is egocentric and expressive of one's indifference to the joy of others," Rabbi Dr. Norman Linzer proposes that "[an effective way] to combat narcissism is to enter into social relationships that require mutual dependency and empathy. Each meaningful relationship requires interdependence, as each partner gives and cares for the other. . . . ." (Linzer, 167). Learning how to relate to others can bring manifold benefits to the recovering homosexual. I remember attending a workshop in which a well-known ex-gay spokesman related how he was unable to perform sexually in his marriage until he stopped worrying about his own performance and started focusing on giving pleasure to his wife.

> Mature object relations presuppose that self-love can be transcended in the person of the other. This is not merely a modern, humanistic approach, but an essential feature of Jewish consciousness and values. This consciousness is not individualistic, lonely, and defeated, but inter-subjective, relational, and interdependent. (Linzer, 167)

JONAH strongly believes that the various experiential weekends it recommends[16] can help men reintegrate themselves into the society of men from which they feel alienated and ostracized. The reactions of our JONAH men who attend these weekends show very clearly how these events have profoundly influenced their lives, alleviated their sense of foreignness with respect to ordinary male society, and thus overcome their alienation toward the community. Here is a

---

16. These include *Shabbatons* and other support programs sponsored by the JONAH Institute for Gender Affirmation; "Journey into Manhood," sponsored by People Can Change; "Tender Loving Care Healing Seminar," sponsored by the International Healing Foundation, "Seasons of Transformation;" sponsored by Call of the Shofar; and, for men who are very secure or have a strong ego structure, the "New Warrior Training Adventure," sponsored by the Mankind Project.

testimonial by the same (anonymous) struggler whose expressions of loneliness and disconnection we quoted above (p. 338):

> I came back feeling extremely connected to the Community of Men. I finally felt being part of a community... of just men among men. Forget religious or sexual orientation... neither mattered. We [*i.e.*, all attendees] were all initiated in our roles as men, just for the sake of being a man. That's it. I finally felt like I belong to a community, finally felt like I belonged and was part of a race of people. The next day as I came to work, I looked at all men with a newfound sense of sameness and one. I am him, he is I. I could no longer dishonor or disrespect my fellow man, for we are the same.[17]

Another struggler commented:

> I continue to be amazed at what I experienced. The kindness, compassion and love from each man was apparent. All of them courageous—choosing to fight this battle. I can honestly say I slaughtered several of the demons inside of me which have been blocking my growth for years. I know that I am a different person now. I feel different. I think different and one of the guys even told me that I look different. I am so certain that this battle can not only be fought but actually won.[18]

---

17. Email addressed to the author, November 3, 2004.

18. Quoted in Berk and Goldberg, "JONAH's Psycho-Educational Model for Healing Homosexuality," <www.narth.com> and <www.jonahweb.org>.

A third struggler reported:

I will be doing some mundane chore when I'll bust up laughing because I know I'm a man! This is such a powerful thing for me to realize. It's what I've lusted for in others for so long, and I now know I have it myself. This is so-o-o cool! I am a man among men. NEVER did I think I could say that, or know it in the core of my being, but I'm there . . . and I LOVE IT! I welcome it and own it, and feel it. (Berk and Goldberg)

The Jewish communal idea involves family life, marriage, and children. The Torah emphasizes the benefits of communal life. It is virtually impossible for a Jewish man to live even a rudimentary, observant life in a community containing less than ten Jewish men. Weddings and circumcisions are occasions for community rejoicing in which strangers are welcome and the poor are honored guests. The community has an obligation to feed and house the poor, to provide schooling for the children, and to fulfill the obligation of proper burial for the dead.

Other examples could be cited. However, in contrast to societies past and present in which individual happiness is sacrificed for the benefit of the community, Torah performs a delicate balancing act, moderating between the needs of the individual and the needs of society, recognizing the humanity and uniqueness of the individual—deserving of love, support, and compassion—while decisively rejecting behaviors deemed antithetical to the welfare of the individual and the community.[19]

---

19. *See, e.g.,* Psalms 104:35: "Let evil deeds cease from the earth and the wicked will be no more." According to the Talmudic interpretation of this verse, King David is praying here for the eradication of the Evil Inclination, after which, obviously, sinners will be no more. (*Berakhot* 10a) The Talmud asks, "Is it written that 'sinners' (*chot'im*) shall cease from the earth? No, it states 'evil deeds' (*chata'im*)—should be eradicated." Remember that according to Jewish tradition, no sinner is ever beyond redemption. This is explained in depth in Chapters 11 through 13.

No society can long survive without appropriate restraints on individual behavior, or without equal application of such restraints to all members of society, irrespective of ethnic origin or economic stratum. Unregulated sexual conduct—whether among the populace as a whole, or even just predominantly among the ruling classes—has long been recognized by historians as a hallmark of the decline and fall of once great civilizations.[20] On the other hand, sexual repression has also proved harmful to society and the individual, driving sex underground and leading to much misery, and widespread moral corruption. Thus the *halakhah* sets clear boundaries of propriety, designed both to minimize egocentric impulsiveness and to foster community harmony, while honoring the full enjoyment of sex and eroticism between husband and wife in an atmosphere of holiness and mutual fulfillment.

It needs to be emphasized that in the Torah view, the marital relationship is not only the very foundation of appropriate sex, but the only permitted ambit for sexual activity. Rabbi J. David Bleich notes how this places an equal responsibility on heterosexual and homosexual alike:

> Man is a corporeal being and as such is subject to various and sundry desires. Some objects of desire are forbidden to man; others are consecrated and commanded; virtually all are subject to regulation. Man, by nature, is a sensual and sexual being. Fornication, extramarital liaisons and adultery would not necessarily be foresworn by heterosexuals if not for divine decree. It may well be that, for some persons... homosexuality is yet another aspect of human nature in which natural tendencies must be confronted and

---

20. *See* pp. 173-74, note 33, and p. 181, note 6.

subdued . . . . The challenge may be onerous in the extreme, but it may not be ignored.[21]

The other side of this coin is the challenging burden on the community to understand and accept those who are struggling in good faith with SSA. Jewish communal attitudes toward the individual struggler need to be reexamined. All too often, the community commits its own errors of neglect, exclusion, and hatred, on the one hand, or condonance on the other. People do not generally ask to be burdened with a homosexual orientation. We must try to keep in mind what we believe the Talmud bids us remember: the SSA individual was initially "led astray" by circumstances outside his control. The homosexual man or woman is simply seeking to meet normal, legitimate unfulfilled emotional needs, but in an immature and counterproductive manner.

Thus, the appropriate community response would seem to be to help educate the struggler as to the options available to him, encourage him to make the right choice, and offer him guidance, understanding and support during the challenging process of change.

And not only that! Moved by the plight of the avowed homosexual, the Lubavitcher Rebbe, Menachem Mendel Schneerson—certainly one of the great pillars of contemporary "Ultra-Orthodox" Judaism—went so far as to urge the community to assume a more proactive stance:

> We must keep in mind that the vehement and vociferous arguments presented by a patient, that he is really well and that his condition is a healthy instinct—or as least not destructive—do not change the severity of the "ailment." In fact, this attitude on the part of this individual indicates how serious his malady really is for this person, how deeply it has

---

21. Rabbi J. David Bleich, *Bioethical Dilemmas: A Jewish Perspective,* Hoboken: KTAV Publishing House, Inc. (1998), p. 136

penetrated into his body and psyche, and how perilous for him it really is. And so, special action must be undertaken to heal the person and save his life. And again, there is no insult at all, no disrespect involved, only a true desire to really help.

The Rebbe compared society's current catering to homosexual whims to the spoiling of children by over-indulgent parents:

> They [*i.e.,* the children] themselves will eventually very strongly complain against those who misled them, and also against those who saw what was going on and did not do all that was possible for them to do, to prevent it from happening.[22]

Many rabbis have tried to articulate more specifically just what society needs to do in order to do "all that is possible." For example, Rabbi Reuven Bulka suggests that the appropriate response to those who are struggling with the issue is to welcome them into the community—without condoning either their homosexual behavior or their gay identity. In other words, distinguish between what a person is and what a person does.[23] Rabbi Michael Gold recommends that we hold to an ideal standard of behavior without becoming judgmental; and, at the same time, that we show compassion towards

---

22. Rabbi Menachem Mendel Schneerson, "Rights or Ills," <www.jonahweb.org. *Compare* Richard Cohen, *Coming Out Straight,* Winchester: Oakhill Press (2000) p. 237: "The modern-day priests of the American Medical Association, American Psychiatric Association, and American Psychological Association are telling us that homosexuality is natural, normal, and simply an alternate lifestyle. Educational institutions, social organizations, many religions, the media, and the entertainment industry have all jumped on the bandwagon, following what our 'experts' have taught them. How angry and hurt these homosexual men and women will be when they learn that they have once again been abused and neglected through miseducation and misinformation."

23. Rabbi Reuven P. Bulka, *One Man, One Women, One Lifetime: An Argument for Moral Tradition,* Lafayette: Huntington House Publishers (1995) p. 118.

people without becoming permissive.[24] Rabbi J. David Bleich suggests that "[those] more fortunate in not having been burdened in this manner, are duty-bound to show compassion and solicitude and to provide all those endeavoring to overcome their SSA with all possible support and encouragement. But to understand is not to condone, to be solicitous is not to approve." (Bleich, 136) Rabbi Norman Lamm argues that, although "under no circumstances can Judaism suffer homosexuality to become respectable,"[25] we must never stint in compassion and lovingkindness toward the individual homosexual—even despite society's "currently permissive atmosphere." This is how Rabbi Lamm sums up his recommendations:

> (1) Society and government must offer its medical and psychological assistance to those whose homosexuality is an expression of pathology, who recognize it as such, and are willing to seek help. We must be no less generous to the homosexual than to the drug addict, to whom the government extends various forms of therapy upon request. (204)
>
> (2) In remaining true to the sources of Jewish tradition, Jews are commanded to avoid the madness that seizes society at various

---

24. Rabbi Michael Gold, *G-d, Love, Sex & Family*, Northvale: Jason Aronson, Inc. (1998) p. xix.

25. Rabbi Norman Lamm, "Judaism and the Modern Attitude to Homosexuality," *Encylopaedia Judaica,* Jerusalem: Keter Publishing House (1974) p. 203.

times and in many forms, while yet retaining a moral composure and psychological equilibrium sufficient to exercise that combination of discipline and charity that is the hallmark of Judaism. (205)

Richard Cohen, a psychotherapist and recovered homosexual, advocates an even more proactive attitude:

> Let us promote true healing and restoration by getting involved, reaching out, and being there for those who wish to change. Remember this is a behavior, not an identity. Each man and woman who experiences same-sex attractions is somebody's son or daughter. Let us reach out and spread the truth with love. Let us mentor one another." (*Coming Out Straight*, 236)

Significantly, Cohen characterizes "gay rights legislation" as a downright betrayal of those it purports to protect:

> We must not sell them out by making new laws or modifying religious doctrine. Homosexuality is out of balance with nature and an incomplete reflection of G–d. Those who are experiencing homosexual thoughts, feelings, and desires truly need much love and support. Many have given up or quit trying to change . . . . (236)

With regard to the more complex question of how to behave toward those of us who do not follow G–d's Commandments at all, Rabbi Jeffrey M. Cohen, spiritual leader of one of England's largest Orthodox synagogues and a cabinet member of the Chief Rabbi of the United Kingdom, invoking the Talmud (*Arachin* 16b), urges: "We must regard all evil-doers as those who have not yet received proper, sensitive, and loving rebuke; and, as such, one may not treat them as transgressors or hate them."[26] This particular approach stems from

---

26. Rabbi Jeffrey M. Cohen, *1001 Questions on Rosh Hashonah & Yom Kippur*, Northvale: Jason Aronson (1997), p. 51. *See also,* Rabbi Chaim Rapoport, *Judaism and Homosexuality: An Authentic Orthodox View,* London: Vallentine Mitchell (2004), p. 49: "For those who reject the Divine nature of the Torah; disregard the

Leviticus 19:17: *You shall love your neighbor as yourself.* Rabbi Cohen notes that the community is obligated to show respect, compassion and sensitivity for the person engaged in the struggle. "The Talmud regards as biblically mandated the prohibition against causing embarrassment to a penitent." (*1001 Questions,* 39)

As for our attitude toward those who simply do not wish to change, there is a fine line between inclusion and approval or encouragement, between repudiating the behavior, the philosophy and the politics on the one hand, and driving the individual further into alienation and isolation, on the other. Clearly, a door must be left open for even the most recalcitrant, for the *halachah* is clear that we must always presume that a sinner will do *teshuvah*—if he or she has not already done so.

Gay and Lesbian Synagogues: An Inappropriate Response to Non-Acceptance by the Community.

Many in the gay community have responded to rejection by the more traditional-minded religious and social groups by forming their own communal institutions to replace those of the broader community. These include a gay establishment press, cable TV stations catering to gays, gay financial service providers, gay tourism,

---

laws of family purity (*taharat hamishpachah)*; do not condemn masturbation, fornication and numerous other biblical and rabbinic prohibitions, cannot truly appeal to biblical or rabbinic texts as a justification for their absolute condemnation of illicit homosexual behavior. It appears to this author that to do so smacks of sheer hypocrisy."

gay clinics, gay legal aid, gay pride parades, and yes, gay bars, spas and porno theaters—in sum, the whole gay network. Gay-and-lesbian synagogues are another example, and they are growing in number.

Of course, at first glance it may seem irreverent to lump gay synagogues in the same category as gay bars or gay cinemas. After all, a synagogue is a place of holy worship. But let us look more carefully. A gay synagogue is where gay men and women gather to serve, to pray, and to express devotion to the very G–d whose Torah forbids homosexual conduct and homosexual liaisons! As Rabbi Bulka explains, "Having a homosexual congregation makes as much sense as having a Shabbat desecrators' synagogue or a ham-eaters' congregation. But we have been lulled into accepting this as a reality, without protesting its absurdity." (*One Man, One Woman,* 117)[27]

Admittedly, homosexuals have as much right and obligation to pray to G–d as any one else. Who among us is free of sin? Who can stand before Him without trembling? The real point is that by seceding from the rest of the congregation of Jews, some Jewish homosexuals have confined themselves to a ghetto of self-deception from which cries of rejection and discrimination sound particularly false. In Rabbi Bulka's words, "[T]he rabbis that I know do not have any sentry at the door asking all those who enter to prove their heterosexuality."(*One Man One Woman,* 117) On the other hand, if

---

27. Rabbi Norman Lamm phrases his objection along the same lines: "[T]o assent to the organization of separate 'gay' groups under Jewish auspices makes no more sense, Jewishly, than to suffer the formation of synagogues that cater exclusively to idol worshipers, adulterers, gossipers, tax evaders, or Sabbath violators." (*Enc. Jud.* 205)

the rest of the community accept such acts of secession, they are equally guilty. Rabbi Hillel Goldberg discusses this aspect in an article well worth reading:

> The homosexual house of worship is the most retrogressive of homosexual institutions because it marks the religious acceptance of homosexuality and the religious inequality of the homosexual—*just the opposite of what is religiously required: the rejection of homosexuality and the acceptance of the homosexual.* The homosexual house of worship . . . is as coherent as "Temple Emanuel: a Heterosexual Congregation." Most serious of all, the assent to segregation in worship is an admission of indifference, tantamount to saying: *We prefer not to make the effort to include you or to offer regenerative counseling. We are content for you to remain apart, as you are.* A house of worship, however, is for imperfect people seeking holiness and inner healing in conjunction with other imperfect people. [. . .] Inclusiveness is not a matter of accepting a status—a deviant sexual orientation—but of accepting a person, and the house of G-d may not put any qualification on that acceptance. Every sinner—that is, everyone—must be welcome in that house . . . .[28]

As Rabbi Bulka notes,

> It is admittedly a delicate tightrope, welcoming without condoning. But, we do it with those who do not observe the Shabbat, we do it with ham-eaters. Why should we not be able to do it with so-called homosexuals? And, unlike the case with non-Shabbat observers or ham-eaters, failure to create a climate wherein self-declared homosexuals feel they can take part in congregational activity may

---

28. Rabbi Hillel Goldberg, "Homosexuality: A Religious and Political Analysis," *Tradition*, vol. 27, no. 3 (Spring, 1993), p. 34. Reprinted in Dr. Seymour Hoffman (ed.), *Issues in Psychology, Psychotherapy, and Judaism,* Lanham: University Press of America (2007), pp. 20-27.

drive them into the homosexual subculture." (*One Man, One Woman*, 118)

Certainly, it is true that if a gay person feels unwelcome or uncomfortable at a traditional synagogue, that may not always be due to his or her own insecurities. Prejudice is a real factor, and must be taken into account. In that regard, public displays of affection between gay couples, or other obvious manifestations of gayness are not calculated to arouse the good will of non-gay congregants.

Nevertheless, gay secession from the community at large is certainly not a forward-looking movement from any angle. Such segregation means making peace with an agonizing fracture in human society, one based—more's the pity—on false information and distorted reasoning. The matter is all the more disheartening in that the dissension is over an issue so fundamental to Jewish teaching and faith.

The question still remains: how do we handle the "self-declared homosexual"—the man or woman who has openly adopted a gay lifestyle, sees nothing wrong with what he or she is doing, and even goes around aggressively advertising his/her views? It is true that, as Rabbi Bulka observes (118), excluding such a person from the Jewish community will almost certainly drive him/her further into the homosexual subculture. However, it is clear that the counterpart of social inclusion is the discretion of the included. It is not simply a matter of "Don't ask, don't tell." Good manners and decent behavior are standards that apply across the board. There is no reason why behavior disrespectful of the community should be tolerated just because the person doing the misbehaving happens to be gay. Clearly, the community of Torah-observant Jews has just as much right as any other to bar or expel those who would come to *shul* (synagogue) to scoff, to shock, or to provoke trouble. Moreover, little can be done, in the short term, for the militant homosexual who angrily rejects all efforts of outreach and reintegration.

On the other hand, we still need to remember that expulsion, excommunication, social ostracism, are devastating measures that cause deep and lasting wounds. People tend to take such measures unnecessarily and impulsively, because they give one an immediate sense of vindication and power. However, such actions often backfire, with consequences that are long-lasting and very hard to undo. Thus, they should be avoided at all costs. JONAH encourages *all* communities—not just the Jewish—to develop coherent programs for the SSA individual *before* he or she feels compelled to withdraw from the fellowship. We must never shut the door of welcome. The community must become part of the solution, rather than part of the problem. We must develop healing programs—not only for adults, but even more critically for adolescents and children as well.

It goes without saying that healing programs cannot coexist side-by-side with gay advocacy programs disguised as "diversity training." As now taught in the elementary, middle and high-school systems, several "diversity" courses actually encourage students to experiment with homosexual acts, and even counsel them where to go for homosexual encounters. (*See* Chapter Three, pp. 67-88, above)

Moreover, it should be obvious that a society that honors Torah-based sexual morality cannot support legislation that attempts to establish, or results in the establishment, of homosexuals as a special protected class. "To enact special legislation legitimizes the unhealthy behavior of broken men and women in need of true love and understanding. The ultimate solution is not laws, but love." (Cohen, 236) What *is* needed is a stronger national campaign against ethnic or cultural violence and hate, and, of course, more programs for re-educating society as to the true causes and treatment of SSA.

Within the religious community, support programs such as JONAH need financial aid, cooperation, and encouragement. Contact such organizations to learn more about their programs, to make a donation, to volunteer assistance, to engage a speaker for your synagogue, church, or other place of worship. As part of a multi-faceted community whose moral and ethical frame of reference is derived from the Jewish Bible, and even more particularly as Jews for whom the Torah constitutes our special Heritage, we owe a special duty to those who are struggling bravely—despite painful emotional handicaps—to establish their authentic gender identity, to demonstrate the understanding, love and concern of the community for these individuals—especially through synagogues and other houses of worship.

The Lubavitcher Rebbe, Menachem Mendel Schneerson, was a great visionary who often saw the solutions before the rest of the world even recognized that there was a problem. In his 1986 *Sichah* ("Talk") (published under the title "Rights or Ills") the Rebbe urged the Jewish Community to reexamine the issue of homosexuality in terms of healing those who are ailing and in pain. (*See above,* pp. 344-45, this chapter). Clearly, the Rebbe understood that homosexuality is a symptom of certain unresolved emotional traumas, and a product of severe alienation. Citing the great risks to both the individual and society, the Rebbe urged that "a special responsibility lies on the parents, educators and counselors to educate those afflicted with this problem," and at the same time, "to take a *loving,* and *caring* attitude by extending a helping hand."

Alienation of the Relationship Between the Individual and G–d.

The third and most extreme level of alienation affects the relationship between the individual and G–d. Viewing themselves as undeservedly and unjustly rejected by the Bible and the religious community, many homosexuals turn angrily away from G–d and religion. The detachment is compounded through the repeated violation and rejection of a specific injunction from the Heavenly Father—namely, *You shall not lie with a man as with women. It is a* to'eivah. (Lev. 18:22) Like any *chet* or *aveirah* (sin or transgression)—especially one that becomes a habit or, even worse, a way of life—it ultimately erodes the spiritual foundations of a person's life. As phrased by Rabbi Moshe Spero, a leading therapist presently living in Israel, "Judaism recognizes that the problem of the deviance of homosexuality resides not solely in a pathology within the individual or society, but also in the complex relationship which exists between the individual who demonstrates behavior labeled as *to'eivah,* and the One who labels such behavior as *to'eivah.*" [29]

There is more. The fact that G–d characterizes this particular sin as a *to'eivah* indicates that the resultant erosion is deeper, more radical, than would be the case with an "ordinary" transgression. Whether or not the individual actually knows about Leviticus 18:22, the awareness of being "different," "deviant," or "abnormal" is inevitable, along with concomitant feelings of guilt, shame, insecurity, anger, resentment, rebelliousness, *etc.*—all of which are greatly aggravated when the subject is actually aware of the Biblical attitude towards homosexuality.

Such intensified feelings are only symptomatic of a deeper, spiritual disharmony, amounting to an actual break between man and G–d. To characterize this in (at least partly) Freudian terms, "Homosexuality represents the acceptance of a neurotic resolution of conflict with the oedipal father in a way which will eventually distort one's relation to the Heavenly Father." (Spero, 168) How this distortion or alienation develops can vary. It may manifest in anger and deliberate rebellion against His laws. It may involve despondency, despair, and loss of *emunah* (faith in G–d) owing to an apparently unanswered plea for salvation. Or, it may involve recourse to intellectual sophistry in an attempt to "reinterpret" the words of Torah and Talmud so as to make homosexuality appear consistent with G–d's will.

Whatever form it takes, this is what the Prophet is alluding to in Isaiah 59:2: "Your iniquities have separated you and your G–d."

---

29. Rabbi Dr. Moshe Halevi Spero, *Handbook of Psychotherapy & Jewish Ethics,* Jerusalem: Feldheim (1986), pp. 167-8

Indeed, this third level of alienation enables the homosexual to consider his/her own lifestyle, fantasies, and same-sex attractions as more important than G–d. This is a form of idolatry.

Reparative psychiatrist Dr. Richard Fitzgibbons stresses the importance of addressing any estrangement between the individual and his or her Maker. Fitzgibbons finds that entrusting one's body and soul to G–d's healing power is a critical component of effective therapy for SSA.[30] This is all the more important in that, as Fitzgibbons confirms, SSA strugglers tend to fear confronting their loneliness "in part, because they do not believe it can be healed." (Fitzgibbons in Harvey, 311)

This is not to suggest that only "believers" can be healed. Belief, in Jewish teaching, is founded on the Tradition embodied by Torah and Talmud and corroborated by personal understanding and experience. (It is, of course, fundamental to Judaism that one's "personal understanding" be nurtured by daily study of Torah and Talmud!) All that is required is sufficient trust to turn to the Creator in complete humility, recognize one's own powerlessness, plead for help, and promise to acknowledge G–d's hand in the healing as it

---

30. This is somewhat akin to the Higher Power concept that is used to treat drug and alcohol abuse. Although the two concepts appear at first blush to be virtually identical, there is a fundamental difference: While "Higher Power" is sometimes used as a periphrasis for G–d, the inherent ambiguity of the phrase allows it to be understood as a reference to some unspecified natural force. Hence the tendency to adopt this phrase in religiously neutral contexts, such as Alcoholics Anonymous. However, while drugs and alcohol are not specifically forbidden by Jewish Law, homosexual conduct is. Thus, G–d Himself—the very Source of Torah—and not just some vague "higher power," is a key factor in the SSA healing equation.

comes. By turning to G–d for help, the Struggler is certain to discover within him- or herself undreamed of resources for overcoming prior limitations and for repairing the severed connection to the Source of his G–d-given *Nefesh Elokis* (Divine Soul, or spiritual vitality).

What this accomplishes, in essence, is a partnership between the individual in question and G–d. The struggler, formerly weighed down by unbearable sorrow, guilt, and a mind-boggling challenge, is suddenly relieved of a tremendous weight. He or she is no longer the sole bearer of the burden. What seemed impossible yesterday appears today as not only possible, but already in progress. So universal is this phenomenon that it has been discussed in the most widely disparate circles, both religious and secular. The People Can Change website does a very good job of describing it:

> A man with homosexual attractions will usually maintain them unless he consciously surrenders them. [. . .] [S]urrender is letting go. It is choosing to release specific obstacles—whatever is holding you back and hurting you. It is a deliberate mental, emotional, and spiritual attitude of giving away these obstacles to G–d . . . in a spirit of humble trust in the wisdom, strength and goodness of the Divine Power. When we talk of surrender, we mean, first and foremost, the yielding of own own self-will to a Higher Power or a Higher Good. It is the essential experience of submitting to and trusting in Divine Will—living for something better or nobler than one's own selfish pleasure."[31]

Just how this partnership between a man or a woman and G–d is formed and how long it takes to solidify cannot be predicted. It has to do with how the two "partners" interact. At one extreme, there is even such a thing as *spontaneous healing*.

> Sometimes the A–mighty aids the penitent and causes a sudden revolution to take place in his way of thinking,

---

31. <http://www.peoplecanchange.com/Surrender.htm>.

transforming his world view, affecting the total essence of his being . . . . Through a sudden ray of illumination, he discovered the focal point of his existence, and he was transformed into another person.[32]

Indeed, as explained in the Jewish mystical literature, when a penitent does *teshuvah* and seeks, with burning emotional intensity and deep and agonizing introspection, to come close once again to G–d, it can arouse a corresponding *teshuvah* (or turning) on high. "Stimulus from below causes a stimulus from above" (*Zohar* II, 135b): the Master of the Universe turns to the penitent as the penitent turns to G–d.

Recovered homosexual Alan Medinger is one who describes his healing as "sudden" and "miraculous." (*Growth into Manhood*, 238) Rav Soloveitchik would probably describe Medinger's rebirth as a "repentance which stems from the spontaneous eruption of the divine flame which possesses man's soul." (*On Repentance*, 319) However, most SSA strugglers advance slowly, step-by-step, in a manner similar to religious penitents. This is not to say that "ordinary"

---

32. Pinchas H. Peli, *On Repentance: the Thought and Oral Discourses of Rabbi Joseph Dov Soloveitchik*, Northvale: Jason Aronson (1996), p. 318. According to Dr. Jeffrey Satinover (in private discussion), this claim is supported by clinical data presented in Laumann, Gagnon, Michael and Michaels, *The Social Organization of Sexuality: Sexual Practices in the United States,* U. Chicago Press (1994), showing a substantial number of individuals experiencing spontaneous remission of homosexuality. Testimonials (published on the internet) by Michael Glatze, a Mormon, and Charlene Cothran, a Christian, all of whom were visible gay activists prior to their religious transformation, corroborate this rare phenomenon.

teshuvah is not a great, powerful and holy accomplishment. Through cognitive understanding, recognition of internalized emotions, and the gained insight into one's experiential feelings, every one can reach a high level of *teshuvah* and spiritual awareness.

One remarkable example is Jill Postell, a singer/songwriter based in San Antonio, Texas. Jill was about to undergo surgery to change her sex from female to male. Fortunately, she decided to seek spiritual counsel before taking such a drastic step. A sensitive woman and spiritually aware, Jill felt depressed and hopeless about her SSA. "I wanted God, but sexual thoughts just kept coming back, over and over again. I didn't know how to deal with them, so I gave in. I remember wondering if there would ever be a day that I wouldn't have a thought about a woman in a sexual way."[33] To overcome her estrangement from G–d, Jill finally agreed to surrender to Him and to "allow G–d to change me from the inside out." ("No More Hiding") As Jill healed, she soon learned how much more effective it was to change her inner being and reunite with G–d than to change her physical being and live as something she was not.

The formula for what Jill Postell did is expressed, in its original Jewish formulation, in the *Shema* prayer.

Hear, O Israel, the Lord is our G–d, the Lord is One!

The observant Jew recites this affirmation and its concomitant text three times a day as a statement of basic faith and personal commitment. It is a statement of complete and unreserved submission to the One G–d who in turn shepherds the conflicted soul and the broken person into an integrated and harmonious whole.

---

33. Jill Postell, "No More Hiding," *Exodus Update*, (February, 2002).

Sexual Idolatry and Alienation from G–d.

We come now to the central component of alienation from G–d, namely, the idolatrous role of sexual desire itself (or of the object of such desire) in disrupting the relationship between a man or woman and G–d. It is here that the discussion of homosexuality overlaps with sexuality—with sexual brokenness—in general, and the habitual abuse of interpersonal relationships for mere sexual gratification. Nevertheless, in the present subsection, we discuss the idolatrous aspects of sex mainly as they apply to homosexuals only—not because we want to minimize the relevance of these aspects to heterosexuals, but because this book focuses on homosexuality; and also because in the course of our research as well as in personal interviews with SSA men and women, we have found express references to body worship and sexual idolatry to occur with significant frequency.

One of Judaism's central teachings is that, as the *Aleinu* Prayer declares, "The L–rd is G–d; in the heavens above and upon the earth below there is nothing else." In fact, in the very First of the Ten Commandments, G–d commands us:

You shall have no other gods before Me.

Hence, the ultimate transgression in Judaism is idolatry, the worship of something—anything—other than G–d. While the Bible evidences particular animosity toward the worship of idols of wood or of stone, our Tradition defines idolatry much more broadly to encompass *even an idea, a force, a habit or obsession to which we have surrendered sufficient authority or power to interfere with our observance of the Commandments.*

What happens when sexual gratification becomes an obsessive need to the point of predominating over every other consideration—as it does when a person adopts a homosexual lifestyle, whether covertly or overtly? Most people do not think of the idolatrous dimensions of same-sex attraction. But if one understands the roots of SSA, if one observes the way homosexuals live, one sees very clearly how a created thing—not the Creator—becomes an object of outright worship.

Alan Medinger describes quite candidly the idolatrous component of homosexual relationships. In fact, he discerns two different types of idolatry, one more commonly found in SSA men, the other in SSA women:

> In men the idolatry typically involves the worship of those things that exude the masculine: muscles, physical strength, authority, male genitalia. Whether he is longing for his own sense of manhood or for a masculine contact that was denied him in childhood, he longs to make contact with—see, touch, smell, be encompassed by, even be entered into by—that which he feels exemplifies true manhood.... In the midst of passionate sexual acting out, the homosexual man imagines he is with a "real man" rather than with another whose manhood is as empty and undeveloped as his.[34]

According to Medinger, the idolatry assumes a different form in female homosexuality:

> In women the idolatry is more likely directed towards a specific person, that one woman who the hurting or empty woman believes can meet all of her needs. Sometimes this is rooted in childhood deficits in the mother relationship. In other situations women who were deeply hurt in their earlier life—usually by a man or men—are left with extraordinary needs to feel protected and secure. They crave someone to meet these deep needs in their heart, and they develop patterns of looking to other women to meet them. Each new woman who meets certain criteria becomes the one who can answer all of these needs. She becomes an idol.... The lesbian woman, not yet knowing the other's weaknesses and neediness, imagines that

---

[34]. Alan Medinger, "What is Idolatry?" *Regeneration Newsletter* (August, 2003), pp. 1-2.

the other woman truly can provide the love and security she needs. (*Regeneration Newsletter,* 2)

Naturally, the fantasy (in either form) is usually short-lived.

> Eventually reality breaks through and the idol's feet of clay become too obvious to ignore and the worship ceases. But the idol did meet needs for a time, and not knowing any other way to go, the needy person doesn't abandon idolatry, but seeks out another idol. (2)

In the early 1970s, psychotherapist Patty Wells-Graham, a former lesbian, surrendered herself to the life-force of feminism, practically worshipping it as a deity.

> Feminism appealed to me very much at this point because it promised personal power to women. It provided emotional support at a time when I was convinced that only other women could understand me. With my damaged self-esteem, that counterfeit power and emotional strength was inviting. The step into lesbianism from there was easy as my determination to identify with women grew. I eventually became sexually involved with my best friend of ten years. We were fighting together for our rights as women. Since she had been the person in my life most able to understand my intimate thoughts and feelings, she seemed the ideal partner for me.[35]

She recalls,

> If you had asked me when I was in lesbianism what was the most important thing, I would have said, "intimacy." But it really wasn't intimacy I was seeking at that time. It was emotional dependence, which had become a god for me. Now that I'd left that behind, standing on my own was really important. It was also key for me to

---

35. Patty Wells-Graham, "Words of Wisdom, Words of Love," in Bob Davies and Lela Gilbert, *Portraits of Freedom,* Downers Grove: Intervarsity Press (2001), p. 99.

have close and caring relationships with a variety of godly women—not just with one woman and not a sexual relationship. That's how I learned what G-d intends for relationships with the same sex. Perhaps most indispensable to my new life was healing for my wounded relationship with my mom, or what is sometimes called "mother wounding." (104)

Dr. Carol Ahrens explains:

[W]hen a woman is emotionally dependent, she feels as though she literally cannot exist without the object of her dependency. She needs constant reassurance from the other woman, consistent displays of affection, and large quantities of time with her. In short, emotional dependency is a bit like idolatry: Another person, in this case a woman, has become a sort of god.[36]

Rich Wyler is among a number of men who have written about their idolization of other males and maleness.

Feeling deficient as males, we pined to be accepted and affirmed by others, especially those whose masculinity we admired most. We began to idolize the qualities in other males we judged to be lacking in our selves. Idolizing them widened the gulf we imagined between ourselves and so-called "real men," the Adonis-gods of our fantasies. In idolizing them, we increased our sense of our own masculine deficiency. It also de-humanized the men we idolized,

---

36. Dr. Carol Ahrens, "Emotional Dependency and Lesbianism," in Joe Dallas, *Desires in Conflict: Answering the Struggle for Sexual Identity,* Eugene: Harvest House Publishers (1991), p. 204.

putting them on a pedestal that deified them and made them unapproachable. (<www.peoplecanchange.com>)

The cyclical pattern of infatuation and disillusionment described above is found in both male and female homosexuals, and meets the definition of neurosis. As such, the behavior is not entirely voluntary. Nevertheless, to the extent that the struggler has some awareness and control over his/her obsessions, the behavior directly contravenes the commandment to have no other gods.

Comparisons between homosexuality and idol worship are not new. We find in the Talmud, (*Sanhedrin* 82a) that when Rav Kahana inquires of Rav the punishment for a man who has sex with a Cuthean (*i.e.,* promiscuous) woman, Rav answers with the following quotation from the Prophets (Malachi 2:11): "Judah has dealt treacherously, and a *to'eivah* has been committed in Israel and Jerusalem . . . . ." The Talmud interprets this quotation as alluding to idol worship and homosexual relations, respectively. Rav's answer implies that the punishment for having sex with a Cuthean woman is the same as for idol worship and homosexual relations. What is interesting about this from the perspective of this chapter is that Rav's response likens promiscuous sex and homosexual relations to idol worship.

Another interesting Talmudic comparison is found in a *Mishnah* discussed in Talmud, *Shabbos* 82a, where Rabbi Akiva draws a *halachic* analogy between idol worship and the ritual impurity of a menstruant woman. According to Jewish Law, there are various ways by which a person can contract ritual impurity from another person or object. One of these ways is called *tumah bemasa* ("impurity by carrying"). A menstruant woman falls into this category. This means that her ritual impurity (*tumah*) can be transmitted not only by touch, but by carrying. In practical terms, this means that if one or more men use a chair or a couch to transport her from one location to another, they will contract her *tumah* even if there is no direct physical contact. In the *Mishnah* referred to above, the great Sage Rabbi Akiva concludes from Isaiah 30:22 ("You shall cast [your idols] away as a menstruous thing") that idols belong in the same category of impurity. In other words, idols are *tamei bemasa*—they transmit their impurity not only through touching, but also through carrying.

Obviously, there are several physical ways to carry an idol without physically touching it, and I am certainly not proposing a new *halachah* by extending Rabbi Akiva's analogy into the realm of metaphor. Nevertheless, it is no great stretch to say that one way to carry an idol without touching it is to harbor it within one's thoughts and desires—in other words, to fantasize about that which has become the idol.

The great Sage Rabbah understands Isaiah 30:22 a little differently, but agrees, in substance, with Rabbi Akiva (*Shabbos* 82b): "You must distance yourself from an idol as you would from a stranger," says Rabbah, alluding to the dangers of traveling alone on the road. Thus, if homosexuality is akin to idol worship, and if we must distance ourselves from idolatry as from a "stranger," then it follows that we must flee from homosexual fantasies as we would from a potential robber encountered alone on the road. Note that *halachah* already forbids thinking lewd thoughts: it is one of the *chataos* (plural of *chet*, "sin") for which we expressly beg forgiveness on *Yom Kippur*. In light of the foregoing, it would seem incumbent upon us to work to eliminate same-sex fantasy, arousal, and other sexually obsessive thoughts from our minds.

The analogy between homosexuality and idol worship is more than just a figure of speech. Alan Medinger notes the extraordinary role fantasy plays in homosexual relationships: "The same sex attracted person makes the other person whoever he or she needs them to be, makes them his or her idol." ("What is Idolatry?" 1) Medinger is being absolutely up front. Several of our strugglers in the JONAH program report having experienced feelings akin to idolatry *before* they became aware of any sexual attraction. According to these individuals, it would start with envious feelings about a certain person's attributes, would progress into an excessive, adoring admiration for that person, and culminating in a same-sex attraction that would lead in turn to a homosexual act.

In a healthy sexual relationship (and "healthy" implies heterosexual, married, and regulated), sex takes its rightful place as one of various modes of communicating love, caring and understanding between two individuals who complement each other's gender attributes physically, emotionally, and spiritually. It is part of a complex, ongoing, living relationship. When the sexual, physical component becomes obsessive and consuming, other essential aspects of the relationship suffer or never develop. In the Torah view, one of the most vital facets of the heterosexual union is the relationship of both partners, and of the marriage itself, to G–d. When the sexual motivation is so uncontrolled as to cause the partners to ignore G–d's presence in the relationship—and, consequently, to cause G–d to leave it, that is, by definition, idol worship. It also describes the *homosexual* dynamic very accurately. The partners know very well that the relationship is forbidden by all major religious traditions, and frowned upon by a large part of human society; very often, they also sense that this kind of relationship is incompatible with "who they are." All of this may give rise to feelings of guilt, self-loathing and shame; yet the sexual element has been allowed to become paramount, to the exclusion of all other considerations.

Clearly, there is much wisdom in extending Rabbah's injunction regarding idols to homosexual fantasies: Distance yourself from them as from a "stranger." On the other hand, by advising strict observance and piety as an antidote for SSA, some religious leaders—both Jewish and non-Jewish—may be carrying the concept too far. What they are prescribing, in effect, is to change the psychological terrain through spiritual or religious involvement so that lustful fantasies find no place to take root. There is no question that intense involvement with Torah and *Mitzvos* can "change the spiritual terrain." However, in my judgment, without dealing with the root sources of the forbidden attractions, it is nearly impossible to eliminate them. Father John Harvey, founder of Courage, the Catholic "ex-gay" ministry, is a major proponent of the "choir boy" approach.[37]

---

37. This approach is known in the secular world as "white-knuckling it." *But see*

Although Father Harvey and others have achieved some notable successes with this method—and they certainly have the best of intentions—their approach, in my opinion, contains two significant flaws. In the first place, it is highly simplistic, and thus likely to be simplified even further, and misinterpreted and misapplied as word filters down the grapevine: "Just don't think about it." But without teaching effective techniques for "not thinking about it," or addressing the root causes, this approach can be not only futile, but actually damaging. In the second place—and more importantly—the prescription serves at best to suppress only the *behavior* and the fantasies, without resolving any of the underlying symptoms, such as arousal and gender identity.

Thus, the "choir boy" method offers at best an incomplete healing in which the suppressed behavior will keep popping up, much like a balloon that is held under water. Because of the greater potential for recidivism in those strugglers who are simply attempting to repress the behavior, this approach provides unnecessary ammunition for those who believe change is not possible.

Although the desire for sex is normal in most healthy men, it tends to become obsessive in homosexuality, as well as in other forms of sexual brokenness. And, while the pursuit of one's physical needs is not seen, in Jewish tradition, as negating the possibility of a personal, loving, and intimate relationship with G–d, the opposite is

---

Harvey, p. 120, note 6: "A seminarian who makes no effort to purge himself of homosexual fantasies and affections has only a minimal chance of remaining chaste." A number of Orthodox rabbis hold analogous views.

often the case with homosexuals. As we have explained, this is because the homosexual's need for sex is a kind of mirage. The act itself can never really fulfill the need. At best, it can only palliate (and at worst, actually exacerbate) the conditions out of which the need is born. In this, homosexuality is strikingly analogous to other SB conditions, such as nymphomania or pornomania.

Envy.

Aside from the kinship between homosexuality and idolatry, perhaps the most compelling analogy would be with envy. The psychology of envy is generally that one "covets"—*i.e.,* desires for oneself—one's neighbor's house, wife, or donkey (read "automobile")—simply because it is the neighbor's. The moment one has taken possession of it, it loses its principal attraction. In fact, the coveted object may never have had any real allure for the coveter: its attractiveness may have been altogether illusory.

Perhaps not surprisingly, intense envy of others of the same sex is one of the early indicators of homosexuality. Envious persons look elsewhere for something that they believe is lacking within themselves. Envy is a covetous spirit within, an intense desire to acquire what they see in someone else, be it a physical possession, a physical attribute, or a personality trait, *etc.* Those who have successfully healed from the homosexual condition find they no longer own this envy, and certainly no longer sexualize it. They have found within themselves what they formerly looked for in others.

D.B., a struggler in the JONAH program, found that the antidote for his own envy-idolatry syndrome was to develop "an attitude of gratitude" about himself. He and others in our program learned how to experience comfortable day-to-day relationships with others of the same sex. D.B. found our sports clinic particularly helpful. It allowed him and others to experience a sense of "sameness" with their peers that had hitherto eluded them. Another JONAH Struggler, M.R., 33 years old, commented to the author, "For the first time in my life, I felt like I had a 'legitimate' reason for being on or near a basketball court . . . . I am now ready to take the steps to find my innate masculinity."

Many JONAH men first begin to understand G–d's plan of creation only after experiencing and internalizing non-sexual, male bonding activities.[38] During the healing process, they find that their sense of gender emptiness is replaced by a feeling of gender fulfillment. A gender *congruity* results. They begin to perceive the opposite sex as complementary to themselves, and it feels good. Their physiological gender starts to "feel right," and this "rightness" banishes the envy, the idolatry, and the SSA.

With the idolatry abated, it should come as no surprise that, through gender fulfillment, many of these individuals find that their connection to G–d has been strengthened. What does this mean in practical terms? It means that also in other areas of their lives, where obstacles once barred the way to greater success or fulfillment or achievement or simply happiness, those obstacles have now been lifted, clearing the way to unanticipated progress in spiritual practice, in work and in life. Repossessing one's gender identity and control over one's sexual behavior can bring a new and deeper awareness of self worth, personal dignity, and achievement.

An Aside on Sexual Addiction.

As we have indicated, homosexual sex often (but not always) tends to fall into the category of sexual addictions. Rich Wyler describes this phenomenon eloquently on the People Can Change website (<www.peoplecanchange.com>):

> Sexual gratification can be immensely intoxicating to men. As soon as some of us started using lust or pornography to anesthetize our emotional pain, we were on the fast track to sexual addiction—perhaps one of the easiest addictions for men to fall into, and

---

38. *See* Medinger, *Growth into Manhood,* pp. 6-7.

certainly one of most difficult to emerge from. Those of us who became addicted to sex or pornography found that, to emerge from a homosexual addiction, we often had to work at least two "recovery programs" simultaneously—a 'detox' program to withdraw from our sex habit, and a program of masculine affirmation and inner healing to resolve the emotional pain.[39]

Another recovered homosexual discovered that

> To be sexually addicted is to literally rely on sex to stabilize you. It's a state in which the rush of sexual pleasure, with all its accompanying chemical forces, has become to you like what a drug has become to an addict. And like a drug, it begins to interfere with all parts of life.[40]

Sex addicts have a compulsive desire for sex.[41] The need to entertain lust and sexual stimulation are prime characteristics of obsessive sex. It is a mind set in which fantasizing about sexual and other self-centered desires or superficial relations replaces one's awareness of reality. The causes of obsessive sex tend to overlap with the causes of SSA. For example, lack of positive self-image, perceived inability to have meaningful relationships, a persistent perception that emotional needs cannot be met, the delusional conviction that sex will meet their needs—all are factors that often give rise to homosexuality as well as sexual addiction.

---

39. <www.peoplecanchange.com>.

40. Joe Dallas, *Desires in Conflict: Answering the Struggle for Sexual Identity*, Eugene: Harvest House Publishers (1991) p. 63.

41. For more information on sexual addiction, *see* Carnes, *Out of the Shadows: Understanding Sexual Addiction*, Center City: Hazelden Foundation (1994), and Schaumburg, *False Intimacy: Understanding the Struggle of Sexual Addiction:* Colorado Springs: NavPress Publishing Group (1992).

Heterosexual and homosexual persons are equally susceptible to becoming "sexaholics." Common behavior patterns include harmful co-dependent relationships, compulsive masturbation, use of pornography, prowling the internet, promiscuous sexual relationships, adulterous or secretive affairs, compulsive exhibitionism, and sexually abusive relationships.

Thus, as Joe Dallas observes,

> Breaking the cycle of sexual addiction is not just a matter of will in this case; it is more a matter of *strategy*, *consistency*, and *patience*. But *repentance* begins that process. Without it there can be no growth, no freedom, no change. And repentance is an act of the will. [. . .] To put away sexual idolatry, you need to call it what it is: a form of sexual expression that has come between you and G–d...." (Original emphasis.) (63)

However, once the addiction is broken, the inclination to engage in these activities no longer stands in the way of deeper healing, and the path to G–dliness lies open.

Sexual Politics as Idolatry.

The 20th century has seen great strides in the progressive liberation of western society from the oppressive "isms" that discriminated against different classes of human beings on the basis of race, color, creed, nationality, economic class and gender. Such movements of liberation are in harmony with the Laws of Noah, which call upon each nation of the world to establish and maintain a fair and equitable system of justice. Such movements appeal to the noblest human qualities of dedication, self-sacrifice and loyalty; but their own momentum often transforms them into new instruments of oppression. The same "party" loyalty that makes a member valuable to his or her noble cause can also lead that same individual to betray family, friends, and, obviously, him- or herself. As one commentator explains, "The deification of the human—which was an exaggeration of the trends for human empowerment—turned various constructive liberation processes into new forms of totalitarian control."[42]

Thus, it should not surprise that movements of sexual and gender liberation can also induce adherents, on a much deeper level, to trample those values that define us as human beings. When the agendas, theories, and ideologies of feminism, gay liberation, or multiculturalism—in short, of Political Correctness—begin to eclipse our relationship with G–d and the moral and civic obligations that relationship places upon us, then we, too, cross the line into oppression, intolerance—and idolatry.

A society that perceives the human being, rather than G–d, as the ultimate measure of morality will soon lose its precious freedoms without even realizing what is happening. We saw this most recently in the former Soviet Union. An earlier generation saw it in the French Revolution. Similarly, in its insidious efforts to institute a new "morality" of licentious hedonism, gay liberation (which started as a movement to end the persecution of, and discrimination against, homosexuals), has not shrunk from intimidating and defaming those who support traditional standards of sexual morality. In the same way, feminism, which started as a movement to liberate women from male-chauvinist bias and economic oppression, went on, in its most extreme version, to envision and advocate a society devoid of males. The more fanatical adherents of this movement openly and aggressively degrade men *qua* men—even while mimicking masculine behavior and espousing lesbianism—a practice that altogether repudiates and degrades the very basis of their purported feminism, that is, their femininity and the quality of being a woman.[43]

---

42. Rabbi Irving Greenberg, *Living in the Image of G–d: Jewish Teachings to Perfect the World*, Northvale: Jason Aronson (1998), p. 118.

43. "The true feminine, I think, has been lost," writes Diane Eller-Boyko. "Today's feminist is angry, aggressive, masculinized, and has lost her sacred place in the home." "Touching the Feminine Soul," <www.jonahweb.org> and <www.narth.com>.

We have already seen how one recovered lesbian, Patty Wells Graham, attributed her long excursion into lesbianism to a political feminism carried to the extreme. Jan Clausen, cast out of the lesbian community by "enforcers of ideological purity"[44] for falling in love with a man, is another example. Her more than twelve years of "intensive lesbian feminist activism on literary and political fronts" did not shield her from the vituperation of her former colleagues when she repudiated homosexuality.[45] According to Eller-Boyko, militant feminism combines with "a rebellious attitude toward the idea of receptivity . . . . Yet receptivity is the very core of the feminine." ("Touching the Feminine Soul")

Where does all this lead? To an understanding that any process of liberation needs to be calibrated and regulated against some absolute standard of ethics and morality. Otherwise, "liberation" ends up as nothing more than a shift in the balance of power and leads inevitably to further oppression and injustice.

From Idolatry to G–d: the Way Back.

The key to overcoming addictions and other deeply ingrained patterns of behavior and emotional response is surrender: surrendering your will to His. Resisting sin certainly favors G–d's

---

44. *See* Jan Clausen, *Applies & Oranges: My Journey Through Sexual Identity,* Boston: Houghton, Mifflin Company (1999).

45. As far as political correctness is concerned, Clausen's abandonment of her female lover for a man was a "fall from grace." It was "transgressing the party line," morphing "into the tender villain of the classic lesbian nightmare," and committing "the lesbian equivalent of mortal sin." She became alienated from her own support structure, a form of totalitarian control where "policing identity" was not only justified but became commonplace. (*Apples & Oranges,* 233). For further information, *see also* Tammy Bruce, *The New Thought Police: Inside the Left's Assault on Free Speech and Free Minds,* Roseville: Prima Publishing (2001) and Tammy Bruce, *The Death of Right and Wrong: Exposing the Left's Assault on our Culture and Values,* New York: Three Rivers Press (2003).

intentions for us; but resistance means "fight or flight," and that is hardly a happy mode of life. In our holy Tradition, G–d wants us to be happy—truly fulfilled and happy, and grateful to be alive. Accentuating the positive helps eliminate the negative. As our souls focus on who G–d wants us to be and what we can become, we are able to take our weary eyes off of our sins and let them rest upon the upward path to sexual wholeness and sexual holiness.

Rav Soloveitchik stresses self-restraint and adherence to *halachah* as the appropriate context for implementing this surrender.[46] How does this differ from mere resistance? When a defeated general surrenders to a conquering army, he gives up his command and the army's autonomy. Both he and his army become entirely subject to the will of the victors. However, that does not affect the nationality of the vanquished. Surrendering to Caesar (cessation of resistance) does not *per se* make one a Roman. With G–d, it is a different story. Surrendering to G–d (trusting in G–d and carrying out His will with intention and devotion) *changes one's entire nature*—indeed, endows us with something of G–d's own power to recreate and to heal and to make grow.

How shall we surrender to G–d? Here, in his own words, is how one struggler did it:

> When I was in the throes of withdrawal from my lust cycles, I had to learn a whole new way of responding to lust. Instead of gritting my teeth and clenching my fists, trying to force the feeling away, as I had always done before, I would close my eyes and imagine a channel of light going up from my body to the heavens. I would open my palms toward heaven and say something like, "G–d, I release this feeling over to you. If I try to resist and fight it, I will lose, because it is stronger than I am. So I give it to you, and trust

---

46. *See* Peli, *On Repentance,* pp. 77-88, and Abraham R. Besdin, *Man of Faith in the Modern World: Reflections of the Rav,* vol. 2 Hoboken: Ktav Publishing House (1989), p. 42.

you to handle it for me instead." In submitting my desires to G–d's greater power, the urgency and control they held over me lessened enough that I could make a phone call to a mentor or friend, and ask for support. I would immediately then make plans to meet my authentic needs for companionship and connection in a non-sexual, fulfilling way.[47]

Besides faith and humility, a third element of surrender is prayer. Speaking to G–d, pouring your heart out in your own words, privately yet audibly, to Him Who is patient, understanding and forgiving toward all His creatures; reciting the *Tehillim* (Psalms) of King David with concentration and meditation on the meaning of the words, and saying the prayers of the traditional Jewish liturgy—all of these create a pathway directly to *Hashem*. Certainly, for a Jewish man, putting on *tefillin* (the prayer phylacteries) and reciting the *Sh'ma* is directly connected with the concept of surrendering to G–d.

Perhaps it is not at all strange that many strugglers find special meaning in the language of Jewish prayer. This is surely because prayer is the vehicle of *teshuvah*, and *teshuvah* begins with a broken heart.

Mike Haley is a recovered homosexual, formerly a male prostitute who worked the gay community over a period of twelve years. Till recently, he served as the manager of the Homosexuality and Gender Issues Department at Focus on the Family. He has also served as Chairman of the Board of Exodus International and Exodus North America (the Evangelical ex-gay ministry).[48] In remembering his struggle with homosexuality, Mike recalls how the words of Jeremiah 15:18-19 not only inspired him to undertake his journey of healing,

---

47. <http://www.peoplecanchange.com/Surrender.htm>.

48. He is also the "Dear Mike" of Jeff Konrad's letters in *You Don't Have to be Gay: Hope and Freedom for Males Struggling with Homosexuality, or for those who Know of Someone who Is*. Hilo: Pacific Publishing House (1987). *See* Exodus International, "From Prostitute to Pastor: the Mike Haley Story," <http://www.exodus.to/content/view/350/151>.

but also unfailingly sustained him along the way. The Prophet cries out to *Hashem:* "Why has my pain become everlasting and my wound acute? It refuses to be healed. You have become like a disillusionment to me, like unfaithful waters." And *Hashem* replies, "If you repent, I will bring you back."

Mike was indeed brought back. In his informative book, he tells how "mountains of hurt and rejection melted as I found a freedom I hadn't known before."[49] He and his wife Angie are the parents of two young sons. He now lectures all over the country about the ability to grow out of homosexuality.

Richard Cohen, cited innumerable times in this book, is another recovered homosexual with a deep reverence for the Heavenly Father. During his struggle, Cohen was moved to compose his own beautiful prayer, which he graciously shared with me:

> O G–d, please show me the meaning of my homosexual desires. L–rd, please help me bring healing to my wounded parts. Allow me to complete my journey into wholeness. Bring loving men and women into my life so that I may experience Your love through them and enable them to help lead me back to your path of righteousness.

---

49. Mike Haley, *101 Frequently Asked Questions About Homosexuality,* Eugene: Harvest House Publishers (2004), p. 17.

Chapter 11:

Teshuvah, or Return to Innocence: the Jewish Process of Return, Rebirth, and Healing.

What is *Teshuvah*?

To answer this question, we might start with the words of Rabbi Menachem Mendel Schneerson, the seventh Lubavitcher Rebbe:

> Chassidic thought teaches us that within each of us resides a Divine soul, a spark of G–d. This infinite G–dly potential represents the core of our souls, our genuine "I". From this perspective, sin and evil are superficial elements that can never affect our fundamental nature. *Teshuvah* means rediscovering our true selves, establishing contact with this G–dly inner potential and making it the dominant influence in our lives.[1]

---

1. Rabbi Menachem M. Schneerson, "Two Different Dynamics," <http://www.sichosinenglish.org/books/timeless-patterns/06.htm>.

The Hebrew word *teshuvah* has been mentioned many times. Commonly translated as "repentance," it more accurately denotes a process of growth and renewal that invigorates and changes one's inner being. "Seen in this light, our motivation to do *teshuvah* is not an awareness of our inadequacies, but rather a sensitivity to this infinite potential within our souls." (Lubavitcher Rebbe, "Two Different Dynamics") *Teshuvah* is a rebirthing of the soul, a returning to the pure spiritual state in which we were created. It is the undertaking of a solemn commitment to live according to the code of conduct set forth by G–d at Sinai. Rav Soloveitchik uses the term "restoration" as a way to convey all these meanings with one simple word.[2] Thus, *teshuvah* means something much broader than "repentance," as it is usually translated.

Even so, the English word "repentance" can also mean more than it is usually given credit for. Joe Dallas, an expert on gender recovery and himself a former homosexual, understands just how valuable this hackneyed little word can be for strugglers. Attempting to impart this deeper definition of "repentance," Dallas, albeit unwittingly, describes very accurately the Jewish concept of *teshuvah*.

> Now "repent" is a word we associate with loony old men in sackcloth warning about the coming doom. (Thanks again, Hollywood.) That's too bad because repentance is a valuable concept. It means "to think differently, reconsider, turn around." No real changes are made without it. Repentance is the willful act of discontinuing a thing which is destructive, followed by an earnest effort to do what is constructive and right. Without confession nothing is forgiven, but without repentance nothing is changed.[3]

---

2. Rabbi Pinchas H. Peli, *On Repentance: The Thought and Oral Discourses of Rabbi Joseph Dov Soloveitchik*, Northvale: Jason Aronson (1996), p. 83.

3. Joe Dallas, *Desires in Conflict: Answering the Struggle for Sexual Identity*, Eugene: Harvest House Publishers (1991), p. 54.

The author of these insights is a Pastoral Counselor in Tustin, California, and a former president of Exodus International, a faith-based organization that for more than thirty years has been working to help homosexuals heal. After many years of uninhibitedly acting out his homosexual fantasies, Dallas sought out and embraced his Christian heritage, began digging up the root causes of his SSA, and courageously embarked on a journey of emotional and spiritual growth that he had put off since early adolescence. Joe Dallas's transformation from an avowed and practicing homosexual to a stable and happy partner in a heterosexual marriage is a perfect example of what *teshuvah* means and what it can accomplish. True repentance is impossible without authentic evaluations of oneself. Unwanted behaviors can only persist if we lie to ourselves—in particular, by telling ourselves that G–d will "shut an eye" to our "foibles." As explained in Chapter Six, there is always a way to rationalize behaviors we know to be "problematic." The process of *teshuvah* helps us identify "the rationalizations that lie at the root of our mistakes: recognizing them, dealing with them and eliminating them."[4]

Let's take a closer look. Rabbinic literature is replete with references to and information about *teshuvah*. The basic theory behind the idea of *teshuvah* is that G–d is merciful and desirous of doing good; and so would not have endowed us with the capacity to sin unless He had also provided us with the ability to cleanse ourselves of wrongdoing and to correct our errors. If we did not have the ability to "do *teshuvah*," we would not have the ability to sin. If we did not have the capacity for sin, there would be no freedom of

---

4. Rabbi Shimon Apisdorf, *Rosh-Hashanah-Yom Kippur Survival Kit,* Baltimore: Leviathan Press (1992), p. 102. JONAH's literature highlights and rephrases Rabbi Apisdorf's statement when it explains that "Change is Possible. These freeing principles [referring to *teshuvah*] enumerate a specific formula for personal growth and change. First, by recognizing a true desire for change, dealing with issues, and then, eliminating the unwanted patterns."

choice; and if there were no freedom of choice, then there would no merit in striving to improve.

The first systematic and comprehensive treatment found in our literature about *teshuvah* is the Rambam's *Mishneh Torah*. He introduces the subject thus: "This section contains one positive commandment, namely, that the sinner should repent before *Hashem* [G–d] and confess." He further explains in the first chapter of the Laws of Repentance:

> All of the commandments of the Torah, whether positive or negative—if a person should violate one of them, whether willfully or inadvertently—when he repents and turns away from his sin, he is obligated to confess before G–d, Blessed is He, as it is written: "A man or a woman, when they do any sin . . . they shall confess the sin that they did." This refers to verbal confession. This confession is a positive commandment. How does one confess? He says: "Please, *Hashem*! I have erred, sinned, and rebelled before you, and I have done such and such. Now I am regretful and embarrassed by my behavior and I will never return to this thing again." This is the essential confession. And anyone who makes a more lengthy confession and elaborates on this topic is praiseworthy.

Note how the Rambam mentions "repents *and* turns away from his sin." These words are not superfluous; they do not mean the same thing. While one might initially assume that the key issue is simply abandoning the inappropriate behavior which violated one of G–d's commandments, the conjunction "and" actually connects two separate and distinct aspects of the *mitzvah* of doing *teshuvah*. Indeed, it is quite common to feel remorse over one's mistakes and wrongful actions, and then go ahead and do them all over again. Rambam's explanation makes it clear that there is no *teshuvah* without a solemn commitment not to repeat the *aveirah* (transgression).

Rabbi Joshua Maroof, spiritual leader of Magen David Synagogue in Rockville, Maryland, and a frequent contributor to the weekly news journal, *Mesora,* explains further:

> Specifically, we must consider the fact that a person who violates one of the commandments is doing a lot more than *acting* inappropriately. His sin is not a random occurrence that can be viewed separately from his personal beliefs and convictions. On the contrary, through his action he is demonstrating something about his entire value system: he is making a statement about what he envisions—or does not envision—as his purpose in life.[5]

There is an amazing similarity between the process of *teshuvah* and the gender-affirming processes (GAP) advocated by JONAH. One can easily apply the theory of *teshuvah* to GAP. For example, read how Rabbi Maroof defines *teshuvah,* and then substitute the phrase "change of sexual orientation" for the word *teshuvah* in the following passage from the above-quoted article:

> It is the internal, transformational *process of self-reflection, value clarification and study* that constitutes true *teshuvah*—the behavior change is, as it were, a by-product of this monumental effort. (Emphasis added.)

Although *teshuvah* might begin with a single, cathartic up-welling of remorse, coupled with a bold resolve to change, all the classic sources recognize that *teshuvah* is indeed a process, not a simple act. As one writer phrases it, "For most people, transformation takes time and occurs gradually."[6] It is not a light thing to restore one's purity of

---

5. Rabbi Joshua Maroof, "The Concept of *Teshuva,*" <http://www.mesora.org/teshuva1.htm.>.

6. Rabbi Irving Greenberg, *The Jewish Way: Living the Holidays,* Northvale: Jason Aronson (1998), p. 203. A long cleansing process is generally required to transform the dynamics of sin in general, and of homosexuality in particular. This gradual dynamic of change applies equally to the processes of *teshuvah* and GAP. Rarely is

soul. There is no proverbial "silver bullet." One doesn't normally change deeply ingrained emotional responses, behavior, and feelings in a single day. It is for this reason that I have coined the term "gender-affirming processes" (GAP) as a reflection of the gradual progress of healing that occurs in sexual reorientation.

Many recovered homosexuals would agree. Reviewing his clients' files, Joe Dallas reports that their main common characteristic "had to do with process versus [instantaneous] transformation."

> Homosexuality doesn't just vanish when a person decides he or she doesn't want it. None of my counselees were insincere or undecided on that point: They no more wanted to be gay than they wanted a third eyeball. They were willing to do anything to be free. The answer in all cases has been to go through a process of growth rather than to expect a quick change. And there's the rub—"process" is a word foreign to the vocabulary of modern Americans. (*Desires in Conflict,* 8)

Indeed, observes Dallas, referring to the culture of instant gratification, "this mentality can be lethal. It's led many a person to try shock treatment, exorcism, and sexual experimentation with the opposite sex in hope of a quick cure. The result is always the same: failure and disillusionment." (9) Why? Because "Homosexuality . . .

---

there a sudden change. Rather, both processes involve the need to recognize deeply repressed feelings and to understand their import at emotional, intellectual, and spiritual levels.

is symptomatic of other problems that are deeply ingrained and often hard to detect. Like the red light on a dashboard, it indicates that something under the hood needs to be checked." (9)

Similarly, *teshuvah* takes place on several levels, all of them integral to the process. Rav Soloveitchik identifies three: the emotional, the experiential, and the instinctive. (*On Repentance*, 22). Other characterizations are possible, some of them encompassing more than three levels: for example, emotional, behavioral, psychological, cognitive, and spiritual. One way or another, the struggler's process of *teshuvah* runs along the following lines: the struggler recognizes his/her need to change a pattern of undesired feelings and/or behavior. He/she learns that the initial behavior came about because of certain emotional patterns. Implementing the desired changes gives rise to new emotional responses. As these new and old emotions are explored, they can lead to deep psychological insights concerning—and ultimately illuminating—the underlying causes that gave rise to the unwanted behavior in the first place. As has been known and accepted ever since Freud, understanding the root causes of a psychological adaptation, both cognitively and emotionally, can be the turning point in the process of radical healing. Moreover, since "you can't heal what you can't feel," the cognitive insights one acquires need to be internalized to the point where they evoke an emotional response. Owing to the mind-body connection, it is often helpful to work with the body (bio-energetics, massage, athletic training, *etc.*) in order to access those emotions.[7] The ensuing healing in turn gives rise to a new level of spiritual awareness and closeness to G–d.

The essential point is that all these different levels of transformation work together and reinforce each other. Discovering the causes of the unwanted behavior promotes the establishing of a new, more positive pattern. Recognition of behavioral progress increases

---

7. In simple terms, the mind has thoughts, the body has sensations, and both the mind and the body have impulses to act.

confidence in the process, hence, reinforces the spiritual motivation to pursue it. Thus, *teshuvah* operates in a context of holistic healing, in which not only the behavior is changed, but its underlying causes are dealt with; not only the deep and hidden wounds from the past are confronted, but also feelings that propel the sense of perpetual frustration and emptiness left by the unwanted behavior.

Every human being has spiritual as well as physical needs. The soul yearns for its pristine state of innocence and purity. However, the human psyche has many ways of suppressing, ignoring, or rationalizing away the needs of the soul. One of the most common ways of rationalizing away the soul's longing to do *teshuvah* has always been to convince oneself that change is either impossible or just too hard. In recent times, the gay lobby has seized upon the "gay gene" theory as a way of "proving" that gender recovery is impossible. However, in Chapters Three and Four, we exposed the untruth of this assertion. Moreover, we saw in Chapters Nine and Ten that a "straying off course"—even a *to'eivah*—can be corrected, as long as the will to change is not undermined. We saw that Talmudic tradition, as attested by Bar Kappara, recognizes that there is indeed a road back from homosexuality—and, so far as *teshuvah* is concerned, the practice of homosexuality is no different from any other sin.

Once this is understood, once the struggler understands that nothing obstructs his way back to a life of wholeness and holiness, the next logical step is to actually "do" *teshuvah*. For if G-d has given us the means to do *teshuvah*, it is certain that this includes the means to turn away from homosexual impulses and behavior. Viewed in this light, Bar Kappara's interpretation—witty and original as it is—is not an innovation at all, but a poignant reminder of something absolutely fundamental to Jewish teaching. Thus, Bar Kappara comes to offer a positive message of hope, a signpost for strugglers, pointing the way out of the gender double bind in which they find themselves.

In the context of gender-affirming processes, *teshuvah*, if properly undertaken, can provide the struggler with an intellectual, emotional, and spiritual environment favorable to personal growth and the closing of long-neglected developmental gaps. Analogous to the process of gender restoration taking place deep within the subject's unconscious, "the process of *teshuvah* is an event which takes place in the deepest recesses of the human mind and psyche." (*On Repentance,* 9) In seeking redemption from sin on Yom Kippur, the Day of Atonement, the Jew asks G–d for the strength to change his/her inner being. And indeed, the deepest level of *teshuvah* redirects the inner person, changes its essence, and purifies it. As explained by Rabbi Irving Greenberg, a former student of Rav Soloveitchik,

> In Soloveitchik's view, *teshuvah* goes beyond elimination of sin to a complete renewal of the individual. Habit and conditioning often combine with the structures of individual life to keep the person torn between evil and ethic, between apathy and ideal, between inertia and desire for improvement. Against these powerful forces which proclaim that humans cannot change, *Yom Kippur* teaches that there is capacity for renewal and unification of life. (*The Jewish Way,* 211)

Defining Sin.

Yom Kippur is a special day that can inspire *teshuvah* in a person who, as suggested above, is "torn between evil and ethic, between apathy and ideal, between inertia and desire for improvement." How shall we apply that special something to help the struggler overcome the barriers that keep him or her from reaching his/her true gender-self?

Without touching on the mystical aspects of the day, we can say that Yom Kippur, the Day of Atonement, was instituted to be a day of moral regeneration, a day concerning which the Torah tells the Jewish People,

> . . . *for on that day He will forgive you, to cleanse you, that you may be clean from all your sins before the L–rd.* (Lev. 16:30)

Yom Kippur is a day devoted to communal fasting, intense prayer, painful introspection, and trusting invocation of G–d's boundless mercy. One of the most characteristic liturgical elements of the day is the repeated confession of our sins. We remind ourselves that the G–d who has judged us on Rosh Hashana is always open to receive our wholehearted repentance (*teshuvah*), for He is a merciful and loving G–d, who desires not our punishment but that we should return to Him. Thus the Sages who composed the special prayers for Yom Kippur have underscored that *teshuvah, tefillah,* and *tzedakah* ("repentance," "prayer," and "charity") can change the entire direction of a person's life, alter his or her destiny, and lead him/her on the path to perfection of character. As the prophet Isaiah urges, "Let the wicked one forsake his way, and the iniquitous man his thoughts; let him return to *Hashem,* and He will show him mercy; to our G–d, for He is abundantly forgiving. (Isaiah 55:7.)

It is important, however, to understand that, as the Lubavitcher Rebbe explains, "The true Jewish meaning of *teshuvah, tefillah,* and *tzedakah* . . . is a Jew returning to his true self (*teshuvah*); a Jew achieving union with G–d (*tefillah*); and a Jew acting justly [toward his fellows] (*tzedakah*)."[8] In other words: authenticity, bonding with G–d, and acting justly. The foregoing are key aspects of an SSA recovery model.

Many strugglers are tormented by the idea that, since the Torah's language in connection with the prohibition of "lying with a man as with a woman" is so strong, perhaps anyone who commits this sin is beyond the pale of redemption. The concept of wanting to repent but being disqualified from doing so by the nature of the sin is not entirely foreign to Jewish Tradition. It is said, for instance that one who says, "I will do this sin, and repent later," will never be able to

---

8. Rabbi Yosef HaLevi Loebenstein (trans.), "*Teshuvah, Tefillah, Tzedakah—the Ten Days of Repentance,*" <http://www.sichosinenglish.org/books/days-of-destiny/03.htm> (adapted for *Sichos in English* from *Likkutei Sichos*, Vol. II, pp. 409-11).

do *teshuvah*.⁹ Another example is the Talmudic account of Elisha ben Abuya, one of the great Sages of the Talmud, who despite the refinement of his soul, went astray from Torah and *Mitzvos*. So far had he wandered from observance that he acquired the nickname of *Acher*—"that other one." When urged by his student, Rabbi Meir, to repent, he would reply, "There is no *teshuvah* for *Acher*." He explained that one Yom Kippur, as he rode his horse (in defiance of the Law!) in the vicinity of the Holy Temple, he heard the singing and was moved to repent and enter; but then he overheard a *Bat Kol* (Voice from Heaven) saying, "Turn back to me O lost children—except for *Acher!*"

In a beautiful *drosh*, ("sermon") Rabbi Dov Greenberg, Executive Director of Chabad at Stanford University, and a contributing editor of the *Algemeiner Journal* and Algemeiner.com, explains that Rabbi Elisha, weighed down by guilt and shame, missed the true meaning of G–d's call:

> Come to me O lost child, leave *Acher* behind! You are not *Acher*. You are my beloved child; stop thinking of yourself as *Acher!* In

---

9. The psychology behind this opinion appears to be that once a person has sinned with the intention of repenting later, what is to persuade him that he cannot postpone his repentance in perpetuity? The sin becomes "permitted" to him. *See* Talmud, *Yoma* 87a. However, the Alter Rebbe and other sources insist that even such a sin *is* amenable to repentance if the desire to do *teshuvah* is sufficiently intense. "But if he pressed forcefully and overpowered his evil impulse and did repent, then his repentance is accepted." Rabbi Schneur Zalman of Liadi ("the Alter Rebbe"), *Igeret Hateshuvah*, Chapter 11, in *Likutei Amarim Tanya*, Brooklyn: Kehot Publication Society (bilingual ed. 1984), p. *383; See* also *Likutei Amarim, Chapter 7, p. 31*, and *Yoma* 86b. The psychology behind this contrasting opinion seems to be that once the sinner realizes that he has been deluding himself, what is to prevent him from repenting? According to this analysis, the barrier to repentance would be the component of self delusion itself. As phrased in a *midrash* quoted by Rabbi Joseph H. Hertz, *Daily Prayer Book* (rev. ed.) New York: Black Publishing Co. (1965), p. 839, "The moment a man is willing to see himself as he is, and make the confession, 'I have sinned,' from that moment the powers of evil lose their control over him."

other words, G-d meant to challenge Elisha to cast off *Acher*, the Other One, the foreign personality, the false identity. What G-d was saying to him is that "You are not *Acher*. The source of your conflict stems from the fact that you have identified your essence as '*Acher*'" ... The tragedy is when we begin to identify the wrong we have done with our essence; when we replace our souls with the identity of "*Acher*."

Although nothing in our tradition indicates that Rabbi Elisha suffered from SSA, the "*Acher*" syndrome is typical of many homosexuals: "I have strayed so far that G-d will never accept my *teshuvah!*" The truth is the opposite: G-d is always ready to accept a sincere *Ba'al teshuvah* ("penitent"), regardless of the gravity or the category of his/her sin. The proof of this lies not only in countless quotes from Torah, *Tanach*, Talmud and later commentaries, but in the very structure and content of Jewish prayer.

In the first place, the *Shemoneh Esreh*—the "Eighteen-Blessing Prayer" in which we ask G-d for all of our communal and individual needs, *precedes* the *Tachanun*, or *Viduy*, (Confessional Prayer) in which we beg forgiveness for all of our sins. Surely this shows that even *before* we request forgiveness, G-d does not bar sinners from His presence. Second, the daily *Viduy* comprises a long list of sins— some specific, some very general—culminating in the cry,

Merciful and Gracious One, we have sinned before You. Have mercy upon us and save us.

The list is meant to be comprehensive, and in the *Al Chet* ("For the Sin") Prayer recited on Yom Kippur and communal fast days, it is greatly expanded. However, it is also clear that G-d's forgiveness is available with respect to all categories of sin through the channels of *teshuvah*. Indeed, Torah and Jewish liturgy appear to classify sin in four different ways: (1) according to intent, (2) according to gravity, (3) according to the type of sacrifice that would have been necessary to atone for it in the days of the Holy Temple, and (4) according to the type of punishment that would have been exacted for it at that time. All of the categories so created are addressed on Yom Kippur (and the other public fast days) in connection with repentance and forgiveness.

The daily liturgy, on the other hand, appears to classify sins on the sole basis of intent. Indeed, the terms *aveirah* and *avón* (mentioned in the Morning Blessings), and *chet* and *peshah* (mentioned in the *Shemoneh Esreh* and the *Viduy*) indicate four separate categories of sin, all of which are expressly mentioned in connection with repentance. Though it is not at all certain what kinds of actions those terms are meant to include, their root meanings plausibly refer to the various levels of intent that can be implicated in the process of sinning. Intuitively, we understand that a wrong can be done either intentionally or unintentionally, or, if intentionally, either rebelliously or impulsively. According to some commentators, the four terms—*chet*, *aveirah*, *peshah*, and *avón*—correspond to these categories. Let us briefly take a closer look.

Chet.

According to Rabbi Nosson Scherman, "*chet* . . . used in conjunction with other words for sin, such as *avón* or *pesha* . . . refers to unintentional sins that could have been avoided. Where *chet* appears alone [as in the *Al Chet* prayer] . . . it is a general term for sin."[10] According to Rabbi Louis Jacobs, *chet* comes from a root word meaning "to miss"—as in "to miss the mark" in archery. Thus it denotes a sin done through carelessness or ignorance.[11]

---

10. Rabbi Nosson Scherman, *The Complete Art Scroll Machzor: Yom Kippur*, Brooklyn: Mesorah Publications (1988), p. 855.

11. Rabbi Louis Jacobs, "Categories of Sin," in Rabbi Dov Peretz Elkins (ed.) *Moments of Transcendence: Inspirational Readings for Yom Kippur*, Northvale: Jason Aronson (1992), p. 44.

Aveirah.

Aveirah, on the other hand, is the most generic term normally used in conversation to describe any kind of sin. *Aveirah* means "to pass the mark," "cross over," or "transgress." Hence, an *aveirah* is a "transgression," a sin done, not out of ignorance, but without due care or consideration. (*Moments of Transcendence,* 44)

Peshah

According to Rabbi Jacobs, "[*Peshah*] refers to the attitude of mind through which a man sets himself as the sole judge of his actions, recognizing neither G–d nor the Law." (*Moments of Transcendence*, 44) Rabbi Nosson Scherman agrees, suggesting that the term refers to "willful sins" or "sins committed rebelliously, because of a lack of belief in the Torah or in the validities of a particular commandment." (*Machzor*, 855) For someone who lacks such a belief system, no external standards of right or wrong exist. Everything is relative. As Rabbi Jacobs observes, "Right is the name he gives to those actions which please him and further his aims, wrong to those which displease him and frustrate his aims." (*Moments of Transcendence*, 44)

Avón.

Malbim (Rabbi Meir Loeb ben Yechiel Michal, the great 19th century *midrashic* and *halachic* scholar) defines *avón* as involving "a distortion of the intellect, resulting in the neglect of a Torah commandment."[12] Nosson Scherman explains it as "an intentional sin, but one that was not committed in a spirit of rebellion." (*Machzor*, 855). According to Rabbi Jacobs, *avón* comes from a root

---

12. Malbim, as referenced in Rabbi Avrohom Chaim Feuer, *Tehillim*, Brooklyn: Mesorah Publications (1991), p. 652.

word meaning "to be twisted," or "to be crooked or bent." (*Moments of Transcendence,* 44) Thus, "It refers . . . to the twist in a man's character which seems to impel him to do wrong . . . ." (44)

How Different Categories of Sin Relate to Homosexuality.

From the above, we see that homosexuality, though characterized by the Torah as a *to'eivah,* does not necessarily confine itself to a single category of sin. Indeed, discussing the foregoing categories with Dr. Joseph Nicolosi, I apparently inspired him to correlate them, in the context of reparative therapy, to different types of SSA client personality. Intrigued by the different degrees of culpability implicit in these subdivisions of sin, Dr. Nicolosi observes:

> *Chet* fits the reparative understanding of homosexuality. The connotation [of *chet*] is of a problematic behavior one falls into "by accident"—through lack of knowledge. *Chet* could have been avoided with the exercise of greater care. But when the man understands his authentic needs, this "shifts his aim" to the true target, which is intimate, non-erotic same-sex friendships.
>
> [. . .]
>
> *Aveirah* is closely related to *chet* in that it also refers to missing the mark or transgressing, but it connotes more of an act done with intention. Although the homosexual man's sense of gender and self come about by a series of circumstances over which he has little or no control and thus reflect his psychological adaptation to emotional pain, he does have free will to choose his lifestyle and subsequent actions. Similarly, in reparative drive theory, someone with same-sex attractions retains the choice of either acting upon those feelings (acting through intention; in Jewish law *aveirah*), or working to overcome them.
>
> [. . .]

[O]ne thinks of *pesha* as applicable to gay activists who work for the normalization and propagation of homosexuality so their own rebellion will be shared and spread to others.[13]

My own take on *avón* is that the average SSA individual (as opposed, *e.g.,* to the gay-pride extremist) fits in this category because his/her intellect has been distorted by all the "mythology" surrounding homosexuality in today's climate of political correctness. Interestingly, Michael (formerly Michelle) Danielle, the ex-gay-identified transvestite discussed in Chapter Six (*see above,* pp. 210-13), noted that members of his former community often referred to themselves as "bent" (as opposed to "straight")—the root meaning of the word *avón*. However, we saw in Chapters Four and Six that people are not generally born "bent." As Dr. Nicolosi observes:

> Both [*aveirah* and *avón*] reflect the reparative concept that homosexuality is *not a choice* one consciously makes, but an emotional adaptation to the pain of emotional wounding.

It reasonably follows, as pointed out by leading psychiatrist Jeffrey Satinover, that "someone who has been raised to believe that homosexuality is not wrong commits less of a sin than does someone raised in the knowledge of its sinfulness and who then deliberately rejects the Torah's standard of behavior."[14] This is entirely consistent with the principle of *tinok shenishba* ("the Jewish infant captured and raised by Gentiles"), which requires "that we take into consideration the educational climate in which the individual was raised, before

---

13. Dr. Joseph Nicolosi, "A Jewish Understanding of Levels of Moral Responsibility," <http://narth.com/docs/junder/html>. Note that Dr. Nicolosi's reference to "reparative therapy" is subsumed under the broader term of Gender Affirming Processes (GAP) used in this book.

14. Dr. Jeffrey Satinover, *Homosexuality and the Politics of Truth,* Grand Rapids: Baker Books (1996), p. 219.

deeming him responsible and accountable for his or her religious failings."[15]

Teshuvah does not Distinguish Among Categories of Sin.

Nevertheless, while the degree of culpability may relate to the severity of the punishment, our focus here is on *teshuvah*, not punishment; and genuine *teshuvah* is always a total commitment of body and soul. Whether our misbehavior manifests as an inadvertent or impulsive act or as a deliberate "transgression;" whether it stems from weakness or carelessness, or from a "bent" or "twisted" character trait, we all have a duty to do *teshuvah*. In that regard, what is important here is: the pathway of *teshuvah* can start from any one of the four categories. Indeed, with regard to the category of intent, we see in our daily prayers:

Forgive us, our Father, for we have sinned (chata'anu); *pardon us, our King, for we have transgressed* (pesha'anu).

— *Shemoneh Esreh.*

L–rd, L–rd, benevolent G–d, compassionate and gracious, slow to anger and abounding in kindness and truth; He preserves kindness for two thousand generations, forgiving iniquity (avón) *transgression* (peshah) *and sin* (chata'ah), *and He cleanses.* (Ex. 32:12)

— *Viduy*

---

15. Rabbi Chaim Rappoport, *Judaism and Homosexuality: an Authentic Orthodox View*, London: Valentine Mitchell (2004), p. 76. This concept is discussed in the Talmud (*Shabbat* 68b and *Shavuot* 5a) in connection with the Jewish infant captured and raised by Gentiles; and in Rambam, *Mishneh Torah Hilchot Mamrim* 3:3, in connection with a second-generation Karaite child.

From the perspective of the ancient sacrifices of atonement, the *Al Chet* prayer, said on Yom Kippur and other fast days, lists all of them, incorporating by reference all the sins for which such sacrifices were prescribed.

Similarly, the *Al Chet* lists the four forms of capital punishment in use during the existence of the Holy Temple, incorporating by reference all the sins for which such punishments were prescribed.

Why do we recite this long litany of terrible sins? Surely, so that we may plead, on behalf of ourselves and the entire community:

For all these sins, G–d of pardon, pardon us, forgive us, atone for us.

Is There *Teshuvah* for *To'eivos?*

There still remains the category of *to'eivah*, which, as we have seen, sets apart certain transgressions as especially offensive to *Hashem*. Is there no *teshuvah* for one who is culpable of such a sin? Answers Rabbi Aharon Feldman, Dean of Ner Israel Rabbinical College in Baltimore: "Although it is a serious sin, all humans by nature have spiritual shortcomings and this is why *teshuvah* was given to them."[16] In the daily *Viduy,* we recite:

We have committed evil, we have acted perniciously, we have acted abominably, we have gone astray, we have led others astray.

---

16. Rabbi Aharon Feldman, "A Letter to a Homosexual *Baal Teshuva.*" *The Jerusalem Letter* 1:5 (March 24, 1998), <http://www.jerusalemletter.co.il/archives/March24,1998/homow.htm.> This letter, with a slight change, appeared in *Jewish Action* 58:3 (Spring, 1998), pp.69-70. Some clarifications appear in Rabbi Aharon Feldman, "Letters from Homosexual Friends," The Jerusalem Letter, 3:1 (June 22, 2000). Available at <http://www.jerusalemletter.co.il/archives/Jun22,2000/friends.htm>.

The Hebrew word translated as "we have acted abominably" is *ti'avnu,* which comes from the same root as *to'eivah.* Nor can we fail to recall Bar Kappara when we read, directly after *ti'avnu,* the similar, perhaps cognate, words *ta'inu* (we have strayed) and *ti'eta'nu* (we have caused others to stray). Thus we see clearly from the Confessional Prayer itself that one who has committed a *to'eivah* may repent and seek forgiveness. Indeed, as we must understand from the communal voice of the prayer ("we"), it is our obligation as a community to do so.

Sin as Pathology.

The noted Chassidic Rabbi, Simon Jacobson tells us that "when a person does not follow an element in the Torah, it's not just a crime against society, it's a crime against yourself."[17] Rabbi Jacobson warns that when sexuality is abused or misused or improperly channeled or set free of all restraints, because it is such a potent force, it can give rise to extremely destructive internal tendencies. Like any other potent force (such as nuclear energy) sexuality can foster both much good and much destruction. Left unattended, or improperly guarded, it can drive people to behave in completely irrational and self-destructive ways.

We saw in Chapter Four how SSA can develop as a psychological band-aid for painfully deep emotional wounds, and how, instead of falling off in time like a real band-aid, it can grow into, become a part of, the person, impeding the development of authentic gender identification. Homosexuality represents an unconscious effort by the individual to assuage the pain caused by his/her having been deprived of the early same-sex bonding so essential to psychological gender formation. In other words, as sometimes happens with addictive

---

17. Rabbi Simon Jacobson, "Toward a Meaningful Life," Radio Show Transcript, May 7, 2000, <http://www.meaningfullife.com/social/sexuality/Homosexuality.php>.

medication, the "cure" may become the disease, or in this case, the emotional adaptation defensively employed to protect against childhood pain becomes normalized as an "alternative lifestyle," instead of allowing the genuine, core personality to break through those defenses once the pain has been palliated.

It is fascinating to compare these thoughts with the Prophet Hosea's appeal for repentance. He exhorts us (14:2):

Return, Israel, to the L–rd, your G–d, for you have stumbled in your sins.

Rav Soloveitchik comments on this verse: "[T]he sins in which you were caught up became your stumbling block, they threw you off your course." (*On Repentance,* 64)

What precisely does the Rav mean? Sin has a strange power over a person. It is not merely the power of temptation (the power to draw one into it), but the power to undermine a person's belief in his or her ability to do *teshuvah* (to pull him- or herself out of it). This may happen either through addiction or habituation, but it may also happen simply through feelings of guilt, self-blame, self-hatred, and loss of self-respect. It may even occur through an unconscious desire to punish oneself by sinning more. As the Rav explains, "It is no use abstaining from sin to evade its punishment because sin is its own true punishment." (*On Repentance,* 64).

This is clearly related to the etiology of SSA. We saw in Chapter Four that certain emotional wounds received during early childhood—such as rejection (perceived or actual) by same-sex parent, enmeshment with the opposite-sex parent, peer wounds, body-image wounds, *etc.,* may later be internalized by the individual, giving rise to SSA and becoming "the causal nexus of sin." (*On Repentance,* 64). Psychological events of this type can become the boulders over which a person may stumble. The SSA can lead a person into homosexual activity, and shame, guilt, alienation, addiction and confusion all conspire to keep him or her there.

Our view is that SSA is a stumbling block that can be removed through *teshuvah,* thus clearing the way for the gender affirming process. *Teshuvah* can repair the road upon which a person travels. In the phraseology of Bar Kappara, SSA "leads a person astray." One loses one's way; *teshuvah* can help one find it again.

Rav Soloveitchik characterizes sin as a pathology. "As there are pathological, physical illnesses in which the tissues cease to function normally and the cells begin to grow wild, so sin is a sign of spiritual pathology whose outcome is the disintegration of the whole personality." (*On Repentance,* 20) The analogy is instructive in regard to homosexuality. The active homosexual has far greater health risks (including such psychiatric illnesses as suicidal tendencies, depression, and substance addictions, and such physical illnesses as AIDS, anal cancer, rectal and throat gonorrhea, syphilis, viral hepatitis types B & C, and other STDs) than the active heterosexual.[18]

On the other hand, Rabbi Dr. Spero suggests that homosexuality is not simply pathological. Rather, according to Spero, homosexuality needs to be thought of as an "inauthentic state of existence" in which the affected individual either "errs through the proscribed behavior" or exhibits "bad faith."[19] Either way, however, the homosexual ultimately retains the power to alter this emotional adaptation and to change sexual orientation through a transition strategy analogous to the process of *teshuvah.* Indeed, combining appropriate psychotherapy with the spiritual modalities of *teshuvah* can offer a powerful boost to a homosexual striving to move back into an authentic state of existence.

To illustrate how this transpires, Spero asks us to visualize two intersecting lines on a chart. The first line represents *teshuvah* or what he refers to as a "sin-repentance continuum." The second line

---

18. John R. Diggs, M.D. "Health Risks of Gay Sex," <www.catholiceducation.org/articles/homosexuality/ho0075.html>.

19. Rabbi Dr. Moshe Halevi Spero, *Psychotherapy and Jewish Ethics,* Jerusalem: Feldheim (1986), p.167.

represents the therapeutic process, or what Spero calls the "psychiatric illness-psychotherapy continuum." When the two lines (processes) come together, there is often a kind of explosion of awareness, insight and sense of accomplishment and self-mastery. What was previously internalized as a gender deficiency ("I don't see myself as a man") is re-integrated into a new sense of gender identity ("I see myself as a man among men"). A new, self-sustaining personality paradigm is created wherein the individual is now better able to integrate (1) his self-image and physiological gender; (2) his need for personal identity and need for gender affiliation; and (3) his painful memories and objective understanding of past relationships. When this occurs, the struggler is then able to leave his "unheroic state of being" (Spero, 167) and rediscover his authentic self.

Sin and Mourning.

This process of rediscovery is by no means painless. Healing from SSA involves not only repentance, but also an intense focus on re-integrating the dismembered personality and re-examining old wounds, agonizing memories, and reinterpreting the events which gave rise to them.

In some respects, this process is similar to the emotional healing a person goes through after suffering a devastating loss. Indeed, Rav Soloveitchik compares the emotions felt by a person who violates a Biblical Law to mourning the loss of a loved one:

> The mourner mourns a kindred and loved person who was once and is no more, while the sinner mourns that which has been lost. What has been lost is man's soul, which is like losing everything, for he has lost his closeness to his Creator, that proximity which allowed him access to purity and sanctity, to perfection and spiritual richness; he has lost the inherence of the holy spirit in man and that which gives meaning and the significance of life to human existence. (*On Repentance,* 21)

In the Introduction to his study of Rav Soloveitchik, Rabbi Peli cites two biblical examples of this relationship between sin and mourning. (21) The first is the sin of the golden calf (Ex. 33:4):

And when the people heard these evil tidings, they mourned . . . .

The Children of Israel were overcome by an overpowering sense of grief and loss. They had lost their closeness to G–d. Likewise, when, the Israelite scouts returned from their mission to "spy out the territory," and sinned by reporting ill of the Promised Land,

. . . the People mourned greatly. (Num. 14:39)

Of course, there is one great difference between mourning and sin: mourning cannot bring back the dead; but genuine *teshuvah* not only erases the sin, but brings one back to a state of original purity. However, for this to happen, we must not only acknowledge that we have committed a sin, but also recognize and assess the power of sin so that we can learn how to avoid its tendrils as we attack its roots.

We know that people *can* change. Rich Wyler gave that name to an entire organization of former homosexuals. "People can change," writes Wyler.

> We know because we have. By "coming out" of our homosexual pasts, we finally found the peace and freedom, the love and healing, and the joy and self-esteem that we had been seeking all our lives. [. . .] [T]o those who do want more than anything else to change their lives, we testify from first-hand experience that change is real. It is within reach. It has brought us joy. In fact, it saved our lives.[20]

More relevant to the context of this chapter, Wyler comments: "We couldn't be truly spiritually whole and emotionally broken, or

---

20. <www.peoplecanchange.com>.

emotionally whole and spiritually broken. Healing had to come about in both." (www.peoplecanchange.com)

We know people can change because we see a growing number of individuals who have successfully changed their sexual orientation. We know because of the more than one hundred studies authenticating change of sexual orientation. We know because of our own successes, and those of our associates and colleagues, in helping strugglers return to their physiological gender. Thus, despite the massive suppressive efforts of the gay lobby, the truth is, *Baruch Hashem* (Blessed be G–d), beginning to percolate down to the grass roots levels of society. Even the Orthodox community has begun to take note. For example, Rabbi Basil F. Herring, Executive Vice President of the Rabbinical Council of America, writes:

> This is a case in which popular or conventional wisdom has followed a path that is politically correct rather than scientifically sound or statistically borne out. [. . .] Indeed, many in the traditional community itself are not aware . . . that homosexual thoughts and behaviors can be successfully treated and permanently changed (or, at the very least, individuals can significantly reduce their homosexual feelings or behavior) in as many as two-thirds of those homosexuals who seek help. [F]indings such as these . . . go a long way to support the biblical and rabbinic prohibitions in this regard.[21]

Many in the broader Jewish and other communities are simply unwilling to hear what Mr. Wyler and so many others are saying. Community leaders, prominent business persons, symphony fundraisers, "society people"—even ordinary people conscious of their public or social "image," all alike are simply so terrified of being

---

21. Rabbi Basil F. Herring, "Choice Diminished Behavior and Religious Communal Policy," in Yitzchok Berger and David Shatz (eds.), *Judaism, Science, and Moral Responsibility: Orthodox Forum*, Lanham: Rowman & Littlefield (2006), pp. 162, 168.

labeled "intolerant" or smeared as "bigoted" that they find it far easier to simply believe what political correctness says should be believed. Many are simply people without political agendas or "vested interests," whose human frailties deaden their perceptions and concerns.

Among these are many male and female homosexuals whose deep wounds and agonizing insecurities prevent them from seeing beyond their immediate needs and involvements. Rabbi Greenberg characterizes their situation very well:

> People despair of their ability to change and give up the capacity to grow or renew. The promise of repentance and the model of G-d challenge this hopelessness. There *is* a process of rebirth, but it needs attention, effort and help. The first step is to become conscious of one's life, to overcome the routines that block the capacity to evaluate, correct, and change." (*The Jewish Way*, 201)

Teshuvah Presupposes Freedom of Choice.

By affirmatively taking responsibility and performing *teshuvah* — in other words, by recognizing, dealing with, and eliminating the rationalizations that lie at the root of a person's sexual brokenness, many formerly SSA-affected people have successfully changed their sexual orientation. A great many more can do so. *Teshuvah* can provide the intellectual, spiritual, and emotional support that will help change their lives.

It is a basic precept of Judaism that men and women have free choice over their actions, and freedom of choice is integrally related to the process of *teshuvah*.[22] Those who feel imprisoned by their SSA, those who have been told again and again that they were "born that way," that they cannot change, need not feel discouraged.

---

22. "Belief in man's freedom of choice is inexorably linked to the concept of repentance in Judaism." Rabbi Raphael Pelcovitz, *Sforno: Commentary on the Torah*, Brooklyn: Mesorah Publications (1997), p. xvii.

Implicit within the concept of *teshuvah* are the realities of free will and free choice. Rabbi Peli explains:

> Free choice, which is part of man's being, means that man can create himself at will and, as it were, be born anew. Rabbi Soloveitchik does not completely reject the law of causation which governs mankind . . . . But, employing the principle of free choice, Soloveitchik demonstrates that man can fashion for himself a new law of causation which will take effect from a specific moment onward, *i.e.*, the moment of repentance-salvation, when a complete transformation occurs from within. (*Soloveitchik on Repentance*, 31).

Those of us who have experienced the full blinding force of sexual desire might well think: "Fine and good. But how can a scholarly and saintly rabbi understand the power such desires can have over ordinary people?" And how wrong we would be! Jewish tradition views all sinful urges as "natural" impulses—the product of the animal component of the human being, the part that wants, craves, lusts, covets *for itself.* Writing from the perspective of *"Mussar"* theory (the Ethical Movement founded by the great 19th-century sage, Rabbi Israel Salanter), Rabbi Hillel Goldberg, editor-in-chief of the highly respected *Intermountain Jewish News* elaborates:

> To Rabbi Israel [Salanter], nature is nothing more than the unique, individuated constellation of a person's environmental influences and psychic forces, at least some of which are in-born. For a homosexual to claim that his sexual desires define his existence, or alternatively, to argue that the demand to alter his homosexualaity is a reductive attempt to change him into something he is not, would meet no quarrel from Rabbi Israel. He posits that *everyone* must redefine himself at his very root, moment by moment, that precisely in those specific, unique ways in which a person finds his psychological existence opposed to the religious norm, the individual must change. In terms of psychological principle, it makes no difference to Rabbi Israel whether the in-born desire is for adultery, unethical monetary gain, homosexual sex, or any other

violation of the religious norm. The in-born desire—call it "nature" if you will—must be tutored and transfigured.[23]

Recognizing that all human impulses are "natural," in that they stem from the nature of the human psyche[24] enables one—even a scholarly and saintly rabbi—to see how homosexuality is essentially no less "natural" than heterosexual promiscuity, adultery, or other forms of sexual misconduct. Thus, from a clinical-penitential perspective, far from discriminating hatefully against homosexuals, Torah actually views the homosexual with an egalitarian even-handedness: the homosexual urge is just another (or different) manifestation of the animal component striving against the spiritual.[25]

Indeed, there is a constant, raging battle going on between the *yetzer hara* ("evil inclination") and the *yetzer tov* ("righteous inclination")—between the physical needs and pleasures and the spiritual yearnings—of nearly everyone. Without this constant battle, our commentators explain, there could be no such thing as freedom of choice: without temptation, we would automatically choose the path that brings us closer to G–d, and no more merit would accrue to us for taking that path than would accrue to a compass needle for pointing north.

On the other hand, without some essential attraction to the spiritual good, we would automatically gravitate to purely physical rewards and gross and evanescent pleasures. For that very reason, there is implanted within each of us what Rav Soloveitchik calls "an

---

23. Rabbi Hillel Goldberg, "Homosexuality: A Religious and Political Analysis," *Tradition Magazine*, Vol. 27, No. 3 (Spring,, 1993), p. 31.

24. One is reminded of the famous line by the Roman comic playwright, Terence: "Nothing human is alien to me."

25. This is one reason why any purported analogy between homosexual activity in animals (as claimed by gay activists) and in humans is untenable. Jewish Tradition teaches that animals do not have a "divine soul" capable of resisting the impulses of its "animal soul." Unlike animals, humans have the ability to make moral choices.

inner sense of sin ... that feeling of inner disquiet, of that bothersome ache which attacks the sinner, any sinner." (*On Repentance,* 148) The Rav describes this feeling with devastating accuracy:

> The sense of sin accompanies the sinner without any possibility of evasion. Intoxication and the blunting of the senses do not allow him to escape from his reaction to sin. "On the morrow," when soberness sets in, the sinner begins to feel the pain caused by sin—not an acute, penetrating pain, but rather a nagging feeling of bereavement, a mood of depression and melancholy. (149)

Logically, one would suppose that the sinner, having obtained what he or she was lusting for, should be satisfied, pleasantly fulfilled, and at peace. What causes the sinner to feel depressed, disappointed, or empty? Our Teachings explain that it is the Divine Soul: it has been sullied and shamed by the sinful deed.

Rav Soloveitchik credits Aristotle with recognizing long ago that "pain is perhaps the Creator's most important gift to His creatures, serving as an alarm-bell to alert man of approaching danger." (147) But what good does this pain do if we do not heed its warning? What kind of "gift" is this pain if the Creator does not also give us freedom to choose, to turn away from the source and cause of the danger and to heal?

Of course, to be truly free, the choice has to be a fair one. Pain must have its compensations. Accordingly the Creator has provided many means and mechanisms for choosing to continue in pain, if that is what we want. Unfortunately, by raising up counter-emotional defenses such as depression and anxiety, or inhibitory responses such as lust, over-intellectualization, and addiction, people do grow numb to their pain or inured to its cause. They allow themselves to become imprisoned by their circumstances. They learn how to endure and nurture the harmful emotional adaptations that could otherwise be healed and discarded. Rabbi Hanoch of Alexander is reputed to have said, "The real exile of Israel in Egypt was that they learned to endure it."[26]

The inhibitory responses of our psyche—designed to shield us from unavoidable pain—can also serve to numb us to avoidable, self-inflicted or self-caused pain. Whether through use of addictive drugs, alcohol, or sex, or by rationalizing or over-intellectualizing or by disavowing authentic emotional responses such as anger, fear, and sadness, a person can adapt to a life of unnecessary misery.

Of course, it is true that breaking through such self-destructive responses and facing one's true feelings openly and honestly can also be extremely painful. However, it is a cathartic pain, like the lancing of a boil. Indeed, authentic emotional breakthroughs also provide immediate relief and healing by releasing the repressed and bottled up feelings in much the same way as cutting open an infected, physical wound releases pus and relieves pressure. Moreover, the liberation of such powerful emotions after years of suppression is a necessary condition for complete healing and recovery. One can only heal what one feels.

Acknowledging that freedom of choice is an intrinsic part of the human soul, and, hence, that homosexuals, too, are intrinsically free to choose their sexual identity, is truly an act of redemption; for it permits SSA strugglers (as well as others who struggle with any kind of emotional adaptation) to connect with their innermost truth, their Divine Soul—where body, mind and spirit meet as one. The religious literature is replete with references to a connection between spiritual pain—perhaps appropriately called "the illness of sin"—and the liberating experience of healing which is implicit in deep repentance, particularly when accompanied by psychological insight. Isaiah 6:10 suggests that if people would only "see with their eyes, and hear with

---

26. Quoted in Estelle Frankel, *Sacred Therapy: Jewish Spiritual Teachings on Emotional Healing and Inner Wholeness,* Boston: Shambhala Publications, Inc. (2003), p. 119.

their ears, and understand with their heart, and return," (*i.e.,* "do *teshuvah*"), they would be healed. We need to remember that seeing, hearing, understanding, and returning are all acts of free will.

It is precisely in this regard that Dr. Jeffrey Satinover points out a fascinating feature of gay psychology exemplified by the "gay gene" theory:

> The example of homosexuality has one stunning feature .... Most of the gay activists in the United States *do not want* to find any freedom and choice involved in their way of life, and they are fiercely determined to prove that there is no way out of it either. Thus, the debate is lined up in the reverse way of most debates over the medical basis of human behavior. People usually *resist* the idea that their behavior is driven by unchangeable, biological factors, as in feminist arguments over innate differences between men and women, or in the firestorm over the genetics of IQ and a potential correlation to racial groupings. But in the case of homosexuality, many people rush to embrace scientific research, however flimsy ... to the end point that no choice is involved at all.[27]

In this manner, the gay movement chooses to sacrifice on the altar of ideology the essence of what makes us human—our free will.

How Homosexual Politics Obstructs Freedom of Choice.

The lesson of *teshuvah* is that it is within our power both to control and to redirect our thoughts and actions. However, the gay lobby has expended enormous efforts to convince us otherwise. Rabbi Barry Freundel writes: "The mass media and most mental health professionals ... publicly portray the goal of 'acceptance of one's orientation' as the optimum, while downplaying or denying the possibility of change."[28] Both the mass media and the mental health

---

27. Dr. Jeffrey Satinover, *Homosexuality and the Politics of Truth,* Grand Rapids: Baker Books (1998), p. 125.

professions do this without acknowledging in any way their utter disregard for clinical findings concerning the effectiveness of the change process, nor is there any willingness to engage in bona-fide discussion of the political dynamics that have engulfed them both.[29]

As we made clear in Chapter Three, gay activists "want to shape 'what everyone knows' and 'what everyone takes for granted,' even if everyone does not really know and even if it should not be taken for granted."[30] They had such faith in the eventual success of their subliminal agenda that they publicly predicted that a decision to legitimize homosexuality would be "ultimately made without society ever realizing that it has been purposely conditioned to arrive at a conclusion that it thinks is its own." (Rondeau, 485)

An unspoken component of such dynamics was the popular enthusiasm for any theory that purported to clothe a licentious lifestyle with the dignity of civil-rights politics and social science. What a relief, in this enlightened age, after centuries of sexual repression, to be able to give expression to every sexual whim, and to do so fearlessly, by the light of day, as a matter of right, with the backing of educators, legislators, scientists, doctors, and psychologists! Small wonder that the efforts of practitioners of reparative therapy and the testimony of successful graduates of GAP have encountered such vicious hostility from gay activists and their allies![31]

---

28. Rabbi Barry Freundel, "Homosexuality and Judaism," *Journal of Halacha and Contemporary Society*, Spring (1986), Vol. XI, p. 76.

29. For a comprehensive study summarizing the intervention outcomes literature on change of sexual orientation, *see* Dr. James Phelan *et. al.* "A Comprehensive Response to the American Psychological Association's Objections to the Treatment of Homosexuality," NARTH (2008). As Phelan observes, extensive documentation on the subject exists since the late 19th century.

30. Paul E. Rondeau, *Selling Homosexuality to America*, 14 *Regent U. Law Review* (2001-02), pp. 424-5.

31. Examples are legion. Kevin Jennings, a former private school teacher in

Notwithstanding the "stonewall,"[32] there has been no lack of criticism. Psychiatrist Jeffrey Satinover has been in the front line of protest. In *Homosexuality and the Politics of Truth,* Satinover details the Gay Task Force's successful political manipulation of the APA, concluding: "The APA vote to normalize homosexuality was driven by politics, not science." (32) Dr. Joseph Nicolosi explains bluntly how this happened: "The combined effects of the sexual revolution and the 'rights' movements—civil rights, minority rights, feminist rights—have resulted in an intimidating effect upon psychology."[33]

In a book based on his post-doctoral research at Hastings Center, Dr. Ronald Bayer lambastes the APA for its decision to delete homosexuality from its official classification of mental disorders.

Massachusetts and founder of the Gay Lesbian Straight Education Network (GLSEN) declares: "Ex-gay messages have no place in our nation's public schools. A line has been drawn. There is no 'other side' when you're talking about lesbian, gay and bisexual students." George Archibald, "Changing Minds," *The Washington Times,* July 27, 2004, <http://www.narth.com/docs/ changingminds.html>. When an Ex-Gay Educators Caucus representative appeared at the National Education Association (NEA) 2005 convention, a delegate wearing the rainbow emblem of the NEA Gay Lesbian Bisexual Transgender Caucus told the delegate, "I'm really offended that you're even here," and another Ex-Gay Delegate was told that a special place in hell is reserved for ex-gays and suggested that her presence was akin to having the Ku Klux Klan present. *Ibid.* In October, 2004, a resident assistant at Indiana University sent packets of scientific data on the causes and healing strategies for homosexuality to more than 25 other resident assistants at the University. His director ordered him to stop doing so. The "diversity programming" head characterized the material he sent as "insulting and factually outrageous," and wondered how the resident advisor "got hooked into this dangerous and bogus group [referring to NARTH]." Further, the "diversity programming" chief ordered the resident advisor immediately to sever relations with any such organization. Michael Knapp, "Former Indiana University Student Describes Efforts to Challenge Pro-Gay Ideology on Campus," <http://www.narth.com/docas/indiana.html>.

32. *See below,* Chapter 14, p. 504, note 5.

33. Dr. Joseph Nicolosi, *Reparative Therapy,* Northvale: Jason Aronson (1997), p. 9.

The entire process, from the first confrontation organized by gay demonstrators at psychiatric conventions to the referendum demanded by orthodox psychiatrists, seemed to violate the most basic expectations about how questions of science should be resolved. Instead of being engaged in a sober consideration of data, psychiatrists were swept up in a political controversy. The American Psychiatric Association had fallen victim to the disorder of a tumultuous era, when disruptive conflicts threatened to politicize every aspect of American social life. A furious egalitarianism that challenged every instance of authority had compelled psychiatric experts to negotiate the pathological status of homosexuality with homosexuals themselves. *The result was a conclusion not based on an approximation of the scientific truth as dictated by reason, but was instead an action demanded by the ideological temper of the times.*[34] (Emphasis added.)

According to Bayer, "most psychoanalysts viewed the 1973 decision to delete homosexuality from DSM-II as a misguided, even tragic capitulation to extra-scientific pressure." (208)

In an article published in the *American Journal of Psychotherapy,* Dr. Charles Socarides lamented the "tragic consequences of the politicizing of the sexual area of diagnosis," noting that the deletion of homosexuality from the Diagnostic and Statistical Manual of Mental Disorders (2nd ed.) (DSM-II) "misinforms psychiatry, the medical profession, individual homosexuals, their families and governmental agencies which are responsible for mental health policies and third party payments."[35]

---

34. Dr. Ronald Bayer, *Homosexuality and American Psychiatry: The Politics of Diagnosis,* Princeton U. Press (1987), pp. 3-4. More recently, at the 2008 American Psychiatric Convention in Washington, D.C., the vociferous objections of gay activists caused the last-minute cancellation of a panel symposium impartially put together by Dr. David Scasta, a former president of the Association of Gay & Lesbian Psychiatrists, to discuss "Homosexuality and Therapy: the Religious Dimension."

35. Charles W. Socarides, M.D., "The Sexual Deviations and the Diagnostic Manual," *American Journal of Psychotherapy,* Vol. 32, No. 3, July, 1978, <www.

Dr. Socarides makes an important point: the DSM of the APA has considerable economic, clinical, social and political impact. The DSM creates the standards applicable to the diagnosis, treatment, and health-insurance coverage of mental disorders. Considered the "billing bible" for therapists, it is the diagnostic coding guide for insurance claims. Most licensed clinicians either bill a patient's health insurance company directly or provide the client with a statement permitting him/her to claim reimbursement after payment. Unless a formal DSM diagnosis exists, neither the mental health counselor nor the client can receive third-party reimbursement.

The diagnostic classification of homosexuality in the manual evolved over time. In 1952, it was classified as a "sociopathic personality disturbance," in 1968 as a "sexual deviation," and in 1973 (that is, until it was deleted) as a "sexual orientation disturbance." The DSM-III-R (3rd edition revised) and the current DSM-IV-TR (4th edition, text revised) edited homosexuality *per se* out of the disordered category. For those seeking treatment for unwanted SSA (ego-dystonic homosexuality), their conditions are referenced discreetly in DSM-IV-TR as "Sexual Disorder NOS" ("Not Otherwise Specified"). The code number for insurance purposes is 302.9. This switch effectively prevents treatment of those gays who, once fully comfortable with their homosexuality (ego-syntonic homosexuality), have now begun to consider change. Once "homosexuality" was removed from the DSM, a gay man who does not exhibit "persistent and marked distress about sexual orientation," may not qualify for insurance reimbursement for psychotherapy because he does not meet the criteria for "Sexual Disorder NOS." As a result many therapists will refuse to treat a gay man or woman with moral, religious, or "mid-life" reservations about their homosexuality.

---

narth.com>.

Some therapists even refuse as a matter of policy to process their clients' insurance claims. This, even though the client's sexual ambivalence may reasonably require treatment.

Given the climate of political correctness, however, gay-affirmative therapists will not hesitate to treat a moderately conflicted client under the rubric of "Sexual Disorder NOS" as if it passed the threshold of "persistent and marked distress about sexual orientation."[36] On the other hand, many therapists will actually withhold GAP treatment from an ego-dystonic homosexual under the misapprehension that the DSM prohibits it.[37] Gender-affirmative therapists who do not refuse such treatment often feel constrained to

---

36. For example, Joe Kort, a gay-identified psychotherapist specializing in gay-affirmative therapy, opines "The Sexual Disorder NOS" diagnosis is in the DSM-IV for those gays and lesbians who are closeted and struggling with coming out. It is used wrongly by those doing RT [reparative therapy] for those trying to "behave as heterosexuals." "Insurances do pay for Reparative Therapy." <www.exgaywatch. com/wp/?paged=142&req1=2003> (posted July 9, 2005).

37. Several therapists screened by JONAH claim they "cannot" ethically engage in reparative therapy either because they misread statements by the mental health organizations, or because they accept the more extreme positions of gay-identified therapists. The above-cited Joe Kort, for example, claims: "Therapists must, from the beginning, strongly affirm the inherent naturalness and okay-ness of homosexuality. The clinician also has an obligation to educate clients about the large body of research disproving [*sic!*] overall the idea that sexual orientation can be changed by psychotherapy." <http://www.exgaywatch.com/wp/2004/08/ psychotherapist/>. Although the American Psychiatric Association has not taken a formal stand on treatments that attempt to change a person's sexual orientation, the APA Board of Trustees has issued a position statement (December, 1998), reaffirming the exclusion of homosexuality *per se* from the DSM: "The American Psychiatric Association opposes any psychiatric treatment, such as 'reparative' or conversion therapy, which is based upon the assumption that homosexuality per se is a mental disorder or based upon the a priori assumption that a patient should change his/her sexual homosexual orientation." However objectionable, this is a far cry from "prohibiting" reparative therapy! <http://www.psych.org/psych_pract/ copptherapyaddendum 83100.cfm>.

cite alternative diagnoses such as depression, anxiety, or other underlying mood disorders, for insurance billing purposes.

Not content with their success in getting the term "homosexuality" removed from the list of psychological disorders, gay extremists are now pressuring the American Psychiatric Association to remove even the term "Sexual Disorder NOS." On another front, in 2002, the gay lobby nearly succeeded in stampeding the American Psychological Association into approving a motion that would have made it *unethical* to provide any treatment whatsoever for unwanted (ego-dystonic) homosexuality! Former Association President Nicholas Cummings registered his alarm:

> Vigorously pushed by the gay lobby, [the motion] was eventually seen by a sufficient number of Council members as runaway political correctness and was defeated by the narrowest of margins. In a series of courageous letters to the various components of APA, former President Robert Perloff referred to the willingness of many psychologists to trample patients' rights to treatment in the interest of political correctness. He pointed out that making such treatment unethical would deprive a patient of a treatment of choice because the threat of sanctions would eliminate any psychologist who engaged in such treatment. Although the resolution was narrowly defeated, this has not stopped its proponents from deriding colleagues who provide such treatment to patients seeking it.[38]

---

38. Rogers Wright & Nicholas Cummings (eds.), *Destructive Trends in Mental Health: The Well-Intentioned Path to Harm,* New York: Routledge (2005), p. 17. Cummings points out a curious contradiction in the position of these activists: During the years when homosexuality was considered a mental illness, "there was no counterargument against psychological interventions conducted by gay therapists to help patients to be gay." (p. 17). These activists apparently view diversity, tolerance, and inclusiveness as a one-way street. It is worth noting, however, that some therapists are so outraged by these encroachments on their freedom of practice that they have felt impelled to express publicly their desire to treat ego-dystonic homosexuals. *See, e.g.,* Dr. Paul Popper, "Coming Out of the Closet: Why I Decided to Treat Homosexuals Who Want to Change their Orientation," *Collected Papers* from 1995 NARTH Annual Conference (July 29, 1995).

Protesting this constant harassment of the therapeutic community by gay activists and their allies, well-known Canadian homosexual spokesman John McKellar proclaims that, as an active homosexual, he cannot understand the gay hysteria at the mere mention of sexual reversion therapy. "Is gay identity so fragile," asks McKellar, "that it cannot bear the thought that some people may not want to be gay?"[39]

If the answer to McKellar's question is too obvious to be stated, the scientific and medical community has hardly shown more backbone. The healthcare professions have simply caved in to the threat of being labeled "un-American," "Fascist," "sexist," "racist," "homophobic"—in short, "politically incorrect."[40]

Politics, pressure and public relations have been allowed to corrupt the scientific process. As a result, those seeking to change their sexual preferences are now faced with a type of reverse discrimination. "Forgotten is the homosexual who, out of a different vision of personal wholeness, legitimately seeks growth and change through the help of psychotherapy." (Nicolosi, *Reparative Therapy*, 12). The SSA struggler must now not only fight the inner battle between the Divine soul and the animal soul, but must also wage a constant, defensive war against the New Bigotry.[41]

---

39. "There's Hope for the World," Address, REAL Women Conf., March, 2003, <http://www.theroadtoemmaus.org/RdLb/22SxSo/PnSx/HSx/MckellarJ%20HOPE01.htm>.

40. Even Dr. Robert Spitzer, one of the practitioners responsible for removing homosexuality from the DSM says, "[F]or healthcare professionals to tell someone they don't have the right to make an effort to bring their actions into harmony with their values is hubris . . . ." <http://www.latimes.com/news/nationworld/nation/la-na-exgay18jun18,0.4259057.story?coll=la-home-center>.

41. "David J," an active member of JONAH, makes the point that "to the extent that one must push away the cultural and behavioral baggage of modern society's definition of 'adulthood' and connect to older, better definitions of maturity, we need to understand that every one of our private SSA healing paths has become politicized. And, that struggle—a struggle over values—is the most definitely politicized in our time: it defines the Right/Left split in America, Europe, and Israel

Victims of Homosexual Politics Speak Out.

Obviously, as Dr. Nicolosi observes, "This is extremely demoralizing for the client, and it makes his struggle to overcome homosexuality that much more difficult." (*Reparative Therapy*, 13) Here are some fairly typical examples of the messages we get at JONAH:

➜ All those years of pain, confusion (even fleeting thoughts of suicide)—inflicted on me, not because there isn't an alternative voice to the gay propaganda, but because this alternative is being viciously stifled, censored and de-legitimized.

➜ Hello. I'm 15 years old and have same-sex attractions. Sometimes I worry that I could be gay because so many people talk about it as just another part of life. But it is the last thing I want to be. Just the thought that I may be gay makes me depressed. To overcome these feelings of inner sadness, I decided to do some research on my own. I used the google search engine for the last six weeks to type in things like, "How do you know if you're gay?" and "Can you become straight if you're gay?" I became so much more depressed because so many articles said if you have such feelings, there is nothing you can do about it except to accept them. The stuff I read said if you feel that way, you were born gay. There is nothing you can do about it—just accept who you are! Because I lack self-esteem, confidence, and a strong sense of myself as masculine, these web sites made me even more depressed. A friend at school committed suicide because of these messages. He saw no way out. But I wanted to fight against the

---

(and probably other areas with which I am not as familiar)." E-mail to author.

large volume of naysayers. So I decided to keep looking for resources that might help me. I typed in "Jewish help for homosexuals" and the first two articles referenced JONAH. [. . .] After calling and speaking with you, I now realize help is really available [. . .] Although I am unhappy that you insisted I talk with my Mom about this issue and get her permission to get counseling, I am so much calmer and happier just knowing . . . that I am not condemned by G–d to live my life this way. My depression has lowered considerably. You have given me hope. I now know that nothing is impossible. I will be back in touch with you after I speak with my Mom.

→ When your're "gay and proud," as I was for ten years, you generally don't go around looking for information to test yourself whether in fact you <u>are</u> really gay and proud (and happy). I resigned myself to the "fact" I was born that way and there was nothing I or anybody else could do about it. I believed the messages fed to me, accepted them, and made the best of things. To even think there was evidence out there to the contrary goes against all the rules of being gay and proud. Hence I didn't give any thought to leaving the gay lifestyle until I heard someone from JONAH speak on a radio program. I couldn't believe what I heard and wondered why I never heard about the many professional studies cited that explain how change is possible. My life was almost ruined by the pro-gay propaganda that I accepted hook, line, and sinker. The gay world in which I spent my teenage years preaches tolerance and diversity but never applied that philosophy to me when I decided to get out of the life. However, true tolerance is recognizing our right to leave behind our unwanted same sex attractions, a thought that is apparently beyond the ken of most folks I knew in the life.

→ When I learned from an article I read in the *South African Jewish Report* about my ability to be free of same sex attractions (gayness) and to be treated for a maladaptative development process, I nearly flipped. [. . .] [T]here is much more "rights discourse" within our fledgling democracy than in more established democracies. But the "rights" question has been hijacked by the mainstream media and gay propagandists. [. .] If I wanted help to learn how to be a better gay, there is plenty of help available. However, the help I desire to not be gay is virtually nonexistent in this country. Can you help me find appropriate resources?

➜ . . . I was told for many years—first in school and most recently by my now gay identified father (who left my mom to live with one gay lover and then another lover and then another) that homosexual feelings are normal and that change is simply out of the question. The school feeds me "scientific studies" to prove that I'm born gay. It is not possible to change, says my father: I received his gay gene. (Of course, he never said from whom he received his gene and there are no other known gays in our paternal line). But he and society make me question whether real change is possible. I am confused. Who do I believe? Why does the world say that we can't change these feelings? I mean, there are so many intelligent people out there constantly repeating loudly and clearly: homosexuality and change—NO WAY! Whenever I hear these messages, I feel so lost, out of touch with my real self, and incapable of dealing with emotions I cannot control and cannot do something about. I feel like I am about to lose a war—even though I have never acted out with another man. When these feelings take control of my mind and body, I feel complete craziness. When I feel so bad, I feel different, I feel strange. I feel I'm not worth anything.

➜ At low points in my life I listen more intently to the cultural messages that exhort me to do whatever feels good, to involve myself in uncontrolled sex and to find other escape mechanisms. I watch *Will and Grace* and other gay shows and then fantasize how they portray me. I tried to tell myself that I am gay and should accept it . . . but it never feels right. On the other hand, whenever I feel connected to other men in healthy non-sexual ways, I find myself having zero desire to identify as gay or to act out with other men. Conversely, when I feel disconnected and emotionally downtrodden, I seek out other men for sex (never for a relationship) as a way to help me feel connected to others of my same gender. It is a blessing that I am introspective enough to realize the truth but it is a curse in that my battle is so hard.

➜ Once I let go of the false identity and obsession of SSA, I find my OSA feelings begging to come back. But I need to block out the pervasive messages all around me that gay is beautiful.

➜ [F]eeling rejected by so many other children/teenagers while in school, I decided to withdraw and to isolate myself. But then I heard about the Gay Straight Alliance at school. I joined and felt immediate acceptance in that Club. It gave me a feeling of being valued, a place where other outcasts like me could feel at home. Having a lesbian mom gave me special status there. Interestingly, the messages being drummed into me initially by the club advisor and subsequently by the teachers to whom the advisor spoke was that I accept myself as gay. In fact, I was given a pamphlet that suggested "if you haven't tried gay sex, how do you know you won't like it.?" This turned me off. I wanted to wait until marriage for sex, any kind of sex (whether gay or straight). I became conflicted. I wondered what ever happened to the Jewish concept of *kiddushin*, a sanctified relationship of one man and one woman for one lifetime together? After all, this was the value structure I learned in Hebrew school and in *shul* [synagogue]. [...] When I began voicing these concerns at school, [...] I was put down by the [gay, lesbian, bisexual and trans-gender] club members and told by the club advisor to go to the school counselor who could help me better accept myself as a gay man. (But my problem was I never considered myself gay.) "Why do you want to change?" was the question I was constantly asked. But in reality I wasn't seeking change because I thought of myself as straight, not gay. If I needed counseling it was simply to feel more confident, more self-affirmed, and more part of the world, to stop isolating myself. I did not believe that identifying myself as gay would accomplish any of those goals nor get me out of my lonely life.

Strugglers are not the only victims of steamrolling by political correctness. Teachers and guidance counselors who oppose the message are ostracized, persecuted, or threatened. Professor Chris Kempling writes on the NARTH members listserve:

> I am facing disciplinary action from the British Columbia College of Teachers for writing a January 2005 letter to the editor. The letter explained my opposition to the proposed same-sex marriage legislation. In that letter, I quoted the McWhirter and Madison study as well as the Xiridou study [*see* Chapter 14, pp.516, n. 25, and 515, n. 22, respectively] showing that infidelity was common in same-sex relationships. I then made a parenthetical comment suggesting that even if same-sex marriage was granted, adultery would become widespread in those relationships (basically making an extrapolation of the existing data). Believe it or not, my teacher's association is now claiming that I associated homosexuality with 'promiscuity, perversion, and immorality' (I didn't use any of those terms) and that my letter was defamatory.
>
> A colleague with an adult gay son in another town claimed that my letter to the editor "personally harassed" her (I never communicated with her in any way). My school district hired an out-of-town lawyer to interview her and me, and he concluded, "Yep, he harassed her!" It still boggles my mind. When I filed a human-rights complaint alleging discrimination based upon religious belief, it was dismissed without a hearing. Meantime, I have already endured a 3-month suspension without pay imposed by my school board and the College of Teachers is still entitled to impose an additional penalty if they wish. The worst sanction possible is full cancellation of my license to teach.

A *frum* (Torah-observant) guidance counselor in the Baltimore public school system reported to me over the telephone that while she agrees with the work JONAH is doing and would like to help students in her school troubled with SSA issues, she was cautioned to stay away from anything having to do with gender-affirming processes (GAP). *She was expressly warned to "keep her mouth shut" or she would be fired from her job.* She apologized for not fighting for Torah values by opposing the prevalent political agenda, but felt helpless to do anything as long as her job was threatened.

So sure has the gay lobby grown of its power over the channels of information that gay extremists have even managed to convince a significant portion of the lay public that the *Diagnostic & Statistical Manual* (DSM) actually *outlaws* homosexuals from having recourse to reparative therapy, or to any other form of gender-affirming processes. How many of you reading this book believed this to be true? It is utterly false.

What to Do?

What must we do to counteract the all-pervasive political correctness infecting the public's perception of this vitally important subject matter? Rabbi Barry Freundel, former Chairman of the Ethics Committee of the Rabbinical Council of America and a congregational rabbi in Washington, D.C. spells it out:

> Our task must be to publicize the possibility of change, and the relevant statistics that now become the statistics of hope. We also should encourage the mental health community to develop new and even more effective methods to alter the sexual orientation of those striving to live a Torah-true lifestyle. (*Homosexuality and Judaism*, 79)

While I totally agree with Rabbi Freundel's suggestions, several other possibilities need to be considered to combat the political virus rampant within the broader society. For example, just as when I worked as a "cooperating attorney" with the NAACP Legal Defense Fund, we must seek out appropriate "test cases" to reinforce the freedoms of speech, religion, and association and the equal protection of the law. Viewpoint discrimination has been held to violate First Amendment freedom of speech.[42] We need to initiate law suits

---

42. *CRC & PFOX vs. Montgomery County Public Schools No. 05-1194* (D. Md. May 5, 2005). *See* Chapter Three, *above,* note 61.

against those who, in violation of their professional and ethical duties, misinform or disinform, and thereby cause harm to the people under their care, by representing that homosexuality is not amenable to change. The potential defendants include therapists, doctors, school teachers and counselors, college and university officials, *etc.* The APAs and other mental health organizations, the media, and the public school systems should also be made aware that by fostering a climate of fear and suppression, they are making themselves potential targets for vigorous legal and legislative action.

Legislators and jurists need to be made aware that, while violent crimes characterized by ethnic, religious, or gender hatred may well need the extra deterrence of special laws, by creating a special homosexual classification with special rights and privileges, they—the lawmakers and the courts—are laying the foundation for an undemocratic society in which those whose legitimate interests lie outside the special classification are subject to discrimination, suppression, intimidation, defamation and persecution. For example, would it be "OK" to beat up or discriminate against an ex-gay man or woman or a non-gay-identified struggler?

Make sure you know what your schools are teaching in their sex-education curricula. If you find the material objectionable or age-inappropriate, be prepared to confront teachers, principals, school boards. Write letters to local newspaper editors. Organize protests. If need be, file class action lawsuits based on religious or viewpoint discrimination.

If there is a gay and lesbian student club in your school system, help organize a club for those who believe in change of sexual orientation. We have a right to equal protection of the laws and equal access to public forums.

Those of us who have studied the subject matter need to take the time to educate our fellow citizens, our legislative representatives, policy makers at all levels of government that change is possible. It is crucial to identify speakers' forums and media outlets with public access. If your workplace, city police or park authority, public school or other public venue permits or hosts a gay pride event, insist that an ex-gay speaker be included, or that an ex-gay event have equal access to the same venues.

Use the telephone, the mail and e-mail to challenge, rebut and expose the lies, misrepresentations, distortions and disinformation disseminated through the media. Do not be afraid to file formal or informal complaints with the FCC when radio and TV stations stonewall your objections. Remember that viewpoint discrimination is a recognized violation of First Amendment protections.

To those of our readers who have successfully transitioned out of homosexuality, we say, you need to be more vocal. Speak out and tell your stories. People need to know of your existence.

A Word of Caution.

On the other hand, we want to remind you and all our readers: do not try to pressure those who claim to be happy with their homosexuality into reparative therapy. Insistence generates resistance, and will invariably arouse antagonism toward the idea of change. Speak with kindness, understanding and knowledge, and use good judgment before attempting to proselytize. When others embroil you in debate on the subject, encourage your antagonists to explore all options, and by all means let them know about this book.

To mothers and fathers and brothers and sisters who are agonizing over their kin's homosexuality, know that forcing, pressuring, "noodging" someone to try this or that therapy will rarely work and often create resistance and hostility.

To straight men and women as well as former strugglers: we need more mentors. If you care deeply about this subject, have strong gender identity, good ego-strength, are emotionally mature, emotionally available, physically affectionate, and willing and able to participate in group activities and to be a friend, why not volunteer to mentor one of our strugglers?

Do not be afraid to welcome those with known or surmised SSA into your circle. One can love the person without endorsing the behavior. Your acceptance can be a life-line for someone struggling to stay afloat. As the Beruriah, the wife of Rabbi Meir said, "Let sin be eradicated, not sinners." Remember that feeling rejected is one of the primary factors leading to SSA.

Overcoming Homosexuality: Escalator to a New Level of Spiritual Awareness and Accomplishment.

It is an oft-quoted precept of the Talmud that "Where a *ba'al teshuvah* ("penitent") stands, even a *tzaddik* (totally righteous person) cannot stand." (*Brochos*, 34b) How is it possible for transgression and sin to lead to such a high level of holiness? The sinner who has struggled with his *yetzer hara* ("evil impulse") his weaknesses, his bad habits, his addictions, his complacency and his inertia—and has overcome them, has achieved something truly awesome, something which is not available even to the perfectly righteous to achieve.[43] The *tzaddik* has a weak or nonexistent *yetzer hara*, and is thus able to keep to the righteous path and avoid sin without struggling, but such a person wins no special merit for resisting evil or adhering to the Negative Commandments: it is simply in his nature to do so.

The war between the *yetzer hara* and the *yetzer tov* has its counterpart in GAP. In its Jungian version, the human psyche is always striving for wholeness, and in the process gyrates between a "shadow side" and a "golden side," both of which are within us. Jung's idea was that by increasing our awareness of these opposing energies, we can make better choices about our behavior. In

---

43. There are positive attributes to the *yetzer hara* (the evil inclination). Psychologist Aaron Rabinowitz explains "that the reason for the creation of the *yetzer hara* is not merely or solely that man-woman resist its blandishments and thereby be rewarded. On the contrary, the *yetzer hara* is indispensable, it motivates behavior. . . . [I]t [the *yetzar hara*] creates the condition, it affords the opportunity, for man-woman to transform evil into good. The ability to do so is uniquely human—angels cannot do so—and, in a very real sense, is the reason for man's-woman's creation." Aaron Rabinowitz, *Judaism & Psychology: Meeting Points*, Northvale: Jason Aronson (1999) p. 32.

developing their theory of "men's work," Robert Bly, Robert Moore, and Douglas Gillette applied this concept to a program for developing self-awareness and "mature masculinity" through confronting one's inner conflicts.[44] The essential idea is this: all that we hide, deny, fear or repress within ourselves is collected within the "Shadow Self," whereas the "Golden Self" contains all our positive qualities like love, trust, loyalty, faith in a Higher Being, and the desire to do good. As Jung points out, both sides ultimately desire the same thing; their difference lies in the means they choose to obtain it. Both sides desire well being, fulfillment and harmony, but the shadow, choosing the shorter and easier path, propels us into sinful, immoral, harmful and destructive activity. For example, the shadow may seek to protect the struggler from feeling shame. However, instead of encouraging him or her to overcome the shame in a healthy and productive way, the shadow may, among other options, push the struggler into withdrawal and isolation. Similarly, desiring to alleviate the intense emotional pain felt by the struggler, the shadow may induce him/her to drink heavily, do drugs, or use sex as a distraction from the pain. "Men's Work" refers to this "end-justifies-the-means approach" as "the gold *within* the shadow." Like "men's work," GAP helps the struggler see

---

44. *See* Robert Bly. *Iron John: A Book About Men,* New York: Addison-Wesley (1990); and Robert Moore and Douglas Gillette, *King, Warrior, Magician, Lover: Rediscovering the Archetypes of the Mature Masculine,* San Francisco: Harper (1990).

how changing one's behavioral response to a legitimate need can lead to emotional wholeness and spiritual holiness—in other words, how it can *take the gold out of the shadow*.

Because the *ba'al teshuva* has a *yetzer hara*—the ability to sin— he or she possesses within him-/herself the key to a powerful dynamic that is only waiting to be accessed in order to release an unlimited spiritual potential. "It is the memory of sin," says Rav Soloveitchik, "that releases the power within the inner depths of the soul of the penitent to do greater things than ever before. The energy of sin can be used to bring one to new heights." (*On Repentance,* 254-5). The penitent's status as *ba'al teshuvah* enables him/her to convert evil to goodness. The bitter memories of wrongdoing enhance his or her longing for, and attachment to, holiness. Thus the true penitent does not attempt to wipe out the past nor does he/she tear out the pages of sin from his/her memory. Rather, he/she builds an entirely new being upon the foundations of the past.

Of course, as the Rav comments, "[A]ll humans by nature have spiritual shortcomings—and this is why *teshuvah* was given to them." The truth is that even the *tzaddikim* (the perfectly righteous) do *teshuvah*; except that their shortcomings are imperceptible to the eyes of ordinary people. The simple fact is that, through genuine *teshuvah,* sin has the potential to be turned into a powerful force propelling the *ba'al teshuvah* toward a dynamic state of holiness and joyfulness. It is the extra motivation, the overpowering urge to do better and to reach higher, the heroic and oftentimes painful struggle against all odds and obstacles, that enables the *ba'al teshuvah* to reach higher than even a perfectly righteous person.

Genuine *teshuvah* has the power not only to repair the spiritual, emotional, and psychological damage wrought by sin and transgression—even by rebellious conduct—but to completely transport the *ba'al teshuvah* to a higher spiritual level. It is no different with SSA. Rabbi Bulka explains, "[T]he person who wrestles with the homosexual demon within and overcomes it is considered much more praiseworthy than one who never had to wrestle with such feelings."[45] Adds Rabbi Feldman, "*Teshuvah* has the capacity to return a person to a state even higher than that which he had before the sin." (*Jerusalem Letter*)

Reparative psychiatrist Jeffrey Satinover is convinced that these Torah-inspired insights are "not mere sentiment. Those of us who have worked closely with men and women who have successfully emerged out of homosexuality cannot but be struck by the depth of their compassion and wisdom, acquired at great cost, and by their strength of character." (*Homosexuality and the Politics of Truth*, 219). "When people turn [*i.e.,* change]," comments Rabbi Irving Greenberg, "they come out stronger . . . . Out of our brokenness we become stronger than when we claimed to be whole." (*The Jewish Way*, 210) Rabbi Greenberg invokes the example of the Ten Commandments, which were given not once, but twice to the Jewish People. The first Tablets were broken by Moses, lest they testify against the Children of Israel in regard to the sin of the golden calf. The second Tablets endured as a symbol of the indestructible bond between G–d and the Jewish People. We might also mention the example of Reish Lakish, one of the great Sages of the Talmud—and a reformed highway robber. Many other examples could be cited of men and women who left grievous sins behind to achieve spiritual greatness. In every instance, this was accomplished through *teshuvah*.

---

45. Rabbi Reuven P. Bulka, *One Man, One Woman, One Lifetime: An Argument for Moral Tradition*, Lafayette: Huntington House (1995), p. 35.

Shame.

Although it is proper to feel ashamed of one's sins, and though shame can be a good motivator for doing *teshuvah*, it is important for the sinner to come out of the closet of shame during this healing process. Wallowing in secrecy and shame is counter-productive to *teshuvah* and is thus strongly discouraged. As Rav Soloveitchik taught, "The torment of his soul and the feeling of shame in themselves block the way of the sinner." (*On Repentance,* 201)[46]

There are two aspects of shame: (1) an internal sense of self-loathing, and (2) an outward manifestation which can result in social or peer rejection. Arising out of an internalized belief that we are noticeably flawed, sullied, disgraced, the painful feeling of shame is often projected out to others. Though a person may hide this "shame experience" from him- or herself (often out of a fear of rendering oneself unacceptable either to others or to oneself), others often see a person looking upon him- or herself as blameworthy or as a failure. Though we try to conceal shame out of a fear that we would otherwise render ourselves unacceptable, others invariably see it long before we ourselves recognize it.

As opposed to guilt, which generally relates to some specific act, shame represents a sense of failure of the whole self. This sense of failure shows up in victims of sexual abuse, generally speaking, as

---

46. Shame can freeze a person into inaction by causing him or her to become self-preoccupied as though he or she were the center of everyone's disapproval—much as a deer caught in the headlights of an oncoming car may stand frozen in inaction. By destroying self esteem, shame can also lead one further into sin. On the other hand, an overwhelming sense of shame before G-d and one's own *neshamah* (soul) can also be a primary motivating force for *teshuvah*.: "In the early stages of *teshuvah,* when the *baal teshuvah* is torn by conflicting emotions and is still drawn to his former life-style, extreme self-affliction in the forms of shame, remorse, and fear of punishment may be the only way to overcome his passions." Rabbi Chaim Nussbaum, *The Essence of Teshuvah: A Path to Repentance*, Northvale: Jason Aronson (1993), p. 174.

well as in SSA individuals. As we saw in Chapter Four, these two groups overlap. Both groups tend to show an inability to trust others or to engage in secure attachment. They often become consumed with shame, self-hatred, and low self-esteem. They tell themselves a story in which they figure as not only unworthy and unlovable, but even deserving of the abuse to which they have been subjected. At the same time, they will seek to shield themselves from the pain of shame and its many manifestations—such as inferiority, passivity, sense of failure, and defective self-image—by raising psychological defenses. Typical defenses against shame may involve depression, manic rage, envy, or contempt. Narcissism, too, is a common defense mechanism against shame.

Such negative emotions sap one's strength of character and drain the penitent of the will to reform and heal. However, as Rabbi Chaim Nussbaum observes, in *The Essence of Teshuvah*, one who overcomes these limitations can transform the memory of sin into a motivation for spiritual improvement and the shame into a vehicle for healing. Rabbi Nussbaum insightfully recognizes in Psalm 51 a paradigm for genuine *teshuvah*. In that Psalm, David expresses deep remorse for having sinned. "I am ever conscious of my sin," he cries. David begs G–d to forgive him and to wash him "whiter than snow." (Psalms 51:9) He promises to make up for his transgression, if forgiven, by teaching others how to do *teshuvah*, and by praising Hashem. At the same time, David is not ashamed to beg, not merely for forgiveness, but for the gift of wisdom and joy. David's acknowledgment of *Hashem's* loving-kindness and readiness to forgive enabled him to reach an even higher level of spirituality and joy. (Nussbaum, 49-50)

As noted before, without forthright confession to oneself and to G–d, genuine *teshuvah* does not occur, because any impulse toward real repentance is hindered by excuses, rationalizing and blaming of others. Thus the complete process needs to involve first shame, then grief, then confession, then resolve, then cognition and understanding, then, transformation, and finally, as in Psalm 51, expressions of praise and thanks to G–d, and using what one has learned to help others in their struggle. Only then is the shame completely banished; replaced by a sense of pride and accomplishment.

So while shame is an essential first step toward *teshuvah*, dwelling on shame undermines self-image and destroys self-esteem—the very components needed to sustain the repentant sinner on his journey of return to a state of purity. "Man is not required to cover-up and conceal the bad years, the years of sin; rather he has the capacity to sanctify and purify them . . . ." (*Soloveitchik On Repentance*, 264) Rav Soloveitchik points out that it is G–d "Who created the possibility that purity might be born out of abomination." (*On Repentance*, 37) To overcome the stasis of unresolved guilt and shame, the penitent needs to discover through his very sin

> new spiritual forces within his soul, a reservoir of energy, of stubbornness and possessiveness whose existence he had not been aware of before he sinned. Now he has the capacity to sanctify those forces and to direct them upward. The aggression which he has discovered in himself will not allow him to be satisfied with the standards by which he used to measure his good deeds before he sinned; it will rather push him nearer and closer to the Throne of Glory. (*On Repentance*, 263)

When this is accomplished, the genuine *ba'al teshuvah* does not say, "I have made a break with the past and now I am a different person." Rather—and more accurately—he or she will say, "I have freed myself from the chains of my past, I have discovered my true self, and I am on the road to recovery." Thus, the true penitent does not throw away the experience of sin; he or she *uses* the errors of the past to achieve and fortify a new moral consciousness and spiritual potential.

Recidivism.

What if a person backslides? Is *teshuvah* still effective? Is exoneration still possible? Temporary relapses are fairly common during any kind of recovery process. Such episodes can stem from hunger, anger, loneliness, or tiredness. These causes are known as the "HALT" (H-A-L-T) warnings. When exposed to these and other stress factors, the struggler risks falling back into old, familiar behavioral patterns—including homosexual fantasies or conduct. When this occurs, the repentant struggler may become extremely discouraged and depressed. After all, this is what "struggling" means. The person who is working hard to improve himself is bound to be much more vulnerable to despair and a perception of failure than those who are stuck in complacency and inertia.[47] Anyone who has attained the level of self-awareness that comes with *teshuvah*, is likely to become extremely self-critical at times. At such times, the struggler will need the support and encouragement of the therapist and fellow strugglers, may even need supervision; and most rehabilitative programs are structured to provide those very needs.

Strategies to avoid relapse emphasize the need for strugglers to take responsibility for their actions, identify their high-risk situations, develop techniques of self-management and independent external control (particularly if porno addiction is involved). Most important, however, are the education and therapy components. They help the struggler identify unsatisfied core needs and fulfill them in healthy, non-sexual ways.

However, a relapse or an episode of recidivism does not mean failure. On the contrary, such lapses can strengthen a person's resolve to succeed. All too often, critics of GAP focus on the few who have quit the process rather than the many who really did *teshuvah* and successfully completed their gender-affirmation. Gay activists love to

---

47. Recovered struggler Rich Wyler found it particularly hard to work with strugglers who were "laid back" or "stuck:" "I find the victim mentality or helplessness of some of these guys to be frustrating. I want to just shake them and say, 'Look, here's all this information. Here are all these resources. Here are all these books.' And often times they say, 'Well, it looks like a lot of work. If there were a magic pill I'd take it, but I'm not really sure I want to change that much if it's going to be hard work." "Roads to Recovery," <www.jonahweb.org.>.

point to the relatively few "ex-ex-gays" who have returned to the "life style." The success rate of GAP is many times higher than that of diet-exercise weight-loss programs (DEWLP).[48] Does the medical establishment dismiss DEWLP as "unethical" or "a fraud"? Do overweight people dismiss successful dieters as "fakes"? Should DEWLP be outlawed because so many dieters fail? Should criminal, drug and alcohol rehab programs be abandoned because of the high rate of recidivism? The success rate of GAP methodologies is generally estimated at more than 66% reporting either total elimination of SSA characteristics or significant improvement. Moreover, as therapeutic approaches are refined and new ones developed, there is high expectation of even better numbers.

Critics as well as strugglers need to understand that the process takes time. We are not talking about an instant make over. Familiar patterns are hard to change—especially when the sexual drive is involved. Inappropriate desires and overpowering urges do not suddenly disappear. Thus, as cogently noted by Rabbi Dr. Moshe Spero, "many of the so-called 'unsuccessful techniques' or 'untreatable' cases of homosexuality are in fact instances of incomplete or inadequate treatment." (*Psychotherapy and Jewish Ethics,* 158-9)

Paradoxically, recidivism can also be an earmark of unusual spiritual potential. The Talmud acknowledges, "The greater the man,

---

48. *See, e.g.,* "Methods for Voluntary Weight Loss and Control," National Institutes of Health, Technology Assessment Conference Statement, March 30-April 1, 1992.

the greater his evil inclination." (*Sukkah,* 52a) Rabbi Adin Steinsaltz elaborates:

> A great person who falls back may still be on a much higher plane than others. In both the material and spiritual realms, "the righteous man may fall down seven times and yet arise." Though he falls again and again, he continues to grope his way upward. Indeed, this is the strength of the righteous: their ability to endure crisis, to bounce back, and to turn failure into a source of strength. "The thoroughly wicked man," on the other hand, "falls once and for all; once down, he cannot get up." His way is blocked, and there is no way for him to renew his ascent.[49]

Rav Soloveitchik teaches that once one has achieved complete healing—as opposed to partial healing—it is unlikely that he or she will fall back to old patterns. This may sound tautological, but "healing" is not merely the disappearance of overt symptoms but something far deeper, a new state of being in which one's perceptions and responses change.

> If the penitent utilizes the power of free choice to form a new way of life for himself and establish a new set of rules which

---

49. Rabbi Adin Steinsaltz, *Teshuvah, a Guide for the Newly Observant Jew,* Northvale: Jason Aronson (1996), pp. 35-6.

will affect all his natural reactions, if he succeeds in shaping a radically new personality for himself, then he is not in danger of backsliding to his former sinfulness. And, indeed, why should he revert to the way of sin? After all, the desires and inclinations which nurtured his sinfulness no longer pertain to him; they no longer play a role in the fabric of his newly-fashioned personality, which is animated by a different set of laws of cause and effect. Those things which once ignited in him the fires of lust . . . have now totally vanished and consequently there is no longer any danger of his reverting to sinfulness. His desires now lead him to another place entirely. (*On Repentance*, 174)

Rav Steinsaltz's insights into this phenomenon are even more radical: According to Steinsaltz, the person who never slipped and fell "never existed, except as figments of the imagination and of literary invention. No Jew," insists Steinsaltz,

> even the greatest leader, saint, or prophet, has ever been free of religious problems, failings, heartaches, and doubts. [. . .] It is not merely that "there is no one so righteous that he does only good and never sins," but more than this: temptation, doubt, pain, and transgression are the inevitable lot of those who would ascend higher. (*Teshuvah*, 35)

The propensity for *teshuvah* is so fundamental to the Jewish *neshamah* ("soul") that in Jewish Law there is a presumption that someone who, the day before, committed a sinful act—even a *to'eivah*—has already done *teshuvah* and achieved spiritual rebirth. This can be illustrated by the following. Rabbi Abraham Isaac Kook, former Chief Rabbi of the British Mandate of Palestine, was consulted on a rather delicate matter. A certain *shochet* ("ritual slaughterer") was reported to have committed a homosexual act. Should he be disqualified from his position? Rav Kook ruled that the *shochet* need not be dismissed from his position. Even if the accusation were true, the man must be presumed to have done *teshuvah,* and thus no stigma could attach to the performance of his religious duties, nor should any repercussions ensue.[50]

The annual recurrence of Yom Kippur (the "Day of Atonement") as well as the thrice-daily repetition of the *Shemoneh Esreh* Prayer (containing the prayer, "Pardon us, our Father, for we have sinned, *etc.*") presumes that recidivism is a part of human nature that must be acknowledged and dealt with in a forthright manner. As Rav Steinsaltz observed, *teshuvah* is a constant process—indeed, it must be so in order to be successful. "[N]o one is safe from temptation; consequently, no one is in a position to despise backsliders." (36)

By no means are we conceding that there is no complete recovery from SSA. "Over the years, one learns one's own weaknesses and how to overcome or at least circumvent them. One learns to create for oneself those inward and outward circumstances most conducive to continued progress . . . ." (Steinsaltz, 36) The essence of complete recovery is the ability to live a normal life free from the torments of unwanted SSA, and with full enjoyment of one's innate masculinity or femininity. We are not talking about a lobotomy in which all memory of one's previous experiences is excised, but rather a resizing and reframing of those experiences in the context of a wholly reintegrated personality.

---

50. David M. Feldman, "Homosexuality and Jewish Law," *Judaism,* vol. 32 (Fall, 1983), p. 427. The presumption that a person has done *teshuvah* for his or her sins may be rebutted by reliable evidence submitted to judicial process.

The *Oness* Argument: Homosexual by "Duress".

Introduction.

Some Jewish members or allies of the pro-gay camp have attempted to justify the acceptance of homosexuality through a legalistic loophole they somewhat naively call *oness*. The term *oness*, meaning "duress" or "compulsion," actually represents a legitimate *halachic* principle that exempts a person from punishment for the commission of a sinful or an immoral activity on the grounds that the transgression was committed under absolute compulsion or duress. In other words, although the act may have been a *ma'aseh aveirah* ("forbidden act"), the one who committed it cannot be held legally culpable, since he or she was compelled by forces beyond his or her control.

Note however that even though *oness* may exempt a person from "legal" accountability (*i.e.,* no punishment or fine may be imposed), the person is still considered to be morally accountable. This can be seen on Yom Kippur (the "Day of Atonement") where the very first plea for absolution in the *Al Chet* (great confessional) prayer includes the sin committed against G–d under compulsion or duress. An example of this principle is the law that a woman who was raped cannot be punished for having had intercourse with a man who is not her husband. (Deut. 22:26) Yet, she, too, would be included in the above-mentioned plea.

The Talmud extends the principle of *oness* to circumstances in which someone commits any other transgression under the threat of death or extreme physical torture. Note, however, that financial duress (as opposed to physical) is not within this exemption. In fact, rather than commit the transgression, the victim must be willing to forego all his or her wealth, as, for instance, through payment of a ransom or bribe to the one trying to force him or her to commit the prohibited act.[51] Indeed, one is obligated to do everything possible—

---

51. *See* Maimonides, *Hilchot Yesodei HaTorah 5:4; Ritva & Meiri,* Commentary to

short of sacrificing one's life—to avoid committing the transgression. Where feasible, one must attempt to escape rather than give in to the duress. Generally, however, when faced with death, we are not only permitted to yield to force, but actually required to. The legal justification for this is found in the Torah itself:

You shall therefore keep my statutes, and my judgments: which if a man do, he shall live by them. (Lev. 18:5)

In other words, "rather than die by them." (Talmud, *Yoma* 85b).

Why *Oness* Cannot Justify Homosexuality.

However, there are three exceptions—three categories of sin for which *oness* does not constitute an excuse. These categories are idol worship, murder, and certain sexual prohibitions, including *machshav zachar* (homosexual relations). Rather than commit any such transgressions one is required to resist even at the cost of one's own life.

Talmud, *Yevamot 53b;* Rivash Simanim 4, 11, and 387. See also *Encyclopedia Talmudit,* Jerusalem: Talmudic Encyclopedia Publishers, Ltd. (1973), *s.v. Oness.*

Unfortunately, many in the Reform and Conservative camps believe that homosexual attractions are so deeply ingrained as to constitute *oness,* and thus that those who act upon their same-sex attraction should be treated like any other person committing a transgression under duress. They argue that homosexuals "act out" under a psychological compulsion, and hence are unable to control their passions. Thus, they insist, that homosexuality is a form of duress even though the duress does not come from a third party (such as having a gun held to one's head), but from within one's very own self. This is extremely ironic: gay activists have lobbied strenuously and successfully for the removal of homosexuality from the APA's Diagnostic Statistical Manual (DSM), yet in raising the defense of *oness,* they are admitting, in effect, that homosexuality is an anxiety disorder—listed in the DSM as "obsessive-compulsive disorder" (OCD)—and therefore treatable under APA guidelines![52]

Clearly, those who attempt to apply the *oness* exemption to homosexual behavior are relying on the "gay gene" theory, or at a minimum, presuming that the condition is congenital and unchangeable. In other words, what these advocates are saying is that gays have no choice in the matter: their sexuality is predetermined, and they have no free will to choose to live as heterosexuals.[53] They are also saying, in effect, that there are no treatment options available for those who would change if they could. This, as we have seen, is an out and out misrepresentation.

Conservative rabbi Hershel Matt is an oft-quoted proponent of this argument. In his view, homosexuals are simply not able to choose or to change their sexual conduct, identity, or their fantasies and arousals.[54] Steven Greenberg is another who has publicly espoused

---

52. OCD is treatable most typically through cognitive-behavioral therapy (CBT).

53. Also implied is the assumption that sexual abstinence is not a reasonable option for homosexuals, even though it is taken for granted among observant Jews that an unmarried Jewish man or woman will not engage in sexual activity of any kind.

54. Hershel Matt, "Sin, Crime, Sickness or Alternative Life Style? A Jewish

this view. "If same-sex desire is an embodied fact for most homosexual people," postulates Greenberg hopefully, "then *oness* might be the imposing duress of a different sexuality, a compelling force."[55] Similarly, Jay Michaelson, Director of *Nehirim*: A Spiritual Initiative for GLBT [gay, lesbian, bisexual and transsexual) Jews, writes: "[Gays and lesbians] are like obsessive-compulsives who can't help themselves, and whose sin is therefore virtually excused."[56]

Conservative rabbi Elliot N. Dorf, Vice-Chairman of the Rabbinical Assembly's Committee on Jewish Law and Standards, and Rector of California's University of Judaism, has been arguing *oness*

Approach to Homosexuality," *Judaism*, Vol. 27, No. 1 (Winter, 1978), pp. 13-24. *But see* Spero, *Psychotherapy and Jewish Ethics,* pp. 158-9: "Matt, along with others, errs in heavily basing his interpretation of homosexuality as *oness* on the assumption that there are no treatment options available for homosexuals. This lack renders the homosexual 'compelled' to remain in his present state. Unfortunately, Matt's review of the relevant psychiatric literature is less than cursory. Successful treatment is actually far more than a 'rarity,' with different therapeutic modalities reporting different types or levels of change, ranging from the mere elimination of homosexual anxiety to complete orientation reversal."

55. Steven Greenberg, *Wrestling with G–d and Men: Homosexuality in the Jewish Tradition,* Madison: U. Wisconsin (2004), p. 250. At a Miami Beach screening of "Trembling Before G–d" on March 24, 2002, Greenberg personally responded to this author that those with SSA "cannot help themselves." The desperate absurdity of Greenberg's thesis shines forth from his own argument: "Perhaps when heterosexual men have intercourse with men, such sexual excess is abhorrent. When homosexual men do so, it is not." (250) Greenberg then proposes a "scientific" test for determining which type of homosexual intercourse falls under the exemption of *oness:* "Galvanic skin responses, perspiration, certain kinds of brain activity, and heartbeat are all associated with sexual arousal. Were two men, or two women, one ostensibly straight and the other gay, hooked up to sensors to detect arousal and if an array of visual stimuli were displayed before them, we would undoubtedly be able to discover which was gay and which was straight." (251).

56. Jay Michaelson, "It is Not Good for Man to be Alone," *Forward,* April 30, 2004, and <http://www.globalgayz.cim/jewishgay.html>.

to push recognition of gay marriages and admission of openly gay individuals to the Conservative rabbinate.

> Since legal demands or prohibitions only make logical sense if the people being commanded can fulfill them, and since the Torah and Jewish tradition clearly assumed the homosexual's ability to choose to be heterosexual . . . homosexuality should no longer be considered an abomination, for that implies that the person could choose to do otherwise.[57]

Such arguments are not merely inconsistent with Jewish Law and Tradition; they go against universal principles of jurisprudence. In the first place, jurisprudence universally recognizes a distinction between thought and action, between feelings and acts. A man might be ravenously hungry, but he is still guilty of theft if he steals a loaf of bread. A pederast might harbor a strong desire to commit pederasty (G–d forbid!) with a certain child, but in most civilized countries he can be arrested if he follows his impulse. Thus, no matter how strong an individual's libido might be, it is ludicrous to say that he is being "forced" to have sex. Jewish Law forbids adultery: should a *Beis Din* (Jewish Rabbinical Court) exempt an adulterous couple because they had a compulsive obsession for each other?[58] At best, Matt, Greenberg, Michaelson, Dorff, *et al.* can only claim that homosexuals are "under duress" as far as their sexual orientation, not that they are compelled to act upon their desires. Even assuming that the immediate arousal could be considered an *oness,* the decision to act

---

57. Elliot N. Dorff, *UCSJ Review* (Spring, 2004), <http://www.uscj.org/cgi-bin/print.pl?CounterpointDorff6332.html.>.

58. *See* Rabbi Josh Yuter, "Lonely Men of Faith: Homosexuality and Orthodox Judaism," <http://yutopia.yucs.org/ archives/ 2004/ 06/>: "Were rabbis to grant homosexuals a special dispensation, then there is no reason not to apply the principle of *oness* to every biblical or rabbinic prohibition. Anyone could claim that their sin was merely the result of the way that G–d created them, and this would be why they committed adultery, murder, or any other transgression."

upon it is clearly not. Jewish Law presumes that, barring mental incapacity, human beings are endowed with the ability to control their impulses.

Another problem ignored by Greenberg, Dorff, and company, is that, as noted, when it comes to violating certain prohibitions—homosexual activity among them—the *halachah* specifically requires us not to succumb to *oness,* but to resist at the cost of our very life! Thus, even if it were true that gays and lesbians only perform homosexual acts under compulsion, that would hardly qualify as an exemption.

A third problem is that in sexual cases—irrespective of sexual orientation—Jewish Law recognizes the excuse of *oness* only with respect to the "passive partner," as opposed to the "active partner," who is said to "perform intercourse with intent." (Talmud, *Yevamot* 53b, and Maimonides, *Yad Sanhedrin* 20:3.) Thus, the "active" male is considered a willing participant in the sexual act. As Rabbi Norman Lamm explains, "[T]he claim of compulsion by one's erotic passions is not valid for a male, for any erection is considered a token of his willingness."[59]

Another basic *halachic* principle, as articulated by the revered 20th-century halachic authority, Rav Moshe Feinstein, is that "any pleasure derived from a forbidden act performed under duress increases the level of prohibition."[60] Applying *oness* to consensual homosexual acts directly violates this *halachic* principle, since

---

59. "Judaism and the Modern Attitude to Homosexuality," *Encyclopedia Judaica,* (*1974 Yearbook*), Jerusalem: Keter Publishing House (1974), p. 202. *See also* Maimonides, *Hilchot Issurei Biyah* 1:9; *Sanhedrin.* 20:3; and *Encyclopedia Talmudit, s.v. "Oness,"* note 21.

60. Lamm, 202, *citing* Rav Moshe Feinstein, *Iggerot Mosheh* (1973) on *Yoreh Dea,* No. 59. There is only one exception to that rule: the case of "a married woman who was ravished and who, in the course of the act, became a willing participant.... However, this holds true only if the act was initially entered into under physical compulsion." Citing *Kesef Mishneh* to *Yad. Sanh.* 20:3.

presumably such acts provide pleasure to the participants. Gay activists rejoin that just as a heterosexual is entitled to sexual pleasure, so too are homosexuals. That claim, however, is disingenuous. Gay advocates cannot have it both ways: they cannot raise "duress" as a legal exemption while simultaneously claiming their right to the enjoyment produced by that very same activity.

Finally, *oness* is at best a *post facto* exemption, not a license to engage in a prohibited behavior. In other words, it does not *permit* the behavior; it simply *exonerates* the individual from legal liability. As mentioned previously, one who is subjected to *oness* must do everything in his power to avoid committing the transgression, including, if necessary, using up all of his/her wealth to buy his/her freedom.[61] This hardly squares with "setting up house" with one's illicit lover—whether they be of the same or opposite sex—and then claiming that whatever occurs in the bedroom thereafter is all a matter of *oness!*

Some who have attempted to argue *oness* have also claimed that it is unfair to compare heterosexual passion to homosexual passion. After all, they argue, in the case of homosexuals, an individual with no attraction to the opposite sex is being asked to deny his/her sexual drive forever, whereas the religiously observant *hetero*sexual always has the option to get married to fulfill his or her sexual needs. While this "celibacy argument" might be true in part, it only means that the challenge of the homosexual is greater, not that their suffering gives them special permission to act. Moreover, the whole truth must take into account that even heterosexuals sometimes go through life without ever finding a willing or suitable marriage partner. Is their suffering less than the non-performing homosexual's?

For all of the reasons mentioned, we find it very difficult to understand how someone even remotely acquainted with legal

---

61. As will be seen, this ruling effectively sets forth an affirmative obligation on the part of the homosexual to spend whatever money he has for therapeutic assistance.

thinking—let alone Jewish Law—could suggest that the homosexual act is excused by *oness*.

Some Unexpected Ramifications of the *Oness* Argument.

Ironically, the *oness* argument is anything but flattering to those who would exempt homosexuality from the sexual prohibitions. Even if one were to concede that SSA is innate and unchangeable, *halachah* still conclusively presumes that the homosexual remains capable of exercising resistance. The concept of *teshuvah* is built upon the premise that individuals are responsible for their own actions and have within themselves the ability to choose between what is permitted and what is forbidden. This is the fundamental basis of all legal systems—not just *halachah*. The argument that one's drive to transgress is innate and irresistible is familiar to the legal profession as a common formulation of the insanity defense. For example, a person on trial for murder may be entitled to a verdict of "not guilty by reason of insanity" if it is established that when the accused shot the victim, he or she was acting under an "irresistible impulse." Similarly, a kleptomaniac convicted of shoplifting may receive a lenient sentence on condition that he or she undergo psychiatric treatment. Thus, like the criminal invoking the insanity defense, a homosexual claiming immunity on the grounds of *oness* would seem to be placing him- or herself—beyond the bounds of personal accountability owing to some pathological condition that prevents him or her from conforming to admitted social norms. This is a very surprising argument from a class of individuals that has devoted so much energy to *removing* homosexuality from the DSM's listing of psychiatric pathologies! Indeed, when it comes to the question of psychological treatment they reject the pathology label, but invoke it to exempt themselves from the religious proscription.

As we mentioned above, Jewish Tradition does in fact recognize SSA as "natural," and Jewish Law certainly regards the homosexuals as "normal"[62]—hence capable of choosing between right and wrong, and personally accountable for their actions. We explained earlier that, in general, where a person is being forced to transgress a sexual prohibition, he or she must do everything within reason to avoid yielding to the compulsion. If the compulsion comes from within, this duty should include the obligation to seek professional help. There can be no doubt that a person driven to compulsive behavior of any sort owes it to him- or herself to pursue treatment rather than passively suffer the consequences. If a person is physically ill and there is a medicine that can help him, the person has a *halachic* obligation to take the medicine. This principle applies equally to psychological assistance.[63] True, these things cost money, perhaps a great deal of it. However, as we learned above, effective therapies certainly exist, and one must be prepared to spend even every dollar one has in order to liberate oneself from a compulsion to sin. Thus, even if it were not possible to repair one's gender identification, the SSA individual would still be obligated to seek help in learning how to restrain his impulses and control his actions.

In this regard, it is important to point out that according to Jewish teaching, the critical time to resist temptation is *as soon as* the person first becomes conscious of it. At that moment, the person has the ability to redirect his/her thoughts to something positive and enlightening. That moment is an opportunity to do a tremendous *mitzvah*—the *mitzvah* of converting evil into good. Once that moment

---

62. By "natural," we mean that SSA is just one of the several manifestations of the *yetzer hara* to which human beings are susceptible by nature; by "normal," we mean that homosexuals are no more and no less susceptible to such manifestations than anybody else.

63. Rabbi Moshe D. Tendler, "The Halachic Import of the Psychological State," in Fred Rosner (ed.), *Medicine and Jewish Law,* Vol. 2, Northvale: Jason Aronson (1933) pp. 67-75.

passes, however, the window of opportunity narrows. The door to obsession is opened, and it becomes much harder to resist.[64]

The congruence of this ancient teaching with modern psychology is remarkable. Based on his own clinical observation and experience, Dr. Joseph Nicolosi has identified a "grey zone"—a moment in time where the struggler has an opportunity to divert his thoughts before the unwanted desires overtake and control his actions. Thus, even assuming, for the sake of argument, that *oness* were a viable *halachic* defense to homosexuality, the individual would still be held responsible for creating the circumstances leading to his or her own subjugation by forbidden desires.

G–d's Role in the Struggle to Overcome SSA.

Thought-diversion techniques and "grey zones" have little relevance unless a person has already commenced the process of *teshuvah* and has found the necessary support from within and without. The plight of the strugglers is that they have already been caught in the web of obsessive desire. They have already been weakened by ineffective resistance and discouraged by repeated failure. They are drowning and in no condition to pull themselves out. What can they do?

Michael Danielle, whose life is partially profiled in Chapter Six, is very open about his dependence on G–d not only for his own healing, but for assistance in helping others to heal:

---

64. *See* Rabbi Joseph B. Soloveitchik, *Family Redeemed: Essays on Family Relationships,* New York: Toras HaRav Foundation (2000), pp. 74-5; and Rabbi Basil Herring in Berger & Shatz, 156-9;

> So many gays are searching. They're searching for something so deep they don't even know what it is. [. . .] Many of the gays want out of that lifestyle. A lot of them feel they must clean themselves up first. "Well, when I get rid of this"—"Well, when I get rid of that"—"then, I'll come to G–d." I tell them the truth. "G–d takes you just as you are. He's the One who cleans you up. It is His power and His spirit." All He needs is to know the desire that's in your heart, and He'll do the rest. He'll take the garbage and give you beauty for ashes. Look! I've been there. I've walked in your shoes. I've gone through what you're going through. I've searched and searched. I went to parks and bars looking for the perfect lover that we could settle down and live together happily ever after . . . .[65]

Alan Medinger is another former homosexual who recounts his "true encounter with the L–rd." After years of failure, Medinger finally admitted his utter inability to control his unwanted behavior. At the end of his resources, he put all his broken heart into words of quiet resignation: "G–d, I give up. My life is a total mess. I can't handle it anymore. I don't care what You do. You take over. And He did."[66] Because of his acceptance of G–d and his total reliance on His loving-kindness, Danielle was able to strengthen his will power to the point where the unwanted behaviors gradually fell away, allowing him to complete the growth-into-manhood that until then had eluded him.

Those who, like Alan Medinger, wish to change their lives and free themselves from enslavement to their desires can find inspiration and encouragement from the words G–d spoke to Cain after rejecting Cain's offering (Gen. 4:7):

---

65. Marie S. Rice, *Michelle Danielle is Dead*, Nashville: Jonathan Publishers (1985), p. 69.

66. Alan Medinger, *Growth into Manhood: Resuming the Journey*, Colorado Springs: Shaw (2000), p. 237.

> *Surely, if you improve [yourself], you will be lifted. But, if you do not improve [yourself], sin rests at the door. Its desire is toward you, yet you can conquer it.*

According to the great medieval Torah commentator Rabbi Ovadiah Sforno, this verse means that the more we allow our *yetzer hara* (unholy inclination) to influence our behavior, the stronger it will grow; nevertheless, we always retain the power to master it, if we so desire. What makes this possible is our Divine Image—*i.e.,* the fact that we were created in G–d's image. (Pelcovitz, 31) G–d's goodness is infinite, and knows no bounds. Similarly, the Divine goodness reflected within each of us is potentially limitless. As explained in many sources, the *yetzer hara* exists only to goad us toward perfection. That is its true mission and ultimate purpose.

Michael Danielle combined the lesson of G–d's admonition to Cain, with his own personal understanding of Isaiah 60:21: "Your people will all be righteous; they will inherit the land forever; a shoot of My planting, My handiwork, in which to glory." (Rice, 123) Jewish Tradition understands this prophecy to refer to the Chosen People and their unique destiny. Michael Danielle chose to be chosen when he let this verse speak to him personally. To Michael, the words meant that he, as an individual created being, was unique, special and precious to G–d. By turning his back on the freedom of choice which G–d gives to every human being, Danielle had degraded his body, besmirched his soul, and messed up his life.

Danielle advises his fellow journeyers: "You're not going to find true love or happiness, or the perfect lover, or peace of mind in a bar, or on a street, or in a bottle, or in a joint, or in . . . any other things that the world has to offer . . . ." (Rice, 69-70) By reestablishing his relationship with G–d and going through a gender-affirming process to fill in his developmental gaps, Danielle was at last able to conclude his harrowing journey of sexual brokenness. By reaffirming the gender of his birth and allowing himself to be Michael instead of Michelle, he was able to come closer to G–d.

Danielle's, Medinger's and Wyler's intensified belief in G–d served as both a catalyst and a power source for their courageous decision to commit to their respective gender-affirming processes. We shall see this chemistry again in the testimonials of Daniel and Scott (*see* Chapter 15, pp. 562-69), each of whom sought Divine help for their journey into sexual wholeness and holiness. Acknowledgment of the One G–d and careful observance of all His Commandments not only weakens the power of the *yetzer hara,* but unleashes unsuspected reserves of strength and determination in the penitent, leading to still greater and higher levels of observance and spiritual connection. Thus, *teshuvah* (*i.e.,* approaching ever closer to G–d) is a self-reinforcing process that entails, in its very momentum, the conquest of sin and the relief from all the pain and misery that goes with it. What all this means is that *teshuvah* and psychological healing are not just parallel processes, but natural allies in the quest for gender recovery—and indeed, for sexual wholeness in general.[67]

---

67. *See* Michelle Friedman & Rachel Yehuda, "Psychotherapy and *Teshuvah:* Parallel and Overlapping Systems for Change," in Berger & Shatz, 175-188.

Chapter 12:

"Doing *Teshuvah*" and Healing From SSA: Parallel Processes.

Jewish teaching regards the commission of an *aveirah* ("sin" or "transgression") as both a symptom and a cause of spiritual illness or debility. The process of healing that spiritual illness or debility is called *teshuvah*—a return to the purity of the soul with which G–d originally endowed us. This process of return takes the penitent through successive stages of shame, regret, confession, resolve, *etc.,* as discussed in the previous chapter. A person who "does *teshuvah*" makes a life-determining choice to repair or heal a breach that has come between him- or herself and G–d through the violation of a commandment.

Teshuvah and *Refuah.*

Thus *teshuvah* can be thought of as a special category of a more general process called *Refuah* ("healing"). *Refuah* is the process by which we overcome any physical, psychological, or spiritual weakness. *Refuah sh'leymah* or "complete recovery" is something we ask G–d to grant us in our everyday prayers. *Refuah* restores our body, mind, and/or soul to a state of health, wholeness, and vigor. Thus, in Jewish teaching, there is a deep and intrinsic connection between *refuah* and *teshuvah*.

Both *teshuvah* ("repentance") and *refuah* ("healing") are commandments of the Torah.

Teshuvah:

When you are in distress and all these things have happened to you, you will finally return to G–d your Lord and obey him. (Deut. 4:30).

You will return to G–d your Lord . . . (Deut. 30:2)

Refuah:

Only he [who caused the injury] *. . . shall cause him to be thoroughly healed.* (Ex. 21:19).

Only take heed to yourself. . . . (Deut. 4:9)

Take therefore good heed to yourselves. (Deut. 4:15)

Let us examine the relationship of these two concepts a bit further, for although *teshuvah* and *refuah* are similar and closely related, they are not identical. Indeed, whereas *teshuvah* always involves healing at some level, *refuah* need not always involve *teshuvah.* For example, if an individual breaks a leg, the leg generally heals even without *teshuvah*—assuming it has been properly set and placed in a cast. However, when the healing involves overcoming a sin or transgression that has affected the physical or spiritual health of the wrongdoer, it follows that if complete healing is to take place, any medical treatment, psychological assistance, or spiritual counseling must necessarily be accompanied by *teshuvah.*

It is also important to recall that according to Torah, the spiritual illness caused by the commission of sin produces an uncleanness or stain upon the soul that must be washed away before the person can heal. We find an example of this in Leviticus, 14:1-32, in which we are taught the laws of purification from *tzara'as*—the "leprosy" that appears in the skin of one who (as Rashi explains) has spoken *lashon hara* ("gossip" or "slander") about another person.

Once we acknowledge that committing a homosexual act does indeed violate a Torah prohibition, and recognize that homosexuality is neither benign nor immutable nor incapable of healing, the confluence of *refuah* with *teshuvah* in the context of SSA becomes obvious. In Chapters Three and Four, we explored a multitude of reasons why SSA presents issues of grave concern with respect to one's physical, emotional, psychological and spiritual health. In Chapters Nine and Ten, we also confirmed (over the strident protests of the pro-gay camp) that homosexuality is indeed a *to'eivah*—an extremely serious level of transgression. Thus it follows that healing from SSA necessarily involves at least some level of *teshuvah*.

Moreover, when an SSA struggler repents of his or her past homosexual behavior and makes a solemn and firm commitment to do *teshuvah*, not only does that very commitment reflect an incipient stage of healing, but the ultimate transformation is most effectively attained by combining the processes of *teshuvah* and GAP at their deepest levels. When *refuah* and *teshuvah* coincide in this manner, it also becomes clear why there is a very deep structural correspondence between the two. Let us now examine this correspondence, starting with a simple analysis of the structure of *teshuvah*.

Kapparah and *Taharah*.

We have already seen that *teshuvah* is a kind of cleansing or purification of the soul. As explained by Rav Soloveitchik, genuine and complete *teshuvah* generally comprises two distinct levels, which the Rav calls "Repentance of Acquittal," and "Repentance of

Purification"[1] Acquittal (*kapparah*) and purification (*taharah*) are both necessary elements of *teshuvah* because the commission of a sin affects more than the sinner's relations with any wronged parties and with G–d: it attacks the very essence of the sinner's spiritual being. "[S]in places man under the burden of culpable liability and it defiles him as well." (Peli, 49) The sinner may have been punished for, or absolved of, a misdeed, or may have received a pardon or a suspended sentence; but to be restored to his or her pristine state of innocence, he or she must still undergo a process of purification. Thus, acquittal from liability for the commission of the sin and purification from the resulting defilement of our souls are essential components of a spiritual process in which the sinner is not only forgiven his or her transgression, but is actually returned to his/her previous state of innocence and spiritual purity.

Let us examine the difference between these two levels of *teshuvah*. As taught by Rav Soloveitchik,

> *Kapparah* means forgiveness or withdrawal of a claim. This is a legal concept, borrowed from the laws of property. Just as one may release his fellow man of a debt owed to him, so may G–d absolve one of a penalty to which he is liable due to sin. *Kapparah* removes the need for punishment. (50) [. . .] The moment acquittal is granted and punishment wiped from the books, man's liability is terminated. (51)

Taharah ("purification"), on the other hand, means totally abandoning the path of sin.

---

1. Rabbi Pinchas H. Peli, *On Repentance: the Thought and Oral Discourses of Rabbi Joseph Dov Soloveitchik,* Northvale: Jason Aronson (1996), p. 49.

> Repentance of purification necessitates a complete breaking away from the environment, the contributing factors and all the forces which created the atmosphere of sin (56) [...] If a man regrets his sin but does not yet abandon the path of sin, he is not considered cleansed of the pollution within him (59).

We saw near the beginning of Chapter Eleven that Yom Kippur, "the Day of Atonement," can procure an acquittal "even for those who have not repented individually." (Peli, 52) Indeed, *kapparah* ("atonement," or as Rav Soloveitchik defines it, "acquittal," "exculpation" or "pardon") need not depend on the repentance of the sinner, but may also be procured by someone or something other than him- or herself. Just as a father may forgive his stubborn child, so may G–d choose to forgive an unrepentant sinner.

On the other hand, because the stain left by the sin is personal to the sinner, investing the intimacy of his very soul, *taharah* ("purification") can never be procured "by proxy," but only through the efforts of the sinner himself. Without such personal efforts, the sinner may remain in a state of pollution that, as the Rav explains, not only affects his personality, but his *halachic* (legal) status as well: "An Israelite who has transgressed . . . is also discredited as a witness in a court of Jewish Law. This does not constitute further punishment but is rather indicative of a change in his personal status. As a result of sin, man is not the same person he was before." (51-2)

Thus, the process of *teshuvah*—and hence, of healing—is not complete until the sinner has been both pardoned for, and cleansed of, his transgression.

> [T]rue *teshuvah* (repentance) not only achieves *kapparah* (acquittal and erasure of penalty), it should also bring about *taharah* (purification) from *tum'ah* (spiritual pollution), liberating man from his hard-hearted ignorance and in-

sensitivity. Such *teshuvah* restores man's spiritual viability and rehabilitates him to his original state.[2] (52)

Purification through Understanding.

We can see now how this simple anatomy of *teshuvah* corresponds closely to the process of healing from SSA. Consider, however, the following: a struggler might decide—for one reason or another—to put a complete stop to his/her homosexual activity, and prevent him- or herself—by one means or another—from engaging therein; and might thereby obtain *kapparah* ("acquittal" or "pardon") for past sins. The reason for the cessation might range from an overwhelming moral sense of shame and a heroic resolve to reform, to purely utilitarian considerations (*e.g.,* fear of public exposure, fear of contracting AIDS) or to the force of external circumstances (*e.g.,* lack of freedom or opportunity). So far as *kapparah* is concerned, it makes no difference *why* the struggler ceased the activity. However, as long as he or she retains a frustrated desire for homosexual contact, he/she retains a vestige of spiritual pollution. Such a person will rarely be a good candidate for marriage, or feel totally comfortable with others of his/her own sex. He or she will most likely remain sexually and emotionally frustrated, repressed and in pain.

To be sure, there are those who believe they can overcome their SSA by "white-knuckling" it—in other words, through sheer will power. However, aside from the harsh fact that this approach is rarely effective, "abandoning the act of sin is only a partial remedy." (Peli, 57) Without addressing the underlying causes of the aberration (note: the word comes from the Latin for "wandering away"), the repentant struggler can rarely, if ever, totally redeem him- or herself from either the behavior or the arousals and fantasies that lead to it. It is only by

---

2. Of course, where one person has wronged another, *teshuvah* alone is not enough. The wrongdoer must first make reparation and seek forgiveness from the wronged party.

daring to discover and probe the underlying and long-hidden emotional wounds and, at long last, addressing them and healing them, that the struggler can free him- or herself of all desire for same-sex activity and thus regain the former purity of his or her *neshamah* (soul).

Thus, the advice often given by well-meaning rabbis and other spiritual counselors to strengthen their faith in G–d and persist in prayer is often—without something more—woefully ineffectual. The struggler who prays, "G–d, please take this curse away from me," accomplishes little. The more appropriate supplication would be, "Father in Heaven, please help me understand the causes of my suffering, so that I may be empowered to do what is necessary to heal my wounds, and learn to think and feel and live in harmony with the gender you have bestowed upon me, and so that I may sanctify myself with the Commandments which you have commanded." Clearly, the approach that is needed to get things moving is a combination of coming closer to G–d, through *teshuvah,* and to oneself, through self-understanding.

We saw earlier that even after a man has been punished for transgressing a commandment, one residual consequence of his transgression is his disqualification to testify before a Jewish Tribunal.[3] Rav Soloveitchik used that example to illustrate the difference between the legal culpability and the spiritual pollution emanating from a single sinful act. Now, to show the meaning of purification from sin, the Rav (56) cites a passage from the Talmud (*Sanhedrin* 25b) in which the Sages seek to define the moment when a gambler, for example (gambling is forbidden by Jewish Law), may be reinstated as a witness: "When is their repentance?" asks the Talmud. "When they break up their dice and repent so completely that they do not even play for free." In other words, the sinner attains purification only when he or she loses the inclination to engage in the

---

3. Is it merely coincidental, in this regard, that the witness's competence to testify depends predominantly on an evaluation of his or her capacity to *understand*?

forbidden activity. It is no longer a matter of repression: the desire is simply not there any more.

Healing from same-sex attraction is no different. Healing and purification remain incomplete until the struggler loses sexual interest in persons of the same sex. When that happens, the "ex-gay" man or woman has made a "complete return" to the sexual innocence and purity of soul with which he or she was born. Only then can he or she begin to develop a normal, healthy interest in the opposite sex.

Such a dramatic turn requires much more than atonement for forbidden acts and thoughts. Homosexual feelings, fantasies and desires are tell-tale signs of deep and long-hidden emotional wounds. Because these wounds affect the individual—both consciously and unconsciously—on all levels, namely emotional, experiential, spiritual, and cognitive, the healing process must likewise be engaged at these same levels.

The Reparative Drive.

Why is it necessary to reopen and painfully probe those old, festering wounds? The answer lies in something Drs. Elizabeth Moberly and Joseph Nicolosi call "the reparative drive." The reparative drive is the psyche's attempt to repair the deficit in one's gender identity—to bridge the gap between one's sense of self and sense of gender.

One of Freud's most fundamental discoveries was that, just as the body is able to heal itself from many kinds of injuries and illnesses, the psyche, too, has this same, amazing power to repair or heal itself from emotional, psychological and spiritual trauma. However, just as a broken leg needs to be set correctly in order to heal properly, the psyche's reparative drive must be guided in the right direction in order to achieve genuine healing, as opposed to makeshift or palliative remediation. In other words, the reparative drive is a blind force that will use whatever means may come to hand in order to shield the person from psychological pain; it cannot distinguish between the causes and symptoms of the underlying trauma. Hence, to be truly effective, the reparative drive must be consciously, rationally guided along the most effective pathway to true healing—namely, the pathway to the underlying causes.

In the case of homosexuality or any other kind of psychological wounding, the shortest route to the causes is the courageous path of introspection, self-examination and self-knowledge. Thus, self-understanding at all levels of conscious and unconscious experience is essential to guiding the reparative drive to its optimal goal of genuine, complete healing. As Sexual Reorientation Specialist Richard Cohen observes,

> The more a person is unaware of his thoughts, feelings, and needs in present relationships, the stronger the need and energy attachment will be to engage in or fantasize about homosexual behavior. Sex then becomes a way back to the body and soul, either through masturbation (self-sex) or sex with another person. Therefore, seeking sex or compulsive masturbation represents a reparative drive to restore the broken self. The frustration is that this never works.[4]

So the key to authentic gender healing is to help the SSA individual's reparative drive find effective ways of accomplishing its purpose. Clinical reports published by gender-affirming clinicians regularly point out that homosexuality is a manifestation of the reparative drive as it labors to repair a gender deficit perceived by the homosexual as within him- or herself.[5] It was Freud who first suggested that the typical male homosexual focuses his emotional energy on—in other words, becomes emotionally attached to—those in whom he perceives the masculine traits or characteristics that he feels are lacking in his own persona. Let us recall (*see* Chapter Four,

---

4. Richard Cohen, *Coming Out Straight*, Winchester: Oakhill Press (2000), p. 53.

5. Dr. Nicolosi cites a number of such studies in his text, *Reparative Therapy for the Male Homosexual: A New Clinical Approach*, Northvale: Jason Aronson (1997), pp.70-76.

above) that every male child naturally desires and needs healthy, non-sexual intimacy with his male role models ("male bonding"). This desire or need emerges in early childhood and is ordinarily satisfied initially by the father, later by male peers. When the pre-homosexual boy's need for bonding is frustrated for whatever reason, the reparative drive prompts him to "defensively detach" from his father and same-sex peers. The boy's sexual attraction for other males eventually manifests as a way to compensate for the loss of masculine identity brought about by his defensive detachment. The objects of the boy's sexual or emotional interest typically possess the physical and/or personality characteristics that he perceives as lacking within himself.

In effect, the homosexual transforms his same-sex partners into an externalized symbol of his abandoned masculinity. He perceives in the other his own ego ideal. Sexual "union" with the same-sex partner permits the homosexual to possess *vicariously* (however fleetingly) what he feels is missing in himself.

Internalizing what we Learn about Ourselves.

Freud's theory of homosexuality was independently confirmed by his daughter, Anna Freud, who reported that several of her homosexual patients were able to attain full heterosexuality once they successfully internalized the realization that the masculinity they coveted in their partners already inhered naturally within themselves.

The key word here is *internalized*. What does it really mean? One can understand something intellectually without being able to act upon it. This is so because the faculty of understanding has no natural connection with the will to act. To "internalize" something, in psychological or philosophical parlance, means to forge a link between the intellectual grasp of a concept and the vital desires, needs and aspirations that stimulate a person to action. Once that link is established, the person not only understands with his/her intellect, but is able to relate and apply the new knowledge to those vital needs and desires, and to act accordingly to fulfill them. It is here that the relevance of *teshuvah* is most obvious: *teshuvah* enables the penitent to *internalize* what he/she has learned about him- or herself through intensive introspection and self-examination. Thus *teshuvah* enables him/her to apply that new knowledge toward achieving the transformation he/she so desperately longs for.

Repentance of Redemption.

What happens when this internalization is fully and completely accomplished? The sinner attains a whole new level of *teshuvah*, transcending both *kapparah* and *taharah*. As Rav Soloveitchik describes it,

> [T]hose things which once ignited in him the fires of lust, when he had his other personality, have now totally vanished and consequently there is no longer any danger of his reverting to his sinfulness. His desires now lead him to another place entirely. This repentance which brings about a radical transformation of a whole way of life leading to a rebirth of the personality is *repentance of redemption* [. . .] [This type of repentance] is higher than all the gradations of acquittal and expiation, for in it the sinner vanishes and is replaced by a new man who essentially has never sinned and is in no need of expiation, of cleansing, of purification. He is in a wholly liberated and redeemed state. (174-5)

The loftiness of this level is not to be downplayed. The expressions used here by the Rav—"higher [level of *teshuvah*]," "another place entirely," "radical transformation of a whole way of life"—indicate that Rav Soloveitchik is referring here to what the mystical teachings call *teshuvah ila'a*, the "superior return." This is how the Alter Rebbe describes it:

After the cleansing spirit passes over and purifies them, then their souls are enabled [*i.e.,* they have the *potential*] to return unto G–d Himself, literally, to ascend the greatest heights, to their very source, and cleave to Him with a remarkable unity. This is the original unity, the ultimate in union, that existed before the soul was blown by the breath of His mouth to descend and be incorporated within the body of man.[6]

We have seen that the basic structures of gender-affirming processes and *teshuvah* are virtually identical. In the following chapter, we shall explore their congruence in more detail.

---

6. Rabbi Shneur Zalman of Liadi, *Likutei Amarim Tanya,* Brooklyn: Kehot Publication Society (bilingual ed. 1984), *Igeret HaTeshuvah,* Chapter 8, p. 373.

Chapter 13:

Teshuvah & Healing: Spiritual Elevation & Sexual Transformation Proceeding in Lock-Step.

Rabbi Adin Steinsaltz, internationally recognized as one of the leading rabbinical scholars of our time, makes a fascinating but highly pertinent observation: "All forms of *teshuvah*, however diverse and complex, have a common core: the belief that human beings have it in their power to effect inward change."[1] Thus, if someone feels the need to "effect inward change," *teshuvah* would seem to be a highly promising approach, given that "all forms of *teshuvah*" are based on the belief that change is possible.

On the other hand, as Rabbi Irving Greenberg observes,

> The power of sin—and of bad patterns—is that it convinces people that change is impossible. People despair of their ability to change and give up the capacity to grow or renew. The promise of

---

1. Rabbi Adin Steinsaltz, *Teshuvah: A Guide for the Newly Observant Jew*, Northvale: Jason Aronson (1996), pp. 3-4.

repentance and the model of G–d challenge this hopelessness. There *is* a process of rebirth, but it needs attention, effort, and help.[2]

Indeed, as explained by Rabbi Jeffrey Cohen, spiritual leader (recently retired) of the famous Stanmore Synagogue of London,

> On the graph of repentance, there is no single, uninterrupted, vertical line from the first stirring of remorse or recognition that one's life is going in the *wrong* direction, to the peak of complete repentance. It is invariably punctuated by interludes of regression. One starts with good intentions to repent, and then one is overwhelmed by the blandishments of habit.[3] There are times when great energy is expended in the battle against the evil inclination and in the tortuous uphill climb toward moral cleansing. And there are other times—which can be protracted—when the exercise of repentance is put on hold while the person gets on with other aspects of life.[4]

There is in fact a momentum to life that translates into a kind of deadening inertia that requires considerable force to change or reverse direction. Both *teshuvah* and gender-affirming programs are life-affirming processes. They counteract a kind of death-in-life, a psychic numbing.

One way to wake up from our spiritual and emotional torpor is to remember that we are all judged for our deeds, and that G–d is merciful and desires our repentance, not our punishment. Thus, though the Day of Atonement can atone even for the unrepentant, the

---

2. Rabbi Irving Greenberg, *The Jewish Way: Living the Holidays,* Northvale: Jason Aronson (1998), pp. 201-2.

3. Or sometimes, as some of our strugglers would say, by a desire to "tease the disease."

4. Rabbi Jeffrey M. Cohen, *1001 Questions and Answers on Rosh Hashanah and Yom Kippur*, Northvale: Jason Aronson (1997), pp. 55-6.

main theme of the ten Days of Awe from Rosh Hashanah through Yom Kippur is a call to do *teshuvah* and procure atonement through our own efforts.

The Book of Jonah: a Paradigm for *Teshuvah* and Healing.

From the perspective of someone struggling to heal from homosexuality, it is profoundly significant that in the afternoon service of Yom Kippur, the public recital of the Book of Jonah follows immediately after the reading of Leviticus 18 (the "Holiness Code"). The Book of Jonah tells us of the repentance of the city of Nineveh from sins which the commentators liken to those of Sodom and Gemorah—including sexual perversion, robbery and violence.[5] Indeed, when the people of Nineveh hear Jonah's prophecy of approaching destruction they repent. And since their repentance resulted in their salvation, the Prophet takes pains to describe how they repented: they fasted, they donned sackcloth, they sat amid ashes, and they implored *Hashem* to be merciful. But was that all?

The Prophet also tells us that "G–d saw their *deeds* [emphasis added] . . . and G–d relented." On this verse, the Talmud comments (*Taanis* 16a): "The verse does not read: *and G–d saw their sackcloth and their fasting*, but *G–d saw their 'deeds'*—that they repented of their evil ways." In other words, all well and good to regret, to mourn and to implore forgiveness; but the true test of *teshuvah* lies in "shaping up," in changing one's ways—in short, in reform. It takes more than the outward trappings of repentance to change the character of a person or to avert the punishment of Heaven.

Basic to the whole idea of repentance is that G–d stays His hand at the sound of tearful prayer and mourning, but waits for more enduring signs of change before tearing up the decree of punishment.

---

5. *See* commentary in, *e.g., Yom Kippur: The Complete Artscroll Machzor* (*Nusach Ashenaz*), Brooklyn: Mesorah (1986), pp. 634-45.

As we saw above, in Chapter Eleven, (pp. 397-98), the violation of a Commandment effects a separation between the sinner and G–d. Thus, to annul the separation and restore our closeness to the Heavenly Father we need to commit to observance of that Commandment from now on, and to evidence our commitment through our actual conduct. It goes without saying that to reform certain types of habitual or addictive behavior can require a profound transformation on a spiritual, psychological, and emotional level.

Can this be accomplished overnight? Not likely. Personal transformation at the deepest levels takes time. Moreover, as we have already seen, gender recovery does not usually occur in an instant. Yet, as the Book of Jonah assures us by implication, the "gay community" of Nineveh "went straight." How did that happen?

Both *teshuvah* and gender-affirming programs involve personal transformation, empowerment, and growth—they are processes. Both evolve through several phases or stages. Both involve intensive intellectual, psychological and behavioral work. Rarely is a single dramatic act decisive. Indeed, there is a structure to *teshuvah,* and like any structure, it needs to be built from the ground up. In *The Jewish Way,* Rabbi Irving Greenberg suggests a methodology for changing deeply ingrained behavior patterns. Reviewing Maimonides' structural division of *teshuvah* into three components—Regret, Rejection, and Resolution (the "Three Rs")—Greenberg gives these categories a chronological connotation:

> Regret deals with the past, nullifying conditioning by repelling it. Rejection deals with the present; not doing the sin keeps the present free and clear. Resolution deals with the future, preventing sin from coming into life again. Only when all three dimensions are in place will the full process of repentance occur.[6]

---

6. Rabbi Irving Greenberg, *The Jewish Way,* Northvale: Jason Aronson (1998), p. 204, *citing* Maimonides, *Mishneh Torah, Hilchos Teshuvah,* 1:1.

Different paradigms are possible. Rabbi Dov Peretz Elkins proposes two alternative formulas. He suggests a different "Three Rs" (Realize, Repent, and Regret) for sins against G–d and a fourth R (redress) when the sin is against a fellow human. He goes on to suggest "Four Cs": Consciousness, Confession, Contrition, and Cessation.[7] Rabbi Elkins also cites yet another "Three Rs" by Rabbi Sidney Greenberg: Recognition, Recitation, and Renunciation, for sins against G–d. Greenberg adds a fourth R—"reparation" when the sin is against another person. (Elkins, 121)

Rabbi Shimon Apisdorf, a modern *ba'al-teshuvah*-oriented rabbi, proposes that we divide Maimonides' "Regret" phase into two distinct steps: Regret and Confession. Thus, Rabbi Apisdorf's "four steps to greatness" (still based on Maimonides' division) consist of: (1) Regret; (2) Abandonment; (3) Confession; and (4) Resolve.[8]

Recognizing that these steps may not necessarily follow a set order (individual approaches may vary), we shall use, for illustrative purposes only, Rabbi Apisdorf's fourfold scheme to show the remarkable correspondences between the various stages of *teshuvah* and the phases of gender-affirming processes (GAP) as practiced by our cooperating professionals and support groups. In much the same way as *teshuvah* rests on recognizing, dealing with, and eliminating the rationalizations that mask our deficiencies, so, too, do gender affirming processes. We shall examine these correspondences step by step, in order to bring out the remarkable congruence of these two independently evolved processes.

---

7. *See* Rabbi Dov Peretz Elkins (ed.), *Moments of Transcendence: Inspirational Readings for Rosh Hashonah,* Northvale: Jason Aronson (1992), p. 121.

8. Rabbi Shimon Apisdorf, *Rosh Hashanah-Yom Kippur Survival Kit* (Rev. Ed.), Baltimore: Leviathan Books (2000), p. 102.

Step 1: Regret (*Charatah*).

Before one can do *teshuvah*, one must first recognize in the depths of one's own soul that one has lost something precious and acknowledge the need for transformation. In the case of SSA, when one senses the loss of one's innocence, the incompleteness of one's sexuality, or the missed opportunity of having a spouse and children, or when a homosexual man or woman fears sexual intimacy with a person of the opposite sex, such feelings can motivate the unmarried homosexual to take the first step of *teshuvah*. A married person may fear losing his or her spouse or children. Alternatively, such individuals may simply come to see a link between their SSA and the emotional adolescence they never grew out of, or else they may simply get tired of the gay "scene." These people may recognize the need to enlist the aid of a professional GAP specialist as they attempt to reexamine their lives.

In the course of their treatment, they will learn to reinterpret not just things that have happened to them, but their own reactions and feelings. What kind of feelings are we referring to? For Rabbi Apisdorf, the characteristic emotion of Step 1 is a deep, abiding, sometimes torturing, regret—a sense of having lost something of value. Others—several Christian theologians among them—theorize that guilt, not regret, is paramount in laying the groundwork for a change of sexual orientation.

Interestingly, strugglers often identify "guilt" and "shame" as emotions that have *impeded,* rather than inspired, their drive to do *teshuvah*. Ben Newman, for example, writes:

> Our lusts and obsessions led many of us to deep feelings of guilt and shame that pulled us down even further. We didn't want to be gay. We didn't want anyone to know of our feelings. Some of us drowned in guilt to the point of contemplating suicide. Others decided guilt was the problem and tried to stamp it out by ignoring our conscience, discarding our religious faith, breaking ties to

family, giving ourselves permission to indulge our lusts with abandon, looking for "Mr. Right" and embracing "gay pride."

Did it work? It seemed to, for a time. But those of us who tried it found that silencing our conscience seemed to lead us inevitably deeper and deeper into the dark side of "gay life," where we needed more and coarser sexual experience to deliver the same "high." It broke our spiritual yearning for G-d and for goodness. Those of us who took this course eventually hit bottom and, humbled at last, turned for help.[9]

Clearly there are two different ways of looking at guilt and shame. One way is to view them as indelible stains on one's character and soul, and thus to wallow in them in perpetual misery. The other way is to use them as fuel for repentance and self-improvement. The latter approach is in full agreement with Jewish Teaching.[10] So negatively does our Tradition regard the psychological state of guilt that the Hebrew language does not even have a specific word for it.[11] Indeed some Jewish commentators talk about "guilt" as an altogether foreign concept. In Rebbetzin Feige Twerski's view, for example,

> There is a great difference between conventional guilt and the Jewish concept of guilt. Conventional guilt keeps one enmeshed in the past, wallowing and repeatedly obsessing about past wrongdoing and misdeeds. In contrast, Jewish guilt

---

9. <www.peoplecanchange.com>.

10. *See, e.g.,* Rabbi Joseph B. Soloveitchik, *Family Redeemed: Essays on Family Relationships,* (David Shatz and Joel B. Wolowelsky editors), New York: MeOtzar HoRav (2000), pp. 82-3. *See also* Rabbi Schneur Zalman of Liadi, *Likutei Amarim Tanya,* Brooklyn: Kehot (Bilingual ed. 1984), *Igeret Hateshuvah,* Ch. 11, p. 383: "'My sin is before me always' (Ps. 51:5) does not imply that one ought constantly be melancholy, humiliated, G-d forbid . . . ."

11. Rabbi Yaakov Haber, *Pardes Project of the Orthodox Union,* New York (1998), p. 4. The Hebrew word *ashem* means guilty in a juridical sense; it does not convey the anxiety felt when a person believes he/she committed a sin.

means regretfully admitting inappropriate behavior and moving on to assimilate and integrate the insights gained into subsequent living. It is present and future oriented. It maintains that to err is human and no experience in life is a failure if we learn from it and are modified by it.[12]

Dr. Joseph Nicolosi clearly shares the view expressed above: "Although guilt may have been a strong motivator that originally propelled the client into therapy, it is *never* the foundation for successful treatment."[13] (Emphasis added.)

> Excessive guilt locks a man into the old, self-defeating thought patterns that reinforce a sense of weakness and self-pity. Excessive guilt erodes self-esteem, which is essential to meet the initiatory challenges of reparative therapy. Self-acceptance and a sincere desire for wholeness open the way to growth. It is through self-acceptance that the man gains the ability to stay in the pain in the faith that he will get better. (Nicolosi, 153)

We commonly see this "sense of weakness and self pity" in SSA clients, who often perceive themselves as victims in a variety of contexts that have nothing overtly to do with their being "gay."[14] It is easy to observe that this layer of victimhood isolates the subject from a sense of responsibility for his or her own behavior, thus literally blocking the person from even beginning the process of *teshuvah*.

---

12. http://www.aish.com/family/rebbitzen/Appropriate_Guilt.asp.>.

13. Dr. Joseph Nicolosi, *Reparative Therapy of Male Homosexuality: A New Clinical Approach,* Northvale: Jason Aronson (1997), p. 152.

14. The concomitant emotional reactions and resultant self-perceptions include feelings of isolation, differentness and low self-esteem. Extreme counter-emotions of anxiety, guilt, and shame are likewise evident. Common inhibitory responses include self-destructive ideation and behavior, discomfort in social situations, and drug and alcohol abuse.

Thus we can understand how excessive guilt feelings tend to prevent the emergence of genuine regret and remorse. As Nicolosi notes:

> The best part of surrendering excessive guilt is that it frees the mind to see clearly the natural dissatisfaction that results when one's behavior is at odds with one's sense of self. This dissatisfaction emphasizes, simply, what valid guilt is—disappointment with oneself for doing something discordant with what one desires to be. This subtle but deeply felt displeasure with oneself is more effective than excessive guilt in fostering lasting change. (Nicolosi, 152-3)

Therapists have written extensively about clients who construct all kinds of defenses so as not to feel the excruciating pain of guilt. Such defenses can become not only an obstacle to therapy, but even a cause of various emotional disturbances for which one seeks a therapist in the first place.

The convergence of psychological theory with age-old Jewish teaching may be surprising to those not yet familiar with the phenomenal psychological insight of the Sages. The first step towards genuine *teshuvah* is regret, not guilt; for dwelling on guilt, far from inspiring a person to repent and improve, causes one to spiral downwards before one has even begun to approach the healing process.[15] Regret, on the other hand—even an intensely bitter feeling of sorrow or remorse over one's behavior—can be a positive motivator to engage in a healing process. This is because regret is an internalized recognition of one's misdeeds and omissions, and as such is a motivating force for changing one's behavior.[16]

Regret normally concerns an event occurring in the immediate or distant past. It takes us unawares at first, like the sharp point of a

---

15. Interestingly, the dictionary definition for "regret" when used as a noun is "repentance." *Webster's Deluxe Unabridged Dictionary,* p. 809.

16. "The awareness that one has not done enough can motivate a person to action." Rabbi Abraham J. Twerski, M.D., quoting Rabbi Aharon of Karlin. *The Zeide Reb Motele,* Brooklyn: Mesora Publications (2002), pp. 155-6.

knife. Only later, when we have localized the source of the pain, do we look back and consciously pass judgment on what we have done or are doing.

Those who refuse or are unable to feel regret or remorse over their SSA are obviously not likely candidates for a change of sexual orientation. Thus many therapists and gay advocates actively counsel those who are struggling with their SSA to *avoid* regret and remorse as symptoms of "homophobia," and instead learn to accept themselves and identify as "gay," and to regard SSA as healthy and normal!

It is not always easy to arouse feelings of regret and remorse for our behavior, even if we understand *intellectually* that we have done wrong. Indulging our physical desires (even in a manner that is *halachically* correct and kosher!) can deaden or dull our responsiveness to deep spiritual and emotional needs. For those of us who are unable to feel genuine regret for our sins, the Alter Rebbe, the great 18th-century Sage and founder of the Chabad school of Chassidic Judaism, counsels us (1) to meditate on the great love with which *Hashem* has provided for all our needs, kept us alive, and given us opportunities to make the right choices; (2) to arouse our mercy for the Divine soul that has been exiled into our physical bodies where it must suffer separation from the Divine Essence in which it formerly resided in bliss; and (3) to realize that, since the *neshamah* (soul) of every Jew is rooted in G–d's ineffable essence, our sins drag the *Shechinah* (G–d's holy Presence in the physical world) down into the mud and filth! (*See, Tanya, Igeret Hateshuvah*, Chapter 7.)

Step 2: Abandonment (*Azivah*)

Rabbi Apisdorf sees the stage of abandonment in terms of confronting one's rationalizations. "[R]ationalization is the enemy and *azivah* is an internal mission of search and destroy." (103) The first step to abandoning the unholy activity or desires is to "identify the rationalization, see what it was that enticed you into that cerebral snare and understand the basic untruth that is the nucleus of the rationalization." (103) This means dropping the mental mask we tend to put on when looking at ourselves in our mental mirror. It means getting past the regret, shame, and self-isolation so often attendant upon our unholy/unworthy activities, and learning how we project and transfer onto others our own impulses and perceptions. Only then can the struggler "understand the basic untruth that is the nucleus of rationalization." (103)

Once the struggler grasps the "basic untruth" that formed the nucleus of the rationalization, he or she will be ready to explore the causes of homosexuality in general, and, in particular, those causes that apply to him- or herself, including such underlying issues as extreme sensitivity to perceived or real rejection, low self-esteem, fear of relationships, a tendency to withdraw or hide from criticism and/or abuse, and denial or repression of authentic feelings.

The next step would be to allow oneself, at last, to feel the feelings that were bottled up during infancy or childhood and to access and utilize the authentic core emotions of anger, fear, sadness, and joy. Anger, for example, can be a gateway to empowerment, sadness a gateway to tenderness, and fear a pathway to courage. Unless we make contact with the core emotions, joy often remains inaccessible to us. Feelings that have been buried alive never die, but live on in the form of emotional blocks that prevent a person from fully experiencing and learning from the joys and sorrows of life. The past fossilizes into something hard and heavy to carry around—an impediment to attaining genuine fulfillment and success.

One of the most powerful rationalizations nurtured by the gay lobby and their allies is the claim that homosexuality is inborn, genetic, and unchangeable. The gay propagandists who disseminated this myth knew very well beforehand that it could not be substantiated (*see* Chapter Three, *above,* pp. 58-9), but chose to make it the central point of their movement for its tremendous rationalizing potential— just as they chose to blame strugglers' discomfort with their SSA on their own "internalized homophobia," as well as on the purported "homophobia" of western culture (*see* "J"'s Case, *above,* Chapter Two, pp. 27, ff.). Once we have seen through such rationalizations, we are ready to take the next step: taking charge of our own life. Good intentions are simply not enough. We must definitively abandon the regretted sin and return to the path of Torah and *Mitzvos*. Once we have taken that pivotal step, we quite naturally attain the spiritual balance necessary for continued growth and the establishment of new and healthier patterns of living.

According to Rabbi Jeffrey Cohen, abandonment must be done "in a way that it will be possible to resist any subsequent enticements," leaving the struggler "morally strengthened." (*1001 Questions*, 24) What is this "way" to which Rabbi Cohen alludes? What Rabbi Cohen means is keeping one's motivation alive and not simply going through the motions of acknowledging sin or renouncing unacceptable activities. One must literally do as the word *teshuvah* ("return") tells us, that is, one must "go back," not just to the righteous path, but to the actual moment when one first began to lose one's way,

> undertaking a wide-ranging and thorough-going review of one's sin and the circumstances that prompted it, consciously working at constructing a mental block to the pleasurable sensations that attended its original commission, and filling the emotional vacuum created thereby in one's imagination with a sense of shame and regret. Only then will one be morally strengthened in a way that it will be possible to resist any subsequent enticements. (Cohen, 24)

Note well: The trick is to maintain one's motivation—to keep moving forward (the word "motivation" comes from the Latin *moveo, movi, motum*, "to move").

One cannot change one's behavior and emotional responses without identifying the satisfaction provided by the old behavior patterns and comparing that against the chain of consequences unleashed thereby. As Rabbi Yehuda HaNassi said, "Consider... the gain derived from a sin against the loss that will follow." (*Pirkei Avos* 2:1)

This cost-benefit analysis must come from the struggler himself, deep within his own soul. Although guidance can be provided, no one can do it for him—neither his parents, nor his spouse, nor his therapist or counselor, nor any of his siblings or friends. There is a story in the Talmud (*Sanhedrin,* 37a) about Rabbi Zeira, who befriended a group of hoodlums and prayed for mercy on their behalf, all in the hope that they would repent. When he died, they asked "Now who will pray for mercy on our behalf? After much thought, they realized that only they could ask G–d to forgive them, and so they did *teshuvah* and changed their ways.

Of course, Rabbi Zeira had befriended these hooligans only to inspire them to do *teshuvah.* Rabbi Zeira knew that, ultimately, the motivation to "shape up" would have to come from within themselves and from nowhere else. This did not happen until the delinquents realized that they no longer had Rabbi Zeira to intercede for them. Rabbi Dov Peretz Elkins retells this story to show that, "ultimately, if there is to be a change, people have to change themselves."[17]

We see here a beautiful lesson about not betraying one's authentic self: not only do people have to change themselves—like the hoodlums in Rabbi Zeira's story—but someone must first teach them that *change is possible*—possible not only from a clinical perspective, but also spiritually—because holiness is intrinsic within our souls and can never be totally lost.

Indeed, Rabbi Zeira's faith in the ability of his hoodlum friends to repent was consistent with his belief that "even the empty ones among you are as full of *mitzvos* as a pomegranate is full of seeds." (*Sanhedrin* 37a) Rabbi Zeira derived this view from the story told in Genesis 27: 27: When Ya'akov, disguised as his sinful brother Esav, approached their blind father Yitzchak to receive the blessings intended for Esav, Yitzchak believed Ya'akov to be Esav because he smelled in the garments of Esav that Ya'akov was wearing, "the field which G–d has blessed." (Gen. 27:27). Because the Hebrew word for

---

17. Rabbi Dov Peretz Elkins, *Moments of Transcendence, Inspirational Readings for Rosh Hashonah,* Northvale: Jason Aronson (1992), p. 91.

b'gadav ("his garments") can also be read as *bog'dav* ("his betrayers"), Rabbi Zeira concluded from this that even those who betray G–d with their sins retain a scent of holiness about them.[18]

Note that Rabbi Zeira did not pressure his delinquent protégés, nor did he lecture them: he *befriended* them and he *prayed* for them, thus giving them a sense of personal worth and an intimation of spiritual dimensions in which strength, encouragement, and inspiration were always to be found—even after the loss of their original guide and mentor. They trusted Rabbi Zeira, and trust is the key to unlocking old belief systems so that defense mechanisms, counter-emotions and inhibitory responses can be broken down and the struggler can access his/her goodness and become the kind of person he/she wants to be. Because Rabbi Zeira did not preach to them, all they got from him initially was his unconditional love and the sense of self-worth engendered by his friendship and words of wisdom. As so often happens, Rabbi Zeira's friends did not initially realize how deeply they had internalized what Rabbi Zeira had given them. However, once their mentor was gone, they themselves found within them the power and the will to give up their old ways for a new life that was more compatible with their new-found self respect.

The foregoing paradigm of Abandonment—the second stage of *teshuvah* in Rabbi Apisdorf's schematic, is remarkably congruent with modern clinical approaches. For "behavioral changes" (a clinical term akin to Step 2—"Abandonment") to take root in the gender-affirming process, strugglers must accomplish three things besides cutting themselves off from the undesirable activities: (1) they must build a support network; (2) they must develop a sense of self-worth sufficient for them to seek a personal relationship with G–d;[19] (3) they must actually seek and develop a personal relationship with G–d.

---

18. See Rabbi Mendel Weinbach, *Weekly Dafnotes,* No. 65 (Oct. 26, 2002) *Sanhedrin* 37-43), Ohr Somayach, <http://ohr.edu/yhiy/article.php/502>.

19. *See* Richard Cohen, *Coming Out Straight,* Winchester: Oakhill Press (2000), p. 73.

Of course, abandonment does not necessarily mean "stopping cold turkey." This is all the more true when dealing with a complex, deeply ingrained intricately woven gestalt (pattern of experiences) like SSA. Total cessation can rarely be achieved without a soul-searing descent into the maelstrom of underlying issues. As Jeff Konrad wrote (*see* Chapter Nine, note 27): "Bringing [my] root issues to the surface, I began working through past hurts, misconceptions and my wrong responses. I no longer felt I was a helpless victim of past circumstances."[20] Those who doubt their own ability to abandon homosexual behavior should also emblazon on their minds Richard Cohen's resounding words: "For those who wish to make this transition from homosexual to heterosexual, I am certain that it is possible. My personal journey and the experience of the many men and women whom I have had the privilege to assist support this claim." (*Coming Out Straight*, 17)

Abandonment through Prayer: Benefits and Limitations.

A well-intentioned but misguided prescription for healing those with a homosexual condition is the advice that if one prays hard enough, G–d will take away one's homosexual desires. Certainly, prayer is an amazing medium for introspection, enlightenment and healing. There is no doubt that prayer can elicit heavenly assistance for those on the path of *teshuvah* and healing; but prayerful utterances alone, however fervent and sincere, are rarely enough. This is not to

---

20. Jeff Konrad, *You Don't Have To Be Gay: Hope and Freedom for Males Struggling with Homosexuality Or for those Who know of Someone Who Is*, Hilo: Pacific Publishing House (1998), pp. 11-12.

say, (G–d forbid!) that prayer doesn't always work—for Judaism teaches that G–d is never deaf to sincere prayer—but rather that G–d's fundamental connection with human beings is through the performance of the *Mitzvos* and the knowledge of His Laws. Thus, the million dollar question isn't how often or how hard we pray, but whether our conduct is in line with His will as expressed through the Commandments.

Why is this so? Judaism teaches that this is because G–d has created a world which requires our active participation, not one in which He does our work for us. If this were not true, we would become physically and spiritually stagnant. This teaching is related to the precept that any burden that G–d puts on our shoulders is ultimately for our own good, and further, that G–d does not test us with any burden that we are not capable of overcoming.

It took Richard Cohen a long time to understand why prayer alone was not enough:

> I wish it could have been that simple, but it was not. I prayed and prayed for G–d to take the desires away, but He did not. I married, hoping it would straighten me out, but the same-sex desires only intensified. I came to understand that I had been praying the wrong prayer for nearly twenty years. What I needed to pray was: "G–d, please *show me the meaning* of my same-sex desires." [Emphasis added.] [. . .] [B]ecause they had a deeper meaning that I needed to discover, heal, and ultimately fulfill in healthy, non-sexual relationships. (*Coming Out Straight*, 64)

Praying for a miraculous healing, like wishing for a bolt of lightening to zap away our unwanted desires, while understandable, can actually be counterproductive and is inconsistent with the normal process of *teshuvah* and gender affirmation. *Teshuvah* and Jewish prayer certainly do invoke G–d's miraculous assistance, but in a manner that presumes *the active participation of the penitent.* Thus, both *davening* (praying to *Hashem*) and doing *teshuvah* challenge us to look upward to G–d and inward at our deeds, our thoughts and our feelings. The ability to heal from a same-sex gender deficit is dependent on uncovering deep emotional injuries that have long lain buried under all the rationalizations and other protective artifacts that our "shadow self" could manufacture. As Rabbi Jeffrey Cohen admonishes, "Just going through the motions of acknowledging that one has sinned, especially when one can hide comfortably behind the plural formulation in which the prayer book confessions are couched, does not constitute a proper act of *teshuvah*." (*1001 questions,* 24). Nor does it provide a basis for resolving one's homosexual issues.

Step 3: Confession (Viduy).

Feeling regret and taking action to abandon the behavior do not by themselves lead to complete *teshuvah.* One has to be able to verbalize one's regret, as well as put into words the behavior one is seeking to abandon. Although Maimonides includes confession—the verbalization of sin—under the rubric of Step 1 (Regret), Rabbi Apisdorf sets confession apart as a separate and distinct third step. As Rav Soleveitchik explains,

> Feelings, emotions, thoughts and ideas become clear, and are grasped only after they are expressed in sentences bearing a logical and grammatical structure. As long as one's thoughts remain repressed, as long as one has not brought them out into the open, no matter how sublime or exalted they may be, they are not truly yours; they are foreign and elusive. [. . .] [M]an does not know for sure what is in his own heart until his feelings and thoughts become crystallized and are given shape and form in the usual modes of expression. Repentance contemplated, and not verbalized, is valueless.[21]

---

21. Rabbi Pinchas H. Peli, *On Repentance: The Thought and Oral Discourses of Rabbi Joseph Dov Soloveitchik,* Northvale: Jason Aronson (1996), pp. 91-2.

In other words, verbalization and emotional release are essential to the process.[22] People have feelings. Feelings come and go. People need to communicate how they feel in words in order to give them cognitive confirmation. This is true of all emotions. Even love for another human being remains nebulous and uncertain until expressed in words to the beloved. How then shall we express regret for our own misguided actions? Even confessing out loud to oneself is too much like thinking aloud: one has to confess to *another* in order to register the emotion indelibly on one's *own* consciousness.

Judaism teaches that the spoken word has a special power. The Book of Genesis tells us that G–d created the world with ten *utterances*. A vow has no legal validity unless verbalized *out loud*. Yeshiva students study Talmud by reciting and analyzing *out loud*. Similarly, repentance remains in the realm of wishful thinking until verbalized out loud. Confessing one's sins out loud—even to one's self—requires one to overcome the barrier of shame that stands in the way of true *teshuvah*. This is all the more true when confessing to another person—especially one whose moral probity places our iniquities in sharp focus. Thus, confession helps liberate us from the negative constraints of shame and self-loathing. Moreover, confessing to one who is a *tzaddik* (righteous person) and a *chocham* (a person learned in Torah and Talmud, one who is expert in the intricacies of Jewish Law and Ethics)—or to a professional skilled in GAP, can help us understand the full implications of our misconduct and set us on the road to outgrowing our same-sex attractions.

---

22. Many learned rabbis, including Rabbi Adin Steinsaltz, consider verbalization to be the crucial *first* step in the process of *teshuvah*: "When a vague feeling of discomfort turns to clear recognition that something is wrong, and when that recognition is expressed in words spoken either to oneself, to G–d, or to another person, the first step in the process of turning has been taken, the part that relates to one's previous life and character." Rabbi Adin Steinsaltz, *Teshuvah: A Guide for the Newly Observant Jew*, Northvale: Jason Aronson, Inc. (1996), p. 6.

The Torah, cognizant of the workings of the human emotions, commands:

When a man or woman shall commit any sin . . . then they shall confess their sin which they have done. (Num. 5:6-7)

Maimonides explains that the Torah is telling us "to confess all our sins and transgressions against G–d and to *recite them at the time of our repentance.*" (Emphasis added.) As summarized by Rav Soloveitchik, "Maimonides rules [*Hilchos Teshuvah,* 1-2:3] that even after a man has truly repented spiritually, and even after he has brought a sacrifice of atonement, and even after he has died, his repentance remains incomplete if confession has not taken place." (*On Repentance,* 91), Thus, confession is not only the "ultimate act in the process of repentance," (92) but it is "the act that brings man acquittal" (92)—freedom from shame, self-hatred, regret and fear of punishment.

Rambam tells us very clearly [*Hilchos Teshuvah* 1:1] how we are to confess. We are to articulate very specifically what it is that we did or did not do, and why it was wrong for us to do or not do it. We are required to express our regret, shame, and remorse, and promise never to do—or, as the case may be, never to omit doing—it again.

Confession: Catalyst for Healing.

How does confession apply to gender-affirming processes? Virtually all GAP professionals consider verbal confession an integral part of the therapeutic process. The human being has an infinite capacity for self-justification. We refuse to admit—or even recognize—our own wrongdoing. Steve Greenberg's book *Wrestling with G–d* is a perfect example of "rationalizing away the prohibitions against homosexual acts."[23] Rich Wyler draws a devastating picture of this kind of rationalizing:

---

23. Rabbi Asher Lopatin, "What Makes a Book Orthodox: *Wrestling With G–d and*

We sometimes felt that it would tear us apart. Our inner selves craved emotional healing and wholeness. Our spiritual selves craved a Higher Power and purpose. Our social selves craved unity with heterosexual men and acceptance into the masculine world. But, fueled by our lusts, our sexual selves threatened to overpower them all. Our sexual selves lied to us that we could satisfy all our desires and find joy and healing by having sex with other men. Ultimately, someone had to win. We could not live in this state of internal warfare forever.[24]

Confession is the exact opposite of rationalization. Rationalization offers the comfort of self delusion. Confession provides catharsis—a powerful emotional release from the tyrannical bind of one's internal conflicts. To confess is to stand naked before oneself and acknowledge to oneself the true nature and implications of one's conduct.

One of the most vivid illustrations of the power of confession is found in the Biblical account of David's sin in the matter of Bathsheba. After submitting to the harsh censure of the Prophet Nathan, David exclaims, "I have sinned against the Lord." Nathan responds, "The Lord also has removed your sin." (II Samuel 12:1-13) The great king's spontaneous cry captures the very essence of confession. All said, confession serves as a release of bottled-up emotions under terrible pressure. Lacking such release, the repentant homosexual will usually find him- or herself blocked from further progress.

Men by Steve Greenberg," *The Edah Journal,* Vol. 4, No. 2 (2004), p. 8.

24. <www.peoplecanchange.com>.

In actuality, a number of JONAH's strugglers get stuck at this juncture. Because there is a mind-body connection in the makeup of every human being, the residual pain of emotional injury can become "stored" in the body, ultimately blocking (or suppressing) the emotional pain and even interfering with the normal neuro-mechanical and organic functions. It is remarkable that more than two centuries ago, the great Chassidic Master, Rabbi Nachman of Breslov, taught that

> [C]onfession gives frank and honest expression to one's often conflicting thoughts and feelings. This is what lays the foundation for more positive attitudes and behavior in the future. Until one gives verbal expression to one's negative thoughts and feelings, they remain inscribed on one's bones and may continue to give rise to actual physical symptoms.[25]

This is obviously all the more true in the case of SSA, which, according to the principles espoused herein, actually arises as a result of repressed emotional pain. The body is an inseparable part of the psychological process. It follows that therapy designed to remove the neuro-muscular blockages can be extremely helpful in bringing about the emotional release that characterizes genuine confession. This phenomenon is well known to chiropractors, osteopaths, massage therapists, and practitioners of many other related physical and psycho-physical therapies.

---

25. Rabbi Yaacov Haber, "Guilt," *The Pardes Project of the Orthodox Union* (1998), p. 10. Rabbi Haber is Rosh Yeshiva of Yeshivat Orchos Chaim, Jerusalem, and President of TorahLab.

Physical-Emotional Release as a Form of Confession.

JONAH believes that an essential part of the confession process goes deeper than just verbal confession.[26] Emotional release work, often expressed physically, for example by enacting a psychodrama around masculine shadows, or by miming how his life has been touched by the feminine, provides each participant with an opportunity to replay—and hence, *to reframe*—painful, frightening, or degrading experiences. This playacting enables him or her to identify genuine needs and emotions long walled up behind a brick wall of fossilized protective devices. This form of confession is an important step toward authentically meeting the struggler's long-neglected vital needs. My experience as a facilitator at Journey into Manhood and Call of the Shofar, as a developer of JONAH's *Shabbatons,* and as a participant in the New Warrior Training Adventure and other similar experiential weekends, has shown me that this form of bodily confession effectively shortens the time needed for a struggler to heal. My facilitator colleagues (many of whom are licensed therapists) and I agree that one successful weekend program can be worth six months of weekly counseling in a therapist's office.

The emotional-release process ("guts work") often enables the participant to deal emotionally (rather than intellectually) with a core issue that may have been impeding his healing. First, we help the participant identify a specific personal conflict, crisis, feeling or

---

26. Arthur Janov, the originator of Primal Therapy observes that simply verbalizing the problem is of limited effectiveness because the cerebral cortex (the higher reasoning area of the brain) cannot affect the sources of psychological pain emanating from other areas of the brain. The emotional response initially triggered by the original traumatic stimulus gets trapped in the "reptilian" sector of the brain, which has no awareness of time or place. Without the reprocessing offered by confession or other means, the original trauma continues to be felt in the present tense. See Janov's *The Primal Revolution: Toward a Real World*, New York: Simon & Shuster (1972), and *The Primal Scream: Primal Therapy: The Cure for Neurosis*, London: Abacus Books (1973).

impulse by posing a series of probing questions. At some point, the responses provide enough information for us to recreate the conflict scenario. The simulation enables the participant to make contact with his or her repressed feelings by way of the physical sensations associated with those emotions. We then encourage the participant to externalize or "act out" (*i.e.,* bodily confess)—and thus release ("let go")—those feelings, be it anger, grief, fear, or shame. At the same time, by accessing those repressed feelings, the participant revivifies his/her ability to experience genuine emotions that have become atrophied through years of disuse.

The next stage of the process is to help the struggler identify what he needs in order to replace the pain, the shame, the helplessness that have just been released with a new vision of himself as a strong adult male with real choices and responsibilities—in short, a new-found ability to fend for himself and meet his authentic needs. Using Jungian terminology, the struggler replaces his shadow with gold, or—in Jewish terms—he overcomes his *yetzer hara.* He is now ready to move on to the next step.[27]

---

27. Among the various therapeutic modalities based on the same general principles, Eye Movement Desensitization and Reprocessing (EMDR) is a relatively new form of psychotherapy that reframes a person's thoughts, physical sensations and behaviors relating to the memory of traumatic events in his or her life. EMDR has been used to treat depression, phobias, recurrent nightmares, post-traumatic stress disorders, anxiety, stress, addictions, *etc. See* Francine Shapiro & Margot Silk Forrest, *EMDR: the Breakthrough "Eye Movement" Therapy for Overcoming Anxiety, Stress and Trauma,* New York: Basic Books (1997). Drs. Norman

"Sharing" as a Form of Confession.

Also helpful is just plain "sharing." Richard Cohen emphasizes the importance of availing oneself of a friend to express one's inner pain, to give voice to one's inner child as a prelude to healing:

> G–d has built into each one of us the ability to completely heal and grow. Simply put, this is called the *process of grieving*. If you watch a child when he gets hurt, he will scream and cry and let you know how he feels. After releasing his pain, he wants comfort and a kiss, and then he is on his way to play. That is the long and short of it, how every person is meant to deal with pain. (*Coming Out Straight*, 156)

Note that Richard Cohen mentions both "release" and "comfort." Have you noticed that people tend to cry when retelling a "hurt"—a personal tragedy—that happened even many years ago? Is that because they never "let go" of the pain until this moment? Or is it because there is a unique connection between speech and feeling? To relate something painful is to re-feel it. "Sharing" with a friend can awaken feelings that have long lain dormant and forgotten, thus enabling the speaker to reinterpret with new insight the painful events that gave rise to those feelings.

Moreover, uncovering, verbalizing, and "re-feeling" with a trusted *same-sex* friend the underlying pain that has alienated them from their own gender and from G–d, can put strugglers on the path to *teshuvah*

Goldwasser, of Miami, Florida, Paul Miller, of Belfast, Ireland, and Esly Regina de Carvalho, of Brasilia, Brazil, have independently adapted EMDR for use in SSA cases.

and healing by helping them fulfill their unmet need for involvement in healthy, nonsexual same-sex relationships.

Finally, it is only by verbalizing the sadness and pain that the struggler can evoke from his fellows the consolation and comfort he or she so desperately craves.

Lack of Sincerity Voids the Confession.

Obviously, if the confession is insincere, if the words of regret are merely mouthed, then the exercise is pointless. Rather, one must expatiate through body and soul one's thoughts and feelings—as conflicted as they may be. Otherwise, there is no real taking of responsibility for one's actions. "When *teshuvah* becomes a token gesture and mere lip service without a change of heart, it cannot create the momentum that causes a sinner to mend his ways. A confession that lacks any trace of shame and regret is not a true repentance."[28] In other words, to be effective, confession has to be something more than what Rav Soloveitchik calls "merely a perfunctory verbalization of a set formula."[29] (*On Repentance,* 93)

Conflicted Confession: Confession as Prayer.

It is surprising how difficult it can be to confess one's mistakes, particularly when the desires and needs of the soul and the body are locked in a constant contest. As Rabbi Apisdorf tells it, "There is a basic tension in life which we all feel. That tension is between what we *want* and what we *feel* like doing." (*Rosh Hashanah-Yom Kippur,*

---

28. Rabbi Chaim Nussbaum, *The Essence of Teshuvah: A Path to Repentance*, Northvale: Jason Aronson (1993), p. 107.

29. Joe Dallas sets forth the same thought in the specific context of healing from same-sex attractions. He states, "The question isn't whether or not we *claim* to love G–d, but whether or not *our actions are in harmony with His expressed will.*" *Desires in Conflict: Answering the Struggle for Sexual Identity,* Eugene: Harvest House Publishers (1991), p. 275.

100) To illustrate these internal dynamics, Rabbi Apisdorf offers the analogy of a horse and rider: the rider represents our soul and our spiritual desires; the horse represents our body and our material needs and cravings. Rabbi Apisdorf asks: "Who is in control? Is this a skilled rider leading a faithful obedient horse, or is this a rider who has lost control and is at the mercy of his horse's every whim and desire?" (*Rosh Hashanah-Yom Kippur,* 101)

The point is that in such a situation, even a conflicted confession is better than an insincere one. Conflicts between one's intellectual/spiritual aspirations and one's physical drives are inevitable. There are moments when even the bravest, most stalwart penitent can feel incapable of resisting. Yet especially at such times is it true that confession can be helpful. How often have strugglers shared with me the prayers they have offered that go along the following lines:

> O L–rd! I don't feel ready to give up my homosexual lifestyle, because I crave it, but I know it is wrong, and this causes me terrible pain and continual suffering. Please help me understand why this has happened to me, and how to make it stop. You have created me and You have created my desires. Please give me also the strength and the wisdom to live in accordance with the Laws which, in Your great lovingkindness, You have given to us to live by.

Such words are far from empty, and they are anything but a "set formula." They are a cry for help which cannot go unanswered. That is another reason why it is so important for one's confession to be heard by another person.

Indeed, it has become quite the norm for therapists to suggest that their clients arrange for one or two friends to participate in their confessional process. Richard Cohen refers to this step as "accountability/confession," because it ensures that the subject undergoing a gender-affirming process will not only verbalize what he or she has been doing, but also remain accountable to others for his or her actions. This principle has become an essential component of every twelve-step program like Alcoholics Anonymous and Overeaters Anonymous, *etc.*, as well as of many different kinds of therapy. Richard Cohen suggests involving more than just one or two friends, if possible, so as to minimize the danger of developing an unhealthy emotional dependence.

Dr. Joseph Nicolosi strongly favors support groups, where one can share common challenges and concerns in a safe and supportive atmosphere of mutual understanding and acceptance. He believes that support groups should not be used as a substitute for individual counseling, but rather as an adjunct to it. According to Nicolosi, such group support can make all the difference, especially when dealing with a subject who is shy or reticent. "Unlike conventional psychotherapy, which prohibits outside meetings between group members, reparative therapy encourages friendships in order to counter the isolation characteristic of the condition."[30] Indeed, as Nicolosi reports (and I can confirm this from my own experience as a JONAH lay-counselor), virtually every conflicted male homosexual client resists attending a group meeting out of fear of speaking openly about himself before other men who share his struggle. "There is the dreaded thought, 'G–d forbid I should meet someone I know!'" (*Reparative Therapy*, 205)[31] Such fears are almost always allayed by

---

30. Dr. Joseph Nicolosi, *Healing Homosexuality: Case Stories of Reparative Therapy*, Northvale: Jason Aronson (1993), p. 198.

31. The fear is reasonable, and has two distinct aspects: (1) the struggler who has not "come out" to family and friends fears that his homosexuality will be exposed—whether inadvertently or on purpose—by one of the other participants; and (2) the struggler who has previously "come out" fears that his gay comrades will learn of his desire to change sexual orientation, thus exposing him to their ridicule and harassment, as in Jeff's Case, discussed in Chapter Two, above, pp. 20-27.

Publicizing a person's homosexuality or discomfort with his/her SSA without that person's consent can have devastating consequences for everyone involved. For that very reason, gay activists have used "outing" as a weapon of political blackmail. As John McKellar warns, "We can't ignore the intimidation tactics which gay activists have honed to perfection, and with which I have plenty of firsthand experience." "There's Hope for the World," REAL Women Conference,

the confidentiality statement all participants are required to sign as standard procedure in all such group settings. The statement prohibits disclosing the identity of any other participant without his express informed consent. The problem remains getting them to overcome their fears enough to come to the meeting in the first place.

In any case, after attending three or four such meetings, or an experiential weekend, the usual result is the evaporation of the struggler's sense of isolation and the weakening and gradual disappearance of his defensive detachment from other men. "The reason I never made much progress before," says one of Dr. Nicolosi's clients, "was that I was working in a vacuum, was all alone, and wasn't talking to anyone about it. As soon as I found some camaraderie here with guys that felt the same way and had the same troubles, then I could start discussing solutions." (*Reparative Therapy*, 206-7)

As Nicolosi explains,

> Although ostensibly the subject matter of these groups is homosexuality, the underlying process is the universal one of initiation, growth, and change. While our specific concern here is

---

(March, 2003), http://www.theroadtoemmaus.org/RdLb/22SxSo/PnSx/HSx/MckellarJ%20HOPE01.htm. A tragic example of "outing" occurred during the summer of 2001 in Brooklyn, New York and Deal, New Jersey. An anonymous gay pride activist circulated on the internet a list of local teenagers who were flirting with the gay lifestyle, causing untold shame and disruption to the lives of the young boys and their families.

Perversely, Michaelangelo Signorile argues that "gayness" *per se* is not private: "How can being gay be private when being straight isn't?" *Queer in America: Sex, Media, and the Closets of Power*, New York: Random House (1993), p. 80. Gay journalist Randy Shilts writes, "[T]he greatest impediments to homosexuals' progress often [are] not heterosexuals, but closeted homosexuals." Warren Johansson & William A. Percy, *Outing: Shattering the Conspiracy of Silence*, New York: Harrington Park Press (1994), p. 226. Note the self-righteous posturing exemplified by the title of the latter book. Indeed, the authors' thesis is expressly that loyalty to the "collective Queer Nation" is a "superior good" overriding any concerns about privacy.

the cessation of a certain behavior, these groups are committed to the common human task of growing toward wholeness. The men see that we are all challenged to move forward into fullest adulthood, and each one of us has his own personal obstacles to overcome, based upon past developmental failures. The distinctly human abilities to self-reflect, to evaluate oneself, and to choose positive change are true miracles of human nature. (210)

More will be said on this subject below, this chapter (pp. 492 ff.) in the subsection entitled "The Need for a Supportive Environment."

Step 4: Resolve (*Kabbalah*).

Rabbi Apisdorf's fourth stage of *teshuvah* is Resolve—a solemn commitment to a definite course of action toward change and actual involvement in the process of personal transformation. "Resolve" means more than mere "intention;" rather, it involves specific action, *i.e.,* initiating and following a "treatment plan." Thus, by "resolve," Rabbi Apisdorf means both "determination"—and "resolution." Indeed, according to Rabbi Apisdorf, this is a process that permits one to say, "It won't happen again. With this final act of commitment never to repeat the same mistake, you have come full circle. You have returned." (*Rosh Hashanah-Yom Kippur,* 103) In other words, the struggler in the fourth stage of *teshuvah* not only resolves to change, but also resolves the underlying issues that led him or her to SSA in the first place. As he does so, the struggler's essential self remains intact, free of the masks previously used. The subject effectively reverses his/her direction in life and overcomes his/her detachment from self, from others, and from his/her own physical gender. Aaron, one of JONAH's strugglers, put it this way:

> I grew up emotionally by engaging in a process of gender affirmation (by utilizing bibliotherapy, private counseling, and group support). Through it, I successfully synthesized my chronological and emotional ages. I accepted the strengths and weaknesses of my core personality while learning new skills and

insights that enabled me to grow up. The residual and authentic masculine power locked up inside of me was freed. I liberated my natural masculine instincts. I was finally able to relate healthily both to myself and to others.

Another struggler, Baruch, cited experiential weekends and group support as key factors in alleviating his previously ever-present feelings of inferiority and insecurity around other men. According to Baruch, these activities provided him with "permission" to experience intimate, non-sexual relationships with other men—something he truly craved.

"How Long Does it Take?" The Value of Time.

How long does the process of healing take? There is no magic time frame. For some, it can be short journey; for others, a lengthy one. Remember, it took many years for a man or a woman to develop inappropriate fantasies, arousals, behaviors or gender identity. Time is needed for the process of deconstruction and reconstruction to take place.[32] What makes the wait worthwhile is how rewarding the process itself can be. It is a journey of self-discovery made of many modest victories, each one a small but exhilarating step toward a new life of promise, fulfillment, and spiritual awareness. For many, it will become the first time in their lives that they feel accepted as a man by other men or as a woman by other women.

Anne Paulk, a married mother and, for over 20 years, a recovered lesbian, leads women's support groups and serves on the board of Exodus International. Paulk tells how her resolve to undo her lesbian feelings and activities was continually tested until she was able to resolve the "underlying issues in my life that were so relevant to my struggle against homosexuality, such as forgiving my parents,

---

32. In the context of *teshuvah*, Rabbi Jeffrey Cohen explains, "Judaism believes in the gradual approach, moving forward and upward steadily and firmly, on the basis of conviction and the new vistas that [Torah] study and increased observance open out before the true searchers for truth." *1001 Questions,* p. 47.

grieving the loss of former lovers, and learning about emotional dependency."³³ Learning to forgive, to confront grief, to achieve emotional independence are all incredibly important stages of self-realization for anyone, whether homosexual or heterosexual. Even though completing these stages did not *per se* mean that she had successfully transitioned from gay to straight, still, Anne Paulk was able to internalize those lessons *as a result* of her quest for genuine womanhood.

There is no question that in learning to overcome one's limitations, whether physical, spiritual, or psychological, one taps into a tremendous reserve of power and insight. We all have it. Where does it come from? What is one to do with it after the change?

Anne Paulk describes how the momentum gained from her gender transformation from lesbian to straight carried over into her day-to-day spiritual consciousness. "The following months were filled with joyful intimacy with G–d. Something had changed deep inside of me. I realized that the L–rd had truly changed my sexual orientation from ex-gay to godly woman." (*Love in Action*). Once Anne had gained an understanding of the causes of her gender disidentification, she was able to increase her level of religious observance far beyond where it had stagnated for years.

Overcoming the Shadow Self.

Each of us carries a shadow in our life. The shadow is made up of beliefs and behaviors that we unconsciously create to deal with our shame and our unmet needs. The shadow is that part within each of us that we seek to hide, repress, run away from, and deny. It is associated

---

33. *Love in Action Newsletter*, 1993.

with dark, destructive, and painful sensations. However, if we expose this shadow to the light, the shadow evaporates, and the shame, the undesirable longings and behaviors, the miserable feelings, the rationalizations and foolish contortions of logic, gradually dissolve.

Paradoxically, this shadow is actually the work of the reparative drive, that blind but well-meaning force whose only purpose in life is to protect us from emotional harm. (*See* Chapter12, above, pages 453-455) The trouble is, being blind, the reparative drive can't distinguish between cause and effect. Instead of urging us to change our shameful ways, it may prompt us to hide from shame. Instead of encouraging us to make true friends, it may prompt us to drown our loneliness in drugs, alcohol, or illusory encounters. Instead of leading us to the cure, it may prompt us to suppress the symptoms. Why, one might ask, did G–d create a reparative drive without eyes to see? And one might answer, because He also created a *driver*. G–d created men and women with eyes to see and brains to think, and a heart that knows the difference between good and evil. When G–d designed the human "automobile," He did not put the motor in the driver's seat! Who would?

No matter how inextricably we may have entangled ourselves with our shadow self, Judaism teaches that G–d gives each of us the power to choose the path of genuine wellness, and—provided that we put in the necessary effort—the assistance we need to get there. This *Siyatta diSh'maya* ("help from Heaven") comes through Torah, which is a contract of reciprocity between man and G–d. Hence, it follows that the abolishment of unhealthful or sinful life patterns and their replacement by healthful and harmonious ones is an appropriate form of spiritual practice and religious observance.

Why Band-Aid Marriages Can't Cure Homosexuality.

Anne Paulk mapped out her voyage of realization from "active lesbian" to "ex-gay" to "godly woman." It was only during the final stages of her transformation that she found herself "having a new interest in men." (*Love in Action,* 1993).

It bears repeating: "Transformation takes time and occurs gradually." (Greenberg, *The Jewish Way,* 203) Thus, those who suggest that gay men and women can "straighten themselves out" once they find an opposite-sex partner may be well-intentioned, but they clearly lack knowledge about the process of healing SSA individuals. Richard Cohen couldn't have stated it more cogently:

> Marriage is not the solution of anyone who has homosexual feelings, because a woman can never meet the homo-emotional needs of a man, and a man can never meet the homo-emotional needs of a woman. In the process of recovery, first a man must heal with other men, and a woman must heal with other women. (*Coming Out Straight,* 63)

What Cohen means here is that gay men and women have a normal need to form legitimate bonding relationships with their same-sex peers, and those needs can *only* be met through normal, *non-sexual* bonding with those of their own sex. Pushing a struggler into marriage before he or she is ready is like trying to mend a broken bone with a band-aid: it can't work. For example, if a man is psychologically and emotionally stuck in the pre-adolescent stage where "all girls have cooties," how can he have a meaningful relationship with a woman? Just as hunger and thirst are entirely different, so too is the dissimilarity between the need for same-sex connection and the need for opposite-sex connection. One cannot simply transform sexual desire for men into sexual desire for women (or vice-versa).

Well-intentioned parents and clergy often make this mistake with usually unfortunate—if not tragic—results. Mental health professionals, too, have contributed to these naïve assumptions. "One main cause for past psychoanalytic failures," writes Dr. Nicolosi, "was the premature encouragement of heterosexual relations." Nicolosi explains why forcing heterosexual relations on homosexual men doesn't work:

Ironically, it is actually his fear of *men* that leaves the [male] homosexual developmentally unready to approach a woman sexually. Although it might be very easy for the client to become friends with a woman, it may be impossible for him to sexualize the friendship. On the other hand, the sexual attraction to men will be immediate, but he will have to work on the friendship. (*Reparative Therapy*, 202)[34]

Though their approaches may differ in a number of respects, both Cohen and Nicolosi accord here with the Jewish precept that, as Rabbi Steinsaltz advises *ba'alei teshuvah* (new returnees to Jewish practice), "It is best from both a religious and psychological point of view to begin with the negative precepts—avoiding what is forbidden—rather than with the burden of positive obligations." (*Teshuvah*, 23) In our context, this means that the struggler's first priority needs to be shedding forbidden thoughts and acts, rather than plunging into marriage and family. The power of habit often makes this initial abstinence difficult. Moreover, as so eloquently expressed by Anne Paulk, sexual attraction for the opposite sex does not generally develop before the underlying emotional issues have been

---

34. Dr. Jeffrey W. Robinson, a Utah-based cognitive-behavioral therapist who treats SSA, lists seven "blocks" to heterosexual attraction commonly experienced by SSA men: (1) Moral Anxiety—a belief or "feeling" that sex with a woman is immoral or incestuous; (2) Performance Anxiety—the struggler fears he will prove sexually inadequate with a woman; (3) Heterosexual Incompetence—the struggler has no idea how to handle a woman sexually; (4) Homosexual Flooding—the struggler is so preoccupied with desire for men that he has no "room" to fantasize about women; (5) False Beliefs—the struggler has so internalized the cultural message that "change is impossible" that he cannot "allow" himself to feel attracted to women; (6) Heterosexual Perfectionism—a "defensive" belief that arousal can only come from the "perfect woman", or the one who meets all his idealized criteria for marriage; (7) Heterosexual Disgust—an obsessive-compulsive repugnance for the female body. Of all the foregoing, only the OCD may be a deep psychological construct; its manifestation as heterosexual disgust is not. Thus, all of these "blocks" are amenable to the kind of treatment discussed in this text. *See* Dr. Jeffrey Robinson, *Developing Heterosexual Attractions* (compact disc), Address, Evergreen Annual Conference (Sept. 2001), transcribed at <www.jonahweb.org>.

dealt with and resolved. For example, in many cases, transferences and projections based upon prior negative, opposite-sex experiences will need to be surrendered before a male struggler can engage in an intimate relationship with a woman—or vice versa. *P'ru ur'vu* ("Be Fruitful and Multiply") may be the first *mitzvah* of the Torah, but it is a dual *mitzvah*: we must *ripen* before we can multiply. Indeed, the effects of an *unripe* marriage are almost always disappointment, failure and divorce. The results can be especially disastrous when homosexuality is a factor.

The most successful gender recovery programs are designed to address the struggler's homo-emotional wounds so that his or her unmet needs for same-sex acceptance can be fulfilled in healthy, non-sexual relationships. For authentic heterosexuality to emerge, the struggler must connect internally to his/her own innate masculinity or femininity, as the case may be. Only then can he or she begin to experience healthy attraction to the opposite sex. Good recovery programs will also seek to strengthen the struggler's self-confidence and self-affirmation—in short, his/her emotional independence. Only by closing these developmental gaps can the struggler begin to emerge from his/her SSA and begin to develop normal heterosexual attraction.

The Need for a Supportive Environment.

Success in recovery is often a function of one's environment: the more supportive the environment, the better the chance of success. We have already seen that support groups can be an effective—even an essential—component of the "confessional" phase of *teshuvah*. But support-group meetings do not constitute the entire environment. "Environment" means something that is all-encompassing. In this context, "supportive" means more than just "sympathetic": it means "influencing the positive." Let us turn once again to the Bible for an illustration.

The Torah describes Noah as being "completely righteous in his generations." (Gen. 6:9) The commentators offer two interpretations for the phrase "in his generations." One is that Noah was only righteous in comparison to the rest of his generation. Had he lived in a less corrupt generation, he would not have been considered particularly righteous. Another way of looking at it is that the Torah's praise is without reservation: Noah was a righteous man *despite* being surrounded by evil and corruption; had he lived in a more praiseworthy generation, he would have been even more righteous, thanks to the positive influence of his contemporaries. "This is a fundamental lesson on the importance of being in the presence of elevated people," writes noted Talmudic scholar and psychologist Rabbi Zelig Pliskin, who heads the counseling center at Aish haTorah in Jerusalem.[35] "We are all influenced by our surroundings. When you are close to people who act in an elevated manner, you are automatically influenced in positive ways." (Pliskin, 31)

Of course, the opposite is also true. The very first chapter of *Tehillim*—the Book of Psalms—observes:

> *Praiseworthy is the man that walked not in the counsel of the wicked, and stood not in the path of the sinful, and sat not in the session of scorners.*

"Keep away from an evil neighbor and do not associate with a lawless man," counsels Rabbi Nittai the Arbelite, one of the Sages quoted in the *Ethics of the Fathers* (*Pirkei Avos* 1:7) Can it be far-fetched to suggest that the struggler distance him- or herself from unhealthy peer pressure and from an environment where the perverse is considered normal? We most emphatically and most urgently encourage the struggler to become part of a morally sound and healthy social environment.

But how? How do you transplant a struggler from an unhealthy environment into which he or she may have invested years of adaptation and acclimatization to another that, benign as it may be, he

---

35. *Growth Through Torah*, Brooklyn: Benei Yakov Publications (1988), p.31.

or she perceives as unfamiliar and uncomfortable? Sexual Reorientation Specialist Richard Cohen answers with a profoundly ingenious proposal.

The Four Masculine Relationships.

Cohen reasons that the most efficient way for a male struggler to build a completely new social network is to start with a basic mix that contains at least one male representative—but preferably several more than one, from each of four distinct categories of relationships.[36]

> The individual in recovery needs to have at least four solid relationships with other men: (1) a mentor, an elder who can teach him the ways of men; (2) a fellow struggler, someone else on the journey towards healing; (3) a friend who is secure in his gender identity, is supportive, and knows about his struggle; and (4) a friend who is secure in his gender identity, is supportive, and *unaware* of his struggle. [Emphasis added.] With these and other men, he is accountable for his stated goals. They stand by and around him in order to lend support and love. By learning to be open and honest, deeper feelings, thoughts, and needs will emerge and healing will ensue. He also needs to be a giver, not just a receiver. Through giving, he experiences his own gifts to the community. He has been endowed with many spiritual gifts from G–d. Learning about his gifts and sharing them with others brings more positive energy and feedback into his life. (Cohen, 125).

---

36. JONAH advises its male strugglers to initially incorporate at least ten men from among the four categories into their lives. This is symbolic of the ten men that are minimally required for a *minyan* (prayer quorum); we suggest that for optimal healing, a minimum of ten men be brought into the ambit of the struggler. Subsequently, we try to increase the number to 18 or multiples thereof, to represent the Hebrew word *chai* which means both the number 18 and "life." The principle behind this advice is having the struggler create a community of men to whom he can relate. Transformation occurs by changing one's relational experiences with the self and with others.

Cohen wrote this passage for homosexual men, but obviously the foregoing applies to lesbians as well.

Cohen's outline of the archetypal forms of companionship and their therapeutic benefits is tremendously insightful. Let us examine each in turn.

1. The Mentor. The first archetype has to be the mentor. "A boy cannot change into a man without the active intervention of older men." (Cohen, 199). Mentoring represents an attachment model, "a means whereby one may restore the parent-child relationship, but may also be employed to heal other relationships, *i.e.*, with siblings, relatives, and friends." (199). This is because the mentoring process helps uncover buried feelings that stand in the way of male trust and male bonding and thus lead to homosexuality. As Nicolosi propounds, "All homosexuality is the *sexualization of the natural need for a mentor*." (Original emphasis.) (*Reparative Therapy,* 137)

Mentoring is critical to the process because successful gender repair depends in large part on the formation of intimate, *nonsexual* relationships with other males—typically one of the areas of human relations with which the struggler has had least experience. Since same-sex attraction began as the "shadow's" misdirected response to that unfilled need, its resolution can come about only through *redirecting* the response toward its genuine fulfillment—*i.e.,* healthy, nonsexual bonding relationships. This is exactly what a good mentor will do. The mentor will be his guide through uncharted territory.

Who should be the mentor? Clearly, neither the therapist nor the counselor. Such a duality of roles would create confusion. Nor can another struggler be the mentor, for one cannot give what one has not received. A personal friend or acquaintance of the struggler—perhaps a former struggler who has successfully completed the process of recovery, or any other person of the same sex who is secure in his or her gender identity—can make an excellent mentor for the struggler.

2. The Fellow Struggler. While the mentor-pupil relationship is comparable in some ways to that between father and son, a friendship between strugglers is a relationship between equals. It is here, very likely, that the struggler will experience his first appropriate, non-sexualized friendships. As the struggler seeking to grow out of his same-sex attractions gets to know fellow strugglers and makes friends in the process—whether from within a support group or through a network of peers—he finds—often for the first time in his life—that he can legitimately and authentically express deep unresolved issues, conflicts, and unful-filled needs to another person. Because SSA men tend to be such a bundle of insecurities, conflicts and trepidations, the process of learning to trust other men begins with getting to know others with similar feelings.

Conversely, the trust-building process helps break down the barriers of fear, suspicion and self-doubt that work to keep individuals isolated from one another. With trust, the struggler, instead of viewing other men as threatening, suspect, or rejecting, begins to see men as safe, honorable and welcoming. Experiencing the camaraderie among those who share similar doubts and fears, he begins to understand he is no longer alone and isolated. The following was Ami's response after joining the JONAH Internet support group:

> The validation of my fears, my judgments, and my misperceptions of other men and of manhood in general by men who have encountered similar situations made me feel, *Baruch Hashem* [thank G–d] much better about myself. I am not alone anymore with these feelings. I can join a *minyan* of [*i.e.,* pray together with] kindred spirits.

With these new friends, the struggler is able to share valuable information about the recovery process, learn coping skills through the experiences of others, share common concerns, receive and give emotional support, affirmation, and validation for the struggle he and his friends have chosen to undertake.

3. The Straight Friend Who Knows. When the struggler takes the next step and decides to tell a straight friend about his struggle, an even greater validation occurs, because the straight friend who accepts him may be someone he previously feared, or believed would reject him, or who he assumed would have nothing in common with him. Benny explains how elated he felt when . . .

> For the first time, I told someone OSA (Opposite-Sex Attracted) who was not a rabbi or a therapist about my struggle. I knew it was an important step in my overall journey but I couldn't find anyone that I felt close enough to tell. Then last Thursday I was talking with my *chavrusa* (study partner). We sit across the table from each other for about 6 hours a day studying Jewish texts. He is a nice guy, a year older than me, married, with kids, and, thank G-d, I have a zero charge about him. We learn well, and he's very understanding but I never felt that close to him. He told me that he recently got a job and will be moving next year. During our conversation, he mentioned in passing, "Don't worry Benny I won't let our friendship fizzle out. I intend to call you and maintain contact."
>
> From my end, I had chosen to always maintain a distance from him but I saw by his comments and body language that he genuinely cared about me and valued my friendship. I decided I could trust him and decided to tell him about my SSA. We scheduled a time to talk further. I carefully explained my situation to him. He was totally understanding and supportive. He is not an effusive guy, nor very demonstrative of his feelings. But I felt he cared and supported me in my struggle and would be there to hear me out and offer advice when needed. Most importantly, during this past week, NOTHING has changed. We still spend 6 hours a day across the table from each other. He doesn't treat me any differently. My fears of rejection and excommunication evaporated and I now recognize that straight men who know about my issues can be friends.

Benny's breakthrough is not to be underestimated. Conditioned by their long history of same-sex peer rejection to fear reaching out to another man in friendship, non-gay-identified SSA men are extremely apprehensive about trusting other men. On the other hand, gay-identified men often find it difficult to separate friendship from sexuality. For them, friendship with another man often has a sexual connotation. They attempt to use sex as a way to mask their gender alienation—their defensive detachment if you will, as a pathway around their fears of confrontation, criticism, and aggression, or as a means of expressing their own repressed aggressive impulses.

The struggler's diffidence of non-gay men has other grounds as well. Well-intentioned but ill-informed or insensitive "straights" may significantly impede the struggler's recovery by failing to appreciate his commitment to change and by disregarding his need for validation. Mark well the words of Ari, a JONAH struggler active on our listserv:

> My only negative experience telling the few people that I did was not rejection but the "wrong" kind of encouragement. Out of a misguided desire to offer support, my friends tried to get me to "accept" my gay/bi self. I would patiently explain why they're wrong, but after a while it gets exasperating. It says something about our current cultural climate that people are perfectly willing to accept you as pretty much any sort of a sexual deviant, but are not willing to legitimize your struggle with unwanted urges.

4. The Straight Friend Who Doesn't Know. The struggler enters the final recovery stage when he can at last recognize and comfortably accept himself as just another man. He no longer looks at himself as different or "detached" from other men, but rather can relate to other men in a relationship characterized by positive contact, reciprocity, loyalty and confidence, mutual sympathy and esteem, a similarity of interests, and a sense of equality. Dr. Nicolosi believes that these friendships are so therapeutic that, even without psychotherapy, they are "central to the repairing of homosexuality." (*Reparative Therapy*, 194)[37]

---

37. I have been told innumerable times by JONAH's Israeli strugglers that they did not experience SSA while doing military service. To me, this is a remarkable validation of the phenomenon discerned by Nicolosi. The inherent need for non-sexual male bonding, unfulfilled in these men since infancy, found fulfillment in the soldierly companionship of the corps. This made them feel for the first time in their

Associating with other men who are secure in their gender identity reinforces, rather than undermines, the struggler's own sense of masculinity. Each of the foregoing four categories represents a different pattern of healthy friendship. Each is designed to overwrite behavior patterns of detachment typically found in SSA men, whether conflicted or gay-identified. Men engaged in homosexual relationships often substitute the false "high" of sexual activity and the allure of special attention offered by the gay world as a way to meet unfilled needs for masculine connection, rather than work at developing the healthy non-sexual friendships suggested above.

Homosexual relationships, when not purely haphazard encounters, are typically cemented by a casual convenience of overlapping egocentric needs, and are thus characterized by a shaky co-dependence in which the needs of one partner are subordinate to the needs of the other. Thus, many homosexual partnerships are challenged by boundary and power struggles, and/or by one partner overvaluing or undervaluing the other. (The same is true, of course, of many *heterosexual* relationships—including most foolishly contracted marriages.) It is critical to the process of gender affirmation that strugglers learn to assume and to expect equal responsibility for the friendships they undertake with their same-sex peers.

Through working with "The Four Friends," the struggler's perceptions about himself and about other men, and about his interactions with other men will change. In turn, the struggler's beliefs and ideas based on those perceptions will also change. These changes invest and affect the struggler's entire emotional reality.

Thus, as happens with *teshuvah,* the struggling homosexual is no longer the same at the end of the process as he was when he began it.

---

lives that they belonged to the fraternity of men. On their discharge into civilian society, these men experienced a relapse into their homosexuality.

"*Teshuvah* is a change, sometimes a complete reversal of direction," writes Rabbi Steinsaltz. By changing his perceptions of the world, the struggler has not only changed himself but also his reality. He has discovered his real self. Nevertheless, Rabbi Steinsaltz emphasizes that this change is "*not* the creation of a new being. In the final analysis, one's fundamental qualities, talents, and stores of knowledge go with him wherever he goes." (*Teshuva,* 54).

The Four Friends and *Teshuvah*.

I found it amazing to realize that Cohen's four archetypal relationships ultimately correspond to the four stages of *teshuvah:* Regret, Resolve, Confession and Abandonment. Let us see how:

(1) The Mentor's function is to guide, encourage, and chastise—in short, to help sustain the struggler's sense of contrition or *Regret,* as the struggler sees the gulf between his reality and his reflected ideal self. (In turn, these interactions provide him with direction and the desire to improve.)

(2) The Fellow Struggler represents *Resolve,* because the two reflect, reinforce and watch over each other;

(3) The Straight Friend Who Knows—*i.e.,* who is aware of the struggler's situation—fulfills the struggler's need to *Confess* his or her failings to a righteous person; and

(4) The Straight Friend Who Doesn't Know corresponds to *Abandonment:* the struggler's sexual issues play no role whatsoever in the dynamics of this relationship. The relationship is natural, spontaneous, and not specifically related to the therapeutic environment. Hence, this friendship represents the struggler's full reentry into a world where he is no longer an outsider, where he both feels, and in fact is, "one of the guys." As Michael H. said, after experiencing such acceptance and confirmation as a man, "For the first time in my life I actually like myself." (Jeff Konrad, 280-81)

Chapter 14:

Homosexuals, "Marriage," and the Family.

Background.

The need to rationalize, and hence intellectualize or dignify as natural, harmless and respectable, the various drives toward aberrant or promiscuous sex has long led to the commingling of simple notions of "sexual liberation" with highly developed theories of social reform. In the context of homosexuality, it is obvious that many gay-identified men and women aspire to be able to express their sexuality without reproof, guilt, ambivalence, or hindrance of any kind. Thus, for many gay activists it is essential to fight not merely for the freedom to *engage* in homosexual relations, but for the ability to *sanctify* them via the institutions of marriage and parenthood.

As quaintly phrased by National Gay and Lesbian Task Force Policy director Paula Ettelbrick, "Being queer means pushing the parameters of sex and family, and in the process transforming the very fabric of society."[1] This transformative process has long passed

---

1. *See* Stanley Kurtz, "Beyond Gay Marriage: the Road to Polyamory." *The Weekly Standard,* August 4, 2003, <http:www.weeklystandard.com/Utilities/printer_preview.asp?idArticle=2938&R=ECBD33>.

the stage of incipiency, with Belgium, Canada, the Netherlands, and South Africa asserting themselves as the established leaders in the international trend towards legalizing and normalizing "same-sex marriages" (or "civil unions") and gay parenting—all in a context of radical sexual "liberation" and sweeping social reform. Within the United States, Massachusetts, Vermont and, more recently, California have served as the advance guard in the same battle.

The constant push for social and legal ratification of the gay-oriented household has inevitably exacerbated the inherent conflict between traditional Jewish religious principles and the secular culture of political correctness. The intensification of this conflict has led to two important consequences of interest to the Jewish community at large: (1) it has prompted secular and reformist Jews to question the "rightness" of traditional Torah-based attitudes toward homosexuality,[2] and (2) it has encouraged the more extreme elements of the gay lobby to "demonize—and then punish—faith communities that refuse to bless homosexual unions."[3]

Since essentially the same dichotomy exists between Torah and heterosexual promiscuity as between Torah and homosexuality, it

---

2. The most recent manifestation of this conflict can be seen in the Conservative Movement of Judaism, which hotly debated the question and, in a paradoxical split, approved totally contradictory responses.

3. Pepperdine University law professor Doug Kmiec, in Tom Strode, "Gay Marriage will Cause Church-State Clashes," BP News, June 2, 2006, <http://www.bynews.net/printerfriendly.asp?IC=23383>. In a shocking example of this vindictiveness, two lesbians sought to reserve the Methodist Ocean Grove Camp Meeting Association's seaside property (which the Church had dedicated for public recreational use) for a private commitment ceremony. After their request was denied as inconsistent with Methodist Church doctrine, the lesbians filed a civil rights complaint with the State of New Jersey. Ultimately, the State revoked the Association's long-standing tax exemption on the basis of the Association's refusal to permit a same-sex civil union on its property. *See, e.g.* Julia Vitullo-Martin, "On the Boardwalk," *Wall Street Journal,* Oct.12, 2007, p. W11.

may be instructive to consider the reasons why the sexual revolution of the 1960s did not define this issue in terms of sexual freedom versus freedom of religion, as we see happening today within the gay and lesbian camp.

The sexual revolution of the '60s separated previously inseparable life-choices such as sexual relations, sexual fidelity, childbearing, and childrearing from marriage and lifelong commitment; but as long as the movement remained predominantly heterosexual, each separate component could potentially lead to the fulfillment of Biblical *mitzvos*. Marriage could and often would result if nature were allowed to take its course.[4] Moreover, young lovers did not, by merely appearing together in public, throw down the gauntlet to Biblical morality—as inevitably happens when two young men walk down the street in provocative attitudes—or when activists organize gay pride demonstrations in Jerusalem or at the Vatican.

Jewish society as a whole is unprepared to deal with the anti-religious animus being nurtured in some quarters of gay and lesbian

---

4. "In the Jewish view, it is insufficient to affirm that the [sexual] act must have meaning: it must also have value. For Judaism, value in human sexuality comes only when the relationship involves two people who have committed themselves to one another and have made that commitment in a binding covenant recognized by G-d and society. The act of sexual union, the deepest personal statement that any human being can make, must be reserved for the moment of total oneness." Rabbi Maurice Lamm, *The Jewish Way in Love and Marriage,* Middle Village: Jonathan David Publishers (1980), p. 31.

society. Thus it is important that Jewish communities and spiritual and policy leaders understand exactly what is entailed by the gay lobby's insidious efforts to redefine marriage and the family.

Before we address that topic, however, it should be noted that even the gay movement is divided over the issue of "gay marriage"— namely, over whether to lobby for "legalization," or to oppose the institution of marriage altogether. Indeed, many elements of the gay leadership cling to a "pre-Stonewall"[5] philosophy that perceives gays essentially as outsiders expelled from society, and desire no part of absorption into straight society. They therefore opt for an anti-bourgeois and radical stance. (*See* Chapter 3, *above,* pp.117-20.)

The competing philosophy senses a new opportunity to raise the status of homosexuality to an integral part of mainstream, bourgeois society. In the process, "a need to rebel has quietly ceded to a desire to belong."[6] Which philosophy is more prevalent can perhaps be seen

---

5. The term "Stonewall" bears an iconic significance for the gay liberation movement arguably comparable to the Boston Tea Party in American history. The term owes its origin to a June 28, 1969 incident in which, shortly after gay icon Judy Garland's funeral, the NYC police and Alcoholic Beverage Control Board, during a routine crackdown on gay bars, targeted The Stonewall Inn, a mafia-owned bar whose clientele consisted mainly of drag queens and kings, gay men, and lesbians. Instead of meekly submitting, several patrons put up a struggle, transforming the atmosphere from the customary passivity to one of defiance and protest. A sympathetic crowd collected outside the bar, cheering on and even assisting the gay protesters. Encouraged by the showing of public sympathy, the protest spread to other gay bars. Prior to "Stonewall," many gays and lesbians viewed themselves as a radical revolutionary group who deliberately excluded themselves from society and rejected its rules. The post-Stonewall mentality aspired to social inclusion and political empowerment, and began to use sophisticated public relations to win over middle America to their cause. One example was their ideological transformation of the "Christopher Street Riots," as the newspapers initially styled them, into the "Stonewall Uprising," as the event has been enshrined in gay history. See Toby Marotta, "What made Stonewall Different?" *Gay & Lesbian Review Worldwide,* March-April, 2006.

6. Andrew Sullivan, "Here Comes the Groom: A Conservative Case for Gay Marriage," <http://www.andrewsullivan.com/print.php?artnum=19890828.>.

from a spring, 2006 study conducted by the Institute for Marriage and Public Policy. The authors examined the trend data to determine the proportion of gay- and lesbian-identified individuals who chose to marry in jurisdictions where same-sex marriage was legal. Their study showed that only a small fraction—between 1% and 5% of gays and lesbians—had entered into a same-sex marriage in those jurisdictions.[7]

Despite the passionate pleas for "marriage equality," the evidence continues to mount that the vast majority of homosexuals do not even consider marriage a blip on their radar screen. For example, once the initial thrill of the gay legal victories in Massachusetts and Canada had worn off—along with all the attendant publicity—there was a rapid downturn in the number of gay "marriages." In Massachusetts, for example, where homosexual "marriage" has been legal since the middle of 2004, 6,121 gay and lesbian marriages took place in the remainder of that year. However, in the entire year 2005, the number fell by more than two-thirds: only 2,060 same-sex couples tied the knot. In 2006 the number dropped by nearly half again to 1, 427, and in the first third of 2007, only 86 gay or lesbian couples marched down the aisle. This out of a total estimated gay population of circa 200 thousand![8] In the same time-period (January through April, 2007), in Toronto, Canada, reputed to have one of the world's largest homosexual populations, just one Canadian homosexual couple chose to get married.[9] If these numbers show anything, they show that marriage is not the real goal of gay politics.

---

7. Maggie Gallagher & Joshua K. Baker, "Demand for Same-Sex Marriage: Evidence from the United States, Canada, and Europe," IMAPP Policy Brief, Vol. 3, No. 1 (April 26, 2006), p. 1.

8. Based on the 1996 Census Bureau estimate of 6,437,193 for the total population of Massachusetts, and on the assumption that 3% of the population is gay or lesbian.

9. J. Matt Barber, "Gays Don't Want Marriage After All," *World Net Daily*, July 6,

A front-page *New York Times* article on the legalization of gay marriage in Canada confirms this phenomenon. "Many gays," says the article, "express the fear that it [same-sex marriage] will undermine their notions of who they are. They say they want to maintain the unique aspects of their culture and their place at the edge of social change." The article quotes a gay Canadian who sees marriage "as a dumbing down of gay relationships. My dread," he continues, "is that soon you will have a complacent bloc of gay and lesbian soccer moms."[10]

In fact, if what knowledgeable commentators have been telling us is accurate, "this campaign is not really about marriage at all. Instead, it is about the desperate desire of homosexuals for society at large to affirm that homosexuality (not just homosexual individuals, but homosexual sex acts) is the full equivalent of heterosexuality in every way—morally, socially, and legally."[11] It is both ironic and predictable, of course, that proponents of homosexual "equivalency" should seek to legitimize—if not "sanctify"—the homosexual union via the very institution which, in a more general context, it hopes to destroy.

2007, <http://www.worldnetdaily.com/hws/printer-friendly.asp?ARTICLE_ID=565217>.

10. Clifford Krauss, "Free to Marry, Canada's Gays Say, 'Do I?'" *New York Times*, August 31, 2003, p.1.

11. Peter Sprigg, *Outrage: How Gay Activists and Liberal Judges are Thrashing Democracy to Redefine Marriage,* Washington, D.C.: Regnery Publishing (2004), p. 86. Homosexual activist writer Michelangelo Signorile goes further, suggesting that the real goal of the fight for same sex marriage is ultimately to destroy the institution altogether: "To fight for same-sex marriage and its benefits and then, once granted, redefine the institution of marriage completely, to demand the right to marry not as a way of adhering to society's moral codes bur rather to debunk a myth and radically alter an archaic institution." Timothy J. Dailey, "Homosexual Parenting: Placing Children at Risk," Family Research Council, <http://www.frc.org/get.cfm?i=IS01J3.>, citing M. Signorile, "Bridal Wave," *Out*, December, 1994.

The sanctity with which G–d views marriage applies as much to non-Jews as it does to Jews, and non-Jews have universally recognized it and practiced it in one form or another. The Talmud (*Chullin* 92b) recalls how non-Jews, too, honored G–d's prohibition against male homosexual marriage.

Generally speaking, the institution of marriage has been severely weakened in recent years. A June, 2006 study by an independent research organization identified divorce, illegitimacy, "living together," and same-sex marriage as four troubling phenomena that portend "serious negative consequences for society as a whole."[12] Religious institutions play a critical role in sustaining a marriage culture in civil society; in fact, the majority of Americans still marry in religious ceremonies. (Witherspoon Institute, 15)

Why Gay "Marriage" is No Marriage.

As we examine the homosexual relationship in this chapter, it will become apparent why it has been described as "radically and peculiarly non-marital."[13] Openly gay author Andrew Sullivan admits that homosexuals have a "*need* for extramarital outlets."[14] (Emphasis added.) Lesbian writer Camille Paglia notes how gay magazines glamorize "the bigger bang of sex with strangers" and advocate "monogamy without fidelity" in same-sex couplings. (Sears & Osten, 95)

---

12. "Marriage and the Public Good: Ten Principles," Princeton: The Witherspoon Institute (2006), p. 5.

13. John M. Finnis, "Law, Morality, and Sexual Orientation," *Notre Dame L. Rev.* Vol. 69 (1994), pp. 1062-63.

14. Alan Sears & Craig Osten, *The Homosexual Agenda: Exposing the Principal Threat to Religious Freedom Today,* Nashville: Broadman & Holman (2003), p. 95, citing Andrew Sullivan, *Virtually Normal: An Argument about Homosexuality,* New York: Knopf (1995).

Loneliness and isolation are key characteristics of the homosexual lifestyle. Dr. Robert J. Hatterer explains:

> Isolation is often a product of the homosexual man's ambivalence—his rejections, disloyalties, transient promiscuities, and the impersonal nature of his lifestyle.... Tiring of the chase or the seduction or of having too often failed at achieving permanency in a one-to-one relationship, he can turn to totally depersonalized, emotionless, masturbatory sexual contacts that replace all intimacies. In so doing, he cuts off his emotional contact with others and remains alone and vulnerable to a variety of psychiatric symptoms such as panic, acute anxiety, depression, and impulses toward suicide.[15]

The committed homosexual is typically extraordinarily narcissistic. Dr. Van Den Aardwag refers to this personality trait as infantile ego-centeredness.[16] A common expression of this emotional adaptation is a sexualized envy of another person of the same sex. The homosexual envies those traits he admires in another but lacks (or believes he lacks) within himself. In sexualizing this envy, he endeavors to acquire—take possession of—the characteristics he desires for himself. It can't work. As Genesis 2:18 observes, *It is not good for man to be alone*—or, in Rabbi Meiselman's apt paraphrase, "G–d however said that it is not good for a human being to be totally self-sufficient and devoted only to himself."[17]

---

15. Dr. Lawrence J. Hatterer, *Changing Homosexuality in the Male: Treatment for Men Troubled by Homosexuality,* New York: McGraw-Hill (1970), p. 406.

16. Dr.Gerard J.M. Van Den Aardweg, *The Battle for Normality: A Guide for (Self) Therapy for Homosexuality,* San Francisco: Ignatius Press (1977), pp. 132-3. The narcissistic personality is oversensitive to failure and is prone to extreme mood swings between self-admiration and insecurity.

17. Rabbi Moshe Meiselman, *Jewish Woman in Jewish Law*, New York: Ktav and Yeshiva U. Press (1978), p. 9.

Most human beings feel incomplete without a mate and it is through marriage that their completion is achieved. "The completion and perfection of the human personality occurs when man and woman live for each other, give to each other, and function together as one unit, each performing his or her own unique tasks." (Meiselman, 10) In fact, the Hebrew word for bride, *kallah,* derives from *kalot,* meaning "completion." The union of two men or two women mocks at this wholeness and completion: in reality, such unions are just doubly *in*complete.

Indeed, to be complementary, the sexual anatomy of the marital partners must fit together and complete the whole. The anatomical facts of male/female organs are self-evident. In that regard, the Torah view is fully consistent with that expressed by two Christian writers:

> *G–d designed sex so that man and woman can become one.* Notice the beautiful symmetry illustrated here [Gen. 2:24]—that which was taken out of man returns to him. Man is completed in woman and woman is completed in man. There is a union spoken of here that is much deeper than a mere physical act."[18] (Original emphasis.)

---

18. Terry Wier & Mark Carruth, *Holy Sex: G–d's Purpose and Plan for Our Sexuality*, New Kensington: Whitaker House (1999), p. 30.

In the absence of this wholeness, there is incompleteness or brokenness. The special wholeness or completeness of the male-female bond is also related to the spiritual challenges imposed upon each partner by virtue of their physiological and psychological differences. The man must learn to respect the menstrual cycle and changing moods of his wife by exercising restraint at the appropriate times. Each partner must rise above his or her own frustration and hurt to learn and adapt to the gender (as well as personality) patterns of thought, speech, and behavior of the other. Moreover, in Jewish marriage, each partner must learn to "de-sexualize" the relationship during the twelve days of *niddah* (menstrual period plus the mandatory seven days of abstinence) and to become the other's "platonic" friend while remaining sexually faithful to him or her. It is this very ability to transcend egocentrism and gender-chauvinism that true marriage demands. When achieved, it is this transcendence that confers upon the relationship the "holiness" that the Sages attribute to it.

This is the opposite of the homosexual union in which—even when characterized by genuine mutual caring—each partner "loves" narcissistically an idealized replica of himself, and, typically, must at times divert his sexual attention outside the union in order to keep the relationship alive.

The ability to control one's sexual desire clearly benefits the persons affected as it provides a sense of personal mastery, autonomy, and competency in one's life, while opening up new "vistas" of non-physical communication between the sexes. Susan Weidman Schneider, editor of *Lilith,* observes, "He, as well as she, must yoke passion to the dictate of a higher authority. A marriage that cannot withstand this kind of self-control is *ipso facto* a marriage based on sexual slavery and is contemptible in the eyes of Judaism."[19] Typically, those who learn to control their sexual drives also manage

---

19. Susan Weidman Schneider, *Jewish and Female: Choices and Changes in Our Lives Today*, New York: Simon and Schuster (1984), p. 205.

to keep themselves away from harmful or self-destructive behaviors such as drug use and alcoholism. In short, in a true marriage, each spouse learns to relate to his or her mate as a multi-faceted human being and not as a mere object for his or her own gratification.

By contrast, sexual promiscuity is a common feature of the male homosexual lifestyle, and one that typically carries over to some significant degree in the relatively rare instances in which the partners overcome their characteristic inability to maintain an enduring relationship. There is little, if any, question that the frequency of sex outside of homosexual long-term relationships is significantly greater, and the duration of such relationships is significantly shorter, than that of heterosexual long-term relationships. Indeed, to most observers, the homosexual lifestyle is characterized by self-indulgence and unrealistic expectations of immediate gratification—factors that militate strongly against enduring partnerships.[20]

Duration does not a Marriage Make.

One point that is often overlooked is that even in the exceptional cases of stable relationships, homosexual coupling is simply not

---

20. Professor Thomas E. Schmidt cites numerous studies suggesting that "the vast majority of homosexual activity, particularly among males, occurs outside the context of quasi-marital partnerships." *Straight and Narrow?—Compassion and Clarity in the Homosexual Debate,* Downers Grove: InterVarsity Press (1995), p. 110, *and see* pp. 105-8. "In short," concludes Schmidt, "there is practically no comparison possible to heterosexual marriage in terms of either fidelity or longevity. Tragically, lifelong faithfulness is almost nonexistent in the homosexual experience." (110) *Compare* Edward O. Laumann, *et. al., The Social Organization of Sexuality: Sexual Practices in the United States,* U. Chicago Press (1994), p. 216: "Seventy-Five percent of married heterosexual men and 85% of married heterosexual women report never having had extramarital sex." *See* also Chapter Three, *above*, at pp. 91-2, and note 53.

marriage. Gay propagandists assiduously propagate a sanitized picture of gay coupling by drawing a veil of charity over characteristic homosexual practices that vary considerably—at least in frequency and emphasis—from those associated with heterosexuality. Thus, there is a widespread public perception that homosexual couples enjoy stable, sexually monogamous relationships. The reality is quite the opposite.

Indeed, according to Professor Thomas Schmidt (*see above,* this chapter, note 20), the grim realities of gay sex typically include some pattern of brief, anonymous encounters, not infrequently resulting in physical trauma and/or sexually transmitted disease. What goes on during such encounters, writes Schmidt, "is very *unlike* what happens between heterosexual partners, especially in terms of susceptibility of participants to physical harm and disease." (Emphasis added.) (110)

This is true even on the purely mechanical level of the sexual relationship. Schmidt catalogues only the most common sexual techniques performed by homosexuals (listing them in order of frequency) and suggests that they differ radically and quantitatively from heterosexual techniques to achieve orgasm. Among male homosexuals studied, 95% had engaged in oral-genital contact, 80% in mutual masturbation, 80% in "insertive anal intercourse," and 70% in "receptive anal intercourse." "Mutual masturbation," Schmidt clarifies, "is not limited to genital stimulation but includes a variety of anal stimuli, involving the fingers and other objects." Among homosexual women, the most popular techniques were mutual masturbation 80% and oral-genital contact 80%. The report concludes, "Males named insertive anal intercourse as their favorite sexual activity, with receptive oral-genital contact a close second. Females named receptive oral-genital contact as their favorite sexual activity, with receptive masturbation a distant second." Twenty-nine percent of subjects studied engaged in orgies and sexual encounters that are often crowded in sequentially, "such that some participate in a dozen or more sexual transactions in the course of a single day or evening."(Schmidt, 108-9).

More generally, studies cited by Schmidt show a direct correlation between the number of partners and drug use, on the one hand, and the incidence of unsafe sex on the other. The studies also reported a significantly higher rate of substance abuse by homosexual men and women as compared to heterosexuals. A 1989 San Francisco study, for example, showed 89% of homosexuals using marijuana as compared to 25% of the heterosexual control group, and 50% using cocaine, versus 6% of heterosexuals. Thirty-three percent used barbiturates, as compared to 9% of heterosexuals. Fifty percent used LSD as against 3% of heterosexuals, and 72% used poppers, versus 2% of heterosexuals. For those who have never heard of "poppers," they are amyl and butyl nitrate inhalants, used almost exclusively by male homosexuals as recreational drugs "to enhance sexual performance by relaxing smooth tissues, engorging blood vessels, lowering blood pressure, causing dizziness and heightening skin sensitivity." (Schmidt, 110-11)

Out of the Closet and into the Clinic.

"For the vast majority of homosexual men," writes Schmidt, "and for a significant number of homosexual women—even apart from the deadly plague of AIDS—sexual behavior is obsessive, psychopathological and destructive to the body." (Schmidt, 130) The physical and mental disorders which accompany homosexual activity are numerous. The most common *non-viral* physical infections are often caused by pathogens that are transmitted by oral-genital contact, genital-anal contact, and oral-anal contact and include, in order of frequency, amebiasis (25-40%), giardiasis (10-30%), gonorrhea (40-80%), shigellosis (10-20%), chlamydia (5%-15%), syphilis (30%), and ectoparasites (scabies, 22%; pubic lice or "crabs," 69%). (Schmidt, 119-120)

As for viral infections, condylomata (anal warts) (30-40%), herpes (10-20%), hepatitis B (16% or more), hepatitis A (5-7% annually, or three times the rate of the general population!) In all these cases, the number of carriers is two to three times higher than the number of infected. (Schmidt, 120-22)

Looking at the incidence of STDs in general, male homosexuals were found to have a lifetime incidence rate of 75% as compared to 16.9% for the general population. (121-22)

A disproportionate number of male homosexuals are affected with depression, suicidal ideation, and other mental health issues. Forty percent of male homosexual subjects were found to have a history of major depressive disorder as compared to only 3% of males generally (Schmidt, 113), while 18% of male homosexuals, and 23% of female homosexuals, had actually attempted suicide, as compared with 3% and 11% of male and female heterosexuals, respectively. (Schmidt, 113-114)

Another distinction concerning the physical and psychological dangers facing homosexuals relates to the assignment and manner of performance of male and female roles in homosexual intercourse. Hatterer found that

> Acute and chronic problems occur in establishing a balance between and sustaining submission and dominance or passivity and aggressivity, that is, male-female role-playing in the committed homosexual's relationships. [. . .] They often result in sado-masochistic patterns of behavior between homosexual partners which generally threaten or even destroy [*i.e.,* psychologically] one partner or the other. When this happens, frequent evidences of self-destructiveness or violence emerge in the form of hysterical behavior or suicide threats or attempts. [. . .] [B]ecause of the ambiguity of assigned sexual and gender roles and rapid shifts in sado-masochistic roles, the destruction is greater [than in destructive heterosexual relationships], and less obvious to each member of the 'marriage.' (397-98)

Thus, as Hatterer observes, even conceding the rare case of duration and stability, the homosexual union is still so loaded with other "vicissitudes" as to render comparison with true marriage highly inappropriate. Indeed, as Schmidt concludes, "If there were no specific biblical principles to guide sexual behavior, these considerations alone would constitute a compelling argument against homosexual practice." (Schmidt, 130)

A Sober Look at "Stability" and "Duration."

Studies by Stephen Ellingson & Kirby Schroder working under Edward Laumann, an acknowledged expert on the sociology of sexuality, show typical gay males spending most of their adult lives in "transactional markets" (defined as relations forged purely for pleasure and involving commitments of less than six months) as opposed to "relational markets" (defined as longer term, more stable relationships)[21]

An oft-cited Dutch study by the Amsterdam Municipal Health Service not only shows the promiscuous nature of male homosexual relationships but also dramatically highlights the transience of gay coupling. The study found the average male homosexual partnership lasting only one and a half years.[22] This is compared to a CDC study that found 50% of heterosexual marriages lasting fifteen years or more.[23]

A 2004 study of same-sex divorce in Sweden reported that gay and lesbian couples divorced at a higher rate than heterosexual

---

21. "Race and Construction of Same Sex Markets in Four Chicago Neighborhoods," Chapter Four in Edward Laumann, et. al., *The Sexual Organization of the City*, U. Chicago Press (2005), pp. 93-123.

22. Maria Xiridou et al., "The Contribution of Steady and Casual Relationships to the Incidence of HIV Infection among Homosexual Men in Amsterdam," *AIDS Journal* (2003), p. 17.

23. National Center for Health Statistics, Centers for Disease Control, "Forty-Three Percent of First Marriages Break up Within 15 years," <http://www.cdc.gov/nchs/releases/01news/first-marr.htm>. *See also* Sprigg, 97.

couples (and, contrary to common assumptions, the lesbian divorce rate was higher than for male couples)[24]

These findings are supported by the well-known research of McWhirter and Mattison (a homosexual male couple—the one a psychiatrist, the other a psychologist). Questioning the premise that gay male relationships are promiscuous and transient, McWhirter and Mattison surveyed 156 male couples in relationships that had lasted from 1 to 37 years. The results show that only one half of one percent (*i.e.*, seven couples) of the sample group maintained sexual fidelity but *none* of those seven couples had been together for longer than five years. In other words, contrary to the authors' stated desire to refute the thesis that gay male relationships are not monogamous, the researchers were unable to find a single male couple that had actually maintained sexual fidelity for more than five years. McWhirter and Mattison candidly concluded: "The expectation for outside activity was the rule for male couples and the exception for heterosexuals. Heterosexual couples lived with some expectation that their relationships would last 'until death do us part,' whereas gay couples wondered if their relationships could survive."[25]

---

24. Gunnar Andersson, Turid Noack, Ane Seiestad, and Harald Weedon-Fekjair, "Divorce-Risk Patterns in Same-Sex Marriages in Norway and Sweden," Paper presented at the Annual Meeting of the Population Association of America, April 3, 2004, <http://paa2004.princeton.edu/download.asp?submissionId=40208>. *See also* Sprigg, 97.

25. David P. McWhirter and Andrew M. Mattison, *The Male Couple: How Relationships Develop*, Englewood Cliffs: Prentice-Hall (1984), p. 3. Former homosexual William Aaron explains why monogamy is not part of the gay lifestyle, even in so-called committed relationships: "In the gay life, fidelity is almost impossible. Since part of the compulsion of homosexuality seems to be a need on the part of the homophile to 'absorb' masculinity from his sexual partners, he must be constantly on the lookout for [new partners]. Consequently the most successful homophile 'marriages' are those where there is an arrangement between the two to have affairs on the side while maintaining the semblance of permanence in their living arrangement." William Aaron, *Straight*, New York: Bantam Books, (1972), p. 208.

As their data would not support their intended thesis, these two social scientists felt compelled to recast their premise: "Many [gay] couples learn very early in their relationship that ownership of each other sexually can become the greatest internal threat to their staying together." (256) Fidelity is thus redefined to mean "emotional dependability": "We found that gay men *expect* mutual emotional dependability with their partners and that relationship fidelity transcends concerns about sexuality and exclusivity." (285)

Questioning how partners in a relationship not based on sexual fidelity could remain "emotionally dependable," Dr. Joseph Nicolosi rightly proposes, "the agreement to have outside affairs precludes the possibility of trust and intimacy."[26] Even in the rare instances where sexual fidelity is intact, other factors conspire to undermine the male-male union. As Nicolosi astutely observes,

> Two men can never take in each other, in the full and open way. Not only is there a natural anatomical unsuitability, but an inherent psychological insufficiency as well. Both partners are coming together with the same deficit. Each is symbolically and sexually attempting to find fulfillment of gender in the other person. But the other person is not whole in that way either, so the relationship ends in disillusionment. (109-10)

After reviewing the McWhirter and Mattison study, and several other investigations, Professor Thomas Schmidt concludes, "If we project these numbers out over several years, the number of homosexual men who experience anything like lifelong fidelity becomes, statistically speaking, almost meaningless." (*Straight and Narrow?* 108)

A contention often espoused by gay activists and their well-meaning allies is that gay marriage will purge the gay lifestyle of its objectionable appurtenances. In other words, if we allow gays to marry, they will change their sexual behavior and adopt heterosexual

---

26. Dr. Joseph Nicolosi, *Reparative Therapy of Male Homosexuality: A New Clinical Approach*, Northvale: Jason Aronson (1997), p. 113.

standards of sexual fidelity, hygiene, and commitment.[27] However, we have just seen that long-term relationships are not an effective antidote for gay promiscuity. Moreover, we saw earlier (this chapter, at p. 505) that gay couples have not exactly been falling over each other in a rush to the altar in those jurisdictions which allow gay marriages. Further, those who do marry are subject to a tellingly higher rate of divorce than heterosexual couples. Thus, to prognosticate a sanatory influence on the gay lifestyle from the legalization of gay marriage is extremely unrealistic.

---

27. *See, e.g.,* Dale Carpenter , "The Traditionalist Case for Gay Marriage" (October 31, 2005) <http://www.volokh.com/posts/chain_1131164649.shtml>: "(1) Marriage will help support and stabilize gay families, including the many such families raising children; (2) it will help channel these families into traditional patterns of living, providing them and their communities some measure of the private and public goods we expect from marriage; (3) it will, over time, tend to traditionalize gay individuals by elevating respect within gay culture for values like commitment to others and monogamy at the expense of hedonism and promiscuity; (4) it will make available the most moral life (in a traditionalist sense) possible for a sexually active homosexual; (5) and it will do all of this without hurting traditional families or marriage, (6) perhaps even helping to a limited extent with the revival of marriage." One may be surprised that Professor Carpenter did not add as a seventh point the establishment of world peace and the elimination of poverty and hunger!

On the contrary, if there is any influence at all, it is more likely to be destructive and to flow in the opposite direction. As Peter Sprigg, Director of the Family Research Council's Center for Marriage and Family Studies, suggests, "If homosexual relationships, promiscuity and all, are held up to society as being a fully equal part of the social ideal that is called 'marriage,' then the value of sexual fidelity as an expected standard of behavior for married people will further erode." (*Outrage*, 96)

Perhaps the most remarkable feature of marriage, anthropologically speaking, is that it did not require a Commandment of Heaven to establish it. In all cultures, the need for marriage arose out of the natural physical and psychological constitution of man and woman. At some point in the natural (as opposed to the socially sanctioned) marital relationship, the dependency of each partner on the affection, esteem, security, trust and support of the other outweighs the need for adventure and variety. However, we have just seen that this is rarely the case in homosexual unions. The need to "prowl," even if only "occasionally," remains paramount. Thus, the very incentives for staying together (the emotional sustenance and security provided by mutual affection, trust, etc.,) are either missing or illusory.

The Role of "Family" in Gay Politics. (*See also* Ch. 3, pp.117-20.)

Gay and lesbian couples involved in a "stable" relationship are inevitably faced with the issue of family—whether to seek some variant of the family unit, repudiate the notion entirely, or nurture a nostalgic regret for the rest of their lives. Homosexuals who were raised in religious—especially Jewish—households rarely escape this dilemma. In Jewish tradition, family is central to the whole idea of marriage. As phrased by Rabbi Irving Greenberg, "family is the basis of humanization as well as being central to the inculcation and transmission of Jewish values."[28] Indeed, all traditional societies have always kept the reproductive function within marriage. Until the advent of reliable birth control, parenthood was virtually never treated as merely a lifestyle option, but rather as a divine commandment, or at least a societal obligation.[29] Thus, the issues of family structure and parenthood have never been far from gay and lesbian social theory. In reality, however, such theorizing has generally taken on a radical-socialist cast. As Rabbi Samuel Dresner explains this phenomenon,

> Until the influence of normal and traditional families is countered, the gay rights movement will never win the ultimate victory it desires—which is total affirmation by the American people of everything they do. Thus, [say the gay activists,] the family must be bypassed, undermined, and finally eliminated as a way of organizing society. It is a theme that recurs throughout homosexual literature and is voiced by some of the movement's most responsible leaders.[30]

Gay activists and social radicals have often spoken of "the need" to deconstruct family life as an essential prerequisite for full gay liberation. For example, Yale University law professor and gay activist William N. Eskridge, Jr. aspires to "dethrone the traditional family based on blood relationships in favor of families we choose."[31] He also argues, "legally as well as culturally, the norm is up for grabs,

---

28. Rabbi Irving Greenberg, *Living in the Image of G-d: Jewish Teachings to Perfect the World*, Northvale: Jason Aronson (1998), p. 117.

29. *See* Rabbi Michael Gold, *G-d, Love, Sex, and Family: A Guide for Building Relationships that Last*, Northvale: Jason Aronson (1998), pp. 108-11.

30. Rabbi Samuel H. Dresner, *Can Families Survive in Pagan America?* Lafayette: Huntington House Publishers (1995), p.31.

31. William N. Eskridge, Jr. *The Case for Same-Sex Marriage*, New York: The Free Press (1996), as quoted in Sears and Osten, *The Homosexual Agenda*, p. 97.

and as a [gay] community we must contribute to the reformulation of the norm."[32] Others, like Kirk and Madsen, recommend "a whole panoply of possible choices for the integration of one's own life with those of others and of society as a whole."[33]

Since alienation from family is one of the recognized earmarks of the homosexual condition, the vituperative horror expressed by some gay activists in regard to the idea of "family" should come as no surprise. "[S]pawning ground of lies, betrayals, mediocrity, hypocrisy and violence." "[D]efective, the source of much suffering and neurosis."[34] "[T]he nuclear family has been the most destructive influence on all our human relationships. [. . .] [A]ny notion of family being defined by direct biological links is a nonsense."[35]

Such exclamations are more of a window into the past family life of the "theorist" than a preamble to an actual social theory. It may be observed that the only known genuine experiments in communal parenting were done by heterosexuals, and the idea never really caught on even in socialist countries.[36] Thus, it seems reasonable to

---

32. William N. Eskridge, Jr., "A Social Constructionist Critique of Posner's *Sex and Reason:* Steps Toward a Gaylegal Agenda," 102 *Yale Law Journal* (Oct., 1992) 374-5.

33. Marshal Kirk and Hunter Madsen, *After the Ball: How America Will Conquer Its Fear and Hatred of Gays in the 90's*, New York: Doubleday (1989), p. 366.

34. Michael Swift, *Gay Community News*, Feb. 15, 1987, as quoted in Kirk and Madsen, p. 365.

35. Susan Mitchell, "Let Love Determine Who is Part of a Clan," *The Australian*, June 5, 2000, p. 13, quoted in Bill Muehlenberg, "Deconstructing the Family," <http://www.marriage.org.au/deconstructing_the_family.htm>.

36. Israel's kibbutz movement offers a classic example of a failed effort to have children raised by the community rather than their biological parents. "Israeli *kibbutzim* are rapidly dismantling their collective child care centers and returning children to live with their families—because both the families and the community established that even a limited disassociation of children from their parents at a tender age is unacceptable." Amitai Etzioni, *The Spirit of Community*, London:

conclude that gay and lesbian rhetoric about revolutionizing the family structure is largely academic. The real focus of gay activism is sexual freedom—a circumstance that makes the notion of homosexual parenting all the more alarming.

Homosexual Parenting.

The drumbeat of "born that way" and "normalize homosexuality" has led to a plethora of studies attempting to show that child rearing by same-sex couples is no different from traditional heterosexual parenting. Consider for example the following finding in a New Hampshire judicial decision: "The overwhelming weight of professional study on the subject concludes no difference in psychological and psychosexual development can be discerned between children raised by heterosexual parents and children raised by homosexual parents."[37] How true are such types of findings? Is there a result orientation in the studies? Are they really unbiased? Are the studies themselves designed to be misleading? Some analysts have found serious deficiencies both in the data analysis and in the interpretation of the findings.

It is important to note that because most researchers locate articles through computer retrieval systems which set forth the title and abstract of the study in question, false information set forth in the abstract can totally mislead other researchers. Thus, a result-oriented

---

Fontana Press (1985), p. 59. A decade later, "nearly all *kibbutzim* have overthrown the communal childrearing practices that were once at the heart of their efforts. Infant care has shifted back to parents. Children's houses are disappearing. Single-family dwellings have sprung up, and the private family dinner has returned. Parent-child intimacy and closeness are enjoying a great revival." Karl Zinmeister, "Villages are Lousy at Raising Pre-school Children," *The American Enterprise*, Vol. 7, No. 3 (May-June 1996), p. 54.

37. *In Re: Opinion of the Justices*, 525 A. 2d 1095 at 1102 (New Hampshire, May 5, 1987).

study by Richard Green *et al.* comparing children reared by lesbian and heterosexual mothers has the following erroneous statement in the abstract: "No significant differences were found between the two types of households for boys and few significant differences for girls."[38] On the contrary, the body of the article cites numerous significant differences. Here are some examples concerning the boys: (1) 32% of lesbians' sons wanted to play at both sexes' activities equally as opposed to only 10% of heterosexuals' sons (Green, 178); (2) More children of lesbian mothers showed a considerable interest in playacting and role-taking than did children of heterosexual mothers (177); (3) Sons of heterosexual mothers were more likely to have experienced more than one period of separation from father, whereas sons of lesbian mothers typically had experienced a single separation (174); (4) 73% of heterosexual mothers encouraged truck play compared to only 30% of lesbian mothers (179); (5) During the child's first year of life, the majority of lesbian mothers reported having spent fewer daytime hours holding or touching their infant sons than did heterosexual mothers. (174)

As far as the girls are concerned, some reviewers found "many statistical differences between the daughters from the two types of households, including: compared to daughters of heterosexual mothers, the daughters of homosexual mothers had significantly more cross-dressing, more rough and tumble play, more playing with trucks, more playing with guns, more play with boys' activities, greater preference for both masculine and feminine activity, and greater preference for taking masculine adult roles."[39]

While some might applaud the crossing of gender lines described in the Green study, no one can rightly claim that the differences

---

38. Richard Green *et al.*, "Lesbian Mothers and their Children: A Comparison with Solo Parent Heterosexual Mothers and their Children," 15 *Archives of Sexual Behavior* (1986), 167, 180.

39. George Rekers and Mark Kilgus, "Studies of Homosexual Parenting: A Critical Review," 14 *Regent University Law Review* 342, 368 (2002).

observed by the authors are "insignificant." Unfortunately, both the courts and the media have heavily relied upon the numerous examples of illegitimate conclusions and generalizations to be found in such articles, often representing little more than "self-presentation bias."[40] University of South Carolina Professors George Rekers and Mark Kilgus carefully analyzed a host of articles on homosexual parenting, and found that almost all of them were not only replete with methodological deficiencies but, more egregiously, "many of the authors make illegitimate generalizations or unwarranted conclusions from their flawed research studies."[41] (Rekers & Kilgus, 382)

Ever since the early 1970s, The American Psychological Association has been a strong advocate of "gay rights." It should be no surprise, therefore, to see their official statement on homosexual parenting claiming that "Not a single study has found children of gay or lesbian parents to be disadvantaged in any significant respect relative to children of heterosexual parents."[42] Really? Not so, if we

---

40. Timothy J. Dailey, "Homosexual Parenting: Placing Children at Risk," *Family Research Council,* No. 238, <http://www.frc.org/get.cfm?i=IS01J3>.

41. A case in point: the abstract of Fiona Tasker & Susan Golombok, "Adults Raised as Children in Lesbian Families," 65 *Am. J. Orthopsychiatry,* Vol. 65 (1995), p. 203, claims: "The commonly held assumption that lesbian mothers will have lesbian daughters and gay sons was not supported by the findings." In direct contrast to that claim, Rekers and Kilgus found: "The actual data in this study not only indicated a statistically significant greater percentage of sons and daughters of lesbian mothers having been involved in homosexual behavior and identifying as homosexuals as young adults, but further indicated that none of the sons and daughters of the heterosexual single mothers had been involved in homosexuality." (*Regent U. Law Rev.,* 373-4)

42. Charlotte J. Patterson, "Lesbian and Gay Parenting," *American Psychological Association Public Interest Directorate* (1995), p. 8. Buried however in the very next paragraph is an unheeded caveat: "It should be acknowledged that research on lesbian and gay parents and their children is still very new and relatively scarce. [...] Longitudinal studies that follow lesbian and gay families over time are badly needed."

actually read the several studies that did find such children to be disadvantaged! In one carefully controlled Australian study, Dr. Sotirios Sarantakos looked at children raised in three different family styles: married heterosexual parents, unmarried cohabiting parents, and homosexual parents. Sarantakos concluded that the children raised by heterosexual married couples were the best adjusted in the nine of the thirteen academic and social categories measured; while children of homosexual couples were the least well adjusted in the same nine categories, and children of cohabiting heterosexual couples were in the middle. These nine categories were language, mathematics, sports, sociability, attitude to school and to learning, parent-school relationship, sex identity, school-related support (such as parent's help with homework), and parental aspirations. One of the few exceptions where children of homosexual parents emerged best was social studies, where there was relatively little differential between the three categories (7.0- 7.6, on a scale of 9). However, in the nine categories where children of heterosexual parents did best, the differentials were significantly larger.

Sarantakos utilized the children's teachers, as well as personal interviews with the children, to help him rate the children's academic adjustment in language, mathematics, social studies and athletics, and to assess them in terms of sociability, learning attitudes and parental support. A total of 174 children, 58 from each family type, were studied. Children of 11 male couples and 47 female couples were matched with children of married and cohabiting heterosexual parents whose education, occupation, and socio-economic status were similar. Sarantakos concluded that "overall, the study has shown that children of married couples are more likely to do well at school, in academic and social terms, than children of cohabiting heterosexual and homosexual couples"[43]—*a direct contradiction of the APA's official statement on homosexual parenting!* Dr. Timothy J. Dailey,

---

43. Sotirios Sarantakos, "Children in Three Contexts: Family, Education, and Social Development," *Children Australia*, Vol. 21, No. 13 (1996), p. 23.

Senior Research Fellow at the Center for Marriage and Family Studies of the Family Research Council, concurs: "The importance of the traditional family has been increasingly verified by research showing that children from married two-parent households do better academically, financially, emotionally, and behaviorally. They delay sex longer, have better health, and receive more parental support."[44]

Of all the medical and mental health organizations, the American College of Pediatricians (ACP) is one of the few that have not jumped on the bandwagon of policymakers, social scientists, media and health-related organizations lobbying for the lifting of bans on homosexual parenting. The ACP rightly observes that

> In making such far-reaching, generation-changing assertions, any responsible advocate would rely upon supporting evidence that is comprehensive and conclusive. Not only is this not the situation, but also there is sound evidence that children exposed to the homosexual lifestyle may be at increased risk for emotional, mental, and even physical harm.[45]

---

44. "Homosexual Parenting." *See also:* "Same-Sex Parenting is Harmful to Children," REAL Women of Canada, <http://www.realwomenca.com/newsletter/2004_mar-apr/article_1.html>; Sara McLanahan & Gary Sandfeur, *Growing Up with a Single Parent: What Hurts, What Helps,* Harvard U. Press (1994), p. 45; Pat Fagan, "How Broken Families Rob Children of Their Chances for Prosperity," *Heritage Foundation Backgrounder,* No. 1283 (June 11, 1999), p. 13; Dawn Upchurch *et al.,* "Gender and Ethnic Differences in the Timing of First Sexual Intercourse," *Family Planning Perspectives,* vol. 30 (1998): 121-7; Jeanne M. Hilton and Esther L. Devall, "Comparison of Parenting and Children's Behavior in Single-Mother, Single-Father, and Intact Families," *Journal of Divorce and Remarriage,* Vol. 29 (1998), pp. 23-54; Jane Mauldon, "The Effect of Marital Disruption on Children's Health," *Demography,* Vol. 27 (1990), pp. 431-46; Frank Furstenberg, Jr., & Julien Teitler, "Reconsidering the Effects of Marital Disruption: What Happens to Children of Divorce in Early Adulthood?" *Journal of Family Issues,* Vol. 15 (June, 1994); Elizabeth Thomson *et al.,* "Family Structure and Child Well-Being: Economic Resources vs. Parental Behaviors," *Social Forces,* Vol. 73 (1994), pp. 221-42.

45. American College of Pediatricians, "Parenting Issues: Homosexual Parenting: Is it Time for Change?" <http://www.acpeds.org/?CONTEXT+art&cat=22&art

Believing that children raised in traditional families by a mother and a father are happier, healthier, and more successful than children raised in non-traditional environments,[46] the ACP summarizes in one paragraph, with detailed footnote citations for each of their conclusions, several of the risks of the homosexual lifestyle to children:

> Violence among homosexual partners is two to three times more common than among married heterosexual couples. Homosexual partnerships are significantly more prone to dissolution than heterosexual marriages with the average homosexual relationship lasting only two to three years. Homosexual men and women are reported to be inordinately promiscuous involving serial sex partners, even within what are loosely-termed "committed relationships." Individuals who practice a homosexual lifestyle are more likely than heterosexuals to experience mental illness, substance abuse, suicidal tendencies, and shortened life spans. Although some would claim that these dysfunctions are a result of societal pressures in America, the same dysfunctions exist at inordinately high levels among homosexuals in cultures where the practice is more widely accepted. Children reared in homosexual households are more likely to experience sexual confusion, practice homosexual behavior, and engage in sexual experimentation. Adolescents and young adults who adopt the homosexual lifestyle,

=50>.

46. A 2007 study from the U.K. Office of National Statistics concurs. Steve Doughty, "Married Couples are Healthier and Live Longer—and so do Their Children," *Daily Mail,* October 5, 2007 <http://www.dailymail.co.uk/pages/live/articles/health/thehealthnews.html?in_article_id=485790&in_page_id=1797>.

like their adult counterparts, are at increased risk of mental health problems, including major depression, anxiety disorder, conduct disorder, substance dependence, and especially suicidal ideation and suicide attempts.

To the same effect, the Spanish Association of Pediatrics (SAP) endorsed a report noting the following conditions among children raised by same-sex couples: a significant decrease in self-esteem, increased stress, confusion regarding sexual identity, an increased incidence of mental illness, drug use, promiscuity, STDs, and homosexual behavior. In addition, the report set forth statistics showing a significantly higher instance of separation and break-up in homosexual relationships than in heterosexual relationships, with deleterious consequences for the children.[47]

State and Federal courts and administrative agencies, as well as state legislatures, consistently manage to avoid focusing on negative data such as those cited by the ACP and the SAP. A simple example may help to bring this point home. Wayne Tardiff and his partner Allan Yoder were the first homosexuals in the State of New Jersey to become adoptive parents—with the official approval of all State authorities involved. Two years after the adoption Tardiff died. A few months later, Yoder died. The unfortunate result was an orphaned five year old child.[48] Since the life span of gay men averages 20 years less than that of heterosexual men (see chapter 3), the foregoing example can hardly be called exceptional. "Our parents often die early," reports Dawn Stefanowicz, author of a recently published book on her

---

47. "Experts Worldwide Find Gay Adoption Harmful for Children," Life Site News. com (May 31, 2005) <http://www.lifesite.net/ldn/2005/may/ 05053106.html>. The original Spanish-language report can be found at <http://www.fides.org/spa/approfondire/ 2005/spagna_noesigual>.

48. *The Washington Blade,* July 16, 1992, Obituaries.

experiences growing up as the daughter of a gay man (her own father died of AIDS in 1991). Those experiences are worth highlighting:

> My father's partners and ex-partners, who I had deep caring feelings for and associated with, had drastically shortened lives due to suicide, contracting HIV or AIDS. [. . .] I was at high risk of exposure to contagious STDs due to sexual molestation, my father's high-risk sexual molestation, and multiple partners. Even when my father was in what looked like monogamous relationships, he continued cruising for anonymous sex.[49]

Stefanowicz demurs to the countless gay activists supporters who claim that sexual orientation of the parents has no bearing on the psychological and psychosexual development of children.

> Over two decades of direct exposure to these stressful experiences caused me insecurity, depression, suicidal thoughts, dread, anxiousness, low self-esteem, sleeplessness and sexual confusion. Every other family member suffered severely as well.

One factor Stefanowicz found she shared with the approximately 40 other adult children of homosexuals with whom she has been in touch was their negative attitude about life in general. They all felt that the gay parenting they had received left them pitted against "insurmountable odds." Indeed, Stefanowicz was so pained by her childhood experiences that she originally vowed she would never have children." It took many years, much therapy and a happy marriage to change her mind.

Jakii Edwards, who has written about her experiences growing up with a lesbian mother, laments: "I have never heard of one program or

---

49. Dawn Stefanowicz, "The Sad Side of Gay Parenting," Mercatornet (April 25, 2007) <http://www.mercatornet.com/articles/the_sad_side_of_gay-parenting/>. *See also* Stefanowicz's autobiography, *Out From Under: the Impact of Homosexual Parenting,* Enumclaw: Annotation Press (2007). Her web site is <www.dawnstefanowicz.com>.

read a book from any psychologist or counselor who has addressed the hurts, doubts, and fears a child faces when growing up in a homosexual environment, and I have been asking myself why."[50] In the same vein, Dawn Stefanowicz rues:

> I feel sorry for [these] kids today, because they can't even go to most counselors or teachers without hearing the gay rights rhetoric. The professional may try to change your negative perspective about your parent's lifestyle choices as if you, as the child, have the problem. There's no really safe place to get help.

In that regard, the position of the American College of Pediatricians is unequivocal:

> The research literature on childrearing by homosexual parents is limited. The environment in which children are reared is absolutely critical to their development. Given the current body of research, the American College of Pediatricians believes it is inappropriate, potentially hazardous to children, and dangerously irresponsible to change the age-old prohibition on homosexual parenting, whether by adoption, foster care, or by reproductive manipulation. This position is rooted in the best available science.[51]

Why would the courts and legislatures of our country ignore the opinion of the American College of Pediatricians and other dissenting organizations? Children are the most vulnerable—and valuable—individuals in our society. They have enormous potential, and enormous emotional and developmental needs. The damage done to them by ill-advised social experiments and sexual adventurism will

---

50. Jakii Edwards, *Like Mother, Like Daughter? The Effects of Growing Up in a Homosexual Home*, Vienna: Xulon Press (2001), p. 193.

51. "Parenting Issues: Homosexual Parenting: Is it Time for Change?" American College of Pediatricians, <http://www.acpeds.org/?CONTEXT+art&cat= 22&art =50>.

not be easily reversed. Both the children and society as a whole will pay a huge price for the "liberal" politicking that is willing to sacrifice the welfare of children on the altar of political correctness.

Chapter 15:

What the Strugglers Have to Say: Testimonials.

Before concluding this study, I think it is only appropriate to let our readers hear from the strugglers themselves. They are the ultimate source of everything we know about the change process. Some of them have completed their transformation, others are still in process, but all of them understand GAP and are fully qualified to talk about it. Some of them are JONAH's own, others are not. However, they are all known to me personally. They are a remarkable group of people, and what they have to say about the process of their recovery is worth hearing. Here is their testimony.

Ben Newman: A Natural Leader of Men Steps into his Masculine Power.

Ben Newman, as indicated by the professional pseudonym that Rich Wyler chose for himself, sees himself as a "new man." Ben's chosen first name is Hebrew for "son," indicating that he is what he is today thanks to his own hard work and determination, but also that as the "new man" he is, he has "fathered" nearly a thousand "sons" who have successfully completed Journey Into Manhood, the experiential weekend program that Rich Wyler inspired and oversees. Rich took risks, overcame shame, and stepped into his masculine power. In fact, Rich has emerged as one of the intellectual leaders of the SSA masculinity movement. His influence in helping other men heal, one by one, has been awesome.

Rich is the founder and driving force of the largest non-denominational on-line support group in the world for men seeking to grow out of homosexuality (<www.peoplecanchange.com>). After successfully healing from his own emotional wounds, Rich, working together with therapist David Matheson, developed the high-impact weekend of experiential exercises and inner-healing processes for men who are serious about overcoming and resolving their unwanted same-sex attractions. I have been privileged to serve as a senior facilitative guide on many of those weekends.

Rich's story, compiled here from autobiographical material published on the People Can Change website, describes a process of self discovery in which Rich came to understand the roots of his same-sex attraction, overcame his homosexual attractions, and matured into a happily married husband and father.

> Even though I married at age 26, held a strong belief in my faith and enjoyed heterosexual family life, I was so desperate for male love, I would do anything to feel it, even for a moment, even if it were counterfeit. I lived in shame, fear and isolation. My wife knew something of my struggles, but I lied and minimized them, and she wanted to believe me.
>
> I resented the suggestion that the only politically correct solution for me was to abandon my wife and children and throw myself into the gay life. I had the opportunity to do that before I met Marie and had children with her. Back then—when the stakes were much lower—I realized that was not what I wanted.
>
> While dating men, briefly adopting a gay identity, and throwing myself into the gay lifestyle had been exhilarating at first, it had soon felt like it was killing my spirit, alienating myself from my

goals in life, from G–d and a sense of higher purpose. I had realized then that I didn't want to be affirmed as gay; I wanted to be affirmed as a man.

It began with hope, when I met a reparative therapist, David, who had made the transition from homosexual attractions himself. I finally understood that it was really possible to change. David was the first real live human being I had ever met who said, "I felt gay, and thought I wanted to live my life that way, but I found a way out that gave me more happiness and peace by healing rather than indulging." I didn't know what that meant, exactly, but I trusted that he, more than anyone else I had ever met, could help me find a way out of the pit I was in.

I went into reparative therapy weekly for two and a half years, including 14 months of weekly group therapy with other men who were seeking change. Therapy became my lifeline as I began withdrawing from sexual addiction, digging underneath to discover and heal the underlying fear and hurt that I been anesthetizing all this time through homosexual lust. With David working with me every step of the way, I began to build new relationships, take new risks, release long-suppressed anger and hurt, and come out of my shame.

The first order of business on Rich's initial visit with David was signing a release form designed to make sure (and, if necessary, document) that Rich's choice of reparative therapy was informed and uncoerced. Among other things, the form disclosed that the APA's official stance was that sexual orientation could not be changed, and that attempting to do so might even cause psychological harm.

Yeah, right, I thought, as if the double life I was living was not causing psychological harm enough. I knew I had dug myself into a very deep pit out of which I saw no escape. I was living a complete double life. On the surface, I appeared to be a happy husband and father, a religious individual, and a successful professional. On the inside, however, I was hiding secret lusts and addictive behaviors. After 14 years of this pattern, I had surrendered myself to it, convinced that I was going to have to live my life this way, somehow hoping the inside and outside would never collide nor destroy my life.

In our first session, I blurted out the whole story with a frankness and abandon that was unprecedented for me. David was safe to tell. I didn't have to worry about seeking his approval or about there being any consequences in my life for divulging my story to him. He responded with candor: "Your life is a mess." I was surprised at his bluntness, but knew it to be true. "I can help you work through the immediate crisis," he said, "but unless you go a whole lot deeper than that, you'll just go back out there and delay the inevitable recurrence—probably with even greater consequences next time." I agreed. I had hit bottom. I was ready to do whatever it took to salvage the mess of my life. Over the next several weeks, I practically ran to David's office each Tuesday evening, finding a place of safety and solace where I could get help and guidance with the darkest secrets of my life. I grieved with him over the intense pain I had caused my wife and her very legitimate hurt and rage at me. How relieved I was that, seeing my resolve to work with David and with hope in this new resource, she tentatively decided not to leave—at least not yet.

The floodgates opened, and in therapy David and I explored a lifetime of perceived rejection from men. In successive therapy sessions, I cried and I raged. To my amazement, David encouraged the full expression of this anger in my sessions with him. But I wanted to freeze up instead, paralyzed with fear and shame. Wasn't anger bad? I thought. Wasn't it out of control? Good boys don't get mad. And worst of all, what might I uncover just underneath the paralysis? But David taught me it was this hidden anger and shame, in part, that I was turning on myself self-destructively and that was driving me to act out sexually. The anger needed to be expressed legitimately. It needed to be honored.

And so the anger spilled out of me: anger at my father for being emotionally checked out of my life; rage at Mike the Bully for his constant ridicule of me in high school; rage at my mother for shaming me over my maleness; hurt that I had been carrying around inside of me my whole life, where it could continue to attack me from within. With David coaching me, I visualized fighting back, ejecting the taunts, shame and rejection from my heart, and then destroying them. Over the months we repeated this process, until at last I could find no more anger stirring within me. At last, having emptied a lifetime of pent-up anger from my wounded soul, I was ready to release and forgive.

At other times, David worked with me on my addictive cycles. We explored in depth what seemed to trigger my acting out—stress, anger, fear, almost any uncomfortable emotion caused me to try to seek solace in the drug-like rush of forbidden sexual experiences. I determined to return to Sexaholics Anonymous, where I had once started to make progress toward breaking my addictive cycles. [It was there] I learned to surrender my will, and my lust, to G–d. Overcoming my "heterophobia"—my fear of straight men—I learned to pick up the phone and ask for help when I was tempted, instead of going into isolation. In the moment of temptation, I learned to seek out unconditional brotherly love from good men, friends who knew of my struggles and loved me anyway, instead of seeking the counterfeit of homosexual lust. The love of true brothers began to replace the lust of counterfeit lovers. As I did, and as I processed my emotional life in depth with David each week, the cycles first slowed and then tapered off dramatically.

David taught me about defensive detachment, and I learned how I had defensively rejected men in order to protect myself from being hurt by them. I pored over a book by the clinic's director, Dr. Joseph Nicolosi, called "Reparative Therapy of Male Homosexuality," and was amazed to find my exact psychological profile, it seemed, complete with defensive detachment, described in his book.

David helped me open my mind and heart to the possibility of finding a heterosexual man or men whom I could turn to for help and support throughout my week. It was terrifying, but I approached Mark, a man about eight years older than I, and asked him to be a spiritual mentor to me. He readily agreed. He knew nothing about homosexuality, but he knew about G–d, and he knew about pain (and shame), and he was more than willing to be there for me. I talked with him at least weekly, sometimes several times a week, baring my soul. I called him when I was tempted to act out. I called him when I stumbled, and he helped lift me back up. He gave me the loving, caring "fathering" I had always longed for but only imagined.

Still, there were plenty of times I froze in fear at the prospect of reaching out to other men in friendship. I was convinced that heterosexual men didn't have friends—didn't even need friends. Their wives or girlfriends were supposed to be enough for them. Certainly, my father never had any friends, and never went anywhere socially without my mother. I could only remember one friend that my three much-older brothers had between them. How could I rely on heterosexual men to be there for me, to be my friends, to meet my needs for male companionship and affirmation? I had always believed the only men who wanted anything to do with other men were gay.

David challenged me to open my eyes, to look beyond my ingrained perceptions. "Your soul demands male connection, and that desire WILL express itself, one way or another. It WILL come out. Suppressing it will only work for a short while, and then the dam will burst. If you don't experience authentic, intimate male connection platonically, the need will absolutely drive you to find it sexually. One way or another, the need will be met."

The words resonated within me: "One way or another, the need will be met." I knew it was true for me. I pushed myself to reach out of my shell. I started observing heterosexual men more. I started to notice men going out to eat together, going to the movies together, going to men's groups, working on cars together. At parties, I noticed the men cluster in groups separate from the women within moments of arriving. They hung out together watching a game on TV as they talked, or playing pool, or some other activity.

I was discovering the world of men as if for the first time. I would come into a therapy session with David and share my discoveries with him as I sought to understand and demystify the world of men. We talked about the things that men do, how they are at parties, how they are with each other and with women. I started to understand them, then appreciate them—then, a bit at a time—to feel that I wasn't so different from them.

David became my surrogate father, my surrogate brother, my mentor into the world of men. At one point, I remember looking deeply into his dark eyes as long silence passed between us. I felt how much joy he experienced in my growth. Just looking into his eyes I could feel him affirming me as a man, and for the first time, I realized, "I am taking in his masculinity, and feeling him affirming mine, and I am not even touching him, let alone having any sexual feelings for him. I can do it through the eyes! I don't need to do it through my genitals, or even my hands. I can feel his love and connect with his maleness silently, without touching him." It was a joyous moment—a moment when I felt completely male, and completely affirmed as a man.

In the last few months of my therapy with David, sensing my need for professional therapy was coming to an end, I took greater command of the sessions to make sure I dealt with everything I needed his help with: lingering feelings of rejection I needed to release; hurts I needed to forgive. More and more, I was coming in to therapy sessions reporting joy instead of hurt, anger or fear, sharing my increased sense of identity and power as a man, reporting on new friendships I was building and new risks I was taking to test my increased inner strength.

As a young man, Rich had been the object of taunting and ridicule by his same-sex peers owing to his lack of athletic ability. As a result, Rich had developed feelings of exclusion and inferiority that contributed to his defensive detachment from other males. So he sought out a sports mentor.

One of my most frightening steps was to ask another man, Rob, to teach me to play basketball. For me, this was a huge risk. The fear I had around sports was nothing short of phobic, but something inside of me demanded that I face this fear. It was hard enough to approach Rob and ask him to teach me, but to actually show up at the basketball court for my first lesson was even more frightening. I was actually more embarrassed about my ineptness around sports than I was about my homosexual past. So I was making myself completely vulnerable to Rob by revealing to him that I didn't know the first thing about basketball.

Rob's non-critical coaching helped me begin to heal my decades-old anxiety over athletics and the fear of being mocked by other boys. One time, I e-mailed David with pride: "I can do a jump shot! For the first time in my life, I did a jump shot!" He e-mailed back that he was thrilled for me, and he could relate. Who else could have understood the significance of that for a 36-year-old man?

As they continued to work together, David encouraged Rich to attend one of the experiential weekends JONAH counsels as beneficial for its strugglers. Rich registered for a New Warriors weekend. It is sponsored by the Mankind Project and is an intensive weekend initiation training for men. Although Rich was hesitant the first couple of times David mentioned it, he warmed up to the idea as his fear of men dissipated. He resolved to go.

> I practically floated into his office my first session after returning from the weekend. "It was awesome!" I reported. "I discovered MEN!" I was like them; they were like me! I was a man among men. The realization sank into me as never before. For the first time in my life, I drank in this awesome realization: men DO feel, men DO fear, men DO care. I saw *at last that I was like other men*, after all, or they were like me. *I belonged.*
>
> I walked out of David's office for the last time on August 25, 1999, 27 months after I had first walked in. I was a different man. Stronger. Happier. More grounded. Whole. I had been "sexually sober" and faithful to my wife for two years—and had found peace and joy in doing so. I didn't need David as a therapist any more, because now I could be in honest relationships with others. I would take the gifts he had given me with me into every other relationship from now on. I could make friends. I could ask for help. I could be real. And more than anything else, I could love. I had learned to give love and receive love from other men as my brothers, and trust them with my heart. In this, I truly had found what I had been looking for all my life.
>
> I have the most positive friendships with other heterosexual men that I've ever had in my life. They give me more joy and masculine affirmation than gay lust ever did. I have overcome a lifetime of shame as a male and fear and distrust of other men. Instead of lusting after their masculinity to fill my emptiness, I now identify with them as men and relate to them as a man among men. Same-sex attraction has been replaced by same-sex affinity. Today, at last, I am a man among men.

I now have a solid identity as a heterosexual man. My marriage is better than ever, my family happier.[1]

In February 1999, acknowledging how much Rich had grown and healed—especially in light of the fact that he had now been faithful to his wife for a year and a half—Rich and Marie decided to renew their marriage vows and exchange new wedding bands.

Josh L.: One Man Shares his Thoughts as he Struggles Through the Process of Change.

An investment banker in his late twenties working in New York City's financial district, Josh grew up in a stringently religious but classically dysfunctional family, with an emotionally stunted and overly disciplinarian father and a deeply frustrated and emotionally needy mother. Once, when Josh was eight years old, his father became angry with him while they were walking to *shul* (synagogue). Dad pulled down Josh's pants and spanked him right there in the street. Josh would sometimes hide in the closet or under his father's desk in order to avoid his father's apparent hostility. Neglected by her emotionally aloof husband, Josh's mother turned to her son for comfort and support. Psychologically speaking, Mom used Josh as her surrogate husband. The pathologically close relationship between mother and son further stunted Josh's psychosexual development.

Hampered by his home environment, and intimidated by his peers, Josh soon developed feelings of inferiority. His awkward attempts to form friendships with other boys were roundly rebuffed.

By the time Josh reached the 11th grade, Josh had openly rebelled

---

1. Sadly, in 2006 Rich's wife died after a courageous struggle with cancer.

against his parents and his religious upbringing. He also found in gay porn a way of coping with his interpersonal dysfunction and gender confusion. Of course, the pornography provided very little relief. Once "used," the magazine or video would lose its fascination and be discarded—a pattern predictive of future promiscuity. Graduating to phone sex, Josh, age 21, grew friendly with the phone-sex operator, Martin, who offered to become Josh's "coming out" coach—meaning that he would "help" him learn how to become actively gay. ("Coming Out" is verbal shorthand for the concept of "coming out of the closet," that is, "raising one's own consciousness" as a self-identifying homosexual and thus accepting and celebrating one's same-sex attractions. It also has the effect of increasing one's commitment to the gay subculture).

Martin introduced Josh to gay New York City, teaching him how to dress, how to act, and where the gay clubs and bars were. During the spring of 2001, the "coming-out coach" convinced the then 23 year-old to try gay sex. After unsuccessfully propositioning him himself, Martin introduced Josh to a group of gay men not involved in the gay bar scene. One of them Josh later recalled as "really good looking—until we finished fooling around. Then he wasn't good looking anymore." Recognizing a pattern similar to that which he had previously established with pornography, Josh noted astutely, "That happened with all the guys I fooled around with."

Trying to explain his own SSA, Josh wrote:

The lure for me is feeling like a person—perhaps it is [owing to] the attention I received from that one guy. At that moment, I [feel] I am actually someone who is worth caring about and loving. It's the physical and emotional connection I feel at the time of messing around. The instantaneous mood change I experience. But, of course, although I never feel so great after the act, I don't think so much about that. To me, it's a need for instantaneous gratification. Society taught me a contemporary meaning of freedom that is free ourselves of any restrictions that prevent us from seeking immediate gratification of our desires.

No one wants to be alone, everyone wants to have someone

there for him. For me, it is like fuel. I will hook up with a guy and feel confident for a while. Then, I feel lonely and needy again. The emptiness returns. So I hook up again. But the funny thing is that I won't want to hook up with the same guy again. No matter how much I think he is my type. I pull back and I'm afraid of that guy. It is not cuz I enjoy anonymous sex. I fear getting too close to him; yet part of me wants that closeness. Sex is physical. It is closeness without having to emotionally connect, something I cannot do. Because I yearn for a closeness—but deep down I am afraid to speak in order to connect—I have found sex as a way to connect without words.

Despite his addictive behavior, Josh remained deeply conflicted. While he believed that his "gayness" constituted the "ultimate revenge" against his parents, his sexual acting out sharply conflicted with his deepest personal values. Moreover, Josh found the many degrading aspects of the gay lifestyle deeply disturbing. Behind the carefree and liberated facade, he could see inner turmoil, anguish, and fear. With his critical faculties aroused, Josh began to chronicle his observations.

Noting Josh's lingering ambivalence, "Coach" Martin invited him to spend a weekend in a large, island vacation house with a group of young men Josh had met previously and knew as successful, contented "yuppies," well adjusted in the gay world. The experience proved to be enlightening.

Arriving before dinner on Friday, Josh noted the weekend roster included four couples besides himself and his coach. Another man, to whom Josh had previously been introduced, was expected, but never showed. Describing the dinner that followed, Josh wrote in his journal:

> Everyone seemed to be so happy, lively, and engaging. The conversation flowed easily. Everyone seemed so erudite. Most of the meals were eaten together. During that time the men talked about life, accomplishments, happy times and that kind of thing. They seemed so carefree, relaxed, and confident. I thought, "This life

can't be so bad. These guys really seem to be cool."

However, as the weekend progressed, Josh's initial impressions were challenged. One of the older men opined: "Guys my age should not worry or even think about THE disease (HIV/AIDS)." Since Josh was likely to catch the disease sooner or later, advised this individual, Josh should "get it over with and catch the disease."[2] Thereafter, suggested this guru, Josh would be able to live the rest of his life with reckless abandon and worry free. The only response noted in Josh's journal: "Dear G–d!"

Josh was also able to observe that many of his fellow guests seemed very clearly to be affected by the "Peter Pan Syndrome"[3]—basking in perpetual adolescence and never expecting to grow old. In stark contrast, Josh also noticed a number of highly visible—and obviously unattached men—wandering around the island. These men were part of the "older" crowd—which Josh defined as "over 40"—and they clearly emitted an aura of loneliness and sadness. They had outlived what Josh called "their 15 years of fun." Josh wrote about these men, "What now? Where do these guys go from here?"

By the time Josh left on Monday night, he had learned a lot about his fellow guests. Josh's journal contrasts his initial impressions of these men with his final assessments on parting. "Friday night confused me cuz everyone seemed so great. Well, Saturday, Sunday, Monday and the weekend rain really allowed me to see another side

---

2. This philosophy is known in the gay community as "chasing the bug."

3. Dr. Don Kiley describes the Peter Pan Syndrome as consisting of men with "a poor adjustment to reality . . . who indulge in an impetuous lifestyle. Narcissism locks them inside themselves, while an unrealistic ego trip convinces them that they can and must do whatever their fantasies suggest. [. . .] Pursuit of other people's acceptance seems their only way to find self-acceptance. Their temper tantrums are disguised as manly assertion. They take love for granted, never learning how to give it in return. They pretend to be grown-ups but actually behave like spoiled children." *The Peter Pan Syndrome: Men Who Have Never Grown Up,* New York: Avon Books (1984), p. xvi.

of them." Here are some of Josh's journal entries:

Person
Joe (30ish)

Initial Impression
Handsome midwesterner who appears to be a financial whiz. Seems to have it made. Lives in a 1600 square foot New York City apt with a wraparound balcony. He ran the place, cooked all the meals and functioned as the responsible "house-mother." He stays in the vacation house most of the summer—his business can be done by telephone. He loves the Island so much that he wants his ashes spread throughout the place when he dies. I was so into him.

Reality
Not only is he HIV positive, but he is fighting several forms of cancer. I'm afraid his wish to have his ashes spread over the Island when he dies will come true . . . all too soon.

Person
Manny (20s)

Initial Impression
Moved in with Joe this past month. Describes himself as a color stylist who charges $135 for what my non-English speaking barber performs for $9. Meditates a lot.

Reality
Also HIV poz. Likes the idea of caretaking Joe. Did not feel entitled to having his own needs met. Sees himself as a burden to others.

Person
Guy (40s)

Initial Impression
Successful attorney. Seems to have it all. Still has the looks and the money to do whatever he wishes. Erudite and intellectual. Reads the NY Times every day, without fail. This guy is great. The anchor of

the group. I envy him.

Reality
HIV Positive.

Person
Robby (30)

Initial Impression
Guy's partner for about a year. Queeny appearance. Seems at ease with himself. Quiet guy. Really nice. Not much to say about him.

Reality
Although coupled with Guy, unsure about his status. Unable to get closer to him.

Person
Donald (35)

Initial Impression
Psychologist. Weekend guest like me. Nice guy with a great job. Has money. Liked to pontificate.

Reality
Although 6 friends of his are HIV poz and 13 died of AIDS-related illnesses, he still believes the gay lifestyle can best actualize a person's potential.

Person
Buddy (25)

Initial Impression
Coupled with Donald. Student/Singer/Writer. Closest to my age. Awesome personality. Seems to have his act all together. Great-looking. Lives it up. Has the looks, the body, the confidence. Appears so happy about life & so comfortable with his sexuality. Truly an inspirational figure.

Reality
Recovering alcoholic and recovering drug abuser. Trembles near liquor or any other kind of substance.

Person
Brian (33)

Initial Impression
Upper West Side computer geek. Coach had introduced him to me in the City. Appeared to be a fun loving guy and a party animal. When he didn't show this weekend, I wondered why.

Reality
He jumped out of his apt window last week. The guys said he was manic-depressive. He flew to San Fran for 2 days before coming home to take his own life. Group blamed it on his being incoherent (perhaps drug-induced).

Person
Martin (38) (My coach)

Initial Impression
Saw his mission as teaching me "all about the ever so happy gay life." Good looking. I was really excited about spending so much time with him. I couldn't wait to go with him, spend quality time, and know him as a real person. I wanted to better understand what makes him tick. I had so many questions for him about this lifestyle and his apparently successful adaptation to it.

Reality
He annoyed the hell out of me by Monday. He is the one who kept trying to convince me that father issues cannot be the cause of SSA because he had a perfect relationship with his father. But the truth differed. He revealed how Dad was quite distant from his family because he traveled a lot. Martin actually craves constant attention and is very immature. The best illustration is an embarrassing tee-shirt he wore that read, "Does this dick in my mouth make me look gay?" My reaction: "No, it makes you look sad and pathetic."

Though he had previously denied that being gay may be hazardous to my health, he reeled off dozens of guys he knows who are either HIV poz or dying of AIDS. By Monday, I was simply nauseous being around him.

The more Josh progressed along the garden path to gaydom, the more confused and conflicted he became.

When I turned 25, I realized that maybe I'm losing sight of that dream where I thought I could have a family. Living a gay life enables me to have 15 years of adolescent fun without serious responsibilities, but then what? While that's a lot of years of fun, where will it leave me? I thought about the following contradictions:

• My straight friends are moving on with their lives, maturing as human beings, falling in love, getting married; I'm living for the moment, emotionally functioning as an adolescent seeking never to grow up.

• My straight friends are rushing their wives to the hospital to give birth; I'm driving to meet two guys who have the number 69 in their internet screen names.

• My straight friends are in the delivery room, experiencing a moment of true intimacy with their wives and achieving G–d's ultimate blessing, the birth of a healthy child; I'm either in the chat room or hooking up anonymously with other guys, thereby creating a false intimacy, that is, a self-created illusion of connection that permits me to connect through my pain.

• My straight friends are taking pictures of their new baby; I'm downloading pictures of masculine bodies which I envy and eroticize.

• My straight friends are naming their kids; I don't even know the name of the guy I'm messing with.

Recognizing the acute state of ambivalence in which he found himself, Josh finally called the JONAH message line. In our ensuing phone conversation, I explained to him the typical causes of homosexuality, some aspects of which he felt corresponded to his own past. When he asked if he could talk with someone who has actually changed, I introduced him to Don and to Marshall (*see below*). Each openly shared with Josh the pain and agony they had gone through for so many years before coming to JONAH. They also congratulated him for waking up a lot sooner than they had, explaining that generally the younger a person is when he starts the process of healing, the easier it is to complete it.

Shortly thereafter, I drove out to Brooklyn to meet Josh in person. We talked for several hours. Noting Josh's hesitancy, I could see that three factors in particular weighed heavily on his mind: (1) Fear of turning his back on all the indoctrination he had absorbed from his coming out coach; (2) Fear of losing his gay friendships and the acceptance he felt he had received from the gay community; (3) and, most pressing of all, his fear of failure. What if he actually went through the entire process successfully and then, for whatever reason, found that he could not realize his dream of wife and family? What if during the recovery process he were rejected by the larger society and could no longer find solace among his former friends?

Yet, the deeper our conversation went, the more Josh realized that the "comfort" he felt in the gay world was counterfeit. On the surface, the gay lifestyle seemed to enhance his enjoyment of life, but in reality Josh could see that it had become a form of bondage. He seemed to understand the importance of grappling with his own self-defeating emotional defense mechanisms.

Josh joined JONAH. He immediately availed himself of our listserv to reach out to fellow members.

> I don't know where I am at or if I am simply going, or if I'm coming and going at the moment. While I'm scared about the future, I want to be part of your struggle, your challenge, your failures, and your successes. At this time, I can't support you guys the way it seems you support each other. Perhaps one day I will be able to do

so. While I fear the future, I think I fear the present even more. Confusion remains. Nevertheless, I keep thinking that you all may be the Proverbial Pill that will enable me to experience true happiness—even though I intellectually and emotionally understand that only I have the power to create it.

On JONAH's recommendation, Josh switched from the gay-affirmative therapist with whom he was then counseling, to one who believed deeply in GAP. JONAH also proposed that Josh follow a self-help program consisting of "bibliotherapy" (reading books and websites by "ex-gays" and reparative therapists), networking with others in the recovery process, and consistent attendance at group support activities, experiential weekends, and other gender-affirming processes. This work enabled Josh to begin tearing down the emotional walls that had previously imprisoned him. These defenses covered up Josh's authentic emotions and masked Josh's true self—the hurting "inner child" he had buried deep within him for so many years.

Josh achieved his first big breakthrough during one of the experiential weekends recommended by JONAH.

> I met someone this weekend. He was 10 years old. He was so afraid. He was scared and hurt. He had no one to turn to. His only friend was fear. I met him a few times. He wanted someone to listen to him and to hold him. He wanted someone to hear his need to give and receive love. He wanted to be held. He wanted to be told that he is OK and that his life will go on. He wanted encouragement and to be told that he will succeed. I met him. I saw him. I held his hand. I told him it was OK. I told him he can be afraid. I told him he can be loved. I told him it will be OK. He was me—and I now know I have the ability to reassure him and tell him everything will be OK . . . Yes!

Three years into the program, Josh has made phenomenal progress. For the first two years, however, he was unable to sever his ties to the gay community. This is how he explained his *then* situation to a fellow struggler just joining the program:

> I am still conflicted, not wanting to fully give in to a gay lifestyle (deathstyle?) but determined to create a traditional family (man + woman + kids + dog named Charlie). I came out to my parents and still retain gay friends who don't know I am in the process of change. I own the gay feelings I have ... yet something holds me back from fully coming out and living gay. The process of change has helped me immensely. My sense of self-confidence, of masculinity, and of seeing a way out of a gender double bind has never been stronger. Yet, I continually question the process. So many times I wish I can just give it all up, go fully gay, and come back here to JONAH when I'm 40 years old, once I have already "enjoyed the best years of my life."
>
> [. . .]
>
> I've come to realize that I can control the acting out sexually but still the attraction persists. Every time I continue to find myself attracted to a man, I tell myself, "I must be gay." Other times, I see the man inside of me and realize that *what I seek in another man is what I am looking for in myself.* I often feel as if I'm in a no-man's land—not gay, not straight. I hate that. I hate this in-between space where I am no longer who I used to be, but am not yet the person I seek to be. I'd rather be a gay man in a gay world or a straight man in a straight world than a no man in a no man's land. I no longer feel gay but I don't yet feel straight. I cannot fully embrace the future because I cannot fully let go of the past. "Some days I just wanna go out and be picked up by dudes—to feel attractive. On those days, I wanna go all-out gay and express this part of me... to see what it feels like to be an all-out Madonna loving, George-Bush hating, Prada worshipping, Desperate-Housewife watching fag. Yet on other days, I just wanna come home to a wife, a crying kid, a family, a home, the Jewish tradition I grew up with, and a reverent spirituality. In sum, a happiness in which my greatest aspirations are fulfilled. What holds me back from fully embracing the latter lifestyle? Some skepticism, some fear, some wondering if a girl will actually know my past and still want me, accept me and marry me.

The story I tell myself is what holds me back.

Will Josh succeed? Six months ago, when I last spoke to him, Josh indicated that he needed to "take a break" from our program. At that time he was still maintaining links with the gay world (though I do not know the extent of his involvement), and still showing ambivalence about completing the change process. Nevertheless, I have good reason to hope that, with time, he will return to complete his journey. Josh's wounds were exceptionally deep, yet he had made a lot of progress. He had come to recognize the sources of pain and rage previously bottled up within him. He had learned to identify the coping mechanisms he had previously used to justify "acting out," and to recognize that those mechanisms were leading him nowhere while leaving his real issues unaddressed. He had *unlearned* the sordid lessons taught him by his coming-out coach, as well as the false information absorbed from a society and media in the grip of political correctness. He was no longer afraid to tell his gay friends about his journey toward sexual wholeness, or to explain to skeptics how his journey had already contributed to his maturity, self-confidence, sense of manhood, and emotional growth. Indeed, in our last discussion, Josh indicated his readiness to speak on behalf of JONAH at any time. Josh was learning to compensate for the incredible loneliness he had experienced during childhood—not by acting out, but in a manner congruent with his intellectual understanding and spiritual beliefs. As Josh himself is aware, it is his fears of rejection by the "straight" world and by a potential bride that are holding him back. Such fears are not unreasonable, and it takes considerable courage to confront them. However, Josh has shown so much courage in successfully overcoming other overwhelming issues that I continue to be optimistic about his chances of ultimate success. Time will tell.

Don M.: One Man's Escape from Personal *Gehennom* (Hell).

One of the men to whom I had referred Josh for advice and

counsel was Don M., then forty-two, married, and religiously observant. Don had been sexually abused at age four, then again at ages eight and eleven. By the time he was twelve years old, Don was hanging out in men's rooms, looking for sex. Like both Jeff (*see* Chapter Two, above) and Josh, Don was defensively detached from his father. His loitering in restrooms was a neurotic expression of his unconscious search for the love he felt he could not receive from his father. His body-image wounds came from his shorter than normal height and a minor birth defect. Don felt inferior to other boys because of his minimal athletic ability and also because of a learning disability that hampered his academic performance. The sordid attentions he received from older men made him feel that he was "somebody." At age sixteen, after four years of such homosexual encounters, Don approached his parents, confessed his homosexuality and asked for help. They had a simplistic "cure." A *shiddach* (arranged marriage) was made, and the discussion was closed. At age eighteen, Don was married to a lovely young girl who did not have a clue about his sexual issues (until more than 20 years later).

Ironically, the marriage was, by all appearances, a success, producing, moreover, five children over the next 24 years. During all that time, however, Don had been leading a secret double life, engaging in homosexual liaisons as many as six or seven times a week. He would start cruising for men from early in the morning before *Tefilla* (prayers), and would run back to *shul* to pray. Sometimes, on *Shabbat*, he would skip *shul* altogether, slink over to the bookstore around the corner, pick up someone for anonymous sex, and then return home—racked with guilt but in time for lunch. He was a genuine sex addict. Then, one day, Don heard about the movie "Trembling Before G–d." Thinking the film's promoters might be able to advise him, he sent an e-mail to their website asking for help. In response, someone called and introduced himself as a gay psychologist who could relate to his pain. Don told him of his anguish. This purported therapist tried to convince Don that the reason for his unhappiness was his so-called "internalized homophobia" and advised Don that if he stopped hating himself for simply being who he is (that is, "a gay man"), everything would be fine. He then invited Don to his apartment for a Hanukkah gathering—certainly unusual conduct for a licensed psychotherapist! When Don asked why he was being invited, the therapist suggested that the cure for his ailment was to meet another Orthodox married man with SSA, and this he might do at the Hanukkah party! In this way, continued the "therapist," Don could have an on-going affair with another man without getting caught. Since both were *frum* (observant) and married, they would share a common interest in maintaining secrecy. Life could go on. Don tried to explain to the man that he wasn't looking for a partner or for more sexual affairs. He had had enough! He wanted out. The "therapist," however, wouldn't let go. As Don told it in a talk he gave at Baltimore's Liberty Jewish Center,

> He kept on talking for another twenty minutes, trying to convince me that this was the answer to my problems, that I was born this way, that G-d created me this way, and that I should accept the gay lifestyle. I asked him whether any therapists could help me change. Not only did he say no, but he represented that such practices were "banned" by both the American Psychological and Psychiatric Associations.[4] Of course, he did not tell me anything about JONAH either.

Thirty-four years of constant emotional conflict between his homosexual desires and his deep spiritual longing for a normal life of

---

4. Even though supporters of the gay agenda state this consistently, it remains a mystery why it is necessary to exaggerate the positions of the two APA's. In 1973, the American Psychiatric Association removed homosexuality as a mental illness from the Diagnostic & Statistical Manual (DSM), but specifically provided that therapists may treat "ego-dystonic homosexuality" (that is, where an individual's same-sex attraction is incongruent with his/her values and beliefs.) The American Psychological Association followed suit shortly thereafter. For more detail on this matter, *see* Chapter 11, pp. 407-11.

Jewish observance and family harmony brought Don to the very brink of suicide. Don described that moment in an article printed in New York's *The Jewish Press* (August 23, 2002):

> I was 10 seconds away from ending all the pain and suffering I had been through. At that moment, *Hashem* (G-d) put a thought in my head: you will not die, but rather simply hurt yourself and others who love you, thereby increasing your own pain and frustration.... So, at the last second, I stopped, and, at that precise moment, realized that I needed to find help somewhere.
>
> I cannot begin to tell you how it hurts to have a problem such as SSA, or to be unable to discuss it with anyone in the entire world, and to feel trapped in a *Gehennom* (hell) that you don't know how to exit. Fortunately, *Hashem* gave me a clue. He gave me the thought that perhaps if I called a particularly competent *Rav*, I might get assistance. I called one of the leading rabbis in my community. He doesn't know me but, of course, I knew who he was and what a *Talmid Chacham* (learned man) he was. I told him about my pain and suffering and all that I had been through. He listened carefully and advised me to call a therapist friend of his in Brooklyn. When I did so, he, in turn, recommended I call JONAH....
>
> [...]
>
> Those in the community need to understand, as the Lubavitcher Rebbe once said in a 1986 *Sicha* (discourse), that "a special obligation lies on the parents, educators, and counselors to educate those afflicted with this problem [and] at the same time, to take a loving and caring attitude by extending a helping hand." To do so does not mean to ignore the issue, or sweep it under the rug. It also does not mean buying into today's politically correct rhetoric that same-sex attractions can lead to a perfectly acceptable alternative lifestyle. Rather, it means that our communal leaders, synagogues and community centers need to look to organizations like JONAH which help educate us how to heal the underlying emotional wounds resulting in personality aspects which retard one's psychosexual and psychosocial development. When the causes of this developmental arrest are revealed, understood, and felt through the head, the heart,

the body, and the soul, only then will an individual so afflicted experience appropriate gender identity, release latent heterosexual desires and fulfill unmet love needs, all in a manner consistent with G-d's plan of creation.

I am pleased to state, *Baruch Hashem* [Thank G-d], that I have changed. I have learned about controlling that which the Torah forbids. I am now authentic and honest with my wife and am working to recreate our relationship as two equal partners.

Don's success is directly attributable to the intensive work he did over a period of approximately 15 months. He was one of those who aggressively took advantage of many of the resources we recommend to strugglers to overcome their SSA. He participated in our regular support meetings, listened to numerous tapes of ex-strugglers and therapists, attended several experiential weekends, and intensively involved himself with a number of different therapists, each with different skill sets, in order to deal with his individual and family issues. Don was a driven person, determined to fill in those gaps in his social growth which had simply stopped during his pre-adolescent and adolescent years. His ability to learn and internalize new developmental skills and, in the process, to reclaim his inherent masculinity, provided him with the necessary tools to stop acting out his pathology and to become one of JONAH's talented mentors and teachers.

Don concluded his speech to the Liberty Jewish Center in Baltimore with the following memorable words:

I now help others as part of my recovery process and, most importantly, am out of the closet of shame and isolation. I am clean, live life without lies and deceit, and am truly engaged in the process of *teshuvah*. G-d challenged me to go through *gehennom* and come out whole. He challenged me to understand, by personal experience, the depths of despair which a person can go through and yet come out whole. He challenged me to understand the difference between sexual brokenness, sexual wholeness, and sexual holiness. The fact that I was successful is a testimony to *Hashem's* wisdom and the resiliency with which He endowed me. I hope others of you who are aware of people conflicted with SSA take to heart my story that change is possible—but only if the person seeking change really wants to and is motivated.

Don and his wife are now grandparents. Don has become a better husband, father, and grandfather because of the gender-affirming processes he engaged. This is not to say, however, that everything will be hunky-dory from here on out. Don must still deal with a variety of other issues, including some residual addictive tendencies, long-term health issues, and periodic flare-ups in his marriage directly attributable to the changes in his personality. For example, he no longer passively accepts his wife's every wish, as he did in the past, when he would try to ingratiate himself with her out of guilt and shame.

Marshall S.: a Feminized Male Recovers his Gender Identity by Discovering Himself.

Marshall S., the other person to whom I referred Josh, a man in his mid-40s, might be the man next door. Twice married, he fathered two boys with his present wife, makes a solid six-figure income as a high-tech sales person, and lives in a spacious, five-bedroom house in the suburbs. He coaches little league baseball for his kids, plays on a co-ed softball team with his wife and neighbors, and studies Torah and Talmud at the local Chabad house. One would never guess that this emotionally together, physically handsome, and financially successful man had a past that involved sexual encounters with hundreds of men, gay pornography, internet chat rooms, and compulsive masturbation.

In fact, when Marshall was in his early 20s, he so identified with the female sex in manner and dress that the patrons of the gay bar where he worked as a bartender voted him the person most likely to undergo a sex change operation. As he told me in a private e-mail,

[They] teased me because I was feminine in so many ways. Although I did not dress like a woman, I wore tight clothing. I had very long hair with a blond pony tail, long painted fingernails, a lightning-bolt earring and dark glasses. Because I wanted status in the bar, and felt I couldn't be masculine enough, I went the other way by copying the mannerisms of other feminized gay guys.[5]

Marshall's childhood profile fits a number of the men with whom I work. He reported that his dad was "a wuss" who was so dominated by his (Marshall's) mother that Marshall spent most of his life "looking for a strong man" to replace Dad. He had body-image problems, viewing himself as a weak and effeminate boy. He was a "compliant child" but maintained "a sneaky rebellious side." He was also sexually molested by "an older neighborhood kid." When that relationship became known in his school and neighborhood, he became identified by the other boys as "the little faggot." To dull the pain he felt, he liberally used drugs and alcohol and had sex with whatever men would have him. He even had a steady affair with a married man in the community where he lived. Not knowing how to live autonomously, he felt he needed other men to validate his existence.

Given the multitude of his problems, Marshall's recovery took nearly a dozen years. During this lengthy process, Marshall availed himself of the resources of several organizations, including New Warriors, People Can Change, JONAH, Sexaholics Anonymous, and Alcoholics Anonymous. His turnaround came when he finally realized that he was sexualizing the envy he felt for other men.

Marshall spoke about his first attempts at changing his sexual orientation:

> I joined a group involved in transformational technologies, a "post-EST" group of people where the emphasis was on being authentic. The woman who ran the group remembers me coming to

---

5. This is a fairly common phenomenon in the gay community.

> meet her before the weekend retreat to inform her, "I am not really gay. My lover is though. And, going to this retreat will make us break up." She recalls the humor of my statement. I was a feminine, slightly built guy and my lover looked like Christopher Reeves. However, she took my feelings at face value and worked with me both during and after the weekend. She showed me how a guy sits, brushes his hair, walks, talks, *etc*. During this time, I also began body building. My female coach also stated that when I was out with her, she saw a strong masculine man. However, when she observed me around others she saw me revert to the little feminine kid image I projected as a teenager.

Through this process, Marshall's masculine energy and identification started to become stronger and more deeply imbedded. Thus at age 23, he "decided to change teams," and believed the way to do so was to "get married." Marshall had become emotionally involved with his "post-EST" group counselor, and after introducing him to heterosexual sex, she ultimately became his first wife.

The relationship did not last long. The marriage, says Marshall, was "a disaster," but, as he realized, the failure was due in large part to his addictions to drugs, alcohol, and internet pornography. Thus, Marshall decided to quit drinking and drugs.

> I joined AA and learned how to be friends with men. It was a safe place to explore relationships. It was there that I learned more about masculine interests such as sports. While I still felt different, I began to feel a sense of acceptance.

After years of living on his own, and still in recovery from drugs and alcohol, Marshall met and married "a strong-willed, hard, closed woman who was deeply devoted to truth, spirituality and change."

> I was 29. Before we slept together for the first time, I informed her about my SSA issues. Her response was, "We all have issues of one sort or another. Hopefully, working together, we can sort them out." [. . .] Because she never saw me as gay or ex-gay, but rather simply as the man she loved, she was invaluable to me in the recovery

process. As I grew in my masculinity, she has softened and opened up more and more. The balance in our relationship changed. Our marital issues weren't about SSA but how a man and a woman react in a relationship. We utilized the services of a great marriage therapist who helped us work on dynamics in the relationship.

Nevertheless, after about seven years of marriage, I started going back to porn and gay chat rooms. I also became obsessive about sleeping with men. I revealed to my wife my belief about this "fall."[6] I had gotten all that I had ever wished for—a loving wife, beautiful children, and lots of money. But I retained a lousy self-image and thus I couldn't handle the success I was having. My insecurities led me to go back to where I had started. I would destroy everything I had achieved! I felt I did not deserve either the success or the happiness I had gained. Even though so much had changed, I still felt like a "little fag" inside. This time, however, the feeling was more like that of a lost little boy than the feminized man I felt as a teenager.

She encouraged me to seek help, to find support for the underlying emotional issues that were forcing me to seek unhealthy ways of fulfilling my most basic needs. I joined SA, found PCC and JONAH and saw that I had not completed my healing process, there was still much more left to do. My defense mechanism enabled me to repress so many feelings of inadequacy. What I should have done instead of retreating (as I did) was to armor myself and walk into my fears, just like any warrior does when he goes into battle.

With his wife's encouragement, Marshall threw himself wholeheartedly into the gender-affirming processes. Marshall's big breakthrough occurred shortly after he returned from one of the experiential weekends recommended by JONAH (Journey into Manhood, sponsored by People Can Change). Catching sight of

---

6. According to Marshall, he did not actually go back to gay sex, but only fantasized obsessively about it.

himself naked in a full-length mirror in his bedroom, Marshall was startled to see himself as "a *man* getting dressed." This was new to him. Previously, he had seen himself as a "paunchy, hairy, grotesque being." But now, as he wrote several years ago on the JONAH listserv:

> I see a 39 year old man and I love what I see. I was used to thinking of myself as a little boy. If I was a boy, however, then the hair and fat and scars would be grotesque. But as a man ... I ... Well, I am just what I am supposed to be. What a freakin' revelation!

Later that same day, while driving his car to make a sales call, Marshall had another revelation.

> I actually heard G–d say to me (way too clearly for comfort) that I am "healed from homosexuality," and further, that "the battle is over—you've won." I pulled off the road and started to sob uncontrollably. Although the sobbing went on and on, I could not deny what was happening. It was all too clear ... G–d granted me a wholeness where the spiritual, intellectual, emotional and physical dimension of my being became integrated. These four different aspects of me reunified with each other, enabling me to feel within me that I was truly a man as G–d had intended.

Like Ben Newman (profiled above), Marshall had gone to New Warriors, where he had gotten to know himself as a man among men.

> I learned that most of the stuff I dealt with in the past and deal with today are exactly the same thing that most if not all men deal with. My conditioning up to now was simply: find a strong man and try to bring that person within me. That was my reflex response. But I found out through the New Warrior program that most men fear their lack of courage and strength. I witnessed other men that are just as, if not more, insecure and fearful as I was. I learned that these are normal fears faced my most men. It is not a "gay issue." I also learned how to *feel* my emotions and to be authentic with other men. It became apparent that I could identify as a man, just like any other

man does, and relate to other men as brothers.

Marshall's transformation affected more than just his self-identification as a man. "My relationships in every aspect of life were strengthened, whether it involves my marriage, family, or others within the world." He reported that he was now able for the first time to "see men as the same sex and women as the opposite sex." To the reader, this may seem quite ordinary; but for Marshall, this insight represented "a total change of perspective."

Today Marshall's demeanor is anything but effeminate. He is happily married to a spiritually and physically beautiful woman. Together they have been blessed with two adorable children. Together, Marshall, his wife, and their children are deepening their connection to G–d through a program of Torah study with their local Chabad rabbi. Marshall has become one of JONAH's mentors, helping other men in the process of transformation.

It is important to note that Marshall's transformation has been much more than merely sexual.

> My transition is completing itself. I profoundly changed my life. For the first time, I felt linked to G–d in a real way. I am clear both as to my choices and as to who I am. Homosexuality is a "non-issue." It has been replaced by a competent, strong masculinity that has been continually growing within me, but which I could neither experience nor feel until recently. I can no longer hide behind my old deceptions and false self. I am floored by the realization how much my growth into manhood was able to release my authentic self out of the prison I alone created for myself. I had stunted my growth because of relational pains in my early years. More and more, I know who I am, what I want and what I don't want. I know how I feel and what I think. I now have relational satisfaction—normal healthy relations with family and friends. None of this used to be true. The feelings, thoughts, and wants of the past were all directed from another place, a place other than from my authentic self.
>
> Through years of hard work and the support of a loving wife, I was able to overcome the emotional maladaptations within me, to rewire the internal structures, and ultimately to triumph over the

inertia or resistance to change within me, permitting a regenerated whole me to emerge.

Daniel's and Scott's Testimony: Incorporating G–d into the Plan of Healing.

Though Daniel and Scott began their journeys from totally different vantage points, they discovered so many parallels along the way that they ultimately combined their respective stories into a joint testimonial that they both identify with.

Daniel is a 40-year-old Canadian, born into a hard-working, nominally Christian family. Daniel's early life is similar to many of the stories already reported: defensive detachment from father, over-involvement with Mother, body image wounds, same sex peer wounds, low self-esteem, bouts of depression, *etc.* Several years ago, as he struggled to find a way out of homosexuality, Daniel discovered a faith that more closely reflected his view of what G–d wanted of him. He chose to live his life as a *Ben Noach,* a non-Jew who lives in accordance with the Seven Laws that Torah prescribes for non-Jews (the Noahide Laws).[7]

---

7. The "Noahide Laws" are the fundamental laws of human society commanded by the Torah to all mankind. The *B'nei Noach* are non-Jews who live in accordance with the Seven Noahide Laws, and study the Written and Oral Torah as their moral frame of reference. A non-Jewish person of any ethnic or religious background who observes the Noahide Laws is referred to as a *ben* (son) or *bas* (daughter) of Noah.

Although Judaism does not actively seek converts, many rabbis will go out of their way to assist a non-Jew who desires to observe the Noahide Laws. Indeed, any non-Jew who lives according to the Seven Laws is known as one of "the righteous among the gentiles." The Talmud tells us: "Righteous people of all nations have a share in the world to come." (*Sanhedrin* 105a) Maimonides tells us that this applies to those who have acquired knowledge of G–d and who behave in accordance with the Noahide laws. The Laws are first mentioned in the Talmud, *Sanhedrin* 56a/b, and in *Tosefta,* 9:4. They are: (1) Do not murder; (2) Do not steal; (3) Do not worship any gods but G–d; (4) Do not transgress the laws of sexual morality; (5) Do not eat the limbs of a living or improperly slaughtered animal; (6) Do not curse G–d; and (7) Establish a fair and righteous system of justice.

Scott, on the other hand, was born into a prosperous, secular, Jewish family in a suburb of metropolitan New York. He is a survivor of long-term (from ages 8 to 16) sexual abuse committed by an older brother, who himself had previously been victimized by another family member in a similar manner. Scott is 22. Like Daniel, he suffered from a triadic family relationship (distant Dad, enmeshed Mom), body-image, same-sex peer wounds, and low self-esteem.

Both strugglers had their high school and college years marred by depression, recreational drugs, homosexual fantasy, and an addiction to internet pornography. Both men initially chose to work on their SSA issues with therapists who would counsel them by telephone. Daniel specifically sought out a Jewish Orthodox therapist since the Noahide understanding of morality and life is based on Torah. He found a Canadian psychologist living in Israel who is learned in Torah and well-versed in the Seven Laws. This therapist not only counseled him on SSA issues but also helped Daniel address crippling issues of guilt, self-condemnation and spiritual confusion.

Scott chose a California therapist who practiced in one of the leading reparative therapy offices in the United States. Scott was not especially concerned about his therapist's religious affiliation as long as his approach did not incorporate any principles contrary to Jewish teachings. However, after getting the help he needed to heal from his SSA, Scott still felt he needed something more. Here is how he describes the aftermath of his successful therapy:

> Whereas I used to be totally preoccupied with my SSA issues, I am now more and more occupied with Torah—G-d's design for creation—and His Teachings for mankind. I am now connected with an inexhaustible well of wisdom that makes a difference in how I live, what I do, and the meaning and significance of everything I encounter in life. And wow, what a difference it has made. I am not just saying this either—people have told me that they have seen me change significantly. (Yes, for the better!) The path He has lit and on which I travel is indeed a journey of discovery, learning, growing, and progressing.

Speaking for himself, Daniel adds:

> Please understand, it is not like being a Noahide has some sort of established religious identity in which I can cloak myself and hide myself from reality. Early on, the Torah made a big difference for me, simply grasping the "moral context" in which I live. That is, I sensed that there was something not right about the same-sex acts I committed. I recognized that it created too much pain in my life to be normal. Not so incidentally, my family did not bring me up to be a religious person nor did my family condemn my homosexuality. In fact, they encouraged me to live my life as a homosexual man, assuming that I was born gay and that is what would make me happy. They bought into the current cultural message about homosexuality, but I sensed deep within me that such attractions were not right for me.
>
> What specifically caused me pain? First, I had a vague but strong sense that such activity was a "sin," that it was inconsistent with G–d's plan of creation. Why? Because whenever I acted out homosexually, it just plain messed me up. I felt unhappy and depressed after such an activity. Moreover, I didn't like the feeling of being "overwhelmed" by the compulsive urges to act out. Something wasn't right. Something wasn't working.

Scott, who felt much the same way, recalls how, instead of obsessing over his problems and his pathology, he began to think about G–d's perfection and to appreciate how getting closer to G–d through an intensely personal relationship could help cleanse his soul. By recognizing G–d's purpose in creation, Scott began to see himself as part of a larger cosmic whole instead of isolated and alienated with his own pain.

> This shift occurred when I came across a Christian book called *The Purpose Driven Life*. Because I identified myself as a Jew (albeit nonreligious), whenever the author used the word "Jesus," I'd replace it in my mind with "G–d." The book allowed me to begin looking at my problems differently. It gave me an insight that, in spite of being sexually abused and compulsively acting out

> homosexual fantasies, I should not feel or see myself as a victim. Rather, I began to see Divine Providence in my life.
>
> The book came into my life about a year and a half ago. I started taking Torah classes eight months ago and that's when things really took off for me. Now I'm here in *yeshiva* [*i.e.,* a Jewish academy of learning]. I have no doubt that everything that led me here to *yeshiva* was Divine Providence. I never had a religious Jewish upbringing. This connection I've established with G–d is so awesome. I'm so happy. If things had been going well in my life, do you think I would have ever turned to G–d? Why would I have done so?

Scott's therapist encouraged him "to relive how I felt in situations when I was younger and to access long-repressed emotions." He recognized the need to walk through those fears and his anger, "almost as if I was reliving it, but for the purpose of getting rid of it." This approach helped Scott become less narcissistically self-centered, yet simultaneously to develop a stronger sense of self.

> The essence of my therapy was to teach me how to feel and not to keep everything locked up inside me. Doing this brings up old and current situations, all of which are processed to create a positive outlet or way of dealing with the by-products of those emotions (in my case, SSA). [. . .] [R]eliving it may cause additional hurt or pain but ultimately I learn how to release it.

An important aspect of the healing process which both Daniel and Scott experienced is the concept of surrendering those things that stand in the way of healing. These may include such counterfeit emotions as anxiety or shame, or defenses such as detachment and falseness. Both men concur that

> There is an incredible tension between the need for self-actualization and the need for self-surrender. Without gaining an ability to balance our individuality and separateness against the awareness of how we are all interconnected, our separateness can become the source of our greatest suffering. We become lonely,

isolated and fragmented. We cannot become whole unless we understand how to surrender. We need to stop resisting connecting with G–d; He is our Higher Power. He helps us create unity and connection and permits us to make ourselves whole.

In Scott's case, he needed to surrender the festering resentment against his abusive older brother and ineffectual parents that led him to assume a victim mentality. In this, Scott was aided by a spiritual process of genuine *teshuvah* that brought him closer to G–d and strengthened Scott's resolve and power to change.

After discovering Torah, I started to decrease my weekly therapy (which I had been doing for nearly two years) to every other week. Judaism enabled me to move more quickly in my therapy by providing a framework in which I could integrate what happened. The therapy doesn't teach or encourage you to blame anyone; nevertheless, my natural tendency was to put the blame on someone, to look for a scapegoat. As I relived my experiences, I figured out where the feelings came from, where they led to, and why I felt this way. If I didn't realize there is a higher purpose to it all, or recognize that what I went through created an incredible form of character building, I certainly would have wanted to blame someone, like my parents. Judaism gave me the foundation that enabled me to rebuild my character, rebuild my essence, and emerge as a reconstructed personality. I now can acknowledge the problem and be open to dealing with it. I am now in a position to let go of it. *My past is no longer my future.*

Part of the challenge implicit in changing one's sexual orientation (and of *teshuvah* in general) is the feeling of passing through a dark tunnel where the end is unknown. (This is one of the primary reasons JONAH has created a mentor system where those who are successfully transforming themselves provide counsel to those who are just beginning). The space through which the strugglers are traveling is one where they know they're no longer who they used to be, but they have not yet become who they will become. As Scott recalls it,

The therapeutic work provided me with incredible new insights, but then the question arises, what do I do with those insights? There is an unknown abyss that inevitably becomes critical during transition times. When we are in this space, we often feel stuck and this can lead to feelings of emptiness and depression. I recognized how hard it was to let go of my old identity before knowing or at least having a sense of what comes next. However, my newly found faith in G-d provided a bridge to walk over the chasm.

I basically re-formed my whole being by tapping into my Divine essence: how I relate to people, how I go out into the world, and what makes me feel comfortable. To gain the inner peace required to not only go on with life's daily chores but to actually start anew and to do things you never thought you could do, the Torah becomes our beacon of light. I feel more connected to G-d, and am more confident in myself. I no longer idolize other guys. I only seek G-d's approval. Before, when I was always trying to gain approval from others, I never felt good enough. I now find instead that by following G-d's commandments, I can actualize my potential and can achieve what He wants me to achieve.

It's very difficult to get to a psychological place where you want to change and then actually go through the pain, struggle, and challenge of changing. It certainly would have been easier to simply accept the alternative of joining gay society, which I could have done a hundred times over. But to do so was inconsistent with my own sense of what I sought out of life. Subsequently, by studying Torah, it became obvious that joining gay society was also inconsistent with G-d's intent for me as a human being.

As a *Ben Noach,* Daniel, too, drew strength and direction from Torah study.

A fundamental premise of the Torah's understanding of a person is that the core of my being is the beautiful, infinitely precious soul which G-d Himself created, and this soul has its own infinitely significant mission for which I was created. With this newfound spiritual perspective of connection to G-d, and understanding His purpose in creating me, I was able to leave behind my previous disconnectedness, a disconnection that emanated from a frame of reference in which my significance (or lack thereof) depended upon how I perceived myself in the eyes of other men. Beginning in the schoolyard, I compared myself unfavorably to other males and the "games of the day" they played. Due to developmental gaps, I always believed I was inferior. I envied other males. However, by incorporating a Torah perspective within my daily life and connecting to G-d, I am no longer detached and unconnected, either to G-d or to other men or women. Understanding G-d's plan of creation enables me to see the meaning and challenge of life, learning how to best return to G-d, striving to embody His teaching in my life work, and somehow to continuously do His will—which is in reality what the Torah lifestyle is all about.

For his part, Scott's Torah study taught him to see his troubled past not as a shameful burden but as a precious opportunity of which he could be proud to have availed himself.

I was coping with the emotional pain of my childhood and coming to terms with its by-product (my SSA). However, the ultimate task involved something more, an ability to rewrite the script. At first, the work was all about me—how I did not want to be a homosexual. It was focused on how I did not want to live that sort of life or to be part of that subculture. But the process became different when I began to look at it from G-d's perspective. I started to understand maybe there was some purpose in the painful experiences and the resultant same-sex attractions. Perhaps *Hashem* visited all this upon me, expecting that I would learn my true purpose in life: to do His will and to follow His commandments. Connecting with G-d not only enhanced my motivation, it allowed me to see a bigger picture.

[E]ven my brother's molestation. If that never happened, maybe I would have homosexually acted out elsewhere. Instead of gravitating toward porn, fantasies, masturbation and incestuous relationships, I may have met my unfilled needs more dangerously elsewhere, like . . . anonymous outside relationships with strangers, or, even worse . . . gay bathhouses and crystal meth. So I'm almost thankful. If my brother and I [had not engaged] in homosexual activity, the sum of my experiences would totally differ. The bottom line is that a huge part of what made me the way I am are those very experiences. Those experiences in turn created within me a certain purpose in life. There are no accidents in life. I started to realize that everything that happened to me enabled me to serve a higher purpose.

For Scott, healing from homosexuality opened doors of opportunity whose existence he never suspected, leading him to life choices he would have never thought possible.

> People need to know that healing from homosexuality is possible. I am living proof of that statement. Perhaps that is my purpose here. I may have been given these struggles and these challenges, not simply to overcome them for myself, but to show by example how other people may likewise overcome. I need to carry Torah's light unto the world. And, in doing so, to have the world see how a person can resume their growth into full mature manhood. Thinking of that purpose, and connecting to *Hashem,* makes whatever problems I had just melt away. When I was able to stop thinking narcissistically so much about myself and why I went through such pain, *Hashem* stepped in to truly help me take care of all my needs. As I started to imbue myself with faith, I found my depression decreasing and my motivation to heal increasing. I came to realize that it was Divine Providence that had me endure everything that I went through. G-d knew that because of those difficulties, I would become a *ba'al teshuvah,* go to a rabbinic yeshiva, and change the entire purpose of my life.

Chapter 16:

Conclusion.

Spearheaded by the media and the discovery of safe and inexpensive birth control, the "sexual revolution" of the '60s and '70s has given rise to a social environment in which growing numbers of people feel free to enjoy their sexuality unfettered by guilt, shame, or traditional boundaries. A large part of society now claims that enjoyment as the right of free people living in a democracy. This atmosphere of sexual freedom, combined with a sexually exploitive culture, has given homosexuals the courage to emerge from the closet of secrecy, fear, and shame to claim what they see as their fair share of the action and the fun.

However, owing to the tension which exists naturally between those in the vanguard and those in the rearguard of change, the emergence of homosexuality into the light has, ironically, become obfuscated by politics, and a propaganda war of disinformation and intimidation. Inspired by the civil rights movement, and riding on the unfounded theory that "homosexuals are born that way," and "can't change," the gay rights movement has placed itself in positions of enormous leverage to influence educational and medical policy, state and federal legislation, and media content and editorial opinion. Thus, the gay movement has been able effectively to silence or suppress information—including clinical data—tending to disprove their fundamental claims, as well as whitewash the sordid realities of gay life. Gay advocates have gone on—in the name of civil and human rights!—to propose (and in some jurisdictions, even to pass) laws that could make it a "hate crime" to propagate the kind of information presented in this book!

While the atmosphere of political correctness so created has been an obvious detriment to freedom of speech, freedom of information, and to the democratic process in general, the primary victims are to be found among the homosexuals themselves, including those who, though practicing *hetero*sexuals, are tormented by same-sex attractions. Since the APA deleted homosexuality from its diagnostic manual in 1973, men and women who have never accepted their same-sex attraction as natural or right have been told and retold that they must learn to live with it: they were "born that way," they "can't change," it's "who they are." They have been told this by their peers, by their family and friends and neighbors, by their therapists, by their legislators, by the courts, by the gay or pro-gay journalists of radio, TV and newspaper. Many who sought help were directed to therapists who proceeded to "cure" them of the "homophobia" that was purportedly keeping them from full enjoyment of life as a gay or lesbian—often without informing the client that alternative therapies were available that could effectively treat their SSA. Many more strugglers continued to live in emotional pain, unable to escape the clutches of a sexual inclination for which they felt a deep-seated "value incongruity" ranging from ambivalence to repugnance. Some committed suicide or died of drug or alcohol addiction. Countless more died of AIDS or other STDs. In our opinion, such travesty raises extremely serious issues of human rights.

The zone of damage created by the gay rights propaganda war extends much further, however, investing all of society in a variety of harmful and disruptive ways, and, most unconscionably, the children, who from grade K onward, are systematically indoctrinated into the new "morality" of promiscuity and bisexual experimentation by public-school "educational" programs that blithely promote the gay agenda.

We have tried to shed some light into this closet of misery—to present a truthful and objective picture of homosexuality, its causes, its social climate and politics, and its consequences in terms of physical, mental and spiritual health. Above all, we have tried to show the humaneness and wisdom of the *halachah's* (Jewish Law's) conclusive rejection of homosexuality, and how the Torah offers those who wish to change a way out, a way back to a life of health, dignity, and to the holiness of marriage, procreation and family in accordance with G–d's plan of creation. We have outlined a tried and tested program of gender affirmation processes and *teshuvah* that has enabled thousands of strugglers to transform themselves from deeply wounded, miserably unhappy and despairing human beings into serene and joyfully productive members of society and loving husbands and wives and mothers and fathers of children.

Our purpose in writing this book has been to help, not to hurt. No doubt some of our readers are prepared to receive this book as a reactionary assault on social progress or to construe it as an attack on homosexuals. It should be clear by now that it is not. Neither I, the author, nor JONAH, the organization I work for, aspire to throw a bombshell into the lives of those who have achieved a measure of contentment and fulfillment in the face of adversity, nor is it our goal to destroy the bonds of genuine affection that can develop between friends—whatever the circumstances that may have originally brought them together. We fully recognize that those who do not *wish* to change, for that very reason will generally be *unable* to change. What we hope for is that those who are *not* contented and *not* fulfilled may know that change *is* attainable; that those who have sought in vain the reasons for their homosexuality may profitably seek them in their early relations with parents and peers, or in the other causal factors listed in Chapter Four; and that those who, for whatever reason, truly wish to change may find in these pages inspiration, motivation, and orientation for doing so.

What we hope for also is that mothers and fathers and teachers and school administrators may learn the importance of proper child-parent bonding, and of nurturing positive peer relations; and that "sex-education" programs will be replaced by programs that teach non-violence, conflict resolution, communication skills, and mutual respect and appreciation among all members of society.

In researching and writing this book, we have been conscious of the reality that despite the outstanding successes achieved by JONAH and other such programs, there will always be some strugglers who will be unable to achieve all of the goals they set out to accomplish. Whether such shortfall be due to causes too deeply ingrained to completely erase, or to an inability to replace SSA with a viable interest in the opposite sex, or to external circumstances, such as not finding a compatible mate, we are nevertheless persuaded, thanks also to the testimonials of our strugglers, that there is no one who cannot benefit from our program in terms of self-discovery, self-respect, social adjustment, and spiritual growth.

To those of you who have totally eliminated or mastered their SSA and have not yet found the pathway to marriage and family, we say that the programs recommended herein will give you the strength and the courage to persevere without those things until, with G–d's help, you find them. Keep in mind the words of one of the great scholars of our time, Rabbi Aharon Feldman, Dean of Ner Israel of Jerusalem:

> The fact is that neither homosexual nor heterosexual activity has the capacity to grant happiness to humans, as even a cursory glance at our unhappy world will demonstrate. The only activity, which can give us happiness, is striving towards reaching the true goals of life. Life is not meant to be an arena for material satisfaction. It is to be used to carry out G–d's will by coming closer to Him and serving Him by keeping His commandments.[1]

Thus, we say to those of you who truly want to change, but are

---

1. Rabbi Aharon Feldman, "Letter to a Homosexual *Baal Teshuva*," *Jewish Action*, Vol. 58, No.3 (Spring, 1998), pp. 69-70, www.jerusalemletter.co.il/archives/March24,1998/homow.htm, and clarifications in Rabbi Feldman's "Letters from Homosexual Friends," *The Jerusalem Letter*, 3:1 (June 22, 2000), <http://www.jerusalemletter.co.il/archives/Jun22,2000/friends.htm.>. *See also* editor's commentary at <www.jerusalemletter.co.il/archives/Jun22,2000/ intro.htm>.

afraid of being rejected by the opposite sex: do not fear. Men and women who are productive, settled and genuinely happy within themselves—and therefore brimming with confidence and self-esteem—are always more attractive to the opposite sex than those who "need" someone else to make them happy. Until you find that special person, seek material and spiritual sustenance through work, through creative expression, through public service, and certainly through studying and practicing Torah or, for non-Jews, the Noahide Laws. In that regard, many who have gone through programs endorsed or run by JONAH have found joy and fulfillment in helping to guide other strugglers through their transformation.

Virtually no secular or religious leaders would take issue with Rabbi Feldman's view that sexual energy is redirectable. Sigmund Freud, who wrote from a totally secular standpoint, observed in 1911 that some of the greatest contributions to society came from those with same-sex attractions who redirected their sexual energy. "[T]hose who set themselves against an indulgence in sensual acts" are often able to distinguish themselves "by taking a particularly active share in the general interests of humanity."[2]

Notwithstanding the above, we emphasize that this book is not written just for strugglers dealing with unwanted SSA. In today's commercially hyped culture of sexual indulgence and exploitation, who can be totally free of illicit thoughts, fantasies, lusts and arousals? The essential message of Leviticus 18 (the "Holiness Code") applies to all who are troubled by any form of sexual

---

2. Sigmund Freud, *Psychoanalytic Notes upon an Autobiographical Account of a Case of Paranoia, Standard Edition* 12:61, quoted in Dr. Joseph Nicolosi, *Reparative Therapy of Male Homosexuality: A New Clinical Approach*, Northvale: Jason Aronson (1997), p. 197.

brokenness, such as those listed in Chapter Six: you can do *teshuvah,* and you can *heal.*

It is vitally important that the Jewish community as a whole recognize that there is no conflict between the prohibitions of the Torah and healing homosexuality. On the contrary, just as Torah commands those who are wounded or ill to heal through *teshuvah,* medicine and counseling, so are we all prohibited from hindering their recovery through hostility, rejection and scorn. Nor can it be countenanced that so many leaders of our communities remain in ignorance of the realities of homosexual lifestyle or of the tools and opportunities for complete healing made available through Torah, *teshuvah,* and modern psychological science. Nor can we stand idly by when those who are afflicted with SSA and "led astray" by public misconceptions are taunted, humiliated and ostracized in the name of Torah, religion, or conventional morality.

Once again, we emphasize that this book is not just for Jews. The prohibitions regarding homosexuality are included in the Seven Noahide Laws which the Torah requires of all the Nations. It is not simply ironic that the gay pride movement has adopted as its symbol the rainbow flag. For the rainbow, with its seven colors—corresponding to the Seven Noahide Laws—is the very symbol G–d chose as a perpetual memorandum to Himself and to all of humanity of the Covenant by which G–d swore never again to destroy the world. The *Tanach* (Torah, Prophets and Writings) tells us in several places that homosexuality is one of the *aveiros* ("sins") leading to the destruction of civilization. Thus, the gay pride movement has inadvertently chosen for its banner the very symbol which G–d chose to admonish the world to abide by the Seven Laws! In this we see the boundless love and mercy G–d nurtures for all His creatures, for in the very moment we are bent on sin, He sends us—through our own words and actions—a gentle warning and a loving reminder.

Shalom!

ABOUT JONAH

JONAH, Jews Offering New Alternatives to Homosexuality, is a non-profit international organization dedicated to educating the world-wide Jewish community about the prevention, intervention, and healing of the underlying issues causing same-sex attractions. JONAH works directly with those struggling with unwanted same-sex sexual attractions (SSA) and with families whose loved ones are involved in homosexuality. JONAH offers access to professional, compassionate help and a wide range of potential resources, both psychological and spiritual.

TO CONTACT JONAH:

Telephone (201) 433-3444

e-mail: info@jonahweb.org

P.O. Box 313, Jersey City, New Jersey 07303, USA

JONAH respects your privacy and confidentiality. Please remember that e-mail is not a suitable medium for communications of a private or confidential nature.

About Red Heifer Press

Red Heifer Press is an independent press devoted to the publishing and audiopublishing of works of unusual interest and merit in literary fiction, poetry, documentary memoirs, belles letters, beaux arts, sheet music, scholarship in the humanities and sciences, and Torah/Judaica in English.

Connoisseurs of classical and contemporary music are invited to become acquainted with our musical recording alter ego, Leonore Library of Musical Masters. Leonore is dedicated to the restoration, preservation and dissemination on compact disc of rare and neglected recordings of special musical and historical significance. We are currently engaged, in association with Cambria Master Recordings, in the restoration and reissue of the many outstanding recordings of Jakob and Bronislaw Gimpel. For more information, please visit the following sites:

www.leonoremusic.com

www.gimpelmusicarchives.com

www.cambriamus.com.

MORE FINE BOOKS FROM RED HEIFER PRESS

Rumours of Bees. Paintings by Tricia Sellmer, Poems by Alexander Forbes. An outstanding new poetic talent teams up with one of Canada's most celebrated painters to pay harmonious tribute to those remarkable denizens of the hive, purveyors to the breakfast table and all-around buzzing wonders: The Bees. An imaginative and thought-provoking dialog between the visual and poetic arts. "A charming holiday gift for that favorite person." —Raymond J. Steiner, *Art Times.*
Soft Cover. 7.5" X 12". 64 pages.
ISBN: 0-9631478-8-9. Price: US $24.95; Canadian $34.95.

If I Could Sleep, a novel by Alex B. Stone. By the fifth day of sitting Shiva for his eldest daughter, Fred Stern has transformed his mourning into a desperately needed opportunity to reconnect with his soul, his past, and his Faith. There's only one problem: his devoted sister has flown in to share his bereavement, *and she's driving him nuts . . .* A brilliant and moving novel about aging, grieving, noodging, and never giving up. "A master of dialog. Authentic. Intriguing." —Patricia Anaya, Co-Founder, Aztlan Prize. "Intensely human." —Julie Jensen, *The Dispatch and Rock Island Argus.* "Beautifully understated and ultimately moving." —Chris Leppek, *Intermountain Jewish News.*
Trade paper. ca 225 pages.
ISBN: 0-9631478-6-2. Price (US): $16.95.

Professor Gansa's Dream, or Science as a Naked Lightbulb: a Jewish Reply to Carl Sagan's **Demon-haunted World: Science as a Candle in the Dark.** By Peter Gimpel. Narrative poem in 75 "stanzos" satirizing Sagan's anti-religious agenda; with a critical exposé of Sagan's fuzzy thinking, sloppy scholarship, and Jewish self-hatred. With 11 "visualizations" by Gerry McGuinness. "Inspired. Even otherwordly. Critical skewering [done] deliciously in rolling, hilarious verse." David Brin, *San Diego Jewish Press Heritage.*
Trade paper. 72 pages (including illustrations).
ISBN: 0-9631478-3-8. Price (US): $12.95.

13 Ways of Looking at Images: the Logic of Visualization in Literature & Society. By Mervyn Nicholson. Marks the beginning of a new era of thinking about images and what they are and do. In discovering, through deceptively familiar literary texts, the laws that regulate the proliferation and organization of mental images, Nicholson shows how society—not just individuals—thinks in images, and how this "imagethinking" informs social constructs, not just literary texts. "Erudite but accessible . . . a fascinating journey not only into the mind of the author but also into the mind of the reader." —Michael G. Cornelius, *The Bloomsbury Review.*
Hardcover. 248 pages.
ISBN: 0-9631478-5-4. Price (US): $29.95.

MORE FINE BOOKS (CONT'D)

The Carnevalis of Eusebius Asch. Edited, Annotated and with an Introduction by Peter Gimpel. This novel of love and friendship set against a background of music, literature, philosophy, art, and Jewish Mysticism won the rare distinction of a review in a journal of philosophy: "An imaginative and perspicuous treatment of Vico's philosophical character and enigmatic relationship to the Jews ...Rewards the reader's labor with insights too varied to be treated in a short review."—Frederick R. Marcus, *New Vico Studies.* "An unusual, educational and ultimately wonderful book."—Chris Leppek, *Intermountain Jewish News.*
A SELECTION OF THE JEWISH BOOK CLUB!
Trade paper. 272 pages. Price (US): $14.95. ISBN: 0-9631478-1-1

Twilight with Halfmoon Rising: Selected Poems by Peter Gimpel. Containing... *POETRY MY ARS!* a hilarious send-up of the academic poetry scene. *ON THE INTERPRETATION OF BEETHOVEN:* Elegy from the ruins of today's mass-media classical-music celebrity culture. *THE QUESTION:* What if the State of Israel had no right to exist? A fable. *CANTO VII:* An unsuccessful bid for the first civilian space ride is transformed into a defiant tribute to the *Challenger VII* Astronauts. *TESHUVA:* A five-poem cycle celebrating the poet's return to Jewish observance in the chassidic tradition of his grandfather. And much more! "A major Jewish poet in our midst. But Major."—Herb Brin, *Heritage Southwest Jewish Press.*
Trade Paper. 72 pages. Price (US): $7.95. ISBN: 0-9631478-0-3

NOW IN PRINT: FIRST WESTERN TRANSLATION!

Brief Rest in the Garden of Flourishing Grace. Poems of Remembrance & Loss by the Manchu Prince Yihuan: Renditions from the Chinese, by Vera Schwarcz. In these wonderful poems by the last patriarch of the Qing Dynasty, Ms Schwarcz probes with her own poetic artistry the consolation of memory, forging a profound link between old and new, east and west, history and poetry.
Trade Paper. 90 pages, (including 7 historical illustrations) and 11 art photographs of Chinese gardens. Price (US): $18.00. ISBN: 978-0-9631478-2-0

AUDIO

For di Amud: Learn Nusach haTefilla with Rabbi Moishe Shur: Weekday and Shabbos (Nusach Chabad/Russian). Learn the traditional melodic chant for Weekday and Shabbos Prayers! Learn the traditional *Nusach* of Chabad-Lubavitch and other Russian Chassidim. Taught by renowned Chazan Rabbi Moishe Shur. With 16-page booklet of detailed notes and explanations.
2-CD set. Jewel Box included. Price (US): $18.00.

ORDER DIRECT FROM THE PUBLISHER: www.redheiferpress.com